# ☙ LHISTOIRE ☙ DE LA
# MORT·DANNE·BOVL
# LENC·ROYNE·DAN
# GLETERRE

L Es cas nouueaux & choses merueilleuses

Tristes aux vns &aux autres ioyeuses

Quadrienus sont en ce loingtain pays

Ont mes espritz tellement esbahiz

Que tousiours suis en pensee profonde

Et si auant a contempler me sonde

Ce que mon oeil me contrainct regarder

Que ie ne puis mon esprit en garder

Ny de ces cas estranges diuertir

Pour les escrire & vous en aduertir

Mais ie vouldrois que les nouuelles fussent

Telles que point de facheries n'eussent

*The Story of the Death of Anne Boleyn*
A Poem by Lancelot de Carle

Medieval & Renaissance
Texts and Studies

Volume 580

———————

French Renaissance Texts in Translation

Volume 3

# The Story of the Death of Anne Boleyn
## A Poem by Lancelot de Carle

*Translation, Edition, and Essays by*

## JoAnn DellaNeva

Arizona Center
for Medieval and
Renaissance Studies

**ACMRS PRESS**

Tempe, Arizona
2021

*This publication was supported by the*
*Institute for Scholarship in the Liberal Arts,*
*College of Arts and Letters, University of Notre Dame*
*and the*
*Nanovic Institute for European Studies,*
*University of Notre Dame*

Arizona Center
for Medieval &
Renaissance Studies

Published by ACMRS (Arizona Center for Medieval and Renaissance Studies)
Tempe, Arizona
ISBN: 978-0-86698-638-0

∞
*Printed in the United States of America*

*For Christine,*
*"fille unique," in more ways than one*

# CONTENTS

# Acknowledgments

During the course of this project, I tread through a great deal of what was, for me, quite unknown territory. The journey would never have been completed were it not for the help of many expert guides who generously gave of their time. I owe a great deal of thanks to my sometime student and now colleague, Greg Haake, who answered a multitude of questions and helped polish the translation, mostly in the congenial atmosphere of Rohr's. I am likewise especially grateful to Lance Donaldson-Evans, who graciously read a draft of the translation and offered many pertinent suggestions. Among my colleagues at Notre Dame, I am indebted to Maureen Boulton for her help in paleographic and bibliographic matters; Jonathan Boulton also generously shared his expertise in matters medieval. Other Notre Dame colleagues helped in countless ways, including Theodore J. Cachey, Peter Holland, Robin Jensen, Encarnación Juárez-Almendros, Elizabeth Mazurek, Margaret Meserve, Christian Moevs, Denis Robichaud, Nicholas Russo, Julie Tanaka, and Sandra Texiera, along with another former student, Walter Scott. Several scholars from around the world kindly answered queries sent by a stranger; these include Tracy Borman, Raphaël Cappellen, Rachel Hile, Sharon Jansen, William Kemp, Raphaële Mouren, Michel Oosterbosch, Remco van Rhee, William H. Sherman, and Alain Wijffels. I am particularly grateful to George Bernard, who generously answered many questions and read a draft of portions of this manuscript, helping me to avoid many inaccuracies. Among my *seiziémiste* friends and colleagues, who kindly shared with me the benefit of their knowledge and for the interest they took when parts of this work were presented at conferences, I must acknowledge Richard Cooper, Kathleen Perry Long, Amy Graves Monroe, Timothy Hampton, Robert Hudson, Reinier Leushuis, Louisa MacKenzie, Cynthia Nazarian, Corinne Noirot, Marian Rothstein, Emily Thompson, Colette Winn, and Cathy Yandell. I am especially grateful for Phillip John Usher's early support of this project, without which it would not have seen the light of day. The two anonymous readers for this press likewise offered an abundance of constructive criticism, for which I am very appreciative.

Research such as this requires the assistance of many libraries, and it is a pleasure to acknowledge their help here. I am indebted to the staff of the following libraries who welcomed me to consult their rare books and manuscripts: the British Library; the Brotherton Library of the University of Leeds; the Bibliothèque nationale de France; the municipal libraries of Soissons, Valenciennes, and Bordeaux; the Vatican Library; and the Royal Library of Belgium. Specifically, I should like to mention Anne-Marie Natanson, Didier Tomes, Cécile Gérard, and Marie-Pierre Dion, who worked on providing me with access to and digital copies of manuscripts housed in Soissons and Valenciennes; Paolo Vian, who facilitated my visit at the Vatican Library; John Smurthwaite, who answered questions regarding the copy of Carle's book held at the library of the University of Leeds; and Juliane Trede, who kindly sent me unpublished material on the Munich copy of Carle's manuscript. Among the staff of the congenial British Library, I would especially like to thank Andrea Clarke, who shared her expertise regarding the British Library copy of Carle's manuscript; Helen Parnaby, who helped me to procure a digital copy of that text and others; Bruna Lago-Fazolo, who facilitated granting permission to reproduce the frontispiece image; and Hannah Graves, who answered a question regarding the BL's copy of Carle's imprint. The staff at the Hesburgh Library at Notre Dame, particularly everyone in its Interlibrary Loan and Document Delivery departments, were exceptionally helpful and efficient.

It is likewise a pleasure to acknowledge those people who aided me in more material ways during the course of this project. The publication of this book has benefitted from a subvention grant from the Institute for Scholarship in the Liberal Arts (ISLA), in the College of Arts and Letters, at the University of Notre Dame. I am grateful to James Brockmole and Alison Rice, the current and previous directors of ISLA, for their support of this project, as well as to Stephanie Hasse and Pat Base, their efficient assistants. Likewise, the Nanovic Institute for European Studies at the University of Notre Dame provided a further publication subvention grant, for which I am very grateful. Special thanks go to Grant Osborn and Clemens Sedmak for their support of my work and to Melanie Webb for her efforts in administering this grant. Additionally, my visit to the Vatican Library would not have been possible were it not for a generous research grant from ISLA, in conjunction with another grant from Notre Dame's Rome Global Gateway; for these, I should like to express my gratitude to my Notre Dame colleagues, Tom Merluzzi and Ted Cachey, who headed these programs at the time of my visit. I would be remiss if I did not especially thank John T. McGreevy, former dean of the College of Arts and Letters, for his continued generous financial support of my research, including funds for materials and related travel. To this end, I would also like to thank my able former assistant, Brenda Teshka, for her administrative support. I should also like to thank Julie Eichinger, Todd Halvorsen, and Roy Rukkila of ACMRS Press for their work in seeing this book into print.

The genesis of this project was a class taught in Notre Dame's London Global Gateway (LGG) in 2014. For the opportunity to teach that class and for the chance to teach again in London and put the finishing touches on this project, I am indebted to Warren von Eschenbach and Michael Pippinger; I should also like to thank my colleagues in London, Alice Tyrell and Charlotte Parkyn, for their invaluable help. David Gregory, also at the LGG, generously answered many questions and read a portion of this manuscript, for which I am grateful. I also owe thanks to Cheryl Periton, who provided good counsel, and, especially, Mimi Ensley, who very generously helped with regard to Early Modern English paleographic matters and other general insights. I should also like to thank Odelia Silver for her library efforts on my behalf at the LGG.

My greatest appreciation goes to my family for their unfailing support throughout the project. My husband, Tom Flint, read (nearly) every word of this manuscript (multiple times) and offered countless wise suggestions; I cannot thank him enough for welcoming Henry, Anne, and Carle into our daily lives. Finally, I dedicate this book to my daughter, Christine DellaNeva Flint, for whom I hope this book brings back fond childhood memories of many visits to Hampton Court Palace. She is loved beyond measure.

# LIST OF ABBREVIATIONS

| | |
|---|---|
| BL | British Library |
| BnF | Bibliothèque nationale de France |
| Cotgrave | *A Dictionarie of the French and English Tongues* |
| CSP | *Calendar of State Papers* |
| DMF | *Dictionnaire du Moyen Français* |
| Fr. | *fonds français* (BnF shelfmark designation) |
| Lat. | *fonds latins* (BnF shelfmark designation) |
| LP | *Letters and Papers, Foreign and Domestic, of the Reign of Henry VIII* |
| n.s. | New Series |
| ODNB | *Oxford Dictionary of National Biography* |
| OED | *Oxford English Dictionary* |

# Chapter 1

## PREFACE

The story of the death of Anne Boleyn—the second of King Henry VIII of England's six wives, who was found guilty of adultery leading to treason and sentenced to death along with her five alleged lovers—is a familiar one. Recent years have seen a proliferation of scholarly works on this subject, not to mention popular histories, novels, films, television series, and theatrical productions, and this phenomenon shows no sign of abating. Yet one might justifiably wonder whether our over-familiarity with the general outline of this story desensitizes us to the full horror of these events and impedes our ability to understand just how amazing all this must have appeared to those who were witnessing it as it happened. For, certainly, prior to Anne's downfall, it would have been unthinkable, in England, to put to death an anointed queen.

But *The Story of the Death of Anne Boleyn*, attributed to the minor French writer Lancelot de Carle, relates this tale with a powerful immediacy that allows its readers to see these events with fresh eyes—eyes that belong to an outsider who is both fascinated and horrified by what is taking place around him. Carle, a young Roman Catholic cleric who was serving as the secretary to Antoine de Castelnau, the resident French ambassador in England, was required to inform the French court of the events of May 1536. Essentially, then, his text is a diplomatic dispatch and was completed within two weeks of the queen's execution. But, uniquely amid the ink that was spilt in foreign embassies at this moment on this topic, this text is in verse. In this way, Carle's "letter," a narrative poem of more than 1300 lines, straddles the historic and literary worlds, though it is far better known to historians than to specialists of sixteenth-century French literature.

Carle's work is unique in one further way: it provides a detailed account of how Anne's downfall came about through an encounter between one of Anne's ladies and this lady's brother, who happens to have been a close advisor to Henry. The brother is embarrassed by what he sees as evident signs of his sister's sexual impropriety and admonishes her to change her ways lest her reputation be sullied. The sister, in defending herself, lets it be known that there is a greater sinner among them, namely Queen Anne, whom she accuses of having entertained numerous courtiers (including a lowly musician named Mark) in her chambers and, most shockingly, of having welcomed her own brother, George, Viscount Rochford, to her bed. In turn, the lady's brother (with great trepidation) informs the king of these matters and thus sets the wheels in motion for Anne's arrest, trial, and execution.

Because Carle is writing for a French audience, he naturally pays particular attention to the peculiarities of the English judicial system, with a remarkable eye for detail; he even attempts to teach his audience some English legal vocabulary. The poem, thus, also constitutes a cross-cultural analysis of the events at hand and serves to document differences between two nations whose relationship was, at this time, far from stable. It might also be called the first biography of Anne Boleyn, as it tells her story from her youthful days in France to her rise and fall in England. Indeed, it is remarkably balanced in its portrayal of Anne. She is certainly not shown to be the deformed and demonized harlot depicted by her detractors; but neither is she the unblemished religious martyr described by her staunch defenders. Like many biographies, it frames its story as a lesson in the art of living, but it also reflects on the art of dying, drawing upon the familiar literary themes of vanity and mutable fortune. As a letter, it participates in the conventions of the epistolary genre and, at the same time, touches on the theatrical in its recreation of dialogue in this inherently dramatic story. It is not without humor, nor is it devoid of pathos. It paints a picture of courtly life that recalls the world of medieval romance. It is imbued with religious conviction and incorporates echoes from Scripture; it speaks of signs and prophecies; and it comments, directly and indirectly, on models of female comportment and gender relations. In short, it is a text worth reading, whether in its original French or in modern English translation.

To say that Lancelot de Carle is the author of *The Story of the Death of Anne Boleyn*, or, to cite one of its original French titles, *L'Histoire de la mort d'Anne Boulenc*, is undoubtedly already to claim to know more about this poem than many of its original readers knew. For, of the sixteen known surviving manuscript versions located in libraries in Europe and England, only one is explicitly ascribed to Carle, and all but one of the others—which appears under a pseudonym (or, more likely, the name of a forger or plagiarist)—are anonymous. Although the poem was ostensibly written primarily for the eyes of the French court, that is, of King Francis I (reigned 1515–1547) and his ministers, it clearly circulated in manuscript throughout France (and even beyond) within a relatively short period from the time of its composition. In 1545, the poem was printed by an unnamed printer who attributed the text to "Carle, almoner of the Dauphin" (that is, the future Henry II of France), the position the poet held at the time. While it is unclear whether or not Carle himself supervised—or even authorized—its printing, he seems to have made no attempt to dissociate himself from it. And, certainly, other evidence points to Carle as the poem's true author, as will be discussed more fully in Chapter 3.

The editorial material presented in this new edition and translation of Carle's poem is aimed at three audiences: (1) scholars of French literature, who may not be conversant with the details of sixteenth-century English history; (2) students of English history, who may not be familiar with literary matters such as the conventions and language of sixteenth-century French poetry; and (3) general readers, who might welcome background material on both these subjects. The chapters are designed such that they can be read independently of each other, allowing readers to focus on the material that interests them most, in any order. Chapter 2 constitutes an essay on the historical background to this story, focusing primarily on incidents that are reflected in the poem but also on some matters that give the larger context behind Carle's work, though this is in no way intended to be comprehensive. Nor is this chapter intended to make an original contribution to historical scholarship, though it might offer the occasional new insight in its evaluation of previous scholarship. Chapter 3 provides an essay on the poet's life and works as well as on the circulation and reception of this poem from the time of its writing to the present day. This is followed, in Chapter 4, by a description of the manuscripts and books in which the poem is found, from the sixteenth century onward. In the guise of an afterword, the last chapter analyzes the literary qualities of the poem and offers a summative interpretation of its meaning. Wherever I quote from Middle English throughout these chapters, I have modified the spelling and punctuation to conform to modern standards for the ease of the reader, and I have provided translations of all foreign language quotations.

The central chapter constitutes an edition of the poem in its original Middle French along with a modern English translation. I have provided all significant variants found in sixteenth-century versions of the poem and translated these when the variant is meaningful. Accordingly, this edition is silent regarding insignificant spelling differences (including variants such as *ne/ni*, *par/pour*, *quel qu'*, *cest'/ceste* or any other instance where the difference is an apostrophe vs. final *e* that would be dropped for elision), but spelling differences that matter for the purpose of versification are given in the variants. I also do not include obvious scribal errors such as repeated words. I have respected the original spelling and retained the copy text's use of the letters *v/u* or *i/y/j*; but I give a single spelling in notes when variants with different spellings are found in multiple manuscripts. I have also added diacritical marks when necessary to distinguish between two words (e.g., *a/à*, *ou/où*, *la/là*) or when an accent mark affects pronunciation (e.g., final *e/é*). Throughout, I have introduced punctuation, including apostrophes, but not stanza divisions except as in my copy text. I do show variant word order, missing words, variant verse order and missing verses. In addition to providing variants and their translations (when substantive), a series of notes keyed to the English translation also gives pertinent explanatory material.

My goal has been to compose a sense-for-sense (and certainly not word-for-word) translation of the poem into modern English in free verse form, that is, without rhyme or set meter. I have tried to respect what Carle emphasizes in his syntax, but I do sometimes rearrange verses in order to bring a part of his sentence into a more understandable modern English word order. Therefore, the reader should not expect there to be a perfect correspondence between the numbered French and English verses, though they will be in close proximity. Carle rarely provides antecedent pronouns (or nouns, for that matter) in his work; hence, I have often silently supplied nouns, including proper names, where needed for clarity. Similarly, I sometimes add explanatory words in the course of my translation when I believe the context is unclear. Additionally, I have used a more precise (and, I hope, more vibrant) wording when Carle's word choice is vague: for example, occasionally replacing *être* [to be] with words such as *exist*, *live*, or the like. In some cases I have altered the original grammatical structure (e.g., subject vs. object, passive vs. active) in order to provide a more agreeable, understandable English rendering. Translation often entails making a choice between multiple potential, equally valid meanings, but when the interpretation of Carle's text is debatable, I provide explanatory footnotes that cite sixteenth-century dictionaries to validate my choice. Moreover, I do want the reader to remember, from time to time, that this is a poem from the sixteenth century; therefore, the word choice or syntax of my translation is not always exactly what is most commonly said today in standard English prose. I also capitalize all references to God, to serve as a reminder that religious matters were taken with the utmost seriousness by the people who figured in this text (as well as its writer); as a side benefit, such capitalization helps to make the referent clearer in some instances.

In short, I have aimed for a translation that reads well in English and that remains true to the meaning of the French text, even if it does stray somewhat from the strict wording of the original. And while the Italian maxim *traduttore, traditore* [the translator is a traitor] highlights the risk of translation as an act of betrayal, I should rather like to think of this work as an act of diplomacy or, rather, of mediation: one that mirrors the intent of the original text, which, written by an outsider at the English court—that is, by a diplomat—to his countrymen back home, sought to connect two nations, two languages, and two cultures. I hope that in this I have done right by Carle—himself a translator from Latin and Greek—and that he would approve of my effort to make his poem better known and better understood in the twenty-first century.

# Chapter 2

## HISTORICAL BACKGROUND TO
## *THE STORY OF THE DEATH OF ANNE BOLEYN*

### Henry VIII before Anne Boleyn

On 24 June 1509, King Henry VIII (1491–1547) was crowned king of England in a magnificent ceremony at Westminster Abbey.[1] At his side was his bride of less than two weeks, a Spanish princess named Catalina, the daughter of the monarchs Ferdinand of Aragon and Isabella of Castile, whose prominence in Europe had been heightened by their success in war, their diplomatic savvy, and their financial support of New World exploration, including that of Christopher Columbus. But Catalina, or Catherine of Aragon (1485–1536), as she would come to be known, was not there merely to witness her husband's accession to the crown: rather, she herself was anointed and crowned Queen of England at the very same ceremony.[2] Yet, less than eight years earlier, such a scene would have been unimaginable. Instead, all eyes were focused on a different ceremony that took place on 14 November 1501 at old St. Paul's Cathedral in London: the marriage of this same Catalina to Henry's elder brother, Arthur, who was the heir apparent to the throne.[3] The fact that Henry came to gain both the crown and

---

[1] For a good general biography of Henry VIII and an overview of the political context, consult the entry "Henry VIII" in the *Oxford Dictionary of National Biography* [hereafter abbreviated ODNB], written by E. W. Ives and available online at oxforddnb.com. See also John Guy, *Henry VIII: The Quest for Fame* (London: Allen Lane, 2014); David M. Loades, *Henry VIII* (Stroud: Amberley, 2013); and Lucy Wooding, *Henry VIII*, 2nd ed. (London: Routledge, 2015). The classic history of Henry VIII remains J. J. Scarisbrick, *Henry VIII* (1968; repr. London: Penguin, 1974).

[2] For the standard biography of Catherine, see Garrett Mattingly, *Catherine of Aragon* (London: Jonathan Cape, 1942).

[3] For specific details regarding the magnificence of these ceremonies (i.e., the marriage of Arthur and the double coronation of Henry and Catherine), see Edward Hall, *The Union of the Two Noble and Illustre Famelies of Lancastre & Yorke* (1548), found in *Hall's Chronicle Containing the History of England . . . to the End of the Reign of Henry the Eighth,*

the bride originally intended for his brother—and the circumstances surround-
ing that fact—would later take on a significance seemingly beyond all propor-
tion and would figure as a central piece of the story of Anne Boleyn.

In the wake of the Wars of the Roses, the Tudor dynasty, if it could be called
that, was a very fragile thing.[4] The Lancastrian Henry, Earl of Richmond (1457–
1509), had claimed his kingship on the battlefield at Bosworth in 1485, having
wrested the crown from the Yorkist King Richard III.[5] With the battle won, the
newly crowned Henry VII looked to secure his throne in a very practical way: he
married into the family of his enemy, with the hope that his marital union with
Elizabeth of York (1466–1503), daughter of Edward IV and niece of Richard III,
would bring together the warring houses of York and Lancaster, represented,
respectively, by the white rose and the red. The union of the two houses would be
symbolized by the commingling of the red and white rose in what would become
known as the Tudors' heraldic badge, but, more importantly, it would be incar-
nate in the future offspring of Henry and Elizabeth.

Soon after their wedding, Elizabeth gave birth to their first son, Arthur, at
St. Swithun's Priory in Winchester on 20 September 1486.[6] The birthing site
was not chosen at random. Instead, Henry sought out Winchester thanks to its
presumed association with the legendary King Arthur (for whom his son was
conspicuously named); clearly, Henry hoped that the Tudor dynasty would foster
a renewal of the glory of Camelot.[7] Other children followed, and Arthur, now
dubbed Prince of Wales, became the older brother of surviving siblings Mar-
garet (1489–1541), Henry (named after his father), and Mary (1496–1533); but
Arthur was raised apart from his brother and sisters and received the education
and training that befitted a future ruler. His household was moved to Ludlow
Castle, on the Welsh marches (or borderlands), while Henry, who had been born
on 28 June 1491, remained near London and was raised with his sisters primarily

---

ed. Henry Ellis (London: Johnson et al., 1809), especially 493–95 and 507–14 (hereafter
*Hall's Chronicle*).

[4] It has been suggested that the name "Tudor" was not used by Henry VII or by his
descendants. But for the sake of convenience, the word will be used here to designate the
reign of three generations of monarchs from 1485 to 1603. See, on this point, C. S. L.
Davies, "Tudor: What's in a Name?" *History* 97.1 (2012): 24–42, and the same author's
review article "Representation, Repute, Reality," *The English Historical Review* 124.511
(2009): 1432–47. For a classic overview of the Tudor dynasty, originally published in
1955, consult G. R. Elton, *England Under the Tudors*, 3rd ed. (London: Routledge, 1991).

[5] For a biography, see the entry "Henry VII" by S. J. Gunn, in the ODNB.

[6] For an overview of Arthur's life, consult the entry "Arthur, Prince of Wales," by
Rosemary Horrox, in the ODNB. For a more extensive biography of Arthur, see Sean
Cunningham, *Prince Arthur: The Tudor King Who Never Was* (Stroud: Amberley, 2016).

[7] David Starkey discusses Henry VII's predilection for Arthurian culture in "King
Henry and King Arthur," *Arthurian Literature* 16 (1998): 171–96, here 180 (issue edited
by James P. Carley and Felicity Riddy).

at Eltham Palace.[8] Henry's education was certainly of high quality—indeed, his first tutor was none other than the poet John Skelton—but he was clearly not raised with the assumption that he would rule England, for that honor would have been thought to belong to his brother.

When Arthur was only a year old, he was promised in marriage to the two-year-old daughter of the Spanish "Catholic Monarchs" in an effort to seal an alliance between Spain and England. Details of this marriage were negotiated over a period of several years, and by 1501 Catherine undertook the treacherous journey to England to meet her fifteen-year-old husband-to-be. Soon after the autumn wedding, the young couple made their way to Ludlow; but by spring, it is thought, both Catherine and Arthur were ill and fighting for their lives.[9] While Catherine survived, Arthur died on 2 April 1502. What happened—or did not happen—in between Arthur's wedding and his funeral was a subject that was to come under great scrutiny before the end of the 1520s. The reason it mattered was that Catherine was soon to be considered the potential bride of her husband's brother, Henry, who was more than five years her junior. Such a union —between a person and a close family member (such as a sibling, parent, or child) of a previous sexual partner, whether or not that sexual act occurred within marriage—constituted an "impediment of affinity" and required a papal dispensation. Even if Catherine's first marriage had not been consummated, however, it would still require a dispensation, but of a different kind, one that removed the "impediment of public honesty."[10] In either case, the dispensation could be routinely granted and would not have been considered a major obstacle to the eventual marriage of Catherine and Henry.

The more pressing obstacle was of a political nature. Although an initial agreement between the monarchs of England and Spain regarding the marriage was signed within a few months of Arthur's death, negotiations frequently broke down and dragged on for years. Catherine was left virtually impecunious and in limbo in a foreign and sometimes hostile environment, while her father and

---

[8] For a study of Henry's early years, see David Starkey, *Henry: Virtuous Prince* (2008; repr. London: Harper Perennial, 2009). For more on various Tudor royal palaces, consult Simon Thurley, *Houses of Power: The Places That Shaped the Tudor World* (London: Transworld, 2017).

[9] There is some uncertainty as to whether or not Catherine's illness coincided with her husband's (thus suggesting that the fatal disease was infectious). See, on this point, Cunningham, *Prince Arthur*, 178; and David Starkey, *Six Wives: The Queens of Henry VIII* (2003; repr. London: Harper Perennial, 2004), 79.

[10] For a thorough explanation of the complicated matter of dispensations for these varying impediments, see Scarisbrick, *Henry VIII*. Also consult Virginia Murphy, "The Literature and Propaganda of Henry VIII's First Divorce," in *The Reign of Henry VIII: Politics, Policy and Piety*, ed. Diarmaid MacCulloch (New York: St. Martin's Press, 1995), 135–58.

father-in-law bickered over financial details, each trying to gain an advantage over the other and neither wishing to let go of Catherine fully. Determined not to end negotiations, Ferdinand ingeniously named Catherine his official ambassador to England so that she could remain on site—and in sight. It was only upon the death of Henry VII on 21 April 1509 that the political obstacles to the marriage were fully overcome, allowing the seventeen-year-old Henry to gain both the throne of England and the hand of a Spanish princess in quick succession.

In the meantime, although Catherine had declared that her marriage to Arthur had not been consummated, the Spanish ambassador working on her behalf in the negotiations with Henry VII decided that it was preferable to seek a dispensation from the impediment of affinity—just in case—which was duly granted. The wedding of Catherine and Henry was celebrated at Greenwich, at the church of Observant Friars, on 11 June 1509, just under two months after Henry's accession to the crown. Although earlier, as a fourteen-year-old, Henry had renounced his betrothal to Catherine, by the time his father had died, Henry seems to have chosen to marry Catherine of his own accord.[11] The pair were evidently well matched: the famed Dutch humanist Desiderius Erasmus wrote in 1519 that theirs was an exemplar of "harmonious wedlock."[12]

A devout and strong woman, Catherine was made regent in 1513 while Henry led an army into France; this meant that she was put in charge of all domestic matters during her husband's absence. Catherine showed her mettle by raising troops against Scotland, which, honoring the "Auld Alliance" between that country and France (based on the principle that the enemy of my enemy is my friend), had predictably attempted to invade England as a distraction to Henry's French war.[13] Under the military leadership of Thomas Howard, Earl of Surrey (1443–1524), and his son, also called Thomas (1473–1554), Catherine's troops were victorious at Flodden, and the Scottish king, James IV, was killed in battle. The victory helped restore the elder Thomas Howard to the family title of Duke of Norfolk (lost when they found themselves on the wrong side of the Wars of the Roses), whereupon Howard's son assumed the title of Earl of Surrey. But

---

[11] See Starkey, *Six Wives*, 93 and 112.

[12] Erasmus wrote: "What family of citizens offers so clear an example of strict and harmonious wedlock? Where could one find a wife more keen to equal her admirable spouse?" See the letter of Erasmus to Henry VIII (1519, no. 964), in *The Correspondence of Erasmus: Letters 842–992 (1518–1519)*, trans. R. A. B. Mynors and D. F. S. Thomson, notes P. G. Bietenholz, Collected Works of Erasmus 6 (Toronto: University of Toronto Press, 1982), 359.

[13] For more on this alliance, see Norman Macdougall, *An Antidote to the English: The Auld Alliance, 1295–1560* (East Linton: Tuckwell, 2001).

the biggest victor was no doubt Catherine herself, who triumphantly sent Henry the blood-soaked coat of James IV as proof of her victory.[14]

Yet all was not always bliss between Henry and Catherine, particularly with regard to the matter of securing the dynasty through the birth of healthy children, especially sons. Catherine conceived at least six times through 1518, but three of these pregnancies resulted in still-births, and two babies died within weeks of their birth. Perhaps the most heart-breaking of these infant deaths was that of their first son, optimistically named Henry, whose birth on 1 January 1511 was cause for great celebration throughout the kingdom. But before February came to an end, the infant Henry was dead. Only one child, their daughter Mary, who was born at the Palace of Placentia in Greenwich (her father's birthplace) on 18 February 1516, was to survive infancy. Catherine, whose mother had been an active and strong queen regnant in her own right, ensured that her daughter would be given an education fit for a princess and engaged her countryman Juan Luis Vives to write a treatise on the education of women that could serve as an outline for Mary's preceptors to follow.[15] While Vives's vision for female education was not nearly so broad as that of his contemporary Thomas More (1478–1535), whose daughter Margaret was an accomplished classicist, there could be no doubt that Mary's education was not neglected and that she became conversant with foreign languages (including Latin), music, theology, and philosophy.[16] Indeed, by the age of twelve, she was receiving compliments regarding her command of Latin.[17]

Nevertheless, it was assumed that Mary, as a female, would be an unsuitable heir to the throne. Technically, of course, there was no law in England that prevented this from happening (as did the Salic Law in France, which prohibited

---

[14] For further details on this episode in Catherine's life, see Starkey, *Six Wives*, 135–49.

[15] For more on Vives's books and their place in the royal library, see James P. Carley, *The Books of King Henry VIII and His Wives* (London: The British Library, 2004), 116. For an English translation of this treatise, see Juan Luis Vives, *The Education of a Christian Woman: A Sixteenth-Century Manual*, ed. and trans. Charles Fantazzi (Chicago: University of Chicago Press, 2000).

[16] For more on Mary's education, see Andrew W. Taylor, "*Ad Omne Virtutum Genus*? Mary between Piety, Pedagogy and Praise in Early Tudor Humanism," in *Mary Tudor: Old and New Perspectives*, ed. Susan Doran and Thomas Freeman (New York: Palgrave Macmillan, 2011), 103–22; see also Loades, *Mary Tudor: A Life* (Oxford: Blackwell, 1989), especially 42–43. For general biographical information on Mary, also consult John Edwards, *Mary I: England's Catholic Queen* (New Haven: Yale University Press, 2011); John Guy, *The Children of Henry VIII* (Oxford: Oxford University Press, 2013); and Anna Whitelock, *Mary Tudor: Princess, Bastard, Queen* (2009; repr. New York: Penguin, 2016). For an account of Thomas More's relationship with his daughter Margaret (or Meg), see John Guy, *A Daughter's Love* (2008; repr. London: Harper Perennial, 2009).

[17] See Edwards, *Mary I*, 14 on this point.

inheritance of the throne by females). But common wisdom held that a woman
—even a queen—was to be submissive to her husband, making him, in effect,
the ruler of the land. And if this husband were a foreigner, England would soon
relinquish its independence to an outside power.[18] The lack of a legitimate male
heir was acutely felt by Henry. The operative word here is *legitimate*: for Henry
had, in fact, fathered a son by his mistress, Elizabeth Blount (one of Catherine's
ladies-in-waiting), in 1519, and this son became known as Henry Fitzroy, the
surname designating the son of a king (*filz du roy*, in sixteenth-century French)
from an illegitimate line. Fitzroy was the only illegitimate child Henry acknowl-
edged as his own; he was raised in and around Henry's court and was made Duke
of Richmond and Somerset—which were royal titles, as John Guy reminds us
—in 1525.[19]

Having a healthy illegitimate son proved, in Henry's view, that there was
nothing amiss with regard to his own reproductive capacities. Instead, the prob-
lem must lie with his wife or, quite possibly, with their marriage itself. And so,
little by little, Henry moved away, emotionally as well as physically, from Cath-
erine, who in 1525 turned forty years old. Henry had come to terms with the
fact that there would be no sons from his marriage with Catherine, who was no
longer fertile and with whom, moreover, he had already ceased having sexual
relations. Henry knew, as well, that there would be no point in fathering any
more illegitimate sons. So, in 1527, Henry began openly to discuss the possibil-
ity of pursuing a "divorce" or, more precisely, an annulment, which meant that
his marriage had, in effect, never been true and valid; this would allow him to
marry a younger, fertile woman with whom he could beget a male heir. Probably
not coincidentally, this was also about the time that he began to pursue another
goal: to marry, in particular, Anne Boleyn, yet another of Catherine's ladies-in-
waiting.

## Enter Anne Boleyn

How Henry came to this point—and more importantly, in what order the mutu-
ally reinforcing but presumably separate thoughts of divorcing Catherine and
marrying Anne entered his mind—is a subject of debate. Publicly, Henry main-
tained that he was burdened by a matter of scruple concerning the dispensation

---

[18] For this opinion, see "A Glasse of the Truthe," a tract thought to be written by
Henry VIII himself in 1532 (though published anonymously); the text is reprinted in
*Records of the Reformation: The Divorce, 1527–1533*, 2 vols., ed. Nicholas Pocock (Oxford:
Clarendon, 1870), 2:385–88. See especially 386: "if the female heir shall chance to rule,
she cannot continue long without an husband, which, by God's law, must then be her
governor and head, and so finally shall direct this realm."

[19] See Guy, *Henry VIII*, 35.

he received to marry his brother's widow. Henry had always been something of an amateur theologian; indeed, in 1521 he published a Latin treatise called the *Assertio septem sacramentorum, or Defense of the Seven Sacraments*, aimed at Martin Luther, for which he earned the papal title of "Defender of the Faith" (a title still used by the English monarchs).[20] This book was an outward sign of his strong adherence to Catholicism, his allegiance to the pope, and his abhorrence of heresies. Henry also, no doubt, thought of himself and his reign as somehow specially blessed by God, as would have been the case for all Christian monarchs. So he may well have been genuinely puzzled as to why God would withhold from him (and from England) a son who could reign over the land after his demise. Accordingly, Henry studied Scripture assiduously and seized on the injunction, found in the Book of Leviticus, against marriage to one's brother's wife. The passage reads thus: "If a man takes his brother's wife, it is impurity; he has uncovered his brother's nakedness; they shall be childless" (Leviticus 20:21).[21] This divine law, he concluded, was the reason that Catherine had borne him no surviving male offspring.

There are, of course, several problems with this argument. The first is that Catherine and Henry were not childless; they had conceived and raised a healthy daughter, Mary. Secondly, the injunction against a man taking his brother's *wife* does not specifically outlaw marrying the *widow* of one's brother. The passage could well be read to obtain only in the case when one's brother is still alive and thus was similar to all biblical prohibitions against sexual relations outside of marriage (as the broader context of this chapter in Leviticus—which condemns adultery, incest, sodomy, and bestiality—demonstrates). Indeed, the prohibition in Leviticus, if taken to refer to a brother's widow, would seem to contradict a command found in the Book of Deuteronomy that *compels* a man to marry his brother's widow: "When brothers reside together, and one of them dies and has no son, the wife of the deceased shall not be married outside the family to a stranger. Her husband's brother shall go in to her, taking her in marriage, and performing

---

[20] For an early imprint of this work, see *Assertio septem sacramentorum adversus Martinum Lutherum* (Antwerp: Michel Hillen, 1522). For the Latin text with English translation, consult *Assertio septem sacramentorum, or Defence of the Seven Sacraments*, ed. Louis O'Donovan, S.T.L. (New York: Benziger, 1908).

[21] English translations of the Bible here and elsewhere are taken from the New Revised Standard Version (hereafter, NRSV) as printed in the *Common Bible* (Nashville: Thomas Nelson Publishers, 1989). Henry would no doubt have read these verses in the Latin version known as the Vulgate of St. Jerome (hereafter, Vulg.), which states: "Qui duxerit uxorem fratris sui, rem facit illicitam, turpitudinem fratris sui revelavit absque liberis erunt." See *Biblia Sacra juxta vulgatam Clementinam nova editio* (Madrid: Biblioteca de autores cristianos, 1977). Henry did not approve of William Tyndale's partial translation of the Bible into English, which was begun in 1522; however, after his split from Rome, Henry did approve the continuation of Tyndale's work by Miles Coverdale, who published his Bible in 1535 and dedicated it to Henry.

the duty of a husband's brother to her" (Deuteronomy 25:5).[22] Thirdly, Catherine had maintained that she left her marriage with Arthur as a "true maid";[23] they were never, in fact, really husband and wife, because their marriage had not been consummated, and so the biblical injunction was a moot point. And, finally —and most importantly—Henry and Catherine were granted a dispensation by the Church precisely to allow for this perceived impediment.

Nevertheless, Henry had an answer for all these objections (including being persuaded that the term "childless" actually meant "without sons"). He particularly held fast to the opinion that his marriage was invalid as a matter of *divine* law, derived directly from Scripture, and not simply *canon* law (which could be righted by means of a papal dispensation). Indeed, he was convinced enough of this position to pursue what came to be known as "the King's Great Matter" through the proper ecclesiastical channels, petitioning the pope to recognize the inapplicability of the previously acquired papal dispensation. In May 1527, a secret tribunal to judge on the validity of his marriage was convened at Westminster Palace in London, presided over by Henry's Lord Chancellor, Cardinal Thomas Wolsey;[24] Catherine was informed of the proceedings only in June. By that time, it was impossible to obtain a favorable ruling from the pope, for Rome had just been sacked by renegade Imperial troops, which held Pope Clement VII prisoner. Since the Holy Roman Emperor, Charles V, was nephew to Queen Catherine, this meant that the pope would be keen to avoid angering the emperor by ruling in favor of Henry. The matter, which was already quite complicated theologically, thus had political implications for both the pope and

---

[22] Vulg.: "Quando habitaverint fratres simul, et unus ex eis absque liberis mortuus fuerit, uxor defuncti non nubet alteri: sed accipiet eam frater eius, et suscitabit semen fratris sui."

[23] This is the expression Catherine herself used during the trials held at Blackfriars in 1529. See, on this point, George Cavendish, *The Life and Death of Cardinal Wolsey*, in *Two Early Tudor Lives*, ed. Richard S. Sylvester and Davis P. Harding (New Haven: Yale University Press, 1962), 3–193, here 84: "when ye [Henry] had me at the first (I take God to be my judge) I was a true maid without touch of man."

[24] For summaries of original historical documents on much of Henrician history, including a summary of the proceedings regarding this matter, see the multi-volume *Letters and Papers, Foreign and Domestic, of the Reign of Henry VIII* (hereafter abbreviated as LP), ed. J. S. Brewer, J. Gairdner and R. H. Brodie (London: Her Majesty's Stationery Office, 1846–1932). These documents are now available through an online searchable database: British History Online (https://www.british-history.ac.uk/). For another searchable database available by subscription, which sometimes gives a digitized copy of the original manuscript in addition to the summary made by these Victorian-era scholars, see "State Papers Online: Early Modern Government in Britain and Europe," https://www.gale.com/intl/primary-sources/state-papers-online. For this particular reference to the proceedings of 17 May 1527, see LP 4.3140.

the emperor. As a result, it dragged on, without resolution, for years.[25] Before it ended, Wolsey would die in disgrace, never having achieved the ruling that Henry so desperately wanted from ecclesiastical authorities.[26]

That Henry's desire to seek a divorce was closely linked to his desire to marry Anne Boleyn can be proven by virtue of a document that Henry himself devised for presentation to the pope this same year. In it, Henry requested papal authorization to enter into another marriage—once his union with Catherine had been annulled—with "any woman, even one related to him in the first degree of affinity, even one whose affinity sprang from illicit intercourse and even one with whom he himself had had intercourse already."[27] As J. J. Scarisbrick goes on to explain, this document is not only "a remarkable acknowledgment by Henry of the scope of papal authority," indicating that at this time, at least, Henry had no intention of denying the pope's ability to rule on marital matters in general and on his marriage in particular; it is also, and perhaps more importantly, "the first document which affirms (implicitly) Henry's intention to marry Anne, a fact which hitherto was not obvious to observers (including Wolsey)."[28] For such was Henry's relation to Anne: he was related to her "in the same degree of affinity as he was related to Catherine," due to the fact that Anne's sister, Mary Boleyn, had previously served as Henry's mistress.[29] But importantly, as Scarisbrick explains, this new affinity—as unholy as it might be—was not subject to the proscription against marrying *a brother's wife* that was implied in the book of Leviticus and thus would not be considered a violation of divine law.[30]

Cardinal Wolsey's presumed ignorance of Henry's particular marriage plans with Anne Boleyn might seem inexplicable in hindsight, but at the time there would have been little reason to think that Henry would not marry, once he was free to do so, a suitably royal partner chosen from Europe's most eligible ladies. Instead, he chose to pursue a well-bred but not high-ranking English subject to be his next bride. Not much is known about Anne's early life: the exact year of her birth is itself disputed, but evidence suggests she was born around

---

[25] For the story of the divorce told from the perspective of the English ambassador to the papal court in Rome, see Catherine Fletcher, *The Divorce of Henry VIII: The Untold Story from Inside the Vatican* (New York: Palgrave Macmillan, 2012). See also Murphy, "Literature and Propaganda."

[26] For a biography of Wolsey, see Peter Gwyn, *The King's Cardinal: The Rise and Fall of Thomas Wolsey* (1990; repr. London: Pimlico, 2002).

[27] Scarisbrick, *Henry VIII*, 215. For this document, see also Pocock, *Records of the Reformation*, 1:22–27.

[28] Scarisbrick, *Henry VIII*, 215. For an argument that Wolsey was indeed aware of Henry's intentions towards Anne, see Gwyn, *The King's Cardinal*, 514–15.

[29] Scarisbrick, *Henry VIII*, 215.

[30] Scarisbrick, *Henry VIII*, 216.

1501.[31] Her father, Thomas Boleyn, had married into the prominent Howard family and served the king in various diplomatic missions while Anne was still a girl.[32] He was evidently quite proficient in French and wanted his daughter to become equally comfortable in that language. Accordingly, he arranged for Anne to travel to the Burgundian court of Margaret of Austria, where she could be given training in French, the language of that court, as well as in other skills appropriate for ladies of that time. A letter from the young Anne to her father, thought to date from 1513—in effect, a linguistic exercise known as a *dictée* whereby the French master would speak and the pupil would write what he or she heard—is in the poorly spelled French and adolescent hand of a twelve-year old.[33] The letter is interesting, not just because of the light it sheds on Anne's age but also because in it Anne reveals her desire to come to court to speak with the queen in French, thus making it all the more important that Anne do well in these language lessons.[34] This has been interpreted, fairly enough, as the ulterior motive behind Thomas Boleyn's desire to have his daughter "finished" at Margaret of Austria's court: he wanted her to be groomed to serve Queen Catherine as a lady-in-waiting.[35]

But Anne could avail herself of this opportunity for only a short time. For in August 1514, Thomas Boleyn wrote to Margaret asking that Anne return home so that she might accompany the king's sister Mary to France, where the latter

---

[31] For more on Anne's early life, see Hugh Paget, "The Youth of Anne Boleyn," *Historical Research* 54.130 (1981): 162–70. For an argument that Anne was born in 1507 and the elder of the two Boleyn daughters, see Retha M. Warnicke, "Anne Boleyn's Childhood and Adolescence," *The Historical Journal* 28 (1985): 939–52.

[32] On the Boleyn family, see Loades, *The Boleyns: The Rise and Fall of a Tudor Family* (Stroud: Amberley, 2011).

[33] See Paget, "The Youth of Anne Boleyn," 164–65, and LP 4.1 for a transcript of this letter, which is now housed in the library of Corpus Christi College, Cambridge (CCCC 119, fol. 21). A digitized copy of the letter is available via The Parker Library on the Web: Manuscripts in the Parker Library at Corpus Christi College, Cambridge, http://parker.stanford.edu. The suggestion that this letter is a *dictée* was also made by Deanne Williams in her presentation entitled "The French Education of Anne Boleyn" at the Sixteenth Century Studies Conference in New Orleans, October 2014.

[34] The pertinent passage of the letter reads: "et m'avertisses que la Rene [la Reine] prendra la pein de visser [de deviser] avecc moy, de quoy me Regoy [réjouis] bine [bien] fort de penser parler avecc ung perscone tante sage et onnete. Cela me ferra a voyr [avoir] plus grante anuy [envie] de continuer a parler bene franssais" [and you advise me that the queen will take the trouble to converse with me, about which I greatly rejoice, in thinking of speaking to such a wise and virtuous person. This makes me all the more desirous to persevere in speaking French well].

[35] See, on this point, E. W. Ives, *The Life and Death of Anne Boleyn, "The Most Happy"* (2004; repr. Oxford: Blackwell, 2005), 19. This work is a revised version of his earlier biography, *Anne Boleyn* (1986; repr. Oxford: Blackwell, 1987).

was to be married to the elderly King Louis XII. Apparently, Mary had specifically requested to have Anne among her young ladies, due to her ability to converse in French.[36] It is thought, therefore, that Anne returned to England and,
soon afterwards, left from Dover for France in October 1514, but the documentation regarding the exact time of her travels to France is unclear on this point.[37]
At any rate, Anne's position in Mary Tudor's court also did not last for long, as
Louis XII died on 1 January 1515, making Mary a young widow; she promptly
married (without Henry's consent) Charles Brandon, the Duke of Suffolk, one
of the king's closest friends.[38] But Anne did not return to England with Mary.
Instead, she was chosen to remain in France to become part of the retinue of
the new French queen, Claude, who was married to the recently crowned King
Francis I.[39] Why this was so is a matter of speculation, but presumably Anne was
amiable and a pleasant addition to the court, as Margaret of Austria had deemed
her to be in a letter written to Thomas Boleyn soon after Anne's arrival in the
Burgundian court.[40] Furthermore, Anne was only a couple of years younger than
her mistress, who was born in 1499; presumably this closeness in age also helps
to explain why Claude was eager to retain Anne in her court.

In any event, Anne lived in France for several years and continued to receive
the kind of European "finishing" her father had hoped she would get with Margaret. Certainly she developed a taste for all manner of things French, and she
continued to read and collect books in French throughout her lifetime.[41] It has
been assumed that she met Marguerite of Angoulême (also known as Marguerite
de Navarre), sister of King Francis, who embraced new ways of religious thinking that proliferated in France at this time, specifically those promulgated by
"evangelicals" and inspired by direct reading of the gospels (*évangiles*, in French)

---

[36] A letter from Thomas Boleyn to Margaret of Austria to this effect, dated 14
August 1514, is displayed at Hever Castle. For a transcript of the original French version, see *Manuscripts of J. Eliot Hodgkin, Fifteenth Report*, Appendix, Part 2 (London: Her
Majesty's Stationery Office, 1897), 30.

[37] See Paget, "The Youth of Anne Boleyn," 167–68, as well as Ives, *Life and Death*,
27–28.

[38] For more on Brandon, see S. J. Gunn, *Charles Brandon, Duke of Suffolk, c. 1484–
1545* (Oxford: Blackwell, 1988).

[39] For a general history of Francis I, consult R. J. Knecht, *Renaissance Warrior and
Patron: The Reign of Francis I* (Cambridge: Cambridge University Press, 1994).

[40] On this point, see Paget, "The Youth of Anne Boleyn," 164–65.

[41] For an example of Anne's interest in French culture, see the manuscript collection
of French songs known as "The Anne Boleyn Songbook," because it bears the inscription "Mres A Bolleyne / Nowe this," thus suggesting Anne's early ownership of the work.
For a facsimile edition of this manuscript, see *The Anne Boleyn Music Book (Royal College
of Music MS 1070)*, ed. Thomas Schmidt and David Skinner, with Katja Airaksinen-
Monier (Oxford: Diamm Publications, 2017).

in the vernacular.[42] Anne's time in France (and her presumed acquaintance with Marguerite and her circle) may explain, in part, her later predilection for religious books written in French, such as Jacques Lefèvre d'Étaples's French translation of the Bible.[43] Additionally, Anne owned another work by Lefèvre—his *Epistres et evangiles des cinquante et deux sepmaines de l'an* [Epistles and Gospels of the Fifty-two Weeks of the Year], which had been condemned as heretical by the Sorbonne. This work comprised an epistle or gospel reading followed by a homily; the copy owned by Anne contained a transcription of the scriptural passage in French followed by English translations of the French homilies thought to have been done by Anne's younger brother, George Boleyn, whose proficiency in French, like that of his father, was honed through his many diplomatic excursions to France.[44]

---

[42] For more on Marguerite and her circle, see Jonathan A. Reid, *King's Sister —Queen of Dissent: Marguerite of Navarre (1492–1549) and her Evangelical Network*, 2 vols. (Leiden: Brill, 2009). There is no definitive evidence to prove a relationship between Anne and Marguerite during the former's early years in France, although the two are likely to have met. See, on this point, Ives, *Life and Death*, 32–33. The disparity in their age while Anne was in France would probably preclude a close relationship, though it is possible that a young and impressionable Anne regarded Marguerite as an example to emulate. For more on Marguerite's relationship with the English court in general, including after Anne's death, see Heather M. Vose, "Marguerite of Navarre: That 'Righte English Woman,'" *Sixteenth Century Journal* 16 (1985): 315–34.

[43] On the French books owned by Anne, see Carley, *Books*, 124–33, who declares that these books "underline [Anne Boleyn's] cultural and religious orientation: France and evangelism. . . . Anne clearly was imitating the reformist atmosphere of Marguerite [de Navarre's] court and visibly aligning herself with reform through the *reading and display* of these impressive manuscripts" (Carley, *Books*, 129). Similarly, William Latymer, a contemporary of Anne's who wrote a biography of the queen that he dedicated to Anne's daughter, Elizabeth I, connects Anne's expertise in French with her "evangelical" interests, noting that she "continually . . . [read] the French bible and other French books of like effect." See William Latymer, "William Latymer's 'Cronickille of Anne Bulleyne,'" ed. Maria Dowling, in *Camden Miscellany* 30, Camden Fourth Series 39 (London: Royal Historical Society, 1990): 23–65, here 63. Latymer's observation is also noted by Carley (*Books*, 124) in his argument referred to above. Here and throughout, I have modified the spelling of Middle English texts to conform to modern standards for the ease of the reader.

[44] This is London, British Library, Harley 6561, "The Pystellis and Gospelles for the lii Sondayes in the yere." For more information on this book, see Carley, *Books*, 128, as well as James P. Carley, "'Her moost lovyng and fryndely brother sendeth gretyng': Anne Boleyn's Manuscripts and Their Sources," in *Illuminating the Book: Makers and Interpreters; Essays in Honour of Janet Backhouse*, ed. Michelle P. Brown and Scot McKendrick (London: The British Library, 1998), 261–80. The dedication from George to Anne is faded and not visible to the naked eye. The folio describing the book's contents

Anne's appreciation of such literature was noted by French men of letters, who dedicated several works to her once she came to be known as the English king's love interest. These included a 1529 manuscript work on letter-writing titled *Un petit traicté en françoys pour bien coucher par escript epistres que l'on dit vulgairement lettres missives* [A Little Treatise in French on Good Letter-Writing], which Loys du Brun dedicated to "Ma dame Anne de Rochefort," as well as a beautiful presentation copy of a French poem titled *Le pasteur évangélique* or "Sermon du bon pasteur" [The Evangelical Shepherd or "The Sermon of the Good Shepherd"], apparently given to the royal couple on the occasion of their marriage.[45] Both of these works bear witness in some way to Anne's perceived evangelical sympathies: the letter-writing treatise refers to her appreciation of the translation of Scripture into the vernacular, while the "Bon pasteur" text (once thought to have been written by Clément Marot but later ascribed to Almanque Papillon) is a virtual pastiche of biblical quotations rendered into French, all driving home the Pauline credo of justification by faith.[46] Furthermore, Anne's general Francophilia was noted in diplomatic circles: Gabriel de Gramont, the Bishop of Tarbes and, at that time, the French envoy to the Roman curia, wrote to Francis I saying that Anne's father had assured him personally that "if his daughter came to be Queen, she would be all her life your very humble servant."[47] In sum, Anne's tastes were, as David Starkey has stated, "French, not only in culture, language and religion but, crucially, in foreign policy too."[48]

---

promises that there will be "after every epistle and gospel a brief exhortation according to the understanding of the same."

[45] The letter-writing treatise is London, British Library, Royal 20 B XVII: 1529–1530; the date 1529 is given in a notation at the end of the work (fol. 46): "Escript a Londres . . . en l'an Mille VC et vingt neufz." For more on this work, including an English translation of the preface, see Ives, *Life and Death*, 268–69. The *Pasteur évangélique* is London, British Library, Royal 16 E XIII.

[46] For more on the attribution of this poem to Papillon, see C. A. Mayer, "'Le Sermon du bon pasteur': Un problème d'attribution," *Bibliothèque d'humanisme et Renaissance* 27 (1965): 286–303; and C. A. Mayer, "Anne Boleyn et la version originale du 'Sermon du bon pasteur' d'Almanque Papillon," *Bulletin de la société de l'histoire du protestantisme français* 132 (1986): 337–46. Although he includes this poem in his edition of Marot's works, Gérard Defaux likewise concludes that the poem was written by Papillon. See Clément Marot, *Œuvres poétiques*, vol. 2, ed. Gérard Defaux (Paris: Classiques Garnier, 1993), especially 54–68 (for the text) and 830–32 for the argument regarding attribution.

[47] See LP 4.6290; the letter is dated 27 March 1530.

[48] Starkey, *Six Wives*, 405. For a further analysis of depictions of Anne's religious beliefs, especially as given by the Protestant martyrologist John Foxe, see Thomas S. Freeman, "Research, Rumour and Propaganda: Anne Boleyn in Foxe's 'Book of Martyrs,'" *The Historical Journal* 38.4 (1995): 797–819. See also E. W. Ives, "Anne Boleyn and the Early Reformation in England: The Contemporary Evidence," *The Historical Journal* 37 (1994): 389–400. For an argument that Anne's evangelical tendencies have been

But relations between France and England were never very stable. Indeed, as early as 1521, only one year after the famous meeting between Henry VIII and Francis I known as the Field of Cloth of Gold (ostensibly a celebration of peace), there was talk of war between the two countries.[49] It is at this point that Anne was recalled from France to England.[50] Anne's years in England between 1522 and 1527 are not particularly well documented, but a few facts emerge from various sources.[51] She participated in an allegorical pageant in March 1522 at York Place (later the royal Whitehall Palace but at this time owned by Cardinal Wolsey, who, among other things, was Bishop of York), where she played the role of "Perseverance." At some point in this period, a courtship developed between Anne and Henry Percy, who was the son and heir of the fifth Earl of Northumberland and was attached to the household of the cardinal. Later, George Cavendish, who also served the cardinal, would write that Wolsey had put an abrupt end to this courtship and arranged for Percy to marry another eligible lady, Mary Talbot. According to Cavendish, Wolsey acted at the request of the king, who, we are to surmise, was already smitten with Anne.[52] But while these machinations might not be provable facts, we do know that, for whatever reason, the relationship between Percy and Anne was terminated.[53]

---

exaggerated for polemical purposes, see G. W. Bernard, *Anne Boleyn: Fatal Attractions* (2010; repr. New Haven: Yale University Press, 2011), 92–96, as well as his earlier article, "Anne Boleyn's Religion," *The Historical Journal* 36 (1993): 1–20.

[49] For more on this major Anglo-French diplomatic event, see Glenn Richardson, *The Field of Cloth of Gold* (New Haven: Yale University Press, 2013), as well as Charles Giry-Deloison, ed., *1520: Le Camp du drap d'or: La rencontre d'Henri VIII et de François I^er* (Paris: Somogy, 2012).

[50] See LP 3.1994, a letter from Francis I, dated January 1522, referring to the departure of "the daughter of Mr. Boullan" amidst rumors of war between the two countries.

[51] For a complete discussion of this period of Anne's life, see Ives, *Life and Death*, 63–80.

[52] See Cavendish, *The Life and Death of Cardinal Wolsey*, 32: "there grew such a secret love between [Anne Boleyn and Henry Percy], that at length they were insured [i.e., engaged] together, intending to marry. The which thing came to the King's knowledge, who was then much offended; wherefore he could hide no longer his secret affection, but revealed his secret intendment unto my Lord Cardinal in that behalf, and consulted with him to infringe the precontract between them."

[53] Tracy Borman, for example, maintains that Cavendish was wrong in seeing Henry's hand behind the breakup of Percy and Anne, saying that "timing makes this unlikely. Their betrothal was broken off by the end of 1523, and it was not for another three years that Anne was talked of as the king's new inamorata." See Borman, *Thomas Cromwell: The Untold Story of Henry VIII's Most Faithful Servant* (New York: Grove, 2014), 67.

Another presumed beau of Anne was Thomas Wyatt, the poet, who lived at Allington Castle, quite near Anne's girlhood home of Hever Castle.[54] Wyatt was separated from his wife, whom he had accused of adultery. He was in service to the king by 1524 and was active on diplomatic missions between 1526 and 1527. Not much is known about Wyatt's relationship with Anne except what can be garnered from a reading of his poems (which literary scholars would scorn as engaging in what is known as the "biographical fallacy"). Yet many readers over the years have claimed that Anne served as the inspiration for some of Wyatt's poetry, which may or may not reflect any actual love affair.[55] Another equally questionable authority for the claim that Anne and Wyatt were lovers is a work written by Wyatt's grandson, George, which elaborates upon family lore.[56] But certainly, the poet Wyatt was a figure at court during the period of Anne's early romance with the king, and there is no doubt that they would have known each other personally, perhaps even as children. Of course this relationship, whatever its status, could not end in marriage either, as Wyatt was already married. Though she was, possibly, the object of attention of at least two lovers, Anne remained unmarried throughout her twenties.

Exactly when Anne met Henry for the first time, or when their relationship began in earnest, is unknown; but certainly, if Henry were toying with the monumental idea of marrying her by 1527, their love affair no doubt began earlier. What exactly attracted Henry to Anne is obviously a matter of speculation.[57] Contemporary reports on Anne's appearance suggest that she was not

[54] For Wyatt, see Patricia Thomson, *Sir Thomas Wyatt and His Background* (London: Routledge and Kegan Paul, 1964), as well as Susan Brigden, *Thomas Wyatt: The Heart's Forest* (London: Faber and Faber, 2012).

[55] For more on the relationship between Anne and Wyatt, see William H. Wiatt, "Sir Thomas Wyatt and Anne Boleyn," *English Language Notes* 6 (1968): 94–102; for another, more recent analysis, see Greg Walker, *Writing Under Tyranny: English Literature and the Henrician Reformation* (Oxford: Oxford University Press, 2005), especially ch. 12. Among the poems by Wyatt that may allude to Anne are "Whoso list to hunt, I know where is an hind," "What word is that that changeth not," "Sometime I fled the fire that me brent," and "If waker care, if sudden pale colour." For these texts, see Sir Thomas Wyatt, *The Complete Poems*, ed. R. A. Rebholz (1978; repr. London: Penguin, 1997).

[56] For this text, see George Wyatt, "Extracts from the Life of the Virtuous Christian and Renowned Queen Anne Boleigne," in *The Life of Cardinal Wolsey by George Cavendish*, ed. Samuel Weller Singer, 2nd ed. (London: Harding and Lepard, 1827), 417–49. Excerpts are also reproduced in Elizabeth Norton, ed., *The Anne Boleyn Papers* (Stroud: Amberley, 2013), 19–32.

[57] For an analysis of this matter, and a critique of modern perceptions that Anne had extraordinary sex appeal, see Tracy Adams, "Anne Boleyn: Seductress or Scholar?," in *The Female Beauty Systems: Beauty as Social Capital in Western Europe and the United States, Middle Ages to the Present*, ed. Christine Adams and Tracy Adams (Newcastle upon Tyne: Cambridge Scholars Publishing, 2015), 48–74.

a great beauty, though she surely was not the deformed creature depicted by her later detractors.[58] Rather, as a Venetian ambassador wrote, Anne was "of middling stature, swarthy complexion, long neck, wide mouth, [and] bosom not much raised"; yet the same report goes on to praise her eyes, "which are black and beautiful."[59] Another foreign report, comparing Anne to Henry's former mistress, Elizabeth Blount, states that Elizabeth was "prettier" but that Anne Boleyn "was more eloquent and graceful, more really handsome, and especially of good family."[60] And indeed, as Hugh Paget reminds us,

> Anne was, in fact, one of a very small number of ladies of royal descent [from Kings Edward I and Edward IV] from whom Henry felt able to select a bride. . . . Anne met an important requirement for a future consort — that she should, by her royal descent, strengthen the claim to the throne of his legitimate heir.[61]

---

[58] For what might be an honest report of Anne's imperfections, see George Wyatt's otherwise favorable account in "Extracts," 423–24: "She was taken at that time to have a beauty not so whitely as clear and fresh above all we may esteem. . . There was found, indeed, upon the side of her nail upon one of her fingers, some little show of a nail. . . . Likewise there was said to be upon some parts of her body certain small moles incident to the clearest complexions." Wyatt is here responding to and minimizing the more serious deformities attributed to Anne by the Catholic polemicist Nicholas Sander in 1585 in his *Rise and Growth of the Anglican Schism*, trans. David Lewis (London: Burns and Oates, 1877), 25: "Anne Boleyn was rather tall of stature, with black hair, and an oval face of a sallow complexion, as if troubled with jaundice. She had a projecting tooth under the upper lip, and on her right hand six fingers. There was a large wen under her chin."

[59] *Calendar of State Papers: Venice* (hereafter abbreviated CSP, Venice), 1527–1533, ed. Rawdon Brown (London: Her Majesty's Stationery Office, 1867–1873). This collection of State Papers is also available in digitized format through State Papers Online, Early Modern Government in Britain and Europe, at https://www.gale.com/intl/primary-sources/state-papers-online as well as "British History Online," https://www.british-history.ac.uk/. For this reference, see CSP, Venice, 4.824 (31 October 1532), "Summary of the interview between the Kings of England and France" (Sanuto Diaries v. lvii, p. 279). The ambassador's expression is: "et li occhj, che sono neri et belli."

[60] London, British Library Add. 28585, fols. 43r–45r, "Helwighen's report concerning the man of Louvain," as transcribed in *Calendar of State Papers: Spain* (hereafter abbreviated CSP, Spain), ed. G. A. Bergenroth, Pascual de Gayangos, and Martin A.S. Hume, vols. 2–7 (London: Her Majesty's Stationery Office, 1866–1899). For this reference, see CSP, Spain, 4, pt. 2 (1531–1533), no. 967. A somewhat different version of this report can also be found at LP 5.1114. The text as written in Add. 28585 reads: "ladite fille [meaning Bessie Blount] estoit plus belle que ladite dame [meaning Anne], mais ladite dame [Anne] estoit bien éloquente et gracieuse, et competamment belle et de bonne maison" (fol. 45r).

[61] Paget, "The Youth of Anne Boleyn," 162.

Since Anne was an English subject, however, there would be no other political advantage to marrying her, as would have been the case in marrying a foreign princess. Henry would have to be satisfied there solely by Anne's French manner, sense of style, and facility in the language, assets upon which contemporaries also commented.[62]

No matter what the original attraction, the courtship of Anne and Henry thus developed against the backdrop of continual discussions regarding the king's divorce; it also took place while Catherine still functioned as queen. The level of intimacy between Henry and Anne during these years is evidenced by a series of love letters penned by Henry himself, who notoriously despised the process of writing, finding it "tedious and painful."[63] Some of these love letters were written in French (presumably to make a good impression on the Francophile Anne).[64] These letters are undated but are thought to cover the early moments of their courtship, through 1528. They are now held in the Vatican Library, and, though no one knows for sure how they got there, it is presumed that they were somehow confiscated or stolen from Anne and brought to Rome to serve as evidence that Henry's request for an annulment was fueled not by (or at least not *just* by) his tender conscience regarding what he viewed as his unlawful marriage to Catherine but, rather, by his fond desire for Anne herself.[65]

In any event, by 1529 it became clear that the pope—in the person of his legate, Cardinal Lorenzo Campeggio, who had (slowly) come to London to hear testimony on the divorce—would continue to hold off making a judgment on

---

[62] See, for example, William Forrest, who noted in the poem he later presented to the king's daughter Mary, upon her accession to the throne, that Anne appeared at court as a young lady, talented in song and dance, who "could speak French ornately and plain"; for this, see *The History of Grisild the Second: A Narrative, in Verse, of the Divorce of Queen Katharine of Arragon* [*sic*], ed. W. D. Macray (London: Whittingham & Wilkins, 1875), 53. Likewise, William Latymer's *Cronickille of Anne Bulleyne*, dedicated to Elizabeth I (and thus highly favorable to Anne), similarly confirms the contemporary view that Anne was "very expert in the French tongue." For this work, see Latymer, "Latymer's 'Chronickille,'" 63.

[63] For Henry's own admission regarding his reluctance to write, see his letter to Cardinal Wolsey, found in London, British Library, Additional 19398, fol. 44. The text is transcribed in LP 3.1.

[64] For facsimile copies and transcriptions of the letters, see Theo Stemmler, ed., *Die Liebesbriefe Heinrichs VIII an Anna Boleyn* (Zurich: Belser, 1988). For an edition with English translation, see *The Love Letters of Henry VIII to Anne Boleyn, With Notes*, ed. J. O. Halliwell Phillips (Boston: John W. Luce, 1906). For an excellent analysis of their content, see Seth Lerer, *Courtly Letters in the Age of Henry VIII: Literary Culture and the Arts of Deceit* (Cambridge: Cambridge University Press, 1997), 87–121.

[65] The original letters can be found at Rome, Vatican City, Biblioteca Apostolica Vaticana, Lat. 3731, pt. A. For a digital version, see https://digi.vatlib.it/view/MSS_Vat. lat.3731.pt.A. I am grateful to Paolo Vian for granting me access to the original letters.

the matter, much to everyone's frustration and to Wolsey's peril. The proceedings Campeggio oversaw, held at Blackfriars in May 1529, allowed Catherine to make her own dramatic and impassioned plea before Henry, declaring that her marriage to Arthur was never consummated, as Henry himself would know. Her testimony, *inter alia*, allowed Campeggio to follow his instructions from Rome not to rule in Henry's favor; but it did not actually induce him to rule definitively *against* Henry, either, despite the weakness of his case from the perspective of canon law. Instead, the court was adjourned for the summer, and Campeggio returned home. In light of this trial, the only offer forthcoming from Pope Clement was to acknowledge that there may have been defects in the earlier dispensation that had allowed Henry to marry Catherine but that he could happily grant another dispensation that would rectify the matter and that would allow the royal couple to live in the state of matrimony without burden to their conscience. This was not the answer Henry wanted to hear, and the matter appeared insoluble, at least from the king's perspective. Soon, Wolsey incurred Henry's full wrath for his lack of success in this matter and was stripped of his political powers, sent off to York to preside over his bishopric, later accused of treason, and died in Leicester on his way back to London to face trial.[66]

Wolsey's successor as chancellor was the famous humanist Thomas More, a renowned legal figure and long-time acquaintance of Henry since the king's childhood days.[67] As a religious conservative, More was, of course, not a proponent of the divorce and was not involved in the continued pursuit of the "King's Great Matter." Thus, when this business continued to languish in Rome, Henry began to take matters somewhat more into his own hands, clearing the way for the decision to be made independently of papal authority. The king seized on an idea suggested to him by an up-and-coming Cambridge theologian named Thomas Cranmer (1489–1556) that he should undertake a systematic canvassing of the universities in Europe to discover their opinion on the matter.[68] This was duly conducted, and it was determined that many theologians would affirm Henry's side of the affair.[69] Cranmer's subsequent rise in prominence at the royal

---

[66] For further details regarding the story of, and, particularly, the political implications behind the "King's Great Matter" as well as Wolsey's downfall, see Gwyn, *The King's Cardinal*, 501–98.

[67] For a biography of More, see John Guy, *Thomas More* (New York: Oxford University Press, 2000).

[68] For a complete biography of Cranmer, see Diarmaid MacCulloch, *Thomas Cranmer: A Life* (New Haven: Yale University Press, 1996); for Cranmer's involvement in the canvassing of the universities, see 45–51.

[69] For the book containing the opinions of the universities on the validity of Henry's marriage, see the original Latin edition *Gravissimae atque exactissimae illustrissimarum totius Italiae et Galliae academiae censurae* (London: Thomas Berthelet, 1530), translated into English as *The Determination of the moste famous and mooste excellent universities*

court coincided with the increasing influence of a man who would go on to become Henry's capable principal secretary and chief minister, Thomas Cromwell (ca. 1485–1540), Wolsey's former faithful assistant.[70] Cromwell was not a theologian and did not involve himself in the religious questions behind the suit to obtain an annulment. Instead, Cromwell forged a political strategy to address the issue and was one of the driving forces making an effort to explore the idea that England was (and always had been) an empire, exempt from foreign rule, including that of the pope.[71] With the rise of Cranmer and Cromwell, the seeds of separation from papal authority were sown but had not yet blossomed into a full-blown schism.

No doubt in an effort to placate Anne during this time of inertia, Henry began to elevate members of her family to the nobility. Thomas Boleyn, who already held the title of Viscount Rochford since 1525, was created Earl of Wiltshire and Earl of Ormond on 8 December 1529, whereupon his son George (who was probably born around 1505) took up the title of Lord Rochford.[72] The bestowal of an earldom on her father carried residual benefits to Anne, who actively used the courtesy title of "Lady Rochford." Her father also became a more central figure in Henry's court and was made Lord Privy Seal around the same time. But beyond the bestowal of these titles and roles, Henry manifested his commitment to Anne by repudiating Catherine once and for all in May 1531. The queen was sent to The More to live apart from Henry and had no further contact with him; she was also separated from her only child, fifteen-year-old Mary, who was sent to Richmond at the same time, and mother and daughter were never permitted to see each other again.[73]

Anne thus began functioning as a queen in all but name, though she and Henry apparently refrained from sexual relations at this time. It has often been assumed that it was Anne who withheld her favors until she could be assured of attaining her crown, but George Bernard provides a compelling argument in

---

*of Italy and Fraunce* (London: Thomas Berthelet, 1531), probably compiled by Edward Fox and possibly translated by Cranmer.

[70] For a biography of Cromwell, see John Schofield, *The Rise and Fall of Thomas Cromwell, Henry VIII's Most Faithful Servant* (2008; repr. Stroud: The History Press, 2011); Michael Everett, *The Rise of Thomas Cromwell: Power and Politics in the Reign of Henry VIII* (New Haven: Yale University Press, 2015); Diarmaid MacCulloch, *Thomas Cromwell: A Life* (London: Allen Lane, 2018); and Borman, *Thomas Cromwell*.

[71] On this matter, Cromwell was to draw inspiration from a document, thought to have been compiled by Cranmer, among others, known as the *Collectanea satis copiosa* [The Sufficiently Abundant Compilation, 1534], which brought together historical arguments on this point. See MacCulloch, *Cromwell*, 143–44. The *Collectanea* is London, British Library, Cotton Cleopatra E.VI, fols. 16–135.

[72] For a biography of both Boleyn men, see Lauren Mackay, *Among the Wolves of Court: The Untold Story of Thomas and George Boleyn* (London: I. B. Tauris, 2018).

[73] See, on this point, Starkey, *Six Wives*, 443.

favor of believing that this chastity was imposed by Henry, who did not want it to be thought that Anne—rather than his conscience—was the catalyst for the divorce he sought from Catherine.[74] Though she was not yet queen, Anne was to travel with Henry to France for another summit between the two monarchs to be held in Calais. And so, to ensure that she would be accorded every dignity while there, Henry ennobled Anne by creating her Marquess of Pembroke. What was remarkable about this elevation (and what earned her the honorific "Marquess" rather than "Marchioness") was that Anne had the right to pass on her title herself, making her fully equal to any other peer.[75] The lavish ceremony was held at Windsor Castle on 1 September 1532, and by October, King Francis I greeted the pair, ostensibly giving official recognition to the as-yet-unwed couple.[76]

In the meantime, new hope was generated that a declaration of nullity would soon be granted, allowing Henry to take Anne as his wife in the near future. This came about because William Warham, then Archbishop of Canterbury, had died in August 1532 and was to be replaced by Thomas Cranmer, who could be counted upon to rule in Henry's favor despite the pope's reluctance to do so. In other words, Cranmer was willing to assert local over universal jurisdiction in ecclesiastical matters. In this he was supported by what became known as the "Reformation Parliament," whose legislative power (which no doubt coincided with the will of the king) now included the domain of the spiritual as well as the secular and whose sphere of influence thus grew exponentially during the 1530s.[77] Little by little, a series of acts were passed that denied papal authority and jurisdiction in England, effecting a separation from Rome. In due course, more legislation was enacted to define the accepted doctrines of what would become known as the Church of England, setting it apart from Roman Catholicism.[78]

---

[74] Bernard, *Anne Boleyn*, 31.

[75] Anne is referred to, in official documents, as both "marchioness" and "lady Marquess." See, on this point, LP 5.1274, which transcribes documents regarding her elevation to this position, including London, British Library, Lansdowne 261, fol. 140; British Library, Additional 6113, fol. 70; British Library, Additional 6297, fol. 27; and British Library, Harley 368, fol. 176. See also LP 5.1370.

[76] For details regarding this meeting between Henry and Francis, see *Hall's Chronicle*, 790–94.

[77] See G. R. Elton, ed., *The Tudor Constitution: Documents and Commentary* (Cambridge: Cambridge University Press, 1960), 229: "the changes produced by the 1530s gave to Parliament a permanent place of political importance and, so to speak, finally incorporated it in the English system of government."

[78] For an overview of Henry's religious policies, consult Bernard, *The King's Reformation: Henry VIII and the Remaking of the English Church* (New Haven: Yale University Press, 2005).

## Queen Anne Boleyn

Emboldened by the support he received from Francis I, as well as by Cranmer's appointment to the bishopric in October 1532, Henry apparently felt confident that the messy business of procuring a divorce would soon end and that he would be free to marry Anne. In light of this, the couple began having sexual relations at least by late 1532, for Anne conceived sometime in mid-December.[79] Once the pregnancy was apparent, it was imperative that Anne and Henry marry so that their child would be born of a legitimate union. A secret ceremony was thus held, though the precise timing of this event is disputed. While one contemporary account (that of Edward Hall) alleges that the ceremony took place on St. Erkenwold's Day (14 November)—and thus that the conception occurred after the couple had been married—many historians dismiss this account in favor of one that places the marriage on St. Paul's Day (January 25), in the west turret of Whitehall Palace (Cardinal Wolsey's former York Place) and performed by the royal chaplain, Rowland Lee, in the presence of only a few witnesses, one of whom was thought to be Henry Norris, the king's groom of the stool and thus an intimate companion.[80] In either event, the marriage long remained a secret even from well-placed observers—and even from Cranmer himself, who had not yet granted Henry a divorce from Catherine. That pronouncement was not made until 23 May 1533, but Anne had already been publicly presented as queen on 12 April, Holy Saturday, that is, the eve of Easter Sunday. Indeed, as early as 9 April, a delegation was sent to Catherine of Aragon to inform her that she must relinquish the title of queen and become known as the "dowager Princess of Wales" (reflective of her marriage to Arthur and subsequent widowhood).

Henry's marriage and Cranmer's ruling were the definitive steps in breaking with papal authority and the Roman church. These actions were supported by the parliamentary Act of Appeals enacted in 1533. This Act declared, in part, "that this realm of England is an empire . . . governed by one supreme head and king" and that, consequently, all "causes of matrimony and divorces . . . shall be from henceforth heard, examined, discussed, clearly finally [*sic*] and definitely

---

[79] Assuming that her due date was somewhere around the actual day of her daughter's birth (September 7), and using the standard formula that ovulation takes place within two weeks of the last menstrual period, which generally occurs 280 days prior to the due date, one can calculate that Anne likely conceived a child sometime between 12 December and 20 December, 1532.

[80] See *Hall's Chronicle*, 794. MacCulloch reviews the matter in *Thomas Cranmer* (Appendix 2, 637–38) and comes down on the side of St. Erkenwold's day but with a priest present only at a second ceremony in January; Loades proposes "some date between 15 and 23 February" in *The Boleyns*, 103. Starkey maintains there were two ceremonies, the official one being in January (see *Six Wives*, 474–76). For the details of a January ceremony, see Ives, *Life and Death*, 168–69.

adjudged and determined, within the King's jurisdiction and authority and not elsewhere."[81] With this separation from Roman authority, all that remained was to formalize Anne's position as queen. The coronation festivities began on 29 May, when Anne was received by the Lords of England as their queen. On 31 May, Anne rode from the Tower of London through the City and, amid much splendor, was anointed and crowned Queen of England with the crown of St. Edward (usually used solely for the coronation of the sovereign rather than the consort) at Westminster Abbey on 1 June, Whitsuntide.[82] On 5 July 1533, Catherine's degradation was publicly announced; within months, her daughter was also stripped of her title of "princess," and it was declared that she was to be known henceforth as "Lady Mary."[83]

Anne's coronation has been described as a "thoroughly ambiguous event."[84] While there was certainly much pageantry, there are unflattering reports of her reception by the people of London. The official English testimonies are rich in detail regarding the sumptuous festivities, but foreign accounts tell of a lack of respect Londoners showed for their new queen.[85] What is more, several high-ranking persons boycotted the ceremony, presumably to make a political statement.[86] Among those notably absent from the celebrations was Henry's former chancellor, Thomas More, who had relinquished that role on 16 May 1532, in the wake of the parliamentary Act for the Submission of the Clergy. According to his biographer and son-in-law William Roper, More received a special invitation to the coronation from leading English bishops along with a gift of twenty pounds to buy a new gown for the festivities. He accepted the money but refused

---

[81] See "The Act of Appeals," (1533: 24 Henry VIII, c. 12), printed in Elton, *Tudor Constitution*, 344–49, here 344 and 346, respectively.

[82] See Charles Wriothesley, *A Chronicle of England during the Reigns of the Tudors from A.D. 1485 to 1559*, ed. William Douglas Hamilton (London: Camden Society, 1875), 1:17–22. Whitsunday is also known as Pentecost Sunday.

[83] For more on how Mary's title changed immediately after the birth of Elizabeth, the new princess, and how Mary was treated by Anne, see Starkey, *Six Wives*, 515–19.

[84] Loades, *Henry VIII*, 230.

[85] For the English accounts, see Wriothesley, *Chronicle*, 1:18–22, and "The Noble Triumphant Coronation of Queen Anne" in *Tudor Tracts, 1532–1588*, ed. A. F. Pollard (Westminster: Archibald Constable, 1903), 9–28 and reprinted in Norton, *Anne Boleyn Papers*, 178–91. For a paraphrase of a now-lost "unfavorable" account, see LP 6.585. For another foreign account, though one that is considered mostly unreliable, see *Chronicle of King Henry VIII of England . . . Written in Spanish by an Unknown Hand*, trans. Martin A. Sharp Hume (London: George Bell, 1889), 13–14. For the original Spanish text, see *Crónica del Rey Enrico Otavo de Ingalaterra* [*sic*], ed. El Marqués de Molins (Madrid: Alfonso Durán, 1874), 17–18. See also, on this point, Starkey, *Six Wives*, 503.

[86] For more on how attendance at the coronation could be construed as a political act, see Alice Hunt, *The Drama of Coronation: Medieval Ceremony in Early Modern England* (Cambridge: Cambridge University Press, 2008), 45.

the invitation.[87] Another conspicuous absence was that of the Imperial ambassador, Eustace Chapuys, whose master, Charles V, it will be remembered, was the nephew of Catherine of Aragon.[88] It is no surprise that Chapuys should therefore be a staunch supporter of Catherine and her daughter Mary and that his letter to the emperor describes the coronation as "a cold, meagre, and uncomfortable thing."[89] Henry's younger sister, Mary, the former queen of France whom Anne had briefly served as a girl, also did not attend the festivities; but, although she vehemently opposed the marriage, her absence is likely due to the fact that she was gravely ill at this time.[90] The French embassy, in contrast, took a leading role in the ceremony, conspicuously heading the procession and "powerfully symbolizing Anne's Francophilia."[91]

On 7 September, Anne gave birth to a daughter and not the long-awaited (and predicted) son Henry had expected.[92] Nevertheless, Henry dissimulated

---

[87] See, on this point, William Roper, *The Life of Sir Thomas More*, in *Two Early Tudor Lives*, ed. Sylvester and Harding, 197–254, here 229–30.

[88] For a brief biography of Chapuys, see the entry "Eustache Chapuys," by Felipe Fernández-Armesto, in *Contemporaries of Erasmus: A Biographical Register of the Renaissance and Reformation*, 3 vols., ed. Peter G. Bietenholz and Thomas B. Deutscher (Toronto: Toronto University Press, 1985), 1:293–95. For a more extensive biography, consult Lauren Mackay, *Inside the Tudor Court* (Stroud: Amberley, 2014).

[89] LP 6.653. Despite whatever bias they might display, Chapuys's frequent dispatches back home, paraphrased in *Letters and Papers from the Reign of Henry VIII*, are an invaluable source of information on the period between 1529 and 1545, his tenure in England. See Ives, *Life and Death*, 56: "The diplomatic reports of Eustace Chapuys . . . provide the only relatively continuous commentary on English politics and the royal court during the lifetime of Queen Anne; on particular episodes they are often the only evidence."

[90] See, on this point, Ives, *Life and Death*, 177.

[91] See Starkey, *Six Wives*, 495: "the procession was headed by twelve Frenchmen — merchants and servants of the French ambassador — all dressed in violet velvet with one sleeve in Anne's colours of violet and blue. Anne's own dress was in the French fashion, and an anonymous Frenchman who wrote an account of the event seems to have acted as a sort of style consultant." While Starkey believes the consultant claimed credit "for the pennants hung with bells in the water," the original text, as found in LP 6.584 (a narration of the coronation dated 2 June 1533), refers only to "rigging . . . adorned with small flags of taffeta" trimmed "by the writer's advice with '*or clinquant*' [gold leaf] as it reflects the sun's rays." There is no indication of any bells used "to make noise," as Starkey claims, a mistake perhaps explained as a misunderstanding of the word "clinquant" in this context.

[92] See Chapuys's letter to Charles V, dated 3 September 1533, as recorded in LP 6.1069: "The King [was] holding it certain by the report of his physicians and astrologers that the Lady would bear a son." See also the letter of 10 September, as recorded in LP 6.1112: "The King's mistress was delivered of a daughter . . . to the great reproach of the physicians, astrologers, sorcerers, and sorceresses, who affirmed it would be a male child."

whatever disappointment he might have felt and ordered lavish festivities to celebrate his daughter's baptism on 10 September.[93] The christening took place at the Church of Observant Friars at Greenwich and was orchestrated by Anne's uncle, Thomas Howard (now himself the third Duke of Norfolk), in his role of Earl Marshal (in effect, a grand master of ceremonies).[94] The child was named Elizabeth in honor of her grandmothers, Elizabeth Howard and, especially, Elizabeth of York, Henry's mother, in an effort to emphasize her royal blood.[95] This was somewhat unusual, as daughters were often named after those who stood as godmother to the infant. But Elizabeth's baptismal godmothers (or "godmothers at the font") were Agnes Tilney, the dowager duchess of Norfolk (that is, Thomas Howard's mother), and Margaret Wotton, the dowager marchioness of Dorset. Elizabeth's godfather was none other than the Archbishop of Canterbury, Thomas Cranmer. The baptismal ceremony was performed by the Bishop of London, John Stokesley. As was customary, right after the christening, the infant received the sacrament of confirmation, where Gertrude Courtenay, the marchioness of Exeter stood as "godmother at the bishopping," which was performed by the Archbishop of Canterbury. In between the christening and confirmation ceremonies, Elizabeth was proclaimed in a loud voice by the Garter King of Arms to be the "high and mighty Princess of England," securing her position as princess of the realm and Henry's sole heir.

Henry did more than merely have Elizabeth proclaimed princess at her baptism. Through the Act of Succession (formally passed in 1534 but begun in 1533), Parliament affirmed that Elizabeth was to be made heir to the throne, should the union of Anne and Henry not bear any male issue, to the exclusion of his first daughter, Mary.[96] In admitting that Elizabeth, even though a female, would be a suitable monarch, should it come to that, Henry was in some sense admitting that Mary could have been so as well, had the circumstances of her birth been different. The point of the divorce was thus refocused on the issue of the legitimacy of marriage to one's brother's widow and not on the perceived necessity of producing a male heir to secure the Tudor dynasty.

But the Act of Succession also included an important preamble that was far more sweeping in its scope and that went considerably beyond the simple issue of choosing a successor to the throne, no matter how important that might be. For

---

[93] For accounts of this ceremony, see Wriothesley, *Chronicle*, 1:22–23, and *Hall's Chronicle*, 805–6. Hall especially notes the lavishness of the setting, including the use of a silver font, fine satins, and other expensive fabrics throughout the ceremony.

[94] For more on Thomas Howard, see David M. Head, *The Ebbs and Flows of Fortune: The Life of Thomas Howard, Third Duke of Norfolk* (1995; repr. Athens: University of Georgia Press, 2009).

[95] On this point, see Ives, *Life and Death*, 185, and Starkey, *Six Wives*, 510.

[96] This is the "Act for the Establishment of the King's Succession," 1534 (25 Henry VIII, c. 22). See Elton, *Tudor Constitution*, 6–12, here 9.

the Act proclaimed once again that the pope's authority in England was "contrary to the great and inviolable grants of jurisdictions given by God immediately to emperors, kings and princes," thus reiterating that the matter of the divorce —among other spiritual issues—was to be decided solely by the king and his designee in the person of the Archbishop of Canterbury, without recourse to Rome.[97] Most importantly, the Act of Succession provided that if anyone "by writing, print, deed or act" did anything "to the prejudice, slander, disturbance or derogation" of the marriage between Henry and Anne, such an offense "shall be adjudged high treason" (resulting in the offender's execution) and that, furthermore, if anyone merely spoke out against the king's new marriage "without writing or any exterior deed or act," that offense "shall be taken and adjudged for misprision of treason," resulting in the offender's imprisonment and loss of property.[98]

Ironically, just as the Act of Succession became law, Pope Clement belatedly issued his sentence on the matter of the divorce and ruled that Henry's marriage to Catherine was valid and true. Henry was ordered to leave Anne and to return to Catherine at once. But the pope's pronouncement obviously carried no weight in England, especially given Henry's determination to rule over the land in spiritual as well as secular matters. Indeed, shortly after the passage of the Act of Succession, Parliament passed the Act of Supremacy, in which the fact that the "King's Majesty justly and rightfully is and oweth to be the supreme head of the Church of England" was formally recognized as having always been so.[99] This was followed by the Treason Law of 1534, passed in November, which spelled out the possible offenses and punishments already implied in the Act of Succession:

> If any person or persons . . . do maliciously wish, will or desire by words or writing, or by craft imagine, invent, practice or attempt any bodily harm to be done or committed to the King's most royal person, the Queen's or their heir's [*sic*] apparent, or to deprive them . . . of the dignity, title or name of their royal estates, or slanderously and maliciously publish and pronounce, by express writing or words, that the King our sovereign lord should be heretic, schismatic, tyrant, infidel or usurper of the crown . . . [they] shall be adjudged traitors. . . .[100]

---

[97] Elton, *Tudor Constitution*, 7.

[98] See Elton, *Tudor Constitution*, 10–11. Elton (482) defines "misprision of treason" this way: "strictly, failure to reveal knowledge of a treason; more generally, association with treasonable activities without direct participation in them; a lesser but still serious offence."

[99] "An Act concerning the King's Highness to be Supreme Head of the Church of England . . ." (1534: 26 Henry VIII, c. 1) in Elton, *Tudor Constitution*, 355–56, here 355.

[100] "An Act whereby divers offences be made high treason" (1534: 26 Henry VIII, c. 13). For this text, see Elton, *Tudor Constitution*, 61–63, here 62.

The penalty for such an infraction would be death. For the first time, mere talk — "even the kind we might typically ignore as harmless gossip, wild rumors, or foolish boasting"[101] — could be construed as dangerous and subject to the pains of death.

That such legislation was deemed necessary suggests that Henry's subjects were not uniformly enthusiastic about the king's new marriage. Numerous contemporary accounts spoke of how women, in particular, "favored the Queen," by which was meant Catherine of Aragon, over Anne.[102] One later report, dated 23 April 1533, described how two women were beaten "because they said Queen Katharine was the true Queen of England and not Queen Anne."[103] These acts of Parliament were thus designed to quell such talk. But the real targets of this legislation were not mainly women; instead, the laws were passed to ensure the conformity of prominent personages who were asked to sign an oath in support of the Act of Succession.

Because the Act of Succession tied together the king's ability to rule in spiritual matters as well as in the secular matter of the succession, it was deemed unacceptable by those who could not in good conscience deny the authority of the pope, no matter what their thoughts might be on the more specific matter of the succession. Thomas More was the most prominent layman to refuse to sign the oath and was imprisoned in April 1534. Soon afterwards, John Fisher (ca. 1469–1535), Bishop of Rochester and a staunch and vocal opponent of the new marriage, followed More to the Tower.[104] In May 1534, a number of Carthusian monks, living at the Charterhouse in London, accepted and swore to the oath; but this was not enough for Henry, who targeted the Carthusians in particular because of their reputation for piety and holiness. Consequently, in 1535, Henry ordered the arrest of their prior, John Houghton, along with several other monks who had refused the oath.[105] In total, ten men (nine of whom were professed reli-

---

[101] Sharon L. Jansen, *Dangerous Talk and Strange Behavior: Women and Popular Resistance to the Reforms of Henry VIII* (New York: St. Martin's Press, 1996), 77; see also Rebecca Lemon, *Treason by Words: Literature, Law, and Rebellion in Shakespeare's England* (Ithaca, NY: Cornell University Press, 2006), 5.

[102] See, for example, *Hall's Chronicle*, 754, which describes early unrest among "the common people" (before the king's marriage to Anne Boleyn) and especially women, "being ignorant of the truth," who "favored the queen" and "said that the king would for his own pleasure have another wife." Jansen also makes note of this and other remarks by women in *Dangerous Talk*, 83–87.

[103] Jansen, *Dangerous Talk*, 85.

[104] For a biography of Fisher, see the entry by Richard Rex in the ODNB.

[105] For more on the Carthusian martyrs, see Dom Maurice Chauncy, *The Passion and Martyrdom of the Holy English Carthusian Fathers*, ed. G. W. S. Curtis, trans. A. F. Radcliffe, intro. E. Margaret Thompson (London: Society for Promoting Christian Knowledge, 1935).

gious or ordained priests) were executed between 4 May and 6 July 1535.[106] An initial group of five—comprising Houghton and two other Carthusian priors, plus a monk of Syon Abbey and one secular priest—were dragged by horses on a hurdle from their prison in the Tower of London to the place of their execution at Tyburn. There they suffered the full penalty assessed for acts of high treason: that is, they were hanged, cut down before reaching the point of asphyxiation, and then, while still at least semi-conscious, were emasculated and disemboweled, had their entrails burned before them, and finally were beheaded and quartered after their death. More, who in his youth lived at or near the Charterhouse over a period of several years, is said to have seen, from his prison cell, Prior Houghton and his confreres embarking upon the three-mile route to their execution.[107] Three more monks from the Charterhouse were executed on 19 June at Tyburn.[108] Two days earlier, John Fisher had stood trial for treason at Westminster Hall and was condemned to death; on 22 June, the prelate (who had been named a cardinal by Rome during his imprisonment) was beheaded at Tower Hill and thus spared the full horror of a traitor's death. On 1 July, More was likewise condemned at Westminster Hall and beheaded at Tower Hill on 6 July.

In the meantime, Anne and Henry lived together in a marriage in which "storm followed sunshine, sunshine followed storm."[109] Reports from the foreign ambassadors and English observers vary regarding the relative degree of their happiness. On the one hand, there were numerous accounts of the couple being "merry."[110] But Chapuys, who, admittedly, was no friend to Anne, reported as early as 1533 (in a letter dated just days before the birth of Elizabeth) that Anne was jealous and was duly reprimanded by the king, who told her to turn a blind eye to his extramarital affairs.[111] In February 1535, Palamède Gontier, then a French envoy to England working on the negotiations that would allow Henry's daughter Elizabeth to marry one of Francis I's sons, wrote that Anne cryptically

---

[106] On this "reemergence of Catholic martyrdom," see Brad S. Gregory, *Salvation at Stake: Christian Martyrdom in Early Modern Europe* (Cambridge, MA: Harvard University Press, 1999), 255–59. These trials and executions are noted in Wriothesley, *Chronicle*, 1:26–29.

[107] On this point, see Gregory, *Salvation at Stake*, 257–58. More's reaction to the sight of the Carthusians *en route* to their executions is recorded by his son-in-law, William Roper, in *The Life of Sir Thomas More*, 242.

[108] In total, there were eighteen Carthusian monks executed between 1535 and 1537. See Chauncy, *Carthusian Fathers*, for more details.

[109] Ives, *Life and Death*, 196.

[110] See, for example, the English reports in LP 7.126, LP 7.682, and LP 7.888 (which date from 1534), as well as LP 9.555 and LP 9.571 (which date from 1535).

[111] See LP 6.1069 for this letter dated 3 September 1533. For other Imperial correspondence referring to Anne's diminishing influence and Henry's new mistress(es), see also LP 6.1054 ("Correspondence of Charles V, 1533"), LP 7.1193 (27 September 1534), and LP 7.1257 (13 October 1534).

urged him to motivate Francis I to help her "so that she may not be ruined and lost, for she sees herself very near that, and in more grief and trouble than before her marriage," adding that "she could not speak as fully as she wished, on account of her fears, and the eyes which were looking at her: her husband's and the lords' present."[112] Furthermore, Antoine de Castelnau, the Bishop of Tarbes, who arrived in England by the end of 1535 to serve as the new ambassador, wrote to his predecessor, Jean de Dinteville, the Bailly of Troyes, telling him to inform Francis I that Henry's "affection for his wife, which is less than it has been . . . diminishes day by day, because he has new *amours* [love interests]."[113] It is true that Chapuys might be biased in his reporting and eager to point out cracks in the marriage of which he and his master, Charles V, vigorously disapproved. But there is no particular reason to doubt the Bishop of Tarbes's observation, for, if anything, the French had been far more tolerant, not to say approving, of Anne and this marriage than the Spanish would ever be. And there is something to be said in favor of the veracity of the reports from foreign diplomats who might have been more at liberty to speak the truth—in dispatches that were not intended to be seen by the English king and that were, moreover, sometimes written in cipher—than the native Englishmen who had to remain at court and needed to show support to retain their favorable positions, not to mention their heads.

Whatever the status of the royal marriage, there were reports of a second pregnancy in early 1534.[114] A planned meeting between Henry and Francis I was postponed at this time due to Anne's delicate condition. However, there was no second child, leaving observers then and historians now to wonder exactly what happened. Anne may have had a miscarriage, a phantom pregnancy, or a stillbirth. According to Chapuys, Henry doubted that Anne had ever been pregnant.[115] Yet all seemed well in 1535, when Henry and Anne went on a Royal Progress through the west of England (returning via the south) to meet with citizens in various places within the realm.

In the meantime, Catherine and her daughter Mary remained separated despite Catherine's increasingly poor health. Although Catherine, who was moved to Kimbolton in 1534, had not been made to swear to the Oath of Supremacy, her living conditions were far below royal standards. Mary fared, in one sense, somewhat worse on that front, as she was sent to live in the same household as her half-sister, Elizabeth, whom she was expected to treat, on Anne's orders, as the royal figure she herself used to be. Catherine succumbed to her final illness on 7 January 1536. The news of her death was greeted with

---

[112] LP 8.174. I have modified the punctuation here for clarity.

[113] LP 9.566; see also Ives, *Life and Death*, 293.

[114] See LP 7.114, a letter from Chapuys to Charles V dated 28 January 1534; see also CSP, Spain, 5, pt. 1. (1534–1535), no. 7.

[115] Bernard, *Anne Boleyn*, 74–75. See LP 7.1193 for the letter from Chapuys to Charles V dated 27 September 1534, as well as CSP, Spain, 5, pt. 1 (1534–1535), no. 90.

relief and, apparently, joy on the part of Anne and Henry, the latter of whom, according to Chapuys, ostentatiously dressed in yellow and celebrated the news with feasting and dance, showing off his daughter Elizabeth to those who had gathered at court for Christmas.[116]

## Marital Troubles

But it is also at this time that Anne's situation became somewhat precarious, at least if we are to believe a series of letters written by Chapuys. The ambassador reported, somewhat incredulously, in a letter dated 29 January 1536, that Henry had already indicated "in great confidence, and as it were in confession" some unhappiness with regard to his marriage to Anne, who, Henry claimed, had "seduced [him] by witchcraft, and for this reason he considered [their marriage] null."[117] The term used by Chapuys, who, as a native Savoyard wrote his dispatches in French, was "sortilèges," but Henry doubtless used an English word (which remains unknown to us) when discussing this matter. Consequently, historians have debated upon the French word's precise significance (and Henry's intended meaning) in this context for years. According to Randle Cotgrave's authoritative early modern French–English dictionary (printed in 1611), the word "sortilège" can mean both "witchcraft" and "divination."[118] Eric Ives favors the latter as its principal meaning in English and believes that "the simple construction is that he was referring to the premarital predictions that union with Anne would produce sons."[119] Retha Warnicke, in contrast, prefers the stronger,

---

[116] See LP 10.141, a letter from Chapuys to Charles V dated 21 January 1536. But *Hall's Chronicle* (818) claims that Anne was the one who wore "yellow for mourning." In any event, yellow was not a color associated with bereavement, either in Spain or in England, and Chapuys's letter makes it very clear that Catherine's death was met with jubilation, reflected in Henry's flamboyant dress.

[117] LP 10.199, letter from Chapuys to Charles V. The date of this letter, 29 January, was actually the very day of Anne's miscarriage, but the dispatch was probably written before that event happened and certainly before Chapuys was aware of it; he writes of that matter only on 10 February. It is, consequently, impossible to know the precise timing of Henry's remarks but, given Chapuys's silence on the more important news of Anne's miscarriage, they probably were not spoken the very day of that event but, rather, predate it. Chapuys avows only that he heard about the king's displeasure with Anne just "this morning" (January 29), but the information was no doubt passed on to Chapuys's informant some time before it made its way to the ambassador. Hence there is strong evidence that Henry's expressed concerns about this marriage predate Anne's miscarriage.

[118] See Randle Cotgrave, *A Dictionarie of the French and English Tongues* (London: Adam Islip, 1611), reproduced in a facsimile edition, introduced by William S. Woods (Columbia: University of South Carolina Press, 1950).

[119] Ives, *Life and Death*, 298.

more literal meaning; she builds a case that Anne was actually thought to have dabbled in witchcraft.[120] A more figurative interpretation—that Henry merely avowed that Anne had "bewitched" or "cast a spell over him" through her feminine "charms"—is by far the more likely meaning of the word, if it is indeed a word that Henry himself used.[121] And, it should be emphasized, witchcraft was *not* one of the charges eventually brought against Anne later that year, making the more figurative meaning seem all the more plausible. Regardless, this story, thought to have been told to Chapuys by Gertrude Blount (the Marchioness of Exeter) and her husband, is a critical piece of evidence that not all was particularly well in this marriage, despite the fact that Anne was, in January, once again with child.

Indeed, as other letters by Chapuys attest, late January 1536 would prove to be a particularly challenging time for both Henry and Anne. On 24 January, Henry suffered a serious riding accident: running at the ring, his horse stumbled, throwing him to the ground and falling on top of him.[122] Chapuys claims, in another letter dated 29 January, that "everyone thought it a miracle he was not killed," though he goes on to say that the king "sustained no injury."[123] Other sources reported that the king had been unconscious for two hours.[124] These reports do not necessarily contradict each other, for it is certainly possible that the king was indeed unconscious and that, upon regaining conscious-

---

[120] Warnicke, *The Rise and Fall of Anne Boleyn: Family Politics at the Court of Henry VIII* (Cambridge: Cambridge University Press, 1989); see especially ch. 8 for these arguments.

[121] For more on this matter, see also Suzannah Lipscomb, *1536: The Year that Changed Henry VIII* (Oxford: Lion Hudson, 2009), 68–70, who believes that, despite Chapuys's report, the royal couple were "upbeat before long" and that there was no serious breach in their relationship at this point.

[122] See Wriothesley, *Chronicle*, 1:33. Whether this was during an actual tournament or merely a practice run at the lists is unclear; there is no reference to a tournament taking place at this time. In his poem, Carle states (vv. 319–320) that this was a hunting accident and makes no mention of the lists. Carle's reference to a hunt, however, may have been motivated by poetic concerns, as it allows him to develop a triple alliteration ("chasse," "cheut," and "cheual") in this passage.

[123] LP 10.200, letter from Chapuys to Granvelle, dated 29 January 1536. See also Wriothesley, *Chronicle*, 1:33, which claims that the king "had no hurt."

[124] See London, British Library, Additional 8715 (hereafter, Add. 8715), fols. 205r–206r, here 205r, a letter from the Bishop of Faenza to the Prothonotary Ambrogio, dated 12 February 1536, paraphrased in LP 10.294: "dicono che per spatio di due hore fu tenuto per morto" [they say that for the space of two hours he was taken for dead]. See also London, British Library, Additional 28588 (hereafter, Add. 28588), fols. 223r–225r (here 224v), a letter from Pedro Ortiz to Isabella of Portugal, dated 6 March 1536 (paraphrased in LP 10.427), which specifies that the king did not speak for more than two hours ("más de dos horas").

ness, he appeared not to be injured (i.e., he had no broken bones or the like). As Chapuys noted, the fall occurred on the eve of the Feast of the Conversion of St. Paul (who, famously, also was toppled from his horse); it was also the eve of the royal couple's third wedding anniversary. The Duke of Norfolk was charged with informing Anne of the accident. The news apparently gave Anne quite a shock, and five days later, that is, on 29 January—the very day that Catherine of Aragon was buried at Peterborough Abbey (now Peterborough Cathedral)—the queen miscarried. Reports indicated that the child was a boy, and that Anne had carried him for about fifteen weeks.[125] According to Chapuys, in a subsequent letter dated 25 February, the king, no doubt worrying that the pattern of still-births and miscarriages he had endured with Catherine was re-establishing itself with Anne, had said "that he saw clearly that God did not wish to give him male children."[126] Anne shot back that the miscarriage was due to her distress over the accident. But, Chapuys reports in the same letter, she added that "her heart broke when she saw that he loved others." Now, Henry was known to take a mistress during the inconvenient time he was expected to refrain from sexual intercourse with his pregnant wives. But perhaps this love was different. For, in another dispatch, Chapuys indicated that Henry was bestowing "great presents" on one of Anne's ladies named "Mistress Semel": that is, Jane Seymour, who would go on to become Henry's third wife in just over four months' time.[127]

Taken together, Henry's hint that he was "charmed" into marrying Anne (with its overt implication that he thought this marriage was not entered into freely and thus was not valid), along with his inchoate love affair with Jane Seymour—both of which seem to have preceded Anne's miscarriage—point to a growing dissatisfaction with his queen, which could only grow stronger in the wake of the loss of his son.[128] Henry's recent fall, which could have had

---

[125] Wriothesley, *Chronicle*, 1:33: "three days before Candlemas [that is, on 29 January], Queen Anne was brought abed and delivered of a man child, as it was said, afore her time, for she said that she had reckoned herself at that time but fifteen weeks gone with child." See also Chapuys's letter to Charles V, LP 10.282 (dated 10 February), which says that the miscarriage occurred on the day of Catherine's burial and that the fetus "seemed to be a male child which she had not borne three and one half months." Chapuys here also mentions that Anne blamed the miscarriage on the fright Norfolk gave her regarding the king's fall, but he discounts this reason.

[126] LP 10.351, letter from Chapuys to Charles V, dated 25 February 1536.

[127] LP 10.282, dated 10 February 1536. There is no way of knowing, of course, whether it was to Jane Seymour that Anne was referring in her reference to Henry's new loves, but this does seem to be a reasonable assumption.

[128] For a particularly persuasive argument, see Schofield, *Rise and Fall*, 155: "Henry's confessions . . . and his anxiety about divine disapproval, and his belief that his marriage to Anne was null, and even his intention to marry again, were not a set of knee jerk reactions to the tragic news of the miscarriage, as is commonly supposed." Schofield goes on to say (157) that "Once [Henry] got attached to another woman, he had to make her

catastrophic consequences, no doubt also contributed to a sense of urgency in the matter of producing a male heir to secure the throne. And Catherine's recent death meant that Henry could entertain the thought of moving on from Anne without any expectation of reconciling with his first wife. Indeed, according to Chapuys, Anne herself expressed her fear "that the King treat her like the late Queen," that is, that he would leave her for another woman, ironically one who turned out to occupy the same position of lady-in-waiting that she herself had held in Catherine's court.[129]

It certainly appears that Henry was considering a divorce—but nothing more than a divorce—from Anne by spring of 1536. Chapuys reports that Richard Sampson, a canon lawyer and dean of the Chapel Royal, conferred with Cromwell for a period of four days in April.[130] A canon lawyer, especially one such as Sampson who had participated in the ecclesiastical proceedings against Catherine, would be of great use in making the case for a divorce.[131] He would be of little or no use in outlining criminal charges against Anne, such as those that were to be formulated later. But at some point in April, something dramatic occurred that shifted the focus from a divorce to a full-blown charge of treason against Anne and five alleged accomplices. Exactly what that something was is a matter of debate: but Lancelot de Carle's poem identifies it as a chance argument between siblings that led one of Anne's own ladies to reveal that the queen had engaged in multiple acts of adultery.[132]

Putting Carle's poem aside for the moment, there is no hard and fast proof that anything more than a divorce was in the works as late as 24 April and possibly even through 28 April.[133] Much has been made of the fact that a commission of *Oyer* and *Terminer* ("to hear and determine") had been appointed by Thomas Audley, the Lord Chancellor, on 24 April for the counties of Middlesex (where London and the royal palaces of Westminster and Hampton Court are located) and Kent (the location of the royal palaces of Greenwich and Eltham), the pre-

---

his queen. By January or February 1536, therefore, the reign of Anne Boleyn was effectively over." Anne's downfall was thus due, in Schofield's view, primarily to his interest in Jane Seymour and was the work not of some court faction but, rather, of "Henry personally" (156). The timing of Henry's interest in Jane is uncertain, but it does seem to be the case that, as Anne herself complained to Henry at the time of her miscarriage about his extra-marital affairs, Henry was pursuing some other woman before that tragic event, leading to Anne's heartbreak.

[129] LP 10.282.

[130] LP 10.753, letter from Chapuys to Granvelle, dated 29 April 1536.

[131] See, on this point, Schofield, *Rise and Fall*, 190.

[132] Carle's take on this matter, along with other supporting evidence, will be discussed later in this chapter and in the Afterword.

[133] Schofield, *Rise and Fall*, 192: "Right up to the last days of April, all the well-versed diplomatic and court gossip focused on the king's divorce and Anne's 'dismissal,' but nothing more."

cise counties where the later indictments place the crimes of Anne and her lovers; yet, there is little agreement among historians regarding the significance of this fact. The popular historian Alison Weir, for example, believes that the establishment of these commissions in the particular counties of Kent and Middlesex "shows that this commission was specifically appointed to examine the evidence [of adultery] against [the queen]."[134] But Ives argues that these commissions were generally not formed to *investigate* charges of treason but, rather, "were begun against the accused only *after* arrest and interrogation."[135] Nevertheless, most historians agree that such commissions were fairly rare and reserved for very serious matters; indeed, there were only seventeen during the whole of Henry VIII's reign.[136] It is possible, of course, that the commission was set up early to expedite matters for a trial to come. One specific — and quite plausible — explanation is that, as John Schofield proposes, "Henry, Cromwell, and now Audley were preparing the ground in the more than likely event that Anne would not depart meekly" after a divorce.[137] If this were the case, the commission would not have any connection to the eventual treason trial but, rather, would be part of the divorce proceedings Henry appears to have been contemplating. In short, Schofield suggests, the establishment of this commission may be merely a red herring in terms of the timetable of Anne Boleyn's ultimate downfall, and it is good to be reminded that "no allegations of the queen's infidelity had yet been reported."[138]

## Accusations

What is indisputable, however, is that something larger than a divorce was afoot by Sunday, 29 April, when a planned royal trip to Calais, via Dover, was cancelled. Still, a celebratory May Day joust, featuring Henry Norris (the king's groom of the stool) leading the defenders and Anne's brother George, Lord Rochford, leading the challengers, was *not* cancelled, this despite the fact that, as tradition holds, one man had already been held for questioning.[139] That man was Mark Smeaton, a Flemish musician attached to the king's privy chamber,

---

[134] Alison Weir, *The Lady in the Tower: The Fall of Anne Boleyn* (2009; repr. New York: Ballantine Books, 2010), 91.

[135] Ives, *Life and Death*, 322.

[136] On this point, see Ives, *Life and Death*, 322, and Bernard, "The Fall of Anne Boleyn: A Rejoinder," *The English Historical Review* 107.424 (1992): 665–74, here 670.

[137] See Schofield, *Rise and Fall*, 188.

[138] Schofield, *Rise and Fall*, 188.

[139] Wriothesley (*Chronicle*, 1:35) attests: "on May Day, 1536, being Monday, was a great jousting at Greenwich, where was challengers my Lord of Rochford and others, and defenders Mr. Norris and others."

who eventually confessed to having had illicit intercourse with the queen.[140] The day following Smeaton's interrogation, as soon as the joust had ended, Norris was personally questioned by the king, who presumably was informed of Mark's confession and, according to some observers, left the festivities suddenly, and "of this sudden departing many men mused."[141] Norris was certainly the most intimate and trusted of the courtiers who attended to the king's very body: his position required him to assist the king at his stool (or toilet) and thus put him into close contact with the king's person at a moment of vulnerability.[142] This intimacy and trust could explain why, as Carle's poem will suggest, Henry would have wanted to question Norris personally and offer him the possibility of a pardon in exchange for the truth.[143] But Norris did not confess and consequently was arrested.[144]

On 2 May, a full-fledged investigation was underway, which saw Anne herself questioned at Greenwich by key members of the king's Privy Council — namely, Cromwell, Norfolk, Audley, and William Kingston (Constable of the

---

[140] The timing of Smeaton's questioning (i.e., before the May Day jousts) is less than certain, though traditional. The main source that alludes to Mark's arrest before 1 May is the very unreliable *Chronicle of King Henry VIII*, 60; see also the document known as "Constantyne's Memorial," printed as "Transcript of an Original Manuscript, containing a Memorial from George Constantyne to Thomas Lord Cromwell," ed. Thomas Amyot, in *Archaeologia, or Miscellaneous Tracts Relating to Antiquity* 23 (1830): 50–78, here 64. Constantyne was a servant of Henry Norris and presumably an eyewitness to these events. However, the authenticity of this manuscript, which purports to be from the library of John Payne Collier, has been questioned by MacCulloch, among others. See *Thomas Cromwell*, 660n44 on this matter: "I am convinced that at all points one must subtract the evidence supposedly provided by George Constantine, since his so-called "memorial" of 1539 is one of the cleverest forgeries of that Victorian master-forger, John Payne Collier." Nevertheless, Carle will also imply that Mark was questioned before the joust (v. 479), and it certainly is plausible that the investigators would begin their questioning with Mark, a vulnerable target. And if we are to believe Carle's poem, certainly the investigators would follow up on the suggestion to seek out Mark for the whole story of Anne's behavior.

[141] *Hall's Chronicle*, 819. Chapuys likewise alludes to the fact that the king had left Greenwich suddenly. See CSP, Spain, 5 pt. 2 (1536–1538), no. 48 and LP 10.782 (letter from Chapuys to Charles V dated 2 May 1536).

[142] For a biography, see the entry "Henry Norris," written by Ives, in the ODNB.

[143] For another testimony regarding Henry's questioning of Norris, see Constantyne's *Memorial*, 64: "And after jousting the King road suddenly to Westminster, and all the way as I heard say, had Mr. Norris in examination and promised him his pardon in case he would utter the truth."

[144] Constantyne goes on to state that although Norris did not initially confess to Henry, he did do so later but ultimately withdrew it, saying that he was "deceived" into confessing by "the Earl of Hampton that now is," that is, William Fitzwilliam, who was created Earl of Southampton in 1537. See Constantyne's *Memorial*, 64.

Tower)—and subsequently brought to the Tower of London. Virtually simultaneously, Anne's brother, George Boleyn, was likewise questioned by the council and imprisoned. Two additional gentlemen, William Brereton and Sir Francis Weston, were taken to the Tower by 5 May.[145] Brereton was a senior courtier close to fifty years of age and married to Elizabeth Somerset, the sister of the Earl of Worcester.[146] Although he was not among those closest to Anne, serving most recently as steward of the marcher lordships far from the court, he had once served in Anne's household. Weston, in contrast, was young—only twenty-five —popular, and athletic, and had been dubbed Knight of the Bath at Anne's coronation.[147] Another pair of courtiers—Thomas Wyatt (the poet) and Richard Page (a member of the king's privy chamber since 1516)—were questioned and imprisoned but never tried (being released not long after the others' execution).[148] A third man, Francis Bryan (a longtime courtier and diplomat as well as a kinsman of Anne), was questioned but not imprisoned.[149]

In total, eight men had fallen under suspicion along with Anne, the vast majority of them interrogated (and in some cases imprisoned) subsequent to her own arrest. And indeed, the timing here is probably not coincidental, for Anne herself may have played a role in the arrests of some of these men, as she related stories about them to her jailor, William Kingston, who duly informed Cromwell of her babblings. Kingston's letters were badly damaged in a fire at the private Cottonian library in the eighteenth century, but not before their contents were described by John Strype in his *Ecclesiastical Memorials*, compiled in 1721.[150] According to these letters, Anne, on the first day of her imprisonment,

---

[145] Constantyne's *Memorial*, 65, indicates that Brereton was arrested "upon Thursday afore May Day . . . afore ij of the clock." If this is true, Brereton would have been the first to be arrested, on 27 April. However, it seems likely that Constantyne meant to write the Thursday *after* May Day (and the context makes it clear that the story had already broken by this time), which would have been 4 May, the day historians do in fact believe to be that of Brereton's arrest. Indeed, given the difficult art of reading ancient handwriting, it is perfectly possible that Constantyne perhaps *did* write "after," but was misread subsequently by his editor, Amyot, assuming, once again, that this text is not a forgery created by Collier. But the misreading of "afore" for "after" might lend some credence to the case that Amyot's text was based on an original sixteenth-century manuscript (unless, of course, the misreading is part of Collier's strategy to pass the work off as a genuine Tudor text).

[146] See the entry "William Brereton," in the ODNB, by Ives.

[147] See the entry "Sir Francis Weston," in the ODNB, by Jonathan Hughes.

[148] For a short biography, see "Sir Richard Page," in the ODNB, by Catharine Davies.

[149] For a short biography, see "Sir Francis Bryan," in the ODNB, by Susan Brigden.

[150] See John Strype, ed., *Ecclesiastical Memorials, Relating Chiefly to Religion, and the Reformation of It . . . Under King Henry VIII*, vol. 1, pt. 1 (Oxford: Clarendon Press, 1822). The letters have subsequently been transcribed, with lacunae, by Henry Ellis in

after enquiring with regard to the whereabouts of her brother, intriguingly said: "O! Norris, hast thou accused me? Thou art in the Tower with me. And thou and I shall die together. And Mark, thou art here too."[151] The next day, one of her attendants in the Tower, Mrs. Cosins, asked her why, on the previous Saturday, Norris had approached the queen's almoner and swore that Anne "was a good woman."[152] In response, Anne revealed that she herself had asked Norris to do so. Pressed further by Mrs. Cosins as to why she had made such a request, Anne explained: "For I asked him, why he did not go through with his marriage," presumably to his betrothed, Mary (or "Madge") Shelton; to this, Norris answered that "he would tarry a time."[153] Crucially, Anne had countered with this well-known, incriminating accusation: "You look for dead men's shoes. For if aught should come to the King, but good, you would look to have me."[154] Anne added that a presumably horrified Norris had said "if he should have any such thought, he would his head were off," to which Anne responded that "she could undo him if she would."[155]

But this was not all that Anne said that day. Kingston reports that Anne went on to reveal that she feared Weston more, "for Weston had said unto her, that Norris came more unto her chamber for her than he did for Ma[d]ge."[156] Moreover, on another occasion, Anne had reproved Weston because "he did love her kinswoman," Mrs. Shelton, and not his own wife.[157] Weston's answer to this, which Anne conveyed to Kingston, was that "he loved one in her house better than them both."[158] When asked by Anne who that was, Weston replied "it is yourself."[159] By virtue of these voluntary conversations with Kingston and others in the Tower, Anne had certainly supplied enough reason to place Norris and Weston under suspicion. And, even if Anne had not reminded Kingston of her words, they could have been remembered — and perhaps reported — by others at the court who were likely to have overheard them.

---

his *Original Letters Illustrative of English History*, vol. 2 (London: Harding, Triphook, and Lepard, 1824), 52–60. See also William Cobbett, *Complete Collection of State Trials . . . for High Treason and Other Crimes and Misdemeanors from the Earliest Period to the Present Time*, vol. 1, ed. Thomas Bayly Howell (London: Hansard, 1809), which reprints Strype's texts, 428–34.

[151] Strype, *Ecclesiastical Memorials*, 432.

[152] Strype, *Ecclesiastical Memorials*, 432. The name "Cosins" has often been rendered as "Coffin" by subsequent historians.

[153] Strype, *Ecclesiastical Memorials*, 433.

[154] Strype, *Ecclesiastical Memorials*, 433.

[155] Strype, *Ecclesiastical Memorials*, 433.

[156] Strype, *Ecclesiastical Memorials*, 433.

[157] Strype, *Ecclesiastical Memorials*, 433. Strype renders her name as "Skelton."

[158] Strype, *Ecclesiastical Memorials*, 433.

[159] Strype, *Ecclesiastical Memorials*, 433.

Nor were these the only public confrontations that were incriminating, for Anne herself (as reported by Kingston) admitted to chastising Mark Smeaton the Saturday before the May Day jousts, that is, April 29. In Anne's words, as recorded in Kingston's letter, she

> "found him standing in the round window in my chamber of presence. And I asked him why he was so sad. And he answered and said it was no matter." And then she said, "You may not look to have me speak to you, as I would do to a nobleman, because ye be an inferior person." "No, no," said he, "a look sufficeth me: and thus fare you well."[160]

The implication here is that Mark was somewhat infatuated with Anne. But, as Anne so brutally reminded Mark, he was no gentleman and could not expect her to be interested in him. Perhaps this conversation ignited Mark's jealousy of better-placed suitors for Anne's attention and sparked a desire to see her suffer.[161] Perhaps this was why he alone confessed to having had illicit sexual intercourse with Anne, specifically on three occasions, thereby implicating the queen.[162] Perhaps, as a foreigner who possibly was not conversant with the recently passed treason laws, he did not understand that such a confession would also put his own life in peril. Perhaps he was promised a pardon if he could supply evidence to Anne's adulteries. Perhaps he was, as some have speculated, tortured into making this confession, though this would have been an illegal use of force.[163] Or, alternatively, as Bernard reminds us, quite apart from Mark's possible "desperate

---

[160] Strype, *Ecclesiastical Memorials*, 436. I have added punctuation to this dialogue for the sake of clarity.

[161] This is what is stated in Add. 8715, fols. 252r–254v, the letter of the Bishop of Faenza to Monsignor Ambrogio, dated 24 May (paraphrased in LP 10.956): "dicono questo essersi scoperto per alcune parole dette dall'organista per gelosia dell'altri" [they say that this was discovered through some words spoken by the organist out of jealousy for the others], 252v.

[162] Strype gives this interpretation to Mark's remarks to the Queen after she rebuffed him: "This shows him to be some haughty person; and thought the Queen gave him not respect enough. And so might take this opportunity to humble her; and revenge himself by this means on her; not thinking it would cost him his own life" (*Ecclesiastical Memorials*, 436). Ellis (2:61) also quotes from Edward Baynton's letter to the Treasurer that "no man will confess anything against her, but only Mark of any actual thing." This letter is also summarized in LP 10.799.

[163] Constantyne's *Memorial* (64) asserts: "the truth is he confessed it, but yet the saying was that he was first grievously racked, which I could never know of a truth." Likewise, the less-than-reliable Spanish *Chronicle of King Henry VIII* describes how Mark was tortured by Cromwell using a rope and cudgel (61). But see Margery Stone Schauer and Frederick Schauer, "Law as the Engine of State: The Trial of Anne Boleyn," *William & Mary Law Review* 22 (1980): 49–84, here 79, who comment: "Torture for the purpose of extracting evidence was quite common in the fifteenth century and again in the latter

wishful thinking" that he was the queen's lover, perhaps "Mark and Anne had indeed had a brief affair" that was brought to a close, which "provoked Mark to confess."[164] Mark's motivation in confessing (and accusing the queen) is lost to time and cannot be recuperated. What is known is that Mark was the first to be questioned, and his responses were doubtless enough to continue the investigation that led to the interrogation, arrests, and indictments of the queen, her brother, and three gentlemen of the king's privy chamber in a matter of days.[165]

But what brought all this speculation about adultery to the attention of the authorities in the first place? In a letter dated 14 May and addressed to Stephen Gardiner, Bishop of Winchester, and Sir John Wallop, both serving as envoys to France at this time, Cromwell informs the diplomats thus: The queen's

> abomination both in incontinent living and other offences . . . was so rank and common that the ladies of her privy chamber could not contain it within their breasts. . . . It came to the ears of some of his grace's council, that with their duty to his majesty they could not conceal it from him.[166]

An examination followed, and "the matter appeared so evident that besides that crime [of adultery] . . . there broke out a certain conspiracy of the King's death." Cromwell himself admits that this is vague, saying he "will write no particulars, the things be too abominable," and even after Gardiner pressed him for more details, he chose not to elaborate and reveal the names of the accusers.[167]

---

part of the sixteenth century but was not so prevalent when Anne Boleyn was tried. . . . Smeaton's torture clearly would have violated the law in force at the time."

[164] Bernard, *Anne Boleyn*, 163.

[165] Schofield emphasizes that "it was Smeaton's confession that led to the arrest of the queen and her other lovers" (*Rise and Fall*, 165). He goes on to say that, according to reports circulating at the time, "Smeaton confessed embarrassingly freely because he was jealous of the queen's other lovers. . . . Within hours of [the exchange with Anne in which she reminded him of his low stature], Smeaton was under arrest, and once in the hands of an interrogator as skilled as Cromwell, no racks or knotted ropes would have been needed to get this jealous young lover to open his heart and blurt out a few secrets" (*Rise and Fall*, 195).

[166] London, British Library, Additional 25114 (hereafter Add. 25114), "Original letters and state papers relating chiefly to the embassies of Stephen Gardiner, Bishop of Winchester, to the courts of Francis I and Charles V: 1527–1545," fols. 160r–161r, summarized in LP 10.873; see also Schofield, *Rise and Fall*, 201. For Cromwell's letters, see also Roger Bigelow Merriman, ed., *Life and Letters of Thomas Cromwell*, 2 vols. (1968; repr. Oxford: Clarendon, 2000); for this letter, see 2:12–13.

[167] Add. 25114, fols. 175r–176v; summarized in LP 11.29 (letter from Cromwell to Gardiner dated 5 July 1536). Cromwell states here that the confessions "were so abominable that a great part of them were never given in evidence, but clearly kept secret" (fol. 176v).

Other accounts do, however, name names. The first is found in the note-book of John Spelman, one of the judges at Anne's trial, who writes, in what can best be described as a mangled mixture of French and English, that the matter was disclosed by Lady Wingfield, a former servant to the queen, and this she did upon suddenly being taken ill and shortly before her death.[168] Now, this Lady Wingfield, assuming she has been identified correctly as Bridget Wiltshire, was indeed known to Queen Anne, who addressed a letter to her that still survives.[169] The letter is signed "Anne Rocheford," thus dating the correspondence to the period between her father's and her own elevation to the peerage. But no one knows precisely when Lady Wingfield died, and her death could have been over a year before the trial began, making her deathbed confession an unlikely immediate catalyst of the investigation, unless what set the wheels in motion was someone's later report of this lady's confession, remembered well after her death.[170] Such hearsay evidence could, of course, not be verified, though it would have been admissible in court at that time. As the early historian Gilbert Burnet writes regarding the person who presumably revealed what Lady Wingfield swore,

who this person was we know not, nor in what temper of mind the Lady Wingfield might be, when she swore it. The safest sort of forgery, to one whose conscience can swallow it, is to lay a thing on a dead person's name.[171]

---

[168] *The Reports of Sir John Spelman*, ed. J. H. Baker (London: Selden Society, 1977), 1:71: "nota que cest matter fuit disclose per vn feme appelle le Dame Wingfeilde que fuit seruaunt a le dit Roine et de mesme les qualites et sodenment le dit Wingfeild devient infirme et per petit temps deuaunt son mort el monstra cest matter a vn de ces (etc.) [*sic*]" [Note that this matter was disclosed by a woman called Lady Wingfield, who had been a servant to the said queen and of the same qualities; and suddenly the said Wingfield became sick and a short time before her death showed this matter to one of her (etc.)]. At this point Spelman's tale breaks off, but Ives contends that "the final 'etc.' is not a sign that something is missing, but a lawyer's abbreviation for self-evident matter, in this case, 'who reported the story.'" See Ives, *Life and Death*, 330.

[169] See LP 5.12, "Lady Anne Rochford to Lady Wingfield." For the identification of Lady Wingfield as Bridget Wiltshire, see Ives, *Life and Death*, 330. The original man-uscript is London, British Library, Cotton Vespasian, F XIII, fol. 199 (formerly marked as 109). A digital copy is available via State Papers Online. For another transcription, see Mary Anne Everett Wood, ed., *Letters of Royal and Illustrious Ladies of Great Britain*, 3 vols. (London: Colburn, 1846), 2:74–75.

[170] It has been suggested that Lady Wingfield's confession was belatedly brought to Cromwell's attention by Charles Brandon, Henry's close friend, as the lady's family was among Brandon's clients. See, on this point, Leanda de Lisle, *Tudor: The Family Story* (London: Chatto & Windus, 2013), 204–5, as well as Ives, *Life and Death*, 331.

[171] Gilbert Burnet, *The History of the Reformation of the Church of England*, 2nd ed. (London: Chiswell, 1681), pt. 1, bk. 3, 197. Burnet's work is excerpted in Cobbett, *State Trials*, 1:411–23, here 413.

Another possible informant is Jane Rochford, George Boleyn's wife. But she is not mentioned by name in any source contemporary to the trial, at least none that survives.[172] Jane may be, as Ives seems to think, the mysterious person mentioned in foreign accounts of these events, who acted "more out of envy and jealousy than out of love towards the King, [and] did betray this accursed secret, and together with it, the names of those who had joined in the evil doings of the unchaste Queen."[173] But an analysis of the original text, rather than its translation, makes this unlikely, as this reading would be grammatically impossible: for, the original Portuguese text, as well as its French translation and the related Italian version, all use a masculine pronoun in rendering the expression "the person who."[174] Jane is, however, mentioned by name in George Wyatt's somewhat later account of the matter, where she is referred to as George Boleyn's "wicked wife, accuser of her own husband."[175] Wyatt's allegation was subsequently accepted by Burnet, who referred to her as George's "spiteful" and "jealous" wife who "carried many stories to the King, or some about him."[176] Burnet's history was widely accepted and "is now our only authority for [Jane's] involvement in Anne's

---

[172] Ives reviews the evidence for and against Jane's involvement (*Life and Death*, 331–32), mentioning "the lost journal of Antony Antony" that "probably included words to the effect that 'the wife of Lord Rochford was a particular instrument in the death of Queen Anne.'" For more on Jane Rochford, consult Julia Fox, *Jane Boleyn: The Infamous Lady Rochford* (2007; repr. London: Phoenix, 2008).

[173] The quotation cited here is from an account printed as *Lettre d'un gentilhomme portugais . . . sur l'exécution d'Anne Boleyn*, edited with French translation from the Portuguese by Francisque Michel and with English translation by Viscount Strangford (Paris: Silvestre, 1832), 9. This same English translation of the Portuguese letter was reprinted in Samuel Bentley, *Excerpta historica or, Illustrations of English History* (London: Bentley, 1831), 260–65. The original Portuguese manuscript is housed in the Conventual Library of Alcobaça (MS 475). In his evaluation of this matter, Ives (*Life and Death*, 331 and 418n67) refers to an anonymous Italian account, similar to but not identical with the Portuguese account, reprinted in A. Hamy, *Entrevue de François Premier avec Henry VIII* (Paris: Gougy, 1898), ccccxxxi–ccccxxxvi, but this version has several errors. For a more reliable and contemporary publication of that account, see *Il Successo in la morte della regina de Inghilterra*, of which there are two printed versions: one, produced in Bologna by Giovam Battista di Phaelli, the other printed without place of publication. Both are dated 10 June 1536 and are printed without pagination.

[174] The Portuguese text uses the pronoun "daquelle" and the French text indicates "celui" (both p. 9). The Italian text likewise uses the masculine form "quello" (n.p.). Had they wished to indicate a female agent, the authors of these texts would have been required to use the feminine form of these pronouns.

[175] Wyatt, "Extracts," 446. See also Susan Bordo, *The Creation of Anne Boleyn: A New Look at England's Most Notorious Queen* (2013; repr. Boston: Mariner/Houghton Mifflin Harcourt, 2014), 100–101.

[176] Burnet, *History of the Reformation*, pt. 1, bk. 3, 197.

downfall."[177] Why Jane would falsely accuse her husband and sister-in-law of such an act might not be entirely clear, but Burnet suggests that it was because Jane was jealous of Anne's closeness to George.

Yet another hypothesis regarding Jane's presumed denouncement of her husband has emerged from the pen of Retha Warnicke: namely, that Jane wished to be rid of George because he was homosexual and involved with Mark Smeaton. Warnicke's claim is based on the fact that George owned a French satirical poem on marriage, which he allegedly passed on to Smeaton, thus suggesting that both men abhorred the state of matrimony (and were intimately connected).[178] Boleyn's ownership of the book is certain;[179] Mark's ownership has been surmised from the existence of an inscription on the bottom of the last folio in the book that appears to read "à moy, Marc S," and thus is less surely connected to Smeaton. Moreover, it is a bit misleading to refer to the physical book as evidence of disdain for the state of matrimony on the part of Boleyn and/or Smeaton: for the book in question, a quite lovely and expensive fifteenth-century manuscript, contains both a French translation of a Latin misogynous poem ("Les Lamentations de Matheolus") as well as its palinode (that is, a retraction), called "Le Livre de Leesce."[180] This second work constitutes a long response to the first poem in which the author, Jean Le Fèvre, professes regret for ever having translated the poem by Matheolus, given its misogynistic content, and wishes to set the record straight.[181] Thus, while the first poem is devoted to a satire against women and marriage, the second poem defends them both. There is no reason to

---

[177] See Muriel St. Clare Byrne, ed., *The Lisle Letters*, 6 vols. (Chicago: University of Chicago Press, 1981), 3:380.

[178] This claim can be found in Warnicke, *The Rise and Fall of Anne Boleyn*, 219. The book once owned by Boleyn, whose *ex libris* is still legible, is London, British Library, Royal 20.B.XXI. For more on this exemplar, consult Carley, *Books*, 130 and 133.

[179] The folio immediately preceding the text bears this signature: "Thys boke ys myne. George Boleyn. 1526."

[180] For a modern edition of the text, including the original Latin version, consult Anton-Gérard van Hamel, ed., *"Les lamentations" de Matheolus et le "Livre de leesce" de Jehan Le Fèvre de Ressons*, 2 vols. (Paris: E. Bouillon, 1892–1905).

[181] For an analysis of the two poems, including a discussion regarding the author's success or failure in rehabilitating women in his palinode, consult Renate Blumenfeld-Kosinski, "Jean Le Fèvre's *Livre de leesce*: Praise or Blame of Women?" *Speculum* 69 (1994): 705–25. Ultimately, the poem of Matheolus became the point of departure for Christine de Pizan's *Cité des Dames* [The Book of the City of Ladies], a contribution to the long-running literary and cultural quarrel known as the *"querelle des femmes,"* which debated the nature and status of women. For this text, which begins with a depiction of the author's persona reading the *Lamentations*, consult Christine de Pizan, *The Boke of the Cyte of Ladyes*, trans. Brian Anslay, ed. Hope Johnson (Tempe, AZ: ACMRS, 2014); see especially 4–5 for the role played by Matheolus's text here. For more on the quarrel on women in its medieval context, see Blumenfeld-Kosinski, 706–8.

home in on the first part, drawing from it conclusions regarding Boleyn's sexu-
ality, while ignoring the second part, especially since it is the defense of women
and marriage, after all, that constitutes the last word in this debate, at least as it
is recorded in the book Boleyn owned.[182]

Another source, though not contemporaneous but, rather, dating from the
reign of Elizabeth, maintains that it was Stephen Gardiner, Bishop of Win-
chester and ambassador to France, who promulgated gossip in the French court
against Anne that reached Cromwell's ears and was eventually passed on to the
king. In a document written specifically for Queen Elizabeth, Alexander Ales
(or Alesius) revealed his conviction that Anne's demise was political in nature
and due to her evangelical leanings.[183] According to Ales, Anne had

> persuaded the King to send an embassy into Germany to the Princes who
> embraced the Gospel. . . . On account of this embassy all the Bishops
> who were opposed to the purer doctrine of the Gospel and adhered to the
> Roman Pontiff, entered into a conspiracy against your mother.[184]

These accusations were in turn presented by Cromwell and his associate, the
courtier Thomas Wriothesley, to the king, who was "furious, but, dissembling his
wrath, he summoned Cromwell, Wriothesley, and certain others who . . . hated
the Queen. . . . To them he entrusted the investigation of the whole business."[185]
Those charged with the investigation bribed and cajoled Anne's ladies to provide
circumstantial evidence of her misbehavior, which they then presented to the
king:

> they had seen the Queen dancing with the gentlemen of the King's cham-
> ber, . . . they can produce witnesses who will vouch to the Queen having

---

[182] The book owned by Boleyn eventually made its way to Thomas Wyatt, who
appears to have written not only his name but also several proverbs and mottoes in it.
This marginalia is extensively analyzed by Thomson in *Sir Thomas Wyatt and His Back-
ground*, 39–41, who convincingly argues that one proverb there written in French—"qui
asne est et cerf cuyde bien estre / a sallir une fosse on le puyt bien cognoistre" [who
believes himself to be a hind but is an ass, will become known upon leaping over a ditch]
—is to be understood as a reference to Anne Boleyn thanks to a homophonic play on
the sound "asne" (ass) and "Anne"; but see Carley, *Books*, 130, who believes the jibe was
"directed at the social upstart Smeaton."

[183] See the synopsis of Alexander Ales's "Letter to Queen Elizabeth," in *Calendar
of State Papers: Foreign Series: Elizabeth, 1558–1559*, ed. Joseph Stevenson (London: Her
Majesty's Stationery Office, 1863), 1:1303, 524–34, with online access at https://www.
british-history.ac.uk/cal-state-papers/foreign/vol1.

[184] Ales, CSP, FS, Eliz., 1:1303, 525.

[185] Ales, CSP, FS, Eliz., 1:1303, 526.

kissed her own brother, and . . . they have in their possession letters in which she informs him that she is pregnant.[186]

The most striking evidence that supports Cromwell's vague remark that ladies in the queen's service were instrumental in bringing forth the accusations against her can be found in two letters from John Husee, who corresponded regularly with Lord and Lady Lisle, to whose household he was attached. In a letter dated 24 May 1536 and sent to Lady Lisle, Husee declared that "the first accusers" against the queen were "the Lady Worcester, and Nan Cobham, with one maid more. But the Lady Worcester was the first ground."[187] The following day (that is, 25 May), Husee reiterated this information to Lady Lisle, writing: "Touching the Queen's accusers, my Lady Worcester beareth name to be the principal."[188] It has been difficult to identify "Nan Cobham," but there was a "Mrs. Cobham" who served as one of the "Queen's gentlewomen" in 1534.[189] What is more intriguing is the identification of Lady Worcester as Elizabeth Somerset, who was the sister of Sir Anthony Browne (a member of Henry's privy chamber), the half-sister of Sir William Fitzwilliam (a Privy Council member, later named Earl of Southampton), and the wife of Henry Somerset, the Earl of Worcester (whose sister, also named Elizabeth, was married to William Brereton, one of the accused).[190] Both Browne and Fitzwilliam were among Henry's long-time and most trusted friends. Lady Worcester was herself evidently very close to Anne, from whom she had borrowed £100 (without her husband's knowledge); roughly a year after the queen's execution, she wrote to Cromwell about this matter and the loan was forgiven.[191] Anne also mentions Lady Worcester in her ramblings to Kingston, saying that she much lamented the fact that Lady Worcester's child "did not stir in her body"; when asked why this was, Anne responded that "it was for the sorrow she took for me."[192]

Furthermore, the involvement of Anthony Browne and his sister also figures in a little-known novella, a work that is literary in form and, consequently, has

---

[186] Ales, CSP, FS, Eliz., 1:1303, 526.

[187] Byrne, *Lisle Letters*, no. 703a (3:377–78, here 378).

[188] Byrne, *Lisle Letters*, no. 847 (4:50, also quoted at 3:378).

[189] See Byrne, *Lisle Letters*, 3:381.

[190] For brief but reliable biographies of both Fitzwilliam and Browne, consult the entries in the ODNB, written by William B. Robison. For more on Henry Somerset, Earl of Worcester, and his family, consult W. R. B. Robinson, "Patronage and Hospitality in Early Tudor Wales: The Role of Henry, Earl of Worcester, 1526–49," *Bulletin of the Institute of Historical Research* 51 (1978): 20–36.

[191] See LP 13.1.450. Lady Worcester's correspondence with Cromwell has given rise to speculation that Cromwell was, in fact, the father of the child she was carrying in the spring of 1536. For more on this theory, which was espoused by T. B. Pugh, see Bernard, *Anne Boleyn*, 155.

[192] Strype, *Ecclesiastical Memorials*, 432.

been largely ignored by historians. Its author was Matteo Bandello, an Italian bishop and short-story writer.[193] Bandello's stories were written over a period of years, but the particular novella that relates this incident ends with a reference to Henry as still being alive and married to Katherine Parr, thus dating the composition of this text to the period between 1543 and 1547. In this story, the king is said to be having an affair with the unnamed sister of "Antonio Bruno" [Anthony Browne], who is identified as the king's physician. Angered by this lady's apparent flirtatious behavior, the king orders that Browne evict his sister from the court. In the course of doing so, Browne learns from his sister that the queen has been engaged in numerous affairs of her own, and this information Browne passes on to Henry, who initiates an investigation into the queen's misbehavior. Bandello's story was itself reprised a few years later by the Frenchman François de Belleforest in his adaptation of the Italian's *novelle*, in which he also refers to "Antoine Brun" [Anthony Browne] and his sister.[194] What is more, part of Belleforest's adaptation is transcribed word for word (with some additional interpolations) in a manuscript dating from the reign of Elizabeth I, Lansdowne 105, which has heretofore been treated by historians as a separate historical document without literary pretensions.[195] Clearly, however, it is merely a handwritten copy of part of Belleforest's printed text that traces its origin to Bandello's short story.

These later French and Italian accounts, with their emphasis on the encounter between brother and sister that eventually leads to the discovery of Anne's adulteries, line up quite nicely with the story as presented by Carle, though, of course, there are some differences in detail.[196] Moreover, they also align well both with Husee's letter and Cromwell's own account to Gardiner: for all these stories promote the notion that it was a woman of the court who first revealed the queen's improprieties (though Husee and Cromwell do not mention the role of

---

[193] For a modern edition of this text, see Matteo Bandello, "De le molte mogli del re d'Inghilterra e morte de le due di quelle, con altri modi e varii accidenti intervenuti" (novella 62), in *La terza parte de le novelle*, ed. Delmo Maestri (Turin: Edizioni dell'Orso, 1995), 287–93, here 289–90. For an English translation, see "Of the Many Wives of the King of England and the Death of Two of Them," in *The Novels of Matteo Bandello . . . now first done into English . . . by John Payne*, 6 vols. (London: Villon Society, 1890), 6:103–13, here, 6:107–9.

[194] For this text, see François de Belleforest, "Mort miserable de deux amans, ausquels le Roy d'Angleterre Henry defendit de se marier ensemble, & autres choses sur la vie dudict Roy" (story 36), in *Le second tome des Histoires Tragiques, extraites de l'italien de Bandel* (Paris: Robert le Mangnier, 1566), 433–62. For the passage regarding Anthony Browne, see 457. As is the case with Bandello, Belleforest's story has not been analyzed by historians.

[195] This is "A Scandalous Account of K. Henry 8th," in London, British Library, Lansdowne 105, fols. 18r–19v, found among the Burghley Papers. It is reproduced in Pocock, *Records of the Reformation*, 2:573–75.

[196] Carle's poem will be analyzed in the Afterword.

this lady's brother).[197] Thanks to the alignment between the Lansdowne manuscript, Husee, Cromwell, and Carle, Bernard has put forth the theory that the Countess of Worcester was the unnamed sister of the advisor to the king who, in Carle's account, eventually broke the news to Henry. Bernard, quite reasonably, follows the Lansdowne manuscript and identifies the brother in question as Anthony Browne, who was not on the Privy Council, rather than Fitzwilliam, who was; but it is of little consequence to which brother the Countess of Worcester confided, since Carle's designation of a man who was among the closest of the king's counselors could no doubt apply to either of them, even if Browne did not occupy this position formally.[198] Indeed, it is also known that Fitzwilliam, Lady Worcester's half-brother, was heavily involved in the investigation of those accused with Anne.[199] Furthermore, years later, when Henry's fifth wife, Catherine Howard, a cousin of Anne Boleyn, was also to be accused of adultery, both Browne and Fitzwilliam were chosen by the king to deal with the matter.[200]

It should be mentioned, however, that the very same evidence has been seen to suggest (by Muriel St. Clare Byrne)—indeed, to "confirm"—a conspiracy at whose center was Fitzwilliam acting in concert with Cromwell.[201] Byrne also declares that this "family involvement of Fitzwilliam and Lady Worcester may

---

[197] The claim that it was one of Anne's ladies who revealed the queen's improprieties was also put forth in a 1548 history of England written by Paolo Giovio. The woman, referred to simply by the Latin word for maid, "ancilla," and not by name, was said to have discovered Anne's indiscretions and revealed them to the authorities so as to avoid the punishment that Anne threatened to inflict on her. This is found in Paolo Giovio, *Descriptio Britanniae, Scotiae, Hyberniae et Orchadum* (Venice: Michele Tramezzino, 1548), 23v. Giovio's story is also cited in Joachim Le Grand, *Histoire du divorce de Henry VIII, Roy d'Angleterre, et de Catherine d'Aragon*, 3 vols. (Paris: Martin and Boudot, 1688), 2:163–64.

[198] See Bernard, *Anne Boleyn*, 154. Alison Weir identifies Browne as a member of the Privy Chamber and Fitzwilliam as a member of the Privy Council and, for this reason, believes that "it is more likely that [Lady Worcester] confided in Fitzwilliam." See Weir, *The Lady in the Tower*, 78. Starkey has maintained that there is little difference between courtiers and councilors in Henry's reign and that often these roles are played by the same person. See his "Introduction: Court History in Perspective," in David Starkey, et al., *The English Court: From the Wars of the Roses to the Civil War* (London: Longman, 1987), 1–24, here 13. The reference to Anthony Browne in the French and Italian accounts does appear, however, to make it more likely that it is indeed to him that Lady Worcester turned.

[199] Byrne, *Lisle Letters*, 3:379–80 and 383; Husee, in a letter to Lord Lisle, paints a picture of Fitzwilliam (referred to here as "Mr. Treasurer") as being so preoccupied by the investigation and trial that he has no time for other matters (Byrne, *Lisle Letters*, no. 695, 3:360–61, here 361). Also see Constantyne's *Memorial*, 64, which refers to the questioning of Norris (and the deceptive extraction of a confession from him) by Fitzwilliam.

[200] Byrne, *Lisle Letters*, 3:380.

[201] Byrne, *Lisle Letters*, 3:382.

also have included the latter's husband [Henry Somerset, Earl of Worcester], who was on the jury of peers that tried the Queen and her brother"; and that, furthermore, given Anthony Browne's "closeness to the King it could have been at his suggestion that [Lady Worcester] was drawn into the plot."[202] From this perspective, the conversation between siblings that led to the investigations was not just an accident that had monumental consequences. Rather, if it occurred at all, according to this scenario, it would have been staged; what was needed was simply that Lady Worcester, presumably approached by Cromwell on this matter, stand by the claim that suspicious activities had been going on in the queen's chamber.

Words spoken by Cromwell himself to Chapuys appear, at least at first glance, further to corroborate a view of Cromwell as the mastermind behind a plot to be rid of Anne. In a letter dated 6 June, Chapuys, writing, as usual, in French to Charles V, reveals that Cromwell had confided in him that he had been given the authority to uncover and "bring to an end" the business of the investigations and trials.[203] Chapuys situates the timing of the investigation in conjunction with a diplomatic disappointment he incurred at the hands of the king: Henry's enraged rejection of a specific plan that the ambassador had brought forth, which would achieve a *rapprochement* with Rome, bring Henry's daughter Mary back into the court (and line of succession), and guarantee overall support for Charles V over the French. In describing this complicated relationship between his own failed diplomatic plan and Cromwell's incipient investigation, Chapuys writes this phrase that has caused historians much trouble: "et que *sur le desplesir* et courroux qu'il avoit eu sur la reponce que le roy son maistre m'avoit donnee le tiers iour de pasques, il se mist *a fantasier et conspirer* le dict affaire." There are two standard English paraphrases of this line found in the reference collections of State Papers: (1) "and that, *owing to the displeasure* and anger he had incurred upon the reply given to me by the King on the third day of Easter, *he had set himself to arrange the plot*"; and (2) "*in consequence of the disappointment* and anger he had felt on hearing the King's answer to me on the third day of Easter,

---

[202] Byrne, *Lisle Letters*, 3:380. Later (at 3:382), Byrne concedes that Browne was probably not "an active agent" in this plot, "nor is there any evidence that the Earl of Worcester was personally involved," but she does maintain that Fitzwilliam and Lady Worcester plotted the queen's demise together. Furthermore, Byrne does not attempt to explain why the Worcester-Somerset-Browne-Fitzwilliam alliance would want to work with Cromwell towards the demise of their kinsman by marriage, William Brereton (Henry Somerset's brother-in-law).

[203] CSP, Spain 5, pt. 2 (1536–1538), no. 61 (dated 6 June 1536). See also LP 10.1069 for another summary of the same letter. The original French, as cited in the CSP summary reads: "et que [a] luy avoit este l'auctorite de descouvrir et parachever les affaires d'icelle concubine."

*[he] had planned and brought about the whole affair.*"[204] In both these formulations, Henry's lack of enthusiasm for Chapuys's diplomatic plan, it is implied, angered Cromwell, who wanted to see a shift towards a pro-Imperial policy to the detriment of the French, who were supported by Anne.

Thus, a narrative devised by some historians suggests that, in light of this rebuke, Cromwell—possibly working in concert with the anti-Boleyn faction that had become established among religious conservatives at Henry's court—set out to bring about Anne's downfall, inventing criminal charges against an anointed queen, her brother, and four other innocent men.[205] But other scholars have countered that this scenario seems like a rather extreme reaction to a matter of diplomatic disappointment.[206] And even if Cromwell were here taking credit for creating the case against Anne *ex nihilo*, it is hard to see why he would boast of it to Chapuys at this time.[207] And then one would need to explain why these particular men were chosen as sacrificial victims to Cromwell's Imperialist agenda.[208]

John Schofield is among the most vocal of the historians who do not believe that Cromwell plotted against Anne but, rather, was authorized and charged by the king to prepare the case against her.[209] To make his point, he considers what other meanings Cromwell's words (as reported by Chapuys) could convey and concludes that the expression "sur le desplesir" was merely meant to give a temporal indication of when the investigation began in reference to an incident Chapuys was sure to remember, rather than admitting to a causal relationship between the two events. That is, Cromwell's work began on or about the time

---

[204] The first translation is from LP 10.1069; the second is in CSP, Spain, 5, pt. 2 (1536–1538) no. 61. In both cases, italics are added.

[205] Ives is a principal proponent of this perspective. See *Life and Death*, 315–18.

[206] See, for example, Bernard, *Anne Boleyn*, 146: "Would a king's leading counsellor invent false charges of incest with her brother and adultery with four other men against the queen, simply because he favoured an alliance with the emperor and she did not? It would, to say the least, be a risky proceeding. As a reading of events, it betrays a lack of proportion."

[207] See James Anthony Froude, *The Divorce of Catherine of Aragon: The Story as Told by the Imperial Ambassadors Resident at the Court of Henry VIII* (New York: Scribner, 1891), 414n1, who states that it would be "inconceivable folly" for Cromwell to acknowledge his plot "to Chapuys, the most dangerous person to whom such a secret could be communicated. Cromwell was not an idiot."

[208] Byrne, for example, writes: "Why certain members of the Privy Chamber were selected as victims for the plot is by no means clear, unless we assume that they were generally known to be on terms of greater intimacy with the Queen and to have paid more obvious court to her, as suggested by the reported conversations with Norris and Weston." See Byrne, *Lisle Letters*, 3:383.

[209] Schofield's argument is set forth in *Rise and Fall*, 166–71.

that Henry had given his disappointing response to Chapuys.[210] Schofield bases his claim (that Cromwell's disappointment had not "motivated him to launch an action of his own against Anne") on a point of grammar, relating to the meaning of the preposition "sur," declaring that, according to authoritative dictionaries, the word never means "owing to" or "in consequence of," which is how it is translated in LP and CSP.[211] However, this is not entirely accurate. According to the *Dictionnaire de l'Académie française* of 1694, the preposition "sur" can indeed "mark the cause which instigates action" or "the motivation, the foundation on account of which one does something."[212]

Schofield is on stronger ground when he analyzes other parts of Chapuys's letter, particularly the words "fantasier" and "conspirer." While these words certainly could give the impression that the matter was "invented" and "plotted," they could also simply mean that Cromwell was charged with planning (that is, thinking about) or working with others to organize (i.e., to project how to achieve the desired outcome of) the case.[213] This was indeed his duty, and Chapuys's earlier statement that Cromwell "was given the authority" to investigate and bring the matter to a close certainly implies that it was the king himself who allowed the investigations to proceed: for who else could have given Cromwell such authority? According to Schofield, Cromwell at first was ordered only "to prepare the legal and constitutional case for the king's second divorce and his third marriage. When allegations of Anne's adultery followed some days later, Henry ordered Cromwell to investigate these as well."[214] Schofield thus concludes that "whatever Cromwell did, he did lawfully and properly, acting under orders from Henry. Allegations about Anne have presumably reached Henry . . . and Henry has appointed Cromwell to take charge of the case, which resulted in her prosecution and conviction."[215] Schofield further explains:

---

[210]  Schofield's alternative translation of Chapuys's sentence thus reads: "On (or just after) the third day of Easter, the day when Cromwell was so disappointed and angry on hearing the king's answer to me, Henry authorised and commissioned him to prosecute and bring to an end the mistress's trial. Since then he was the one who planned and brought about the whole affair, which had taken him considerable trouble." See *Rise and Fall*, 169.

[211]  Schofield, *Rise and Fall*, 168.

[212]  The original text indicates that "sur" serves "à marquer la cause qui fait agir . . . le motif, le fondement en vertu duquel on fait . . . quelque chose." The above is my translation. The *Dictionnaire de l'Académie française* (1694) may be accessed online through the site known as the ARTFL Project, www.artfl-project.uchicago.edu.

[213]  See, for example Cotgrave, *A Dictionarie of the French and English Tongues*, which defines "fantasier," among other things, as 'to thinke of' and 'conspirer' as 'to join, or agree, in a plot, or opinion, with others.'

[214]  Schofield, *Rise and Fall*, 171.

[215]  Schofield, *Rise and Fall*, 167.

Chapuys has combined [the divorce and the adultery investigation] together; but also, and in order to foster good Anglo-Imperial relations now that the "concubine" has been disposed of, he has exaggerated Cromwell's role just a little in order to impress Charles V.

Whether this exaggeration was indeed just Chapuys's idea, as Schofield suggests, or Cromwell's own version of the story, meant to impress Chapuys (and in turn, the emperor), it certainly would be quite natural for those most closely involved in this successful prosecution to present themselves, after the fact, as the prime movers behind the affair in order to aggrandize their own importance. But if Cromwell really wanted to take full credit for "inventing" the case against Anne, why did he not make a similar claim in his official dispatch to Gardiner, the English ambassador in France, which clearly stated that the accusations arose from Anne's own inner circle of ladies? Chapuys's letter to Charles V is certainly a puzzle, but it is not a smoking gun that implicates Cromwell as the mastermind behind Anne's downfall.[216]

However the matter arose, even if it were at Cromwell's suggestion, it is clear that Henry himself allowed the case to be investigated and approved of the plan to bring the accused to trial. For it certainly could have been otherwise, if he so chose. When the accusations came to light, Henry could have invoked, against the accusers, the treason laws enacted to protect Anne and the king's progeny from malicious talk. Instead, these same laws were used against Anne and her alleged lovers, since consensual adulterous behavior with a queen was not yet, strictly speaking, in itself a capital crime. It is only by viewing such acts as impugning upon the king's marriage (potentially damaging the dynasty by introducing a bastard into the line of succession) and, more importantly, as providing a motivation for "conspiring and maliciously practicing against the King's life" that what was normally a matter for ecclesiastical courts to adjudicate would come to be regarded as high treason.[217] Certainly, since Henry, by all accounts,

---

[216] A middle ground has been proposed by Froude, who suggests that Cromwell may "have been in possession of important information for many weeks" prior to the king's "unfavorable answer . . . to the Emperor's advances" and then was led by his disappointment "to apply the match to the train" and bring the accusations out into the open. That is, though Cromwell did not himself invent the charges, his disappointment was still the prime motivation for planning criminal charges against Anne. See Froude, *The Divorce of Catherine of Aragon*, 413–14.

[217] See Byrne, *Lisle Letters*, 3:234; see also Ives, *Life and Death*, 344–45 and 420n21, which explains that in this instance the statute of 1351 was "extended" to make consensual intercourse with a queen high treason and that it was only in 1542 that the Crown devised an explicit statute to this effect. Many historians have pointed to the irony of the fact that "the law that was made for her and the issue of her marriage, is now made use of to destroy her"; see, for this quotation, Burnet, *History of the Reformation*, pt. 1, bk. 3, 202. See also John Fox, *Book of Martyrs, or a History of the Lives, Sufferings, and Triumphant*

was already contemplating a divorce from Anne and had also already chosen Jane Seymour as his new queen, he might have been inclined to listen to these charges rather than instinctively protect his wife.[218] He might also have believed that God was indeed protecting him by allowing these charges to come to light. This would especially be so if the accusations had come about through a seemingly chance encounter between siblings, as Carle's poem and other documents suggest; for coincidences, in such important matters, would be deemed providential and not a matter of luck.[219] As Lacey Baldwin Smith has observed, "a lucky happenstance such as the [quarrel between Lady Worcester and her brother] could not be accidental but had to possess moral meaning. God was informing the King and all England of the truth about Anne Boleyn."[220]

## Indictments and Trials

And so the judicial procedure was begun. A grand jury was assembled on 10 May in the county of Middlesex to rule on the criminal activities alleged to have taken place in Westminster Palace and Hampton Court Palace; another grand jury was summoned in Kent to rule on the activities that allegedly took place at Greenwich and Eltham Palace. In the absence of an independent investigatory body (such as a police force or county prosecutors), which would exist today, the grand jury would have been presented with prepared "bills" that outlined only the Crown's evidence in the case.[221] If the grand jury believed there was sufficient evidence to bring the case to trial, it was said that a "true bill" of indictment had been found. These indictments, which were written in Latin, survive today in the National Archives at Kew in a file known as the *Baga de Secretis*.[222] In both

---

*Deaths of the Primitive as well as Protestant Martyrs*, ed. Charles A. Goodrich (Hartford: Eli Hall, 1833), 225: "the act made for her marriage was now turned to her ruin."

[218] Among the many historians who make this point is Charles-Hugues Le Febvre de Saint-Marc in his edition of Paul de Rapin de Thoyras, *Histoire d'Angleterre par Paul Rapin de Thoyras, nouvelle édition augmentée des notes de M. Tindal*, notes by [Nicolas] Tindal, vol. 1 (The Hague 1749), xlix.

[219] Chapuys presumably saw Anne's downfall in this way, as he wrote a letter of congratulations to Henry in which he says that "God has shown special care" towards the king, in revealing these accusations. See LP 10.1071.

[220] See Lacey Baldwin Smith, *Anne Boleyn: The Queen of Controversy, A Biographical Essay* (2013; repr. Stroud: Amberley, 2014), 198.

[221] See J. H. Baker, "Criminal Courts and Procedure at Common Law, 1550–1800," in *Crime in England, 1500–1800*, ed. J. S. Cockburn (Princeton, NJ: Princeton University Press, 1977), 15–48, especially 16–19.

[222] Ives (*Life and Death*, 57) has described this as the "Tudor equivalent of the file marked 'Top Secret.'" More accurately, they contain documents relating to the Crown's case for major state trials, particularly for high treason. In this instance, the documents

instances, a true bill was found, and indictments were drawn up against all the parties involved, namely Anne, her brother George, Norris, Weston, Brereton, and Smeaton.

Wyatt and Page, though still held in the Tower, were not named in the indictments. Indeed, Cromwell had already written to Henry Wyatt, Thomas's father, before this time, assuring him that his son would be released.[223] Nevertheless, there was widespread discussion regarding whether or not Page and Wyatt would stand trial with the others. John Husee, writing to Lord Lisle on 12 May, observed that Page and Wyatt "are in the Tower, but as it is said, without danger of death: but Mr. Page is banished [from] the King's presence and Court forever."[224] But the following day, other rumors prompted him to write again to Lord Lisle: "some . . . say that Wyat [sic] and Mr. Page are as like to suffer as the others."[225] And on 19 May, after the other men's execution, Husee's letter to Lord Lisle affirms that Page and Wyatt "remain still in the Tower. What shall become of them, God knoweth best."[226] Eventually both gentlemen would be released, which could suggest, as Bernard maintains, that "when allegations of Anne's adulteries came to light, they were carefully investigated. And when nothing incriminating was found, men were set free. . . . This should encourage us to take seriously the charges against those who were tried and convicted."[227] Alison Weir, however, notes that it was rather suspicious that Cromwell had written to Wyatt's father *before* the trial had been held.[228] Indeed, it is certainly possible that Page and Wyatt were arrested by Cromwell precisely *to give the impression* that a careful investigation was underway and that the innocent would be let free while the guilty would suffer.

The indictments specify the time and place of the alleged crimes. Anne,

> wife of Henry VIII for three years and more, . . . despising her marriage, and entertaining malice against the King, and following daily her frail and carnal lust, did falsely and traitorously procure by base conversations and

---

regarding the case against the commoners are National Archives KB 8/8, while the documents regarding the trial of Anne and George are National Archives KB 8/9. The documents are transcribed in Latin in an appendix to Wriothesley, *Chronicle*, 1:189–226. For English translations, see LP 10.876, with some reprinted in Norton, *Anne Boleyn Papers*, 338–41.

[223] LP 10.840 records a response from "Henry Wiat" to Cromwell thanking him for this information.

[224] Byrne, *Lisle Letters*, no. 694 (3:359–60, here 360).

[225] Byrne, *Lisle Letters*, no. 695 (3:360–61, here 361).

[226] Byrne, *Lisle Letters*, no. 698 (3:365–66, here 366).

[227] Bernard, *Anne Boleyn*, 175.

[228] Weir furthermore intimates that Page's freedom was perhaps won through the "influence of FitzWilliam, to whom he was related." See on these points Weir, *The Lady in The Tower*, 200.

kisses, touchings, gifts, and other infamous incitations, divers of the King's daily and familiar servants to be her adulterers and concubines, so that several of the King's servants yielded to her vile provocations.[229]

Anne is said to have first "procured by sweet words, kisses, touches, and otherwise" each of the men, "by reason whereof" the men had "illicit intercourse" with her on days subsequent to the seduction, sometimes at their own initiative and sometimes at the queen's invitation.[230] The most sensational and graphic of the allegations involve Anne's solicitation of her own brother: Anne was said to have

> procured and incited her own natural brother, George Boleyn, Lord Rochford, gentleman of the privy chamber, to violate her, alluring him with her tongue in the said George's mouth, and the said George's tongue in hers, and also with kisses, presents, and jewels; whereby he, despising the commands of God, and all human laws . . . violated and carnally knew the said Queen, his own sister.[231]

While dates are indicated in the document, the vague phrase "several times before and after" appears with regularity, offering, in Bernard's words, "a catch-all guarantee," so that the specified days are, in effect, meaningless.[232] In fact, it has been shown that on approximately three-quarters of the given dates, Anne was not in the place alleged by the indictment; or, to put it another way, only six out of twenty dates appear to be possible.[233] Bernard has noted, however, that two of the allegations of relations between Anne and her brother date to November and December 1535. It is possible, according to Bernard, that these two liaisons represent a "desperate attempt at pregnancy" on the part of Anne at a time when the king was thought to be intermittently impotent, a situation that could certainly make it difficult for Anne to present Henry with the son he still was eager to have in order to preserve his dynasty.[234] Anne would know, of course, that the resulting child of intercourse with George would merely look, unsuspiciously, like a Boleyn and not some other man. Thus, according to this scenario, Anne's recourse to the otherwise unlikely act of incest was motivated not by lust or carnal desire but rather by her perceived need to have a son. Anne did in fact conceive around this time, but miscarried in January, which, Bernard speculates, "could be seen as her body's swift rejection of an unnatural pregnancy."[235]

---

[229] LP 10.876; *Anne Boleyn Papers*, 339.

[230] LP 10.876; *Anne Boleyn Papers*, 339.

[231] LP 10. 876; *Anne Boleyn Papers*, 340

[232] See Bernard, "The Fall of Anne Boleyn: A Rejoinder," 667.

[233] See, on this point, Ives, *Life and Death*, 344; and Bernard, *Anne Boleyn*, 165–66.

[234] Bernard, *Anne Boleyn*, 188.

[235] See Bernard, *Anne Boleyn*, 188.

The indictments do not stop with the accusations of adultery. Rather, these are presented as a pretext for the more serious crime of conspiring the king's death, a treasonous act. The document explains that the men, "thus inflamed with carnal love of the Queen, and having become very jealous of each other, gave her secret gifts and pledges while carrying on this illicit intercourse" and that the queen

> and these other traitors . . . conspired the death and destruction of the King, the Queen often saying she would marry one of them as soon as the King died, and affirming that she would never love the King in her heart. And the King having a short time since become aware of the said abominable crimes and treasons against himself, took such inward displeasure and heaviness, especially from his said Queen's malice and adultery, that certain harms and perils have befallen his royal body.[236]

Here the charge may have been informed by Anne's own damning conversation with Kingston regarding how she spoke of "dead men's shoes" with Norris. By specifying these dangers against the king, the indictment allowed the state to try Anne and her alleged lovers as having violated the Treason Law of 1534.

Two separate trial procedures were organized. The first trial—a special commission of *Oyer* and *Terminer* for the four commoners—was arranged for Friday, 12 May, at Westminster Hall, which was the usual venue for state trials. The accused men would have been led through the streets of London from the Tower to Westminster, escorted by the king's guardsmen or archers. One of these archers was charged with carrying a ceremonial axe, with its blade facing away from the accused until such time as a guilty verdict was read, in which case it would quickly be turned toward them. English law—uniquely at the time—required a trial by jury, as specified by Article 39 of Magna Carta: "No free man will be taken or imprisoned . . . save by the lawful judgment of his peers."[237] In the case of the commoners, this meant that the state needed to empanel twelve men "of the county where the indictment was found who were qualified to serve on the jury," that is, who were "freeholders," though not otherwise "'peers' of the accused in any particular sense."[238] The accused normally had the right to make up to twenty peremptory challenges to the jurors as their names were called; that is, the prisoners could request their removal from the jury without showing

---

[236] LP 10.876; *Anne Boleyn Papers*, 340.

[237] See Baker, "Criminal Courts," 21–23, here 21, which posits that a trial by jury was "more or less peculiar to England." For the Magna Carta, see Nicholas Vincent, *Magna Carta: A Very Short Introduction* (Oxford: Oxford University Press, 2012), here 118. For more on the English judicial system at this time, also consult John H. Langbein, *Prosecuting Crime in the Renaissance: England, Germany, France* (Cambridge, MA: Harvard University Press, 1974).

[238] Baker, "Criminal Courts," 23.

cause.[239] But it does not appear to be the case that these prisoners exercised this right, nor was it, in fact, a common practice to do so.

The jurors were then sworn in, one at a time. The oath that was administered to them required them to judge according to the evidence. Once the jury was sworn in, evidence could be presented. It is important to bear in mind that there was no presumption of innocence; indeed, to the contrary, "the preliminary findings of either a grand jury or commission were taken to raise a strong presumption of guilt."[240] These indictments were thus read aloud—paraphrased from the original Latin into English—to the entire courtroom.[241] This would be the first time that the accused would know precisely the crimes charged against them, and "the burden of proof was on the accused to prove their innocence of the charges contained in the indictment."[242] The accused were asked to enter their pleas. Smeaton pleaded guilty to three charges of adultery with the queen, but not guilty to the other charges regarding endangerment of the king. The other accused men pleaded not guilty to all of the charges. No records survive to indicate what evidence was presented at this trial; perhaps these records were destroyed, or perhaps no evidence other than the indictment was presented.[243] Bernard maintains that the lack of surviving evidence "is not in itself suspicious, though it is conceivable that the records were destroyed later, perhaps in Queen Elizabeth's reign."[244] If there were any other evidence, such as the testimony of witnesses, it would normally have been presented not in person but, instead, by reading aloud a deposition of the witness made under oath.[245] There was no right to counsel, hearsay evidence was admissible, and there was no protection against self-incrimination.[246]

The presider of the trial was the Lord Chancellor, Thomas Audley, who asked the jury to consider the evidence and reach a verdict. Customarily, the jurors retired apart from the court while conducting their deliberations, which would take place in the presence of a jury bailiff, "who was sworn to keep them without fire or refreshment and free from outside influence" until a judgment

---

[239] Baker ("Criminal Courts," 36) writes that, by 1555, thirty-six peremptory challenges could be exercised; see also Ives, *Life and Death*, 339, for a further clarification on the matter of challenges.

[240] Schauer and Schauer, "Law as the Engine of State," 73; Baker ("Criminal Courts," 39) likewise states that "it is doubtful whether the presumption of innocence had been formulated" and that the indictment itself would have been considered sufficient evidence to convict.

[241] See Baker, "Criminal Courts," 34.

[242] Schauer and Schauer, "Law as the Engine of State," 61.

[243] See Starkey, *Six Wives*, 575–76.

[244] Bernard, *Anne Boleyn*, 165.

[245] See Schauer and Schauer, "Law as the Engine of State," 73–74.

[246] See Baker, "Criminal Courts," 39, as well as Schauer and Schauer, "Law as the Engine of State," 73–75.

was reached.[247] In this case, the men were found guilty of treason, and, before the judgment was rendered, "an indispensable preliminary known as the *allocutus*" would have taken place, whereby the accused would have been given the opportunity to inform the court of "anything which would prevent the court from giving judgment in their case" (i.e., revealing a pregnancy on the part of a female defendant), but there is no record as to whether or not the defendants exercised that right.[248] At this point, the Lord Chancellor pronounced the required judgment for treason cases: the guilty parties were to be hanged, drawn, and quartered.[249] By first finding these men guilty of committing adultery with Anne, the Crown assured that the queen's own guilt, to be determined in a separate, later trial, would be a foregone conclusion.[250]

The two nobles, Anne and her brother, were entitled, also by the provisions of Magna Carta, to be judged by Peers of the Realm. If Parliament had been in session, the accused would have been tried before the full House of Lords;[251] but Parliament had recently been dissolved, so this necessitated the establishment of a special tribunal, the Court of the Lord High Steward. The trials of Anne and George were held on Monday, 15 May. Extraordinarily, they took place within the Tower of London, which spared the accused the humiliating procession to Westminster undertaken by the commoners and which also offered a measure of additional security. A platform had been constructed in the center of the King's Hall of the Tower (a thirteenth-century structure that no longer exists), with benches to seat the peers and stands to hold at least 2000 spectators.[252] At one end of the chamber could be found a dais with the chair of estate (over which hung a canopy known as the cloth of estate), representing the king even in his absence, to seat Thomas Howard, Duke of Norfolk, who presided over this trial,

---

[247] Baker, "Criminal Courts," 40.

[248] Baker, "Criminal Courts," 41.

[249] The normal judgment imposed in the case of a treason conviction was this: "You are to be drawn upon a hurdle to the place of execution, and there you are to be hanged by the neck, and being alive cut down, and your privy-members to be cut off, and your bowels to be taken out of your belly and there burned, you being alive; and your head to be cut off, and your body to be divided into four quarters, and that your head and quarters be disposed of where his majesty shall think fit." See Baker, "Criminal Courts," 42.

[250] On how the outcome of the first trial would be prejudicial to the second, see Starkey, *Six Wives*, 578; Weir, *The Lady in the Tower*, 204; and Ives, "Faction at the Court of Henry VIII: The Fall of Anne Boleyn," *History* 57.190 (1972): 169–88, here 174, where Ives explains how, by trying the commoners first, "Anne would come to the bar prejudged by their condemnation; the least likely accusation, Rochford's incest, was taken last of all."

[251] See Baker, "Criminal Courts," 26.

[252] Chapuys discloses this detail regarding the potential number of spectators in his letter of 19 May to Charles V. See LP 10.908 and CSP, Spain, 5, pt. 2 (1536–1538), no. 55.

holding the white staff indicative of his office of the Lord High Steward.[253] His
son, the poet Henry Howard, Earl of Surrey, assumed his father's normal role
of Earl Marshall and carried the golden staff of that office.[254] Audley, the Lord
Chancellor, who had presided over the trial of the commoners, also played the
role of director of proceedings in these trials and was responsible for assuring that
the law was followed to the letter.[255] The chief prosecutor was Sir Christopher
Hales, attorney general, who was assisted by Thomas Cromwell.[256] Twenty-six
peers were called by the Lord High Steward to serve as jurors, or, more precisely,
as judges: for, unlike the jurors who served in the trial of the commoners, these
peers were not asked to swear an oath but were formally charged to deliberate
fairly, "upon their honor and allegiance to the King."[257] Furthermore, the prison-
ers did not have the right to challenge any of them.[258] Each peer was called by
name and seated.

Anne, along with two of her ladies, was brought into the makeshift court-
room by the Constable of the Tower, William Kingston, and the Lieutenant
of the Tower, Sir Edmond Walsingham. She was permitted to sit in a chair,
"whether in regard of any infirmity, or out of honor permitted to the wife of the

---

[253] As Janette Dillon has pointed out, the stage directions of Shakespeare's *Henry
VIII* insist that there be "a cloth of state throughout the play" in order to symbolize
the presence of the monarch. See Dillon, *Shakespeare and the Staging of English History*
(Oxford: Oxford University Press, 2012), 111–27 and William Shakespeare, *King Henry
VIII, or All is True*, ed. Jay L. Halio (2000; repr. Oxford: Oxford University Press, 2008).
The inherently dramatic nature of the trial of Anne Boleyn certainly permits an analogy
with the staging of a play.

[254] For these details, see Wriothesley, *Chronicle*, 1:37, as well as the account given in
Cobbett, *State Trials*, 1:409–11. The latter account is a transcription of London, British
Library, Harley 2194 (hereafter Harley 2194 or "the Harleian manuscript," as it is also
called in histories on this subject), fol. 16r–v. This manuscript was also printed in *Ballads
from Manuscripts*, vol. 1, pt. 2, ed. Frederick J. Furnivall (London: Taylor and Co., 1872),
406–7. For a biography of Henry Howard, see Jessie Childs, *Henry VIII's Last Victim:
The Life and Times of Henry Howard, Earl of Surrey* (2006; repr. London: Vintage Books,
2008).

[255] Wriothesley (*Chronicle*, 1:37) also notes that Charles Brandon, the Duke of Suf-
folk, was present, sitting at the left.

[256] Schauer and Schauer, "Law as the Engine of State," 65.

[257] See Edward Coke, *The Third Part of the Institutes of the Laws of England: Con-
cerning High Treason, and Other Pleas of the Crown, and Criminall [sic] Causes* (London:
Flesher, 1644), 29: "the Peers are not sworn, but are charged, *Super fidelitatibus, & ligean-
tiis Domino Regi debitis.*"

[258] See Schauer and Schauer, "Law as the Engine of State," 63n67. See also Coke,
*Institutes*, 27: "in case of a trial of a Nobleman, . . . he cannot challenge at all any of his
Peers."

sovereign," as several sources attest.[259] The indictment against her was then read aloud by the Clerk of the Crown. Like the commoners, Anne would be hearing these charges for the first time in court. She was not allowed any defense counsel but had the opportunity to defend herself. The *Chronicle* of Charles Wriothesley indicates that "she made so wise and discreet answers to all things laid against her, excusing herself with her words so clearly, as though she had never been faulty to the same."[260] According to some sources, she was then formally stripped of her honors; that is, she was asked to hand over the symbols of her queenship.[261] Chapuys maintains that no witnesses were called; but, again, this would not be unusual for the time, as most often testimony was read from previously acquired depositions as opposed to delivered in person by the witness.[262] Spelman, who was a judge at this trial, certainly implies that evidence of some sort was presented; indeed, he writes that "all the evidence was of bawdry and lechery, so that there was no such whore in the realm."[263] While this could be read as an admission that the evidence was exaggerated and that Spelman was summarily dismissing it in his statement, as historians such as Starkey suggest, it is important to bear in mind that Spelman did, like all the other peers, vote in favor of Anne's conviction.[264] It seems unlikely, therefore, that he would draw attention to the fact that he had so voted knowing that the evidence was a fabrication. Rather,

---

[259] See Harley 2194, fol. 16r, printed in Cobbett, *State Trials*, 1:410, and *Ballads from Manuscripts*, 1.2:406; see also Wriothesley, *Chronicle*, 1:37. This assertion was also made by Carle in his poem (v. 950).

[260] Wriothesley, *Chronicle*, 1:37–38; Harley 2194, fol. 16r, also attests that she answered well: "having an excellent quick wit, and being a ready speaker, [she] did so answer to all objections, that had the peers given in their verdict according to the expectation of the assembly, she had been acquitted." See Cobbett, *State Trials*, 1:410, and *Ballads from Manuscripts*, 1.2:406.

[261] On this point, in addition to Carle (vv. 961–962), see Add. 28588, fols. 284r–285r (here 284v), the letter of Dr. Ortiz to Isabella of Portugal, dated 2 June (paraphrased in LP 10.1043), as well as Add. 8715, fols. 252r–254v, here 252r, the letter of the Bishop of Faenza to Monsignor Ambrogio, dated 24 May (paraphrased in LP 10.956), both of which state that the queen was degraded.

[262] See LP 10.908, where Chapuys writes: "no witnesses were produced against either him or her, as it is usual to do, particularly when the accused denies the charge." See also CSP, Spain, 5, pt. 2 (1536–1538), no. 55. But for the custom of reading the deposition rather than presenting witnesses, see James Anthony Froude, *History of England from the Fall of Wolsey to the Death of Elizabeth*, vol. 2 (London: Parker & Son, 1856), 491n2.

[263] Spelman, *Reports*, 71; the original "French" as transcribed by Baker in his edition of Spelman reads: "et tout levidens fuit sur bawdry et lechery issint que ne fuit ascun tiel hore en le realme."

[264] For Starkey's reading of Spelman's statement as being dismissive of the evidence, see *Six Wives*, 580.

perhaps this statement, as Bernard suggests, "should be taken at face value as a reflection of sincere horror at what was revealed."[265]

The matter was then turned over to the peers, who could withdraw for the course of their deliberation, while the prisoner was also removed from the courtroom. When the peers returned from their sequestration, they were polled by Norfolk in open court, beginning with the most junior member, as was required, with the intention of preventing senior members from exercising undue influence over the younger peers.[266] The polling would normally have taken place in the absence of the prisoner, who was then brought back into the courtroom and informed of the verdict by the Lord High Steward. Normally, a simple majority would have been sufficient to convict, but in this case the judges were unanimous in reaching a verdict of guilty.[267] It also fell upon the Lord Steward to pronounce the sentence, which could, once again, be only the penalty of death. But Norfolk surprised everyone in saying to Anne that "thou shalt be burned here within the Tower of London, on the Green, else to have thy head smitten off as the King's pleasure shall be further known of the same."[268] Burning would have been the normal punishment assigned to female offenders.[269] Beheading, since it would result in a far quicker death, was the usual sentence given to aristocrats or dignitaries (as was the case for Thomas More and John Fisher) and would be a mark of kindness on the part of the king. As queen, Anne would surely fall into that category, but as a female she could conceivably still be sentenced to burning.[270] Norfolk was thus probably genuinely perplexed as to which custom to follow in this unique circumstance of treason committed by someone who is both female and a noble.[271] Indeed, according to Spelman, this judgment "in the disjunctive"

---

[265] Bernard, *Anne Boleyn*, 169.

[266] Schauer and Schauer, "Law as the Engine of State," 69–70. See also Coke, *Institutes*, 30: "when [the peers] are agreed, they all come again into the Court, and take their places, and then the Lord High Steward publicly in open Court, beginning with the puisne [i.e., the youngest] Lord . . . said unto him: . . . Is [the defendant] guilty of the Treasons, whereof he hath been indicted or arraigned?"

[267] See Wriothesley, *Chronicle*, 1:38: "the youngest lord of the said inquest was called first to give verdict, who said guilty, and so every lord and earl after their degrees said guilty to the last and so condemned her." For the norms regarding a simple majority rather than a unanimous vote, see Schauer and Schauer, "Law as the Engine of State," 70.

[268] Wriothesley, *Chronicle*, 1:38.

[269] Baker ("Criminal Courts," 42) quotes the normal sentence for women found guilty of treason as reading "to be burned with fire until you are dead."

[270] Spelman, *Reports*, 71, explains: "The judgment against the queen was that she should be burned, for that is the judgment of treason against a woman; but because she was queen the Steward gave judgment that she should be burned or beheaded at the king's pleasure."

[271] For more on the uniqueness of Anne's circumstances, see Nadia Bishai, "'Which thing had not before been seen': The Rituals and Rhetoric of the Execution of Anne

(that is, framed as an "either/or" proposition) "had not been seen" heretofore and caused the judges to murmur.[272] Finally, it was customary for the prisoner to be allowed to say a few words, though normally this allocution took place before the verdict was announced, as described earlier in this chapter.[273] Several sources, including Chapuys and Carle, report that Anne took the verdict bravely and maintained her composure.[274] These sources also note that Anne expressed sorrow for the men who had been condemned with her.[275] Her last request was that she be given adequate time "to prepare her soul for death."[276]

After Anne's trial concluded, the proceedings against Rochford began (though Carle reverses the order of the trials, presumably for dramatic effect). The same peers served as judges in this trial, with one exception: Henry Percy —the Earl of Northumberland and an early suitor to Anne—who was suddenly taken ill and needed to be removed from the courtroom.[277] Rochford, too, pleaded not guilty and was said to have defended himself ably, answering the charges "prudently and wisely."[278] Rochford was perhaps not so prudent in choosing to read aloud another charge that was handed to him in writing and that, according to Chapuys, he was urged to keep to himself: namely, that Anne had told George's wife that the king was impotent.[279] Revealing this information publicly did not, presumably, endear George to the judges who, despite Rochford's eloquent defense, found him guilty.[280] Norfolk pronounced the sentence that Rochford, like the other men, should suffer the full pains of those found guilty of treason and be hanged, drawn, and quartered at Tyburn. Before he left the courtroom, Rochford made the extraordinary plea that those to whom

---

Boleyn, England's First Criminal Queen" in *The Rituals and Rhetoric of Queenship, Medieval to Early Modern*, ed. Liz Oakley-Brown and Louise J. Wilkinson (Dublin: Four Courts, 2009), 171–85, here 172.

[272] Spelman, *Reports*, 71.

[273] Ives (*Life and Death*, 341) believes that Carle's report is "less credible" because it places her allocution after the verdict; however, Chapuys gives the same timing and further corroborates this detail of Carle's poem. See, on this point, LP 10.908; and CSP, Spain, 5, pt. 2 (1536–1538), no. 55, Chapuys's letter to the emperor.

[274] See LP 10.908; CSP, Spain, 5, pt. 2 (1536–1538), no. 55; and Carle's poem, vv. 991–992.

[275] Chapuys writes (LP 10.908) that "what she regretted most was that [the men], who were innocent and loyal to the King, were to die for her." See also CSP, Spain, 5, pt. 2 (1536–1538), no. 55.

[276] Chapuys's letter to the emperor, CSP, Spain, 5, pt. 2 (1536–1538), no. 55; see also LP 10.908.

[277] LP 10.876.

[278] Wriothesley, *Chronicle*, 1:39.

[279] See LP 10.908; and CSP, Spain, 5, pt. 2 (1536–1538), no. 55.

[280] Constantyne's *Memorial*, 66, asserts: "I heard say he had escaped had it not been for a letter."

he owed money should be paid off by the king—who, strictly speaking, had no obligation to do so—with the wealth he would confiscate from the condemned man.[281]

The judicial action against Anne and the five men was now terminated. In addition to all the members of the two grand juries who had found a "true bill," twelve trial jurors had found the commoners guilty, twenty-six peers had voted against Anne, and twenty-five peers against Rochford. Technically, the trials were fair insofar as they followed standard procedures.[282] Yet there were—and still are—lingering doubts about whether or not the accusations were true. For some, the accusations were not credible because their source—whether that be the Countess of Worcester, Jane Boleyn, Stephen Gardiner, or even Thomas Cromwell—was suspect, each having his or her own reasons for telling this story. For others, the sheer number of alleged adulteries made the case preposterous, though Starkey has argued that "the very extravagance of the accusations . . . became an asset to the prosecution, rather than a liability."[283] Yet there must have been enough doubts about Anne's behavior to make these charges somewhat plausible, for certainly no one would have taken them seriously had they been made against a queen such as Catherine of Aragon.[284] Even Gilbert Burnet, who

---

[281] On these points, see LP 10.908; and CSP, Spain, 5, pt. 2 (1536–1538), no. 55.

[282] On the question of whether or not Anne Boleyn received a fair trial, see Schauer and Schauer, "Law as the Engine of State," 79–80: "If fairness means a trial designed to ascertain the facts, do justice, give the defendant an equal chance, convict the guilty, and acquit the innocent, then the answer must be 'no.' If the question is framed in this way, however, then few other criminal defendants of the time received anything close to a fair trial. . . . [But] if fair means, did Anne Boleyn receive as much in the way of 'due process' as anyone in similar circumstances, the answer to the question must be 'yes.' There is little if any evidence . . . that the rules of the time were in any way bent in order to assure Anne Boleyn's conviction." Ives (*Life and Death*, 339), however, believes that the panel of jurors at the trial of the commoners, at least, was "as hostile a panel as could be imagined," suggesting that the crown (in the person of Cromwell) had stacked the deck against these four men. Of course, no one can assess exactly how much pressure was made to bear on the jurors or peers, who may well have felt compelled to return a verdict of guilty so as not to displease the king.

[283] Starkey, *Six Wives*, 576. Starkey goes on to say that the charges that first emerged —the accusations against Norris, Smeaton, and Rochford—"excited incredulity. . . . But increase the tally of Anne's lovers to five . . . and the accusation became almost believable."

[284] See, for example, Schofield, *Rise and Fall*, 198, who declares: "No evidence exists even from court gossip of Elizabeth of York, Catherine of Aragon, Jane Seymour and Catherine Parr . . . flirting with grooms and assorted gentlemen of the king's Privy Chamber; nor were they ever overheard muttering sweet nothings with handsome young musicians by the window at twilight; and none of them ever, either in jest or in earnest, mused aloud on who might bed her if the king were to suddenly die."

believed in Anne's innocence, admitted that Anne's "carriage seemed too free" and that the "freedoms and levities" in her conduct may have been (wrongly) construed as "invitations" to improper behavior.[285] Similarly, Thomas Amyot, in his preface to George Constantyne's *Memorial*, though that text may be a forgery, acknowledges that Anne appeared indiscreet and that the "levity of her manners, acquired during her education in France, might have contributed to influence the decision of her Judges."[286] In other words, Anne enjoyed a reputation for being a flirt, and her flirtatious behavior could be misread and could make these charges sound more plausible than one would otherwise think. Certainly, her reputation abroad, where she could be more freely criticized than in England, sometimes hinted at improprieties. Indeed, a diplomatic report as early as September 1533 reported that "they say in Flanders that the King is abused by the new Queen, and that his gentlemen goeth daily a-playing where they woll [i.e., "desire"]."[287] Later, less than a year before Anne's trial, on 4 July 1535, Ridolfo Pio da Carpi (the Bishop of Faenza who at that time served as Papal Nuncio at the French court) wrote to Monseigneur Ambrogio Ricalcato (the secretary to Pope Paul III) that, just three days before, the French king, Francis I, spoke to him privately of "the new queen of England [and] how little virtuously in all things she has always lived and now lives."[288] This talk of scandal, coupled with her perceived levity of manners, apparently laid the foundation for the serious accusations of adultery that were to follow. In short, as Schofield declares, "it must be as plain as plain can be that something peculiar had been going on in Anne Boleyn's circle" and that enough suspicions were aroused to find the charges against her to be plausible.[289] Yet Schofield is quick to add that we are in no position to speak authoritatively on this matter and that "a tantalizing historical mystery is set to remain."[290]

Henry's behavior from the time of the prisoners' arrest to their trials certainly gave the impression that he believed in their guilt. Chapuys, writing to Charles V, said that the "very evening the Concubine was brought to the Tower, when the Duke of Richmond went to say goodnight to his father, and ask his blessing after the English custom, the King began to weep, saying that he and his sister, meaning the Princess [Mary], were greatly bound to God for having escaped the hands of that accursed whore, who had determined to poison

---

[285]  Burnet, *History of the Reformation*, pt. 1, bk. 3, 206.
[286]  See Amyot's edition of Constantyne's *Memorial*, 54–55.
[287]  LP 6.1065, "News from Flanders" dated 1 September.
[288]  Add. 8715, fols. 84v–89v: "havendomi parlato molto familiarmente dell'essere di questa nuova Regina d'Inghilterra, e quanto poco virtuosamente in ogni cosa sempre è vissuta, et hora vive," 87r–v, paraphrased in LP 8.985.
[289]  Schofield, *Rise and Fall*, 197–98.
[290]  Schofield, *Rise and Fall*, 201.

them."[291] In the same letter, Chapuys reveals that Henry had told the Bishop of Carlisle that he "had long expected the issue of these affairs, and that thereupon he had before composed a tragedy, which he carried with him; and, so saying, the King drew from his bosom a little book written in his own hand, but the Bishop did not read the contents."[292] Clearly, Henry wanted the world to know how offended and hurt he was by the actions of Anne and her alleged lovers. Yet, at the same time, Chapuys reports that the king

> has shown himself more glad than ever since the arrest of the *putain* [whore]; for he has been going about banqueting with ladies, sometimes remaining after midnight, and returning by the river. Most part of the time he was accompanied by various musical instruments, and, on the other hand, by the singers of his chamber, which many interpret as showing his delight at getting rid of [Anne].[293]

This showy carousing, Chapuys felt, did not sit well with most people, "who murmur at the mode of procedure against [Anne] and the others, . . . and it will not pacify the world when it is known what has passed and is passing between him and Mrs. Jane Semel."[294] Chapuys's instinct proved right, for when Mary of Hungary heard that Henry had so quickly married another woman whom he was already courting before Anne's death, she bluntly stated that "some people think [Henry] invented the charge to get rid of her"; such behavior is so ingrained in the king, she goes on to say, that "when he is tired of his new wife he will find some occasion to quit himself of her also."[295]

## Awaiting and Staging Execution

Notwithstanding these suspicions regarding Henry's motivation for playing the role of the wounded husband, the judicial process had run its course; and, once the judgments had been rendered against all the accused, there was no official

---

[291] LP 10.908. See also CSP, Spain, 5, pt. 2 (1536–1538), no. 55.

[292] LP 10.908. See also CSP, Spain, 5, pt. 2 (1536–1538), no. 55.

[293] LP 10.908. See also CSP, Spain, 5, pt. 2 (1536–1538), no. 55.

[294] LP 10.908. See also CSP, Spain, 5, pt. 2 (1536–1538), no. 55.

[295] "Extract from a Letter of the Regent Mary to Ferdinand of Austria," as translated in *The Pilgrim: A Dialogue on the Life and Actions of King Henry the Eighth*, by William Thomas, edited with notes from the Archives at Paris and Brussels by J. A. Froude (London: Parker, Son, and Bourn, 1861), 117. For the original French letter, see [Louis Prosper] Gachard, *Analectes historiques* (Brussels: Hayez, 1856), 17–18. The letter is dated 25 May 1536. Mary goes on to state, however, that Anne was "a worthless person" and that such behavior "has been her character for a long time," thus implying that, in the end, perhaps Anne was not necessarily wrongly convicted.

possibility of appeal. However, for a reason that remains a mystery even now, considerable effort was made on the part of the French envoys, Castelnau and Jean de Dinteville, to free Weston, but their request was denied.[296] Weston also penned a surviving letter to his parents and wife in which he, like Rochford, expressed a desire that his debts to others be paid off; he added a request that they "forgive me of all the offences that I have done to you, and in especial to my wife, which I desire for the love of God to forgive me."[297] This should not necessarily be construed as a confession of adultery with Anne Boleyn, for it is possible that Weston had been unfaithful to his wife in others ways, perhaps with Madge Shelton, the woman with whom Anne had suggested he was in love, as she reported to Kingston in the Tower.[298] Indeed, the offenses to which Weston is alluding may have nothing at all to do with infidelity with anyone. In any event, Weston and the others would no doubt have been preparing to meet their maker and would have been given the opportunity to make a private, sacramental confession of their sins before their execution.

In two days' time, on 17 May 1536, all five men were executed at Tower Hill, their sentences mercifully commuted to beheading in lieu of the common traitor's death at Tyburn.[299] Chapuys states that Anne was made to watch the gruesome affair from the Tower, but he is the only source to say so.[300] It is possible, but not likely, that the event was witnessed by Thomas Wyatt, also still imprisoned at the time, if we are to believe the poems he wrote on this occasion (though he does not supply any details about the executions itself).[301] Rochford

---

[296] See LP 10.908, in which Chapuys describes the "intercession of the bishop of Tarbes, the French ambassador resident, and the sieur de Tinteville [Dinteville], who arrived the day before yesterday, in behalf of one named Vaston [Weston]." See also CSP, Spain, 5, pt. 2 (1536–1538), no. 55 as well as Husee's letter to Lord Lisle date 13 May [no. 695] which states that "in case any do escape it shall be young Weston, for whose life there is importunate suit made" (Byrne, *Lisle Letters*, 3:361). There are, however, no archival records that explain the motivation behind this effort on the part of the French ambassadors to free Weston in particular.

[297] LP 10.869.

[298] See Bernard, *Anne Boleyn*, 181.

[299] For the assertion that Smeaton was hanged, see John Lingard, *A History of England, From the First Invasion by the Romans*, vol. 4, 5th ed. (Paris: Galignani, 1840), 136, as well as Froude, *History of England*, 2:494. But Paul Friedmann rightly shows that this must be an error as there were no gallows at the Tower. See Friedmann, *Anne Boleyn: A Chapter of English History, 1527–1536* (London: Macmillan, 1884), 2:284n2.

[300] LP 10.908; and CSP, Spain, 5, pt. 2 (1536–1538), no. 55.

[301] Wyatt's poem, known by its refrain of "Circa Regna tonat," contains the lines: "The bell tower showed me such sight / That in my head sticks day and night." A longer poem attributed to him, known by its first line of "In Mourning Wise Since Daily I Increase," discusses each of the five condemned men in turn, concluding with a stanza that states: "The axe is home, your heads be in the street." Neither of these poems con-

was given the privilege of dying first without having to witness the horror of the other executions. Mark, as the "inferior person," was the last to be executed.

It was customary for the condemned to be permitted to speak before their execution, though these scaffold speeches would have been rather formulaic in their structure, content, and style. Condemned criminals were expected to acknowledge that they had been judged under a just law, to praise their sovereign, to pray (and ask others to pray) that the king live a long life, to confess their own sins, to ask for forgiveness from those whom they had offended, and to request prayers for the repose of their own soul.[302] As a whole, Rochford's speech followed the typical pattern of discourse uttered by those condemned to die, by recommending the king to his people and by asking them to pray for his long life. But unlike more typical scaffold speeches, as Carle's poem notes, Rochford's address did not include a confession of guilt for the crime he was alleged to have committed towards the king, but merely a general admission of the sinful condition to which all humanity is subject.

There are several versions of Rochford's scaffold speech, both foreign and domestic, most of which are in general accord with one another.[303] The primary theme that emerges from all of these versions is that Rochford intended for his

---

tains information about these specific executions that would not have been common knowledge. Susan Brigden maintains that "from [the Bell Tower's] iron-barred windows prisoners could not, in fact, look north over the walls and ditch, to Tower Hill beyond and its tragic scaffold. But in their imaginations they might." See Brigden, *Thomas Wyatt: The Heart's Forest*, 274–76. It is also possible that the frightful sight beheld by Wyatt in "Circa Regna tonat," if it does refer to an actual lived experience, was Anne's execution (not that of the five men on Tower Hill) which did take place within the confines of the Tower, on Tower Green. For the text of these poems, see Wyatt, *The Complete Poems*, 155 and 255–56, respectively.

[302] For more on the expectations of scaffold speeches, see Bishai, "'Which thing had not before been seen,'" especially 178. Also consult Katherine Royer, *The English Execution Narrative, 1200–1700* (2014; repr. London: Routledge, 2016), 61–84, especially 65.

[303] See, for example, Wriothesley, *Chronicle*, 1:39–40, and Constantyne's *Memorial*, 65, for an account in English. For an anonymous Italian account, see both printings of *Il Successo in la morte della Regina de Inghilterra*, cited above, as well as the Portuguese account (subsequently translated into English and French) which is substantively nearly identical to the Italian account, in *Lettre d'un gentilhomme portugais*, also cited above. For another French account, see "Ce que dist Millor de Rochefort, frere de la Royne d'angleterre sur l'eschauffault à sa mort," Paris, Bibliothèque nationale de France, Dupuy 373 (hereafter Dupuy 373), fol. 111. The Dupuy account is reprinted in Edmond Bapst, *Deux gentilshommes-poètes de la cour de Henry VIII* (Paris: Plon, 1891), 136–37, as well as in Georges Ascoli, *La Grande-Bretagne devant l'opinion française depuis la Guerre de Cent Ans jusqu'à la fin du XVIᵉ siècle* (Paris: Librairie universitaire J. Gamber, 1927), 273. An English translation of an imperialist account (copies of which are in French and Spanish) is printed in the appendix of Froude's edition of Thomas, *The Pilgrim*, 116–17, and is also printed in LP 10.911; it is very similar in content to the Dupuy manuscript.

fall to be seen as a warning to other courtiers not to place too much hope in the vanity and prizes of this world (or, more precisely, of Henry's court) but, rather, to focus on the message of the Gospel. One extensive report of George's scaffold speech can be found in an English-language document known as *The Chronicle of Calais*, a history of that land held by the English on the continent, which has been attributed to a government official named Richard Turpyn.[304] Boleyn's execution was of interest to this author because of the nobleman's position as Warden of the Cinque Ports, the area of England closest to the Channel and thus to Calais. Turpyn records Rochford's words in this way:

> Christian men, I am born under the law, and judged under the law, and die under the law, and the law hath condemned me. Masters all, I am not come hither for to preach, but for to die, for I have deserved for to die if I had twenty lives, more shamefully than can be devised, for I am a wretched sinner, and I have sinned shamefully, I have known no man so evil, and to rehearse my sins openly it were no pleasure to you to hear them, nor yet for me to rehearse them, for God knoweth all; therefore, masters all, I pray you take heed by me, and especially my lords and gentlemen of the court, the which I have been among, take heed by me, and beware of such a fall, and I pray to God the Father, the Son, and the Holy Ghost, three persons and one God, that my death may be an example unto you all, and beware, trust not in the vanity of the world, and especially in the flattering of the court. And I cry God mercy, and ask all the world forgiveness, as willingly as I would have forgiveness of God; and if I have offended any man that is not here now, either in thought, word, or deed, and if ye hear any such, I pray you heartily in my behalf, pray them to forgive me for God's sake.[305]

Rochford's words, as given here, are in remarkable accord with all extant foreign and domestic accounts of his scaffold speech and generally conform to the expectations of that genre, as described above.[306]

---

[304] For an edition of this work based on manuscripts housed in the British Library, see *The Chronicle of Calais in the Reigns of Henry VII and Henry VIII to the Year 1540*, ed. John Gough Nichols (London: Camden Society, 1846).

[305] The *Chronicle of Calais*, 46. I have significantly modified the spelling of this account for ease of reading.

[306] For a very similar account, see, for example Wriothesley, *Chronicle*, 1:39–40, which quotes Rochford as saying: "Masters all, I am come hither not to preach and make a sermon, but to die, as the law hath found me, and to the law I submit me, desiring you all, and specially you my masters of the Court, that you will trust on God specially, and not on the vanities of the world, for if I had so done, I think I had been alive as ye be now. . . . As for mine offences, it cannot prevail you to hear them that I die here for, but I beseech God that I may be an example to you all, and that all you may beware by me, and heartily I require you all to pray for me, and to forgive me if I have offended you, and I forgive you all, and God save the King."

Nevertheless, there is one major discrepancy from the norm that can be noted in the account rendered by the Imperial ambassador, Chapuys, in his report to Charles V: Chapuys asserts that Rochford specifically repented of his "heretical" ways and urged others to do so as well.[307] Now, many versions of this speech have Rochford admitting that he was one who "set forth" the Gospel but did not sufficiently follow it. The above-cited *Chronicle of Calais*, for example, quotes Rochford as adding that people refer to him as

> a setter forth of the word of God, and one that have favored the Gospel of Christ; and because I would not that God's word should be slandered by me, I say unto you all, that if I had followed God's word in deed as I did read it and set it forth to my power, I had not come to this. I did read the Gospel of Christ, but I did not follow it; if I had, I had been a live man among you: therefore I pray you, masters all, for God's sake stick to the truth and follow it, for one good follower is worth three readers, as God knoweth.[308]

Clearly, this is hardly a retraction of belief but rather an admission of failure to live up to an ideal encompassed in that belief. His troubles, Rochford suggests, have come about because he failed to act upon the words of Scripture, trusting too much in the benefits he reaped in this world and forgetting to put God before all earthly and vain things, a lesson he explicitly wants to impart to other "gentlemen of the court." Chapuys, however, who was probably not an eyewitness to these executions, has focused on Rochford's reference to having "set forth" the Gospel and has turned this into a sin in and of itself; for Chapuys, reformed belief of all kinds, including "evangelical" leanings, were often labeled "Lutheran" and were thus heretical.

Undoubtedly, Rochford *was* a proponent of making the Gospel available to readers in the vernacular, an activity that was not sanctioned by the Catholic Church at that time. This is explained further in another version of Rochford's scaffold speech, provided, in Welsh, by Elis Gruffudd, a soldier from Calais, which quotes Rochford as saying:

---

[307] LP 10.908: "Rochford disclaimed all that he was charged with, confessing, however, that he had deserved death for having been so much contaminated and having contaminated others with these new sects, and he prayed everyone to abandon such heresies." See also CSP, Spain, 5, pt. 2 (1536–1538), no. 55.

[308] *Chronicle of Calais*, 46–47. Similarly, George Constantyne, allegedly an eyewitness to the execution, supports this explicitly by stating that Rochford declared: "I desire you that no man will be discouraged from the Gospel for my fall. For if I had lived according to the gospel as I loved it, and spake of it, I had never come to this. Wherefore . . . for God's love, leave not the gospel, but speak less and live better. For I had rather have one good liver according to the gospel than ten babblers." See Constantyne's *Memorial*, 65.

Truly so that the Word should be among the people of the realm I took upon myself great labour to urge the king to permit the printing of the Scriptures to go unimpeded among the commons of the realm in their own language. And truly to God I was one of those who did most to procure the matter to place the Word of God among the people because of the love and affection which I bear for the Gospel and the truth of Christ's words.[309]

But what exactly George Boleyn meant by procuring and promoting vernacular translations of the Gospel is unclear. Perhaps it refers to George's translation of the work of Lefèvre d'Étaples, which he presented to his sister, as Carley has suggested.[310] Or perhaps it refers to the systematic acquisition of translations of Scripture from abroad while serving as an English envoy to France, an activity that can be construed as "evangelical" and that Chapuys would view as "heretical."[311] But in either case, Chapuys's report that George repented of this activity is false.

Few documents record the final words of the three gentlemen who died with George, and, indeed, they might not have said anything, as Carle was to claim in his poem. Constantyne's *Memorial* (of disputed authority, it will be remembered) maintains that Weston admitted that he "had thought to have lived in abomination yet this twenty or thirty years and then to have made amends," expressing the universal belief that death would not strike so soon.[312] Similarly, Brereton proclaimed, again, according to Constantyne, "I have deserved to die if it were a thousand deaths. But the cause wherefore I die judge not: But if ye judge, judge the best."[313] Constantyne noted that, if Brereton were in fact guilty, such words would not make for a good death, adding that Norris said "almost nothing at all."[314] Mark, as Carle and Constantyne both affirm, did alone among the men

---

[309] This is from a manuscript housed in Wales, The National Library, 3054D, part ii, fol. 511r, as quoted in Carley and translated by Peter Roberts, "'Her moost lovyng,'" 277n43. Carley speculates that the source of these words was "probably the hangman of Calais" who, in turn, gave the story to the soldier. But this is problematic because the person known as the "hangman of Calais" was actually a swordsman summoned for Anne's later beheading and was not involved in the execution of the five men.

[310] See Carley, "Her moost lovying," 268, where he suggests that George's scaffold speech "may well provide a reference *inter alia* to the translating activities he so actively espoused." See also Carley, *Books*, 128.

[311] For the suggestion that George procured evangelical books during his diplomatic excursions to France, see Ives, "Anne Boleyn and the *Entente Évangélique*," in *François I<sup>er</sup> et Henri VIII: Deux Princes de la Renaissance (1515–1547)*, ed. Roger Mettam and Charles Giry-Deloison (Lille: L'Institut de recherches historiques du Septentrion, 1995), 83–102, here 99.

[312] Constantyne's *Memorial*, 65.

[313] Constantyne's *Memorial*, 65.

[314] Constantyne's *Memorial*, 65.

specifically confess that he deserved the death he was about to suffer. The others were careful not to admit their guilt regarding the crimes for which they were charged but, rather, confessed to a more generalized state of sinfulness. Yet, at the same time, they did not actively *deny* their guilt, whether because they did not want "to leave the world with a lie on their lips" (as Froude, who believes they were guilty, suggests),[315] or because they feared that potential repercussions could be visited upon their families after their demise, or because, until their moment of death, there was always a chance that their sentence could revert to the more horrible fate of hanging and quartering.[316]

Rochford was laid to rest inside the royal chapel of St. Peter ad Vincula within the Tower, as befitted his status. The others were buried in double plots in the churchyard. Wriothesley states, as does Carle, that Weston and Norris were buried "in one grave," while Brereton and Mark occupied another grave together.[317] Importantly, Wriothesley also specifies that all the men were buried with their heads; this means that Londoners (and, more importantly, close family members) were not subjected to the sight of the severed heads of these men affixed to spikes on London Bridge (as was customary in treason cases and as was the unfortunate fate of both Thomas More and John Fisher).[318]

---

[315] Froude writes (*The Divorce of Catherine of Aragon*, 429–30): "It appears to me ... that these five gentlemen did not deny their guilt, because they knew that they were guilty. The unfortunate Anne was still alive; and while there was life there was hope. A direct confession on their part would have been a confession for her as well as themselves. ... But, if they were really innocent, that they should have suffered as they did without an effort to clear themselves or her is one more inexplicable mystery in this extraordinary story."

[316] Friedmann (*Anne Boleyn*, 2:286) explains their silence this way: "up to the last moment the government ... might interrupt the execution, and order an offender to be hanged, drawn, and quartered; or his family might be made to smart for the violation of his pledge. Hence scarcely any of Henry's victims dared to maintain their innocence." For more on the fear that a sentence of death by beheading could be converted to death by hanging and quartering, see Lacey Baldwin Smith, "English Treason Trials and Confessions in the Sixteenth Century," *Journal of the History of Ideas* 15 (1954): 471–98, here 484.

[317] Wriothesley, *Chronicle*, 1:40.

[318] There is, nevertheless, some disagreement among sources with regard to the treatment of the men's bodies after their beheading. The anonymous Imperial account, for example, claims that Brereton and Mark were quartered (see Froude's edition of *The Pilgrim*, 116). A letter from the Bishop of Faenza to Monsignor Ambrogio (Add. 8715, fols. 252r–254v, here 252v), dated 24 May and also paraphrased in LP 10.956, states that all the men were supposed to be quartered in Anne's presence. A letter from Viscount Hannart (the Imperial Ambassador to Paris) to Isabella of Portugal, dated 2 June 1536, Add. 28588, fol. 286r–288r, here 287v (also transcribed in LP 10.1044), likewise attests that "los otros cuerpos fueron cuarteados" [the other bodies were quartered].

On the same day as the execution of the men, the Archbishop of Canterbury, Thomas Cranmer, ruled that the marriage of Anne Boleyn and Henry VIII was annulled. Precisely what the grounds were to reach this judgment are unknown, as there are no surviving documents on the matter. A letter from Kingston to Cromwell reveals that Cranmer had been to the Tower that day to hear Anne's confession, giving rise to the speculation that something that was said during their private discussion allowed the Archbishop to pursue the divorce that he declared the following day, though this should have been considered privileged information protected by the seal of confession.[319] Wriothesley, Foxe, and Strype all maintain that the grounds were Anne's supposed pre-contract of marriage with Henry Percy, the Earl of Northumberland, who had previously denied that the two were betrothed.[320] Indeed, Percy had sent a letter to Cromwell on 13 May upholding his previous position, giving further evidence in favor of the theory that Anne's earlier betrothal was at least being considered as grounds for divorce at this time.[321] Others, such as Chapuys, suggest that the grounds could have been Henry's prior relationship with Anne's sister, Mary, resurrecting the idea of "affinity" that had been so central to the case for divorce against Catherine.[322] A later theory, promulgated by Retha Warnicke, holds that the reason for this annulment was Henry's conviction that Anne had literally "bewitched" him into his marriage (and enticed the other accused men into having illicit sexual relations with her).[323] But no one seems to believe that the grounds for this annulment were that the king had in fact been lawfully married to Catherine at the time of his marriage to Anne, for that would entail admitting far too much on Henry's part.[324] And yet, given the absence of surviving evidence on the matter of this divorce, perhaps this is precisely what did happen and why all documents relating to this annulment were destroyed, as Henry certainly would not have wished such an admission to become known.

While it may seem, then, that Anne could no longer be guilty of adultery, since she was not the king's lawful wife at the time of the alleged crimes, this annulment was certainly not sought in an effort to save her from the block. Instead, the annulment was necessary so as to remove Elizabeth immediately from the line of succession by declaring her to be a bastard, without, however,

---

[319] For this letter from Kingston to Cromwell, see Ellis, *Original Letters*, 62–63, here 63. See also MacCulloch, *Cranmer*, 158, who believes that the Archbishop would never have broken the seal in this fashion.

[320] See Wriothesley, *Chronicle*, 1:40–41; Fox, *Book of Martyrs*, 225; and Strype, *Ecclesiastical Memorials*, 437.

[321] LP 10.864.

[322] See LP 10.909, a letter from Chapuys to Granvelle, dated 19 May.

[323] See Warnicke, *Wicked Women of Tudor England: Queens, Aristocrats, Commoners* (New York: Palgrave Macmillan, 2012), 41.

[324] See Friedmann, *Anne Boleyn*, 2:287.

actually denying Henry's paternity, just as had been the case with Mary. This could be accomplished only by declaring that the marriage to Elizabeth's mother was invalid from the start. Henry now had three illegitimate children and no legitimate heirs. The crisis was to be addressed by the Succession Act of July 1536, which formally removed Elizabeth from the succession and declared that the issue of Henry's marriage with Jane Seymour, or with his future true wives, would be next in line to throne; barring this, Henry was free to select his own heir, and thus he could have chosen his illegitimate son, Henry Fitzroy, the Earl of Richmond, to succeed him.[325] Unfortunately, this choice, too, was soon to be taken from Henry, as Richmond, who witnessed Anne's execution, was to die on 23 July 1536, at the age of seventeen.

It is assumed that Anne's execution was scheduled for the day after that of the men accused with her, but it was delayed. Kingston had written to Cromwell on 16 May, the day before the men's executions, to inquire as to "the king's pleasure touching the Queen," since several preparations had yet to be made.[326] On 18 May, the day following the men's executions, Kingston wrote again, notifying Cromwell that he had received the order to "have strangers conveyed out of the tower"—that is, to have foreigners barred from witnessing the queen's execution—and that Chapuys's man had been removed from the premises.[327] The queen, Kingston goes on to say in this same letter, had made her preparations to die, receiving the sacrament of Holy Eucharist and swearing her innocence, thinking that her execution was to take place that very day.[328] Kingston tells how Anne was "very sorry" when she learned that, in fact, she would not die that morning, but he does not explain the cause of the delay. Others, such as Paul Friedmann, have entertained the notion that the delay was caused by the late arrival of a special executioner, a French swordsman (known as the "Hangman of Calais"): for Henry had seen fit to execute Anne not by fire but by beheading, and not with the customary axe but with a sword.[329] It is also possible that, as Ives suggests, the execution had never been planned for 18 May and that there was no delay;

---

[325] See Ives, *Life and Death*, 355–56.

[326] See Ellis, *Original Letters*, 63.

[327] Ellis, *Original Letters*, 64; Strype, *Ecclesiastical Memorials*, 436.

[328] See also Chapuys's letter of 19 May to Charles V: "The lady who had charge of her has sent to tell me in great secrecy that the Concubine, before and after receiving the sacrament, affirmed to her, on the damnation of her soul, that she had never been unfaithful to the King." See CSP, Spain, 5, pt. 2 (1536–1538), no. 55, and LP 10.908. A transcription of the French original, found in CSP, Spain, 5, pt. 2 (1536–1538), no. 55n26 reads that Anne "ne s'estait meffaicte *de son corps* envers ce roy," emphasizing sins of the body. Bernard (*Anne Boleyn*, 172) is not persuaded that Anne was innocent despite her solemnly swearing to that effect.

[329] Friedmann, *Anne Boleyn*, 2:291. See also the *Chronicle of Calais*, 47, for a reference to Anne's death "by the hands of the hangman of Calais, with the sword of Calais."

Anne had merely assumed her execution would take place the day following the deaths of the five men.[330] In any event, Kingston's letter provides evidence that Anne had been thoroughly prepared to die on 18 May and that she was disappointed that she was not already "past her pain" but that she continued to spend her final hours in prayer with her almoner.

## The Death of Anne Boleyn

Anne's execution finally took place on the morning of 19 May, upon the green near the White Tower.[331] Although the precise hour had not been announced in advance, there were plenty of observers—as many as a thousand according to one report[332]—including, quite possibly, the foreigners Cromwell had wanted removed. Several foreign accounts of Anne's final moments exist, agreeing substantially with each other as well as with the English reports that have survived.[333] Indeed, an anonymous Imperial account contends that the gates to the Tower were left open despite orders to the contrary.[334] Furthermore, a letter from the Bishop of Faenza to Monsignor Ambrogio states that "all was done in the presence only of the ambassador of the Most Christian King [Francis I]," but it is not clear what the writer means by "all" and whether or not it included the execution of the queen.[335] Still, the implication is that the French ambassador Castelnau (perhaps even accompanied by his secretary, Carle) was privy to a sight that other ambassadors (or foreigners in general) were forbidden to see, thus lending further credibility to Carle's narration of these events.

---

[330] Ives, *Life and Death*, 356.

[331] Wriothesley (*Chronicle*, 1:41) says the execution took place at 8:00 a.m.; Chapuys, as recorded in LP 10.908 and CSP, Spain, 5, pt. 2 (1536–1538), no. 55, says 9:00 a.m.

[332] See the letter of Antony Pickering to Lady Lisle dated 19 May: "this present day the Queen was put to death within the Tower in the presence of a thousand people." See Byrne, *Lisle Letters*, no. 697 (3:365).

[333] These sources include Wriothesley, *Chronicle*; *Hall's Chronicle*; Harley 2194, fol. 16v (printed in *Ballads from Manuscripts* and Cobbett, *State Trials*); *Lettre d'un gentilhomme portugais*; *Il Successo in la morte*; an anonymous Imperial account (housed in the Vienna archives and printed in Froude's edition of *The Pilgrim*, 116–17, as well as in Gachard, *Analectes*, 17n1); and Dupuy 373, fol. 112.

[334] This account is recorded and paraphrased in LP 10.911 and is reprinted in Froude, *The Pilgrim*, 116–17. For the original French, see Gachard, *Analectes*, 17n1, which specifies that the execution site was left "à portes ouvertes" [with open gates].

[335] For this manuscript account, see Add. 8715, fol. 252v (paraphrased in English in LP 10.956); the Italian specifies that "tutto è stato fatto in presenza dell'Ambasciatore solo del cristianissimo," that is, the most Christian king, the title traditionally given to Francis I.

At any rate, Anne was escorted from her chambers in the Tower to the execution site by Kingston and was accompanied by four ladies whose identities remain unknown. Throughout the ordeal, Anne is said (in most accounts) to have been composed, even smiling at the spectators as she delivered her final address.[336] Yet an anonymous Imperial account claims that "she looked frequently behind her, and when she got upon the scaffold was very much exhausted and amazed."[337] According to Hall, the queen pronounced the following words:

> Good Christian people, I am come hither to die, for according to the law and by the law I am judged to die, and therefore I will speak nothing against it. I am come hither to accuse no man, nor to speak anything of that whereof I am accused and condemned to die, but I pray God save the king and send him long to reign over you, for a gentler nor a more merciful prince was there never: and to me he was ever a good, a gentle, and sovereign lord. And if any person will meddle of my cause, I require them to judge the best. And thus I take my leave of the world and of you all, and I heartily desire you all to pray for me. O Lord have mercy on me, to God I commend my soul.[338]

As can be seen, Anne's final words conform to the expected formula for scaffold speeches, as described above, but for two major discrepancies. First, she does not explicitly acknowledge the justice of the law that condemns her. Indeed, some

---

[336] See, in addition to Carle, the account in Harley 2194, fol. 16v, transcribed in *Ballads from Manuscripts*, 1:407, and also printed in Cobbett, *State Trials*, 1:411.

[337] See LP 10.911; and Froude's edition of *The Pilgrim*, 116. Gachard's *Analectes* (17n1), which transcribes the original French, reads: "elle estoit foible et estonnée . . . regardant souvent derrière elle." Anne's looking nervously behind her is also recorded in Dupuy 373, fol. 112.

[338] *Hall's Chronicle*, 819. Similarly, according to Wriothesley (*Chronicle*, 1:41–42), Anne proclaimed: "Masters, I here humbly submit me to the law as the law hath judged me, and as for mine offences, I here accuse no man, God knoweth them; I remit them to God, beseeching him to have mercy on my soul, and I beseech Jesu save my sovereign and master the King, the most goodly, noble, and gentle Prince that is, and long to reign over you." In a like manner, the Harleian manuscript (Harley 2194, fol. 16v) records her speech thus: "I beseech the Almighty to preserve his Majesty long to reign over you; a more gentle or mild Prince never swayed scepter, his bounty and clemency towards me I am sure hath been special: if anyone intend an inquisitive survey of my actions, I entreat him to judge favorably of me, and not rashly to admit any censorious conceit. And so I bid the world farewell, beseeching you to commend me in your prayers to God." This version is transcribed in Cobbett, *State Trials*, 1:410, and reprinted in *Ballads from Manuscripts*, 1:406–7. Cf. Constantyne's *Memorial*, 65, which reports her final words as: "I do not intend to reason my cause, but I commit me to Christ wholly, in whom is my whole trust, desiring you all to pray for the King's majesty that he may long reign over you, for he is a very noble prince and full gently hath handled me."

accounts, such as the Harleian manuscript, have her specifically raising doubts about this very fact.[339] Perhaps more important, she also does not confess to her crime, though, in some versions, she does make a general admission of sinfulness, as did the men before her.[340] Other supposed eyewitness reports indicate that she herself removed her hood, lowered her collar, and knelt upright (as one must do when executed by the sword as opposed to an axe, which required putting one's head down on the block) while one of her ladies blindfolded her in preparation for the sword's blow.[341] Immediately after her death, the ladies accompanying Anne to the scaffold wrapped her head and body in a cloth and carried her to the chapel of St. Peter ad Vincula, where she, like her brother, was buried.[342] Some reports specify that the queen's body was placed in a makeshift coffin that was originally an arrow-chest, for no other provision had been made as a receptacle for her remains.[343]

---

[339] In Harley 2194, fol. 16v, Anne is reported to have said: "Friends and good Christian people, I am here in your presence to suffer death, whereto I acknowledge my self adjudged by the law, how justly I will not say; I intend not an accusation of anyone." For this text, see Cobbett, *State Trials*, 1:410, and *Ballads from Manuscripts*, 1:406–7. Likewise, in *Hall's Chronicle* (819), Anne declares that she will not speak against the law that has condemned her to death. However, in the Italian *Successo in la morte* (no pagination), Anne refers to "la crudel legge del paese che è sola quella che mi condanna," or, the "cruel law of the country" that alone has condemned her. See also Bishai, "'Which thing had not before been seen,'" 178–79, which evaluates Anne's final speech with reference to expectations of the genre.

[340] Dupuy 372, fol. 112, and the Imperial account (Froude, *The Pilgrim*, 116; and Gachard, *Analectes*, 17n1) have Anne asking for pardon from everyone but not admitting specifically to this crime. Carle also has Anne asking for pardon (v. 1229). But these versions are exceptional; see Ives, *Life and Death*, 358, who affirms: "There was no public admission of sin, even in general, and still less any confession that she had wronged Henry."

[341] See the Imperial account printed in Froude's edition of *The Pilgrim*, 117, and Gachard, *Analectes*, 17n1: "One of her attendants gave her a cap into which she gathered her hair. She then knelt; a lady bound her eyes." However, Ales specifies that Anne "herself arranged her hair, covered her eyes, and commanded the executioner to strike." See Ales, CSP, FS, Elizabeth, 1:1303, 529.

[342] See, for example, Add. 28588, fol. 287v, Hannart's letter to the Empress dated 2 June (summarized in LP 10.1044): "The Queen's head and body were taken to a church in the Tower, accompanied by four ladies."

[343] Foxe, writing well after the fact (*Book of Martyrs*, 226), specifies that the makeshift coffin was "a chest of elm-tree, made to send arrows into Ireland"; but the more immediate Italian account, *Il Successo*, specifies that a "barra" (i.e., a plank) was positioned on the scaffold at the time of Anne's execution for this purpose ("lo postarono su una barra ch'era ivi apparecchiata," no pagination) [they placed (her body) upon a plank that had there been provided].

In the immediate aftermath of Anne's trial and execution, according to Carle and Ales, even her enemies were moved to pity.[344] Others clamored for the goods that were to come as a result of the redistribution of the wealth and titles that had been taken from the convicted men.[345] Many notable figures, such as the French humanist Étienne Dolet (1509–1546), who would himself come to be executed as a "heretic," continued to believe, well after her execution, that Anne was falsely accused and wrongly convicted. In a Latin poem that was published in 1538, Dolet wrote of Anne's execution in this way:

> Epitaph on the Queen of Utopia, falsely accused of the crime of adultery, and executed: What! Because a tyrant falsely condemned me and had me put to death, you now praise me less? And you pour insults upon me, as if I were shameful? I am not disgraced by the blow that I received. For, it is doubtless an honorable disgrace to die without sin and yet to yield to this fate.[346]

Dolet's designation of Anne as "The Queen of Utopia" ironically places her in the imaginary landscape envisioned by her nemesis, Thomas More, in his book of that name; yet, as has been noted, had England more closely resembled More's Utopia, Anne would likely not have suffered the penalty of death for such a crime, even if she had actually been guilty of adultery.[347]

---

[344] Ales writes in his "Letter" (CSP, FS, Eliz., 1:1303, 529): "The Queen exhibited such constancy, patience, and faith towards God that all the spectators, even her enemies, and those persons who previously had rejoiced at her misfortune out of their hatred to the doctrine of the religion which she had introduced into England, testified and proclaimed her innocence and chastity."

[345] See, on this point, Byrne, *Lisle Letters*, 3:354–55. See also LP 10.1087 for the parliamentary record regarding the redistribution of the "lands of Lord Rochford, Norris, and others," dated 8 June.

[346] My translation. For the original Latin version, see Étienne Dolet, *Stephani Doleti Galli aurelii carminum libri quatuor [Epigrammata]* (Lyon: Dolet, 1538), 4.162 (poem 13): "Reginae Utopiae falso adulterii crimine damnatae, et capite mulctatae Epitaphium: Quid? Quod Tyrannus crimine falso damnatam / Me iussit occidi, minus me iam laudas? / Necnon velut turpi maledicta suffundis? / Nulla nota turpis sum ob acceptum vulnus: / Nimirum honesta turpitudo est, sine culpa / Mori, & innocentem cedere aliquando Fatis."

[347] See, on this point, Émile Telle, "Étienne Dolet et Thomas More," *Moreana* 9.36 (1972): 33–38, here 37. For the pertinent passage by More, see Thomas More, *Utopia*, trans. Dominic Baker-Smith (London: Penguin, 2012), 94: "Those who violate the marriage bond are punished with the harshest form of slavery. . . . But any repetition of the offence is punished by death." The addition of this last sentence renders Anne's situation less absolute than Telle would like us to believe.

Still others expressed a particular enthusiasm for the hope that the king's first daughter, Mary, would be restored to favor at court.[348] Mary herself petitioned Cromwell at least twice that she be permitted to return to her father's graces;[349] she also wrote directly to Henry on 1 June and again on 8 June asking for his blessing and forgiveness.[350] But it soon became apparent that Mary was not to be restored to favor without formally agreeing to the terms of the Acts of Supremacy and Succession, which specified that the marriage of her parents was unlawful. A letter from Cromwell to Mary is devastatingly frank on this point and calls Mary "the most obstinate woman that ever was," while sending her "a book of articles to subscribe, on receiving which from you again, with a letter declaring that you think in your heart as you have subscribed with your hand, I will venture to speak for your reconciliation."[351] Following Chapuys's advice, Mary did subscribe to these articles and was finally reconciled with her father by July.[352]

Perhaps most important for Henry, Anne's death opened the door for a remarriage, and he was formally betrothed to Jane Seymour on 20 May, the day after Anne's execution. The couple were married 30 May at Whitehall Palace. Jane was particularly kind to Mary and helped ease her transition back to court, where she was eventually received as "second lady" after the queen.[353] Henry finally got his legitimate son when Jane gave birth to the future Edward VI on 12 October 1537. Sadly, Jane died as a result of that birthing, and Henry mourned her loss for years, ultimately choosing to be buried alongside her at St. George's Chapel in Windsor Castle. But before his death on 28 January 1547, Henry went on to marry three more women—Anne of Cleves (whom he divorced on the grounds of non-consummation), Catherine Howard (who, like her cousin, Anne Boleyn, was beheaded after being convicted of treasonous adultery), and

---

[348] See Chapuys's letter to Charles V, dated 19 May, CSP, Spain, 5, pt. 2 (1536–1538), no. 55: "I cannot well describe the great joy the inhabitants of this city have lately experienced and manifested, not only at the fall and ruin of the concubine, but at the hope that the Princess will be soon reinstated in her rights." See also LP 10.908.

[349] See LP 10.968, a letter from Mary to Cromwell dated 26 May in which she writes: "Master Secretary, I would have been a suitor to you before this time to have been a mean for me to the King's Grace to have obtained his Grace's blessing and favour"; she goes on to ask him "for the love of God to be a suitor for her to the King, to have his blessing and leave to write to his Grace." On 30 May, Mary again wrote to Cromwell (LP 10.991) to thank him "for the great pain and labour he has taken in obtaining for her her father's blessing and license to write to him," saying that she "will be as obedient to the King as can reasonably be expected." Another letter to similar effect was sent on 7 June (see LP 10.1079).

[350] See LP 10.1022 and 10.1083, respectively.

[351] LP 10.1110.

[352] For more on this matter, see Guy, *The Children of Henry VIII*, 92–93.

[353] Loades, *Henry VIII*, 271–72.

Katherine Parr (who outlived him). Yet Edward would be Henry's last child. After Edward's death at the age of fifteen in 1553, Henry's two daughters, Mary and Elizabeth, each went on to wear the crown of the sovereign of England. They both were to remain childless, and the Tudor dynasty would be no more.

# Chapter 3

# THE AUTHOR, HIS TEXT, AND ITS RECEPTION

## Life and Works

Lancelot de Carle (sometimes spelled "de Carles" or simply "Lancelot Carle") was born in Bordeaux to Jacquette and Jean de Carle, a local political figure.[1] He was related by marriage to two illustrious Bordelais of the sixteenth century, Michel de Montaigne (1533–1592) and that author's famed close friend, Étienne de la Boétie: for Carle's sister Marguerite married La Boétie after the death of her first husband, and her daughter (the fruit of her first marriage), in turn, married Montaigne's brother, Thomas.[2] The precise date of Carle's birth is unknown; his

---

[1] For a more extensive biography of Carle, consult the seventeenth-century essay by Guillaume Colletet in *Vies des poètes bordelais et périgourdins*, ed. Philippe Tamizey de Larroque (1873; repr. Geneva: Slatkine, 1969), 5–50. See also Émile Picot, *Les Français italianisants au XVI*ᵉ *siècle*, vol. 1 (Paris: Champion, 1906), 235–49; L.-C. [Lewis C.] Harmer, "Lancelot de Carle: Sa vie," *Humanisme et Renaissance* 6 (1939): 443–74; Harmer, "Lancelot de Carle et les hommes de lettres de son temps," *Bibliothèque d'humanisme et Renaissance* 7 (1945): 95–117; and François Rouget, "Un évêque lettré au temps des Valois: Lancelot de Carle (vers 1500–1568)," *Seizième siècle* 11 (2015): 119–34. Recent scholars have preferred the spelling "Carle," as this was how the cleric himself spelled it in a surviving autograph letter. See, on this point, Jean-Pierre Babelon, "Les derniers moments du duc François de Guise, d'après un manuscrit de Lancelot de Carle (février 1563)," *Comptes rendus des séances de l'Académie des Inscriptions et Belles-Lettres* 131 (1987): 597–608, here 598n3.

[2] Montaigne may be alluding to his kinsman Carle when, in his "Apologie de Raimond Sebond" (*Les Essais de Michel de Montaigne*, ed. Pierre Villey and V.-L. Saulnier [Paris: Presses universitaires de France, 1965], bk. 2, ch. 12, p. 579), he laments the fact that England has changed its laws regarding religion several times during his lifetime, which upsets him all the more since "c'est une nation à laquelle ceux de mon quartier ont eu autrefois une si privée accointance qu'il reste encore en ma maison aucunes traces de nostre ancien cousinage" [that is a nation with which the people of my region formerly had such intimate acquaintance that there still remain in my house some traces of our old cousinship]. Montaigne's *Essais* were translated by Donald M. Frame as *The Complete Essays of Montaigne* (1958; repr. Stanford: Stanford University Press, 1975), here 436.

earliest biographer, the literary scholar Guillaume Colletet (1598–1659), is silent on the matter, while Émile Picot suggests 1500.[3] Thanks to a Latin poem written in 1538, which refers to Carle as being a young man at the time of its composition, L.-C. Harmer believes it is more likely that Carle was born around 1510 or, perhaps, even somewhat later.[4] Since the author of the 1538 poem, Ioannes Vulteius (that is, Jean Visagier), was twenty-eight years old at that time, it does seem logical to believe, as does Harmer, that Carle was certainly no older than Visagier and possibly a bit younger.

Little is known about Carle's formal education, but, judging from the works that he produced and translated, it is clear that he was well versed in the classics. It has been suggested that he made his way to Paris to become part of the itinerant court of King Francis I sometime around 1534–1535.[5] By this time, he may well have taken minor orders in the Roman Catholic Church, as he soon became known as a "prothonotary" or ecclesiastical clerk. The practice of taking minor orders was not uncommon among scholars and writers of his era, because it provided a source of income while retaining a great deal of freedom (other than the freedom to marry, of course). It was at this early stage of his association with the French court that Carle became engaged in the writing of poetry.

Specifically, before the end of 1535, Carle took part in a literary competition along with several other French versifiers who wrote *blasons anatomiques*: that is, poems that describe at length various individual parts of the female body. This contest, or "concours des blasons," as it came to be known, was launched by Clément Marot (1496–1544), a court poet whose evangelical inclinations put him in conflict with the religious conservatism of the French authorities. Marot had taken up residence in Ferrara at the more hospitable court of Renée de France (1510–1575), the younger sister of Claude de France (wife of the French king, Francis I). Renée was sympathetic to those who shared her evangelical, humanist leanings, and she had, in fact, also briefly sheltered Calvin along with other religious reformers.[6] Yet her court also encouraged the pursuit of the arts, and it was here in Ferrara that Marot amused himself by writing a *blason* on the

---

[3] Picot, *Les Français*, 235.

[4] Harmer, "Sa vie," 445–46. For more on this Latin poem, see Louis Delaruelle, "Un dîner littéraire chez Mellin de Sainct-Gelays," *Revue d'histoire littéraire de la France* 4 (1897): 407–11.

[5] For these arguments, see Harmer, "Sa vie," 449–50.

[6] For more on this matter, see Charmarie Jenkins Blaisdell, "Renée de France between Reform and Counter-Reform," *Archiv für Reformationsgeschichte—Archive for Reformation History* 63 (1972): 196–225. For an account of Marot's time in Ferrara, see Rosanna Gorris, "'Un franzese nominato Clemente': Marot à Ferrare," in *Clément Marot, "Prince des poëtes françois," 1496–1996*, Actes du colloque international de Cahors en Quercy, 21–25 mai 1996, ed. Gérard Defaux and Michel Simonin (Paris: Champion, 1997), 339–64.

female breast, which he sent to the court in France. His unique poem served as
an invitation for others to follow suit with their own descriptive poems on body
parts as varied as the eyebrow, mouth, and thigh. Needless to say, some of these
poems are rather bawdy, mentioning unmentionable body parts; others, however,
treated less corporeal themes such as the voice, grace, and honor of the lauded
woman.[7]

Carle was one of the earliest participants in this event and produced at least
two poems before 1536: the "Blason du genoil" (on the knee) and the "Blason de
l'esprit" (on the spirit). The young versifier's efforts were noted by Marot himself
in a poem dating from February 1536, in which he awards the prized laurel to
the Lyonnais poet and humanist, Maurice Scève. Carle's two poems were then
included in the earliest collections of *blasons* published in 1536 and reprinted in
1543.[8] But, as the collected poems initially appeared anonymously, there is some
dispute about authorship, and several other *blasons*, including the "Blason du
pied" (on the foot), have sometimes been attributed to Carle.[9] While the knee
is certainly among the less erotically charged parts of the anatomy, Carle does
not shy away from alluding to other, more private areas of the female body in the
course of his poem, and if the "Blason du pied" is indeed Carle's, it can be said
that he certainly was capable of using less than decorous language in his youth-
ful poetry.

Carle's earliest poetic endeavor, while hardly of the highest merit, was impor-
tant because it provided the fledgling poet with an opportunity to work within
the versification structure — rhyming decasyllabic couplets (known in French as

---

[7] For an argument that even an ostensibly erotic poem such as that on the female
breast might have a religious significance, see Lance K. Donaldson-Evans, "'Le Blason
du beau tetin': Une relecture," in Defaux and Simonin, *Clément Marot, "Prince des poëtes
françois,"* 645–55. For a counter-argument, see Cathy Yandell, "Iconography and Icono-
clasm: The Female Breast in French Renaissance Culture," *The French Review* 83 (2010):
540–88, here 551–53.

[8] The poems first circulated in manuscript; after 1536, they also enjoyed several
reprintings throughout the sixteenth century. For the earliest imprint, see the edition of
the *Blasons* printed in *Hécatomphile, Les fleurs de poésies françaises, Blasons du corps féminin*
(Lyon: François Juste, 1536–1537), a digital copy of which is available on the website of
the Bibliothèque nationale de France (BnF) known as Gallica; a digital copy of the 1543
reprint (*Blasons anatomiques du corps féminin* [Paris: Charles Langelier, 1543]) is avail-
able through the University of Virginia's website, "The Renaissance in Print" (https://
explore.lib.virginia.edu/exhibits/show/renaissance-in-print). For a modern edition, see
*Blasons anatomiques du corps féminin*, ed. Julien Gœury (Paris: Flammarion, 2016). For an
extensive review of the complicated printing history of the *blasons*, see Alison Saunders,
"Sixteenth-Century Collected Editions of *Blasons Anatomiques*," *The Library*, series 5,
31.4 (1976): 351–68.

[9] For more on this matter, see Rouget, "Un évêque lettré," 121–23, as well as Picot,
*Les Français*, 235–36.

*rimes plates*)—that he would come to use when writing his narrative verses on Anne Boleyn. It also gives us a glimpse of Carle's lighter side: at this point in his life, he is not a stern and serious cleric but, rather, a young man who sought amusement in the cultural activities—be they poetry or music—of Francis's court. For this, we also have the testimony of the French storyteller Brantôme, who, years later, remembered having heard of Carle as someone who had earned a reputation for being the most accomplished practitioner of the popular (but complicated and decidedly athletic) *galliard* dance step that one could find in the court of Francis I.[10] Another poet, Louis Des Masures, who frequented Francis's court as early as 1533, likewise mentions Carle as one of those who regularly engaged in reciting his verses for the entertainment of the French court.[11]

Within a short period of time after writing his *blasons*, Carle embarked on his diplomatic career, taking on the role of secretary to the resident French ambassador in London, Antoine de Castelnau (d. 1539), Bishop of Tarbes. Castelnau's letter of credence, signed by Francis I, was dated 19 June 1535.[12] But an Italian diplomat, Cardinal Ridolfo Pio, Bishop of Faenza, wrote as early as May 1535 to announce that a new French envoy was soon to arrive, stating that Castelnau was about thirty years old at this time.[13] According to a letter sent by Eustace Chapuys (the resident ambassador representing the Holy Roman Emperor) to his master, Charles V, on 30 June 1535, Castelnau did in fact arrive in London just three days before (coincidentally, then, just before the trial of Thomas

---

[10] Brantôme describes the court of Francis I thus: "in the time of that great king, one saw the prothonotary Carle, from Bordeaux, later bishop of Riez, a scholar and great dignitary, enjoy the reputation, in his youth, of being the best dancer of the 'galliard' who was ever at court" (my translation). See Pierre de Bourdeille, Seigneur de Brantôme, *Œuvres complètes*, vol. 3, ed. Ludovic Lalanne (Paris: Renouard, 1867), 134. Because Brantôme was born in 1535, he did not witness these scenes personally. For this argument and others relating to the timing of Carle's attachment to the French court, see again Harmer, "Sa vie," 449–50.

[11] See the poem addressed to Joachim Du Bellay in Louis Des Masures, *Œuvres poétiques* (Lyon: Jean de Tournes, 1557), 19.

[12] *Letters and Papers, Foreign and Domestic, of the Reign of Henry VIII* (hereafter abbreviated as LP), ed. J. S. Brewer, J. Gairdner, and R. H. Brodie (London: Her Majesty's Stationery Office, 1846–1932), 8.896. These documents are now available through an online searchable database: British History Online (https://www.british-history. ac.uk/). For another searchable database available by subscription, which sometimes gives a digitized copy of the original manuscript in addition to the summary made by these Victorian-era scholars, see "State Papers Online: Early Modern Government in Britain and Europe" (https://www.gale.com/intl/primary-sources/state-papers-online).

[13] London, British Library, Additional 8715, fols. 59v–62v: "è giovane di circa 30 anni, Dottore di legge, del Gran Consiglio, e persona certo di molta espettatione," 61v; the letter is summarized in English in LP 8.753.

More on 1 July).[14] Chapuys also let it be known, in a letter composed on 11 July 1535, that Castelnau's arrival was not greeted with the customary hospitality one might expect to be shown to a foreign dignitary and that he was initially denied access to Bridewell Palace, "where the French ambassadors have resided for five years."[15] Indeed, Bridewell was the setting of Hans Holbein's famous painting of 1533, known as "The Ambassadors," which depicted two French envoys who preceded Castelnau, namely Jean de Dinteville and Georges de Selve, and that palace continued to be used by the French ambassadors until 1539, so initial denial of this residence to Castelnau would have seemed quite extraordinary.

But, although the date of Castelnau's arrival in England has been documented, it is not clear exactly when the ambassador's secretary, Carle, reached London for the first time. Harmer, though cognizant of this lack of evidence, posits that Carle probably joined Castelnau close to the time when the latter began his residency in London, that is, towards the end of June 1535. Unlike Castelnau, however, Carle was not permanently in residence in the English capital. Rather, there is evidence to prove that he shuttled between England and France, in the service of Castelnau, at various points throughout the latter's tenure as resident ambassador (which ended on 11 September 1537, though Castelnau was to serve as a special envoy to England again in 1538–1539).[16] We know that Carle had returned to Paris by 1538 at the very latest, for he is found there in the company of famed humanists, as documented by the Latin poem by Visagier (cited earlier

---

[14] LP 8.948.

[15] LP 8.1018; see also London, British Library Additional 28587, fols. 356r–357r, here 357r (paraphrased in LP 8.1012), for a corroborating foreign report indicating that "the Bishop of Tarbes has since gone as ambassador to England, but has been badly received by the king." Chapuys himself was not always courteous to Castelnau; at a dinner in June 1536 (after the French had declared war on Charles V, Chapuys's master), Chapuys mocked the French ambassador mercilessly. See the *Calendar of State Papers, Spain* (hereafter CSP, Spain), ed. G. A. Bergenroth, Pascual de Gayangos, and Martin A. S. Hume (London: Her Majesty's Stationery Office, 1862–1954), available via the websites "British History Online" and "State Papers Online." For this reference, see CSP, Spain, 5, pt. 2 (1536–1538), no. 70 (letter dated 1 July 1536); see also LP 11.7. For more on this episode, see Lauren Mackay, *Inside the Tudor Court* (Stroud: Amberley, 2014), 181.

[16] In the *Catalogue des actes de François Iᵉʳ*, vol. 3, January 1535–April 1539 (Paris: Imprimerie nationale, 1889), 249 (no. 8669), can be found this entry attesting to Carle's movement between France and England in October 1536: "a mandate to the treasurer of the exchequer to pay 225 pounds to Lancelot de Carle, secretary to Antoine de Castelnau, bishop of Tarbes, who is leaving this very day to carry to England a response from the king, Roanne, 14 October 1536" (my translation). The document that is described here is Paris, Bibliothèque nationale de France, Clairambault 1215, fol. 75. A further entry in this volume (3:421, no. 9456) attests to a payment made to Castelnau for services rendered as ambassador to England between 2 November 1536 and 11 September 1537. That entry is dated 15 December 1537.

in this chapter) describing a dinner at which Carle was present, as well as by a letter, written by Jean Boyssonné, which speaks of another instance where Carle broke bread with other writers in the French capital.[17] It seems likely, therefore, that Carle left England for good in 1537, at or before the moment when Castelnau ceased his ambassadorial duties.[18]

After the death of King Francis I in 1547, Carle was sent on diplomatic missions in Italy by Francis's son, King Henry II, whom the poet had served as almoner when Henri was "Dauphin" or heir apparent to the king (that is, at some point after August 1536—when Francis's eldest son, also named Francis, died—and before Henri's accession to the throne). Carle was named Bishop of Riez in 1550, although he may not have previously been an ordained priest; at least there are no records to indicate that he had been ordained.[19] By the time of Carle's installation as bishop in 1551, however, he would no doubt have been ordained deacon, priest, and bishop, in quick succession, as was an acceptable practice from the Middle Ages until the Second Vatican Council.

Throughout all these appointments, however, Carle was clearly happy to have the opportunity to write both prose and poetry and to continue other scholarly pursuits, including his poem on Anne Boleyn (written in 1536, within two weeks of her execution) as well as his translation from Greek of two books of Homer's *Odyssey* (which, alas, does not survive). He certainly came to the attention of élite French writers—such as Pierre de Ronsard, Joachim Du Bellay, Olivier de Magny, and Pontus de Tyard—many of whom seem to have enjoyed a certain camaraderie with Carle and each of whom lauds him in their own poetry for his learning and writing ability.[20] Du Bellay, in particular, appears to be espe-

---

[17] See Harmer, "Sa vie," 455; and especially Delaruelle, "Un dîner," 411n1.

[18] On this point, see also Harmer, "Sa vie," 454.

[19] The position of "royal almoner" did not require ordination to the priesthood. In France, many poets—including Mellin de Saint-Gelais, Pierre de Ronsard, and Philippe Desportes—served as almoners, having been named to the position "primarily because of their prominence in domains unrelated to the supposed function of the post." See, on this point, Jeanice Brooks, *Courtly Song in Late Sixteenth-Century France* (Chicago: University of Chicago Press, 2000), 77.

[20] For more on these and other poems in praise of Carle, see Picot, *Les Français*, 238–39; Colletet, *Vies*, 16–21; and especially Harmer, "Hommes de lettres." It should be noted that, in the 1555 edition of his poem entitled "Les Daimons" (dedicated to Carle), Ronsard makes an explicit reference to Carle's acquaintance with both England and Italy, garnered through his diplomatic service. See Pierre de Ronsard, *Œuvres complètes*, vol. 8, ed. Paul Laumonier, 3rd ed. (Paris: Didier, 1973), 115–39, "À Lancelot de Carle, Evesque de Rhiez": "Qui pourroit racompter de combien de loüenges / Tu te veis honoré par les païs estranges, / Discourant l'Italie et l'Angleterre, à fin / De te faire un Ulysse accort, prudent, & fin?" (vv. 23–26) [To Lancelot de Carle, Bishop of Riez: Who can tell of the many praises with which you are honored in foreign lands, wandering about Italy and England, so as to become a Ulysses, astute, prudent, and subtle?]. The long reference to

cially taken with this learned cleric, mentioning him in virtually all his works and naming him, in the preface to his earliest sonnet sequence, *L'Olive* (1549), as one of the ideal readers he envisions for his new style of poetry.[21] Yet most of Carle's other literary productions date only from the 1560s, suggesting a hiatus from serious engagement with writing in the early years after his return to France from England. Among these later works can be found a Latin verse exhortation to his nephew to live a virtuous life, which Carle himself translated into French.[22] He also partook of the popular genre of religious poetry, producing a French verse paraphrase of the books of Ecclesiastes and the Song of Songs as well as a collection of "canticles" taken from various books of the Bible.[23] Rendering books of the Bible into French, even as a paraphrase rather than as a translation, was certainly an extraordinary undertaking for a Roman Catholic churchman: for, making the Bible accessible in the vernacular to the laity was a much-debated matter that typically was divided along confessional lines, pitting Catholics against Evangelicals or Reformists. As Marie-Madeleine Fragonard explained, Carle's publication of these vernacular biblical paraphrases, during his term as bishop, makes him a unique figure who united orthodox Catholicism with the "spiritual

---

Carle (vv. 7–46) was removed from the definitive version of Ronsard's poems published in 1567, probably because the great French poet had no further need to flatter Carle.

[21] "It is enough for me to have as my only readers a Saint-Gelais, an Heroët, a Ronsard, a Carle, a Scève" (my translation). See "Au lecteur," *Cinquante sonnetz à la louange de l'Olive*, in Joachim Du Bellay, *Œuvres complètes*, vol. 2, ed. Marie-Dominique Legrand, Michel Magnien, Daniel Ménager, and Olivier Millet (Paris: Champion, 2003), 12. See also the poem "À Carles" (Ode 12) in the same volume's edition of Du Bellay's *Recueil de poésie* (129–31), where Carle is exhorted to "ring out the English tragedy in a hardy voice." While the editors of this edition of Du Bellay's poetry believe this is a reference to the English battle over Boulogne, other readers have seen here a reference to Carle's "tragedy" on the life and death of Anne Boleyn.

[22] [Lancelot de Carle], *Lanceloti Carlæi Rhegiensium pontificis, ad Janum Carlæum, fratris filium, sermo* (Paris: Vascosan, 1560), translated by Carle himself in the same volume as *Exhortation ou parenese . . . à son neveu*. This work is available on Gallica. See also Colletet, *Vies*, 7.

[23] [Lancelot de Carle], *L'Ecclésiaste de Salomon, paraphrasé en vers françois, par Lancelot de Carles, Evesque de Riez, avec quelques sonnets chrestiens* (Paris: Nicolas Edoard, 1561), with a digital copy available on NuBIS (University of Paris digital site); [Lancelot de Carle], *Le Cantique des Cantiques de Salomon paraphrasé en vers françois, par Lancelot de Carle, Evesque de Riez* (Paris: Vascosan, 1562), a digital copy of which is available on Google Books; [Lancelot de Carle], *Les Cantiques de la Bible, traduits selon l'hébreu, par Lancelot de Carle, Evesque de Riez, plus deux hymnes qui se chantent en l'Eglise* (Paris: Vascosan, 1562), with a digital copy available on Gallica. For more on Carle's paraphrase of Ecclesiastes, see Jean Vignes, "Paraphrase et appropriation: Les avatars poétiques de l'Ecclésiaste au temps des Guerres de Religion (Dalbiac, Carle, Belleau, Baïf)," *Bibliothèque d'humanisme et Renaissance* 55 (1993): 503–26.

advantages of the Reformation."[24] Additionally, appended to his paraphrase of Ecclesiastes are about twenty original sonnets on religious themes; a further set of twenty sonnets, which he sent to the Cardinal of Lorraine, remained unpublished in his lifetime.[25] A prose work, "Les derniers moments du duc François de Guise," which is a long letter addressed to King Charles IX, relates the dying words of this famous political figure and member of the staunchly Catholic Guise family, who was assassinated in 1563.[26]

What is of interest in these other works, for our purposes, is how they might relate to the poem on Anne Boleyn. A few observations are thus in order. For one, it is easy to see that Carle held fast to his vocation as a poet throughout his life. Carle continued to use the decasyllabic rhyming couplet form in his French translation of the exhortation to his nephew, as well as in his verse paraphrases of Ecclesiastes and the Song of Songs, just as he had done in *The Story of the Death of Anne Boleyn*. Furthermore, the themes of all these works—including his works in prose—are also similar insofar as they expound on the biblical topos of *vanitas*, which is a major theme of Carle's poem on Anne Boleyn. It is also fair to say that Carle envisioned all his works to be instructive in nature and that he often comments explicitly on their edifying usefulness in his dedicatory prefaces.[27]

Moreover, there are certain idiosyncratic turns of phrase that demonstrate Carle's stylistic consistency throughout his writings. In the dedicatory preface

---

[24] See Marie-Madeleine Fragonard, "Lancelot de Carle, l'institution ecclésiale, la Bible et la poésie," in *Poésie et Bible de la Renaissance à l'âge classique (1550–1680)*, Actes du colloque de Besançon des 25 et 26 mars 1997, ed. Pascale Blum and Anne Mantero (Paris: Champion, 1999), 161–82, here 162 (my translation).

[25] For these, see Henri Chamard, "Sonnets chrétiens inédits de Lancelot de Carle, Évêque de Riez," in *Mélanges offerts par ses amis et ses élèves à M. Gustave Lanson*, ed. Gustave Lanson (Paris: Hachette, 1922), 87–97.

[26] [Lancelot de Carle], *Recueil des derniers propos que dit et teint feu tresillustre prince, Messire Françoys de Lorraine Duc de Guyse . . . prononcez par luy devant son trespas à Madame la Duchesse sa femme, Monsieur son filz, Messieurs les Cardinaulx ses freres, & à plusieurs assistans à l'heure de son trespas* (Paris: Jacques Kerver, 1563), available on Gallica. The letter has been reprinted under the title [Lancelot de Carle], "Lettre de l'Evesque de Riez au Roy, contenant les actions et propos de Monsieur de Guyse, depuis sa blessure, iusques à son trespas," in *Archives curieuses de l'histoire de France depuis Louis XI jusqu'à Louis XVIII*, 1st series, vol. 5, ed. L. Cimber and F. Danjou (Paris: Beauvais, 1835), 171–97, also available on Gallica. For more on the various editions and translations of this work printed in the early modern period, see Picot, *Les Français*, 245–48.

[27] See, for example, his preface to the *Cantique des Cantiques*, addressing the Duke of Orléans (the future King Henry III), where he explains that he used paraphrase in conjunction with simple translation "pour vous en pouvoir, Monseigneur, mieulx instruire & edifier" [to better instruct and edify you], Aiii. A similar expression is used in his dedicatory letter to the king in *L'Ecclésiaste*, Aii. See also Fragonard, "Lancelot de Carle," 172, on this point.

to the king in his paraphrase of Ecclesiastes, for example, Carle offers some general thoughts on his work, acknowledging his inadequacies in undertaking this "œuvre veritablement difficil à mon insuffisance" [work which is truly difficult in light of my insufficiency];[28] yet he is resolved to make this effort to write verse rather than prose in order to provide greater pleasure to his reader, "pour temperer la severité des sentences avecques la douceur des nombres" [to temper the severity of the pronouncements with the sweetness of meter].[29] Carle's use of the modesty topos also appears in the dedication of his letter on the death of the Duke of Guise: "je crains, comme je doibs, que mon imbécilité diminue par trop tant de perfections" [I fear, as I must, that my feebleness too greatly diminishes (the Duke of Guise's) many perfections].[30] Notably, both the explanation Carle provides for using rhyme and his confession of poetic "feebleness" (an unusual use of the word "imbécilité") are elements that had already appeared in the prefatory lines of his poem on Anne Boleyn, where he alludes to his unique choice of writing this dispatch to the French court in verse rather than prose:

> I shall write it in verse (albeit poorly composed),
> Because it seems more suitable to me,
> So that, through my rhyme, the long discourse of this present letter
> Might be less troubling to you,
> By no means supposing that anyone other than you
> Will read what I am writing,
> And that, in your kindness, you will wish
> To cover up my feebleness in this task.[31]

While both of these features may be commonplaces that appear in the works of many authors of the time, it is primarily Carle's consistent articulation of these themes that is most striking and that helps to tie the various works of his corpus together.

Undoubtedly, among all of Carle's works, it is his account of the Duke of Guise's dying words that is most similar to his poem on Anne Boleyn, despite their formal differences. Like that poem, this prose text is explicitly framed as

---

[28] Carle, *L'Ecclésiaste*, "Au Roy," Aii. See also, on this point, Vignes, "Paraphrase," 513–14.

[29] Carle, *L'Ecclésiaste*, "Au Roy," B.

[30] Carle, "Lettre de l'Evesque," 174.

[31] *The Story of the Death of Anne Boleyn*, vv. 29–36: "Ie l'escriray en vers mal composez, / Pour ce que mieux me semblent disposez, / Et que par eux moins gref vous pourra estre / Le long discours de la presente lettre, / N'estimant point que de cest' escripture / Aultre que vous en face la lecture, / Et que vouldrez par vostre humanité / En ce couurir mon imbecilité." For more on this point, see also Koji Takenaka, "Lancelot de Carle et le récit des dernières paroles du duc François de Guise," *Cahiers d'études françaises Université Keio* 19 (2014): 112–28, here 121–22.

a letter to the French court. Again like that poem, it is presented as a true tes-
timony of events that the author personally witnessed or heard about through
reliable narrators. Indeed, Carle insists on the truth of his narration: he will be
meticulous in his storytelling so that

> les autres ne me soupçonneront point de mensonge en choses testifiées par
> la majesté de la Royne, par messieurs les princes et plusieurs autres sei-
> gneurs et personnages d'authorité, de qui j'en ay entendu l'une partie, et
> l'autre je l'ay veuë et ouye moy-mesme.

> [others shall not suspect me in the least of lying with regard to the things
> which were attested by her Majesty the Queen, the princes and several
> other lords and persons of authority, from whom I heard one part of this,
> and the other part of which I saw and heard myself.][32]

Carle's characterization of his text as one that is constructed through a combina-
tion of reports from honorable personages and his own eyewitness testimony is
a feature that, again, had graced the opening verses of *The Story of the Death of
Anne Boleyn*:

> I shall write about what I have heard,
> Through the insights that several people have provided me,
> And then, my lord, about what I have remembered
> Since the time that I arrived here.[33]

Moreover, the very subject of this work is bound to recall, for the reader, the scaf-
fold speeches Carle records for both the queen and her brother, George, in *The
Story of the Death of Anne Boleyn*, just as surely as in hearing and, later, transcrib-
ing the duke's final words, Carle was himself reminded of the gruesome execu-
tions of 1536: for all are vivid examples of the Christian approach to the art of
dying.[34]
    Carle's ecclesiastical, poetic, and scholarly career garnered him attention in
France until the moment of his death, which occurred in Paris in July 1568.[35]

---

[32] Carle, "Lettre de l'Evesque," 174–75.
[33] "J'en escriray ce que i'ay entendu / Par les raisons que plusieurs m'ont rendu, /
Puis, mon Seigneur, ce que i'ay retenu / Depuis le temps que suis icy venu" (vv. 25–28).
[34] It has been suggested that Montaigne was, in turn, inspired by Carle's letter on
the death of the Duc de Guise in several passages of his own letter relating the death
of La Boétie. See, on this point, Roger Trinquet, "La Lettre sur la mort de La Boétie,
ou Lancelot de Carle inspirateur de Montaigne," in *Mélanges d'histoire littéraire (XVIe–
XVIIe siècle) offerts à Raymond Lebègue par ses collègues, ses élèves, et ses amis*, ed. Raymond
Lebègue (Paris: Nizet, 1969), 115–25.
[35] Carle's death in 1568 is affirmed by Harmer ("Sa vie," 471) as well as by Tamizey
in his edition of Colletet's *Vies*, 14–15n2, who cites multiple ecclesiastical sources for this

As might be expected, Carle's demise did not go unnoticed among the *literati* of the time, and several important writers, including Jean Dorat, wrote eulogistic poems marking his death.[36] Yet, as Harmer reminds us, Carle's life and works were relatively soon forgotten, and he became "virtually unknown in the seventeenth century."[37] Although Harmer opines that Carle's literary works "are not worth a great deal," he nevertheless wonders how this prelate so rapidly fell into oblivion.[38] As shall be seen, the story of Carle's fall from fame (and its more recent resurgence) is one that is intimately linked to the fortunes of his poem on the life and death of Anne Boleyn.

## The Early Reception of
### *The Story of the Death of Anne Boleyn*

It should be noted from the outset that Carle's poem on Anne Boleyn, like many works of its time, circulated primarily in manuscript form, though a printed edition (bearing the title *Epistre contenant le proces criminel faict à l'encontre de la royne Anne Boullant d'Angleterre, par Carles aulmosnier de Monsieur le Daulphin*) appeared in 1545.[39] But how much did early readers know about this poem and its author? The answer to this question is quite complicated. Soon after Carle's death, his works were discussed briefly by two important early modern French bibliographers: François Grudé (known as the lord of La Croix du Maine); and Antoine du Verdier, writing in 1579 and 1585, respectively. Their works (called "libraries")—which seek to describe all the printed books of their time (and which sometimes are the only record of the existence of now-lost volumes)—each duly note Carle's literary contributions.[40] While La Croix du Maine refers to the 1545 printed version of Carle's poem on Anne Boleyn, du Verdier, curiously, makes no mention of this book. A little later, Guillaume Colletet, the early modern biographer of Renaissance poets, does refer to Carle's 1545 book along with his other writings.[41] Despite these two early references to the poem, however, it appears that Carle's name was rapidly becoming detached from *The Story of the Death of*

---

information. Colletet himself (14) mistakenly says Carle died "around 1565."

[36] See, on this point, Picot, *Les Français*, 249.

[37] Harmer, "Sa vie," 473 (my translation). The author here offers a summary of Carle's reputation in the early modern period.

[38] Harmer, "Sa vie," 474 (my translation).

[39] For a complete discussion of the manuscript tradition of this poem, see Chapter 4, "Versions of the Text," in this volume.

[40] See François Grudé sieur de La Croix du Maine, *La Bibliothèque du sieur de La Croix du Maine*, vol. 1 (1579; repr. Paris: Abel L'Angelier, 1584), 282 and [Antoine du Verdier], *La bibliothèque d'Antoine du Verdier* (Lyon: Honorat, 1585), 782.

[41] Colletet, *Vies*, 14.

*Anne Boleyn* as early as the late sixteenth century, as its lack of inclusion in du Verdier's catalogue suggests.

Several factors conspired to bring this about, including the growing rarity of the print edition as well as the normal separation of text and author that is part and parcel of a manuscript culture that persisted into the sixteenth century. As Steven W. May and Heather Wolfe maintain, "it was quite easy for a writer and his [manuscript] work to go their separate ways" in the sixteenth century, for "as texts radiated out from the original circle [of readers and copyists], fewer and fewer scribes would recognize the minor courtier or aspiring laureate whose name was subscribed to it, and therefore would not bother to recopy it."[42] The authors go on to explain this loss of "control over their works and even acknowledgement of their responsibility for them" by means of a modern, but apt, analogy to "an oft-forwarded email" whose original author is lost in the continual copying of his or her text.[43]

In the case of *The Story of the Death of Anne Boleyn*, one could certainly also point to the inflammatory nature of the poem's subject as another factor that contributed to the (perhaps intentional) separation of the poet from his text. To understand this point fully, one needs to consider how this poem was received —particularly in England—in the years closely following the 1536 executions. The first we hear of this poem's reception is an ominous mention of it in a letter written (as is customary) in the hand of Henry VIII's secretary, Thomas Wriothesley, but clearly in the voice of the king, whose anger is deafening. This letter is dated 12 June 1537—that is, almost exactly a year after the completion of Carle's poem—and was addressed to the English ambassador in France, Stephen Gardiner, the Bishop of Winchester.[44] The letter acknowledges Henry's receipt of a French book "written in form of a tragedy," sent to him by Gardiner through Sir Francis Bryan, who had recently arrived in London from a diplomatic mission in France.

It quickly becomes apparent that Henry is incensed by what he has read and asks why, when Gardiner "first had knowledge" of this book and its "malice," he did not "immediately" approach the French king, "as it might not only have been suppressed" but also "punished."[45] The letter alludes to the wide dissemination of the text already in France, stating that "sundry copies" of it have got "abroad."

---

[42] Steven W. May and Heather Wolfe, "Manuscripts in Tudor England," in *A Companion to Tudor Literature*, ed. Kent Cartwright (Oxford: Wiley-Blackwell, 2010), 125–39; here 134.

[43] May and Wolfe, "Manuscripts," 134.

[44] This is London, British Library, Additional 25114 (hereafter Add. 25114), "Original letters and state papers relating chiefly to the embassies of Stephen Gardiner, Bishop of Winchester, to the courts of Francis I and Charles V: 1527–1545," fols. 267r–268v. For a synopsis, see LP 12.2.78.

[45] Add. 25114, fol. 267r.

Henry enjoins Gardiner to tell the French king and the Great Master (that is, the French statesman Anne de Montmorency, the Marshal of France and a key player in Francis's court) how unhappy Henry is to have discovered "that it was first written in the house of his ambassador" in London [that is, presumably, Bridewell Palace], "and is now there [i.e., in France] imprinted."[46] The king then urges Gardiner to insure that "all copies and impressions . . . may be taken in and suppressed." The letter goes on to state that Henry understands that the author "was one Carle" who had been in the service of the French ambassador.[47] On the folio following this letter is an annotation, in a later hand, which sums up this letter quite succinctly: "Touching a book set out in France against K. Henry the 8th whereupon our K. of England was offended."[48]

As the context of this letter makes clear, the book in question was certainly not, as some have claimed, a presentation copy of the poem given to Henry;[49] on the contrary, it was no doubt a copy of the work that was confiscated by or carelessly put into the hands of the English ambassadors in France who, in turn, passed it on to their king. Carle was no fool: he would never have imagined that Henry would be gratified to read a poem in which he is portrayed as a love-sick schoolboy with respect to Anne, as a husband and father who is at best indifferent, at worst callous, towards his family, as a king who is duplicitous with his courtiers and subjects, as someone who uses bad judgment and creates bad laws, and as a tyrant who is capable of unspeakable violence towards those who disagree with him. That this book caused a stir in Henry's court that doubtless hurt Anglo-French relations at a critical moment is further attested by a brief, but chilling, allusion to the book within the "remembrances"—that is, a handwritten "to do" list—found among the papers of Henry's chief minister, Thomas Cromwell, dating from exactly the same year as the letter to Gardiner.[50] There,

---

[46]  Add. 25114, fol. 267v.

[47]  Add. 25114, fol. 267v.

[48]  Add. 25144, fol. 268v.

[49]  See, for example, E. W. Ives, *The Life and Death of Anne Boleyn, "The Most Happy"* (2004; repr. Oxford: Blackwell, 2005), 61, who suggests that this is a presentation copy to the king. He is followed by Alison Weir, *The Lady in the Tower: The Fall of Anne Boleyn* (2009; repr. New York: Ballantine Books, 2010), who reasonably wonders why Carle would have wanted to present such an unflattering account to the king and thus concludes that the book Carle presented to Henry was perhaps "not the poem he wrote on the fall of Anne Boleyn, but another work entirely" (356). This is also unlikely to be the case, since there is no record of Carle writing any other poem around this time that he could reasonably want to present to the English monarch. The simplest solution is simply to recognize that the book acquired by Henry in 1537 was not a presentation copy but a confiscated one, as the letter to Gardiner implies.

[50]  London, British Library, Cotton Titus B/I, fol. 457r. A paraphrase is found in LP 12.1.1315, and a digital facsimile can be accessed via State Papers Online: Early Modern

Cromwell reminds himself to get "the answer of the French ambassador touching the slanderer's book."

Carle's poem was still causing a stir the following winter, however, judging from a subsequent letter written by Germayne Gardyner (or, as he is sometimes known, Jermyn or German Gardiner), nephew and secretary to Stephen Gardiner, the recipient of Wriothesley's earlier missive that had conveyed Henry's wrath.[51] In this letter, which Germayne sent to Wriothesley on 21 February 1538, Gardyner chides the French for denying any knowledge of "the malicious book written in the Bishop of Tarbes's house in London and put to be printed in Paris." He further describes the book as a lengthy and carefully constructed piece, constituting "no light suspicion nor lewd words suddenly spoken, but a long, continued, malicious purpose." Gardyner goes on to say that, although this book was "especially complained on by the king to his good brother [King Francis I]," neither "the author [nor] any of the transumers or the printer either had trouble therefor."[52] He marvels how the French can complain of English offenses, yet can be content in "leaving their own malicious art . . . of making rhyme, allowing, divulging, and printing infamous false books unpunished." While Carle is not mentioned by name here, it is quite clear, from the reference to the Bishop of Tarbes's involvement with a lengthy book in "rhyme," that this is yet another indictment of the *Story of the Death of Anne Boleyn*. This letter thus informs us that Henry's outrage regarding this book, presumably dutifully transmitted by Stephen Gardiner to Francis I less than a year before, apparently fell on deaf ears.

But what is most puzzling about these two letters—that is, Henry's letter to Gardiner and Gardyner's letter to Wriothesley—is their references to an imprint of the text: for the earliest printed version that has survived dates from 1545, whereas these letters were written in 1537 and 1538. Certainly, Henry's letter of 1537 could be mistaken in its assumption that the book had already been printed in France. But Gardyner's letter refers explicitly to the involvement of printers. There is little doubt, then, that Gardyner believes the poem to be circulating in print rather than merely in manuscript form. Could this mean that, in fact, the

---

Government in Britain and Europe, at: https://www.gale.com/intl/primary-sources/state-papers-online.

[51] This document is found at the National Archives of the UK, State Papers (SP) 1/129, fols. 71–82. A summary can be found in LP 13.1.327 (which, however, does not transcribe most of the passage pertaining to Carle's book), and a facsimile can be accessed via State Papers Online. I have modernized the spelling of quoted material, which is concentrated on fol. 79r–v.

[52] It is not entirely clear what Gardyner meant by "transumers" of the book, whom he also indicts along with its author and printer. According to the Oxford English Dictionary, the word "transume" signified "to make an official copy of a (legal) document," but a secondary meaning is "to transport." In this context, then, the noun "transumer" might refer to copyists or, possibly, distributors of the book (i.e., booksellers).

work was printed earlier than is thought and that Henry's decree to take and sup-press all copies was (eventually) carried through? Unfortunately, no book match-ing this description is included in the standard printer's inventories of sixteenth-century imprints, but the absence of a surviving copy would not preclude the existence of an earlier printed version.[53] It may well be, therefore, that Carle's poem had been published soon after its composition, probably in Paris (as indi-cated by Germayne Gardyner), perhaps in the form of a pamphlet (the ephemeral quality of which might also help to explain the lack of a surviving copy), and was intended to bring timely news to a wide French audience.

Given Henry's reaction to first encountering the poem in 1537, as well as the continued anger it aroused among the English envoys in France early the following year, it is no wonder that Carle, as far as we can tell, left England around that time, never to return. And, perhaps, the timing of his master Castel-nau's departure from London, within a few short months of the earlier exchange between Henry and Gardiner in 1537, is also not coincidental: for it may well be that Francis I found it prudent to remove Castelnau (as well as his secretary, Carle) from Henry's sight in light of his angry outburst (even if he had no inten-tion of punishing either of them for their role in disseminating the story of Anne Boleyn). Indeed, when Castelnau returned as ambassador in March 1538, Henry was still enraged with the French envoy, "saying that as ambassador he had done a very bad office" between him and Francis I.[54] Now, it is certainly not evident that this is a reference to Castelnau's harboring Carle while he wrote the "scan-dalous" poem on Anne Boleyn. But it is curious that Castelnau's hostile recep-tion at Henry's court in early 1538 came so quickly upon Wriothesley's presumed receipt of Germayne Gardyner's letter (written in late February) that complained at length of the "malicious book" written in the French ambassador's residence, thus reminding Henry and his men of the envoy's deceit. In any event, realiz-ing that he could no longer function as an effective diplomat, Castelnau there-upon wrote to Francis I suggesting he be replaced yet again, and this request was quickly granted.[55]

But this was not the last that the English court heard of Carle's poem, for it resurfaces again about six years later, in 1543, though it is not clear whether this was in manuscript or printed form. William Paget, a member of Henry's Privy Council who served as secretary of state, wrote to his king "from Boulloyn [Bou-logne], the 7th of April" of that year, sending him

> a fantasy, devised by a French Prothonotary, touching the process of the late
> Marquess of Pembroke [the title conferred on Anne Boleyn before she was

---

[53] For the suggestion that the 1545 version could have been a reprint of an earlier lost edition, see also Rouget, "Un évêque," 123.

[54] See LP 13.1.389 and 390.

[55] See LP 13.1.447 for Francis's decision to recall Castelnau.

crowned queen] and of her complices [*sic*], which fantasy and letter albeit it
may be that your Majesty hath already.[56]

Paget appears nervous to admit that he did not send this material sooner, "upon
my departing from the French Court (for then they came to my hands)"; he
explains that he had planned to bring the work to England personally but
encountered delays that hindered his prompt return. Therefore, he "thought bet-
ter to send them, than to keep them any longer from Your Majesty: most humbly
beseeching Your Majesty to interpret, according to your accustomed goodness,
these my doings in gracious part." While Paget does not mention Carle by name,
his description of the writer as a "French prothonotary" clearly points to Carle
and leaves little doubt that this is, in fact, another copy of *The Story of the Death
of Anne Boleyn*, for the one surviving manuscript that explicitly credits the poem
to Carle uses precisely this honorific to identify its poet.[57] Paget's letter thus tes-
tifies that Henry and his ambassadors were not totally successful in eradicating
all copies of the poem in France. It is perhaps this unspoken admission of failure
to comply with the king's wishes that best explains Paget's trepidation in send-
ing this new copy of the poem to Henry. Indeed, not only were there copies of
Carle's poem still remaining in France but also, quite incredibly (from Henry's
perspective), they were to be found at "the French court" itself, as Paget makes
explicit. One can only assume that, far from confiscating and destroying copies
of the poem, at Henry's orders, in 1537, Francis I deliberately retained at least
one copy at court, in open defiance of Henry's wishes.

We know, furthermore, that within two years of Paget's letter, Carle's
poem would be published by an anonymous press.[58] Although the press might
have retained its anonymity, the poem itself was most definitely not printed

---

[56] Kew, National Archives, State Papers (SP), 1/177, fols. 33–35. The text is sum-
marized in LP 18.1.381, and a facsimile is available via State Papers Online. I have mod-
ernized the spelling of the quoted material, which can be found on fols. 34v–35r.

[57] This is Paris, Bibliothèque nationale de France, Fr. 10194 (formerly Supp. Fr.
1514), whose intitulation reads: "Tragedie sur la mort de la royne d'Angleterre, laquelle le
roy son mary feit mourir dans la Tour de Londres pour avoir commis adultere. Composé
par Lancelot de Carles protonotaire" [Tragedy on the death of the queen of England,
whose husband the king made her die in the Tower of London for having committed
adultery. Composed by Lancelot de Carles, prothonotary]. See my Afterword for an
argument that it is this version of the poem—which includes several verses not found
elsewhere—that came into Henry's hands and that incited his rage due to their explicit
description of Anne as having been misjudged.

[58] There is no indication of the responsible printer on the title page other than this
statement: "On les vend à Lyon, pres Nostre Dame de Confort, 1545" [Sold in Lyon, near
Our Lady of Comfort]. Recent scholarship by Raphaël Cappellen indicates that the work
was in fact published by Jean Rousset in Tours, not in Lyon. For more on this point, see
Chapter 4, "Versions of the Text," in this volume.

anonymously, since Carle's name is prominently placed on the title page, identifying him as the almoner of the Dauphin Henry, the position he held at that time. The title attributed to Carle here makes his official connection to the court of Francis I explicit. This printed text, therefore, once again stands in defiance against Henry; for, far from being "punished" for his scandalous text, as Henry had ordered in his letter of 1537, Carle clearly won a coveted position close to the person of the Dauphin within Francis's court. And, even if Carle did not authorize this printing, he made no real attempt, subsequently, to dissociate himself from the work. It may well be that, by 1545, when France and England were once again at war, diplomatic relations between the two countries were perceived to have deteriorated to such a degree that there was no further need to hide behind a mask. Carle, now safely off English soil, could thus let his name be known without grave danger.[59]

## Mistaken Identities

Still, it appears that this printed version did not make Carle a household name as the chronicler of a dramatic moment in English history, for this book, of which there are only three attested copies worldwide, was apparently exceedingly rare even in the seventeenth century. Indeed, when early historians wished to cite this poem, they did so by referring to manuscript versions of the text for their work, and no one, it appears, ever cited the 1545 imprint. This recourse to anonymous manuscripts, instead of the printed book, is the leading factor behind the growing separation of the poet from his text and the persistent confusion regarding the poem's true author. This is because manuscript versions of this text are most often found in collections that include other works from roughly the same time period, some of which are explicitly attributed to known writers; it is, therefore, understandable that early readers might have thought that the Anne Boleyn poem was also the work of these same known writers. Specifically, the Anne Boleyn poem has been attributed to the best-known poet of Carle's generation, namely Clément Marot himself. This error was first made in the work of Joachim Le Grand, which appeared in 1638, in reference to one of the extant French manuscripts, a text that also contains several poems by Marot.[60] Additionally, the manuscript currently housed in Bordeaux was erroneously attributed

---

[59] For this notion, see Tamizey's notation in his edition of Colletet, *Vies*, 33n1.

[60] See Joachim Le Grand, *Histoire du divorce de Henry VIII, Roy d'Angleterre, et de Catherine d'Aragon*, 3 vols. (Paris: Martin and Boudot, 1688), 2:162–63. This misattribution was based on Le Grand's acquaintance with Paris, Bibliothèque nationale de France, Fr. 02370 (formerly 8057), which contains several poems by Marot. Le Grand's error was repeated by John Lingard, *A History of England from the First Invasion by the Romans*, vol. 6, 2nd ed. (London: Mawman, 1823), 540.

to a local nobleman, Jean de Marcille (or, Marcillé), who had authored a prose work and a series of drawings of armorial shields that preceded the Anne Boleyn poem in this book. That attribution was first made in a notice that had appeared in *The Gentleman's Magazine and Historical Review* (written in 1861) and was accepted by an early cataloguer of the Bordeaux library.[61] As was the case with the misattribution to Marot, there is no evidence to support these claims other than the proximity of the Anne Boleyn poem to other texts in the manuscript collections of which it is a part.[62]

But the greatest confusion has been caused by a manuscript version found in the municipal library of Valenciennes, in the north of France (quite near to Belgium), where the poem is ascribed to one "Anthoine de Crespin, escuyer, Seigneur de Miherne," whose name and title are sometimes written as "Crispin" and "Seigneur de Miherve" or "Mihelve." The wide impact of this confusion is due principally to the fact that the Valenciennes manuscript was partially paraphrased in Emanuel de Meteren's influential *L'Histoire des Pays-Bas* of 1618.[63] This French paraphrase was, in turn, summarized in English by the early historian Gilbert Burnet in the seventeenth century, and Burnet's text was later reproduced in William Cobbett's *State Trials* in 1809.[64] From there, Meteren's version was cited and quoted at length in multiple sources up through the present time, including the works of John Lingard (1820),[65] Elizabeth Benger (1821),[66] Agnes

---

[61] See "Poem on the Death of Anne Boleyn," *The Gentleman's Magazine and Historical Review*, ed. Sylvanus Urban [Edward Cave, pseud.], n.s., 10 (January–June 1861): 189–90: "It is supposed . . . that the author of these verses [on Anne Boleyn] is the same as the writer of the foregoing rhetorical compositions, that is to say, a member of the noble family of Marcille who was in England at the time" (189). See also *Bibliothèque municipale de Bordeaux, Catalogue des Manuscrits*, vol. 1, ed. Jules Delpit (Bordeaux: Delmas, 1880): 255–57, notice 675.

[62] A subsequent cataloguer of the Bordeaux collection rectified this misattribution in 1894. See *Catalogue général des manuscrits des bibliothèques publiques de France*, vol. 23 (Bordeaux), ed. Camille Couderc (Paris: Plon, 1894), 174–77, here 176–77, notice 313.

[63] See Emanuel de Meteren, *L'Histoire des Pays-Bas*, translated from Flemish to French by I. D. L. Haye [Jean de la Haye] (The Hague: Jacobz, 1618), fol. 21r–v. Meteren transcribes the putative author's name as "Anthoine Crispin, Sieur de Miherve."

[64] See Gilbert Burnet, *The History of the Reformation of the Church of England*, ed. Rev. E. Nares (New York: Appleton, 1843), pt. 3, bk. 3, 178–81; and William Cobbett, *Complete Collection of State Trials . . . for High Treason and Other Crimes and Misdemeanors from the Earliest Period to the Present Time*, vol. 1, ed. Thomas Bayly Howell (London: Hansard, 1809), 423–26.

[65] Lingard, *A History of England from the First Invasion by the Romans*, vol. 4, 5th ed. (Paris: Galignani, 1840), 133–34.

[66] Elizabeth Benger, *Memoirs of the Life of Anne Boleyn, Queen of Henry VIII*, 3rd ed. (London: Longman, Rees, Orme, Brown, and Green, 1827); see especially 408–9.

Strickland (1840),[67] and P. Fraser Tytler (1854).[68] Strickland, in particular, valued this account penned by "a foreign contemporary who was one of the few spectators who were permitted to witness" Anne's demise, and she further noted that Meteren himself considered Crespin's poem to be "a valuable and authentic historical document."[69] Her work includes several translations from the text into English, and these passages have been frequently quoted by later academic and popular historians as well as by writers of historical fiction.

It is important to note that the Valenciennes manuscript does not differ materially from any of the others (except for its attribution to Crespin); but Meteren's version (promulgated by Burnet and Cobbett) is not entirely faithful to its source and has introduced elements that are of his invention yet are subsequently taken as authentic to *The Story of the Death of Anne Boleyn* by historians who did not examine the poem itself, in any of its known manuscript or print versions. Among these discrepancies between Meteren's version and the Valenciennes manuscript are the following, which Meteren incorrectly states as being explicitly present in the poem: (1) that Anne's accuser, in speaking to her brother, implicates by name all five men who were ultimately charged and tried with the queen; (2) that these allegations were reported to the king "by enemies of the queen"; (3) that the defendants could have no counsel and that the laws invoked were designed to favor the king's jealousy and to conform to the precedent of Caesar's wife who must be above all suspicion; (4) that Mark's confession was obtained under the false pretense of sparing him; (5) that Mark was actually condemned because he knew about the queen's behavior and had told others about it but had not informed the king of it; (6) that Mark complained that one witness should not be sufficient to condemn him but was told that in his case it was sufficient; (7) that Anne behaved humbly at her trial specifically so that the king would look favorably on her daughter; (8) that the magistrates of London found no evidence to support the charges but that they were resolved to be rid of her; (9) that Anne suggests that her jury found her guilty for specific reasons other than those presented at her trial, namely on account of their jealousy towards her; (10) that Anne declared that her final words were intended to defend not just her honor in general but specifically her chastity; (11) that Rochford specifically stated, in his scaffold speech, that he had not offended the king; (12) that Rochford prayed, on the scaffold, that God grant the king a long and happy life; (13) that, on the scaffold, Anne prayed that whosoever examines her case might judge it in the best light; and (14) that Anne was beheaded by an executioner

---

[67] Agnes Strickland, *Lives of the Queens of England*, 4th ed., vol. 2 (London: Hurst and Blackett, 1854), 562–704, especially 680–83.

[68] P. Fraser Tytler, *Life of Henry the Eighth* (London: Nelson, 1854), 313–14.

[69] Strickland, *Lives*, 683.

from Calais.[70] While some of these misrepresentations of the poem are more egregious than others, taken together they can contribute to a somewhat skewed image of the content and tone of *The Story of the Death of Anne Boleyn*. And it is, of course, in its omissions of important material (e.g., verses that pertain to the treatment of Catherine and Mary) that Meteren's version differs most from the Valenciennes manuscript. But, perhaps most importantly, Meteren's paraphrase brought the name of "Crespin" to the fore in place of the poem's genuine author.

While Meteren's history garnered considerable attention among historians, which continues even to the present day, another history, penned by a Frenchman in the eighteenth century, appears to have gone virtually unnoticed among specialists of the Tudor period, though it, too, contributes to the reception history of *The Story of the Death of Anne Boleyn*. This work is *Histoire d'Angleterre*, first published in 1724 by Paul de Rapin de Thoyras, but it is specifically the preface to the first volume of this work, edited by the French literary scholar Charles-Hugues Le Febvre de Saint-Marc in 1749, where the poem features prominently.[71] Unlike Meteren, Saint-Marc does not attempt to paraphrase the Anne Boleyn poem; instead, he provides extensive and accurate excerpts from the original text, which was known to him through a Parisian manuscript, now housed in the Bibliothèque nationale de France.[72] It is clear, however, that though Saint-Marc is familiar with the poem, having it before his eyes as he wrote, the main author of the history, Rapin de Thoyras, was unaware of its existence, as he did not refer to the poem at all and gives a different version of the events leading up to Anne's downfall in the body of his own work, as noted by Saint-Marc.[73] Since the text of the Parisian manuscript is presented anonymously, this presents a series of baffling questions to Saint-Marc, who wonders if the poet was a Huguenot or Catholic, given the fact that Catherine and Mary, on the one hand, and Anne and George Boleyn, on the other hand, are presented in an equally admirable light.[74] While the poem is here transcribed only partially, it was certainly complete enough to have aroused interest among later historians, but, for whatever reason, this was not to be the case.

---

[70] That Meteren had altered *The Story of the Death of Anne Boleyn* in several places, in part to suit his Protestant religious agenda, was noted as early as 1844 by Aimé Leroy, "Manuscrits de la bibliothèque de Valenciennes," *Archives historiques et littéraires du Nord de la France et du Midi de la Belgique*, n.s., 5 (1844): 361–70, here 363–64; Leroy, however, does not list specific discrepancies.

[71] Paul de Rapin de Thoyras, *Histoire d'Angleterre par Paul Rapin de Thoyras, nouvelle édition augmentée des notes de M. Tindal*, ed. Charles-Hugues Le Febvre de Saint-Marc, notes by [Nicolas] Tindal, vol. 1 (The Hague, 1749), xxxix–lxiii.

[72] This is Paris, Bibliothèque nationale de France, Lat. 5934.

[73] See Saint-Marc's preface, xlvii, which points to Rapin, *Histoire d'Angleterre*, vol. 6, 376–84, for Rapin's own account.

[74] On this point, see Saint-Marc's preface, xi.

By 1826, however, another version of the poem was printed that did indeed attract the attention of historians. Unlike Meteren's text, this version retained its poetic form and, unlike Saint-Marc's text, it is complete; yet it still contributed to the separation of poem and author insofar as this text was printed anonymously, under the designation "The Story of Anne Boleyn, written in French verse by a contemporary." The poem is presented almost as an afterthought, in an appendix to a work by Georges-Adrien Crapelet entitled *Lettres de Henri VIII à Anne Boleyn*: at least it certainly is not the featured text of that volume, which comprised Henry's love letters to Anne written during their courtship.[75] Nevertheless, this version should be considered the first modern printing of *The Story of the Death of Anne Boleyn*, even though it does not constitute a scholarly edition because Crapelet did not distinguish variants in his compilation of three manuscripts that he found in the former King's Library, now the Bibliothèque nationale de France. Indeed, Crapelet does not even state explicitly which manuscripts he *did* in fact consult, although this can be determined with a minimum of sleuthing, which reveals that he too made use of the same manuscript version excerpted by Saint-Marc, along with two other anonymous versions of the text.[76] Crapelet did attempt to tackle the question of authorship in his preface, and comes tantalizingly close to solving the mystery, but in the end fails to reach the proper conclusion. He notes that Joachim Le Grand had attributed the poem to Marot and that Lingard had followed suit, but Crapelet is certain that this attribution is incorrect since Marot could not have been residing in England at this time.[77] He also mentions that Guillaume de Bure notes in his sales catalog of the library of the Duke of La Vallière that a poem on the trial of Anne Boleyn was published by "Charles," almoner to the Dauphin, and that, furthermore, La Croix du Maine lists "Lancelot de Carle" as the author of a poem on the death of Anne Boleyn.[78] But Crapelet hesitates to make the connection between this 1545 imprint and the poem he himself publishes in this work, presumably because the early modern printed edition could not be found for his consultation.[79] Importantly, moreover, Crapelet was not aware of the Valenciennes manuscript and thus does not consider the question of Crespin's authorship of the poem, a lacuna for which he was taken to task by Aimé Leroy, who, in a notice written in 1844 about Crapelet's edition of the poem, devoted considerable attention to

---

[75] See "Histoire de Anne Boleyn jadis royne d'Angleterre, exécutée à mort à Londres, le 19e jour de mai, l'an 1536," in Georges-Adrien Crapelet, ed., *Lettres de Henri VIII à Anne Boleyn* (1826; Paris: L'Imprimerie de Crapelet, 1835), 165–214.

[76] For details, see Chapter 4, "Versions of the Text," in this volume.

[77] Crapelet, *Lettres*, xii.

[78] Crapelet, *Lettres*, xii. See *Catalogue des livres de la bibliothèque de feu M. le duc de la Vallière*, ed. Guillaume de Bure, pt. 1, vol. 2 (Paris: de Bure, 1783), 351. The name "Charles" is clearly merely a misprint for "Carles."

[79] See Crapelet, *Lettres*, xii–xiii.

both the Valenciennes manuscript and Meteren's paraphrase of it and concluded that "Crespin" was a real writer from Artois, belonging to the family of Louis-Charles Crespin who flourished in the 1530s, and was thus the genuine author of this poem.[80]

Later nineteenth-century historians—at least those who were comfortable reading sixteenth-century French—thus had two versions of Carle's work at their disposal: a prose paraphrase attributed to "Crespin" and printed by Meteren; and an anonymous verse rendition printed by Crapelet (which overshadowed Saint-Marc's efforts). For some time, the Meteren and Crapelet versions were treated as similar, but not identical, stories (and, given the changes Meteren enacted on his text, perhaps this is somewhat understandable). Still, in retrospect, this persistent confusion is rather puzzling, since the fact that the two texts were versions of the identical poem was established as early as 1826, in an anonymous review of Crapelet's work written soon after its publication. Upon comparing Meteren's paraphrase with Crapelet's version of the poem, this reviewer demonstrated that "two pages of the latter tally exactly with the former" and that "the production in question is the long-lost composition of Crispin."[81] The reviewer further asserts that the poem Crapelet printed

> thus acquires a much higher historical value than its editor was aware of; and must be read with deep interest, as the relation of a foreigner of high rank and distinguished literature resident amongst us at the time, and relating the facts immediately on their occurrence before his own eyes. . . . It has, therefore, the extraordinary merit of presenting us with a fresh and vivid picture of the melancholy events which it describes, while the impression was strongest.[82]

The author goes on to give an English "epitome" of the poem, since "the quaint old French might not be intelligible to many of our readers."[83] What is most remarkable about this poem, according to its reviewer, is precisely the impartiality of the witness whose testimony it presents: "It is so impartial that he intimates nothing to the disadvantage of either Henry or Anne Boleyn. He adds no decided opinion of her guilt or innocence. He describes what he saw and heard, and leaves the facts to make their own impression upon the readers' minds."[84]

Shortly after the publication of this review, Sharon Turner communicated to the Royal Society of Literature that he had compared the Meteren and Crapelet

---

[80] See Leroy, "Manuscrits," 362n1 and 369.

[81] See *Literary Gazette and Journal of Belles Lettres, Arts, Sciences, etc.* (London: Moyes, 1826), no. 517 (Saturday, 16 December 1826): 789–90, for this review of Crapelet's work.

[82] *Literary Gazette*, 789.

[83] *Literary Gazette*, 789.

[84] *Literary Gazette*, 790.

versions of the text and was persuaded that they were the same work, which, he believes, was composed by Crespin.[85] On the basis of these assertions, the Frenchman Jean-Marie Vincent Audin (in 1847) took the author of Crapelet's poem to be Crespin, and the Swiss historian Jean-Henri Merle D'Aubigné concurred.[86] More cautiously, Sir James Mackintosh stated that "this metrical narrative is believed by some, on no certain proof, to be that which Meteren . . . quoted as the work of Crispin, seigneur de Mihelve."[87]

Despite its anonymity, the Crapelet version of the poem, whether or not believed to be the work of Crispin, became well known to English speakers thanks to the fact that it was paraphrased at length (and rather faithfully) in the historian's sourcebook for this period, *Letters and Papers . . . of the Reign of Henry VIII*, published in 1887.[88] As was the case with Meteren's version, readers of this English prose paraphrase likewise could not appreciate the poetic qualities of the work, which still did not bear the name of Carle, as no definitive link had been established between the Crapelet version of the poem and the early modern printed edition that proclaims Carle to be its author.[89] Indeed, the respected bibliographer Jacques-Charles Brunet explicitly stated, in his entry on the 1545 printed version attributed to Carle, that "this epistle is *not*, as we had supposed,

---

[85] Turner's report to the Royal Society of Literature is mentioned in *The Gentleman's Magazine and Historical Chronicle*, ed. Sylvanus Urban [Edward Cave, pseud.], n.s., 97 (January–June 1827): 623. See also Turner, *The History of the Reign of Henry the Eighth*, 3rd ed., vol. 2 (London: Longman, Rees, Orme, Brown and Green, 1828), 434n4 and 461–64n74. In this third edition of his *History* (which postdates the 1826 review of Crapelet's work in the *Literary Gazette*), Turner provides an extensive English paraphrase of the poem as it appears in Crapelet's text. His paraphrase and line of argumentation owe a great deal to that of the anonymous review of 1826, and this fact increases the likelihood that it was indeed Turner who wrote that anonymous piece.

[86] See Jean-Marie Vincent Audin, *Histoire de Henri VIII et du schisme d'Angleterre*, 2 vols. (Paris: L. Maison, 1847), trans. Edward G. Kirwan Browne as *The Life of Henry the Eighth, and History of the Schism of England* (London: Charles Dolman, 1852), 279 and 287. See also Jean-Henri Merle D'Aubigné, *History of the Reformation in Europe in the Time of Calvin*, Vol. 5: *England, Geneva, Ferrara* (New York: Carter, 1876), 132.

[87] Sir James Mackintosh, *History of England, from the Earliest Times, to the Year 1588* (Philadelphia: Carey, Lea, and Blanchard, 1834), 239.

[88] LP 10.1036 (dated 2 June 1536).

[89] Among those historians who relied on this English paraphrase is James Anthony Froude, *The Divorce of Catherine of Aragon: The Story as Told by the Imperial Ambassadors Resident at the Court of Henry VIII* (New York: Scribner, 1891), 414–15. Yet, in his earlier *History of England from the Fall of Wolsey to the Death of Elizabeth*, vol. 2 (London: Parker & Son, 1856), Froude refers to Meteren's account as the story of "a Flemish gentleman [who] was in London at the time, but was not present in court" and dismisses the account as being "of faint importance" (2:491). Thus, presumably, Froude was under the impression that the Meteren account and the paraphrase of Crapelet's text in LP are different sources.

the same thing as the *Story* in verse of Anne Boleyn, printed by Crapelet. This latter work is by Antoine Crispin (or Crespin), sieur de Miherve, who is named in a manuscript of the said *Story*, held in the Valenciennes library."[90]

But Philippe Tamizey de Larroque, in his 1873 edition of Colletet, was finally able to connect the dots between Meteren's paraphrase of Crespin, Crapelet's anonymous Parisian manuscripts, and the 1545 poem printed under Carle's name. Moreover, he explicitly chastises Leroy, who had criticized Crapelet for not knowing about Meteren's Crespin; for Tamizey, Crespin is simply a phantom, "an author that no one — neither among biographers, nor among bibliographers — knows and who is, to my mind, purely imaginary."[91] Tamizey goes on to suggest that "Crespin" may have been a pseudonym initially adopted by the prothonotary Carle, attached to the French embassy in London, as a prudent measure meant to disguise the work's official ties to France. Furthermore, Tamizey discussed several other French manuscripts, located in Paris (including one that also explicitly credits Lancelot de Carle as its author) and Soissons, linking all of them to Carle's authorship.

Despite Tamizey's work, however, Paul Friedmann was still somewhat confused about the attribution of this poem in his monumental biography of Anne Boleyn (1884).[92] While Friedmann refers to Crapelet's text (and to two of the Parisian manuscripts upon which that edition was based) as well as to the 1545 print edition, he notes (without declaring his own view on the matter) that the text has been variously ascribed to Lancelot de Carle, to Marot, and to "Crispin" and that it was published in 1545 by "Charles," almoner to the Dauphin. This mistake suggests that Friedmann never saw the printed edition but was relying on previous descriptions of the title page that erroneously gave the name "Charles" instead of "Carles." More forgivably, given its date of publication only one year subsequent to Tamizey's discovery, William Hepworth Dixon's *History of Two Queens* also repeatedly (and confusingly) refers to Meteren as well as to Carle's print edition, presenting them as distinct texts.[93]

---

[90] *Manuel du libraire et de l'amateur de livres*, ed. Jacques-Charles Brunet, vol. 1 (Paris: Didot, 1860), cols. 1579–1580 (my translation; italics added). For Brunet's initial assessment, where he ascribes the book to Carle and identifies it as the same text as Crapelet's edition, see *Nouvelles recherches bibliographiques pour servir de supplément au manuel du libraire*, vol. 1. (Paris: Silvestre, 1834), 267.

[91] See Tamizey's essay, "Du poème de Lancelot de Carle sur Anne de Boleyn," in Colletet, *Vies*, 29–34, here 32–33 (my translation).

[92] See Paul Friedmann, *Anne Boleyn, A Chapter of English History, 1527–1536*, 2 vols. (London: Macmillan, 1884), 1:40n1 and 2:317.

[93] William Hepworth Dixon, *History of Two Queens: I. Catherine of Aragon, II. Anne Boleyn*, vol. 6 (Leipzig: Bernhard Tauchnitz, 1874). See, for example, 206n4 and 206n7, which cite both Carle and Meteren as independent sources. Dixon does seem to have realized that the two accounts were exceedingly close and indeed states: "Meteren seems to have had Carles' *Epistre* before him" (208n5).

Tamizey is certainly correct in maintaining that the Meteren paraphrase, the 1545 imprint, and the anonymous manuscripts collated by Crapelet are all one and the same text. But his hypothesis that the mysterious "Anthoine de Crespin" is a phantom or a pseudonym deliberately chosen by Carle himself for his protection does not appear to hold up under further scrutiny. For indeed, historical documents (i.e., records of first instance proceedings from the Great Council of Malines [Mechelen], now housed in the General State Archives in Brussels) contain a reference to a man who styled himself "Anthoine de Crespin, escuyer, seigneur de Myherne," the exact same name and title that appear on the Valenciennes manuscript. The document in question is a record of a legal case filed by Crespin and his wife, named Jehanne de Massenconne (or Massencomme), who were married, according to other documents in this file, in 1528. Their suit is against Franchois (or François) de Melun, Count of Épinoy, regarding the payment of a pension (or "rente," that is, a fixed income) that had been bestowed on them as a wedding present by the Count.[94] The litigants describe themselves as "poor foreigners living in Picardy" (that is, Boulogne-sur-Mer) and state that the dispute was filed in May 1536. From these documents one can assert that Crespin is no imaginary figure but a member of the minor nobility who, around the time of Anne's execution, was living in an area not far from where the Valenciennes manuscript eventually surfaced. His name is thus unlikely to have been pulled out of thin air by Carle to use as a pseudonym for his own protection.

This evidence of the existence of an actual Lord of Miherne does not, however, seriously call into question Carle's authorship of the poem. It is certainly possible that Crespin visited England in 1536, stumbling upon the events surrounding Anne's execution, despite the fact that he describes himself as living in Picardy at this precise time (since litigants need not necessarily be present throughout their case, as they could have been represented by an advocate); still, this seems highly unlikely. In any case, Crespin is not known to have been a poet or to have had access to the courts of England and France, as the writer of this poem clearly can claim. Given that Carle's name was attached to the printed text and one extant manuscript version, that he was already a published poet by 1536, that he was known to have served as secretary to the resident French ambassador

---

[94] For a transcript of this document, see the thesis of C. H. van Rhee, "Litigation and Legislation: Civil Procedure at First Instance in the Great Council for the Netherlands in Malines (1522–1559)" (Brussels: Archives générales du royaume et archives de l'état dans les provinces, 1997), Appendix 1: Procedural Documents, 357–91 (no. 22, "Petition for Judgment"), which transcribes part of the case file no. 371, series Eerste Aanleg (EA). The case file can also be found in the Great Council of Malines, Series Aanzienlijke Families [Prominent families], series A, no. 860. I am indebted to the author of the thesis, Prof. Remco van Rhee, as well as to Dr. Michel Oosterbosch (of the Antwerp Archives), for their invaluable help via email correspondence regarding this matter.

in London in this period, that this poem is stylistically consistent with his other known works (in its use of similar rhyme schemes and idiosyncratic phrases), and that Henry VIII himself refers to the poem as having been written by someone named Carle who was serving in the French embassy at the time, it is exceedingly unlikely that the text could have been written by Crespin, as the Valenciennes manuscript claims. If "Crespin" is neither the author nor a pseudonym created by Carle, then it appears likely that the attribution to Crespin is a deliberate and fraudulent act of appropriation, either by Crespin himself, a scribe working for him, or by someone else who wished to grant him an honor he did not deserve. Indeed, a skeptic might justifiably wonder if this misattribution might also be a subterfuge on the part of Meteren: for he could have wanted to add the name to the manuscript in an effort to obfuscate its connection to other versions, where a reader will find a very different image of Anne than the one he presents in his paraphrase. But the evidence does not support this speculative and skeptical claim, for the poem's intitulation in the Valenciennes manuscript appears to be written in the same hand as the text proper and is thus very unlikely to be an insertion by a later reader such as Meteren. In sum, this attribution to Crespin is destined to stay a mystery, at least in the short term; the most that can be said with certainty is that the name "Crespin" seems to have become attached to this particular manuscript locally, in the area of Picardy, for reasons that remain unclear.[95]

Despite the red herring of the Crespin name, a definitive establishment of the text, firmly attributed to Carle, was finally accomplished with the publication of the poem's first scholarly edition by Georges Ascoli in 1927.[96] Ascoli collated four Parisian manuscripts along with two found in Soissons and one each in Bordeaux and Valenciennes, as well as the 1545 printed edition. This has been the most authoritative French language version of the text since its publication, and it is a solid edition complete with (for the most part) carefully noted and properly identified variants. Here at last, after many years of separation, Carle's name was finally reunited with his poem, in all its known manuscript versions as well as the printed text. Given its newfound accessibility, *The Story of the Death of Anne Boleyn* could now be assessed for its historical and literary value by twentieth-century scholars.

---

[95] This misattribution was officially rectified in the *Catalogue général des manuscrits des bibliothèques publiques de France*, vol. 25 (Valenciennes), ed. Auguste Molinier (Paris: Plon, 1894), which, though it gives the author's name as it appears on the manuscript in the body of the catalogue (377, notice 419 [401]), nevertheless corrects this misperception in the index (552), where it lists Carle, "and not Antoine de Crespin," as the author of this poem.

[96] Lancelot de Carle, "Poème sur la mort d'Anne Boleyn, par Lancelot de Carles," in Georges Ascoli, *La Grande-Bretagne devant l'opinion française depuis la Guerre de Cent Ans jusqu'à la fin du XVI^e siècle* (Paris: Librairie universitaire J. Gamber, 1927), 231–73.

### The Story of the Death of Anne Boleyn
### and Modern Historians

Ironically, however, just at the moment when scholars had a reliable French edi-
tion at their disposal (albeit one that was buried in a much larger work), interest
in the poem appears to have waned dramatically. The most authoritative general
history of the reign of Henry VIII, published in 1968 by J. J. Scarisbrick, makes
no mention of the poem in any of its forms.[97] Indeed, Carle's work appears to
be virtually ignored by scholars for two-thirds of the twentieth century. All that
was to change, however, in the last decades of that century with the approach of
the 450th anniversary of Anne's execution (in 1986), a moment that ushered in
a flurry of new publications on the subject. The first major history to use Carle's
poem extensively (via Ascoli's edition) was Eric Ives's *Anne Boleyn*, published in
1986. Ives was generally dismissive of its significance, particularly with regard
to the crucial recounting of the accusation laid against the queen by one of her
ladies, which he suggests is a literary fabrication and elaboration.[98] Following
upon an earlier article in which he outlined his belief that factions at work in
Henry's court contrived to bring about Anne's downfall,[99] Ives maintained that
Anne was an innocent victim of a plot initiated by Thomas Cromwell, who saw
the pro-French queen as an obstacle to improved relations between England and
the Holy Roman Empire. According to Ives, Cromwell acted to remove Anne
from the king's sphere of influence (along with several other courtiers, either as
collateral damage or because he perceived them to be his personal enemies).

This led T. B. Pugh, in a review of Ives's work in 1989, to comment, among
other matters, that few historians have given Carle's poem the attention it
deserves.[100] In that review, Pugh identifies the participants in the quarrel that
precipitated Anne's downfall as Elizabeth Browne, wife of the Earl of Worces-
ter, and her brother, Sir Anthony Browne, and indeed, these identifications had
previously been suggested by Muriel St. Clare Byrne in her edition of *The Lisle
Letters* in 1981.[101] Inspired by Pugh's interest in Carle's poem and the role of
Lady Worcester in this matter, historian George W. Bernard rewrote the story

---

[97] See J. J. Scarisbrick, *Henry VIII* (1968; repr. London: Penguin, 1974).

[98] Ives, *Anne Boleyn* (1986; repr. Oxford: Blackwell, 1987), 70.

[99] Ives, "Faction at the Court of Henry VIII: The Fall of Anne Boleyn," *History*
57.190 (1972): 169–88.

[100] T. B. Pugh, Review of Ives, *Anne Boleyn*, *Welsh History Review* 14 (1989): 638–
40: "Historians have attached little importance to a valuable contemporary source that
soon chronicled these incredible events" (639).

[101] See Muriel St. Clare Byrne, ed., *The Lisle Letters*, 6 vols. (Chicago: University
of Chicago Press, 1981), 3:378–79. Byrne does not cite the poem from Ascoli's edition;
rather, following Friedmann, she refers to Crapelet's anonymous version of the text.

of Anne's downfall using Carle's poem as his centerpiece.[102] Given the plausibility of the scenario set out in Carle's poem, it is not necessary, Bernard asserts, to believe that Anne's downfall came about as a result of "factional manipulation" within the court; nor is it necessary to portray Henry either as an easily manipulated king or as a "monster" who had tired of his second wife and was eager to move on to a third.[103] Instead, "information [about Anne's infidelity] came into the 'public domain' by chance, by the accident of a quarrel between one of the Queen's ladies and her brother";[104] and, once this information reached the ears of the king, Cromwell was compelled to allow a full investigation to proceed. This is precisely how Cromwell himself had explained the matter to Gardiner, who was serving as ambassador in France at that time: the queen's behavior was revealed by her own ladies and duly investigated by the authorities.[105] For Bernard, then, the facts of Carle's poem fit nicely with those that have come down through other sources, and these do point to a guilty, rather than a victimized, Anne.

Ives naturally responded to Bernard, defending his view and continuing to urge "caution" with regard to the historical veracity of Carle's poem.[106] Conceding that Carle's version does indeed dovetail with what Cromwell told Gardiner was the official story, Ives examines a bit of information that Bernard himself exposed in his essay: namely, that Carle's poem was written while the poet was attached to the French embassy. Ives explains that "previous assumptions were that de Carles versified stories from the Court and City" (although he does not clarify who, other than himself, actually held those assumptions).[107] But this "discovery" of new information regarding Henry's reaction to the poem in 1537 (which, as was noted earlier in this essay, had appeared in *Letters and Papers* in the nineteenth century) allows Ives to modify his reason for disbelieving Carle's story: it isn't so much a fabrication derived from court gossip as it is the official party line fed to foreign ambassadors by Cromwell. Ultimately, the French poet "was writing up what was known at the [French] embassy [in London], and the main source for this was, of course, the English government. . . . De Carles is effectively Cromwell with literary embellishments."[108] Either way, he asserts, the information contained in the poem is suspect and not to be trusted.

---

[102] G. W. Bernard, "The Fall of Anne Boleyn," *The English Historical Review* 106.420 (1991): 584–610. See 596n2 for Bernard's acknowledgment of his debt to Pugh regarding his awareness of Carle's poem.

[103] Bernard, "The Fall of Anne Boleyn," 609.

[104] Bernard, "The Fall of Anne Boleyn," 609.

[105] Add. 25114, fol. 160r. This is summarized in LP 10.873.

[106] Ives, "The Fall of Anne Boleyn Reconsidered," *The English Historical Review* 107.424 (1992): 651–64.

[107] Ives, "The Fall of Anne Boleyn Reconsidered," 659.

[108] Ives, "The Fall of Anne Boleyn Reconsidered," 659.

In both his book of 1986 and his article of 1992, Ives demonstrates a good acquaintance with Carle's poem as it was given in Ascoli's edition. Nevertheless, there are moments when he was not a particularly careful reader of the poem, for he occasionally does not summarize it accurately or fairly. For example, Ives claims that "there is reason to believe that the advanced stages of [Anne's first] pregnancy were in fact, difficult," and he bases this on Carle's poem, vv. 148–164.[109] But these verses do not suggest a "difficult" pregnancy; they are instead dripping with sarcasm aimed at Anne, who was pretending to be in severe pain when she merely felt the baby kick, a sensation few women would describe as very painful (though they might describe it as odd). This and other misreadings and misrepresentations of Carle's text have been repeated by subsequent scholars, perpetuating an inaccurate and unbalanced view of what the French poem actually says.[110]

Not long afterwards, Retha Warnicke entered into this debate that had been documented on several pages of the same scholarly journal.[111] Warnicke's take on the situation is unique, as she had previously promulgated the idea that Anne's downfall was not so much engineered by Cromwell as it was the result of Anne's miscarriage of a deformed fetus in January 1536, which, she asserts, pointed to Anne's dabbling in witchcraft.[112] Be that as it may, Warnicke does comment on the known discrepancies between Carle's poem and historical facts derived from other primary sources, specifically the detail that, in Carle's text, George Boleyn's trial precedes Anne's, which she terms "a rather major lapse considering that the verses are thought to have been written . . . shortly after the executions."[113] Warnicke, following Ives, explains these differences in terms of Carle's liberal use of "poetic license" but goes on to "wonder why the entire poem should not be viewed from the perspective of poetic license."[114] In short, in Warnicke's view, discrepancies between the poem and historical fact—be they random mistakes or deliberate recastings for poetic effect—serve to discredit the entire poem as an historical document.

---

[109] See Ives, *Anne Boleyn*, 229. See further his mistranslation of "plus estroict" as "strait-laced" to refer to the close counselor of the king (*Anne Boleyn*, 375) as well as some of the factual claims made in "The Fall of Anne Boleyn Reconsidered," 661.

[110] Surprisingly, in his response to Ives's last volley, Bernard does not take Ives to task for these mistakes. See Bernard, "The Fall of Anne Boleyn: A Rejoinder," *The English Historical Review* 107.424 (1992): 665–74.

[111] Retha M. Warnicke, "The Fall of Anne Boleyn Revisited," *The English Historical Review* 108.428 (1993): 653–65.

[112] See Warnicke, *The Rise and Fall of Anne Boleyn: Family Politics at the Court of Henry VIII* (Cambridge: Cambridge University Press, 1989), especially ch. 8, "Sexual Heresy" (191–233), on the importance of this miscarriage and its connection to a charge of witchcraft.

[113] Warnicke, "The Fall of Anne Boleyn Revisited," 660.

[114] Warnicke, "The Fall of Anne Boleyn Revisited," 660.

Greg Walker, in contrast, supported Bernard's use of Carle's poem as an historical document and pronounced it to be quite plausible in its reckoning of Anne's downfall.[115] Rather than pointing to one catalyst for Anne's fall (e.g., Anne's increasingly tense relationship with Cromwell on matters regarding funds derived from the ongoing suppression of the smaller monasteries as well as larger foreign policy concerns; or the working together of other court factions whose common enemy was the queen; or, indeed, the damage to her marriage resulting from her final miscarriage), Walker sees all these factors (and more) as contributing to a general landscape that "predisposed the king to be more responsive to the accusations of adultery when they came."[116] And they came, Walker claims, in much the way Carle describes them in his poem, "despite its literary form, and the fact that the author was at times clearly shaping his material to fit his wider moral purpose."[117] The crucial evidence of the queen's adultery emerged in the subsequent interrogation of Mark, who was mentioned by Carle (quoting the unnamed sister) as being capable of supplying further details on the matter. And "once Smeaton had confessed, Henry became increasingly convinced that Anne was guilty."[118] That Anne continued to talk to her jailors while in the Tower, implicating still others — which Carle does not mention — further contributed to the final form of the accusations against her. Ultimately, Walker concludes, "we are left with a lot of smoke but precious little fire"; crucially, however, Walker supports Bernard's claim that "Henry did not invent the charges" but did find the accusations — those recorded in Carle's poem as well as those which surfaced in the subsequent investigations — to be credible.[119]

Within a few years, the debate was revisited in several book publications, beginning with Ives, who issued a revised version of his work on the queen (in 2004); likewise, Bernard expanded upon his earlier articles in a book published in 2010, to which Ives responded yet again in a review article in 2011.[120] In his book, Bernard concludes that it is his "own hunch that Anne had indeed committed adultery with Norris, probably with Smeaton, possibly with Weston, and was then the victim of the most appalling bad luck when the countess of Worcester, one of her trusted ladies, contrived in a moment of irritation with her brother to trigger the devastating chain of events that led inexorably to Anne's

---

[115] Greg Walker, "Rethinking the Fall of Anne Boleyn," *The Historical Journal* 45 (2002): 1–29.

[116] Walker, "Rethinking the Fall of Anne Boleyn," 16.

[117] Walker, "Rethinking the Fall of Anne Boleyn," 16.

[118] Walker, "Rethinking the Fall of Anne Boleyn," 29.

[119] Walker, "Rethinking the Fall of Anne Boleyn," 29.

[120] Ives, *The Life and Death of Anne Boleyn, "The Most Happy"*; G. W. Bernard, *Anne Boleyn: Fatal Attractions* (2010; repr. New Haven: Yale University Press, 2011); Ives, "Anne Boleyn on Trial Again," *The Journal of Ecclesiastical History* 62 (2011): 763–77.

downfall."[121] In his review of this book, Ives persisted in his belief of Anne's innocence and in the lack of credibility of Carle's account.

Apart from this sometimes-contentious debate among these scholars, other recent historians occasionally made use of *The Story of the Death of Anne Boleyn* to some extent. In the introduction to her edition of another treatise, written in English, on the life of Anne Boleyn, Maria Dowling alludes to Carle's poem, which she knows through consulting the manuscript now housed in Brussels, and praises it for being the "only early account of her which is free from religious bias; all the others are either Protestant eulogies or Catholic attacks on her morals."[122] Yet, while Dowling admires Carle's "detached" view of events, she too is not a very careful reader of the text and misquotes or misunderstands it on occasion. For example, she reports that Carle "says that the birth of Elizabeth was very painful for Anne."[123] This is not true; indeed, on the contrary, Carle suggests that God gave her the gift of an easy delivery (vv. 168–170). More puzzlingly, Dowling says that Carle "describes Edward Seymour's fraternal advice to Jane on how to deal with the king's advances."[124] This is nowhere to be found in any version of Carle's poem, which barely alludes to Jane (without actually naming her) as the new woman to whom the king has taken a fancy and whom he will probably marry after Anne's execution.

Similar praise for Carle's impartiality was expressed by John Schofield, who makes limited use of the poem in his work on Thomas Cromwell but who notes admiringly that Carle's work

> is not a vulgar anti-Boleyn diatribe of the kind that later appeared, for in parts it speaks quite well of Anne. It is an independent account, because a French diplomat would not compose an obituary of Anne on the say so of the English government; and he would certainly not circulate false propaganda to oblige Cromwell, the chief advocate of the pro-Imperial policy. De Carles wrote poetically and gives some facts that are not found elsewhere, but much of what he says is verifiable from other sources, so there is no reason to imagine that this is a romance or a fantasy. . . . De Carles contains no obvious howlers. His account therefore is a reliable one. One final point: de Carles does not mention Cromwell's name.[125]

---

[121] Bernard, *Anne Boleyn*, 192.

[122] See Maria Dowling's introduction to William Latymer, "William Latymer's 'Cronickille of Anne Bulleyne,'" ed. Maria Dowling, in *Camden Miscellany* 30, Camden Fourth Series, 39 (London: Royal Historical Society, 1990): 23–65, here 37.

[123] Dowling's introduction to Latymer, "William Latymer's 'Cronickille,'" 37.

[124] Dowling's introduction to Latymer, "William Latymer's 'Cronickille,'" 37.

[125] John Schofield, *The Rise and Fall of Thomas Cromwell, Henry VIII's Most Faithful Servant* (2008; repr. Stroud: The History Press, 2011), 193.

Without saying so explicitly, Schofield is here responding point by point to Ives's main criticism of Bernard's original article regarding Carle's poem.

A separate wrinkle in the debate surfaced with the publication of the popular historian Alison Weir's *Lady in the Tower*, which confusedly quotes indiscriminately from Carle as well as Crespin (whom she refers to as "Crispin de Milherve"), clearly assuming these are different writers, and, equally clearly, depending on Meteren as the sole source for her knowledge of "Crispin," rather than the Valenciennes manuscript itself.[126] Weir comments on the way "Milherve" was "more sympathetic" to Anne than many other contemporary accounts, but this is, of course, because Meteren altered what he found in the Valenciennes manuscript to show Anne in a better light.[127] In his review of this work, John Guy rightly points out that the texts Weir believes are different have been known to be the same since the nineteenth century.[128]

More recently, Lacey Baldwin Smith reconsidered the entire academic quarrel among Bernard, Ives, Warnicke, and Weir. While he weighs their arguments carefully (without, however, correcting Weir's misapprehension regarding the Crespin/Carle source), he ultimately endorses Bernard's view, declaring: "It makes the best sense of any of the proposed explanations for Anne's disgrace and destruction."[129] Further, he argues against the assertion made by Ives that the information in Carle's poem was "'government issue' from the start," maintaining that "there is absolutely no evidence that [Cromwell] informed the ambassador, nor is any reason offered [by Ives] why he should have done so. It is all hypothesis, no more or less substantive than claiming that de Carles had his own source of information."[130] Yet he likewise states that "there is nothing to prove the validity of [Carle's] story of the countess's indiscretions and its conveyance to

---

[126] See, for example, Weir, *The Lady in the Tower*, 229–30. Weir further confuses the facts in her "Notes on Some of the Sources" (358–59), where she describes Clément Marot and "Crispin, Lord of Milherve" as "two renowned French men of letters, whose writings are a valuable source of information on Anne Boleyn, whom Marot knew personally. Milherve, who was present at Anne's trial, wrote a separate metrical history, which was published in 1618." There is no evidence that Marot knew Anne, nor did he write about the French queen. Miherne's "separate metrical history" was not published in 1618; that is the date of the French translation of Meteren's history, which, as demonstrated above, incorporates a prose paraphrase of what he purports to be the work of "Crespin, seigneur de Miherne." Weir also gives a long evaluation of Carle's poem, 356.

[127] See Weir, *The Lady in the Tower*, 258, for this remark on "Milherve's" sympathy.

[128] John Guy, "Footnotes on a Scandal," Review of Weir, *The Lady in the Tower*, *The Sunday Times* (London), dated 1 November 2009.

[129] Lacey Baldwin Smith, *Anne Boleyn: The Queen of Controversy, A Biographical Essay* (2013; repr. Stroud: Amberley, 2014), 196.

[130] Smith, *Anne Boleyn*, 208–9.

the king"[131] and maintains that "the twenty-first century . . . must leave the final judgement of guilt or innocence in doubt."[132]

Because of its presence in so many historical accounts of the fall of Anne Boleyn, it is not too surprising that the poem (or, perhaps more accurately, English paraphrases of the poem) figures into artistic representations of this moment in film, television, and historical fiction. Viewers of the Showtime television series *The Tudors*, for example, have heard Carle's rendition of Anne's trial allocution and her scaffold speech—without knowing it, of course—in the dramatic presentation of the queen's beheading.[133] Anne's speech in that television production is taken verbatim from the English version that appears in Agnes Strickland's *Lives of the Queens of England* (where it is translated from Meteren's paraphrase).[134] Likewise, Hilary Mantel displays an acquaintance with the poem (or its paraphrases) in her novel *Bring up the Bodies* (as well as in the spinoff theatrical and television productions of *Wolf Hall* and *Bring up the Bodies*), where incidents that are peculiar to Carle's poem—namely, the fire in Anne's chambers and the unruliness of Norris's horse at the May Day jousts—are featured.[135]

As can be seen, Carle's poem is no doubt a survivor. Given that, before Ascoli's edition, there was little opportunity to consult the few extant copies in print

---

[131] Smith, *Anne Boleyn*, 207.

[132] Smith, *Anne Boleyn*, 214. For other recent works that demonstrate awareness of Carle's poem, see Joanna Denny, *Anne Boleyn: A New Life of England's Tragic Queen* (2004; repr. Cambridge, MA: Da Capo Press, 2006), which notes the British Library and Brussels manuscripts as well as Ascoli and "Crespin" but does not seriously engage with the poem; Suzannah Lipscomb, *1536: The Year that Changed Henry VIII* (Oxford: Lion Hudson, 2009), especially 76–77; Suzannah Lipscomb, "The Fall of Anne Boleyn: A Crisis in Gender Relations?," in *Henry VIII and the Court: Art, Politics and Performance*, ed. Thomas Betteridge and Suzannah Lipscomb (Farnham: Ashgate, 2013), 287–305, whose analysis gives considerable consideration to Carle's poem, in line with Walker's view; and Susan Bordo, *The Creation of Anne Boleyn: A New Look at England's Most Notorious Queen* (2013; repr. Boston: Mariner Books/Houghton Mifflin Harcourt, 2014), which unfortunately perpetuates Weir's confusion regarding "Milherve" and Carle (see 107). An unpublished dissertation by Susan Walters Schmid, "Anne Boleyn, Lancelot de Carle, and the Uses of Documentary Evidence" (PhD diss., Arizona State University, 2009) reviews general issues regarding the poem and Carle's place in the diplomatic landscape of the time; it also provides a rather literal English translation based on Ascoli's text.

[133] This is season two, episode ten.

[134] See Strickland, *Lives of the Queens of England*, 2:682–83.

[135] For the fire in Anne's chamber, see Hilary Mantel's novel *Bring up the Bodies* (2012; repr. New York: Picador, 2015), 157–58; the Royal Shakespeare Company stage adaptation of that book by Mike Poulton in *Wolf Hall and Bring Up the Bodies: The Stage Adaptation* (2013; repr. New York: Picador, 2014), 202 (Act 2, scene 12); and the BBC Two television adaptation (2015), *Wolf Hall*, episode 5. For Norris's unruly horse, see Mantel, *Bring up the Bodies*, 287–88.

or several early modern manuscripts scattered in European libraries, it is some-what amazing that any scholar had stumbled upon it, let alone made note of its importance. While its prominence in historical writing has ebbed and flowed throughout the centuries, it is safe to say that it has certainly received far more attention in recent years than it has at any point since its composition. Its value as an historical document might be debated, but its story seems bound to figure, one way or another, in every subsequent serious work on the rise and fall of Anne Boleyn.

# Chapter 4
## VERSIONS OF THE TEXT

It is not an easy matter to locate exemplars of this text, either in print or manuscript form. For one thing, the poem often appears anonymously and thus is generally not catalogued under the name of its author. For another, the poem bears no uniform title, thus further contributing to the likelihood that it would not be properly catalogued. Keyword searches are hampered by the fact that the name "Boleyn" was given a seemingly endless number of different spellings. Finally, even the poem's *incipit* (that is, its first line), which is often another means of cataloguing anonymous texts in manuscript form, varies significantly enough in spelling such that it could hinder identifying other extant versions of the text. For all these reasons, it is quite likely that there are many more versions of this poem than are listed here, even in public libraries, not to mention in private hands. Nevertheless, this chapter brings to light, for the first time, several manuscripts that heretofore were not known, described, or studied. The purpose of the narrative that unfolds in this chapter is twofold: (1) to elucidate some of the stories behind these exemplars—qua material objects—that have previously been obscured, including issues of provenance; and (2) to ascertain what is unique about the text that these exemplars provide. A schematic description of these exemplars follows at the end of this chapter.

### Early Modern Versions

It should be noted from the start that there is no known autograph version of this poem, that is, a text written in the hand of the author, Lancelot de Carle. Rather, all known manuscripts are the product of scribes who either worked from other manuscripts (perhaps from the author's copy, but more likely from a subsequent copy) or, possibly, even from an early print version of the poem: for, in the sixteenth century, it was not uncommon to copy out a printed book by hand.[1] Such

---

[1] On the matter of using a printed book as the "copy text" for a subsequent manuscript, see Elizabeth L. Eisenstein, "Afterword: Revisiting the Printing Revolution," in Eisenstein, *The Printing Revolution in Early Modern Europe*, 2nd ed. (Cambridge:

a manuscript might not be the work of a professional scribe, and some of the less-carefully executed manuscripts in this list are likely to have been done by an amateur. In any case, with rare exceptions, the name of the scribe for most of these manuscripts is now unknown, as is the name of the patron who commissioned it. It should also be noted that manuscript versions of this text apparently circulated fairly widely, though it is not possible to say with certainty exactly where all of them were produced. Of the sixteen early modern manuscripts listed here, only one is now found in England; seven are located in Paris, four are in the French provinces, and four are housed elsewhere in Europe. In most instances, little is known of their provenance.

One of the chief ways these manuscripts vary one from the other is in the number of verses they include. Carle's poem comprises 1320 "canonical" verses: that is, verses that are attested, albeit sometimes in variant form, in multiple manuscripts. Only the British Library manuscript (London, British Library, Additional 40662 = BL) contains all 1320 "canonical" verses (as well as eight other verses not attested elsewhere). Similarly, one manuscript housed in the Bibliothèque nationale de France (Paris, BnF, Fr. 10194 = BNF4) contains ten lines that are unique to that manuscript. Remarkably, these additional lines have not heretofore been transcribed, although they are highly significant for the interpretation of the poem. Many of the manuscripts also contain unique variants of at least one of the canonical verses, some of which cast a very different reading on the poem. These variations are all noted in the Middle French edition that appears in this book, and other distinguishing features of some of the manuscripts will be described in due course in this chapter.

The copy text for this edition is the manuscript found in the British Library, which was chosen on the basis of its completeness and distinguishing features. This exemplar is indeed unique, not just in terms of its text but also as a material object. Of all the manuscripts here examined, none compares to the rich presentation of this version, which the cataloguers at the British Library speculate could have been a presentation copy, thanks to its combination of vellum, gilt edging, gold intitulation, and fine, distinctive italic or humanist script.[2] The volume also is graced by a red velvet cover, quite often another sign that the work was intended for an important patron; in this case, however, the binding is not contemporary with the manuscript, and the existing red velvet may be a replace-

---

Cambridge University Press, 2012), 313–58, here 342–43. See also Steven W. May and Heather Wolfe, "Manuscripts in Tudor England," in *A Companion to Tudor Literature*, ed. Kent Cartwright (Oxford: Wiley-Blackwell, 2010), 135.

[2] For the notion that "the use of vellum indicates a book with some pretentions to grandeur," see James P. Carley, *The Books of King Henry VIII and His Wives* (London: The British Library, 2004), 29.

ment for an earlier, perhaps similar, covering.[3] To whom this text was presented, if indeed it was a presentation copy, is, of course, an open question, as there is nothing in the manuscript in its current state that speaks to this issue. But since dedicatory pages were often quite beautiful, sometimes incorporating an elaborate coat of arms (as was the case with the copy of *Le pasteur évangélique* presented to Anne and Henry) it is very possible that, if one had existed, it was separated from the rest of this manuscript and valued independently for its aesthetic properties.[4] While the text of this manuscript is by no means perfect, it is a clean copy and shows only a few traces of carefully executed corrections by its professional scribe. There are no missing verses, save for the extra ten that are unique to BnF Fr. 10194. No other exemplar can make this claim for completeness, as all others, including BnF Fr. 10194, are missing at least one canonical line. The British Library text, as mentioned above, also contains two sets of two extra verses within the poem (vv. 275–276 and 341–342) as well as four extra verses at the end (vv. 1324–1328). The British Library catalogue entry, however, makes note only of the four final unique lines and does not mention the earlier four interpolated extra verses. Despite the obvious care taken in executing this manuscript, however, the text is sometimes problematic and requires emendation.

The British Library exemplar also contains additional documentation, affixed to a folio preceding the text proper as well as its back inside cover, regarding its provenance. The first is a page from a Sotheby's catalogue, dating from 26 January 1866, which describes the manuscript and urges that it "be secured for the Nation." A handwritten marginal note on the Sotheby notice indicates that this work had been in the possession of Thomas Thomson (1768–1852), Deputy Clerk-Register of Scotland, an antiquarian and literary aficionado. But rather than being "secured for the Nation" and made available to the public at that time, it was, instead, purchased privately by Sir William Tite, to whom is addressed a handwritten letter, dated 11 May 1866 (now affixed to the back inside cover of the book), from the antiquary John Bruce, who presumably was asked to advise upon its value. Bruce recognized the poem as being a version of the ones published by Georges-Adrien Crapelet and paraphrased by Emanuel de Meteren (which was attributed to "Crispin").[5] He also, therefore, attributed the poem to

---

[3] I am grateful to Dr. Andrea Clarke of the British Library for sharing her assessment of this manuscript, particularly with regard to the matter of the poem's binding. For more on velvet bindings in connection with the libraries of royal or noble patrons, see again Carley, *Books*, 24–25.

[4] The presentation copy of *Le pasteur évangélique* is now London, British Library, Royal 16 E XIII. See chapter 2, above, for more on this work.

[5] See Georges-Adrien Crapelet, ed., *Lettres de Henri VIII à Anne Boleyn* (1826; repr. Paris: L'Imprimerie de Crapelet, 1835), 165–214: "Histoire de Anne Boleyn jadis royne d'Angleterre, exécutée à mort à Londres, le 19e jour de mai, l'an 1536"; and Emanuel de Meteren, *L'Histoire des Pays-Bas*, translated from Flemish to French by I. D. L. Haye

"Crispin" and noted that the work was known by multiple historians. Of course, none of these historians was acquainted with this particular version of the manuscript, but Bruce was correct in making a general identification of these versions as one and the same poem. Decades later, this manuscript was once again put up for sale at Sotheby's and finally purchased by the British Library on 22–23 May 1922. Further documentation with the manuscript shows that it was foliated in August 1930.

Additionally, although the British Library catalogue does not include this information, there is evidence to suggest that this particular exemplar had once been part of the collection of Joseph-Louis, Baron Heiss, an eighteenth-century bibliophile whose library was largely incorporated into the Bibliothèque de l'Arsenal in Paris. Two sources describe a work that matches the British Library exemplar and that was sold on 7 March 1785 at the Hôtel de Bullion in Paris. In the *Catalogue des livres rares et précieux de M. \*\*\* [Heiss]* can be found the following entry: "1041. L'Histoire de la mort d'Anne de Boullenc, royne d'angleterre. In 4°. Manuscrit sur vélin, du XVI. siècle, de 42 feuillets, écrits en *lettres rondes*. L'auteur de cette pièce est un nommé Charles, aumônier du Dauphin, depuis Henri II" [The Story of the Death of Anne Boleyn, Queen of England. In 4°. Manuscript on vellum, from the sixteenth century, consisting of forty-two leaves, written in italic script. The author of this piece is someone by the name of Charles, almoner to the Dauphin, later Henry II].[6] A second work confirms that this same manuscript was sold for 24 *livres* 1 *sol* in 1785.[7] The description of the work as being on vellum, consisting of 42 folios and written in italic script, along with the unique spelling of its title (with a final "c" on the Gallicized spelling of the name "Boleyn") matches the exemplar of the British Library and no other. It seems quite likely, therefore, that the British Library manuscript was once owned by Baron Heiss and that it was in Paris in the eighteenth century before it eventually made its way to the library of Thomas Thomson. It is possible that it was Thomson (who would have been around seventeen years old in 1785) or a member of his family who bought the book from Heiss. In any case, no evidence has come to light to prove that the volume was owned by someone else between Heiss and Thomson, nor is there an extant record of sale between the two parties.

But, assuming that Heiss's volume was indeed the one later owned by Thomson, the question then arises as to the owners of this manuscript before Heiss, that is, between the time of its production in the sixteenth century and

---

[Jean de la Haye] (The Hague: Jacobz, 1618), fol. 21r–v. For a fuller discussion of the attribution to Crespin, see above, Chapter 3.

   [6] *Catalogue des livres rares et précieux de M. \*\*\* [Heiss] . . . dont la vente se fera le lundi 7 Mars 1785* (Paris: de Bure, 1785), 141. The library for sale has been identified subsequently as that of Baron Heiss.

   [7] See *Dictionnaire bibliographique, historique et critique de livres rares . . . dont les auteurs ne sont pas connus*, pt. 2, ed. Abbé R. Duclos (Paris: Cailleau, 1790), 330.

the time of its sale in Paris. Two pieces of evidence might be useful in determin-
ing its whereabouts at that time, but these are less solid than those that help
make the case for the ownership by Heiss. The first piece of evidence is another
sales catalogue, this one published shortly before the sale of Heiss's exemplar,
announcing a sale to take place in Paris in February 1783.[8] The book is here
described as part of the library of the late François-Abraham-Marie Mouchard
(1712–1782), a receiver-general of finances for the region of Champagne, whose
daughter, Fanny de Beauharnais, would go on to run a prominent literary salon
in the eighteenth century. This text is here titled *L'Histoire de la mort d'Anne Boul-
lenc, Royne d'Angleterre*, and thus uses the same unusual spelling of Anne's family
name as the current BL exemplar. Likewise, it is described as being written on
vellum. Surprisingly, however, the book is said to be bound on cardboard and
not in the red velvet it now carries.[9] But, as it is fairly clear that the current red
velvet cover does not date from the sixteenth century, this does not preclude the
identification of this volume as the one currently in the British Library (and, in
some sense, indeed bolsters that case).

It is curious to note that, in this catalogue, the author of the Anne Boleyn
poem is not specified, whereas within two years, in the 1785 sales catalogue
by de Bure referred to above, the work is definitively attributed to Carle (or, at
least, to "Charles, almoner to the dauphin"), using information garnered from
the 1545 imprint of the work. This is no doubt due to the odd coincidence that
the cataloguer de Bure also had access (in December 1783) to the 1545 printed
version of the text, which was part of the library of the Duc de la Vallière.[10] Thus
it can be stated with some certainty that it was Guillaume de Bure who, by 1785,
first made the connection between the anonymous manuscript version of the
Anne Boleyn poem and the 1545 imprint, though he renders the author's name
as "Charles" rather than Carle. Undoubtedly, de Bure was not aware of the full
significance of his finding, since he did not emphasize the connection between
the manuscript and the book versions of Carle's poem in his 1785 catalogue but
merely asserted that the author was named "Charles," clearly a typographical
error that will be repeated by later scholars.

The second piece of evidence regarding the whereabouts of this book before
it passed into Heiss's library (by way of Mouchard), if indeed this is the same
exemplar, is even less solid but still intriguing. This evidence suggests that the
early modern French historian Charles de Bourgueville had access to this volume

---

[8] *Notice des principaux articles des livres de la bibliothèque de feu M. Mouchard . . . dont la
vente se fera . . . le mercredi 12 février 1783*, ed. Guillaume de Bure (Paris: de Bure, 1783),
13.

[9] The full reference reads: "L'Histoire de la mort d'Anne Boullenc, Royne
d'Angleterre, en vers, in-4, manuscrit sur vel., relié en carton."

[10] See the *Catalogue des livres de la bibliothèque de feu M. le duc de la Vallière*, pt. 1, vol.
2, ed. Guillaume de Bure (Paris: de Bure, 1783), 351.

or, more certainly, to the same version of the text when writing *Les recherches et antiquitez de la province de Neustrie*. First, his reference to "Anne de Boullenc" also uses the same unusual spelling of the queen's name as that found in the British Library manuscript. Moreover, he refers to one of Anne's alleged lovers as "Cathon" (a scribal error for "Oaston," that is, Weston), as does the British Library manuscript alone.[11] This is certainly not definitive proof of the British Library exemplar's provenance, since de Bourgueville did not describe the manuscript itself, but it contributes to the circumstantial evidence that traces the work back to the sixteenth century. At any rate, and quite surprisingly, the exemplar now housed in the British Library has heretofore received no scholarly attention, despite its proximity to the majority of historians of the Tudor period, as it is housed on English soil.

While there are compelling reasons to choose the British Library exemplar as the copy text here, many of the other manuscripts have their own fascinating histories. One of the earliest known manuscripts is Paris, BnF, *fonds français* 12795 (= BNF1).[12] This book is a compilation of manuscripts made for Ferry Julyot, a minor poet, political figure, and diplomat from Besançon, as noted on fol. 28r where is found the inscription: "J'ay commencé à escrire les choses contenues en ce present livre en l'an 1536—Julyot" [I began to write the things contained in the present book in the year 1536—Julyot]. The poem on Anne Boleyn (fols. 33r–60v) is preceded by the "Récit de la mort de Thomas Morus (1535)" on fols. 29r–32r and is followed by assorted verses of Clément Marot beginning on fol. 60v. Marot's name immediately follows the word "Fin" at the end of the Anne Boleyn poem, which may have led some readers to ascribe the Boleyn poem to him. The book also contains the text "Le bon pasteur" (beginning on fol. 166r), a poem formerly ascribed to Marot but now credited to Almanque Papillon, mainly on the basis of the fact that it is so ascribed in this manuscript.[13] Given the inscription by Julyot and the dating of other poems included in this collection (by the likes of Marot, Marguerite de Navarre, and François I, all of whom were active in the early 1530s), it appears that this manuscript transcription of the Anne Boleyn poem was made shortly after Carle composed it in 1536. This is the prime reason Georges Ascoli chose this manuscript version as the

---

[11] See Charles de Bourgueville, *Les recherches et antiquitez de la province de Neustrie* (Caen: Jean de Feure, 1588), 123–25, for references to Anne Boleyn, whom the author describes (123), as does Carle's poem, as having been brought up in France, arriving there as one of Mary Tudor's ladies upon her marriage to Louis XII; see also 124 for the reference to Anne's alleged lover, "Cathon" (Weston). The British Library exemplar spells the name "Caton," a slight variation that would have been pronounced in an identical fashion.

[12] Manuscripts at the BnF are categorized by the language in which the majority of their texts are written. Hence, in this instance, the manuscript belongs to the *fonds français* (hereafter abbreviated as "Fr."), as the manuscripts are written in French.

[13] For more on the attribution of this poem to Papillon, see above, Chapter 2.

copy text for his 1927 edition (designated as text "J"), which stands as the best modern edition of the poem produced thus far.[14]

Among the other Parisian manuscripts, BnF Fr. 01742 (= BNF2) is notable for confusing the date of Anne's execution (19 May) with the date of the completion of the text (2 June) in the title of the poem. It is missing forty verses fairly early in the text (beginning at v. 156). As v. 155 is the last verse on its folio, this suggests that the manuscript was doubtless missing an entire folio before it was bound. Otherwise, the text contains all the canonical verses and is meticulously executed. Its *explicit*, or final line, is written in Latin: "Vivant in Christo qui credunt in eo" [Those who believe in Christ shall live in him], which can be read as a testament to the view that the contents of this text are Christian in orientation.[15] Another Parisian manuscript, BnF Fr. 02370 (= BNF3), is also a very clean copy, with only a few corrections made in the same hand, and thus appears to be professionally done. Indeed, Philippe Tamizey de Larroque, in his 1873 edition of Guillaume Colletet's life of the poet, considers this to be the best manuscript version he has seen.[16] The volume is a compilation of manuscripts, comprising poems by Marot and Saint-Gelais along with several *blasons anatomiques* (including Carle's own *blason de l'esprit*). The presence of Marot's poems in this manuscript collection led Joachim Le Grand, mistakenly, to attribute the Anne Boleyn text to him as well.[17]

No doubt the most historically important of the Parisian manuscripts is BnF Fr. 10194 (= BNF4). The Anne Boleyn poem is found here among multiple other texts, including some spiritual poems and nineteen sonnets by Olivier de Magny that do not otherwise figure in his published works.[18] The compilation attests to an interest in Anglo-French affairs, as it includes a piece on the trial of Thomas More, a text against the English claim to the kingdom of France, and a work on the death of Mary, Queen of Scots. The Boleyn poem is densely written in a small and not very careful—indeed, exceedingly difficult to read—cursive script, though it is fairly clean, with only a few corrections. This version distinguishes itself for bearing Carle's name in the title and for the presence of fifteen

---

[14] See "Poème sur la mort d'Anne Boleyn, par Lancelot de Carles," in Georges Ascoli, *La Grande-Bretagne devant l'opinion française depuis la Guerre de Cent Ans jusqu'à la fin du XVIe siècle* (Paris: Librairie universitaire J. Gamber, 1927), 231–73.

[15] This manuscript was used by Ascoli, designated as text "A."

[16] See Guillaume Colletet, *Vies des poètes bordelais et périgourdins*, ed. Philippe Tamizey de Larroque (1873; repr. Geneva: Slatkine, 1969), 34. This manuscript was used by Ascoli, designated as text "E."

[17] See Joachim Le Grand, *Histoire du divorce de Henry VIII, Roy d'Angleterre, et de Catherine d'Aragon*, 3 vols. (Paris: Martin and Boudot, 1688), 2:162–63; for more on this topic, see Chapter 3 above.

[18] These poems were later published by Tamizey as *Sonnets inédits d'Olivier de Magny* (Paris: Lemerre, 1880).

verses, divided between two passages towards the end of the manuscript, ten of which are extra-canonical and five of which are unique variants of verses found elsewhere. It is also missing two other canonical verses. Four of the ten extra verses are highly significant insofar as they paint a scene in which the crowd of onlookers at Anne's execution realize, on the basis of her steadfast manner in facing death, that they have misjudged her life. This version was used by Ascoli in his scholarly edition of the poem (where it was given the designation "O"); inexplicably, however, Ascoli does not mention or transcribe the text's extra lines in his otherwise careful notation of variants. One can only conjecture that the scholar was not able to decipher these nearly illegible verses.

This text (but, of course, not this very exemplar, which no doubt never crossed the Channel) is very likely to have been the one first given to Henry VIII, which engendered an angry letter on his part sent to the English ambassadors in France demanding that the author of the scandalous poem be punished and that all copies of the work be destroyed.[19] Such a claim can be made on the basis of the intitulation of this manuscript, which, uniquely among the extant manuscripts, refers to the author by name and further identifies him as a "prothonotary," a designation also used in the correspondence about this poem on the part of the English court. The manuscript's title also clearly identifies the poem as a "tragedy," another term found in this diplomatic correspondence.[20] The existence of these extra verses that so explicitly portray Anne as wrongly judged (i.e., through an acknowledgment that the witnesses to her execution believed in her innocence thanks to her comportment) appear to be a further justification for Henry's wrath as demonstrated in these letters. The fact that this is the only manuscript with those particular extra verses also raises the suspicion that Henry's demand that the work be destroyed may have been carried out to some extent, at least with regard to works containing that specific passage. The haste with which this copy was executed, as evidenced by the very poor quality of the handwriting, suggests that it was not done by a professional scribe, and a hypothesis could be formulated that the copy was quickly (and perhaps secretly) made when the order to destroy the poem reached the French court. The fact

---

[19] For a full discussion of this matter, see Chapter 3 above. The diplomatic correspondence referring to this manuscript can be found in London, British Library, Additional 25114, "Original letters and state papers relating chiefly to the embassies of Stephen Gardiner, Bishop of Winchester, to the courts of Francis I and Charles V: 1527–1545" (hereafter Add. 25114), fols. 267r–268v. For a synopsis, see LP 12.2.78. For later correspondence on this manuscript, from William Paget, see Kew, National Archives, State Papers (SP), 1/177, fols. 33–35. That text is summarized in LP 18.1.381, and a facsimile is available via State Papers Online.

[20] Henry's reference to this text as a tragedy and to Carle's name are found in Add. 25114, fols. 267r and 267v, respectively. The reference to the author as a prothonotary is found in SP 1/177, fol. 34v.

that other manuscripts do not have these verses also appears to suggest that they were, subsequently, recognized to be the particular scene that ignited Henry's rage and that a secondary form of the poem, with those very verses excised, came to be the one that survived this early threat to its existence.[21] This is, of course, mere speculation; but it is a plausible scenario that explains both the violence of Henry's reaction as well as the uniqueness of these verses to this manuscript. Furthermore, given what was said about the poem in the aforementioned diplomatic correspondence — specifically, that the poem was *imprinted* in France at that time — perhaps what we have here is a manuscript copied from that now lost early imprint.

Another Parisian manuscript, which once was thought to have been lost, is Paris, Bibliothèque nationale de France, Lat. 5934 (= BNF5). The Anne Boleyn poem is here presented anonymously in a collection of several manuscripts, the others of which are in Latin. Hence its shelf number places it among the *fonds latins* rather than the *fonds français* of the BnF. This has caused several scholars, from Tamizey to Émile Picot to Ascoli and beyond, who could not locate the work within the *fonds français*, to assume that it was lost.[22] Happily, this is far from the case, as the text not only survives but also has been digitized and is available on Gallica, the online digital library of the Bibliothèque nationale de France. The volume is extremely rich in its presentation and traces its provenance to the collection of Jean-Baptiste Colbert (1619–1683), a politician under King Louis XIV whose immense private library of manuscripts was sold in 1732 to the Royal Library of France, the precursor to the BnF. Some of the other texts in the volume have red-colored intitulation. The Anne Boleyn poem is done only in black ink, but it is adorned with an elaborate border of shaded animals and foliage at the top of its first folio, before the title. The text proper begins with a drawn figure of a man reading a book, affixed to the first initial ("L"). The Anne Boleyn poem is not complete in this version, however, ending with v. 1240 (written on a folio with only five lines at the top); this last folio of text is followed by three blank pages, as if the scribe had intended to complete the work later but never did. This version of the poem was excerpted extensively by Charles-Hugues Le Febvre de Saint-Marc in the preface to his edition of Rapin

---

[21] It is possible, of course, that these unique verses constitute an *addition* to the manuscript inserted by a later scribe rather than by the author. But the manuscript itself provides no evidence that these lines are insertions, as they are fully incorporated into the text.

[22] See Tamizey, in his edition of Colletet, *Vies des poètes*, 30, as well as Émile Picot, *Les Français italianisants au XVIᵉ siècle*, vol. 1 (Paris: Champion, 1906), 235–49, here 237n1. It was not used by Ascoli, who presumably believed that it was lost, based on Tamizey and Picot.

de Thoyras's *Histoire d'Angleterre*.[23] Tamizey, the editor of Colletet's life of Carle, knew about the existence of this version through Saint-Marc's work but was ultimately puzzled by the manuscript's apparent disappearance.

Two final Parisian manuscripts have also been virtually neglected in recent years. The first, known as Paris, Bibliothèque nationale de France, Cinq cents de Colbert 465 (= BNF6), is a compilation of manuscripts touching Anglo-French relations. Although the poem on Anne Boleyn is indexed in the BnF database page for this volume, this text has received no attention thus far. This is not necessarily a grave loss to scholarship, as this manuscript has no unique features, save for its *explicit*, a scribal addition at the end, written in Latin — "Soli deo onor et gloria" [To God alone be honor and glory] — which may have been inspired by a perceived spiritual orientation of the text or merely by the scribe's own religious convictions. Lastly, Paris, Bibliothèque nationale de France, Fr. 12489 (= BNF7) is an anthology of poems, most of which are introduced by an indication of genre. However, the Anne Boleyn poem has neither a rubric of this kind nor a title; its *incipit* is neither set off in any way nor located at the top of a new folio. For these reasons, the poem can be (and has been) easily overlooked. While the text is available on Gallica, the Anne Boleyn poem is not indexed in the BnF database page for this volume and thus has not been studied by scholars previously. The text is written in two different hands. The name "Sainct Sire" appears towards the beginning of the volume. According to the Joubaud-Sicard database, this may be a reference to the woman, perhaps named Hélène de Saint-Cire, to whom the volume is dedicated or to whom it was given.[24]

While the vast majority of surviving manuscripts of Carle's poem are located in Paris, a significant number are to be found scattered in libraries throughout France and elsewhere in Europe. One of the most interesting of these texts, qua material object, is that found in the Bordeaux municipal library, MS 0313 (= B). Although one online database, namely "Manuscrits Médiévaux d'Aquitaine," implies (by its use of the plural) that there is more than one poem on Anne Boleyn in this volume, this is not the case. The single Boleyn poem is the last piece of the volume, which is a compilation of diverse anonymous manuscripts, many of which are in Latin and treat spiritual matters. Carle's poem is immediately preceded by prose compositions as well as a piece with color drawings on heraldic shields, attributed to Jean de Marcille (or "Marcillé"), and this proximity led to some confusion regarding the proper author of the Anne Boleyn

---

[23] For these excerpts, see the preface by Charles-Hugues Le Febvre de Saint-Marc to Paul de Rapin de Thoyras, *Histoire d'Angleterre par M. Rapin de Thoyras*, vol. 1 (The Hague, 1749), xxxix–lxiii.

[24] See Pascal Joubaud and Claire Sicard, "B.N. fr. 12489," in the online database, Demêler Mellin de Saint-Gelais, Carnet de recherche *Hypothèses*, 29 August 2011.

poem.[25] By 1894, however, the library's catalogue compiled by Camille Couderc definitively ascribed the poem to Carle, who, it will be remembered, hailed from Bordeaux.[26] Thus it is fitting that this city should be home to one manuscript version of the text. The 1894 notice also gives a complete description of the other anonymous manuscripts in the volume. This manuscript was used by Ascoli, who designated it as text "B."

This exemplar was housed in the library of the Discalced Carmelites of Bordeaux (whose *ex libris* appears on the first folio) before its arrival in the municipal library. An inscription on the flyleaf gives the date 1546 as well as the names "Jehan le Faulcheur" and "Petrus Marchant," who may be the scribes of some of the manuscripts contained in this volume. A notice appearing in *The Gentleman's Magazine* attributes the nineteenth-century rediscovery of this manuscript to Francisque Michel; the author of that notice remarks upon the similarity between this text and the anonymous *Lettre d'un gentilhomme portugais*, another early modern account of Anne's execution, which was published by Francisque Michel, a professor of literature at the University of Bordeaux, in 1832.[27]

Scribal and/or reader intervention in the Bordeaux copy of the poem is notable. The title of the poem as rendered here, "La *pitoiable* description de la *vie et mort* de madame Anne Boulant, en son vivant fesme du roy d'Angleterre, Henry .8. de ce nom *en ses secondes noces*, laquelle fust decolee l'an 1536, *le douzieme de juing*" [The *pitiable* description of the *life and* death of Madame Anne Boleyn, during her lifetime wife of the king of England, Henry the eighth of that name, *in his second marriage*, who was beheaded in the year 1536, **the twelfth of June**], is the most expansive of all the informal titles given to this text. It is the work of three separate hands (as marked here by the use of italics and bold script) and contains some misinformation regarding the date of Anne's execution. It also reveals an orientation toward reading the poem as a lamentable, tragic story.[28] At the end of this title, the scribe adds this notation, "L'aucteur de ceste poësie est incognut" [The author of this poetry is unknown], in recognition of the anonymous state of this manuscript. The scribe ends the text with the words "Louenge à Dieu" [Praise be to God], and another hand writes the equivalent phrase in Latin, "Laus deo."

---

[25] See Chapter 3 above for more on how the Anne Boleyn poem was misattributed to Jean de Marcille.

[26] See *Catalogue général des manuscrits des bibliothèques publiques de France*, vol. 23 (Bordeaux), ed. Camille Couderc (Paris: Plon, 1894), 174–77, here 176–77, no. 313.

[27] "Poem on the Death of Anne Boleyn," *The Gentleman's Magazine and Historical Review*, ed. Sylvanus Urban [Edward Cave, pseud.], n.s., 10 (January–June 1861): 189–90. For the other contemporary account of Anne's death, see *Lettre d'un gentilhomme portugais . . . sur l'exécution d'Anne Boleyn*, ed. Francisque Michel, English translation by Viscount Strangford (Paris: Chez Silvestre, 1832).

[28] For a fuller discussion of this title, see my Afterword.

But what is most interesting about this text is its numerous marginal annotations (including drawings), which show a genuine engagement with the poem. The marginal drawings are a combination of conventional signals, such as manicules (pointing hands) and flowers, along with more idiosyncratic images (including a chevron and what appears to be a scroll).[29] But the manicules used here are distinctive insofar as they do not emphasize the pointing index finger but instead join the third and fourth fingers in what could look like a gesture of benediction. Furthermore, a cross marks the passages where the jurors kiss the crucifix, where the prisoners receive Holy Communion in preparation for death, and where Anne attends to her prayers in her oratory. This suggests that the annotator(s) had a special interest in religious matters alluded to in the text, which would not be unusual for readers living in a religious house such as that of the Discalced Carmelites. Other marginalia give corrections to the text or indicate poetically problematic verses as well as some historical details (not all of which are accurate).[30]

The municipal library of Soissons, northeast of Paris, is home to a small family of manuscript versions of the poem: Soissons MS 201 and 202 (= S1 and S2, respectively), only the second of which is complete. Both texts were used by Ascoli, who designated them "Sa" and "Sb," respectively. The provenance of these volumes has been traced to nearby Prémontré Abbey, which was suppressed as a result of the French Revolution.[31] Because Soissons MS 201 is missing hundreds of verses at the end, it seems likely that it is based on Soissons MS 202, rather than the other way around.

In both instances, the Anne Boleyn poem is contained within a compilation of other historical and literary texts. The first exemplar, Soissons 201, contains several poems written by Marot, François I, and Saint-Gelais, all writers who flourished during the 1530s; however, the rubric under which the work of Francis I falls designates him as the "feu roy" [late king], thus revealing that this part of the manuscript, at least, dates from 1547 or later. Soissons 201 also contains two texts—one in prose, the other in the form of a verse elegy—on the death

---

[29] For more on marginalia common in the Renaissance, consult William H. Sherman, *Used Books: Marking Readers in Renaissance England* (Philadelphia: University of Pennsylvania Press, 2008).

[30] There is a nineteenth-century handwritten copy of this version of the poem: Paris, Bibliothèque Sainte-Geneviève, 3986 (4). This copy reproduces some, but not all, of the written marginalia of the Bordeaux text but does not reproduce any of its marginal drawings. Additional documentation indicates that this later manuscript was copied for research leading to the publication of Elizabeth Benger's *Memoirs of the Life of Anne Boleyn, Queen of Henry VIII*, 1821, 3rd ed. (London: Longman, Rees, Orme, Brown, and Green, 1827).

[31] See *Catalogue général des manuscrits des bibliothèques publiques de France*, vol. 3, (Soissons) (Paris: Plon, 1885), 126–28.

of Thomas More, attesting to an interest in events happening in England in the years 1535–1536.[32] Soissons 201 also differs from its sister text with regard to its significant number of marginal annotations in a hand that differs from the scribe's. These annotations also contain a reference to Anne's daughter as the queen of England, thereby dating themselves to the time of the reign of Elizabeth I or thereafter.

The second exemplar, Soissons 202, likewise boasts of poems by Marot and a selection of *blasons anatomiques* that date from the 1530s. Similarly, it also contains the elegy on the death of Thomas More, as well as a piece on the Carthusian martyrs of 1535.[33] Notably, it also features a poem entitled "Les Regretz que Messire Millort de Rocheffort . . . feist sur l'eschauffault" [The Regrets expressed by My Lord of Rochford on the scaffold], which recounts George Boleyn's final words in a way that differs from (but is complementary to) the one provided by Carle.[34]

In most respects, however, the two manuscript versions of the poem are nearly identical in content. This can best be judged by their similar missing and unique variant verses. One curious variant, found in vv. 653–654 of both manuscripts, indicates that the crowds who gathered in the wake of Anne's arrest, seeking the return of Mary to the court, left joyfully, believing Henry's promise of his daughter's imminent return. All the other extant versions of this poem make it quite clear that Henry was duplicitous in this matter and that the crowds soon realized they were duped and left in disappointment. Another way that these two manuscripts differ from other versions is through their designation (in their intitulation) of the men arrested with Anne as "knights," which is not accurate given the fact that only one of the men, Francis Weston, had in fact been knighted. Furthermore, the two manuscripts, uniquely among extant versions, sometimes use a deliberately antiquated French style, as in their use of the adverbial form "illec" in certain variants (e.g., vv. 745, 929, and 1063). Together with the designation of Anne's lovers as "knights," the use of antiquated French forms here lends a decidedly medieval air to both of the Soissons manuscripts.

No doubt the most significant manuscript outside of Paris is the one located in the municipal library of Valenciennes, quite close to Belgium, shelved as MS 419 (= V). This text was also used by Ascoli, who designated it text "V." It is a less than clean copy, with several corrections and interpolated verses, most notably towards the end. This manuscript betrays its northern origin, near Picardy, and its relationship to other northern manuscripts, through its consistent replacement of the letter "ç" (representing a sibilant consonant) with "ch" (represent-

---

[32] For these texts, see Soissons, Bibliothèque municipale, MS 201, fols. 16v–18r. The poem on More is reproduced in Ascoli, *Grande-Bretagne*, 227–31.

[33] See Soissons, Bibliothèque municipale, MS 202, fols. 128v–133r.

[34] See Soissons, Bibliothèque municipale, MS 202, fols. 137v–140v. This poem is reproduced in Ascoli, *Grande-Bretagne*, 274–78.

ing a palato-alveolar fricative sound). The poem is found among a variety of other verse and prose documents, including one that deals with the repudiation of Anne of Cleves.[35] Aimé Leroy, in his extensive description of the text, declares the provenance of the volume to be the library of the Château de l'Hermitage, near Condé, which belonged to the Croy family.[36] Indeed, fol. 2 has the signature "Croy," while the last folio has the signature "Monsieur de Molembays, Jan de Croy 1597," clearly indicating that the previous owner was from this family. Jacques Mangeart, who compiled the Valenciennes catalogue in 1860, believes the manuscript was transcribed by Jean de Lannoy.[37]

The Anne Boleyn poem is here titled "Pour feu dame Anne de Boullant jadis royne d'Engleterre, l'an VC trente trois, fait et composé par Anthoine de Crespin, escuyer, S[eigneu]r de Miherne" [On behalf of the late Lady Anne Boleyn, formerly Queen of England, in the year 1533, made and composed by Anthoine de Crespin, squire, lord of Miherne]. Another hand has interpolated the word "Apologie" before the title. This manuscript thus distinguishes itself for its attribution of the poem to the mysterious "Anthoine de Crespin"; additionally, this version was the basis for a prose paraphrase dating from the late sixteenth century made by Emanuel de Meteren, which circulated widely.[38] The attribution to Crespin, which Meteren did much to promulgate, has caused endless confusion among historians, some of whom believed that the poems attributed to Crespin and Carle are different texts. They most certainly are the same.[39]

Of all the versions of the Anne Boleyn poem in Europe outside of France, the one found in the Bibliothèque royale de Belgique (MS 19378 = BRB) in Brussels has received the most attention. The text itself is clearly related to the Valenciennes manuscript as it also tends to use "ch" for "ç," in the Picardy manner. Additionally, an examination of the variants of this text and the others found in the North (i.e., Valenciennes, Munich, and Karlsruhe) indicate that this is a family of manuscripts, though it may not be possible to ascertain which one is the parent text or if all the extant manuscripts were based on another, unknown,

---

[35] This is "Remonstrance faicte par la sœur du duc de Juilliers au roy d'Engleterre et son conseil . . . au nom d'Anne de Clèves, femme de Henri VIII" [A remonstrance made by the sister of the duke of Juilliers to the King of England and his council . . . on behalf of Anne of Cleves, wife of Henry VIII], beginning at fol. 30.

[36] See Aimé Leroy, "Manuscrits de la bibliothèque de Valenciennes," *Archives historiques et littéraires du Nord de la France et du Midi de la Belgique*, n.s., 5 (1844): 361–70.

[37] See *Catalogue descriptif et raisonné des manuscrits de la bibliothèque de Valenciennes*, ed. Jacques Mangeart (Paris: Techener, 1860), 400 (no. 401).

[38] For more on this matter, consult Chapter 3 above.

[39] For a final correction of this misattribution, see the index to the *Catalogue général des manuscrits des bibliothèques de France*, vol. 25 (Valenciennes), ed. Auguste Molinier (Paris: Plon, 1894), 552, which lists Carle, "and not Antoine de Crespin," as the author of this poem.

exemplar. The title bears the date of 1533, which presumably must be understood as a reference to the year of Anne Boleyn's coronation and not her execution. The poem ends at v. 1318 and renders vv. 1323–1324 in prose, giving the completion date of 2 June 1533. The anonymous text was first described at length and partially transcribed in a note published in 1845 by Baron de Reiffenberg; a review of Leroy's work, published by Reiffenberg the following year, indicates that the baron was persuaded by Leroy's argument that this poem should be attributed to Crespin.[40] Despite this attention, dating from the nineteenth century, Ascoli did not use this manuscript in his edition; nevertheless, Maria Dowling mentions it as her source for the poem.[41] Notes on the inside front cover read: "Acheté par le Ministère de l'Intérieur . . . prix 75 francs" [Bought by the Ministry of the Interior . . . price 75 francs] and "Il y a un extraict de ce poème historique dans le *Bulletin du bibliophile belge*" [There is an excerpt from this historical poem in the *Bulletin du bibliophile belge*], ostensibly a reference to Reiffenberg's article.

Another related manuscript is found in the Bayerische Staatsbibliothek, in Munich (Cod. GALL 105 = M), where the poem is titled "Le Discours de la vie et mort, Dame Anna de Boullant, Roÿnne putative d'Angleterre, et décapité [*sic*] A° 1536" [A discourse on the life and death of Lady Anne Boleyn, the putative Queen of England, beheaded in the year 1536]. An extensive (but unsigned and unpublished) description of this volume, composed in French by someone affiliated with the *Institut de recherche et d'histoire des textes*, notes that, curiously, there is a signature on the final folio of the manuscript that appears to read "James tant Ohens" with the word "Myherne" written underneath the word "Finis." This document speculates that the signature may refer to the name of a scribe or to a motto but hazards no further guesses as to its meaning.[42] The author of this description appears to be unaware that the word "Myherne" may be a reference to the attribution to Crespin (styled "seigneur de Miherne") in the Valenciennes text. Furthermore, it is possible that the motto actually reads "James tant dheur," a deliberately archaic spelling of the words "Jamais tant d'heur" [never so much happiness], though to whom this motto (if that is what it is), belonged remains a mystery. The flyleaf indicates in French that the text was copied by the Scottish antiquary James Dennistoun in the winter of 1836–1837; Dennistoun undertook

---

[40] See Baron de Reiffenberg [?], "Poème manuscrit sur Anne de Boleyn, par un auteur contemporain," in *Le bibliophile belge* 1 (1845): 455–62; see also the same author's review of Leroy in *Le bibliophile belge* 3 (1846): 158 (no. 40). For another description of this volume, see *Catalogue des manuscrits de la bibliothèque royale de Belgique*, ed. J. Van den Gheyn (Brussels: Henri Lamertin, 1907), 44 (no. 4636).

[41] See Dowling's introduction to William Latymer, "Latymer's 'Cronickille of Anne Bulleyne,'" ed. Maria Dowling, in *Camden Miscellany* 30, Camden Fourth Series, 39 (London: Royal Historical Society, 1990): 23–65, here 37.

[42] I am grateful to Juliane Trede of the Munich library, who made this document available to me.

a tour of Italy and Germany at this time for the purpose of copying manuscripts. The provenance of this volume has been traced to the Grand Ducal Library of Bavaria (in the late sixteenth century to early seventeenth century), as shown by a bookplate inscribed with the words "Ex Electorali Bibliotheca Sereniss. Vtrivsq. Bavariae Ducum" [From the library of His Most Serene Electoral Highness, the Duke of one and of the other Bavaria].[43]

The fourth manuscript in this family of northern texts can be found in Karlsruhe, Germany, in the Badische Landesbibliothek (Güntersthal 12 = K). This text, which dates from the seventeenth century, is of very poor quality. The book is a compilation of multiple discrete manuscripts, mostly in French, dealing with a variety of historical matters.[44] The Anne Boleyn poem, here titled "L'An 1533, Traictié de feuë la Royne d'Engleterre" [The year 1533, Treatise of the late Queen of England], is the last text in the volume. Thus, like the Brussels manuscript, this work bears a date that is incorrect. The text is rendered in a very careless cursive script, with whole passages repeated and then crossed out by the scribe. This exemplar of the poem has not been previously noted or studied, nor would such a study be particularly fruitful, given its poor condition.

A final sixteenth-century manuscript located in Europe is that which is housed in the Biblioteca Apostolica Vaticana (Vatican Library) in Rome (Reg. lat. 1652 = Vat). This volume was owned by Pierre Bourdelot, who was a physician to Queen Christina of Sweden. It was presumably gifted or sold to her and then absorbed into the Vatican Library's "fondo Reginense latino" with other works in her collection. The Anne Boleyn poem is the only text in this volume, and it is rendered in cursive script by a late sixteenth-century hand. It is fairly clean, with a few minor corrections in the same hand as the scribe. The name "Bourdelot," indicating the volume's original owner, is written in a different hand from the scribe's on fol. 1.[45]

There is only one (surviving) early modern printed edition of the text, in octavo, entitled *Epistre contenant le proces criminel faict à l'encontre de la royne Anne Boullant d'Angleterre, par Carles aulmosnier de Monsieur le Daulphin* [Letter Containing the Criminal Proceedings Against Anne Boleyn, Queen of England, by Carles, Almoner to the Dauphin = 1545]. Its title page features a woodcut of a king enthroned with several counselors seated on either side; furthermore,

---

[43] For another description of this volume, see *Catalogus codicum manu scriptorium bibliothecae Regiae Monacensis*, vol. 7 (Munich: Regia Palmiana, 1858), 4 (no. 12).

[44] For a full description of this volume, see *Romanische Handschriften der Grossherzoglich Badischen Hof- und Landesbibliothek, Karlsruhe*, ed. Ferdinand Lamey (Karlsruhe: Ch. Th. Groos, 1894), 46–49, no. 13.

[45] For more on this manuscript, consult "Catalogue des manuscrits de Jean et Pierre Bourdelot, médecins parisiens," ed. H. Omont, *Revue des bibliothèques* 1 (1891): 81–103, here 89, no. 79; and "Catalogue des manuscrits de Jean et Pierre Bourdelot: Concordance," ed. Elisabeth Pellegrin, *Scriptorium* 40 (1986): 202–32, here 210, no. 79.

an elaborate floral woodcut is used for the initial "L" of the poem's *incipit*. The text is produced in italic print and features several printed marginal annotations. There are only three known extant examples of this book worldwide: one in the Bibliothèque nationale de France, one in the British Library, and one at the University of Leeds.[46] None of these three exemplars carries any significant features, such as relevant handwritten marginalia showing a reader's engagement with the text. The Leeds exemplar traces its provenance to the Goodwood House Large Library in Sussex, the ancestral home of the Dukes of Richmond. Documentation attached to the book includes a record from Sotheby's catalogue, dated 24 March 1930. The British Library copy indicates that the book belonged to the library of John Towneley, which was put up for sale by 1815.[47] An acquisition invoice from the British Library archives indicates that this exemplar was purchased from Boone booksellers in July 1867.[48] There is no definitive information regarding the book's whereabouts between 1815 and 1867 (and certainly none for the period preceding this timeframe), though annotations on this exemplar refer to a sale by the bookseller Evans (who indeed had a copy for sale in 1835) as well as a reference to a Sotheby's sale in 1854.[49] Even less is known about the provenance of the BnF exemplar, which carries the signature of G. Faylier, who remains unidentified.

The printed edition of the poem is significant because it definitively attributes the poem to Lancelot de Carle, who was, by 1545, serving as almoner to the Dauphin, the future King Henry II. While there is therefore no mystery here regarding the author of the poem, as had been the case with the prior anonymous manuscripts, this book has, however, generated other mysteries of its own. First,

---

[46] These are BnF Rés. Ye. 3668 (with a digital copy available on Gallica), BL 11474 a.14 (with a digital copy available via Google Books), and University of Leeds, Special Collections: Anglo-French 6 1545/CAR.

[47] For a description of the library of John Towneley, including a reference to this exemplar, see *Repertorium bibliographicum, or, some account of the most celebrated British libraries* (London: William Clarke, 1819), 553. See also *Bibliotheca Towneleiana: A Catalogue of the Curious and Extensive Library of the Late John Towneley . . . Sold by Auction by R. H. Evans* (London: Bulmer, 1814), 17, no. 371, where the book is described as "extremely rare." The sale actually took place in 1815.

[48] BLCA/501/26–Department of Printed Books Acquisition Invoices, 18 Dec. 1868–8 Oct. 1869. I am grateful to Hannah Graves of the British Library for locating this information.

[49] See *Catalogue of the Library of the late Richard Heber, Part the Sixth, which will be sold by auction by Mr. Evans* (London: W. Nicol, 1835), 22 (no. 317). The notice indicates that this exemplar has a green morocco binding, though the BL exemplar has a brown cloth cover. For another reference to the 1545 print edition in private English libraries, see *The Bibliographer's Manual of English Literature*, vol. 1, ed. William Thomas Lowndes and rev. Henry G. Bohn (London: Henry Bohn, 1858), 47. It is quite possible that these exemplars are not the ones in London, Paris, or Leeds but are now in private hands.

it is not known whether or not the work was produced with Carle's permission or under his direction. Second, the printer's name is not given, though there is an indication on the title page that the work was sold in Lyon, a major center for printing in the Renaissance.[50] On the basis of this indication, it has traditionally been thought that the book was published in Lyon; indeed, the bibliographer La Croix du Maine so states very clearly in his sixteenth-century *Bibliothèque* (an annotated catalogue of early modern books, some of which can no longer be found).[51] Recent scholarship, however, indicates that this is not the case. Instead, according to Raphaël Cappellen, this book should be considered a counterfeit edition that gives fictitious or misleading imprint information, which was a very common practice in the Renaissance. Cappellen has discovered that the book was actually published by Jean Rousset in Tours. He bases this assertion on typographical similarities found between the *Epistre* and other works known to be published by Jean Rousset in Tours.[52] These similarities, which are quite strong, include the use of the same initial letter "L" in the incipit, as well as the layout and type used on the title page of the respective works, including a characteristic "fleuron" or vine-leaf ornament.

But what still remains unknown is how this manuscript came into Rousset's hands and why he was moved to publish it at this time, nine years after its composition, when the contents of the poem were indeed old news. Cappellen speculates that perhaps this edition was procured for Rousset by Jean Brèche, an advocate in Tours, who provided other texts to the publisher. Or, perhaps the 1545 edition was based not on a manuscript but on a now-lost earlier imprint (whose existence can be surmised from the diplomatic exchange between Henry's court and Stephen Gardiner, Germayne Gardyner, and William Paget, analyzed in Chapter 3 above). Whatever the story here, it is clear that this book was very shoddily (and perhaps quickly) produced. It is not carefully executed and

---

[50] The title page gives the indication "on les vend à Lyon, pres nostre Dame de Confort" [sold in Lyon, near Our Lady of Comfort]. This designation was used by the printing house of Arnoullet, for example, and referred to a very popular *quartier* for printing in Renaissance Lyon.

[51] See François Grudé sieur de La Croix du Maine, *La Bibliothèque du sieur de la Croix du Maine*, vol. 1 (1579; Paris: Abel L'Angelier, 1584), 282. This indication is repeated in the *Catalogue des livres de la bibliothèque de feu M. le duc de la Vallière*, pt. 1, vol. 2, 351 as well as in *French Vernacular Books: Books Published in the French Language before 1601*, ed. Andrew Pettegree, Malcolm Walsby, and Alexander Wilkinson, vol. 1 (A–G) (Leiden: Brill, 2007), 262. For further references to the printed edition, see *Nouvelles recherches bibliographiques pour servir de supplément au manuel du libraire*, ed. Jacques-Charles Brunet, vol. 1 (Paris: Silvestre, 1834), 267; and *Manuel du libraire et de l'amateur de livres*, ed. Jacques-Charles Brunet, vol. 1 (Paris: Didot, 1860), cols. 1579–1580.

[52] I am grateful to Raphaël Cappellen for sharing his discoveries with me via email correspondence. See Cappellen, "Le mystère des origines. *L'Isle Sonante* dans son contexte tourangeau (1544–1562), *L'Année rabelaisienne*, 5 (2021): 49–94, here 72–74.

contains many obvious errors: for example, Henry Norris is consistently referred to as "Maurus," which is the Latinized name of Thomas More, and a study of the variants here noted in the present edition will also confirm that it contains multiple mistakes, many of which are nonsensical misreadings. Furthermore, it is missing two canonical verses.

## Adaptations, Translations, and Modern Editions

After the sixteenth century, two other printed versions of the poem, each based on multiple manuscript versions, were produced. The first was edited by Georges-Adrien Crapelet and was included in his *Lettres de Henri VIII à Anne Boleyn* in 1826. This version of the text does not identify variants, nor does it explicitly identify the manuscripts it uses, but an analysis of the text confirms that Crapelet relied on three Parisian manuscripts: namely BNF3 (which he refers to, in his preface, under its former shelf mark of 8057); BNF1 (identifiable because of its unique rendering of vv. 7–8); and BNF5 (identifiable because of its unique rendering of v. 220). The poem is here printed anonymously. Later, an edition of the poem was included in Georges Ascoli's *La Grande Bretagne devant l'opinion française*, which appeared in 1927. This has been the standard edition of the Anne Boleyn poem for decades and is single-handedly responsible for salvaging the poem from an undeserved oblivion. It is very carefully done (with only a few errors), well-introduced, and features some explanatory notes. Ascoli's base text is BNF1, and he provides variants from BNF2–BNF4, B, S1, S2, V, and the 1545 printed version. However, he does not include the extra verses from BNF4. He unhesitatingly ascribes the poem to Carle.

Aside from these versions of Carle's text, the poem has been adapted in verse form in French at least twice. One version, found in the British Library (Egerton 2403), is clearly a variation of Carle's text, rendered into rhyming *alexandrins* (the 12-syllable verse preferred in France by the second half of the sixteenth century and used frequently by great classical writers, such as Racine). It is contained in a volume that includes a long metrical piece on Mary, Queen of Scots, which was signed by the owner of this book, Thomas Wenman, in 1601. The poem on Anne Boleyn, here entitled (in a manner reminiscent of the Brussels manuscript) "Traicté de Dame Anne Boullam [*sic*] iadis Royne d'Angleterre, par ung gentillome françoys" [Treatise of Lady Anne Boleyn, formerly queen of England, by a French gentleman] is presented in reverse at the end of the other manuscripts, and is accessed by flipping the book over. The text thus begins on fol. 50v and continues to 49r. The poem here appears to be an imitative exercise, perhaps even an assignment from the author's schooldays, which may explain why the poem ends at verse 100: the task may well have been to provide a 100-line version of Carle's poem, at which point the pupil duly stopped writing. Verses 1–26 serve as a preamble that has no counterpart in Carle's text but that demonstrates a similar

Christian orientation (invoking God as the poet's muse) along with the theme of the mutability of fortune. Beginning at v. 27, the poet starts to follow Carle's text fairly closely, alluding to the unprecedented events that have occurred in England, which have left him astounded. He then begins, at v. 46, to tell Anne's backstory, starting with the time she spent in France in the court of Queen Claude, whose virtuous example she failed to follow. The poem ends just at the moment when Anne has succeeded in attracting the king by her seductive glance. There are many close verbal echoes of Carle's text in this section of the poem, but no verse is identical to its model. The poetry is quite mediocre and is clearly not the work of an experienced or gifted lyricist. Nevertheless, the existence of this text is a testament to the survival of Carle's poem in the late sixteenth and early seventeenth centuries, at least in academic circles.

Another French manuscript (BnF Fr. 19886) is also more a variation than a copy, given that many lines are entirely different from any of the early modern manuscripts. The poem on Anne Boleyn, written in a nineteenth-century hand, rather puzzlingly begins under the rubric (fol. 113) "Discours en prose et en vers sur Marie Stuard; autre discours en vers sur l'execution de cette Princesse" [A discourse in prose and verse on Mary Stuart; another discourse in verse on the execution of this princess], the latter title presumably referring to the poem on Anne Boleyn's death (fols. 114r–169v). The work is found amid a variety of other texts, including one printed work. The pages of the manuscript are scored, leaving a very small writing area. Because this later manuscript varies so wildly from the early modern versions, it is not included among the variants of this edition, but perhaps deserves study as a unique imitative exercise.

Additionally, Carle's poem has been rendered in well-known prose para-phrases, both in French and in English. The first was composed by Emanuel de Meteren in his *Historia Belgica*, which circulated in manuscript and was first published in Latin in 1597 and translated into French in 1618.[53] Two English prose paraphrases of Carle's poem, based on Crapelet's edition, have also made their way into print. The first English *précis* of Crapelet's text, made for the benefit of those for whom the "quaint old French might not be intelligible," was offered in the nineteenth century in an anonymous review that was clearly done by a sensitive reader of the text.[54] But the version of Carle's poem that is most widely cited is the prose paraphrase rendered in *Letters and Papers, Foreign and Domestic, of the Reign of Henry VIII*.[55] This is a fairly faithful English paraphrase

---

[53] For more on the importance of this paraphrase, see Chapter 3 above.

[54] See *Literary Gazette and Journal of Belles Lettres, Arts, Sciences, etc.* (London: Moyes, 1826), no. 517 (Saturday, 16 December 1826): 789–90. This review may have been written by the historian Sharon Turner. For more on this matter, see Chapter 3 above.

[55] See the multi-volume *Letters and Papers, Foreign and Domestic, of the Reign of Henry VIII* (hereafter abbreviated as LP) ed. J. S. Brewer, J. Gairdner and R. H. Bro-

of the Anne Boleyn poem, with only a few mistranslations, based on Crapelet's printed version. The author makes an effort to capture some of the phrasing of the original and refrains from adding information garnered elsewhere. But, like all paraphrases, this text cannot reflect the literary form of the poem, and much of the original flavor is lost.

Two other translations into English have been produced. The first was contained in an unpublished dissertation by Susan Walters Schmid.[56] This work reproduces Ascoli's edition and offers a somewhat literal and sometimes inaccurate translation. Some explanatory notes accompany the text, which is set in its historical context and in which the author considers whether or not Carle's text can be used as historical evidence for the events of 1536. The second was a self-published English translation of the poem based on the poorly executed 1545 printed edition, produced by Margaret Bolton.[57] It is highly unreliable and often grossly misreads the sixteenth-century French.

---

die (London: Her Majesty's Stationery Office, 1846–1932). These documents are now available through an online searchable database: British History Online (https://www. british-history.ac.uk/). For another searchable database available by subscription, which sometimes gives a digitized copy of the original manuscript in addition to the summary made by these Victorian-era scholars, see "State Papers Online: Early Modern Government in Britain and Europe," (https://www.gale.com/intl/primary-sources/state-papers-online). For this reference, see LP 10.1036, dated 2 June 1536.

[56] Susan Walters Schmid, "Anne Boleyn, Lancelot de Carle, and the Uses of Documentary Evidence" (PhD diss., Arizona State University, 2009); the poem can be found at pp. 110–75.

[57] See *De Carles' Trial and Death of Queen Anne Boleyn translated into Modern English*, trans. Margaret Bolton (CreateSpace Independent Publishing Platform: 2015).

## Schematic Descriptions of
## Early Modern Versions of the Poem

For complete bibliographical information on the secondary sources listed here, consult the general bibliography.


# I. Early Modern Manuscripts of the Poem

## A. Manuscript in London (British Library)

| | |
|---|---|
| Identification | BL = Additional 40662 (copy text). A digital copy of the first folio is available on the British Library website. |
| Volume Title | *L'Histoire de la mort d'Anne Boulenc, royne d'Angleterre*; catalogue entry reads: L'Histoire de la mort d'Aiine Boullene [*sic*], royne d'Angleterre |
| Poem Title | "L'Histoire de la mort D'Anne Bovlenc Royne d'Angleterre" (fols. 1r–42v) |
| Description | Vellum; 42 fols. + 4 fols.; 21 × 14 cm; red velvet binding, gilt edging; title and first initial in gold ink. Scored folios with 16 vv. per folio with the exception of fol. 1 (which has four lines dedicated to the title and twelve lines of verse, therefore making a total of sixteen) and the verso of the last folio (which has only the four extra lines not found in other manuscripts); irregular division into stanzas; italic script. |
| Attribution | Anonymous |
| Verses | 1328 vv. (including extra-canonical verses 275–276, 341–342, and 1325–1328) |
| Explicit | "Fin" [The End] |
| Provenance | William Tite; Thomas Thomson; Baron Heiss (?); Mouchard (?); Charles de Bourgueville (?) |
| Marginalia | Some notes in French, done in early modern hand other than the scribe's. Some underscoring of verses. |
| Notes | Only MS in book<br>Attestation: BL catalogue; Jonas database; *Catalogue des livres rares et précieux de M. \*\*\* [Heiss]*, 141; *Dictionnaire bibliographique*, 333; *Notice . . . de la bibliothèque de feu M. Mouchard*, 13 |

N.B. All of the following manuscripts are missing the verses that are unique to BL

## B. Manuscripts in Paris
## (Bibliothèque nationale de France)

**1.**

| Identification | BNF1 = Fr. 12795 (= Microfilm 21046); available on Gallica |
|---|---|
| Volume Title | *Recueil* |
| Poem Title | "De la royne d'Angleterre" (fols. 33r–60v) |
| Description | Paper; 623 fols.; 28 × 21 cm; leather half binding; approximately 24–26 lines per folio; not divided into stanzas; fine hybrid hand (combining book script and chancery script) |
| Attribution | Anonymous |
| Verses | 1318 vv. [missing vv. 719–720]; unique reading of vv. 7–8 |
| Explicit | "Fin" [The End] |
| Provenance | Ferry Julyot |
| Marginalia | None |
| Notes | Compilation of manuscripts, including a report on the death of Thomas More (fols. 29–32); assorted verses of Clément Marot; "Le bon pasteur." Full description of contents available on the Gallica website.<br>Attestation: BnF catalogue; Jonas, Gallica databases; Crapelet; Ascoli (J) |

**2.**

| Identification | BNF2 = Fr. 01742 (formerly 6491) |
|---|---|
| Volume Title | *Histoire de la royne Anne Boullant* |
| Poem Title | "Histoire de la royne Anne Boullant d'Angleterre, qui mourut le 2e jour de juing 1536" (fols. 1r–33r) |
| Description | Paper; 33 fols.; 18 × 12 cm; leather binding; small cursive script; approximately 16–20 vv. per folio; divided irregularly into stanzas |
| Attribution | Anonymous |
| Verses | 1280 vv. [missing vv. 156–195 (one entire folio)] |
| Explicit | "Vivant in Christo qui credunt in eo" [Those who believe in Christ shall live in him] |
| Provenance | Unknown |
| Marginalia | None |

| Notes | Only MS in book |
|---|---|
| | Attestation: BnF catalogue; Jonas database; Ascoli (A) |

## 3.

| Identification | BNF3 = Fr. 02370 (formerly 8057) |
|---|---|
| Volume Title | None |
| Poem Title | "Histoire de Anne Boullant, royne d'Angleterre" (fols. 1r–26r) |
| Description | Paper; 109 fols.; 22 × 15 cm; leather binding. Approximately 26–28 vv. per folio; irregular divisions into stanzas; careful hybrid hand |
| Attribution | Anonymous |
| Verses | 1312 vv. [missing vv. 213, 290–295, and 699] |
| Explicit | "Fin" [The End] |
| Provenance | Unknown |
| Marginalia | None |
| Notes | Compilation of manuscripts, including poems by Marot; several *blasons anatomiques*, notably, Carle's own *blason*, "L'Esprit," on vellum; sonnets by Saint-Gelais. |
| | Attestation: BnF catalogue; Jonas database; *Bibliotheca bibliothecarum manuscriptorum nova* 2:795; *Dictionnaire des manuscrits* 1: col. 775; Tamizey/Colletet, 34; Crapelet; Ascoli (E) |

## 4.

| Identification | BNF4 = Fr. 10194 (formerly Supp. Fr. 1514) |
|---|---|
| Volume Title | *Livre d'extraictz pour Monsieur d'Orléans, advocat en Parlement, 1577* |
| Poem Title | "Tragedie sur la mort de la royne d'Angleterre, laquelle le roy son mary feit mourir dans la Tour de Londres pour avoir commis adultere. Composé par Lancelot de Carles protonotaire" (fols. 74v–89r) |
| Description | Paper; 331 fols.; 34 × 21 cm; tree calf binding; dense cursive script; approximately 36–44 vv. per folio; irregularly divided into stanzas |
| Attribution | Carle |
| Verses | 1328 vv. [missing vv. 268, 388; 10 additional verses (plus 5 that are variants of vv. 1241 and 1265–1268)] |
| Explicit | "Fin de la tragedye" [End of the Tragedy] |

| Provenance | Unknown |
|---|---|
| Marginalia | None |
| Notes | Compilation of manuscripts in French and in Latin, mainly legal documents and some poetic texts, including sonnets of Olivier de Magny, a work on the trial of Thomas More, a discourse on the death of the Queen of Scotland<br>Attestation: BnF catalogue; Tamizey/Colletet, 32–33; Ascoli (O) |

## 5.

| Identification | BNF5 = Lat. 5934; available on Gallica |
|---|---|
| Volume Title | *Pauli Aemilii, Veronensis: Gallicae Antiquitates, etc.* |
| Poem Title | "Histoire de Anne de Boulant jadis Royne d'Angleterre executée à mort, à Londres le deuxiesme jour de juin l'an mil cinq cens trente six" (fols. 58r–72r); Title from BnF catalogue: "Histoire de Anne de Boulan, jadis Reine d'Angleterre: elle est écrite en vers de dix syllabes" [title #4 in index] |
| Description | Paper; 86 fols.; cover measures 31 × 22 cm; inner pages measure 30 × 20.5 cm; red leather binding with gold embossing, image of royal salamander on cover; spine reads: "Gallica Antica"; border of shaded animals and foliage at top of first folio of poem; ornamental first initial in black ink; three blank folios at end of poem, which is incomplete; fine hybrid hand and display script at title and *incipit*; approximately 38–44 vv. per folio |
| Attribution | Anonymous |
| Verses | 1239 vv. [missing vv. 208, 451, 690, 1241–1328]; one additional verse after vv. 121 and 452 (the former disrupts the rhyme scheme while the latter completes the missing rhyme); unique variant at v. 220 |
| Explicit | None (incomplete poem) |
| Provenance | Jean-Baptiste Colbert |
| Marginalia | None |
| Notes | Compilation of manuscripts (all others in Latin)<br>Attestation: BnF catalogue; Gallica, Jonas, Schoenberg databases; Saint-Marc, *Histoire d'Angleterre*, 1:xxxix–lxiii, Crapelet |

**6.**

| Identification | BNF6 = Cinq cents de Colbert 465; Microfilm 19610 |
|---|---|
| Volume Title | *Mélanges historiques sur l'Angleterre et L'Ecosse* (general title of Colbert 465–467); *Recueil de pièces sur les relations de la France et de l'Angleterre (1200–1660)* (title attached to Colbert 465) |
| Poem Title | "L'Histoire de la royne Anne d'Angleterre" (fols. 101r–120v) |
| Description | Paper; 278 fols.; red morocco binding with gold embossed arms of Colbert; cover size is 34 × 24 cm with varying size folios; the folios for the Anne Boleyn poem measure 26 × 15 cm; cursive script; approximately 30–34 vv. per folio; not divided into stanzas |
| Attribution | Anonymous |
| Verses | 1318 vv. [missing v. 699; conflates vv. 779–780] |
| Explicit | "Soli deo honor et gloria" [To God alone be honor and glory] |
| Provenance | Jean-Baptiste Colbert |
| Marginalia | Some corrections and notes |
| Notes | Compilation of multiple manuscripts touching on Anglo-French relations<br>Attestation: BnF catalogue; CCFr database |

**7.**

| Identification | BNF7 = Fr. 12489; anc. supp. fr. 2036,51 (Microfilm 34370); available on Gallica |
|---|---|
| Volume Title | *Recueil de poésies amoureuses, épitres, ballades, rondeaux, etc. de divers poètes français du XVI<sup>e</sup> siècle* |
| Poem Title | No title or heading; fols. 135r–163v |
| Description | Paper; 168 fols.; 28 × 20 cm; leather half-binding; cursive script done in three hands; approximately 18–26 vv. per folio |
| Attribution | Anonymous |
| Verses | 1319 vv. [missing v. 1092] |
| Explicit | None other than final lines of poem |
| Provenance | Hélène de Saint-Cire (?) |
| Marginalia | None |
| Notes | Compilation of poems by various authors including Marot and Saint-Gelais<br>Attestation: BnF catalogue; Gallica, Jonas databases |

## C. Manuscripts in France Outside of Paris

**1.**

| | |
|---|---|
| Identification | B = Bibliothèque municipale de Bordeaux 0313 |
| Volume Title | *Discours anonymes et poème de Lancelot de Carle, évêque de Riez, sur Anne Boleyn* |
| Poem Title | "La *pitoiable* description de la *vie et* mort de madame Anne Boulant, en son vivant fesme du roy d'Angleterre, Henry .8. de ce nom *en ses secondes noces*, laquelle fust decolee l'an 1536, **le douzieme de juing.** L'aucteur de ceste poësie est incognut" (fols. 217v–237v). The words in italic are interpolations written in a different hand from the main text, and the words in boldface type are the work of a third hand. |
| Description | Paper; 237 fols.; fols. 209–211 and 214–216 are blank; cover size is 30.5 × 20 cm, writing area is 23 × 14 cm; half calfskin binding; cursive script with multiple corrections; approximately 32 vv. per folio; the ink and hand appear to change at v. 420 and then again at v. 621 |
| Attribution | Anonymous |
| Verses | 1318 vv. [missing vv. 336, 452, 489, 822]; extra verse added after v. 1119 and v. 1120; unique variants at v. 1066 and v. 1218 |
| Explicit | "Louenge à Dieu" and "Laus Deo" [Praise be to God], written in two different hands |
| Provenance | Ex libris Carmelitarum Discalceatorum Burdigalensium S. Ludovici (as indicated on fol. 1) |
| Marginalia | Multiple drawings and annotations; at least some marginalia written after the accession of Mary and Elizabeth |
| Notes | Compilation of multiple anonymous manuscripts done in different hands. Many of the works are in Latin and treat spiritual matters; 19th-century copy located in Bibliothèque Sainte-Geneviève, Paris (MS 3986). Attestation: Jonas, CCFr, Schoenberg, Manuscrits Médiévaux d'Aquitaine databases; *Bibliothèque municipale de Bordeaux, Catalogue des Manuscrits* 1:255–57; *Catalogue général des manuscrits des bibliothèques publiques de France*, 23 (1894): 174–77; *Gentleman's Magazine* 10 (1861): 189–90; Ascoli (B) |

**2.**

| Identification | S1 = Bibliothèque municipale de Soissons 201 (formerly 189A) |
|---|---|
| Volume Title | *Mélanges de vers et de prose* |
| Poem Title | "Ensuyt le proces de la royne d'Angleterre, de son frere et de quatre chevaliers decapitez en Engleterre, l'an mil cinq cens trente six en may"; this heading is written in a different hand from the main text; fols. 18v–26v |
| Description | Paper; 122 fols.; volume size 31 × 20 cm with smaller pages (26 × 16 cm) pasted onto larger pages; brown calfskin half-binding; small, rough, and irregular cursive script; change of hands to a denser script at v. 59; approximately 48–58 vv. per folio; water stained; has multiple indications of foliation (the foliation used here refers to the numbers in red that appear on the outer folio) |
| Attribution | Anonymous |
| Verses | 930 vv. [missing vv. 449, 623–624, 841, and 933–1328, with an additional verse after 450 and 842 to complete the missing rhyme]; unique variants at vv. 178, 182, 453 653–654, and 908 |
| Explicit | None (incomplete poem) |
| Provenance | Prémontré Abbey |
| Marginalia | Some explanatory annotations in a hand different from the scribe's |
| Notes | Compilation of historical and literary texts, including poems by Marot, Saint-Gelais, François I, and two texts on the death of Thomas More<br>Attestation: Jonas, CCFr, databases; *Catalogue général des manuscrits de bibliothèques publiques de France*, 3 (1885), 126–28; Ascoli (Sa) |

**3.**

| Identification | S2 = Bibliothèque municipale de Soissons 202 (formerly 189B) |
|---|---|
| Volume Title | *Mélanges de vers et de prose* |
| Poem Title | "Ensuyt le proces de la royne d'Angleterre, de son frere et de quatre chevaliers decapitez en Engleterre, l'an mil cinq cens trente six en may"; fols. 141r–163v |

| Description | Paper; 232 fols.; volume size 32 × 20.5 cm, with a smaller writing area (25 × 15.5 cm) pasted onto larger papers; brown calfskin half-binding; cursive script, approximately 24–29 verses per folio |
| --- | --- |
| Attribution | Anonymous |
| Verses | 1316 vv. [missing vv. 182, 449, 623–624, 841, 1052, 1157, with verses added after 450, 1050, and 1158 to complete the rhyme]; unique variants at vv. 178, 182, 453, 653–654, and 908 (shared with its sister text, S1) as well as v. 1061 |
| Explicit | "Fin" [The End] |
| Provenance | Unknown |
| Marginalia | None |
| Notes | Compilation of works, including poems by Marot and some *blasons anatomiques*; several additional works regarding the English events of 1535–1536, including a piece on the Carthusian martyrs, an elegy on the death of Thomas More (as in S1), as well as "Les Regretz que Messire Millort de Rocheffort . . . feist sur l'eschaffault" [The Regrets expressed by My Lord of Rochford on the scaffold] (fols. 137v–140v) Attestation: CCFr, Jonas databases; *Catalogue général des manuscrits de bibliothèques publiques de France* (1885), 3:128–30, Ascoli (Sb) |

4.

| Identification | V = Bibliothèque municipale de Valenciennes 419 (formerly 400) |
| --- | --- |
| Volume Title | *Anne de Boull* [*sic*] (from spine) |
| Poem Title | From title page of MS: "Apologie pour feue Dame Anne de Boulain" [written in different hand from MS proper]; Poem title (from fol. 2r): "Apologie" [written in a different hand from MS and well to the left of the rest of the title]; "Pour feu dame Anne de Boullant, jadis royne d'Engleterre, l'an VC trente trois, fait et composé par Anthoine de Crespin, escuyer, S[eigneu]r de Miherne" [this is in the same hand as the MS]; fols. 1v–27r |

| Description | Paper; 74 fols. (fols. 51–74 are blank), 33.5 × 21 cm with scored interior margins of 27 × 15 cm; brown calfskin binding with gold lettering on spine; cursive script in a northern hand (with consistent use of "ch" for "ç"); approximately 30 vv. per folio, divided irregularly into stanzas |
|---|---|
| Attribution | Anthoine de Crespin, seigneur de Miherne |
| Verses | 1309 vv. [missing vv. 60, 146, 208, 384–385, 482, 623–624, 808, 852, 1026, and 1081; adds verse after 386] |
| Explicit | "Fin" [The End] |
| Provenance | Château de l'Hermitage, Jan de Croy |
| Marginalia | None |
| Notes | Compilation of poems and prose documents, including a work on the repudiation of Anne of Cleves, beginning at fol. 30 Attestation: Jonas, CCFr databases; *Archives historiques et littéraires* (1844), 5:361–75; *Le bibliophile belge* (1846), 3:158; *Catalogue descriptif et raisonné des manuscrits de la bibliothèque de Valenciennes* (1860), 401 (n. 400); *Catalogue général des manuscrits des bibliothèques publiques de France* (Valenciennes), 25:377–78; Ascoli (V) |

## D. Manuscripts in Europe Outside of France

### 1.

| Identification | BRB = Brussels, Bibliothèque Royal de Belgique, 19378 |
|---|---|
| Volume Title | *MSS. sur Anne de Boulen* |
| Poem Title | "Traictié pour feue dame Anne de Boulant jadis Royne d'Engleterre, l'an Quinzecens trente troys" (fols. 1r–19v) |
| Description | Paper; 38 fols.; poem preceded by six blank folios and followed by thirteen blank folios at end of MS; all the blank folios bear a watermark with the inscription "Pro Patria" along with primitive renderings of figures, including a crowned lion; 28 × 18 cm; red morocco half binding with gold embossed title; careful cursive book script, with few corrections or interpolations done in the scribe's hand; approximately 28–40 vv. per folio; divided irregularly into stanzas |
| Attribution | Anonymous |

| Verses | 1299 vv. [missing vv. 60, 67–68, 385, 623–624, 717–718, 752, 771, 852, 1026, 1179–1182, 1261–1264, 1319–1328; adds verse after 386] |
|---|---|
| Explicit | [After v. 1318] "Fin. Cecy fut fait à Londres en Angleterre, le deuxiesme du mois de juing en l'an Trentetroisiesme" [The End. This was done in London in England, on 2 June in the year (15)33]. |
| Provenance | Unknown |
| Marginalia | None |
| Notes | Only text in the volume<br>Attestation: Schoenberg Database; *Bibliophile belge* 1:455–62; *Catalogue des manuscrits de la Bibliothèque royale de Belgique* (1907), 7:44 (4636) |

## 2.

| Identification | M = Munich, Bayerische Staatsbibliothek, Cod. GALL 105; Microfilm 11821; digital copy available through library website |
|---|---|
| Volume Title | *Le Discours de la vie et mort Dame Anna de Boullant, Roÿnne putative d'Angleterre, et décapité* [*sic*] A° 1536 |
| Poem Title | "Faict pour deffuncte Anne de Boulland jadis Roynne d'Angleterre" (fol. 2); fols. 1r–22r |
| Description | Paper; 24 fols., including two blank folios; original brown calf binding, decorated with *fleur de lys* design; cover dimensions 30 × 24 cm; folio dimensions 29.5 × 20.5 cm; fine, cursive sixteenth-century script, with the exception of the text heading, first three words and final signature, which are done in a display script; approximately 26–29 lines per folio, divided irregularly into stanzas |
| Attribution | Anonymous |
| Verses | 1317 vv. [missing vv. 385, 778, 1172, 1302, with an additional line added after v. 386 to complete the missing rhyme]; unique variant at v. 1301 |
| Explicit | "Finis" [The End] |
| Provenance | Grand Ducal Library of Bavaria (late sixteenth century to early seventeenth century), as shown by bookplate |

| Marginalia | Two short explanatory marginal notes in French; final folio shows a signature which perhaps reads "James tant dheur" [= Jamais tant d'heur] with the word "Myherne" written underneath the word "Finis" |
| Notes | Only text in the volume Attestation: Jonas, Munich online catalogue; *Catalogus codicum manu scriptorum bibliothecae Regiae Monacensis*, 7:4, no. 12 |

**3.**

| Identification | K = Karlsruhe, Badische Landesbibliothek, Güntersthal 12 |
| Volume Title | *Kollektaneen zur Geschichte von Burgund, Frankreich, und England, Belgien/Niederlande, ca. 1670/80* |
| Poem Title | "L'An 1533. Traictié de feuë la Royne d'Engleterre" (fols. 372r–394r) |
| Description | Paper; 396 fols.; 32 × 21 cm; careless cursive script; hand changes at v. 661, becoming less dense; approximately 28–34 verses per folio |
| Attribution | Anonymous |
| Verses | 1313 vv. [missing vv. 60, 385, 534, 623–624, 852, 918, 1026; adds verse after 386] |
| Explicit | "Finis" [The End] |
| Provenance | Unknown |
| Marginalia | None, but whole passages are repeated and then crossed out by the scribe |
| Notes | Compilation of multiple discrete manuscripts, mostly in French, dealing with a variety of historical matters Attestation: *Romanische Handschriften Badische Landesbibliothek Karlsruhe* (1894), 49, no. 13; *Die Handschriften der Badischen Landesbibliothek in Karlsruhe* (2000), 231 |

**4.**

| Identification | Vat = Biblioteca apostolica Vaticana, Reg. lat. 1652 |
| Volume Title | *Tragedie de la femme du Roy d'Angleterre, Anne Boulans* [in a different hand from the scribe's] |
| Poem Title | "Tragedie de la femme du Roy d'Angleterre, Anne Boulans" [in the scribe's hand]; fols. 1r–23v |

| Description | Paper, 23 fols., plus three blank folios; 25.5 × 17.5 cm; gilded brown leather binding; late sixteenth-century cursive script; approximately 27–30 lines per folio |
|---|---|
| Attribution | Anonymous |
| Verses | 1317 vv. [missing vv. 77–78 and 841] |
| Explicit | None other than final lines of poem |
| Provenance | Pierre Bourdelot; Queen Christina of Sweden |
| Marginalia | None |
| Notes | Only text in the volume<br>Attestation: Jonas, Schoenberg databases; Pellegrin, "Catalogue des manuscrits de Jean et Pierre Bourdelot," 210; Omont, "Catalogue des manuscrits de Jean et Pierre Bourdelot, médecins parisiens," 89. The title as given in the Schoenberg database (which is based on the way it appears in the two articles above) is: "Tragœdie D'Anne De Boulain, Femme De Henry VIII, Roy D'Angleterre." |

## II. Early Modern Printed Text

| Identification | 1545 |
|---|---|
| Volume Title | *Epistre contenant le proces criminel faict à l'encontre de la royne Anne Boullant d'Angleterre, par Carles, aulmosnier de Monsieur le Daulphin* |
| Poem Title | "Epistre de la royne d'Angleterre" [Epistle of the queen of England] |
| Description | 47 pp., 8°. Title page features a woodcut of a king enthroned with several counselors seated on either side. The first page of the text proper (p. 3) gives the heading: "Epistre de la Royne d'Angleterre." An elaborate floral woodcut is used for the initial "L" of the poem's incipit. Italic print. Paginated. |
| Attribution | Carle |
| Verses | 1318 vv. [missing vv. 280 and 440] |
| Explicit | "Fin de l'Epistre, & Proces criminel de Anne Boullant, Royne d'Angleterre" [The end of the epistle and criminal trial of Anne Boleyn, queen of England] |

| Publication | On les vend à Lyon, pres nostre Dame de Confort. 1545. [A false imprint for Tours, Jean Rousset] |
|---|---|
| Marginalia | Occasional printed explanatory marginal notes |
| Notes | Three extant copies:<br>1. BnF Rés. Ye. 3668 (digital copy available on Gallica)<br>2. BL 11474 a.14 (digital copy available via Google Books)<br>3. University of Leeds, Special Collections: Anglo-French 6 1545/CAR<br>Attestation: BnF, BL, and Leeds library catalogues; World-Cat, Universal Short Title Catalogue; Jonas database; *Catalogue des livres de la bibliothèque de feu M. le duc de la Vallière* (Paris, 1783), pt. 1, vol. 2, p. 351, no. 3108; Brunet, *Nouvelles recherches bibliographiques pour servir de supplément au manuel de libraire; Manuel du libraire* (Paris, 1860), 1:1579; La Croix du Maine, *La Bibliothèque* (Paris, 1584), 1:282; and Pettegree et al., *French Vernacular Books*, 262, no. 8932; Ascoli (I) |

# Key to Manuscripts

BL = London, British Library, Additional 40662
BNF1 = Paris, BnF, Fr. 12795
BNF2 = Paris, BnF, Fr. 01742
BNF3 = Paris, BnF, Fr. 02370
BNF4 = Paris, BnF, Fr. 10194
BNF5 = Paris, BnF, Lat. 5934
BNF6 = Paris, BnF, Colbert 465
BNF7 = Paris, BnF, Fr. 12489
B = Bordeaux, Bibliothèque municipale, 0313
S1 = Soissons, Bibliothèque municipale, 201
S2 = Soissons, Bibliothèque municipale, 202
V = Valenciennes, Bibliothèque municipale, 419
BRB = Brussels, Bibliothèque royale, 19378
M = Munich, Bayerische Staatsbibliothek, Cod. GALL 105
K = Karlsruhe, Badische Landesbibliothek, Güntersthal 12
Vat = Rome, Vatican City, Biblioteca apostolica Vaticana, Reg. lat. 1652
1545 = Imprint [BnF Res. Ye 3668; BL 11474 a.14; University of Leeds, Special Collections: Anglo-French 6 1545/CAR]

*Chapter 5*

# THE FRENCH TEXT AND THE ENGLISH TRANSLATION

# L'HISTOIRE DE LA MORT D'ANNE BOVLENC
# ROYNE D'ANGLETERRE[1]

| | | |
|---|---|---|
| 1 | Les cas nouueaux & choses merueilleuses, | [1r] |
| 2 | Tristes aux vns & aux autres ioyeuses, | |
| 3 | Qu'aduenus sont[2] en ce loingtain pays, | |
| 4 | Ont mes espritz tellement[3] esbahiz | |
| 5 | Que tousiours suis en pensee profonde. | |
| 6 | Et si auant à contempler me fonde | |
| 7 | Ce que mon œil[4] me contrainct regarder,[5] | |
| 8 | Que ie ne puis mon esprit engarder,[6] | |
| 9 | Ny de ces cas estranges diuertir, | |
| 10 | Pour les escrire & vous en aduertir. | |

---

[1] BL: Marginal note reads: "2e femme de HENRI VIII 1535. Avoit repudié sa premiere femme, tante de l'empereur, nommee Catherine, l'an 1527. A eu six femmes. La Troisiesme Jeanne de Seymour." Title variations are as follows: BNF1: De la royne d'Angleterre; BNF2: Histoire de la royne Anne Boullant d'Angleterre, qui mourut le 2e jour de juing 1536; BNF3: Histoire de Anne Boullant, royne d'Angleterre; BNF4: Tragedie sur la mort de la royne d'Angleterre, laquelle le roy son mary feit mourir dans la tour de Londres pour avoir commis adultere. Composé par Lancelot de Carles protonotaire; BNF5: Histoire de Anne de Boulant jadis Royne d'Angleterre executée à mort, à Londres le deuxiesme jour de juin l'an mil cinq cens trente six; BNF6: L'histore de la Royne Anne d'Angleterre; BNF7: text has no title; B: La *pitoiable* description de la *vie et* mort de Madame Anne Boulant, en son vivant fesme du roy d'Angleterre, Henry .8. de ce nom *en ses secondes noces*, laquelle fust decolee l'an 1536, **le douzieme de juing**. L'aucteur de ceste poësie est incognut. [The words in italics are interpolations written in another hand and ink from main text, boldface is written in yet a third hand]; S1/2: Ensuyt le proces de la Royne d'Angleterre, de son frere et de quatre chevaliers decapitez en Engleterre, l'an mil cinq cens trente six en may; V: Title page (fol. 1): Apologie pour feue dame Anne de Boulain; fol. 2: Apologie (left margin); Pour feu dame Anne de Boullant, jadis royne d'Engleterre, l'an VC trente trois, fait et composé par Anthoine de Crespin, escuyer, S[eigneu]r de Miherne; BRB: Traictié pour feue dame Anne de Boulant jadis Royne D'Engleterre. L'an Quinzecens trente troys; M: title page: Le discours de la vie et mort Dame Anna de Boullant, Roÿnne putative d'Angleterre et decapité [*sic*] A° 1536; heading, fol. 1: Faict pour deffuncte Anne de Boulland jadis Roynne d'Angleterre; K: L'an 1533. Traictié de feuë la Royne d'Engleterre; Vat: Both title page and fol. 1 read: Tragedie de la femme du Roy d'Angleterre, Anne Boulans; 1545: title page: Epistre contenant le proces criminel faict à l'encontre de la royne Anne Boullant d'Angleterre, par Carles aulmosnier de Monsieur le Daulphin; p. 3: Epistre de la Royne d'Angleterre

[2] BNF4: Que veues j'ay

[3] BNF6, 1545: Ont nos espritz tellement; S1/2: Ont tellement mes espritz

[4] BNF6: Ce que mon dueil

[5] BNF1: Verse missing

[6] BNF1 adds, in another hand and ink: Mon corps d'aller, mes yeulx de regarder (effectively replacing the missing v. 7 and completing the rhyme, though with a corrupted reading).

# THE STORY OF THE DEATH OF ANNE BOLEYN, QUEEN OF ENGLAND[1]

| | |
|---|---|
| 1 | The unprecedented events and wondrous things, |
| 2 | Sad to some and to others joyous, |
| 3 | That have occurred[2] in this distant country |
| 4 | Have so astounded my wits[3] |
| 5 | That I am still in deep thought about them. |
| 6 | And, yet, I set out to reflect further |
| 7 | On what my eye[4] forces me to see |
| 8 | And on what I cannot keep from my mind, |
| 9 | And I intend not to turn away from these strange events, |
| 10 | So as to write them down and advise you of them. |

---

[1] BL marginal note reads: "Second wife of Henry VIII, 1535. Had cast off his first wife, the emperor's aunt, named Catherine, in the year 1527. Had six wives, the third Jane Seymour"; BNF1: On the Queen of England; BNF2: The story of Queen Anne Boleyn of England, who died the 2nd day of June 1536 (an error in dating that confuses the date of the poem's composition with that of the queen's execution); BNF3: The Story of Anne Boleyn, Queen of England; BNF4: Tragedy on the death of the Queen of England, whose husband, the king, made her die in the Tower of London for having committed adultery. Composed by Lancelot de Carle, prothonotary; BNF5: The story of Anne Boleyn, formerly Queen of England, put to death in London on the second day of June in the year 1536 (dating error); BNF6: The story of Queen Anne of England; BNF7: this text has no title; B: The *pitiable* description of the *life and* death of Madame Anne Boleyn, during her lifetime wife of the king of England, Henry the Eighth of that name, *in his second marriage*, who was beheaded in the year 1536, **the twelfth of June**. The author of this poetry is unknown. (Contains a dating error that misreads the date of the composition of the poem, confusing "deuxieme" and "douzieme," and that further mistakes this for the date of Anne's execution. The words in italics are interpolations written in another hand and ink from the main text; boldface is written in yet a third hand); S1/2: Here follows the trial of the Queen of England, of her brother, and of four knights, beheaded in England, in the year 1536 in May; V, fol. 1: An apology on behalf of the late Lady Anne Boleyn; fol. 2: Apology. On behalf of the late Lady Anne Boleyn, formerly Queen of England, in the year 1533, made and composed by Anthoine de Crespin, squire, lord of Miherne (dating error); BRB: A treatise for the late Lady Anne Boleyn, formerly Queen of England. 1533; M, title page: A discourse on the life and death of Lady Anne Boleyn, the putative Queen of England, beheaded in the year 1536; fol. 1: Done for the deceased Anne Boleyn, formerly Queen of England; K: The year 1533 (dating error); Treatise of the late Queen of England; Vat: Both the title page and fol. 1 read: Tragedy of the wife of the king of England, Anne Boleyn; 1545, title page: An epistle containing the criminal proceedings made against Queen Anne Boleyn of England, by Carle, almoner of the Dauphin; p. 3: Epistle of the Queen of England.

[2] BNF4: Which I have seen

[3] BNF6, 1545: our wits

[4] BNF6: my grief

| 11 | Mais ie vouldrois que les nouuelles fussent | |
|----|---|---|
| 12 | Telles que[1] point de facheries[2] n'eussent, | |
| 13 | Et que du ieu le triste[3] acheuement | [1v] |
| 14 | Fust respondant à son commancement. | |
| 15 | Certes, ie croy qu'en auriez grand plaisir.[4] | |
| 16 | Mais bien scauez qu'on ne scauroit choisir | |
| 17 | Aucun plaisir en ce monde muable | |
| 18 | Qui longuement y puisse[5] estre durable: | |
| 19 | Car toute chose,[6] en sa mutation, | |
| 20 | D'vne[7] autre faict la[8] generation, | |
| 21 | Et plus[9] souuent nous produyt son contraire,[10] | |
| 22 | Comme en ce cas pourrez iugement faire,[11] | |
| 23 | Qui de ioyeuse & belle comedie | |
| 24 | Fut conuerti[12] en triste tragedie. | |
| 25 | I'en escriray ce que i'ay entendu[13] | |
| 26 | Par les raisons que plusieurs m'ont rendu,[14] | |
| 27 | Puis, mon Seigneur,[15] ce que i'ay retenu | |
| 28 | Depuis le temps que suis icy[16] venu. | |
| 29 | Ie l'escriray en vers mal composez, | [2r] |
| 30 | Pour ce que mieux me semblent[17] disposez, | |
| 31 | Et que[18] par eux moins gref vous pourra[19] estre | |
| 32 | Le long discours de la presente[20] lettre, | |

---

[1] BRB: Telles, et que

[2] All others but M: fascherie

[3] BNF2: Et que de jeu et triste; BNF6, 1545: Et que le jeu du triste; S1/2: Et que du faict le triste; V: "le" missing

[4] BNF1: aurez grant desplaisir; 1545: grand desplaisir

[5] B: peust; V: peult; M, K: puist

[6] M: toutes choses

[7] BNF2, BNF4–5, BNF7: D'ung; BNF6: En une

[8] BNF6, BRB: sa; V: de

[9] BNF4: Et bien

[10] BNF6, 1545: plus souvent produit effect contraire

[11] 1545: pourrez avoir veu faire

[12] BNF1, V: S'est convertie; BNF3, BNF5: Fut convertie; BNF4, BNF7, BRB, M, K: S'est converti

[13] B: originally had "Je escripveray en vers mal composez"; this is crossed out and replaced with "… ce que j'ay entendu"; S2: j'en ay entendu

[14] B: "rendu" is added in a different hand and ink; V, BRB: m'en ont rendu

[15] BRB: Et puis, Monsieur

[16] B: que je suis cy; 1545: que ie suis icy

[17] BNF1–3, BNF6–7, S1/2, V, BRB, M, Vat, 1545: m'y semblent

[18] B, V: "que" missing

[19] 1545: pourroit

[20] All others: de ma facheuse

11 But I should wish that the news were such
12 That it brought no displeasure at all,
13 And that the sad conclusion of this play
14 Were in keeping with its beginning.
15 Certainly, I believe you would take great pleasure[1] in that.
16 But you know very well that one cannot choose
17 Any pleasure at all, in this changeable world,
18 That might be long-lasting:
19 For everything,[2] in changing,
20 Gives rise to some other thing,
21 And most[3] often produces for us its opposite,[4]
22 As you will be able to judge in this case,[5]
23 Which, from a joyous and fine comedy,
24 Was turned into a sad tragedy.
25 I shall write about what I have heard,
26 Through the insights that several people have provided me,
27 And then, my lord,[6] about what I have remembered
28 Since the time that I arrived here.
29 I shall write it in verse (albeit poorly composed),
30 Because it seems more suitable to me,
31 So that, through my rhyme, the long discourse of this present[7] letter
32 Might be less troubling to you,

---

[1] BNF1, 1545: displeasure
[2] M: for all things
[3] BNF4: And quite
[4] BNF6, 1545: produces an opposite effect
[5] 1545: As you will be able to have seen done in this case
[6] BRB: And then, Sir
[7] All others: of my unpleasant

---

13: Carle introduces here the network of imagery surrounding spectacles, plays, and perfor-
mance that will reappear throughout the text. See the *Dictionnaire du Moyen Français*
[hereafter, DMF], which defines "jeu" as "représentation théâtrale d'une pièce en vers."

33    N'estimant point que de cest'[1] escripture
34    Aultre que vous en face la lecture,
35    Et que vouldrez par vostre[2] humanité
36    En ce couurir mon imbecilité.
37          Or, mon Seigneur,[3] ie croy que bien[4] scauez,
38    Et de longtemps[5] la congnoissance auez,[6]
39    Qu' Anne Boullenc[7] premierement sortit[8]
40    De ce[9] pays quant Marie en partit[10]
41    Pour s'en aller trouuer le roy en France,[11]
42    Pour[12] accomplir des[13] deux roys l'alliance.
43    En ce temps, la Boullenc, qui ieune estoit[14]
44    Venue en court,[15] sagement escoutoit
45    Dames d'honneur, s'efforçant inciter[16]                          [2v]
46    Tous ses[17] espritz à bien les[18] immiter,
47    Et employa ses sens de[19] tel couraige
48    Qu'en[20] peu de temps elle apprint le[21] langaige.
49    Apres que fut[22] Marie reuenue

---

1  BNF1: celle
2  BNF1: Qui bien saurez par doulce; BNF2–3, BN5–6, V, BRB, M, K, Vat, 1545: Qui bien saurez
   par votre; BNF7, B, S1/2: Qui bien scavez par vostre; BNF4: Qui bien scavez par vraye
3  BRB: Monsieur
4  BNF3: je croy bien que scavez
5  BNF1, BNF5: Et des longtemps; S2: Et que de long
6  This verse is underscored in BL.
7  BNF1, BNF5, S1/S2: Anne Boulan; BNF2–3, BNF6, B, 1545: Anne Boullant; BNF4, Vat:
   Anne Boulans. Henceforth, variants in the spelling of this name will not be noted. V, BRB, M,
   K: Qu'envie vollant (a defective reading).
8  BNF5: partit; 1545 printed marginal note reads: "Anne Boullant"
9  BNF5: son
10  BNF5: sortit; V: "quant" missing
11  BNF2: Pour s'en aller estre royne de France; BNF3, BNF6: Pour s'en aller trouver la royne en
   France; S1/2, V, BRB, K: roy de France; 1545 printed marginal note reads: "Marie d'Angleterre,
   royne de France, mariée au Roy Loys XII"
12  BNF4, S1, V, BRB, M, K: Et
13  M: de
14  BNF1: En ce temps-là, voyant que; BNF5, B: "la" missing; B marginal note reads: "Nourriture
   de Anne Boulant"
15  BNF6: originally reads "en France" with marginal correction "en court"; 1545: en France
16  BL: s'efforçoit inciter (emended to the reading provided by all others, for grammatical clarity);
   BNF6, B, S1/2, 1545: s'efforçant d'inciter; K: "inciter" missing
17  BNF2: les
18  B: les bien
19  BNF3: en
20  1545: Qu'à
21  BNF2: ce
22  BNF6: fusse

| | |
|---|---|
| 33 | By no means supposing that anyone other than you |
| 34 | Will read what I am writing, |
| 35 | And that, in your kindness,[1] you will wish[2] |
| 36 | To cover up my feebleness in this task. |
| 37 | Now, my lord,[3] I believe that you know well,[4] |
| 38 | And for a long time have known, |
| 39 | That Anne Boleyn first left[5] |
| 40 | This[6] country when Mary departed[7] |
| 41 | To meet up with the king in France,[8] |
| 42 | In order to[9] bring about the alliance of the two kings. |
| 43 | At that time, the Boleyn girl, who was young[10] |
| 44 | When she arrived at court,[11] would wisely listen |
| 45 | To the ladies-in-waiting, endeavoring[12] to engage |
| 46 | All her wits to imitate them well, |
| 47 | And she set her mind to it with such alacrity |
| 48 | That in very little time she learned the[13] language. |
| 49 | After Mary came back |

---

1   BNF1: in sweet kindness; BNF4: in true kindness
2   All others: you will know how
3   BRB: Sir
4   BNF3: I well believe that you know
5   BNF5: first departed from; 1545 printed marginal note: Anne Boleyn.
6   BNF5: Her
7   BNF5: Mary left
8   BNF2: To go off to be queen of France; BNF3, BNF6: To meet up with the queen in France; S1/2, V, BRB, K: To meet up with the king of France; 1545 printed marginal note reads: "Mary of England, queen of France, married to King Louis XII"
9   BNF4, S1, V, BRB, M, K: And to
10  B marginal note reads: "Upbringing of Anne Boleyn"
11  1545: in France
12  BL: [and] she endeavored
13  BNF2: this

---

36:     Cf. Carle's similar use of the word "imbécilité" in his "Lettre de l'Evesque" [Letter on the Duc de Guise], 174, regarding his poetic inadequacies: "I fear, as I must, that my feebleness too greatly diminishes [the Duke of Guise's] many perfections" [je crains, comme je doibs, que mon imbécilité diminue par trop tant de perfections].

39:     V, BRB, M, and K all carry the same nonsensical defective reading here, suggesting that they are related manuscripts. Similar instances of comparable corrupt readings can be found throughout the text.

42:     Carle is referring to the marriage of King Henry VIII's sister, Mary Tudor, to King Louis XII of France in 1514. Louis died on 1 January 1515, leaving Mary a young widow. Previously, Anne had spent time in the court of Margaret of Austria in the Low Countries.

48:     Anne Boleyn's command of French was notable, but Carle may be referring more generally to the "language" of courtly behavior.

50    En ce pais, elle fut retenue[1]
51    Par Claude, qui Royne[2] apres succeda,[3]
52    Où tellement ses graces amenda
53    Que ne l'eussiez onques[4] iugee Angloyse
54    En ses façons,[5] mais naïfve Françoyse.[6]
55    Elle scavoit bien chanter & danser,[7]
56    Et ses propos sagement adiancer,[8]
57    Sonner de[9] Lutz & aultres[10] instrumens,
58    Pour diuertir les tristes pensemens.
59    Oultre ces[11] biens & graces tant exquises[12]
60    Qu'auoit en France heureusement acquises,[13]
61    Elle[14] estoit belle & de taille elegante,                    [3r]
62    Mesmes des yeulx encor plus attreante,[15]
63    Lesquelz scauoit bien conduyre à propos,
64    En les tenant quelque fois en[16] repos,
65    Aulcune fois enuoyant[17] en message
66    Porter du[18] cueur le secret tesmoignage.
67    Et pour certain telle estoit leur puissance
68    Que maintz[19] rendoit en[20] son obeissance.[21]

---

1   This verse is underscored in BL. S1/2: En France fut noblement retenue
2   BNF4, V, BRB, M, K: Royne qui; 1545: qui puis
3   1545 printed marginal note reads: "Claude de France, Royne de France"
4   BNF2, BNF4, Vat: onc
5   BNF4: En tous ses faictz
6   BL: mais vne vraye Françoyse (emended for purposes of versification); V, K: mais natisve
    Françoyse; 1545: mais née fine Françoyse; S1 marginal note in another hand reads: "Occupations
    d'Anne Boullant"
7   S1/2: bien chanter, bien danser; V, BRB: bien danser et chanter
8   BL: adresser (emended to reading of all other manuscripts to maintain rhyme)
9   BNF1–4, BNF6–7, M: du
10  BNF6, BRB, 1545: d'autres
11  BNF2, BNF4–5, M, Vat, 1545: ses
12  S1: Hand changes here
13  V, BRB, K: Verse 60 missing
14  BNF1–3, BN5–7, B, BRB, M, K: S'elle; V: Celle
15  BNF1–3, BNF6–7, M: Estoit des yeulx encor plus attirante; BNF4: Estoit des yeulx encore plus
    attrayante; BNF5, B, V, BRB, K, Vat: Estoit des yeulx encores plus attirante; S1/2: Et de ses yeux
    encor plus atraiante; 1545: Estoit des yeulx au cheoir plus attirante (a corrupt reading)
16  BNF4–5, B, S1, 1545: à
17  1545: envoyoient
18  BNF2: de
19  BNF2: nous
20  V: à
21  BRB: Verses 67–68 missing

| 50 | To this country, Anne was retained[1] |
|---|---|
| 51 | By Claude, who afterwards succeeded as queen,[2] |
| 52 | In whose court she so refined her gracious abilities |
| 53 | That you would never have judged her to be English |
| 54 | In her manners,[3] but a natural-born Frenchwoman.[4] |
| 55 | She knew how to sing and how to dance well, |
| 56 | And how to fit words together handsomely,[5] |
| 57 | How to play the lute and other instruments, |
| 58 | So as to drive away sad thoughts. |
| 59 | Beyond these[6] assets and such exquisite graces |
| 60 | Which she happily acquired in France, |
| 61 | She was beautiful and of elegant stature, |
| 62 | And even more attractive were her eyes,[7] |
| 63 | Which she knew quite well how to wield appropriately, |
| 64 | Sometimes keeping them still, |
| 65 | Other times using them to send a message |
| 66 | To bear the secret testimony of her heart. |
| 67 | And, to be sure, their power was such |
| 68 | That many a man yielded to her his obedience. |

---

1  S1/2: She [Anne] was nobly retained in France
2  1545: Printed marginal note reads: "Claude of France, Queen of France"
3  BNF4: In all her actions
4  BL: a true Frenchwoman; V, K: but a native Frenchwoman; 1545: but born a refined Frenchwoman; S1 marginal note reads: "The pastimes of Anne Boleyn"
5  BL: how to address her words wisely
6  BNF2, BNF4–5, M, Vat, 1545: her
7  BNF1–3, BNF5–7, B, BRB, M, K: Verses 61–62 read: "If she were beautiful and of elegant stature / She was even more attractive in her eyes"; 1545 is corrupt

---

51:  After Louis XII died, Francis I gained the crown of France. His wife, Claude of France, retained Anne as a lady-in-waiting, after Mary Tudor returned to England.
62:  The Venetian ambassador likewise commented that Anne's eyes were "black and beautiful." See *Calendar of State Papers* (hereafter CSP), Venice, 4.824.

69    Estant ainsi[1] de tous telz biens[2] remplie,
70    D'honnesteté & graces[3] accomplie,
71    Si tost que fut retournee[4] en ses[5] lieux
72    Ell' employa la force de ses yeux,
73    Et son regard vint en si hault[6] lieu mectre[7]
74    Qu'en peu de temps elle pleut à son maistre.
75    Ô![8] que tenue elle estoit à l'honneur[9]
76    De France qui luy causoit[10] ce bon heur.
77    Ô![11] quel honneur, quelle obligation                    [3v]
78    Elle debuoit[12] à la perfection[13]
79    De ceulx de[14] qui elle apreint[15] tant de biens,
80    Qui l'ont depuys faicte[16] royne des siens.
81    Heureuse estoit, mais encor plus heureuse[17]
82    S'elle eust suyuy la voye[18] vertueuse,
83    Et du chemin eust sceut tenir l'addresse[19]
84    Que luy monstroit[20] sa prudente maistresse.
85    Mais les honneurs & grans exaulcemens
86    Changent souuent les bons entendemens,[21]
87    Et[22] plusieurs fois altere[23] la nature

---

[1]  1545: aussi
[2]  All others: de tant de biens
[3]  This verse is underscored in BL. BNF2: grace; BNF4, V: D'honnestetés et de grace; BRB: et des graces
[4]  M: revenue
[5]  BNF1, BNF3–4, B, BRB, Vat, 1545: ces
[6]  S1/2: regard en si haultain
[7]  BNF7: lieu se mectre
[8]  BNF3: Et
[9]  Verses 74–75 are underscored in BL. BNF3, S1/2: à honneur; BNF4: en honneur
[10]  B: luy avoit causé
[11]  BNF3: Ah!
[12]  B: Elle doibt
[13]  BNF1, BNF7: profession; BNF2: profection; BNF5: à ceste nation; Vat: Verses 77–78 missing
[14]  V, BRB, M, K: à
[15]  S1/2: desquelz elle a prins
[16]  B, V, BRB, M, K: faict
[17]  BL, B, M, K: encore(s) plus heureuse (emended for versification); BNF4: estoit, encores plus heureuse; BRB: encor plus faustueuse
[18]  BNF1: vye
[19]  K: eust bien l'adresse; all others: eust bien tenu l'adresse
[20]  BNF1–2: monstra
[21]  BNF4: les grands contentemens; S1 marginal note: Mot doré (with quotation marks surrounding vv. 85–86)
[22]  V: En
[23]  BNF1, BNF5, BNF7: alterent; 1545: attirent

69    Having thus been filled with all such gifts,[1]
70    And having become accomplished in courtesy and social graces,
71    As soon as she returned home
72    She employed the power of her eyes,
73    And she cast her glance on such a high[2] place
74    That in no time at all she came to please her master.
75    Oh,[3] how beholden she was to the glory
76    Of France that brought about this happiness!
77    Oh what credit, what obligation
78    She owed[4] to the accomplishment[5]
79    Of those from whom she learned[6] so many good things
80    That have since made her queen of her own people!
81    Happy was she, but happier still[7] would she have been
82    If she had followed the virtuous way[8]
83    And if she had been able to stay the course
84    On the path that her prudent mistress had shown her.
85    But honors and great exaltation
86    Often change one's good judgment,[9]
87    And, many times, a change from one's good upbringing

---

1    All others: filled with so many gifts
2    S1/2: on such a noble
3    BNF3: And
4    B: owes
5    BNF1, BNF7: to the quality; BNF5: to this nation
6    S1/2: from whom she took
7    BRB: but still how very false
8    BNF1: life
9    BNF4: great satisfaction; S1 marginal note reads: "A golden saying"

---

71:    Anne returned to England around 1521.
74:    That is, King Henry VIII.
84:    Presumably Claude of France, though an argument could be made for this as a reference to
       Catherine of Aragon.

|     |     |     |
| --- | --- | --- |
| 88  | Le[1] changement de bonne nourriture, | |
| 89  | Mesmement[2] quand d'vne subiection | |
| 90  | Soubdain on vient à[3] domination. | |
| 91  | Or, vous diray de ce qu'il en aduint:[4] | |
| 92  | Premierement, tant amoureux deuint | |
| 93  | D'elle le Roy son maistre qu'il la mist[5] | [4r] |
| 94  | En plus hault lieu qu'onques aultre[6] ne fist. | |
| 95  | Pour commancer, d'vn[7] conté[8] l'honora, | |
| 96  | D'vn[9] marquisat apres la decora, | |
| 97  | En[10] la faisant comme Royne obeyr | |
| 98  | Et de tous biens à son soubhait iouyr. | |
| 99  | Ne luy suffit: il ne voulut[11] laisser | |
| 100 | Vn poinct d'honneur qui la peust[12] aduancer, | |
| 101 | Et, n'estimant[13] que fust assez grand Dame,[14] | |
| 102 | Il la fist Royne & la print pour sa femme. | |
| 103 | L'an trente troys[15] la premiere iournee[16] | |
| 104 | Du moys de Iuing[17] elle fut couronnee | |
| 105 | Aux lieux qui sont pour ce faire[18] ordonnez. | |
| 106 | Les grans seigneurs[19] du pays assignez | |
| 107 | Pour s'y[20] trouuer feirent de leur presence[21] | |

---

1  BNF1: Et
2  BNF6: Mesmes
3  BNF2–6, B, S1/2, 1545: en
4  BNF1: diray d'elle qu'il en advint; BNF5: "de" missing; BNF6: "luy" in margins; B: "en" missing;
   S1: diray puys ce qu'il en advint; V: de ce qui en advint; 1545: diray ce qui luy. B marginal
   notation of asterisk; S1 marginal note reads: "Grant amour"
5  BNF2, BNF5, BRB, M, K, 1545: qui la mist
6  BNF2–3, BNF6: qu'oncques à autre; BNF4: que nul autre; BNF7, B: qu'onc à autre; S1/2, BRB,
   M, K, 1545: qu'onc aultre
7  BNF1–5, B, S1/2, V, BRB, M, K, Vat: de; 1545: Et pour l'advance, du
8  BNF7: à comptes
9  BNF1, BNF4–7, B, V, BRB, M, K, Vat: De; 1545: Du
10 BNF3: Et
11 BNF1, S1/2, Vat: Il ne suffit, car ne voulant; BNF2–7, B, V, M, K, 1545: Il ne suffit, car ne
   voulut; BRB: Il ne suffit, car il ne vouloit
12 BNF1, BNF 3–5, BNF7, B, BRB, M, K: où la peut; BNF2: où le peult; V: où la pense
13 BNF2: Et ne sçavant; 1545: Et mesmement
14 This verse is underscored in BL.
15 BNF2: L'an 33; BNF4, BNF6–7: trente et troys
16 BL: Marginal note: premier juin 1533; B: Marginal note: 1533 premier de Juing; S1: Marginal
   note: courronement d'Anne Boullant; V: this verse is underscored
17 S1/2, Vat, 1545: de May
18 BNF1–3, BNF5–7, B, S1/2, V, BRB, M, K, Vat, 1545: pour cet acte; BNF4: pour telz actes
19 B: milors (interpolated in a different ink)
20 BL: si; all others as emended except BNF2: De se; BNF3, BNF5–6: De s'y; BNF7, 1545: Pour se
21 BNF4: puissance

88    Alters one's character,
89    Especially[1] when, from being a mere subject,
90    One suddenly becomes a ruler.
91        Now, I'll tell you what came of this:[2]
92    First, the king, her master,
93    Fell so deeply in love with her that he raised her
94    To a higher position than he ever had anyone else.
95    To begin with,[3] he honored her with an earldom,
96    And afterwards he graced her with a marquisate,
97    Making her like a queen to be obeyed,
98    And to enjoy all good things according to her wishes.
99    Nor was this enough for him: he didn't want[4] to leave aside
100   A single honor that might promote her,
101   And, not judging that[5] she was already a great enough lady,
102   He made her queen and took her for his wife.
103   In the year 1533, on the first day[6]
104   Of the month of June,[7] she was crowned
105   At the locations that are ordained for doing this.[8]
106   The great lords of the country who were appointed
107   To be there gave, by their very presence,[9]

---

[1]  BNF6: Even
[2]  BNF1, 1545: what happened to her; S1: what then came of this; S1 marginal note reads: "Great love"
[3]  1545: In the first place
[4]  BNF1, S1/2, Vat: It wasn't enough, for not wanting; BNF2–7, B, V, BRB, M, K, 1545: It wasn't enough, for he did not want
[5]  BNF2: And, not realizing that; 1545: And, especially because
[6]  BL and B marginal notes read: "1 June 1533"; S1 marginal note reads: "Coronation of Anne Boleyn"
[7]  S1/2, Vat, 1545: May [this is an error]
[8]  BNF1–3, BNF5–7, B, S1/2, V, BRB, M, K, Vat, 1545: for this act; BNF4: for such acts
[9]  BNF4: by their power

---

95:    Anne herself was not made a countess, a title usually given to the wife of an earl. Instead, it was her father, Thomas Boleyn, who was created Earl of Wiltshire and Earl of Ormond in 1529. Anne actively used the title "Madame de Rochford," though not necessarily the title of "countess." Thomas Boleyn had been elevated to the title of "Viscount Rochford" in 1525. Once he gained an earldom, his son, George, assumed the title of "Viscount Rochford."
96:    Anne was made Marquess of Pembroke on 1 September 1532 at Windsor Castle.
102:   The date of their marriage is disputed, but most scholars agree that some sort of wedding ceremony was held on the feast of St. Paul, 25 January 1533.
105:   Anne was crowned Queen of England in Westminster Abbey in June 1533. Other coronation festivities were held in Westminster Hall.

| 108 | À la Princesse honneur & reuerence, | |
|---|---|---|
| 109 | Et n'eussent sceu en faire dauantage | [4v] |
| 110 | S'elle eust esté de Royal parentage. | |
| 111 | L'inuention[1] des maistres & millors, | |
| 112 | Petitz & grans,[2] bien apparut alors:[3] | |
| 113 | Car les espritz des Angloys n'auoient[4] cesse | |
| 114 | Pour honorer la[5] nouuelle Princesse: | |
| 115 | Non qu'il[6] leur pleust ainsi, comme ie croy,[7] | |
| 116 | Mais, pour complaire au vouloir[8] de leur Roy, | |
| 117 | Danses & ieux de diuers appareil,[9] | |
| 118 | Chasses es[10] boys de plaisir nompareil,[11] | |
| 119 | Excercitoient[12] seigneurs[13] & damoyselles. | |
| 120 | Plusieurs tournois s'entreprenoient[14] pour elles;[15] | |
| 121 | Chascun mettoit sur la[16] cuisse la lance[17] | |
| 122 | Ou combattoit[18] de[19] l'espee à oultrance. | |
| 123 | Finablement tous plaisans excercices[20] | |

---

[1] B, S1/2: L'intention
[2] S1: Grandz et petitz
[3] BL: apparurent lors; all others as emended except BNF5: apparoissoient lors
[4] BNF6, 1545: n'eurent
[5] BNF4, S1/2, BRB: leur
[6] BNF2, M: qui
[7] B: Marginal manicule with elaborate cuff
[8] BNF1, S1: plaisir
[9] BNF1: et divers appareilz; BNF4: de nouvelz appareilz
[10] BL, 1545: & (emended for sense); all others as emended except BNF6: de
[11] BNF1: et plaisirs non pareilz; BNF4: de plaisirs non pareilz
[12] S1/S2: executoient
[13] 1545: Dames
[14] BNF6, S2: s'entretenoient; 1545: entreprenoient
[15] BNF5: elle
[16] BNF1, BRB: sa
[17] After v. 121, BNF5 adds: Où plusieurs receurent mort seulle (a verse that upsets the rhyme pattern)
[18] BL, BNF3–4: On combattoit; all others as emended except BNF2: Et combatoit; V, BRB: Et combatoient
[19] 1545: à
[20] BNF1–2, BNF4, V, 1545: tous plaisirs, exercices

108    Honor and reverence to the princess,

109    And they couldn't do more for her

110    If she had been of royal parentage.

111    The duplicitous ingenuity[1] of some lords and counselors,

112    Both great and small, then became quite apparent:

113    For English hearts never ceased

114    To honor the[2] new princess:

115    Not that it pleased them to do so, I think;[3]

116    But, in order to conform to the will[4] of their king,

117    Dances and games of various design,[5]

118    Woodland hunts of unparalleled pleasure,[6]

119    Were taken up by gentlemen and maidens.[7]

120    Several men engaged in tournaments for the women;[8]

121    Each one would set his lance at his thigh for a joust,[9]

122    Or[10] fight vigorously with his sword to the brink of death.

123    In sum, they considered every fine sport[11]

---

1  B, S1/2: The intention
2  BNF4, S1/2, B: their
3  B: marginal manicule with elaborate cuff
4  BNF1, S1: pleasure
5  BNF4: of new designs
6  BNF1: hunts and unparalleled pleasures
7  1545: by ladies and maidens
8  BNF5: for her
9  After this verse, BNF5 adds: Where several men met only their death
10  BNF2, V, BRB: And
11  BNF1–2, BNF4, V, 1545: considered all pleasures, sports

---

108:    Other prominent dignitaries, such as Thomas More, boycotted Anne's coronation as a political statement.

110:    By this remark, Carle is alluding to the fact that the king had, extraordinarily, married beneath himself by not making a royal alliance.

111:    The translation "duplicitous ingenuity" is a rendering of the term "invention" (used in all versions but B and S1/2), which, according to Cotgrave, can mean 'trick.' The DMF suggests 'idée, moyen ingénieux.' The context here affirms a negative connotation regarding the courtiers' ability to imagine a way to act (or, to put it another way, to "perform") so as to please their king even when their hearts were not in it.

122:    The expression "à oultrance" (here translated as "to the brink of death") designates a confrontation that is pursued to the point of complete defeat or even death of one of the adversaries. See Cotgrave's definition: "To fight it out, or to the uttermost; not to spare one another in fighting."

124    Et tous esbatz leur[1] estoient lors propices.
125    Oultre ces beaulx & ioyeux passetemps,                              [5r]
126    Tous se rendoient fort soigneux & attentz[2]
127    À bien seruir leur nouuelle maistresse.[3]
128    Mesmes le Roy, par gratieuse addresse,[4]
129    En grand[5] honneur souuent l'entretenoit,
130    Et maintz propos gratieux luy tenoit,
131    Non comme Roy, ou seigneur, ou mary,
132    Mais, desirant estre d'elle[6] chery,[7]
133    Diuertissoit[8] l'ennuyeuse pensee,
134    Ou l'appaisoit[9] s'elle estoit offensee,
135    Et ne taschoit[10] qu'en tout luy[11] satisfaire.[12]
136    Tous les moyens cherchoit de[13] luy complaire:[14]
137    Il colloqua aux lieux plus apparentz
138    De ses estaz[15] ses principaux parentz,[16]
139    Et de faueur telle enuers[17] elle vsa
140    Que iamais riens il[18] ne luy reffusa.
141    Pour augmenter sa grand prosperité,[19]                             [5v]
142    Dieu luy donna celle felicité[20]
143    Qu'en peu de temps vne fille conceut,

---

1    BNF3: luy; Vat: leurs
2    BNF1: joyeux et entens; BNF7: joyeux et attentz; V, BRB, M, K: à temps
3    BNF4, BRB: princesse
4    S1 marginal note reads: "Admirable amour du Roy d'Angleterre envers Anne Boullant"
5    1545: En gros
6    BNF1, BNF7: desiroit d'estre d'elle; BNF2, BRB: desirant d'elle estre; BNF3–4, B, 1545: desirant d'estre d'elle
7    S1/2: choysy
8    S1/2: Divertissant
9    B, S1/2: l'appaisant
10   All others but V, BRB, M, Vat: Et ne taschant
11   B: qu'en tous lieux
12   BRB: complaire
13   BNF4, B, V: pour
14   This verse is underscored in BL. BRB: Tous moyens cherchoit pour luy satisfaire
15   BNF4: son estat
16   S1/2: d'elle tous les parens
17   BNF7: tel envers; B: telle vers
18   BNF1–7, BRB, V, M, K, Vat, 1545: Que pour jamais riens; B: Que pour faveur rien; S1: Qu'aucune chose oncq ne; S2: Qu'aucune chose on ne
19   BL: Pour l'augmenter en sa prosperité (emended for sense); BNF3: Pour augmenter sa grand felicité; 1545: Pour augmenter si grand prosperité
20   This verse is underscored in BL. BNF1–2, BNF4–6, S1/2: telle felicité; BRB: celle prosperité

| 124 | And every game suitable for that moment. |
|---|---|
| 125 | Beyond these lovely and happy pastimes, |
| 126 | Everyone became quite diligent[1] and solicitous |
| 127 | About serving their new mistress[2] well. |
| 128 | Even the king, with gracious skill,[3] |
| 129 | Would often entertain her in great honor |
| 130 | And held many a courteous conversation with her, |
| 131 | Not like a king, or a lord, or a husband, |
| 132 | But, desiring to endear himself to her,[4] |
| 133 | He would distract her from any troubling thought, |
| 134 | Or would appease her if she were offended, |
| 135 | And he endeavored[5] solely to satisfy her in all things. |
| 136 | He would seek every means to please her:[6] |
| 137 | He bestowed on her close relatives[7] |
| 138 | The most notable places of his estates, |
| 139 | And he showed such favor toward her |
| 140 | That he never refused her anything.[8] |
| 141 | To increase her great prosperity,[9] |
| 142 | God granted her the happiness[10] |
| 143 | To conceive, in short order, a daughter, |

---

[1] BNF1, BNF7: joyous
[2] BNF4, BRB: princess
[3] S1 marginal note reads: "Admirable love of the king of England towards Anne Boleyn"
[4] S1/2: desiring to be her chosen one
[5] All others but V, BRB, M, Vat: And endeavoring
[6] BRB: Verses 135–36 read: "And he endeavored only to please her in all things. / He sought all means to satisfy her"
[7] S1/2: on all her relatives
[8] S1: That never did he refuse her a single thing
[9] BNF3: happiness
[10] BNF1–2, BNF4–6, S1/2: such happiness; BRB: that prosperity

---

124:  For details on Anne's coronation events, see especially Wriothesley's *Chronicle*, 1.17–22, which states (1:22): "On the morrow after was great jousts [*sic*] at the tilt done by eighteen lords and knights, where was broken many spears valiantly." Here and throughout, I have modified the spelling of Middle English quotations to conform to modern conventions. In his poem, Carle is describing two components of the tournament: the joust proper, performed with lances and on horseback, and the tourney, performed on foot with swords.

138:  No doubt a reference to the numerous benefits bestowed on Anne's father and brother in the 1520s and 1530s.

143:  Anne was already pregnant by the time of her January wedding ceremony and June coronation. She must have conceived sometime in December 1532.

144    Dont en l'esprit[1] tresgrand ioye receut,[2]
145    Cuydant que fust[3] vn gaige d'asseurance
146    De l'amytié[4] & certaine esperance[5]
147    Pour l'aduenir d'ainsi[6] continuer.
148    Quand commença de sentir remuer[7]
149    Les petitz piedz & qu'elle se veid prinse,
150    Ô![8] qu'elle estoit bien sagement[9] apprinse
151    De bien se[10] plaindre & faire la dolente,
152    En voix piteuse & parolle tremblante,[11]
153    Pour demonstrer[12] la doulleur qu'elle auoit!
154    Ô! quel[13] ennuy le Roy en receuoit[14]
155    De veoir s'amye[15] en si piteuse sorte![16]
156    Ie croy qu'il eust voulu sa fille morte.
157    Mais, qu'elle en fust deliuré[17] sans tourment,      [6r]
158    Tant[18] la faisoit traicter soingneusement,
159    Se trauaillant d'entendre son envye[19]
160    Plus qu'il n'eust faict[20] pour conseruer sa vie.

---

[1] BNF3–4, V, K: Dont en esprit; BNF5, 1545: Dont en espoir; BNF6: Dont en espoir (corrected in margin to "en esprit"); S1: Dont à l'esprit; S2: Donc à l'esprit; Vat: Dont en l'espoir

[2] BL: tresgrande ioye receut (emended for versification); BNF1–2, BNF4–5, BNF7, Vat: tresgrand aise receut; BNF3, 1545: tresgrand aise en receut; V, BRB, K: grant aise il en receut; M: grant ayse il receut

[3] V: que ce fust

[4] S1/2: Perpetuelle

[5] V: missing v. 146

[6] BNF1–2: ainsi

[7] BNF5: commença sentir et remuer; BNF6, S1/2, 1545: à sentir remuer; V: le sentir remuer; BRB: la sentir remuer

[8] BNF3, BNF5: Et

[9] BNF4: estoit soigneusement; B, V, Vat: estoit sagement

[10] BNF1: se bien

[11] V: parolles tremblantes

[12] B: vertical line in margins marking vv. 150–152; S1/2: Pour myeulx monstrer; K: Pour monstrer

[13] BNF3: Et quel; M: Auquel

[14] BNF4: Et le roy lors par moings n'en supportoit

[15] All others but BRB, M: sa mye

[16] This is the last line of BNF2 until v. 195; it is the last verse on its folio.

[17] All others but BNF3, S2, and Vat: delivree (which disrupts the versification)

[18] BL: Et; all others as emended

[19] BL: Se trauaillant comme pour son amye (emended for sense and to maintain rhyme); BNF1–2: S'y travaillant de toute son envye; B, Vat: Soy travaillant d'entendre son envie; S1: Se travaillant de scavoir son envye; S2: Se travaillant de scavoir son ennuy; 1545: Se trauailler d'entendre son envie

[20] BNF1–3, BNF5–7, M: Qui n'eust tant faict; BNF4: Qui eust tant faict; B, S1/2, V, BRB, K, Vat, 1545: Qu'il n'eust tant faict

| 144 | Which brought very great joy[1] to her heart,[2] |
|---|---|
| 145 | For she believed that it was a guarantee |
| 146 | Of love and of the sure and certain hope[3] |
| 147 | That the future would continue in this way. |
| 148 | When she began to feel the movement |
| 149 | Of little feet and knew she was with child, |
| 150 | Oh![4] how easily[5] she learned |
| 151 | To whine a lot and pretend she was hurting, |
| 152 | In a pitiful voice and with trembling words, |
| 153 | To show[6] what pain she was suffering! |
| 154 | Oh![7] What anxiety the king would draw from this,[8] |
| 155 | To see his beloved in such a pitiable state! |
| 156 | I believe he might have wanted his daughter dead. |
| 157 | But, so that she might be delivered without difficulty, |
| 158 | He would treat her so solicitously, |
| 159 | Taking greater pains to know her every whim[9] |
| 160 | Than he would have done to save his own life. |

---

1  BNF1–5, BNF7, Vat, 1545: very great comfort; V, BRB, M, K: brought great comfort
2  BNF5–6, Vat, 1545: Which in hope brought her very great comfort [joy]
3  S1/2: Of perpetual and certain hope
4  BNF3, BNF5: And
5  BNF4: carefully
6  S1/2: To show better
7  BNF3: And
8  BNF4: And the king then could barely stand
9  BL: Taking greater pains for his beloved; BNF1–2: Taking greater pains in this with all his desire; B, Vat: Taking greater pains to understand her desire; S1: Taking greater pains to know her desire; S2: Taking greater pains to know her anxiety

---

146:  Carle's language here is reminiscent of many scriptural passages regarding the Christian's joyous and confident hope (and, indeed, assurance) of eternal life (see, for example, Romans 12:12 and Hebrews 7:20–28). I have tried to render this more explicit by echoing a phrase— "sure and certain hope"—that is frequently found in funeral services of the Anglican and Catholic traditions. Carle's use of these expressions is meant to suggest that Anne's "hope" in a secure future, based on her ability to provide Henry with an heir, is misplaced. A similar expression reappears in v. 1261, this time in the more appropriate context of hope for eternal life.

149:  The DMF defines "preins" as "enceinte" [pregnant]. The root is the Latin "praegnas," from which the English "pregnant" is derived. It was thought that it was at the moment of quickening, which Carle describes here, that a woman would know for sure that she is pregnant.

| 161 | Or, pensez donc,[1] puys que le Roy luy mesme |
| 162 | Estoit en dueil[2] &[3] soulcy tant[4] extresme, |
| 163 | Si vn[5] chascun s'efforçoit de trouuer |
| 164 | Mille[6] moyens pour plaisir[7] recouurer. |
| 165 | Estant venu le terme desiré,[8] |
| 166 | Tellement eut le couraige asseuré |
| 167 | Qu'au[9] grand trauail sans peur se disposa. |
| 168 | Dieu en ses faictz tant la[10] fauorisa |
| 169 | Qu'elle produyt,[11] sans extresme[12] douleur, |
| 170 | Vn bel enfant de naifue couleur,[13] |
| 171 | Et de ses traictz[14] bien ressemblant au[15] pere, |
| 172 | Mieux, pour certain, qu'à[16] la Royne sa mere. |
| 173 | Fille elle estoit, belle en[17] perfection,                                        [6v] |
| 174 | Et de visage & de proportion, |
| 175 | Tant qu'on iugeoit[18] des astres l'influence |
| 176 | Fauoriser du tout à sa naissance. |
| 177 | De vous compter[19] la sumptuosité |
| 178 | De son baptesme &[20] grand solemnité[21] |
| 179 | Il n'est besoing: Car prolixe sera |
| 180 | Ce long[22] discours, parquoy me[23] suffira |

---

[1] S1, V, BRB, M, K: doncques
[2] S1/2: en peine
[3] Vat: en
[4] V, BRB, M, K: si
[5] BNF5: qu'un
[6] V: Mil; BRB, M: Nul (a transcription error); K: Milz
[7] BRB: santé
[8] S1 marginal note: Premier enfant d'Anne Boullant La Royne d'Angleterre
[9] BNF4, BNF6, V, 1545: Qu'à; BNF5: Qu'en
[10] BNF4: Dieu ses souhaitz ainsy; V: Dieu ses souhaitz en elle; all others: Dieu ses souhaitz en ce
[11] BNF4: Car elle eust; all others: Car elle feist
[12] BNF5: sans trop grande
[13] B marginal note reads: "1534 Naissance de la Roinne Elisabeth Roinne d'Engleterre" (actual date is 1533)
[14] S1: son traict; S2: son traictz
[15] BNF4: traictz resemblant à son; B: bien resembloit au
[16] M, K: que
[17] BNF1: Elle estoit belle en grant; BNF7: Fille estoit, belle en; B, 1545: Fille estoit elle, belle
[18] B: jugeroit
[19] V, BRB, K: De vous compter du tout
[20] BNF3: en
[21] S1/2: De ce triumphe et superfluité
[22] BNF4: grand
[23] BNF7: m'y; V, BRB, K: m'en

161     Now, imagine, then, since the king himself
162     Felt such extreme concern and grief,[1]
163     How everyone tried so hard to devise
164     A thousand ways to find enjoyment[2] again.
165     When the end of her term arrived,[3]
166     So confident was she
167     That she gave herself over to her great labor without fear.
168     God so favored her in these matters[4]
169     That she produced,[5] without great[6] pain,
170     A beautiful baby of healthy coloring[7]
171     Who quite resembled her father in her features,
172     Certainly more so than she did her mother, the queen.
173     It was a girl, perfectly beautiful[8]
174     In both face and form,
175     Such that people thought[9] the influence of the stars
176     Favored her in all things at her birth.
177     To recount for you the excessive cost
178     And great solemnity of her baptism[10]
179     Is not necessary: For that long[11] discourse
180     Would be tedious, which is why it will suffice

---

1   S1/2: pain
2   BRB: to recover health
3   S1 marginal note: "First child of Anne Boleyn, the Queen of England"
4   BNF4: God thus favored her wishes; all others: God favored her wishes in this matter
5   All others: For she had
6   BNF5: without very great
7   B marginal note reads "1534, Birth of Queen Elizabeth, Queen of England." The correct date is 1533.
8   BNF1: She was beautiful in great perfection
9   B: people would think
10  S1/2: To recount for you the excessive cost / And extravagance of this pompous public show
11  BNF4: great

---

170:    Anne's daughter, Elizabeth, was born on 7 September 1533. By virtue of the annotation found in B, which refers to Elizabeth as queen, it is clear that this reader engaged with the manuscript sometime after November 1558, when Elizabeth acceded to the throne.
178:    Elizabeth's baptism took place on 10 September 1533 in the Church of Observant Friars at Greenwich. Hall's *Chronicle* (805–6) gives an account of the lavishness of the ceremony; for another description of these rites, see Wriothesley's *Chronicle*, 1:23.

181     Vous[1] dire icy que tant[2] estoit exquis
182     Tout l'appareil[3] que riens n'y fut requis.[4]
183     Dame Ysabeau, marquise d'Exester,[5]
184     Qui bien voulut[6] de cecy s'exempter,
185     Marrine[7] fut, pour au Roy ne desplaire,
186     Et eut le Duc de Norfort pour compere.[8]
187     Ysabeau, donc,[9] au baptesme[10] nommee
188     Fut en tous lieux Princesse renommee,
189     Et, par le grand parlement d'Angleterre,                    [7r]
190     Apres[11] le Roy dame de ceste terre,
191     Et seulle fut declairee heritiere[12]
192     Contre le droict de la[13] fille premiere.
193     Continuant sa supresme puissance,[14]
194     Ce parlement feit vne aultre ordonnance:[15]
195     On exempta le prince[16] de l'eglise
196     Pour mieux mener à[17] fin son entreprise,[18]
197     Pour ce que[19] point le Pappe n'accordoit[20]
198     À son vouloir, mais tousiours pretendoit[21]
199     Que ce seroit[22] iniustice et oultrage

---

[1]   BNF3: De
[2]   BNF4: tout
[3]   BNF5: Tout appareil; 1545: Tant l'appareil
[4]   This verse is underscored in BL. BNF4: et rien ne fut requis; S1: Comme appartient à royne de hault pris; S2: Verse missing; B: Marginal manicule and note: Isabeau ou Elisabeth Royne d'Angleterre
[5]   BL, B6, S1/2, Vat, 1545: de Pester (emended for accuracy); BNF1, BNF7: de Parester; BNF3: d'Exselter; BNF4: de Selter; BNF5: de Prester; B: d'Excelter; V, BRB, M, K: d'Exaster
[6]   S2, K: Qui voulait de; all others: Qui bien vouloit
[7]   This is merely a variant spelling of "Marraine," which most of the other manuscripts use.
[8]   Verses 185–186 are underscored in BL.
[9]   1545: Daire (a transcription error)
[10]  BNF1: doncq estant ainsi
[11]  1545: A prins (a transcription error)
[12]  This verse is underscored in BL.
[13]  S1/2: sa
[14]  S1 marginal note reads: "Ordonnance contre l'eglise faite par le Parlement d'Angleterre"
[15]  BL: Verses 193–194 are underscored
[16]  BL: Faisant le Roy le Prince (emended to avoid redunancy with vv. 201–202); BNF5: L'on exempta du prince; all others: Où exempta le prince
[17]  B: en
[18]  This verse is underscored in BL. Vat: reverses order of vv. 195–196
[19]  S1/S2: Pour quoique; BNF2: Penser que
[20]  BNF2: n'attendoy
[21]  BNF6: originally reads "et tousiours pretendoit"; marginal correction reads "mais tousiours contendoit"
[22]  S1/2: ce estoit

| 181 | For me to tell you here that all the preparations |
|---|---|
| 182 | Were so exquisite that nothing was wanting in them.[1] |
| 183 | Lady Elizabeth, marchioness of Exeter, |
| 184 | Who truly wanted to excuse herself from this, |
| 185 | Was the godmother, so as not to displease the king, |
| 186 | And the Duke of Norfolk stood as godfather. |
| 187 | Thus, named Elizabeth at her baptism,[2] |
| 188 | She was acclaimed[3] everywhere as princess, |
| 189 | And, by the great Parliament of England, |
| 190 | Became known, after the king, as Lady of the Realm, |
| 191 | And was declared his sole heir, |
| 192 | In opposition to the rights of the[4] first daughter. |
| 193 | Furthering its supreme power,[5] |
| 194 | This Parliament created another statute: |
| 195 | The prince was freed from the rule of the Church,[6] |
| 196 | To better carry out his enterprise, |
| 197 | Because the Pope did not concur at all |
| 198 | With his will, but always claimed |
| 199 | That it would be an outrage and injustice |

---

1 S1: For me to tell you here that it was so exquisite, / As befits a queen of great worth
2 B: marginal manicule and note: "Isabelle or Elizabeth, Queen of England"
3 BNF1: Elizabeth, thus, being so named / Was acclaimed
4 S1/2: his
5 S1 marginal note reads: "Decree against the church made by the Parliament of England"
6 BL: Making the king the prince of the Church

---

185: Carle is wrong on these details. The marchioness of Exeter *did* serve as godmother "at the bishopping," that is, for Elizabeth's confirmation ceremony, but her name was Gertrude Courtenay (née Blount). Carle probably assumed that the godmother's name was Elizabeth because that was the name given to the child, but Anne's daughter was named after her grandmothers. Two other participants were Margaret Wotton, the dowager Marchioness of Dorsett, and Agnes Tilney, the dowager duchess of Norfolk, who were godmothers "at the font" for Elizabeth's baptism. Carle is, however, correct in implying that Gertrude Courtenay was not partial to Anne or happy with the new marriage.

186: Thomas Howard, the third Duke of Norfolk, did not serve as godfather; rather, he bore the responsibility of serving as Earl Marshall. Elizabeth's godfather was Thomas Cranmer, the Archbishop of Canterbury, who later performed the confirmation ceremony. See Hall's *Chronicle*, 805–6, and Wriothesley's *Chronicle*, 1:23.

188: This proclamation took place between the baptism and confirmation of the infant Elizabeth. See Hall's *Chronicle*, 806: the "Garter chief king of arms cried aloud 'God of his infinite goodness, send prosperous life and long, to the high and mighty Princess of England Elizabeth.'"

192: This is a reference to the Act of Succession of 23 March 1534.

| 200 | Contreuenir au[1] premier mariage. |
| 201 | Puis, ordonna que le Roy seroit chef |
| 202 | De son Eglise, & que[2] pareil meschef |
| 203 | Seroit[3] venir[4] contre l'authorité |
| 204 | Que[5] delinquer en lese[6] maiesté, |
| 205 | Ce que depuys fut monstré par effect:          [7v] |
| 206 | Car puny fut Maurus[7] pour ce meffaict[8] |
| 207 | Et cinq[9] Chartreux, mesprisans leurs edictz, |
| 208 | Tous vifs ouuertz, seullement estourdiz.[10] |
| 209 | Le peuple, esmeu de veoir la nouueaulté |
| 210 | De ceste grande & dure[11] cruaulté, |
| 211 | En[12] murmurant de ces faictz[13] deuisoit, |
| 212 | Et plussouuent[14] la Royne Anne accusoit[15] |

---

[1] V: à

[2] B: "que" missing

[3] BNF1: Feroit

[4] BNF2: venu

[5] BNF2–3, BNF6: Et

[6] BNF1: royal; BNF2: royale; BNF4: ceste

[7] BNF1, BNF3, BNF6: fut Morus; S1/2: Morus fut pugny; Vat: furent Maurus

[8] Verses 205–206 are underscored in BL. BNF5 gives "MAURUS" in large letters; BNF7: pour son meffaict; B marginal note reads: "T. Maurus"

[9] BNF4: six

[10] BNF1: seullement eslourdiz (a transcription error); BNF3, BNF6: ouvers furent et estourdiz; BNF5, V: Verse 208 missing; BRB, M, K: ouverts sans entendre leurs dictz (a corrupt reading)

[11] BNF4, V, BRB, M, K: ceste dure et grande

[12] BNF2: Et

[13] BL: ses faictz (emended for sense); BNF6, 1545: ce faict; B: ces cas; V, M: telz faictz; BRB: de telz propos

[14] BNF3: plus avant

[15] BL: la Reine en accusoit (emended for grammar); all others as emended except BNF1, M: la Royne accusoit; BNF4: la Royne on accusoit; B: Marginal drawing which may represent a scroll

200    To nullify the king's first marriage.

201    Then, Parliament decreed that the king would be the head

202    Of his Church, and that it would be a comparable misdeed

203    To oppose this authority

204    As it would be to commit high treason,

205    Which was since demonstrated in actual fact:

206    For More was punished for this[1] crime,[2]

207    And five[3] Carthusians who scorned Parliament's edicts

208    Were cut open alive, after being only dazed.[4]

209    The people, who were filled with emotion by the unprecedented sight

210    Of this great and harsh cruelty,

211    Spoke in whispers about these deeds,[5]

212    And most often they would accuse Queen Anne[6]

---

[1] BNF7: his

[2] B marginal note: "T. More"

[3] BNF4: six

[4] BNF3, BNF6: Were cut open alive and dazed

[5] BL: his deeds; BNF6, 1545: this deed; B: these events; V, M: about such deeds; BRB: about such topics

[6] BL, BNF1, BNF4, M: they would accuse the queen; B: marginal drawing which may represent a scroll

---

200:    Pope Clement VII refused to annul Henry's marriage to Catherine of Aragon. The 1533 Act of Appeals allowed the divorce to be determined by Henry himself, without recourse to Rome, via Thomas Cranmer, his Archbishop of Canterbury, by declaring that "all causes of matrimony and divorces ... shall be from henceforth heard, examined, discussed ... and definitely adjudged and determined within the King's jurisdiction and authority and not elsewhere." See Elton, *Tudor Constitution*, 346.

202:    This is the Act of Supremacy of 1534, which reads: "Be it enacted by authority of this present Parliament that the King our sovereign lord ... shall be taken, accepted, and reputed the only supreme head in earth of the Church of England called *Anglicana Ecclesia*." See Elton, *Tudor Constitution*, 355.

204:    A reference to the Treason Act of 1534, which was enacted "to prohibit, provide, restrain, and extinct all manner of shameful slanders." See Elton, *Tudor Constitution*, 61–62.

206:    Thomas More, formerly Henry's Chancellor, was beheaded for treason in July 1535, after he refused to sign the oath upholding the Act of Succession, whose preamble denied the authority of the "Bishop of Rome" over the "jurisdictions given by God immediately to emperors, kings, and princes." See Elton, *Tudor Constitution*, 6–7.

207:    Carle errs in speaking of "five" Carthusians who were martyred. Initially, three Carthusian priors plus two other ordained priests were executed in May 1535; in June, an additional three Carthusian monks were executed at Tyburn. All these religious were hanged, drawn, and quartered. More and Bishop John Fisher were beheaded at the Tower of London.

213     D'auoir esté cause de telle horreur.[1]
214     Pour comprimer du peuple la fureur,[2]
215     Le Roy voulut[3] que qui mesdiroit d'elle
216     Seroit puny d'vne peine mortelle.
217     Donc,[4] close fut la bouche aux mesdisans,
218     Qui[5] bien estoient en nombre suffisans,
219     En[6] vn besoing, pour remplir vne armee.
220     Elle fut lors de tous craincte ou[7] aymee:[8]
221     Car[9] qui scauoit ce qu'on ne doit[10] celer                    [8r]
222     Contrainct estoit de le[11] dissimuler.
223     Telle estoit[12] lors la[13] parfaicte fiance[14]
224     Qu'avoit le roy en sa grande prudence.[15]
225     Pendant ce[16] temps, la Royne Catherine,[17]
226     Lors qui viuoit, supportoit[18] la ruyne
227     De son estat le plus patiemment
228     Que permettoit humain[19] entendement,

---

1   BNF1, V, BRB, K: de tel erreur; BNF2, BNF4–7, B, S1/2, M, Vat, 1545: d'un tel erreur; BNF3:
    Verse missing
2   S1 marginal note reads: "Ordonnance pour Anne Boullant Royne"
3   BNF1: voullant; BNF5: ordonna
4   All others but BNF2 and BNF4: Dont
5   V: Que
6   BNF1–3, BNF5–6, S1/2: À
7   BNF1, BNF3–4, S1/2, Vat, 1545: et
8   BNF5: Car moult estoit grande leur assemblee
9   BNF5: Et
10  BNF1: ce qui ne doit; BNF2: ce qu'il ne doibt; BNF4: ce qu'on debvoit; B: ce qu'on ne debvoit
11  BNF2: ce; S2: d'elle
12  BL: D'elle; all others as emended except BNF1: Et telle estoit
13  BNF2: sa
14  BNF4: science
15  BL: Plus sur le Roy qu'en la sienne prudence. This verse is underscored; it is emended here
    to conform with all others with the following exceptions: BNF4: Qu'advouet le roy en grande
    prudence; BNF5: Qu'en eut le Roy en sa grand' prudence; BNF7: Qu'avoit le roy en sa grande
    puissance; B: Qu'avoit le Roy en sa tresgrande prudence
16  BNF2: le
17  BNF6 marginal note: Catherine premiere femme; B marginal note: Catherine Reine; S1 marginal
    note: Contemnement de la Royne Catherine premiere femme du roy d'Angleterre
18  BNF2: Seule vivant, supportant (a corrupt reading); BNF5–6: Seule vivait en supportant; all
    others: Seule vivoit, supportant
19  BNF3, BNF5–6, Vat, 1545: l'humain

213    Of being the cause of such horror.[1]

214    In order to hold the people's rage in check,[2]

215    The king willed[3] that whoever spoke badly of her

216    Should be punished by pain of death.

217    Thus,[4] closed were the mouths of her detractors,

218    Who were quite sufficient in number

219    To fill an army, if need be.

220    She was then feared or[5] loved by everyone:[6]

221    For[7] whoever knew something that one ought not[8] conceal

222    Was forced to disguise it;

223    Such[9] was, then, the complete confidence

224    That the king had in her great prudence.[10]

225    Meanwhile, Queen Catherine,[11]

226    Who was alive at that time, tolerated[12] the collapse

227    Of her condition as patiently

228    As humanly possible,

---

1  All others: of such an offense.

2  S1 marginal note: "Ordinance for Anne Boleyn, Queen"

3  BNF5: decreed

4  All others but BNF2 and BNF4: About this matter

5  BNF1, BNF3–4, S1/2, Vat, 1545: and

6  BNF5: For their company was very great

7  BNF5: And

8  BNF4: that one ought to

9  BNF1: And such

10  BL: Surer was the king in his perfect trust of her / Than he was in his own prudence; BNF7: Such was then the perfect confidence / That the king had in his great power; B: Such was the perfect confidence / That the king had in her very great prudence

11  BNF6 marginal note: "Catherine, the first wife"; B marginal note: "Catherine, Queen"; S1 marginal note: "The scorning of Queen Catherine, first wife of the king of England"

12  All others but BNF2: Was living alone, tolerating

---

213:    For examples of such accusations against Anne, see Chauncy's account of the Carthusian martyrs (48–49); the *Mémoires* of Michel de Castelnau, 56–57; and Chapuys's letter to Charles V, dated 15 April 1535, in *Letters and Papers, Foreign and Domestic, of the Reign of Henry VIII* [hereafter LP] 6.351.

216:    The Treason Act of 1534 prohibited slanderous speech against the king and queen: "if any person or persons ... do maliciously wish, will or desire by words or writing ... bodily harm to be done or committed to the King's most royal person, the Queen's or their heir's apparent ... or slanderously and maliciously publish and pronounce, by express writing or words, that the King our sovereign lord should be heretic, schismatic, [or] tyrant ... shall be adjudged traitors; and that every such offence ... shall be reputed accepted and adjudged high treason." See Elton, *Tudor Constitution*, 62–63.

228:    Catherine of Aragon was repudiated by Henry in 1531 and forced to live in exile from the court.

229     Et tant estoit de tous honneurs[1] priuee
230     Qu'elle viuoit comme femme priuee.[2]
231     Mais qui des[3] maux siens estoit[4] le plus fort,
232     On separa d'elle tout son confort:[5]
233     Sa fille vnicque en sa[6] saige ieunesse,
234     Le seul repos de sa triste vieillesse.
235     Le maternel[7] cueur ne sceut longuement[8]
236     Porter l'ennuy de son esloignement,[9]
237     Qui par langueur[10] tellement la[11] myna                    [8v]
238     Qu'en peu de temps à la mort la mena.
239     Sa fille, alors, qui seulle ainsi[12] viuoit,[13]
240     En son esprit grand[14] patience auoit,
241     Et mesprisoit[15] la[16] fortune contraire
242     Comme si fust vn bien[17] petit affaire,
243     Et tellement se reposoit en[18] Dieu
244     Qu'ennuy ne dueil en son cueur n'auoit[19] lieu.
245     Mesmement quand on dit que[20] trespassee
246     Sa mere estoit,[21] n'en troubla[22] sa pensee,
247     Mais louoit Dieu & l'estimoit[23] heureuse

---

1   BNF1, S1, V: tout honneur
2   BL: femme laisee (emended for rhyme); BNF1: Qu'el se trouva de tous habandonnee; BNF2:
    Qu'elle se trouva du tout habandonnee; B: vivoit de tous honneurs privée
3   BRB: de
4   BNF4: Mais ce qui estoit de ses maux; S1/2: Mais qui estoit de ses maux
5   This verse is underscored in BL.
6   BNF2–5, BNF7, B, S1/2, V, K, Vat: la
7   BNF4: naturel
8   S1/S2: Adoncq le cueur maternel longuement; V: ne sceut plus longuement; Vat: n'a seu
    longuement
9   S1/2: Ne sceut porter ce dur esloignement
10  BNF1, BNF4: longueur
11  BNF3: se
12  BN 1–4, BNF7, S1/2, B, V, BRB, M, K, Vat: aussi
13  B marginal note: Marie Reine; S1 marginal note: Occupations de la premiere fille du roy
    d'Angleterre, prisonniere
14  BNF4, V: grande
15  BNF2: mesprisant
16  BNF1–7, B, S1/2, V, BRB, M, K, Vat, 1545: sa
17  BNF1, B, S1/2, V: Comme ce fust un bien; BRB: Comme sy ce fust un bien; M, Vat, 1545:
    Comme se fust un bien; K: Comme si ce fust bien
18  BNF1–3, BNF5–7, B, S1/2, BRB, M, K, Vat, 1545: s'asseuroit avec; BNF4, V: s'asseuroit envers
19  BNF4, 1545: avoit; BRB, K: n'avoient
20  S2: quand ont dit que; M: quand sceut que
21  BNF4, B: Estoit sa mere
22  B: ne troubla
23  1545: s'estimoit (a scribal error)

229 And she was so deprived of every honor
230 That she lived like a private citizen.[1]
231 But what was the hardest of her troubles
232 Was that she was separated from her every comfort:
233 Her only daughter, who, wise beyond her years,
234 Was the sole consolation of her sad old age.
235 Her motherly[2] heart could not bear for long
236 The anguish of her estrangement,[3]
237 Which, in her pining,[4] did so drain her
238 That it soon brought her to death.
239 Her daughter, then, who thus[5] was living alone,[6]
240 Was greatly patient in spirit,
241 And scorned her adverse fortune
242 As if it were quite a little thing,
243 And found such rest[7] in God
244 That anxiety or grief had no place in her heart.
245 Even when they told her[8] that her mother
246 Had passed away, her thought was not troubled;
247 But she praised God and deemed her mother to be happy

---

1 BL: That she lived like a woman who was cast off; BNF1: That she found herself abandoned by everyone; BNF2: That she found herself totally abandoned; B: That she lived stripped of all honors
2 BNF4: natural
3 S1/2: Verses 235–236 read: Then her motherly heart could not bear for long / Her harsh estrangement
4 BNF1, BNF4: Which by its length
5 BNF1–4, BNF 7, B, S1/2, V, BRB, M, K, Vat: also
6 B marginal note: "Queen Mary"; S1 marginal note: "The pastimes of the first daughter of the king of England, held prisoner"
7 All others: And found such assurance
8 M: when she learned

---

233: Catherine's daughter, Mary, was the only surviving child of her marriage with Henry.
238: Catherine died on 7 January 1536 at Kimbolton.
244: In a letter from Chapuys to Charles V, dating from the time of Elizabeth's baptism, the Imperial ambassador noted that Mary, "like a wise and virtuous princess as she is, … takes matters patiently, trusting in the mercy of God." See LP 6.1125. The same letter notes that Mary was publicly stripped of her title of princess at this time.

| 248 | Qu'elle fust hors de vie[1] douloureuse, |
|-----|------|
| 249 | Pour receuoir le certain refrigere |
| 250 | Et viure[2] mieux au celeste repaire. |
| 251 | Souuent vacquoit aux[3] diuines leçons, |
| 252 | Souuent cherchoit des instrumens les sons, |
| 253 | Ou s'occupoit[4] à faire quelque ouurage, |
| 254 | Ou apprenoit quelque estrange langage. |
| 255 | Cecy ne dy pour ses perfections, |
| 256 | Mais pour monstrer ses occupations: |
| 257 | Car ses[5] biens sont de tous tant[6] estimez |
| 258 | Qu'en les louant[7] ils seroient reprimez.[8] |
| 259 | Ainsi passoit patiemment ses iours, |
| 260 | Mectant en Dieu l'espoir de son secours. |
| 261 | Et ce pendant, la Royne florissoit,[9] |
| 262 | Et son vouloir du tout[10] accomplissoit, |
| 263 | Ayant loysir, moyen, & liberté |
| 264 | À son souhait[11] prendre sa volupté.[12] |
| 265 | Elle pouuoit aller en toute part, |
| 266 | En compaignie,[13] ou bien seulle à l'escart, |
| 267 | Et,[14] s'elle estoit, par fortune, saisie[15] |
| 268 | De quelqu' Amour[16] de personne choisie,[17] |
| 269 | Il luy[18] estoit entierement permis |

[9r] (at line 253)

[9v] (at line 269)

---

1 BNF5–6, 1545: Qu'elle estoit hors de la vie; BNF7: Qu'elle fust hors da sa vie; S1/2, V, BRB, M, K: Qu'elle estoit hors de vie
2 BNF5: vivant
3 BNF5: vaguoit en; 1545: vacquoit en
4 BNF1: s'occupant
5 BNF2: ces
6 BNF4: Car ses vertuz sont tant de tous; BNF5: Car ses vertuz sont de tous
7 BNF2: la louant; V: le louant; 1545: les voyant
8 BL: ne sont assez louez (emended for rhyme); BNF2: ils seront reprouvez; BNF3, BNF7, S2, Vat: ils seront reprimez; BNF4: ne seroient reprimez; B: ils sont reprimez; V, BRB, M, K: ils seront exprimez; 1545: ils seroient reprouvez
9 S1 Marginal note: Grand habandon donné à Anne Boullant Royne d'Angleterre
10 BNF2–7, S1/2, V, M: Et son vouloir en tout; BRB: En son vouloir en tout; 1545: Et son vouloir en soi
11 BNF4: semblant
12 BNF5: volonté
13 BNF4: Acompagnié
14 V, BRB, K: Ou
15 BNF4: choisie
16 BNF3: A quelqu' Amour; S1/2: D'avoir l'Amour
17 BNF1: par fortune choisye; BNF4: Verse missing
18 BNF5: À ell'; 1545: Il y

| 248 | To be beyond this sorrowful life, |
|---|---|
| 249 | Believing that she would obtain sure refreshment |
| 250 | And live better in her celestial abode. |
| 251 | Often, Mary would apply herself to[1] spiritual readings; |
| 252 | Often, she would seek the sounds of instruments, |
| 253 | Or would occupy herself by doing some needlework, |
| 254 | Or would learn some foreign language. |
| 255 | I do not say this to show her accomplishments |
| 256 | But, rather, to show how she spent her time, |
| 257 | For her[2] virtues are so highly valued by all |
| 258 | That in praising them[3] they would become diminished.[4] |
| 259 | And so she patiently passed her days, |
| 260 | Placing in God the hope of His assistance. |
| 261 | And, in the meantime, the queen was flourishing,[5] |
| 262 | And her will in all things was fulfilled, |
| 263 | Having leisure, means, and freedom |
| 264 | To take her pleasure[6] as she wished.[7] |
| 265 | She could go everywhere, |
| 266 | Either accompanied or alone and out of sight, |
| 267 | And[8] if, by chance, she was seized |
| 268 | By some Love[9] for a favored person, |
| 269 | It was entirely permitted to her |

---

[1] BNF5: would wander through

[2] BNF2: these

[3] BNF2: in praising her

[4] BL: they are not adequately praised; BNF2: they will be blamed; BNF3, BNF7, S2, Vat: they will be diminished; BNF4: they would not be diminished; B: they are diminished; V, BRB, M, K: they will be expressed; 1545: they would be blamed

[5] S1 marginal note: "Great license given to Anne Boleyn, Queen of England"

[6] BNF5: To do her will

[7] BNF4: as she saw fit

[8] V, BRB, K: Or

[9] S1/2: To have love

---

250:  Perhaps an echo from Psalm 23:3 ("He refreshes my soul") and other scriptural passages that describe the heavenly refreshment of the celestial banquet.

254:  In a letter to her daughter dated 1533, Catherine of Aragon writes that she will be sending Mary additional spiritual readings in Latin and urges her to play, for recreation, her virginals or lute. See LP 6.1126.

270    À son plaisir de[1] traicter ses amis:
271    Car,[2] le moyen de la[3] grande licence
272    Que luy donnoit la[4] publicque deffence
273    Que nul n'osast,[5] sur peine de martyre,
274    Aucunement de la royne mesdire,[6]
275    Fut cause apres de la fortune aduerse,
276    Qui de bien hault promptement la renuerse.[7]
277    Mais telle[8] loy n'eut pouuoir[9] d'asseurer
278    Que l'amytié peust longuement durer,
279    Car par le temps elle s'amoindrissoit,
280    Et tous les iours plus se reffroidissoit[10]
281    Le Roy de sa premiere affection.
282    Ie n'en scauroys[11] dire l'occasion,
283    Si ce n'estoit par[12] la raison commune
284    De l'inconstante[13] & muable fortune,
285    Ou que Dieu veult nous monstrer bien[14] souuent          [10r]
286    Que grandz honneurs & biens ne sont que vent,
287    Lesquelz il donne[15] à ceulx qu'il veult[16] punir
288    De leurs meffaictz, pour[17] les faire venir
289    D'un grand plaisir apres à grand[18] souffrance,[19]
290    Comme verrez[20] icy l'experience.
291    Mais dire veux les derniers[21] accidens

---

[1]   BRB: "de" missing; K: "de" inserted interlinearly
[2]   All others: Par
[3]   BNF6, 1545: sa
[4]   BNF1–2: sa
[5]   BNF7: n'osoit
[6]   M: maldire
[7]   Verses 275–276 are unique to BL.
[8]   BNF1–3, BNF6–7, B, S1/2, V, BRB, M, K, Vat, 1545: celle; BNF4–5: ceste
[9]   V, BRB, M, K: moyen
[10]  1545: Verse missing
[11]  BNF1: Je ne scaurois; B: originally had "Je ne scay dire," later corrected to "Je ne scaurois dire"
[12]  BNF3: de
[13]  V: l'inconstance
[14]  BNF1, BNF2, BNF4, BNF6–7, S1/2, Vat: Ou que Dieu veult nous monstrer plus; BNF3: Ou
      que nous veult monstrer le plus; BNF5, B: Ou que Dieu veult monstrer le plus; V, BRB, K, M:
      Ou que Dieu nous veult monstrer plus; 1545: Ce que Dieu nous monstre plus
[15]  1545: Lesquelz donne
[16]  BNF7: que veult; M, Vat, 1545: qui veult
[17]  BRB: pour apres
[18]  BNF1–3, BNF5–7, B, S1/2, M, K, Vat: D'un grand plaisir apres en grand; BNF4: De grandz
      plaisirs en tres grande; V: D'un grand plaisir en grande; BRB: D'un grand plaisir en grand
[19]  BNF3: missing vv. 290–295
[20]  BNF2–3, S1/2: Comme en verrez; B: Comme on voirra; 1545: Comme voyez
[21]  All others: divers

270   To treat her lovers as she pleased:
271   For,[1] the great license given to her
272   By the public prohibition
273   That no one dare, under pain of martyrdom,
274   Speak ill of the queen in any way at all[2]
275   Became the device that afterwards led to her adverse fortune,
276   Which promptly brought her down from great heights.
277   But such a law[3] did not have the power[4] to assure
278   That love could long endure,
279   For, in time, it diminished,
280   And, every day, the king grew colder
281   From his first infatuation.
282   I couldn't tell you the circumstances surrounding this,
283   Unless it were due to the ordinary reason
284   Of inconstant[5] and mutable fortune,
285   Or that God quite[6] often wants to show us
286   That great honors and wealth are but wind,
287   Which He grants to those whom He wants to punish
288   For their misdeeds, to make them go[7]
289   From great pleasure to great[8] suffering afterwards,[9]
290   As you shall see[10] in the proof provided here.
291   But I want to tell you about the most recent[11] incidents

---

1   All others: Through
2   All but BL end the sentence here and are missing vv. 275–276, reading vv. 269–274 (with its variant at v. 271) as one continuous phrase
3   All others: this law
4   V, BRB, M, K: the means
5   V: Of inconstancy
6   All others: most
7   BRB: go afterwards
8   BNF4: very great
9   BNF4, V, BRB: missing "afterwards"
10  1545: you see
11  All others: the various

---

281:   On the cooling of Henry's infatuation with Anne, see the Imperial correspondence in LP 6.1054, LP 6.1069, LP 7.1193, and LP 7.1257; see also the letter of Palamède Gontier in LP 8.174, and Castelnau to Dinteville in LP 9.566.
286:   For wind as a scriptural symbol of delusion and disappointment, see Isaiah 26:18 and 41:29.
290:   See the DMF, which defines "voir l'experience" as 'voir la preuve … la réalité' [to see the proof, the reality].

Qui furent pour[1] pressaiges euidens
De la fortune[2] & malheur aduenir:
Car souuent Dieu, pour faire reuenir
Vn grand pécheur au faict de[3] penitence,
Et luy donner quelque recongnoissance,
Permect qu'il[4] tumbe en[5] peril de sa vie.
Et si tant est la personne[6] asseruie
À son péché que, pour punition
De Dieu ne veult faire correction,[7]
Et qu'à[8] tousiours en ses vices empire,[9] [10v]
Dieu monstre alors[10] la fureur de son ire,
Et recepuoir luy faict honteusement
De ses meffaictz[11] le dernier payement.
Ainsi aduint par deux precedens signes[12]
Que la Royne eut de son malheur insignes,[13]
Se trouuant[14] fort en son espoir[15] confuse.
Le premier[16] fut par flambe furieuse
Qui[17] soubdain l'eust en sa chambre surprise,[18]
Si ne fust vn qui promptement l'aduise[19]
De s'exempter[20] du feu qui se[21] prenoit

1 V, K: Que demonstroient; all others: Qui demonstroient
2 BNF2: l'infortune
3 BNF4: à faire; BNF6, S1/2, 1545: au fruict de
4 BNF3: que
5 BNF6–7, S1/2, Vat, 1545: au
6 B: la personne est
7 BNF1–2, S1/2: ne veult prendre correction; BNF3, BNF6, Vat, 1545: n'en veut faire correction; V, M: n'en veuille faire correction; BRB: n'en veuille faire satisfaction; K: ne veuille faire correction
8 All others: que
9 BNF1–2: en vices il empire
10 BNF1, M: lors
11 BNF3: orginially had "pechez," which is then crossed out and changed to "meffaictz"; V: mesus
12 All others: advint que par deux ou troys signes; S1 marginal note: Signes merveilleux qui advindrent à la Royne d'Angleterre
13 BL: enseignes (spelling emended to maintain the rhyme for the eye); BNF3: royne par merveilleux insignes; BNF5: royne eut de merveilleux insignes; BNF7: eut merveilleuses insignes; all others: eut merveilleux et insignes
14 BNF1–4, BNF6, B, V, BRB, M, K, 1545: trouva
15 All others: esprit
16 1545: prouver
17 BNF2, S1/2: Que
18 M marginal note: feug [*sic*]; this is also how the scribe renders "feu" in vv. 311 and 314
19 BNF4, BNF6, 1545: s'advise; V: que promptement advise; BRB, M: qui promptement advise
20 BNF4, V, BRB, M, 1545: De l'exempter; S1/2: De se tirer
21 BNF4: la

| 292 | That were intended as[1] obvious portents |
|---|---|
| 293 | Of the misfortune and unhappiness to come: |
| 294 | For often God, in order to bring |
| 295 | A great sinner back towards an act of repentance[2] |
| 296 | And give him some understanding of his situation, |
| 297 | Allows him to fall in peril of his life. |
| 298 | And if the person is so enslaved |
| 299 | By his sin that, even considering God's punishment, |
| 300 | He still doesn't want to amend his ways[3] |
| 301 | And forever worsens[4] in his vices, |
| 302 | God then shows the full fury of His anger |
| 303 | And makes him shamefully receive |
| 304 | The ultimate payment for his misdeeds.[5] |
| 305 | And so it happened that by two earlier signs[6] |
| 306 | The queen encountered omens of her misfortune,[7] |
| 307 | Finding[8] herself sorely confounded in her hope.[9] |
| 308 | The first was by furious flames |
| 309 | That would quickly have taken her by surprise in her chambers,[10] |
| 310 | Were it not for one person who promptly warned her |
| 311 | To escape[11] from the fire that was |

---

1  V, K: That were demonstrated by; all others: That demonstrated
2  BNF4: back to do penance; BNF6, S1/2, 1545: towards the fruit of repentance
3  BRB: to make satisfaction
4  All others: And still worsens
5  BNF3: originally reads "sins"
6  All others: two or three signs; S1 marginal note: "Wondrous signs that happened to the Queen of England"
7  BNF3: That the queen by wondrous omens; BNF5, BNF7: That the queen encountered wondrous signs; all others: That the queen encountered wondrous things and omens
8  BNF 1–4, BNF6, B, V, BRB, M, K, 1545: [and] found
9  All others: sorely troubled in spirit
10  M marginal note: Fire
11  S1/2: To withdraw

---

298:  The concept of being a "slave to sin" is expounded primarily by St. Paul in Romans 6:6–20.
304:  V uses the Old French word "mesus," meaning "faults or abuses." See DMF: "abus, manquement contre un règlement, une loi."
308:  Carle is the only surviving source of information on this fire.

312    Desia au lieu ou elle se tenoit,
313    Tellement que si tost n'en fut partie,[1]
314    Iamais du feu ne s'en[2] fust garantie.
315    Vn temps[3] apres, vn[4] enfant luy croissoit
316    Dedans le ventre, &[5] fort s'esiouissoit,
317    Plus que iamais estant[6] reconfortee,                    [11r]
318    Prenant espoir du fruict de sa portee.
319    Adonc le Roy, s'en allant à la chasse,
320    Cheut du cheual rudement à[7] la place.
321    Donc, l'on[8] cuydoit que, par cest[9] aduenture,
322    Il deust payer le devoir de[10] nature.
323    Quant la Royne eut la nouuelle entendue,
324    Peu s'en fallut que[11] ne cheut estendue
325    Morte d'ennuy,[12] tant que fort offensa[13]
326    Son ventre plain, & le fruict[14] aduancea,
327    Et enfanta vn beau filz auant[15] terme,
328    Qui nasquit mort, dont versa[16] maincte larme.[17]
329    Mais pour peril ne perturbation[18]

---

[1]  BNF1, B: si lors elle ne fust partie; BNF2–3, BNF6–7, S1/2, M, Vat, 1545: si lors n'en fust partie; BNF4, BRB: si lors ne fust partie; BNF5: que si hors ne feust sortie; V, K: que lors n'en fust partie

[2]  BNF1, BNF3–7, S1/2, BRB, M, Vat: du feu ne se fust; B: du feu elle ne se fust; V: du feu ne fust; 1545: de feu ne se fust

[3]  BNF3: peu

[4]  BNF4: qu'un

[5]  BNF5: dont

[6]  BNF4–5, B: estoit

[7]  BNF1: de cheval rudement en; BNF3: rudement de cheval en; BNF5–7, B, V, S1, M, K, Vat, 1545: du cheval rudement en

[8]  BNF1: Dont bien; BNF3, BNF6, B, V, BRB, M, K, Vat, 1545: Dont l'on; BNF4, S1/2: Dont on

[9]  B: par celle

[10]  BNF1, BNF6, B, S1/2, V, BRB, M, K, 1545: tribut de; BNF4: tribut à

[11]  BNF1: s'en faillut qu'el; BNF2, BNF4, S2: s'en fallut qu'elle; BNF5–6, S1: s'en faillit que; B: se faillut que; V, BRB: s'en faillut qu'elle; Vat, M: s'en faillit qu'elle; K: s'en failloit qu'elle; 1545: s'en failloit que

[12]  V: devint

[13]  BNF5: efforça

[14]  BNF1–2: et son fruit; BNF4: qui le fruit; S1/2, Vat: et l'enfant

[15]  BNF4: un filz avant son

[16]  B: usa

[17]  M: mainctes larmes

[18]  BNF4: tribulation

| | |
|---|---|
| 312 | Already spreading to the place where she was staying, |
| 313 | Such that, if she hadn't left quickly,[1] |
| 314 | She would never have been saved from the fire. |
| 315 | A while[2] later, a baby was growing |
| 316 | In her belly, and[3] she greatly rejoiced, |
| 317 | Being[4] comforted more than ever before, |
| 318 | Taking hope from the fruit of her womb. |
| 319 | Then the king, who had gone hunting, |
| 320 | Fell hard to the ground from his horse. |
| 321 | Therefore, it was thought[5] that, by this mishap, |
| 322 | He would have to pay nature its due.[6] |
| 323 | When the queen heard the news, |
| 324 | She barely kept from falling flat out |
| 325 | Dead from anxiety, such that she greatly hurt[7] |
| 326 | Her full belly and hastened its fruit,[8] |
| 327 | And she gave birth prematurely to a fine son[9] |
| 328 | Who was stillborn, for which she shed[10] many a tear. |
| 329 | But on account of neither peril nor disquiet[11] |

---

1  BNF5: if she hadn't gotten out; all others: if she hadn't left then
2  BNF3: A little
3  BNF5: for which
4  BNF4–5, B: [And] was
5  BNF1: For which it was truly thought; all others but BNF2, BNF5, BNF7: For which it was thought
6  BNF1, BNF4, BNF6, B, S1/2, V, BRB, M, K, 1545: duty
7  BNF5: forced
8  S1/2, Vat: the child
9  BNF4: a son
10  B: spent
11  BNF4: tribulation

---

318:  Cotgrave defines "portée" as "The burthen [*sic*], or fruit of a woman's womb."

320:  Chapuys indicates that the fall came about as a result of an accident while riding at the lists (not while hunting), which occurred on 24 January 1536. See LP 10.200 for Chapuys's letter; see also the letter of the Bishop of Faenza, LP 10.294, and that of Pedro Ortiz, LP 10.427, on the aftermath of this incident. Wriothesley's *Chronicle* (1:33) likewise indicates the king was running at the ring (though it is not evident that he was engaged in an actual tournament at this time). It is possible that Carle wanted to evoke the hunt rather than the list merely to develop a stronger alliteration in this and the following verse ("<u>ch</u>asse," "<u>ch</u>eut," "<u>ch</u>eual").

328:  Anne was told of Henry's accident by the Duke of Norfolk. Her miscarriage occurred on 29 January 1536, the day of Catherine's burial. See Wriothesley's *Chronicle*, 1:33 and Chapuys's letter to Charles V, LP 10.282, both of which provide the detail that the child was a male and the miscarriage was caused by the "fright" Anne took upon being told of the king's accident.

| 330 | Ne delaissa la[1] conuersation |
|---|---|
| 331 | De sa premiere & mauuaise coustume, |
| 332 | Et, comme vn feu qui peu à peu s'allume, |
| 333 | Venant en fin par sa[2] grande rigueur[3] |
| 334 | À demonstrer l'effect de sa vigueur,[4] |
| 335 | Ainsi[5] le mal dont estoit[6] entachee, |
| 336 | Et[7] la malice en son esprit[8] cachee,[9] |
| 337 | Tousiours croissant, en si hault[10] degré monte |
| 338 | Qu'elle en[11] rendit[12] euidente la honte, |
| 339 | À son malheur &[13] grand confusion, |
| 340 | Comme en verrez la disposition. |
| 341 |     De celles dont la Royne se seruoit,[14] |
| 342 | L'vne estoit seur d'vn Seigneur qui auoit |
| 343 | Cest[15] honneur d'estre au[16] conseil plus estroict, |
| 344 | Qui, la voyant qui[17] mainctz signes monstroit[18] |
| 345 | D'aymer aucuns par amour deshonneste, |
| 346 | Par bon conseil fraternel[19] l'admonneste |
| 347 | Qu'elle acqueroit vne honteuse fame |
| 348 | De mal viuante &[20] impudicque femme, |
| 349 | Et grandement son honneur blesseroit,[21] |

[11v] is marked at line 333.
[12r] is marked at line 349.

1  BNF1, BNF4, B, V, BRB: Ne delaissa sa; M: N'en delaissa la; K: Ne laissa sa
2  BNF1–2, BNF4: Vient à la fin par si; BNF3: Venant à la fin par sa; BNF5: Vient à la fin de si;
   BNF6: Vient à la fin de sa; BNF7, S1/2: Vient à la fin par sa; B: Vint en la fin par sa; V: Vint à la
   fin pour sa; BRB, K: Vient à la fin pour sa; M: Vient à la fin par grande; Vat: Vient en la fin par
   sa; 1545: Vient en la fin de si
3  BNF4: vigueur
4  BNF4: rigueur
5  BNF1, BNF2, BNF4, BNF6–7, S2, M, Vat, 1545: Aussi
6  BNF4: c'estoit
7  BRB, V, K: À
8  BNF1–2: dedans son cueur; V, BRB, M: de son esprit
9  V: cachés; B: Verse missing (marginal note: faute d'un vers)
10 BNF2, 1545: grand; BNF3: gros
11 V, BRB: Qu'en
12 BNF5: a rendue
13 S1/2: en
14 Verses 341–342 are unique to BL, and v. 341 is underscored.
15 BL: C'est (emended for sense)
16 All others: Ung des seigneurs du; S1 marginal note: Declaration du crime de la Royne faicte par
   une demoyselle d'Angleterre; M marginal note: noise
17 BL: que; all others: Voyant sa seur qui
18 BNF6, 1545: faisoit
19 M: fraternelle
20 BNF7: "et" missing
21 BNF3: besseroit

330    Did she forsake engaging in
331    Her first—and bad—way of living,
332    And, like a fire that, little by little, begins to burn,
333    Coming[1] finally, by its[2] great rigor,[3]
334    To demonstrate the full effect of its vigor,[4]
335    So, too, do the evil that tainted her
336    And the malice hidden in her spirit,[5]
337    Ever growing, reach such a height
338    That it made her shame evident,
339    To her misfortune and great dismay,
340    As you shall see it here laid out.
341        Among those women in service to the queen,
342    There was one who was the sister of a gentleman who held
343    The honor of being a close advisor to the king,[6]
344    Who, upon seeing that his sister was showing many signs[7]
345    Of loving some men with an impure love,
346    Admonishes her, with good brotherly counsel,
347    That she might acquire a shameful reputation
348    As a lewd and immodest woman
349    And might greatly injure[8] her honor

---

1  BNF1–2, BNF4–7, S1/2, BRB, M, K, Vat, 1545: Comes; B, V: Came
2  BNF1–2, BNF4–5, 1545: so
3  BNF4: vigor; M: by great rigor
4  BNF4: rigor
5  BNF1–2: hidden within her heart; V, BRB, M: the hidden malice of her spirit; B marginal note: Missing verse
6  All others missing vv. 341–342; v. 343 reads: One of the gentlemen among the king's closest advisors; S1 marginal note: "Declaration of the queen's crime, made by an English lady"; M marginal note: "quarrel"
7  BNF6, 1545: Seeing his sister who was giving many signs; all others: Seeing his sister who was showing many signs
8  BNF3: debase

---

343:  The sister has been identified as the Countess of Worcester, whose brother was Anthony Browne, a gentleman of the Privy Chamber, and whose half-brother was William Fitzwilliam, a member of Henry's Privy Council. The expression Carle uses, "conseil plus estroict," could perhaps refer to the Privy Council, but the poet uses the expression "le conseil privé" later in the poem (v. 745) to refer to that body. Given this distinction, I have chosen to translate the phrase here more generically as "close advisor." See the definition provided in the DMF for "estroit conseil": "conseil privé, restreint, intime" and for "au plus estroit du conseil": "au point le plus fort, le plus important, au cœur du conseil," both of which emphasize intimacy of counsel though not necessarily in a formal capacity.

346:  At this point in the narration, Carle extensively uses the present tense (for dramatic purposes), especially, but not exclusively, in reporting dialogue. This translation will generally reflect the use of present tense in the original poem.

| 350 | Si de[1] péché tost ne se retiroit. |
| 351 | Adonc, voyant congneue[2] son offence, |
| 352 | "I'aperçoy[3] bien," dit elle, "que l'on pense |
| 353 | Que i'ay faulsé de loyauté les[4] droictz. |
| 354 | Le vous nier, mon frere, ne[5] vouldrois. |
| 355 | Mais on voit bien vne petite[6] faulte |
| 356 | En moy, laissant vne beaucoup[7] plus haulte[8] |
| 357 | Qui porte effect de plus grand preiudice. |
| 358 | Et s'il falloit[9] que le[10] tout ie vous disse, |
| 359 | Vous cognoistriez que moins[11] de seureté |
| 360 | Y a, plus où l'on pense[12] loyauté. |
| 361 | Mais vous, messieurs, iugez les collombeaux,[13] |
| 362 | Et[14] pardonnez aux infames corbeaux." |
| 363 | Ainsi[15] vouloit ses faultes amortir |
| 364 | Pour ses péchéz[16] en aultruy[17] conuertir, |
| 365 | Pensant qu'vn[18] mal plus grand effaceroit[19] | [12r] |
| 366 | Vn plus petit quand declairé seroit. |
| 367 | Puis,[20] commença asseurer[21] son excuse, |
| 368 | En luy disant que la plus malheureuse |
| 369 | Qui oncques fut femme[22] dessoubz les cieulx |

---

1  BRB: du
2  BNF2: voyant et congneu; BNF4: voyant qu'il congneust; BNF5: l'oyant, recognut; B: voiant estre cognue; S1/2: Or congnoissant qu'on scavoit
3  BNF6, 1545: Je cognois
4  BNF1–2: la loyaulté des
5  1545: le
6  S1/2: on veult bien pugnir la moindre
7  S1/2: Et pardonner à une bien; M: En delaissant une beaucoup
8  Vat: originally read "plus grande," corrected to "plus haulte"
9  BNF6, M: si failloit
10  BNF6, 1545: du
11  BNF2–3: cognoistrez que moins; BNF4: cognoisteriez moins
12  BNF1–3, BNF5, S1/2: Y a, où plus on pense; BNF4: Et où pensez plus grande; BNF6: Y a vue où plus on pense; B: Là où plus l'on pense de; changed to "Y a" in another hand and ink; V, BRB, M, K: Y a, où plus on pense de; Vat: Y a où plus on en pense; 1545: Y a une plus on pense
13  BL: messieurs les iuges collombeaux (a corrupt reading)
14  BL: Vous
15  BNF6: Aussy
16  BNF4: Pour son péché; BNF6, 1545: Par ses péchés
17  1545: aultre
18  BNF1: que mal; 1545: qui mal
19  BNF2: "effaceroit" missing; "trieroit" added in different hand and ink in the margin
20  All others: Et
21  BNF4: d'asseurer; B: commence à asseurer
22  BNF4: Qu'oncques fut femme estant; BNF5, V, BRB: Que oncques fut femme; 1545: missing "fut"

350  If she didn't soon withdraw from sin.
351  Then, seeing that her offense was known,[1]
352  She says: "I fully realize[2] that people think
353  That I have been untrue to the duties of loyalty.
354  I would not want[3] to deny this to you, my brother;
355  But people easily see a small fault
356  In me, allowing[4] a much higher one
357  That carries the potential of greater harm.
358  And if I am required to tell you everything,
359  You would learn that there is less surety there
360  Where one thinks there to be more loyalty.
361  But you, gentlemen, condemn doves,
362  And pardon infamous ravens."
363  And so she wished to deaden the impact of her faults
364  By changing the subject from her sins[5] to another's,
365  Thinking that a greater evil would efface[6]
366  A lesser one when it was openly declared.
367  Then,[7] she began to defend herself
368  By telling him that the most wretched woman
369  There ever was under the sun

---

1  BNF2: seeing and knowing her offense; BNF4: seeing that he knew her offense; BNF5: hearing him, she recognized her offense [and]; S1/2: Now realizing that one knew her offense
2  BNF6, 1545: I fully know
3  1545: I would like
4  S1/2: But people truly want to punish the slightest fault / And pardon; M: Setting aside
5  BNF4: sin
6  BNF2: would sort out from (this is written in the margin)
7  All others: And

---

356:  Carle here uses the poetic technique of "enjambment" (the continuation of a thought from one verse to the next without a pause at the end of a line) to put the words "in me" in greater relief.
362:  This is a variation of a quotation from Juvenal, *Satires*, 2.63: "Dat veniam corvis, vexat censura columbas" [That's a judgment that acquits the ravens and condemns the doves]. The phrase became proverbial and made its way into the *Adages* of Erasmus.
363:  The verb "amortir" can be rendered "to attenuate," but I have chosen the locution "deaden the impact" to preserve the etymological sense of the French verb, meaning "to bring to death."
368:  Carle's epithet, "la plus malheureuse," may be a deliberate inversion of Anne's chosen motto, "the most happy." It is also meant to contrast with Carle's earlier declaration of Anne as "happy" in v. 81.

| 370 | Estoit[1] la Royne, "& pour le scavoir mieulx, |
|-----|------------------------------------------------|
| 371 | Si ne[2] voulez mon asseurance croire,[3] |
| 372 | De Marc scaurez" (dit elle) "ceste histoire.[4] |
| 373 | Mais ie ne veux[5] oublier à vous dire |
| 374 | Vn poinct de tous[6] qui me semble le pire.[7] |
| 375 | C'est que souuent son frere eut[8] auec elle, |
| 376 | Dedans son lict, accoinctance[9] charnelle. |
| 377 | Du demeurant Marc vous en comptera, |
| 378 | Et le discours de sa vie fera."[10] |
| 379 | Le frere, apres auoir bien[11] escouté |
| 380 | Ce dont iamais il ne se[12] fust doubté, |
| 381 | Tant se troubla de ces[13] propos entendre |
| 382 | Qu'il ne scauoit quel conseil deuoit prendre. |
| 383 | Car, d'vne part, s'il faisoit ce rapport[14] |
| 384 | Au Roy, & qu'il ne vint pas[15] à bon port |
| 385 | De faire croire effectz & entreprises,[16] |

[13r]

---

[1] BRB, M: C'estoit

[2] BNF6: Si n'y; 1545: Si n'en

[3] This verse is underscored in BL.

[4] BL: cest affaire. This reading is a rhyme for the ear, according to sixteenth-century pronunciation; but all other versions read "histoire," maintaining a rhyme for the eye as well. BNF1–2: De Marc (deist elle) vous en saurez l'histoire; V, BRB, K: (dit elle) l'hystoire; Vat: (dist elle) tout l'histoire

[5] K: Mais ne veulx

[6] B: point tout seul; BRB: poinct de tout; K: poinct du tout

[7] This verse is underscored in BL.

[8] BNF1: son frere souvent a; BNF5, B, V, BRB, M, K: son frere a; BNF6–7, 1545: son frere est

[9] BNF2: son frere avec elle / Dedans son lict a acointance; BNF4: son frere avec elle / A dans son lict accointance; BNF5: Dedans ung lict accoinctance

[10] BNF1, BNF4, BNF6: vie vous fera; B: originally "de sa vie fera"; this is crossed out and replaced, in a different hand, with "de sa vie vous dira"

[11] V, BRB, K: apres bien l'avoir

[12] B: il ne s'en fust (with "il" added as correction); BRB: iamais ne se fust; K: il ne fust

[13] BNF1–2, BNF4, BNF7, S1/2, V, M, K: ses; BRB: des ces

[14] BNF3, BNF6: le rapport; M: sy faisoit ce rapport; Vat: son rapport

[15] BNF4: et qui ne conduist; BNF7, BRB, M, Vat: et qu'il ne conduist; B: et qu'il ne se conduyst pas; V: missing v. 384; all others: et qu'il ne conduist pas

[16] BL: entreprinses (emended to maintain a rhyme for the eye with v. 386); BNF1–2: Tous les effectz du premier entreprinse; BNF3, B: Tous les effets des primes entreprinses; BNF4: Tous les effets des entreprises; BNF5: Tous les essaiz des premieres entreprinses; BNF6–7: Tous les effects des premieres entreprinses; S1/2: Tous les effets de telles entreprinses; V, BRB, M, K: missing v. 385; Vat: Tous les effectz des premiers entreprises; 1545: Tous les effets les premieres entreprinses

370 Was the queen, "and to get a better grasp of this,
371 If you don't wish to take my word for it,
372 You can learn about this story"[1] (she says) "from Mark.
373 But I don't want to forget to tell you
374 One point[2] that seems to me to be the worst of all,
375 Which is that her brother has often had[3]
376 Carnal knowledge of her in her own bed.
377 Mark will recount the rest to you,
378 And will make[4] the speech of his life."
379 The brother, after carefully listening to
380 That which he would never have suspected,
381 Was so troubled in hearing these[5] words
382 That he didn't know what course of action to take.
383 For, on the one hand, if he made this[6] report
384 To the king, and he didn't successfully arrive[7]
385 At making these undertakings and developments believable,[8]

---

1 BL: this business; BNF1–2, V, BRB, K: the story; Vat: learn all the story
2 B: A single point
3 BNF1–2, BNF4–5, B, V, BRB, M, K: her brother often has
4 BNF1, BNF4, BNF6, B: And will make for you
5 BNF1–2, BNF4, BNF7, S1/2, V, M, K: her
6 BNF3, BNF6: the; Vat: his
7 All others: And if he didn't steer to a good conclusion
8 BNF4: All the effects of the undertakings; BNF5: All the efforts of the first undertakings; S1/2: All the effects of such undertakings; all others, except V, BRB, and K, where this line is missing: All the effects of this first [these first] undertaking[s]

---

372: Mark Smeaton, a court musician.
375: George Boleyn, Viscount Rochford.
378: "Sa vie" can mean "his life" or "her life." Thus, another possible translation might be: "and will give testimony about her [Anne's] life." My inclination, however, is to see it as a way of indicating that Mark's words will put him center stage, such that he will make the speech of a lifetime.

386     Il se liuroit aux grandz peines promises[1]
387     Aux mesdisans par la Loy[2] apprestees,[3]
388     Que ie[4] vous ay cy deuant recitees.[5]
389     Ne le faisant,[6] le deuoir l'assailloit
390     Qu'envers le Roy desloyaulment failloit,
391     Et si par temps on s'en[7] fust aperceu,
392     Cruelle mort il eust aussi receu.[8]
393     Parquoy voulant satisfaire au deuoir,
394     Deslibera de le faire scauoir[9]
395     À deux amiz les[10] plus fauorisez
396     Du Roy, afin que plus[11] authorisez
397     Fussent ensemble, & que plus de creance[12]                    [13v]
398     Receust de troys que d'vn[13] seul l'asseurance.
399     Ainsi,[14] vn iour que l'opportunité
400     Estoit[15] duysante à leur commodité,[16]
401     Les deux presens, luy pour tous commença,[17]

---

[1] BNF3, S1/2, BRB: peines commises; BNF4: Se livreroit à grand peine promises; B: Il se livreroit; S1/2: Il se mectoit; 1545: peines que mises. V adds this verse after v. 386: Du parlement bien et au long icy mises; BRB and K add this verse after v. 386: Du parlement bien au long icy mises; M adds after v. 386: Du parlement icy dessus au long mises. Again, the similarity among these last four variants demonstrates that this is a manuscript family.

[2] V: par loy

[3] BNF1, BNF6: par la loy arrestés; BNF2-3, BNF7, B, V, BRB, M, K, Vat, 1545: par la loy arrestée; BNF5: par le Roy arrestées; S1/2: par la loy arretées

[4] BNF1-3, S1/2: ja

[5] BNF1: recités; BNF2: arrestée (a transcription error); BNF3, BNF7, B, S2, V, BRB, M, K, Vat, 1545: recitée; BNF4: Verse 388 missing

[6] BNF1-3, S1/2, Vat, 1545: S'il se taisoit; BNF4-5, V, BRB: S'il le taisoit; BNF6: Si se taisoit; BNF7: Sy le faisoit; B: S'il ne le faisoit; M, K: Si le taisoit

[7] BNF4, BNF7, B: on se; V: Et par temps l'on s'en; BRB, M: l'on s'en

[8] BNF1, BNF5: Voyoit qu'il eust aussi la mort receu; BNF2: Voyoit aussy qu'il eut la mort receu; BNF3, BNF7, Vat: Veoit qu'il eust la mort aussi receu; BNF4: Voiant qu'il eust la mort ainsy receu; BNF6, 1545: Croyez qu'il eust la mort aussi receu; B, S1/2: Voyoit qu'il eust la mort aussi receu; V, BRB, M, K: Verité est qu'il eust la mort receu

[9] BNF3, BNF5-6: assavoir; 1545: à sçavoir

[10] S1/2: Aux deux amis des; all others: À deux amis des

[11] All others: mieulx

[12] V, BRB, M, K: credence

[13] BNF1-3, BNF6, B, BRB, M, K, Vat, 1545: Receust des trois que d'un; BNF4: On eust des trois que d'un; S1/2: Receust aux trois qu'à ung

[14] BNF6, BRB, K: Aussy

[15] BRB: C'estoit

[16] BNF4-5: la commodité; B: originally "leur conduicte" then changed to "commodité" in another ink

[17] BNF1-3, M, K, Vat, 1545: l'ung pour tous prononça; BNF4: l'un pour tous commença; BNF5, BNF7, B, V, BRB, S1/2: luy pour tous prononça

386    He would open himself up to the serious penalties promised[1]
387    To the queen's detractors, as provided by the law,[2]
388    And which I told you about earlier.[3]
389    But in not doing so,[4] he would be beset by his
390    Treacherous failure of duty towards the king,
391    And, if, in time, the matter became evident,
392    He, too, would receive the penalty of a cruel death.[5]
393    For this reason, wanting to fulfill his duty,
394    He resolved to make it known
395    To two of the most favored friends
396    Of the king, so that together they might hold more authority
397    And that the testimony of three men
398    Might be given greater credence than that of one man alone.
399    And so, one day, when the opportune moment came
400    That was suitable for them,
401    With the two men present, he[6] began speaking for everyone,[7]

---

[1]  V, BRB, K are all missing v. 385 but add another line after 386 to read (with slight variations): He would open himself up to the serious penalties / At length put into place by Parliament. M is also missing 385, but the line added after 386 is corrupt.

[2]  BNF1–3, BNF6–7, B, S1/2, V, BRB, M, K, Vat, 1545: For the queen's detractors arrested under the law; BNF5: For the queen's detractors arrested by the king. The variant readings of all but BNF1 and BNF6 are grammatically problematic. The reading of BL makes it clear that it is the "serious penalties" that were both readied by Parliament and recounted by Carle above.

[3]  BNF1–3, S1/2: And which I already told you about

[4]  BNF7: If he did it; B: If he didn't do it; all others: If he were silent

[5]  BNF1–2, BNF5, B, S1/2: He saw that he too would receive the death penalty; BNF3, BNF7, Vat: He sees that he too would receive the death penalty; BNF6, 1545: Trust that he would also receive the death penalty; V, BRB, M, K: The truth is that he would receive the death penalty

[6]  BNF1–4, M, K, Vat, 1545: one man

[7]  BNF1–3, BNF5, BNF7, B, S1/2, V, BRB, M, K, Vat, 1545: spoke for everyone

---

396:   These men remain unidentified, though it is possible that Browne and Fitzwilliam together informed the king along with an unknown associate (perhaps even Thomas Cromwell).

| 402 | Et sagement ce propos aduança:[1] |
| 403 | "Si ce n'estoit,[2] Sire, que vous nous estes |
| 404 | Beaucoup plus cher que noz biens &[3] noz testes,[4] |
| 405 | Et que nous est plus en affection[5] |
| 406 | De vostre honneur la conseruation |
| 407 | Que ne craignons[6] la rigueur du tourment |
| 408 | Qui ordonné[7] fut par le[8] parlement, |
| 409 | Iamais n'eussions prins ceste[9] hardiesse |
| 410 | Vous desclairer ce que vostre honneur presse.[10] |
| 411 | Mais nous[11] vouldrions tous trois plustost[12] mourir |
| 412 | Que n'entreprendre en[13] ce vous secourir. |
| 413 | Sire, ce cas vostre[14] maiesté touche                    [14r] |
| 414 | Et[15] si auant, que vous seroit reprouche[16] |
| 415 | Si ne mettez[17] en bonne heure[18] remede |
| 416 | Au parauant que plus oultre procede.[19] |
| 417 | Et qui[20] plus est, cecy craincte nous[21] donne |
| 418 | D'vn grand danger touchant vostre personne: |

---

1 BNF1, S1/2: Et sagement son propos commença; BNF2–3, BNF7, B, M, K, Vat, 1545: Et sagement ce propos commença; BNF4: Et sagement ce propos prononça; BNF5, V: Et ce propos saigement commença; BNF6: Et sagement le propos commencea; BRB: Et sagement ses propos commença; S1 marginal note: Accusation contre la Royne d'Angleterre, son frere et quatre autres chevaliers

2 BNF1, V: Si n'estoit

3 BNF2–5, BNF7, V, BRB, M, K, Vat: ni; B: ou

4 K, 1545: bestes

5 BNF1–7, B, S1/2, V, BRB, K, M, Vat: Et qu'avons plus en commendation; 1545: Et qu'avons plus à recommendation

6 K: Quoique craignons

7 BNF4–5: Qu'ordonné

8 BNF2, BNF5: vostre; BNF4, V, BRB, K: le grand; B: originally read "le," then changed to "vostre"

9 All others: prinse la

10 BNF1–2, BNF4, BNF7, S1/2, V, BRB, K: blesse

11 All others: Tant que

12 BNF5, BNF7, B, S1/2, V, BRB, M, K, Vat: vouldrions plustost tous troys

13 BNF6, 1545: à

14 BNF1: le cas vostre; 1545: ce cas que vostre

15 1545: Est

16 BL: reproche (spelling modified to maintain rhyme for the eye); BNF4: Et cy apres vous seroit ung reproche

17 BNF3, BNF6, B, S1/2, Vat, 1545: Si n'y mettez; V, BRB, K: Sy ne mettiez; M: Se n'y mettyez

18 BNF6: de bon heure; all others: de bonne heure

19 BNF5: oultre on procede; BRB: Avant que plus oultre on procede

20 K, 1545: que

21 BNF4: vous; V, BRB, K: me

| | |
|---|---|
| 402 | And discreetly brought forth[1] these words:[2] |
| 403 | "If it were not, Sire, that you are much dearer to us |
| 404 | Than our own goods and[3] our own heads,[4] |
| 405 | And that we are more desirous of[5] |
| 406 | The preservation of your honor |
| 407 | Than we are fearful[6] of the rigor of punishment |
| 408 | That was ordered by Parliament,[7] |
| 409 | We would never have taken this[8] bold step |
| 410 | To declare openly to you something that lies heavy against[9] your honor. |
| 411 | But[10] we three would all rather die |
| 412 | Than not undertake to help you in this situation. |
| 413 | Sire, this matter touches upon your majesty |
| 414 | And is so far along that you would be remiss |
| 415 | If you do not rectify it in a timely manner, |
| 416 | Before it proceeds[11] any further. |
| 417 | And what is more, this matter leads us[12] to fear |
| 418 | A great danger touching your very person. |

---

1 BNF4: discreetly pronounced; all others: discreetly began
2 S1 marginal note: "Accusation against the Queen of England, her brother, and four other knights"
3 B: or
4 K, 1545: beasts
5 All others: we are more committed to care for
6 K: Although we are fearful
7 BNF2, BNF5, B: your Parliament; BNF4, V, BRB, K: the great Parliament
8 All others: taken the
9 BNF1–2, BNF4, BNF7, S1/2, V, BRB, K: something that injures
10 All others: Such that
11 BNF5, BRB: Before one proceeds
12 BNF4: you; V, BRB, K: me

| 419 | Celle, à qui tant auez faict[1] d'honneur, Sire,[2] |
|-----|------|
| 420 | Qu'il luy debuoit,[3] par raison,[4] bien suffire, |
| 421 | S'est[5] tellement de[6] son honneur demise |
| 422 | Qu'enuers vous a maincte faulte commise. |
| 423 | C'est à[7] la Royne à qui cecy s'adresse,[8] |
| 424 | Qui tous les iours auec[9] plusieurs ne cesse |
| 425 | Prendre desduictz[10] & volupté lubricque |
| 426 | En la façon d'vne femme publicque: |
| 427 | Car, quand l'vn[11] a achevé sa iournee, |
| 428 | Vn autre[12] apres vient à l'heure[13] assignee, |
| 429 | Et puis vn aultre. Ainsi[14] passe le iour |
| 430 | En ce lascif &[15] infame seiour; |
| 431 | Et quand la nuict à part[16] vous retirez, |
| 432 | Elle a soubdain ses mignons attitrez.[17] |
| 433 | Son frere n'est entre[18] iceulx le dernier. |
| 434 | Norris[19] & Marc ne vous scauroient nier |
| 435 | Qu'ilz n'ayent souuent avec elle[20] passee |
| 436 | Mainte nuict seulx,[21] sans l'auoir pourchassee,[22] |

[14v] appears at line 429.

---

1   BNF2: avez tant faict; V: avez fait tant

2   S1 marginal note: Declaration des crimes proposez contre la Royne et les autres chevaliers par ung chevalier de la court du Roy

3   BNF1, BNF5–7, S1, Vat: Qui luy debvoit; BRB, K: Qu'il luy debvroit; M, 1545: Qui luy debvroit

4   BNF2: pour orayson; B: hand and ink change at this verse

5   BNF2, BNF6–7, 1545: C'est; S2: Ces

6   V: en

7   BNF5, V, BRB, M, K: "à" missing

8   BRB: cecy j'adresse

9   Verses 422–424 are underscored in BL. B: Qui tousjours avecq

10  BNF5: plaisir; BNF6, BRB: deduyt

11  Vat: quand ung

12  BNF4: L'autre

13  B: à heure; S1/2: Ung apres vient tout à l'heure; V, BRB: Un autre vient apres l'heure; M: Un autre vint apres l'heure; K: Un autre prent à propos l'heure (a corrupt reading)

14  BNF2, BNF6: Aussy

15  BNF2: Dans ce lascif et; BNF6, 1545: En son lascif et; V, BRB, M, K: En cela fait son

16  BNF6: apres

17  BNF1–3, B, S1/2, V, BRB, M, 1545: attirez; BNF4–5, Vat: atiltrez

18  V: en

19  BL, BNF5, S1, Vat: Nourriz (emended for accuracy as in BNF1–2); BNF3–4, B: Nourris; BNF6: Naurriz; BNF7, M: Narois; S2: Nourroiz; V: Maurys; BRB: Naurys; K: Nauroy; 1545: Maurus. Hereafter, this name will be given in the text as "Norris," and later variations will not be noted.

20  BNF5: Que souvent n'ayent avec elle

21  BNF1–2: Beaucoup de nuytz; BNF4, S1/2: Maintes nuictees; BNF5, BNF7, B, BRB, M, K, Vat, 1545: Maintes nuictz seuls

22  BNF1–2, BNF4–5, BNF7, B, S1/2, BRB, K, Vat: pourchassé; 1545: prochassée

| | |
|---|---|
| 419 | That woman, on whom you have bestowed so much honor, Sire,[1] |
| 420 | That it ought, by all rights, to satisfy her, |
| 421 | Has so set aside her honor |
| 422 | That she has committed many a fault towards you. |
| 423 | It is the queen about whom I speak, |
| 424 | Who, every day,[2] with several men, does not cease |
| 425 | To take sensual delight and wanton pleasure |
| 426 | In the manner of a street-walker: |
| 427 | For when one man finishes his job |
| 428 | Another comes along at the appointed hour,[3] |
| 429 | And then another. Thus she spends her day |
| 430 | In this[4] lascivious and infamous[5] employment. |
| 431 | And when at night you retire apart from her[6] |
| 432 | She quickly summons[7] her little darlings. |
| 433 | Her brother is not the last among these men. |
| 434 | Norris and Mark cannot deny to you |
| 435 | That they have often spent with her |
| 436 | Many a night alone,[8] without having to pursue her, |

---

[1] S1 marginal note: "Declaration of the crimes proposed against the queen and the other knights by a knight of the king's court"

[2] B: Always

[3] S1/2: One afterwards soon comes along; V, BRB, M: Another comes [M: came] after that hour

[4] BNF6, 1545: her

[5] V, BRB, M, K: In this she makes her infamous

[6] BNF6: retire afterwards

[7] BNF1–3, B, S1/2, V, BRB, M, 1545: invites

[8] All but BNF3, BNF6: Many nights

---

432: Carle uses the word "mignons," which might be translated as "minions," insofar as that was a term used to designate the gentlemen of the privy chamber and would also connote the men who are eager to do the queen's bidding. But the word also carries the connotation of "lovers" and can be used as a term of endearment (e.g., "darling"), though, if so, it is clearly being used derisively here.

434: Henry Norris, the king's Groom of the Stool.

437    Car elle mesme à ce[1] les incitoit,[2]
438    Et par presens et caresse inuitoit.[3]
439    Sire, plusieurs sont comprins en ce nombre[4]
440    Lesquelz, pourtant, pour cest heure[5] ne nombre,[6]
441    Car par le temps vous entendrez[7] les choses
442    Qui de present sont en silence[8] encloses.
443    La plus grand part par Marc au vray[9] scaurez.
444    Et ce pendant, Sire, vous garderez[10]
445    Que mis[11] ne soit à[12] execution                    [15r]
446    Le triste effect[13] de leur intention.
447    Car Norris a à[14] la Royne iuré
448    De l'espouzer, i'en suis bien asseuré."
449    De ce recit[15] nouueau & bien[16] estrange[17]
450    Le roy s'estonne & la couleur luy change,[18]
451    Et demeura en[19] son esprit doubteux[20]

---

[1] Vat: mesme adont

[2] B: invitoit

[3] BNF6: et par presens et largesse excitoit; B: et par presens et caresse incitoit; V, BRB, M, K: et par caresse et presens invitoit; 1545: et par presens et caresse excitoit

[4] V, BRB, K: sont en ce nombre comprins (a corrupt reading that disrupts the rhyme)

[5] BNF4: Lesquelz pourtant à cest heure; BNF5: Desquelz pourtant pour ceste heure; S1/2: Lesquelz partant pour ceste heure

[6] V, BRB, K: Lesquelz pour ceste heure ne nomme; 1545: missing v. 440

[7] BNF1, BNF3, BNF5, BNF7, B, S1/2, V, BRB, M, K, Vat: par le temps descouvrirons; BNF2, BNF4, BNF6, 1545: par le temps descouvriront

[8] BNF1–7, B, S1/2, V: Qui sont encor en grant secret; BRB, M, K, Vat: Qui sont encores en grant secret; 1545: Qui sont encor' en secret

[9] BNF5, S1/2: La plus grand part de Marc au vray; BNF6: La plus grand part par vray de Marc; Vat originally reads "par Marc apres scaurez," but "apres" is crossed out and "au vray" interpolated interlinearly.

[10] V, BRB, K: Et ce pendant faire, vous garderez

[11] V, M: nulz

[12] BNF3: en

[13] S1: triste faict

[14] BL: marginal annotation of cross to left of verse, perhaps to note the awkward hiatus (succession of two vowels); BNF4: Car ilz avoient; V: Car Nauroye a ja; K, Vat, 1545: missing "à"

[15] BNF1–2, B: regne (a corrupt reading); V: ce vent

[16] BNF1–7, B, BRB, M, Vat, 1545: tant; K: nouueau et estrange

[17] S1/2: Verse 449 missing

[18] S1/2 add after v. 450: D'avoir oy ung propos si estrange (the first part of this substituted verse, added to complete the rhyme, repeats v. 452)

[19] BNF4: à

[20] BNF5: Missing v. 451

437    For she herself incited[1] them to this,[2]

438    And, with gifts and welcoming gestures,[3] invited them in.[4]

439    Sire, several men are included in their number,

440    Which, for the moment, however, I will not tally.[5]

441    For, in time, you will hear about things[6]

442    That are, at present, shrouded in silence.[7]

443    Most of this story you will learn, assuredly, from Mark.

444    And, in the meantime, Sire, take care[8]

445    That they don't carry out

446    The sad end[9] that they intend,

447    For Norris has sworn[10] to the queen

448    That he[11] will marry her, I'm quite sure of it."

449    By this unheard of and quite[12] outlandish tale,[13]

450    The king is astounded, and his color changes,[14]

451    And he remained perplexed in spirit

---

1  B: invited

2  Vat: them then

3  BNF6: and generosity

4  BNF6, 1545: excited them; B: incited them

5  V, BRB, K: Which, for the moment, I will not name

6  BNF1, BNF3, BNF5, B, S1/2, V, BRB, M, K, Vat: we shall discover things; BNF2, BNF4, BNF6, 1545: they will discover things

7  1545: That are still covered in secret; all others: That are still covered in great secret

8  BRB, V, K: And while doing this, take care

9  S1: sad deed

10  BNF4: For they have sworn; V: For Norris has already sworn

11  BNF4: that they

12  BNF1–7, B, BRB, M, Vat, 1545: so

13  V: rumor

14  S1/2 are missing v. 449 but add another line after 450 so that the passage reads: "The king is astonished, and his color changes / From having heard such strange talk"

---

438:   The language here echoes that of the indictment against Anne in which it was said that she "did falsely and traitorously procure by base conversations and kisses, touchings, gifts, and other infamous incitation, divers of the King's daily and familiar servants." See LP 10.876. The word translated here as "welcoming gestures" is "caresse," which does not necessarily carry the connotation of physical contact but, rather, implies, as Cotgrave notes, "a cheering, cherishing, welcoming, friendly intertainment [sic]."

440:   The readings of BL and all other texts for verses 439–440 is an example of equivocal rhyme ("nombre" used as a noun and then as a verb). As for this extravagant claim of multiple lovers, Chapuys wrote, in a letter to Granvelle dated 18 May, that "the king has been heard to say that he believes that upwards of 100 gentlemen have had criminal connexion" with Anne. See CSP, Spain, 5, pt. 2, no. 54.

448:   The indictment likewise states that the men "conspired the death and destruction of the King, the Queen often saying she would marry one of them as soon as the King died." See LP 10.876.

452   D'auoir ouy vn propos si[1] honteux.[2]
453   Mais à[3] la fin parlant aux gentilzhommes[4]
454   Leur[5] dit ainsi: "Dieu, à qui subgectz[6] sommes,
455   O mes[7] amys, m'a monstré au besoing
456   Qu'il a de moy[8] & de mon honneur soing,
457   Puis qu'[9] a voulu à ce vous[10] inspirer,
458   Que voulussiez[11] ces cas[12] me declairer.
459   En ce m'auez faict seruice aggreable.
460   Mais s'il aduient que[13] ne soit veritable
461   Vostre rapport, ce que croire ne veux,                    [15v]
462   Peine de mort vous aurez[14] en[15] lieu d'eux."
463   Ainsi le Roy, peu à peu, donnoit[16] foy
464   À ses[17] seigneurs, sans regarder la loy
465   Aux mesdisans de la[18] Royne ordonnee,
466   Qui ne se sent tant estre[19] infortunee[20]
467   Que descouuert soit au Roy[21] le mistere
468   De[22] tout le cours de son grand vitupere.
469   Mais comme si elle eust[23] le vent à grey,

---

1   V, BRB, M, K: tant
2   BNF5 adds after 452, to complete its rhyme: "Parquoy de honte il se cacha les yeulx"; B: Missing
    v. 452 (Marginal note: faute d'ung vers)
3   V: en
4   S1/2: Dont se clamoit chetif sur tous les hommes
5   B: Leur a; S1/2: Lors; 1545: Leurs
6   BRB: Dieu qui subject
7   BNF6: Et mes; V: Quy es (a corrupt reading)
8   V: Quy de moy
9   V: Puisqu'il
10  B: voulu en ce vous; S1/2: voulu votre cueur; Vat originally read "voulu adont vous," which is
    crossed out and replaced with "voulu à ce vous."
11  BNF1, BNF3, BNF5–6, S1, V, BRB, M: voulsissiez; BNF4: Que vous eussiez; B: vausisiez
12  BNF1, BNF3–6, B, K, 1545: ce cas; BNF7: ces faiz
13  BNF1–2, BNF5, S1/2, V, BRB, M, K, 1545: qu'il
14  All others: mort recevrez
15  BNF1–7, S1/2, BRB, K, Vat, 1545: au
16  BNF6–7, V, 1545: donna
17  BNF1, BNF4–5, B, BRB, M: ces
18  BNF7: "la" missing
19  BNF7, 1545: Qui ne se sceut tant estoit; V: Qui ne sceut estre tant; BRB, K: Qui ne se sent estre
    tant
20  BNF4: fortunee
21  BNF4: descouvert fut au Roy; BNF5: descouvert au Roy feust
22  BRB: Et
23  S1/2: s'elle eut eu

| | |
|---|---|
| 452 | From having heard such shameful talk.[1] |
| 453 | But in the end, speaking to these gentlemen, |
| 454 | He says to them:[2] "God, to whom we are subject |
| 455 | (O my friends!), has shown me, in my hour of need, |
| 456 | That He takes care of me and my honor, |
| 457 | Since He wished to inspire you[3] in this matter, |
| 458 | So that you should want to speak openly to me of these events.[4] |
| 459 | In this you have done me a fine service. |
| 460 | But, if it should happen that your report |
| 461 | Isn't true, which I wouldn't want to believe to be the case, |
| 462 | You, instead of them, shall suffer pain of death."[5] |
| 463 | And so the king, little by little, began to trust |
| 464 | His[6] gentlemen, without regard for the law |
| 465 | That was ordained for slanderers of the queen, |
| 466 | Who doesn't realize[7] just how unfortunate she was |
| 467 | In that the king had been made aware of the secret |
| 468 | Of[8] the whole range of her shameful conduct. |
| 469 | But, as if she held the wind at her pleasure, |

---

[1] BNF5 is missing v. 451 but adds another line after 452 so that the passage reads: "The king is astonished, and his color changes / From having heard such shameful talk / For which reason he hid his eyes in shame"; B marginal note: "Missing verse"

[2] S1/2: the sentence in 452 continues into vv. 453–454, which read: "For which he declared himself to be the most miserable of all men. / Then he said this"

[3] S1/2: inspire your heart

[4] BNF1, BNF3–6, B, K, 1545: of this matter; BNF7: of these deeds

[5] All others: shall receive the death penalty

[6] BNF1, BNF4, BNF5, B, BRB, M: These

[7] BNF7, V, 1545: didn't know

[8] BRB: And

---

450: Carle describes Henry's reaction in much the same way King Arthur was said to have reacted upon being told of Queen Guinevere's adultery with Lancelot, as recounted in *La Mort le roi Artu*, 109.

456: Chapuys uses similar wording in his congratulatory letter to Henry of June 1536, noting that "God has shown special care for Henry" in allowing the allegations to come to light. See LP 10.1071.

| 470 | Estoit sur[1] iour en vn verdoyant[2] prey, |
|---|---|
| 471 | Ou beau iardin, ou[3] parc, prenant esbat,[4] |
| 472 | À veoir des chiens & bestes[5] le combat,[6] |
| 473 | Le soir plaisir aux[7] melodyes grandes |
| 474 | Des instrumens sonnans[8] en[9] plusieurs bendes. |
| 475 | Le Roy aussi luy faisoit[10] traictement |
| 476 | Comme s'il n'eust eu malcontentement,[11] |
| 477 | Et luy monstroit d'vne façon entiere |
| 478 | Plus que iamais bonne & priuee[12] chere. |
| 479 | Et ce pendant Marc estoit en prison,[13] |
| 480 | Que l'on faisoit desia rendre[14] raison |
| 481 | Du cas estant contre luy imposé, |
| 482 | Et[15] sans tourment, d'vn sens bien reposé,[16] |
| 483 | Dit que d'amour la Royne a[17] poursuyuie, |
| 484 | Et que trois fois[18] à couuert l'a seruie.[19] |
| 485 | On prend[20] ce[21] dit & deposition |

[16r]

---

1   BNF4: ung; BNF5, V, BRB, K: ce
2   B: en verdoiant
3   BNF1, BNF6, V, K: Au beau jardin ou parc; BNF2, BRB: Au beau jardin au parc; S1/2: Ou ès jardins ou parcs; Vat: Ou beau jardin au parc
4   BNF4: jardin, où prenoit ses esbats
5   BNF1: des bestes ou des chiens; 1545: De veoir de chiens et bestes
6   BNF4: les combats
7   BNF1, BNF3, BNF5–7, B, S1/2, V, M, Vat, 1545: Le soir le bal et; BNF2, BNF4: Le soir l'esbat et; BRB, K: Le son, le bal et
8   S1: Les instruments sonnoient; S2: Des instruments sonnoient
9   BNF7: et
10  BNF1, BNF3: faisant
11  BNF5: Comme si d'elle n'eust esté mescontent; BRB, K: Comme si n'eust eu mescontentement; 1545: Comme s'il n'eust nul mescontentement; all others: Comme s'il n'eust eu mescontentement
12  BNF2: jamais a bonne et privee; S1/2: jamais bonne et plaisante; 1545: jamais, et avec privee
13  BL marginal notation of cross. S1 marginal note: Marc emprisonné
14  BNF4: À quy desja rendre on faisoit; S1: À quy on feit bien tost rendre; S2: À quy on feit rendre bien tost; V, BRB, K: À quy l'on faisoit desia rendre; 1545: Que l'on faisoit ja rendre
15  BNF4: Qui
16  BNF5: advisé; S1/2: disposé; V: Verse 482 missing
17  B: d'honeur la Royne a poursuivie; BRB: d'amours la Royne l'a poursuivie; 1545: d'amours a la Royne poursuyuie
18  S1/2: qu'autreffoys
19  V: a couvert sa chaire vive; BRB: à couvert sa servie (an error in transcription); 1545: au couvert l'escripue (a corrupt reading)
20  V, BRB, K: L'on prend; 1545: On peut (an error in transcription)
21  BNF4: son; BNF7: le

470    She would go out in the morning to[1] a verdant field
471    Or beautiful garden, or park, taking[2] delight
472    In watching dogs and[3] other beasts fight,
473    And in the evening taking pleasure in the great melodies[4]
474    Of instruments playing[5] in[6] several bands.
475    The king, too, treated her
476    As if he had no displeasure[7]
477    And showed her, by his whole manner,
478    Friendly good cheer,[8] more than ever before.
479    And meanwhile, Mark was in prison:[9]
480    They were already[10] making him account for
481    The charges imposed against him,
482    And, without duress, and with a sense of great calm,[11]
483    He says that[12] he pursued the queen in love
484    And that three times[13] he serviced her in secret.[14]
485    They take this[15] statement and deposition,

---

1  BNF4: She was one day in; BNF5, V, BRB, K: She was that day in
2  BNF1, BNF6, V, K: In a beautiful garden or park, taking; BNF2, BRB: In a beautiful garden in the park, taking; BNF4: Or a beautiful garden, where she took; S1/2: Or to gardens or parks, taking; Vat: Or a beautiful garden in the park, taking
3  BNF1: or
4  BNF1, BNF3, BNF5–7, B, S1/2, V, M, Vat, 1545: In the evening enjoying dance and great melodies; BNF2, BNF4: In the evening, enjoying sport and great melodies; BRB, K: Enjoying the sound, dance, and great melodies
5  S1/2 end this sentence at v. 473 with v. 474 reading: Instruments played
6  BNF7: and
7  BNF5: As if he had not been displeased with her
8  S1/2: Good and pleasant cheer; 1545: And with friendly cheer
9  BL marks this verse with a marginal cross; S1 marginal note: "Mark imprisoned"
10  S1/2: soon
11  BNF5: and in a greatly circumspect manner; S1/2: and in a well-ordered manner
12  BNF4: Verses 482–483 read: Who, without torment and with a sense of great calm / Says that
13  S1/2: that previously
14  V: three times he covered her living flesh
15  BNF4: his; BNF7: the

---

472:   Agnes Strickland relates (without citing a source) that Anne "would sit for hours in the quadrangle court of Greenwich palace ... seeking a joyless pastime in playing with her little dogs, and setting them to fight with each other." She appears to be basing this on Carle, embellishing it with further details not present in the French text. See *Lives of the Queens of England*, 664.
479:   It is thought that Mark Smeaton was arrested on 30 April.
482:   "Tourment" could also mean "torture," but the context here, which refers to Mark's manner of responding, suggests "torment" or "duress." Clearly, however, in saying that Mark responded calmly, the author is also implying that no torture was involved.

486    Pour faire foy de[1] l'accusation
487    Enuers le Roy, qui alors[2] creut le faict,
488    Et du rapport demeura satisfaict,
489    Mais[3] de cccy[4] ne faict aulcun semblant,
490    Ains[5] s'esiouist, tous plaisirs assemblant.[6]
491    Et mesmement, le premier iour de May,[7]
492    À Grenuy[8] fit[9] dresser vn beau Tournoy,[10]
493    Auquel[11] plusieurs se misrent à[12] deuoir                [16v]
494    De bien combattre &[13] honneur receuoir,
495    Entre lesquelz millord[14] de Rochefort,[15]
496    Frere à la Royne, employa son effort
497    De rompre lance, & faire grand prouesse,[16]
498    Et bien volter[17] son cheual par addresse.[18]
499    Norris aussi, du Roy le mieux aymé,
500    Se presentoit[19] sur les rengs[20] bien armé.
501    Mais son cheual, qui tant[21] estoit propice
502    Pour les tournoys, reffuza lors la lice,
503    Et reculloit, comme s'il eust congneu[22]
504    Le grand malheur à son maistre aduenu.
505    Et qui soulloit estre braue & bien fier[23]

---

1  BNF1–3, V, BRB, K: à
2  V: lors
3  BL, BNF3-6, S1/2, Vat: Qui (emended for clarity); B: Verse 489 missing
4  1545: ce
5  BL and all but BNF1–2, BNF7, V, BRB, M, K: Mais (emended for syntax and clarity)
6  BNF4: s'esiouist à tout plaisir semblant
7  S1 marginal note: Tournoy fait à Gremys
8  BNF1, S1/2: Gremyes; BNF2, B: Grenuitz; BNF3: Greniuys; BNF4: Guynes; BNF5, BRB, M,
   K: Grenuys; BNF6: Grenuis; BNF7: Grenis; V: En Grennys; Vat: Grenny; 1545: Gremie
9  Vat: faict
10 BL and all others but BNF1, BNF4-5, S1/2: un tournoy (emended for versification)
11 BNF1: Ouquel; M, 1545: Ausquelz
12 BNF1-6, B, S1/2, V, BRB, K, M, Vat: en; BNF7: misent en; 1545: au
13 Vat: pour
14 1545: Meilhort
15 BL: Marginal notation of two crosses; B: Marginal note: M. de Rochefort
16 BNF4: lances et faire grandz prouesses; BNF5, BRB, M, K: lances et faire grand prouesse; V:
   lances et faire prouesse
17 B: De bien volter; S1/2: De voltiger; 1545: Et bien voller
18 BNF4: adresses
19 V, BRB, M, K, Vat: presenta
20 BNF7, BRB, 1545: rains
21 1545: mieux
22 BNF7: hand changes here
23 BNF1, BNF5, BNF7, B, V, BRB, M, K, 1545: brave et fier; BNF2-3, BNF6, Vat: tant brave et
   fier; BNF4: sy brave et fier; S1/2: gay, brave et fier

| | |
|---|---|
| 486 | In order to substantiate the accusation, |
| 487 | To the king, who then believed the allegation |
| 488 | And remained satisfied with the report, |
| 489 | But he[1] makes no semblance of this; |
| 490 | Rather,[2] he enjoyed himself, convening all manner of pastimes. |
| 491 | And, specifically, on the first day of May[3] |
| 492 | He set up[4] a fine tournament[5] at Greenwich, |
| 493 | At which several men committed themselves |
| 494 | To fighting well and to gaining[6] honor, |
| 495 | Among whom was Lord Rochford,[7] |
| 496 | The queen's brother, who endeavored |
| 497 | To shatter lances in the joust and to show great prowess,[8] |
| 498 | And skillfully make his horse turn about.[9] |
| 499 | So, too, did Norris, most beloved of the king, |
| 500 | Present himself well armed at the tiltyard. |
| 501 | But his horse, which was so suitable[10] |
| 502 | For tournaments, refused to take to the list then |
| 503 | And recoiled, as if he knew |
| 504 | The great misfortune that had come upon his master. |
| 505 | And he who was customarily brave and quite proud[11] |

---

1  BL and all but BNF1–2, BNF7, V, BRB, M, K: Who
2  BL and all but BNF1–2, BNF7, V, BRB, M, K: But
3  S1 marginal note: "Tournament established at Greenwich"
4  Vat: sets up
5  BL and all others but BNF1, BNF4–5, S1/2 read: a tournament
6  Vat: fighting well in order to gain
7  BL: marginal notation of two crosses; B marginal note: "M. Rochford"
8  V: show prowess
9  1545: horse run swiftly
10  1545: was best suited
11  BNF1, BNF5, BNF7, B, V, BRB, M, K, 1545: brave and proud; BNF2–4, BNF6, Vat: so brave and proud; S1/2: gay, brave, and proud

---

504:  Carle is the only source for this incident. However, Wriothesley (*Chronicle*, 1:22) notes a similar disinclination of certain horses to enter the jousts held in celebration of Anne's coronation: "some of their horses would not come at their pleasure near the tilt, which was great displeasure to some of them that ran."

| 506 | Ne se vouloit[1] alors glorifier. | |
|---|---|---|
| 507 | Le Roy, estant en[2] ce tournoy present, | |
| 508 | Voyant cecy, à Norris fist[3] present | |
| 509 | De son cheual, lequel, pourtant, sçauoit | [17r] |
| 510 | Que le garder longuement ne pouuoit.[4] | |
| 511 | Si[5] toutesfois fist tant[6] d'armes qu'il[7] eust | |
| 512 | Autant d'honneur que nul autre qui fust.[8] | |
| 513 | Maistre[9] Waston,[10] Bruton[11] pareillement: | |
| 514 | Le Roy à[12] tous se iouoyt priuement,[13] | |
| 515 | Et leur faisoit meinte caresse humaine, | |
| 516 | Dissimulant leur[14] ruyne prochaine. | |
| 517 | La Royne[15] estoit en hault lieu, qui voyoit[16] | |
| 518 | Les combatans, & souuent enuoyoit | |
| 519 | Ses doux regards[17] pour accroistre le cœur[18] | |
| 520 | À[19] chacun d'eux de[20] demourer vainqueur,[21] | |
| 521 | Dont nul n'estoit[22] qui[23] n'eust bien entrepris, | |
| 522 | Par grand honneur, d'en emporter[24] le pris. | |

[1] BNF5, B, 1545: voulut
[2] BNF4–6, Vat, 1545: à
[3] BNF1, BNF3: faict
[4] B, 1545: pourroit
[5] All others: Qui
[6] K: missing "tant"
[7] BNF6, V: quy
[8] B: qu'il fust; S1/2: que feust
[9] S1/2: Puys; 1545: Mais
[10] BL: Caton (probably a misreading of the graphically similar "Oaston," a French approximation of the name "Weston." The spelling "Oaston" appears in BNF3, BNF6, S1/2, and Vat. The name will henceforth be rendered as "Waston" (which is as it appears in BNF1–2, BNF5, BNF7, B, V, BRB, M, and K) since that is the closest form to the actual English name. BNF4: Vaston; 1545: Gaston
[11] BL: Marginal notation of cross. BNF3, S1/2: Breton.
[12] 1545: sur
[13] S1/2: doulcement; 1545: premierement
[14] B: la
[15] BL: Le Roy (a scribal error); all others as emended
[16] BNF2: qui en hault lieu voyoit; BNF3, BNF7, B, S1/2, V, BRB, K, 1545: qui veoit
[17] BNF5: Les doux regards; BNF7: Ses doux regretz (a scribal error)
[18] BNF4, BNF7: leurs cueurs; BNF5, B, Vat: les cueurs
[19] BNF1: De; BNF5: À ung
[20] BNF3, BNF6: et; BNF4–5, V, BRB, K, 1545: pour
[21] BNF5: vaincueurs
[22] BNF1–2, BRB, Vat, 1545: estoit
[23] S1, K: qu'il
[24] BNF5: honneur en emporter; V: honneur d'emporter

506 Had no wish, then, to seek glory for himself.

507 The king, who was present at this tournament,

508 Upon seeing this, made[1] a gift to Norris

509 Of his own horse; however, he knew

510 That Norris wouldn't be able to keep it for long.

511 Yet, Norris, nonetheless,[2] performed so many feats of arms

512 That he garnered more honor than anyone else.

513 Master[3] Weston and Brereton, similarly:

514 The king delighted in them all, in an amicable fashion,[4]

515 And made many kind and welcoming gestures towards them,

516 Dissembling their coming ruin.

517 The queen[5] sat up high and watched[6]

518 The combatants and often directed

519 Her sweet glances towards each of them,

520 To encourage them to be the victor;

521 Among these there was not a one who did not fully undertake,

522 As a matter of great honor, to come away with the prize.

---

[1] BNF1, BNF3: makes

[2] All others: He nonetheless

[3] S1/2: Then

[4] S1/2: delighted in them all, tenderly

[5] BL: The king (a scribal error)

[6] BNF3, BNF7, B, S1/2, V, BRB, K, 1545: watches

---

513: The poet consistently refers to Sir Francis Weston alone with the honorific "Maistre"; Weston was indeed the only one of the accused men to have earned the title "Sir," having been made a Knight of the Bath in 1533 at Anne's coronation. William Brereton (sometimes spelled "Bruton"), a senior courtier, was married to the sister of the Earl of Worcester.

515: Once again, the word is "caresses," without physical connotation. See the note to v. 438, above.

| 523 | Mais ne scauoient,[1] les[2] paouures fortunez, |
|---|---|
| 524 | L'extremité où[3] estoient destinez:[4] |
| 525 | Car tost aprez qu'ilz[5] furent departiz[6]        [17v] |
| 526 | De ce tournoy, archers sont[7] aduertiz |
| 527 | De prendre au corps premierement Norris, |
| 528 | Dont furent tous esbahis & marriz, |
| 529 | Veu sa vertu & grande[8] priuaulté, |
| 530 | Ne pouantz croire en luy desloyauté.[9] |
| 531 | Le Roy voulut plustost à luy[10] parler |
| 532 | Qu'il[11] ne le fist à la[12] prison aller, |
| 533 | Et[13] par doulceur grande luy vint[14] offrir |
| 534 | Que mort ne mal[15] ne luy[16] feroit souffrir, |
| 535 | Et le lerroit pourueu[17] de ses estatz, |
| 536 | Combien qu'il[18] fust coulpable de ce cas,[19] |
| 537 | S'il luy vouloit dire[20] la verité: |
| 538 | Ou, aultrement, tant seroit[21] irrité |
| 539 | Qu'il[22] le feroit mourir de mort cruelle, |
| 540 | Si contre droict[23] soustenoit sa querelle. |

---

[1] BNF6: ne sachantz; 1545: non sçachans

[2] BL: le (emended for grammar, to reflect a later reader's correction and as in all others)

[3] BNF5: L'extremité dont; V, BRB, K: De l'extremité où

[4] BNF5, 1545: fortunez

[5] BNF3, BNF6–7, B, V, BRB, M: que; K, 1545: qu'il

[6] S1: Marginal note: Emprisonnement de Norriz

[7] BNF2, B: furent

[8] BNF1, BNF3–4, BNF6, B, V, BRB, M, Vat: et la grant; BNF2, S1/2, K, 1545: et sa grant

[9] BNF1, BNF3, BNF5–7, B, V, BRB, M, K, Vat: Du roy, qu'il eust commis desloyaulté; BNF2: Du roy, qu'il eust commis la desloyauté; BNF4: Au roy, qu'il eust commis desloyauté; S1/2: Qu'avoit au Roy et sans desloyauté; 1545: Du roy, qu'il eust comme desloyauté

[10] BNF1: Le Roy voullant plus tost à luy; BNF2: voulut à luy plustost; V: Le voulut premier à luy ("roy" missing); BRB, V: Le Roy voulut premier à luy

[11] BNF1: Que; BNF2, BNF5, M: Qui

[12] BNF5, S1/2, V, BRB, M, Vat: en la; 1545: en sa

[13] V, BRB, K: Où

[14] BNF3, BNF6: fit; 1545: veult

[15] BNF6: Que mal ni mort

[16] BNF4: le; K: Verse 534 missing

[17] BNF4: Et le laissoit pourvu; V: Et ne laiyroit pourvu; BRB: Et ne l'auroit despourvu; K: Et ne laisseroit pourvu

[18] B: Combien que; M: Combien qui

[19] 1545: des cas

[20] BRB, M, 1545: Sy luy vouloit dire; K: Sy vouloit dire

[21] V: seroit tant

[22] BNF2, M: Qui; V, K: Que

[23] Vat: Dieu

| 523 | But these poor, unfortunate men did not know |
| 524 | The violent end to which they were destined. |
| 525 | For soon after they left[1] |
| 526 | This tournament, the archers were advised |
| 527 | To arrest Norris first, |
| 528 | Which astonished and aggrieved everyone, |
| 529 | Given his integrity and great intimacy with the king, |
| 530 | For they could not fathom any treachery in him.[2] |
| 531 | The king preferred to speak to him[3] |
| 532 | Rather than send him to prison,[4] |
| 533 | And,[5] with great gentleness, he came[6] to propose |
| 534 | That he would not make him suffer death or any harm |
| 535 | And would let him keep[7] his estates, |
| 536 | No matter how guilty he might be in this matter, |
| 537 | If he should wish to tell him the truth;[8] |
| 538 | Otherwise, he would be so angry |
| 539 | That he would make him die a cruel death |
| 540 | If he wrongly[9] maintained his claim of innocence. |

---

[1] S1 marginal note reads: "Norris's imprisonment"

[2] S1/2: intimacy / With the king and [being] without disloyalty; all others [but 1545, which is corrupt]: intimacy / With the king that he would have committed some treachery. BL does not include the words "with the king," but I have provided them here, on the model of the other variants, for the sake of clarity.

[3] B, BRB, K: The king wanted to speak to him first

[4] 1545: to his prison

[5] V, BRB, K: Where

[6] BNF3, BNF6: he arranged; 1545: he wanted

[7] V, K: And would not leave him provided with (a corrupt reading); BRB: would not deprive him of

[8] K: If he wished to tell the truth

[9] Vat: If against God he

---

526: This is a reference to the Yeomen of the King's Guard, a troop of archers, established by Henry VII, who acted as bodyguards to the king.

537: See Constantyne's *Memorial*, 64: "And after jousting the King rode suddenly to Westminster, and all the way as I heard say, had Mr. Norris in examination and promised him his pardon in case he would utter the truth."

541   Et luy monstra[1] qu'il estoit accusé                    [18r]
542   D'auoir souuent auec la Royne vsé
543   De ses plaisirs, & que par plusieurs[2] nuictz
544   Auecques elle auoit prins ses desduictz,[3]
545   À quoy[4] respond Norris[5] qu'on n'ozeroit[6]
546   Luy[7] meintenir, & que preuue feroit
547   De sa personne, en tous lieux, au[8] contraire,
548   Et si le Roy luy deuoit faire traire[9]
549   Le cœur du corps, & l'ouurir[10] tout viuant,
550   Qu'il ne diroit[11] ce dont n'estoit[12] scauant.
551   Ainsi fut pris & serré dans[13] la tour,
552   Dont peu de gens espoirent[14] bon[15] retour:
553   Car c'est[16] le[17] lieu le plus espouuentable
554   De ce pais, & le plus redoubtable.
555   La Royne apres, par[18] le duc de Norfort,[19]
556   Le[20] iour suyuant,[21] fut conduicte en ce fort,
557   Et là[22] luy fut la cause[23] racomptee                  [18v]
558   Pourquoy estoit en la tour arrestee.

---

[1]  S1/2: Luy demonstrant; V: luy monstroit
[2]  BNF5: maintes
[3]  BNF1: Avecques elle il avoit ses desduictz; BNF2: Avecques elle avoit prins ses plaisirs (with "plaisirs" crossed out and replaced by "desduitz"); BNF4: Avecques elle avoit eu ses desduictz; BNF5, M: Avec elle avoit pris ses desduictz; B: Avecqu' icelle avoit prins ses desduictz; V, BRB, K: Avoit prins avec elle ses deduictz; 1545: Avec elle avoir prins ses desduictz
[4]  B: Adoncq; BRB: Ainsy
[5]  BNF5: Norris respond; V: respondit Norris
[6]  BL: Marginal notation of two crosses; S1 marginal note: Defence de Norriz, chevalier
[7]  BNF7: Le
[8]  BNF4: De sa personne apparoir du; all others: De sa personne en tous lieux du
[9]  V, K: luy voullait faire traire; BRB: luy voulut faire traire; 1545: le debvoit faire taire (a corrupt reading)
[10]  BNF7: et couvrir (a corrupt reading)
[11]  BNF4: Il ne diroit; S2, 1545: Qu'il ne disoit; M: Qui ne diroit
[12]  BNF6, V: ce dont il n'estoit; B: ce de quoy n'estoit
[13]  BRB, K: dedans
[14]  1545: esperoient
[15]  BNF2: le
[16]  BNF2: est
[17]  BRB: "le" missing
[18]  BNF2: "par" missing
[19]  BL: Marginal notation of two crosses. BNF2: Noffort; B: Northfort; 1545: Nerfort; S1 marginal note reads: "L'emprisonnement de la Royne d'Angleterre"
[20]  BNF2: Ce
[21]  B: apres
[22]  BNF1-2, V, K: Parquoy; M: Parquilz; all others: Par quy
[23]  Vat: chose (a corrupt reading)

541   And he showed[1] him that he was accused
542   Of having often partaken of the queen's
543   Pleasures and that on several[2] nights
544   He had taken sensual delight with her,
545   To which[3] Norris responds that one would not dare[4]
546   Maintain that of him, and that he would give evidence
547   To prove the contrary on all accounts, with every fiber of his being,
548   And even if the king were to have his heart drawn out
549   From his body, opening it up while he was still alive,
550   He would still never say what he knew nothing about.
551   And so he was taken and locked in the Tower
552   From which few people expect to return safely,
553   For it is the most frightful place
554   In this country, and the most dreadful.
555   Afterwards, the queen was conducted, by the Duke of Norfolk,[5]
556   To this fortress the following day,
557   And there[6] she was informed of the reason
558   Why she was under arrest in the Tower.

---

[1]   S1/2: Demonstrating to
[2]   BNF5: many
[3]   B: Then; BRB: Thus
[4]   BL: marginal annotation of two crosses; S1 marginal note: "Defense of Norris, knight"
[5]   BL: marginal notation of two crosses; S1 marginal note: "The imprisonment of the Queen of England"
[6]   BNF1–2, V, K: For which; all others but M, which is corrupt: By whom

---

547:   Literally, "with his person." Norris seems to be proposing to settle the matter by means of a judicial combat, in which the victor, providentially, is deemed to be the party in the right.
551:   The Tower of London functioned as both castle and prison.
556:   Wriothesley notes (*Chronicle*, 1:36) that Anne was arrested on 2 May, the same day as Norris and Rochford (not the following day, as Carle claims): "the second day of May, Mr. Norris and my Lord of Rochford were brought to the Tower of London as prisoners and the same day, about five of the clock at night, the Queen Anne Bolleine was brought to the Tower of London by my Lord Chancellor [Thomas Audley], the Duke of Norfolk, Mr. Secretary [Thomas Cromwell], and Sir William Kingston, Constable of the Tower." Carle believes that Norris was arrested immediately after his questioning by the king at the May Day jousts.

| 559 | Son frere aussi, ce iour mesme, y fut[1] mis, |
| 560 | Qui n'estoit lors[2] sans plusieurs ennemys, |
| 561 | Disans que bien il auoit merité |
| 562 | De se[3] trouuer en ceste extremité. |
| 563 | Maistre Waston[4] & Bruton le[5] suyuirent, |
| 564 | Paige et Oyet[6] ce mesme chemin feirent: |
| 565 | Vous eussiez dit que par deuotion |
| 566 | On les menoit à[7] la procession. |
| 567 | Soubdain le bruict s'espart par[8] la cité,[9] |
| 568 | Qui s'esiouit de[10] la diuersité,[11] |
| 569 | Esperant que maintenant[12] iouyroit[13] |
| 570 | De[14] sa[15] Princesse, & que mise seroit |
| 571 | En son estat, dont elle fut cassee[16] |
| 572 | Par le moyen de ceste ores leissee. |
| 573 | La ville estoit attendant sa[17] venue,                [19r] |
| 574 | De grand plaisir & ioye[18] toute esmeue,[19] |
| 575 | Et n'eussiez[20] veu iusqu'aux[21] petitz enfans, |
| 576 | Que tous chantans & d'aize[22] triumphans. |

---

1 BL, BNF2: ce jour mesme fut mis (emended for clarity); 1545: ce jour y fut mys; all others as emended

2 BRB: "lors" missing

3 B: soy

4 S1/2: Sire Oaston

5 BNF1, S1: là

6 BNF1: Page, Vyot; BNF2: Paige et Wyort; BNF3: Page et Oyet; BNF4: Paige et Vallot; BNF5: Pages aussi; BNF6, S1/2: Paige et Vyot; BNF7: Page, Wyot; B: Paige et Oyot; V, BRB, M, K: Consequamment; Vat: Page et Oyot; 1545: Parge, et Oy, et

7 BNF6: originally "en," corrected to "à"; 1545: en

8 BNF1–2, BNF6, B: s'estend par; BNF3–4, BNF7, S1/2, Vat, M: s'espend par; BNF5: s'estend dans; V, BRB: s'espandit par; K: s'espandoit par; 1545: s'espend en

9 S1 marginal note: Commotion de peuple

10 V: Quy s'estoit de

11 BNF3: par la diversité; BNF5: de ceste adversité; BNF6: pour l'aduersité

12 BNF4–5: En esperant que bientost

13 V, BRB, K: verroit

14 V, K, BRB: "De" missing

15 BRB, 1545: la

16 BNF3–4, BNF6: fust chassee; BRB: estoit cassee; 1545: estoit chassee

17 M: la

18 B: et de joye

19 Verses 573–574 do not technically rhyme but are, rather, an example of assonance, sharing vowel sounds but not a common consonant.

20 BNF4: l'eussiez

21 BNF4–7, B, S1/2, V, BRB, M, K, 1545: jusques aux

22 BNF4: Qui tous chantoient et dansoient; B: Que sautant et en danses; S1/2: À bien chanter et d'ayse; 1545: Que tous chantans et danse

| 559 | Her brother, too, was taken there this same day, |
| 560 | He who, at that time, was not without several enemies, |
| 561 | All saying that he richly deserved |
| 562 | To find himself in these dire straits. |
| 563 | Master Weston and Brereton followed him;[1] |
| 564 | Page and Wyatt took[2] this same road: |
| 565 | You might have said that |
| 566 | They were led solemnly in a religious procession. |
| 567 | Suddenly a clamor breaks out through[3] the city,[4] |
| 568 | Which rejoiced in this turn of events,[5] |
| 569 | Hoping that now[6] they would enjoy[7] |
| 570 | Their princess and that she would be returned |
| 571 | To the condition of which she was deprived[8] |
| 572 | By means of that woman who is now forsaken. |
| 573 | The town was awaiting her arrival, |
| 574 | Quite moved by great pleasure and joy, |
| 575 | And you would have seen everyone, including small children, |
| 576 | Singing in triumphant delight.[9] |

---

[1] BNF1, S1: followed there

[2] BNF5: Pages also took; V, BRB, M, K: Consequently they took

[3] BNF1–2, BNF6, B: spreads throughout; BNF5: spreads in; V, BRB, K: broke out through; 1545: breaks out in

[4] S1 marginal note: Uproar among the people

[5] BNF5–6: this adversity

[6] BNF4–5: soon

[7] V, BRB, K: would see

[8] BNF3–4, BNF6, 1545: from which she was expelled

[9] BNF4, 1545: All singing and dancing in triumph; B: Jumping and dancing in triumph; S1/2: Greatly singing and in triumphant delight

---

559: See Wriothesley's *Chronicle*, 1:36, quoted above.

564: Richard Page was a member of the king's privy chamber. Thomas Wyatt, the poet, was thought to be a former suitor of Anne's. Neither of these two men was brought to trial.

576: Chapuys wrote on 19 May: "I cannot well describe the great joy the inhabitants of this city have lately experienced and manifested, not only at the fall and ruin of the concubine, but at the hope that the Princess will be soon reinstated in her rights." See CSP, Spain, 5, pt. 2, no. 55; and LP 10.908.

577   Et n'y a cœur si triste qui ne[1] rye
578   En attendant la princesse Marie,[2]
579   Qui,[3] toutesfois, encores[4] ne bougea
580   De son logis, & point ne se[5] vangea,
581   Blasmant la Royne en aulcune maniere,
582   Quand entendit[6] qu'elle estoit prisonniere.
583   Ains dit alors,[7] par humaine pitié:[8]
584   "Or pleust à Dieu que si grande[9] amitié
585   Elle eust porté[10] au Roy qu'elle[11] n'eust point
586   Mis son honneur & sa vie en ce poinct.
587   Mais puis qu'elle est[12] en ce triste accident,
588   Ie prie mon[13] Dieu qu'il luy vueille estre[14] aydant,
589   Et si[15] sa fille est au Roy, ie prometz                    [19v]
590   Qu'en[16] mon pouuoir ne luy fauldray[17] iamais."
591   Ainsi le cueur de ceste bonne Dame
592   Ne s'esiouyt d'ouyr le[18] grand diffame
593   De celle qui plus qu'aultre[19] luy nuysoit.

---

[1]  B, S1/2: qu'il ne
[2]  BL marginal note: Marie
[3]  BNF5, 1545: Et
[4]  BNF2, Vat: encor
[5]  BNF1, BNF3: s'en
[6]  S2: actendit
[7]  BNF5, 1545: alors dict
[8]  S1 marginal note: Vertu admirable en la fille du Roy d'Angleterre
[9]  M: grant
[10] 1545: portée
[11] 1545: qui
[12] BNF4: Mais elle estant
[13] BNF5, V, M, 1545: à
[14] BNF1; Vat: que luy soit; BNF2–6, S1/2, V, BRB, K, 1545: qu'il luy soit; B: que luy soict pour;
      M: qui luy soit
[15] K: missing "si"
[16] BNF1, BNF3–6, B, S1, Vat, 1545: Qu'à
[17] M: fauldra
[18] BNF5: Ne s'esiouist d'ouyr ce; B: Ne s'esjoit de celle; Vat: Ne s'esiouist de veoir le
[19] BNF5, K: plus qu'aultruy; S1/2: D'Anne Boullant qui par trop

577      And there was not a heart so sad that it didn't laugh
578      While awaiting the Princess Mary,[1]
579      Who, nevertheless,[2] still did not move
580      From her lodging and did not avenge herself in the least,
581      Not blaming the queen in any manner,
582      When she heard that she was a prisoner.
583      Rather, she said then with kindly pity,[3]
584      "May it have pleased God that she had borne
585      The king so great a love that she would not have
586      Put her honor and her life at risk in the slightest.
587      But since she is in this sad circumstance,
588      I pray to my God that He should wish to help her,[4]
589      And, since her daughter is the king's, I promise
590      That, to the best of my ability, she should never want for anything."
591      Thus the heart of this good Lady
592      Does not rejoice in hearing of[5] the great disgrace
593      Of that woman who, more than any other, harmed her.[6]

---

[1]   BL marginal note: "Mary"
[2]   BNF5, 1545: And nevertheless she
[3]   S1 marginal note: "Admirable virtue of the daughter of the King of England"
[4]   All others: should help her
[5]   Vat: in seeing
[6]   S1/2: Of Anne Boleyn, who greatly harmed her

---

589:    "Si" most often means "if," which would imply a degree of uncertainty about Elizabeth's parentage. However, in this context, given how much the author insists on Mary's generous response to Anne in her plight, it is clear that the intended meaning is instead another common usage of the word that draws from its etymological origin (< Latin, "sic") to mean 'thus,' 'and yet, as,' 'surely,' or 'since.' See Cotgrave's definition: "In the beginning of a speech now and then implies ... a kind of certainty ... as 'Si advint' ... *Surely it happened*." Certainly, Carle has already made it clear that Elizabeth resembled Henry greatly, and thus it would be odd to interject any doubt about her paternity here, which, of course, Mary would have no way of verifying before making good on her promise. Rather, this entire passage demonstrates Mary's feelings of duty toward her father and his offspring, no matter what Anne may have done, and, as the marginal note of S1 indicates, it thus emphasizes her "admirable virtue." Therefore, the word "si" cannot logically be translated here as "if" but needs to be understood as "since."

593:    Chapuys, in a letter to Charles V, written soon after Anne's arrest, reminds the Emperor that Mary was prepared to accept lawful heirs begotten by the king should he divorce Anne and remarry, stating that Mary did not wish for the king to divorce Anne "out of revenge for the many injuries inflicted on her mother, the late Queen, and herself. Those she had willingly forgiven and forgotten for the honor of God, and she now bore no ill-will to anyone whomsoever." See CSP, Spain, 5, pt.2, no. 48; and LP 10.782. Burnet, however, contended that the "Lady Mary could not so easily pardon these injuries; but retained the resentments of them her whole life." See Burnet, *History of the Reformation*, pt. 1, bk. 3, 204.

594    Mais en tous[1] temps tousiours se conduysoit
595    En mesme estat, tant en l'aduersité[2]
596    Qu'en la saison de la[3] prosperité.
597    Et se monstroit en ses façons toute[4] vne,
598    Fust en[5] contraire ou en[6] bonne fortune.
599    Et qui plus est, pour tristesse ou dommage,[7]
600    Ne changea onc[8] la couleur du[9] visaige.
601    Ains quant l'ennuy plus en elle[10] croissoit,
602    C'estoit[11] alors que plus embellissoit.
603    Et croy que Dieu, qui son bon[12] cueur regarde,
604    L'a tousiours mise & tenue[13] en sa garde:
605    Car sans luy n'eust sceu iamais[14] resister          [20r]
606    Au traictement qu'il[15] luy failloit porter,
607    Paouure viuant,[16] estant du tout[17] bannie,
608    De tout plaisir & bonne compaignie,[18]
609    Tant que parler à elle nul n'ozoit[19]
610    Premierement,[20] si au Roy ne plaisoit,
611    Qui la souloit, auant le changement,
612    Traicter en fille aymee vnicquement.
613    Ainsi[21] viuoit seulle,[22] en passant le temps[23]

---

[1]  V, BRB: tout
[2]  BNF1–2, BNF6, B, S1/2: en adversité; BNF4: en son adversité
[3]  BNF3–5, S1, 1545: sa
[4]  BNF7, 1545: tant; all others but B, S2, and Vat: tout
[5]  BNF1: Ou par; all others: Ou pour
[6]  BNF1: ou par; all others: ou pour
[7]  V, BRB, K: ou pour dommaige
[8]  BNF1: point; BNF4–5, V, 1545: onques
[9]  B: de son
[10]  BNF1–2, S1/2: l'ennuy en elle plus
[11]  1545: Sembloit
[12]  S1/2: qui le vray
[13]  BNF4: mise et tenu; B: mis et tenu; V, BRB, K: mis et tenue
[14]  BNF1–3, BNF5–7, B, V, BRB, K, M, S2: sans luy n'eust jamais sceu; BNF4: Car elle n'eust sceut sans son Dieu; 1545: sans luy jamais n'eust sceu
[15]  M, 1545: qui
[16]  S1/2: Vivoit privee; all others: Vivant privee
[17]  BNF1, BNF6, B: de tout; BNF4, S1/2: de tous
[18]  BNF1–3, BNF5, BNF7, B, M, 1545: Hors du plaisir de bonne compaignie; BNF4: Hors de plaisirs et bonne compagnie; BNF6, Vat: Hors du plaisir de toute compaignie; S1/2: Hors de plaisir de bonne compaignie; V, BRB, K: Et hors du plaisir de bonne compagnie
[19]  BNF1: parler nul à elle n'osoit; BNF2, V: parler à elle nul osoit; BNF4: parler à elle on n'osoit
[20]  B: Premier
[21]  BNF6: Aussy
[22]  BNF4: elle
[23]  BNF5, 1545: seulle, passant le temps; Vat: seulle, en passant temps

| | |
|---|---|
| 594 | But at all times she always conducted herself |
| 595 | In the same way, whether in adversity |
| 596 | Or in the season of prosperity. |
| 597 | And she showed herself to behave completely in a single manner, |
| 598 | Be it[1] in good fortune or bad. |
| 599 | And, what is more, on account of sadness or loss, |
| 600 | The color in her face never changed.[2] |
| 601 | Rather, the more anxious she grew, |
| 602 | The more beautiful she became.[3] |
| 603 | And I believe that God, who sees her good[4] heart, |
| 604 | Placed and held her always in His keeping; |
| 605 | For without Him, she would never[5] have been able to withstand |
| 606 | The treatment that she had to bear, |
| 607 | Living in poverty,[6] banished from everything,[7] |
| 608 | From every pleasure and good[8] company, |
| 609 | Such that no one dared to speak to her |
| 610 | First, if it didn't please the king, |
| 611 | Who, before his transformation, was wont |
| 612 | To treat her solely as a beloved daughter. |
| 613 | And so she lived alone,[9] spending her time |

---

[1] All others: Either in

[2] BNF1: did not change at all

[3] 1545: The more beautiful it seemed she became

[4] S1/2: who sees one's true

[5] BNF4: without her God, she would not

[6] S1/2: She lived deprived; all others: Living deprived

[7] BNF4, S1/2: from everyone

[8] BNF1–3, BNF5, BNF7, B, S1/2, M, 1545: Without the pleasure of good; BNF4: Without pleasures and good; BNF6, Vat: Without the pleasure of any; V, BRB, K: And without the pleasure of good

[9] BNF4: And this is how she lived

614    À prendre[1] tous vertueux passetemps,
615    S'excercitant[2] par vne grand prudence
616    De[3] receuoir de Dieu la cognoissance,
617    Puis à sçauoir[4] raison du mouuement,
618    Et le secret de tout le firmament,
619    Du monde aussi la situation,[5]
620    Des elementz l'association.
621    Puis, sagement, auec mathematicque[6]                    [20v]
622    Mesloit[7] raison moralle & politicque,[8]
623    Puis, aprenoit latine[9] & grecque lettre,
624    Par oraison, par histoire, ou par mettre,[10]
625    Tellement que ces[11] sciences confuses
626    Sembloient en elle estre du ciel infuses.[12]
627    Et combien que semble estre suffisant[13]
628    Petit scauoir, &[14] beaucoup plus[15] duysant
629    Selon l'estat de[16] feminin vsaige,
630    Le[17] faisoit pour asseurer[18] son courage,
631    Et pour garder que[19] sa fragilité
632    Ne se[20] laissast veincre[21] d'oysiueté.
633    Ainsi vertu sa constance asseuroit.
634    Et ce pendant,[22] le peuple demeuroit

---

1  BNF2: Et prendre; V: Apprendre
2  S1/2, Vat: Excercitant; 1545: Se persistant
3  BNF1–4, BNF6, BNF7, B, V, BRB, M, K: À
4  S2: assavoir
5  1545: l'ascention
6  B: Hand appears to change here
7  BNF3–7, B, S2, V, BRB, M, Vat, 1545: Mettoit; BNF2: N'estoit (a corrupt reading)
8  BNF1: raison et moralle et praticque; BNF2, BNF5: raison morale, politique
9  BNF1–2: latin
10 BNF2–6, B, M: oraison, par histoire et par mectre; S1/2, V, BRB, K: Verses 623–624 missing;
   1545: oraison, histoyre et par mettre
11 BNF2, BNF4, BNF7, B, V, S2, BRB, Vat: ses; BNF5, 1545: les
12 BNF1: Sembloit en elle estre du ciel infuses; BNF2: Sembloient du ciel estre en elle infuses; B:
   Semblent estre du ciel infuses
13 BNF1: qu'il me semble suffisant; BNF4: Et qui sembloient estre assez suffisans
14 BNF2, BNF4, BNF7, S2, V, 1545: est; B: estre
15 BNF2: moins; all others but S1/2: mieulx
16 BNF1–4, B, V, BRB, K, Vat: du; BNF5: et
17 BNF4: Et le
18 BNF4: armer
19 V: par
20 BNF1–2, S1/2: la
21 BNF1: vaincque; BNF5, 1545: rompre; S2: vivre (word is crossed out)
22 V: En ce pendant

614    Engaged in[1] all virtuous pastimes,
615    Occupying herself,[2] with great prudence,
616    In gaining knowledge of God,
617    Then learning about the ordered movement
618    And mystery of all the firmament
619    As well as the position of the earth
620    And the relationship among the elements.
621    Then, wisely, with mathematics
622    She blended[3] moral and political philosophy,[4]
623    Then she learned Latin and Greek literature,
624    Through orations, history, or poetry,
625    Such that these diverse fields of knowledge
626    Seemed to be infused in her by heaven.
627    And even though little learning seems[5] to be sufficient,
628    And much more fitting,[6]
629    In accordance with the customary feminine state,[7]
630    She did this to stiffen[8] her courage
631    And to keep weakness
632    From overcoming[9] her through idleness.
633    Thus virtue strengthened her constancy.
634    And, meanwhile, the people remained

---

[1]  V: Learning
[2]  1545: Persisting
[3]  BNF3–7, B, S2, V, BRB, M, Vat, 1545: She placed
[4]  BNF1: moral and practical philosophy
[5]  BNF1: seems to me
[6]  BNF2: less suitable; all others but S1/2: better suited
[7]  BNF5: the feminine custom and state
[8]  BNF4: to fortify
[9]  BNF5, 1545: breaking

---

620:    Carle's description of Mary's intellectual interests is reminiscent of the way William Roper described the king's frequent discussions with Roper's father-in-law, Thomas More, in which they addressed "matters of astronomy, geometry, divinity" and would consider "the diversities, courses, motions, and operations of the stars and planets," thus suggesting that Mary's curiosity about these sciences was shared with her father. See Roper, *The Life of Sir Thomas More*, 202.

632:    A later report (dated 12 October 1541), from the French envoy Marillac to Francis I, confirms that Mary took solace in music and in reading classical literature in times of trouble. See LP 16.1253.

635   Presque[1] rauy d'aize de l'esperance[2]
636   Qu'auoit d'en bref[3] recouurer sa[4] presence,
637   Tant que le Roy ne fut[5] sans auoir crainte,[6]                      [21r]
638   Voyant les gens[7] en[8] assemblee mainte,[9]
639   Qu'il[10] ne suruint quelque commotion.
640   Mais quand il veid que c'est affection[11]
641   Et grand desir de reueoir[12] la[13] princesse
642   Qui cause[14] au peuple vne si grande presse,[15]
643   Pour leur donner quelque contentement,
644   Remercier le fist[16] benignement
645   De ce qu'auoit[17] bien experimenté
646   Leur cueur entier &[18] bonne volunté
647   Enuers sa fille, & enuers luy aussi,[19]
648   Mais qu'il[20] n'estoit besoing auoir[21] soucy
649   De son[22] retour, car auant peu de temps
650   Ilz en seroient satisfaictz & contens.
651   Et ce pendant qu'en[23] ceste confiance[24]

---

1   BNF1: Plus que
2   BNF1–2, BNF4, BNF6: d'aise et d'esperance; B: et d'aise et d'esperance
3   BNF1–2: en bref; BNF3–4, BNF6, V, BRB, M, K, 1545: de bref
4   1545: la
5   BNF1–2: que ne fut le Roy; 1545: le roy ne sceut
6   S1 marginal note: Cautelle du Roy d'Angleterre
7   V: les grans; S1/2: ses gens
8   1545: et
9   V: originally read "grande" but corrected to "mainte" in another hand and ink
10  BNF3, BNF6–7, B, V, BRB, M, K, 1545: Que
11  BNF1: Mais quant il veoit que c'est l'affection; BNF2, BNF5, S1/2: Mais quand il voit que c'est
    affection; BNF3: Mais quand il vid que ceste affection; BNF4, B: Quand il void que c'estoit
    l'affection; BNF6, Vat: Mais quand il voit que ceste affection; BNF7: Mais qu'il veit que c'est
    l'affection; V, BRB, K: Mais puisqu'il voit que c'est l'affection; M: Mais puis qui veit que c'est
    l'affection; 1545: Mais quand il veit que celle affection
12  BNF1–2: desir recevoir; BNF4, B, BRB, K: desir de ravoir; 1545: desir de recepuoir
13  S1/2: leur
14  S1: causoit
15  BL: une si grand presse (emended for verisifcaiton); BNF1–2: si grant ennuy et presse
16  BNF2: la feist; BNF3–6, V, BRB, M, K, Vat, 1545: les feist
17  1545: qu'elle avoit
18  BNF1: Leur entiere et; BNF3, BNF6: Le cueur entier et; BNF4: Leur cueur entier en
19  S1/2: Tant envers luy qu'envers sa fille aussi
20  M: qui
21  All others but V: d'avoir
22  1545: ce
23  BNF4: en
24  B: confidence

635    Almost[1] carried away by delight in the[2] hope
636    Which they had that they would shortly get her back before their
       eyes,
637    Such that the king was not without fear,[3]
638    Upon seeing so many people gathering,
639    That some riot was stirring.
640    But when he sees[4] that it was their affection
641    And great desire to see[5] the[6] princess again
642    That is[7] the reason behind such a great throng of people,[8]
643    In order to give them some satisfaction,
644    He thanked them kindly
645    For their having given strong proof of
646    Their whole-hearted[9] good wishes
647    Towards his daughter and towards him as well.[10]
648    But there was no need to be concerned
649    About her return, for before long
650    They would be satisfied and content.
651    And while, in this confidence,

---

[1]   BNF1: More than
[2]   BNF1–2, BNF4, BNF6, B: and the
[3]   S1 marginal note: "The King of England's ruse"
[4]   V, BRB, K: But since he sees; M: But then he saw
[5]   BNF1–2, 1545: to receive; BNF4, B, BRB, K: to have
[6]   S1/2: their
[7]   S1: was
[8]   BNF1–2: such anxiety and urgency among the people
[9]   BNF1: Their complete
[10]   S1/2: As much towards him as towards his daughter

652    Pour quelques iours[1] ilz eussent patience,
653    Ainsi en dueil l'aize se conuertit[2]                    [21v]
654    Du[3] paouure peuple, &[4] confuz s'en partit[5]
655    Pour le regret[6] de leur bien pretendu,[7]
656    Que[8] tant auoient[9] de bon cueur attendu.
657    Et la[10] princesse encores faict[11] demeure
658    À[12] son chasteau & sera[13] iusque[14] à l'heure
659    Que sera par le[15] parlement remise[16]
660    En[17] son estat où elle est tant requise.[18]
661    Ce temps pendant[19] la royne, estant[20] au lieu
662    Où n'esperoit plus secours que de Dieu,
663    Veoit bien que plus n'est temps qu'elle[21] se fonde
664    Au[22] vain espoir de ce muable monde,
665    Parquoy en Dieu[23] met toute sa[24] fiance,

---

1    BNF5, 1545: quelque iour; S1/2, V, BRB, K: quelque temps
2    BNF1, BNF3: en dueil laissé se convertit; BNF2: en dueil lassé se convertit (a scribal error); B: en dueil liesse convertit; S1/2: L'ennuy du peuple adoncq se convertit; 1545: en dueil laissa ce convertit (a corrupt reading)
3    BNF1–2, B: Le
4    BNF4: qui
5    BNF3: en partit; B: se partit; S1/2: En doulx plaisirs et joyeux se partit
6    S1/2: Car par l'espoir
7    B: d'avoir leur bien perdu
8    BNF1, BNF4, 1545: Qui
9    BNF4: avoit
10   S1/2: leur
11   BNF2: encor faict; BNF4: faict encore; S1: encores feist; K: encore faict; 1545: feit encore
12   All others: En
13   All others: fera
14   BL and all others except BN1–5, S1, Vat: jusques (emended for versification)
15   BL: Qu'elle sera du (emended for sense); BNF2, 1545: Qu'elle sera par le parlement; V, BRB, M, K: Qu'elle sera par parlement
16   BNF4: Que par le grand Parlement sera mise; S1/2: Qu'elle sera par les millortz remise
17   BRB, K: De
18   B: où elle estoit requise; BRB: où elle estoit tant requise; K: after v. 660, K jumps to v. 723 and continues to 750, but these are crossed out and the text resumes at v. 661 in a different ink and hand.
19   BNF4: Pendant ce temps; B: Ce pendant
20   All others: estoit
21   BNF1: Et veoit bien que plus n'est où; BNF2–3, BNF6–7, Vat: Et veoit que plus il n'est temps que; BNF4–5, V, BRB, K: Et veoit que plus n'est temps qu'elle; B: Et voioit que plus n'est temps que; S1/2: Disant que plus ne fault qu'elle; M: Et veoit que plus n'est temps que; 1545: Et veoit plus il n'est temps qu'elle
22   BNF1: Le
23   All others: Mais en Dieu seul
24   BNF4: met tout sa fiance; B: mettoit toutte sa fiance; S1: mecte toute sa fiance; V: met sa fiance

| | |
|---|---|
| 652 | They were patient for a few days,[1] |
| 653 | Even so, the poor people's pleasure[2] |
| 654 | Was changed to grief, and they left dismayed[3] |
| 655 | On account of the loss of the gift they longed for,[4] |
| 656 | Which they had awaited so faithfully. |
| 657 | And the[5] princess still makes[6] her home |
| 658 | In her castle and will do so until the hour |
| 659 | That she is brought back by Parliament[7] |
| 660 | To her estate where she is so earnestly sought. |
| 661 | In the meantime, the queen, who was at that place |
| 662 | Where she could expect help only from God, |
| 663 | Quite realizes[8] that it is no longer the moment to[9] rest upon |
| 664 | The vain hope of this changeable world. |
| 665 | For this reason, she places all her trust in God,[10] |

[1] S1/2, V, BRB, K: for some time

[2] B: gladness

[3] BNF1, BNF3, 1545: Verses 653–654 read: Thus left in sorrow, the poor people were changed / And they left dismayed

[4] S1/2: Verses 653–655 read: The anxiety of the people then was changed / Into sweet pleasure and they departed joyfully / On account of the hope of the gift they longed for

[5] S1/2: their

[6] 1545, S1: made

[7] BNF4: by the great Parliament; S1/2: by the lords

[8] BNF2–6, B, V, M, K, Vat, 1545: And realizes

[9] BNF1: And quite realizes that she is no longer where she could; S1/2: Saying that she must no longer

[10] V: But in God alone she places her trust; B: But in God alone she put all her trust; all others: But in God alone she places all her trust

655: The unique reading of the Soissons manuscripts of vv. 653-655 implies that the people have been taken in by the king's words and are fooled into remaining hopeful.

660: Mary returned to court only after signing the oath recognizing her father as head of the Church. This occurred in the summer of 1536.

664: This verse marks the end of the first half of the "canonical" text and ushers in a more sympathetic portrayal of Anne, who will now turn her thoughts to God.

| | |
|---|---|
| 666 | Comme s'elle eust[1] de sa fin[2] prescience. |
| 667 | Et lors[3] que moins de sa vie se fie[4] |
| 668 | Plus auec Dieu d'espoir[5] se fortifie. |
| 669 | Mesmement[6] quand les seigneurs deputez |
| 670 | Ont tous les[7] cas contre elle recitez, |
| 671 | Qui la rendoient coulpable de la mort,[8] |
| 672 | Rien ne confesse & ne[9] resistoit[10] fort, |
| 673 | Comme voulant presque se veoir[11] deliure[12] |
| 674 | De vie icy pour aux cieux aller viure.[13] |
| 675 | Et l'esperit en elle tant[14] surmonte |
| 676 | Que de la mort ne tient plus aucun[15] compte, |
| 677 | Qui toutesfois n'oublye sa grandesse,[16] |
| 678 | À ces[17] seigneurs parlant comme[18] maistresse, |
| 679 | Et deuant[19] eux se monstre autant[20] constante |
| 680 | Comme estant Royne en honneur[21] triumphante, |
| 681 | Qui ne fut pas[22] sans beaucoup esbahir[23] |
| 682 | Ceux qui estoient là venuz[24] pour l'ouyr;[25] |

[22r] appears to the right of line 669.

---

1  BNF4: Comme celle eust; 1545: Comme si sceust
2  BNF6: sa mort
3  BNF1: alors
4  BNF5, 1545: en sa vie se fie; S1/2: eust espoir de sa vie; V: et sa vye se fye
5  BNF1: Avecques Dieu plus; BNF2–3, BNF5–6, V, K, Vat, 1545: Avecques Dieu lors plus; BNF4, BNF7, B, BRB, M: Avecq Dieu lors plus; S1/2: Avecques Dieu plus fort
6  S1/2: Et mesmes
7  BNF5: ces; V: leurs
8  BNF4, B: de mort
9  BRB, K: "ne" missing
10  BNF1, BNF4: ne resiste; BNF2: et se resistoit; V: missing "et"
11  BNF1, B, S1/2: voulant estre presque; BNF2–3, BNF5–7, V, BRB, M, K, Vat, 1545: voulant presque estre; BNF4: Comme voyant qu'elle est presque
12  BNF2, V: deslivree
13  BNF1, BNF7, V, BRB, M, K: De vie icy pour aller aux cieux vivre; BNF2: De vivre icy pour estre à Dieu livree; BNF5–6, S1/2, 1545: De vivre icy pour aux cieux aller vivre; Vat: De vivre icy pour aller aux cieulx vivre
14  BNF1: Et l'espoir tant en icelle; BNF2: Car l'esperit tant en elle; BNF3, BNF6, B: Et l'esperit tant en elle; BRB: Et l'esprit tant en elle
15  BNF5, BNF7, B, V, BRB, M, K: aultre
16  BNF4: Et toutefois n'oublya; S1/2: Et toutesfois suyvant sa grand haultesse
17  BNF2–3, BNF6–7, V, 1545: ses; B: initially reads "ses," corrected to "ces"
18  BNF7: parlant que; S1: parloit comme
19  BRB: devers
20  S1/2: se monstroit tant
21  BNF6: en estat
22  V, BRB, M, K: point
23  1545: s'esbahir
24  Vat: estoient venuz là
25  S1/2: pour oyr

666    As if she had foreknowledge of her end.[1]
667    And, now that she puts less trust[2] in her life,
668    She strengthens herself the more with hope in God.
669    In particular,[3] when the designated lords
670    Recited all the allegations against her,
671    Which would make her deserving of the death penalty,
672    She confesses to nothing and did not resist[4] strongly,
673    Almost as if she wished to see herself become[5] free
674    From life here,[6] so as to go live in heaven,[7]
675    And the spirit[8] within her is so elevated
676    That she no longer pays any heed to death.
677    Nevertheless she does[9] not forget her greatness,[10]
678    Speaking[11] to these[12] lords as their mistress,
679    And shows[13] herself as steadfast before them
680    As is a queen triumphant in honor,[14]
681    Which happened not without greatly astonishing
682    Those who came there to hear her.

---

[1]  BNF6: her death
[2]  S1/2: she has less hope
[3]  S1/2: And even
[4]  BNF1, BNF4: does not resist
[5]  All others but BNF4, which is corrupt: Almost as if wanting to be
[6]  BNF5–6, S1/2, Vat, 1545: From living here
[7]  BNF2: From living here so as to be delivered to God
[8]  BNF1: the hope; BNF2: For the spirit
[9]  BNF4: did
[10]  S1/2: And nevertheless, following her great nobility
[11]  S1: She spoke
[12]  BNF2–3, BNF6–7, V, 1545: her
[13]  S1/2: And showed
[14]  BNF6: queen in triumphant estate

683    Lesquelz, apres l'auoir interrogee,
684    Pour au proces faire[1] fin abregee,
685    À Rochefort, son frere, presenterent                    [22v]
686    Les dictz de ceux qui au Roy l'accuserent,
687    Dequoy il feit[2] moins compte que de rien,[3]
688    En leur disant[4] que desia scauoit bien
689    La mort luy estre en bref temps preparee,[5]
690    Et que, pour vray, la[6] tenoit asseuree,[7]
691    Parquoy en riens ne dissimuleroit[8]
692    La verité qu'on[9] luy demanderoit.
693    Mais, quant au cas[10] qu'on luy mettoit[11] auant,
694    Par son serment, les yeulx au ciel leuant,[12]
695    Dit qu'ilz sont faux & que[13] ne sont que songes
696    Et[14] meschamment controuuées mensonges.[15]
697    Apres ce faict,[16] à Norris sont venuz,
698    Et[17] telz propos leur a aussi[18] tenuz,
699    Et ne confesse en rien estre[19] coulpable.
700    Waston, Bruton ont faict tout[20] le semblable,
701    Tant que tous ont les cas[21] desaduouez,[22]             [23r]
702    Fors Marc, qui ia les auoit aduouez.[23]

---

1   S1: mectre
2   M: Dequoy y fist
3   B: moins de compte que rien; BNF7: maint conte de rien (a corrupt reading)
4   V, BRB, M, K: Et leur disoit
5   BNF1: separee (a corrupt reading)
6   BNF1: s'en; B: Et que la mort pour vray (a corrupt reading)
7   BNF5: Verse 690 missing
8   BRB: dissimuloit
9   BNF5: de ce qu'on
10  BNF3: aux cas
11  S1/2: mist en; all others: a mis
12  BNF2, BRB, M: aux cieulx levant; BNF7: au ciel tenant; V: au cieulx levant
13  BNF1, BNF7, S1: et qu'ilz; BNF4: faux, que ce ne; BNF5: et ne sont
14  1545: Ont; all others but BNF5: Ou
15  BNF7: contournees mensonges; 1545: de mensonges
16  BNF5, 1545: ces faictz
17  1545: Que; all others: Qui
18  BL: leur ont aussi (emended for sense); BNF1: leur a ainsi; BNF5, 1545: ainsi leur a; S1/2: luy ont
    ainsi; V: aussi (interpolated in a different ink) luy a; BRB: luy ont aussi; K: lui a aussi
19  BNF3, BNF6: Verse 699 missing; S1/2: Mais il confesse en rien n'estre; 1545: rien n'etre
20  BNF4: en font tout; K: missing "tout"
21  BNF3: le cas; BNF4: Car tous ses cas ilz ont
22  BL: Marginal notation of two crosses; BNF6: Marginal notation of cross
23  BNF1–2, BNF7, B: Fors Marc, qui ia les avoit allouez; V, K: Fors Marc, qui là les; BRB: Fors que
    Marc, qui les

| | |
|---|---|
| 683 | Those men, after interrogating her, |
| 684 | To bring the matter shortly to a close, |
| 685 | Presented to Rochford, her brother, |
| 686 | The statements of those who accused him to the king. |
| 687 | He cared less than nothing about this, |
| 688 | Telling them[1] that he already knew quite well |
| 689 | That a death sentence would soon be set for him |
| 690 | And that truly he was sure of it, |
| 691 | For which reason he would in no way disguise[2] |
| 692 | The truth that they would ask of him. |
| 693 | But, as for the charges that they put before him, |
| 694 | By his oath, raising his eyes towards heaven, |
| 695 | He says that they are false and that they are but dreams |
| 696 | And[3] wickedly concocted lies. |
| 697 | After doing this, they came to Norris |
| 698 | And he[4] also maintained the same position, |
| 699 | And he does not confess that he was guilty of anything; |
| 700 | Weston and Brereton did exactly the same thing, |
| 701 | So that everyone denied the charges,[5] |
| 702 | Except Mark, who had already admitted to[6] them. |

---

[1] V, BRB, M, K: And he told them
[2] BRB: he in no way disguised
[3] All others but BNF5 and 1545: Or
[4] All others: Who
[5] BL: Marginal notation of two crosses; BNF6: Marginal notation of cross
[6] BNF1–2, BNF7, B: already avowed

---

694: This gesture is one attributed to Christ in prayer; see Matthew 14:19, Mark 6:41, Luke 9:16, and John 17:1.
699: See Constantyne's *Memorial*, 64 for Norris's interrogation.
702: See Edward Baynton's letter to the Lord Treasurer in which he states: "no man will confess anything against her, but only Mark, of any actual thing" (Ellis, *Original Letters*, 2:61).

703    Apres ce faict,[1] pour tost[2] remedier
704    À vie ou mort &[3] les expedier,
705    Le Roy voulut qu'on en fist[4] iugement.
706    On aduertit ces quatre assemblement[5] —
707    Waston, Bruton, Norris, Marc—que,[6] le iour
708    Celuy suyuant, partiront[7] de la tour
709    Pour receuoir leur[8] condamnation,
710    Ou receuoir[9] leur absolution.[10]
711    Et par cecy, la façon pourrez veoir[11]
712    Qu'ilz ont[12] icy pour à tel[13] cas pouruoir:[14]
713    Premierement, la cause fut[15] monstree[16]
714    À douze[17] estans[18] de la[19] mesme contree
715    Et de l'estat[20] pareil aux accusez,
716    Pour veoir si point deuoient[21] estre excusez,
717    Qui disrent tous que raisonnablement                         [23v]
718    Sont detenuz[22] en emprisonnement,[23]

---

[1]  S1/2: Ung peu apres
[2]  K, 1545: tout
[3]  BNF1: À la vye ou mort les; BNF2: À vye ou mort ou les; S1/2: À vie et mort et; 1545: À vie ou
     à mort et les
[4]  BNF1–4, BNF6–7, B, V, BRB, M, K, Vat: veult qu'on en face; BNF5: si veult qu'on face; 1545:
     commande en faire
[5]  BNF1, BNF3–5, BNF7, B, V, BRB, M, K, Vat, 1545: ensemblement; S1: Tous quatre on mist
     bientost separement; S2: Tous quatre ont mit bientost separement
[6]  BNF7, S1/2: qui
[7]  BNF1–2, BNF4–5, B, V, BRB, M: partiroient; BNF3, BNF6: sortiront; 1545: partiroit
[8]  BNF5, Vat: la
[9]  BNF1: À Wuesmester; BNF2–3: À Oesmaster; BNF4, BRB, V, K: À Wasmester; BNF5, BNF7:
     À Wesmester; BNF6: À Remester; B: À Oesmester (crossed out with "Westmaster" in margins);
     S1/2: À Osmaster; M: À Wastmester; Vat: À cest mestier (a corrupt reading); 1545: À droict ou
     tort
[10] V, S1/2, BRB, 1545: ou absolution; all others: ou l'absolution
[11] K: New folio begins here and resumes previous ink and hand
[12] BNF1, B: Qui sont
[13] BNF2: en telz; BNF6, V, M: à telz; BRB: pour telz
[14] BNF5: prouveoir
[15] BNF1: fut la cause
[16] S1 marginal note: Formes de juger au royaume d'Angleterre
[17] S1/2: À gens
[18] BRB: estats (a scribal error)
[19] B: d'une mesme
[20] BNF4: Et l'estat en; BRB: Et de leur estat
[21] BNF1, Vat: devroient
[22] S1/2: Estoient tenuz
[23] BRB: Verses 717–718 missing

703 After this was done,[1] so as to decide quickly[2]
704 And to send them off to life or death,
705 The king wanted a judgment to be made on this matter.[3]
706 They advised these four together[4]—
707 Weston, Brereton, Norris and Mark—
708 That the following day they were[5] to leave the Tower
709 To receive their conviction
710 Or obtain[6] their acquittal.
711 And from my description, you shall see the method
712 That they have here to look into such a matter:
713 First, the case was brought[7]
714 To twelve men[8] from the same region
715 And of similar standing as the accused
716 To see if any of them should be let go.
717 These men all said that the accused were reasonably
718 Detained[9] in prison

---

[1] S1/2: A little afterwards
[2] K, 1545: decide completely
[3] 1545: commands that a judgment be made
[4] S1/2: They soon placed all four separately
[5] S1/2: Who, the following day were
[6] 1545: For right or wrong, or; all others but Vat (which has a corrupt reading): At Westminster, or
[7] S1 marginal note: "The judicial system in the kingdom of England"
[8] S1/2: To people
[9] S1/2: Held

---

708: The trial of the commoners took place on Friday, 12 May 1536.
716: Carle is here describing the grand jury proceedings, but he is confusing it with the empaneling of a jury of freeholders from the county where the indictment was found. The proceedings of the grand juries of Middlesex and Kent took place on May 10 and 11, and each grand jury consisted of sixteen jurors, not twelve.

719    Et lors sont dictz[1] en ces lieux[2] "inthimez,"[3]
720    Puisque par les douze[4] sont estimez[5]
721    Suspectz[6] d'auoir contre la[7] maiesté
722    Par trahison quelque chose tenté.[8]
723    Apres cela, tous quatre sont menez[9]
724    Par les archiers pour leur garde[10] ordonnez,
725    Ayans[11] tousiours deuant eux vne hache,
726    Qui est le[12] signe à fin que chascun saiche,[13]
727    En le[14] voyant, si l'estat de l'affaire[15]
728    Sera pour eux ou contraire ou prospere:[16]
729    Car en allant, elle[17] tourne le doz
730    Vers eux, & puis est tousiours en[18] repos,
731    Tant que soient tous les[19] iugementz finiz.
732    Et puis, s'ilz[20] sont coulpables diffiniz,
733    Qu'on dit "GUILTY"[21] en ce[22] commun langaige,        [24r]
734    Le[23] trenchant lors se tourne à[24] leur visaige,
735    Qui est le vray & manifeste enseigne[25]

---

[1] BNF2, 1545: fut dict
[2] S1/2: ces motz
[3] BNF2: inhumez; BNF7: Et lors sont en ces lieux intismez
[4] BNF2, BNF5: par ces douze; S1/2: Incontinent par tous; 1545: Puisque les douze
[5] BNF1: Verses 719–720 missing
[6] S1: Certains; S2: Actainctz; V: Subjectz
[7] V: sa; BRB: contr' à la
[8] BNF1, BNF5, S1/2: traicté; BNF3: attempté; BNF4: intanté; BNF6: attenté
[9] K: Marginal notation "X"
[10] BNF2: leurs gardes; S2: leur gardez; V, BRB, K: les garder; Vat: leurs garde
[11] 1545: Ains (a scribal error)
[12] M: la
[13] 1545: le sache
[14] BNF1–4, BNF6–7, B, S1/2, V, BRB, M, K, Vat: la
[15] BNF1: s'il estoit de l'affaire; S1/2: si leur cause ou affaire
[16] BNF1: au contraire prospere; S1/2: malheureux ou prospere
[17] BNF3, BNF6, V, BRB, M, K: s'elle
[18] BNF5, V: toujours est en repos; S2: est toujours à repos; K: Verse 730 interpolated, missing "est"
[19] BNF1: Tant que soient les; BNF4, Vat: Tant que soient tous leurs
[20] V: s'il; M, 1545: si
[21] BL, BNF7: QUILTY (emended for accuracy, as in BNF1, BNF6, B, M, Vat); BNF2, BRB: Guilly; BNF3: Guylti; BNF4: Guelty; BNF5: Guilti; V: Guylty; S1: Guylly; S2: Guytty; K: Gulty; 1545: Gilty
[22] BNF3, BNF6, B: en leur
[23] B: Ce
[24] BNF4: lors se tourne en; S1/2: lors on tourne à; BRB: se tourne lors à; K: lors se tourna à
[25] BNF4, BNF5, S1/2, 1545: signe

719  And then they were, as it is called in these parts, "indicted,"
720  Since they were deemed by the twelve men to be[1]
721  Suspected of[2] having attempted some act
722  Of treason against His Majesty.
723  After that, all four were led[3]
724  By the archers, who were ordered to watch them,
725  Holding an axe before them at all times,
726  Which is the sign used so that each one might know
727  By looking at it if the decision[4]
728  Will be either in their favor or against them.
729  For, going into the court, its back side is turned
730  Towards them, and then it is always at rest,
731  Up until the time when all the[5] judgments are finalized.
732  And then, if they are found to be culpable,
733  Which is called "GUILTY" in this[6] vernacular,
734  The[7] cutting edge is at that time turned towards their face,
735  Which is the true and manifest sign

---

[1] S1/2: And forthwith deemed by everyone to be
[2] S1: Certain of; S2: Attainted for
[3] K: Marginal notation of "X"
[4] S1/2: if their case or affair
[5] BNF4, Vat: their
[6] BNF3, BNF6, B: in their
[7] B: This

---

719:  The word "intimé" is defined by Cotgrave as "cited, summoned, warned to appear (in an Appeal)." The modern equivalent would be "indicted."
733:  Carle uses the English word "guilty" here and in vv. 779–780. The word is fully capitalized each time in BL.

736    Qui leur malheur[1] aux assistans enseigne:[2]
737    Car deuers[3] eux ne se tourneroit[4] pas
738    Le trenchant si absoubz estoient[5] du cas.
739    Ainsi s'en vont pour[6] ouyr leur sentence
740    Les prisonniers[7] en publicque assistence,
741    À se remettre au lieu accoustumé[8]
742    Pour[9] iuger ceulx de qui est presumé,
743    Par quelque effect[10] d'apparente raison,
744    Qu'enuers le Roy ayent commis[11] trahison.
745    Et là, deuant[12] tout le conseil priué[13]
746    Qui pour ce faict[14] y estoit arriué,[15]
747    On leut au long leurs[16] informations
748    Pour faire foy des[17] accusations.
749    Et quand, ce faict, ont assez[18] plaidoyé                    [24v]
750    Les gens du Roy, & ceux cy[19] ont nyé[20]
751    Le contenu aux charges[21] criminelles,

---

[1]  BNF3: Qui les malheurs; BNF4: Que leur malheur; V, K: De la mort; BRB: Et la mort
[2]  BNF4, 1545: assigne; BNF7: s'enseigne; V: en seigne; BRB: asseigne
[3]  1545: davant
[4]  1545: trouveroit
[5]  BNF5: s'absoubz estoient; B: si absolus estoient; S1/2: Le dur tranchant s'estoient absoulz; V, BRB, K: s'ils estoient absoulz
[6]  BRB: "pour" missing
[7]  BL: De ses prisons (emended for grammar and sense); BNF5, S1/2, Vat: Ces prisonniers; B: Ces personnes; all others as emended
[8]  BNF1–3, BNF5, BNF7, B, S1/2, V, BRB, M, K, Vat: À Oesmester [or other spelling variants as above], le lieu accoustumé; BNF4: Ainsy qu'il est de faire accoustumé; 1545: À ce mestier le lieu accoustumé
[9]  BNF5: De; 1545: À
[10]  BNF5: Par quelque faict
[11]  BNF5: Envers le roy commectant; B: D'envers le roy avoir commis; S2, V: aiant commis; 1545: Envers le roy ayant comme
[12]  B: Et l'advouant (a scribal error); S1/2: Illec devant
[13]  B: Marginal drawing of a chevron; Vat: originally repeats vv. 744–745 between vv. 745–746, the former of which are later crossed out
[14]  BNF4, V, BRB, K: faire
[15]  V: y estoient arrivés
[16]  BNF1–3, BNF6, Vat, 1545: Leues leurs sont les; BNF4, B, V, BRB, M, K: Leues leurs sont leurs; BNF5: Leues leur ont; BNF7: Leues leur sont les; S1/2: On leur a leu les
[17]  B: faire foi aux; V, BRB, M: faire fin des
[18]  BNF3, BNF6, BRB, M, K, Vat: assez ont; B: on a assez
[19]  BNF1: "cy" missing; S1/2: roy, tous ceulx-cy
[20]  K: A large "X" follows this verse to cover the remainder of the folio; the text resumes at v. 751 on the next folio.
[21]  Vat: choses

736    By which those in attendance learn of the men's misfortune,[1]
737    For the blade[2] would never turn towards[3] the accused
738    If they were acquitted of the charges.
739    And so the prisoners go out,[4] amid the public,
740    To hear their sentence
741    And to be brought to the accustomed place[5]
742    For judging[6] those who are presumed
743    By some show[7] of evidence
744    To have committed treason towards the king.
745    And there, before the entire Privy Council[8]
746    Who have come there for this purpose,
747    The depositions from witnesses are read in full[9]
748    In order to substantiate[10] the accusations.
749    And, after this is done, and the king's men
750    Have sufficiently pleaded their case, and the accused have denied
751    The substance of the criminal charges,

---

[1]   V, K, BRB: of the men's death
[2]   S1/2: the harsh blade
[3]   1545: be found before
[4]   BL: And so they go out from his prisons; BNF5, S1/2, Vat: And so these prisoners go out; B: And so these persons go out
[5]   BNF1–3, BNF5, BNF7, B, S1/2, V, BRB, M, K, Vat: At Westminster, the accustomed place; BNF4: As it is customary to do; 1545: At the accustomed place for this job
[6]   1545: To judge
[7]   BNF5: some fact
[8]   B: Marginal drawing of a chevron
[9]   All others: are read to them
[10]   V, BRB, M: To conclude

---

738:   The ceremony of the axe is an integral part of Shakespeare's staging of the trial of the Duke of Buckingham in *Henry VIII*, 2.1.
741:   Westminster Hall, where the commoners were tried, was the traditional site for state treason trials, including that of Thomas More.
745:   Carle is wrong here; the trial did not take place in the presence of the Privy Council in any formal capacity, though council members were no doubt in attendance.
747:   The legal term "informations" is used to designate the reports from the examination of witnesses and is most closely rendered by "depositions." These reports would be read into evidence in lieu of having the witnesses testify personally at the trial. See, on this point, Langbein, *Prosecuting Crime*, 28–29.

752  Les accuseurs dient[1] raisons nouuelles,[2]
753  Ausquelz ceux cy respondent, s'il[3] leur semble.
754  Lors le conseil douze encores assemble,[4]
755  De la contree[5] & lieu dont[6] sont natifz,
756  Et de l'estat de ces[7] paouures captifz,[8]
757  Pour veoir[9] si par les proces[10] entendus
758  Les prisonniers sont coulpables rendus,
759  Qui, par raisons,[11] peuuent premierement
760  Les recuser: mais que soit[12] promptement.
761  Ce neantmoins, chascun d'eux[13] se contente
762  Des iuges que le conseil leur presente,
763  Qui font alors[14] solennelle promesse,[15]
764  Sur leur honneur & la foy de[16] noblesse,
765  Mettans la main[17] sur l'escripture saincte,                    [25r]
766  Que pour courroux, par faueur, ou[18] par crainte
767  Nul d'eux sera à iuger incité
768  Que par le droict de[19] congneue equité;

---

[1] BNF1, BNF3–7, B, M, Vat, 1545: disent; BNF2, S1/2: Les accuseurs dirent; V: Les accusateurs disent

[2] BNF1, S1/2: choses nouuelles; BRB: Verse 752 missing

[3] BNF2–4, BNF6–7, S1/2, V, BRB, M, 1545: si

[4] BL: Lors le conseil des douze, encor ensemble (emended for accuracy); BNF1: Lors le conseil encores se assemble; BNF3: Lors le conseil douze encores s'assemble; BNF4: Lors le conseil et douze encores ensemble; B, V: Lors le conseil de douze encores s'assemble; S1/2: Lors le conseil douze seigneurs assemble; BRB: Lors le conseil des douze encores s'assemble; K: Lors le conseil de douze encores assemble; Vat: Lors le conseil douze encores ensemble; 1545: Lors du conseil douze encores ensemble; S1 marginal note reads: "Sentence de mort contre les 4 chevaliers."

[5] V: leur contree ("contree" is interpolated in a different ink)

[6] BNF1–2, BNF5, BNF7, S1/2, V, BRB, K: lieux dont; BNF3: lieux d'où

[7] BL, M: ses (emended for sense as in BNF1–5, B, Vat, 1545); S1: C'est sur l'effect de ces (a corrupt reading); S2: C'est sur l'estat de ses (a corrupt reading); V, BRB, K: des

[8] V: captif

[9] BL: Verront (emended for grammar)

[10] BNF6: par le proces

[11] All others but S1/2: par raison

[12] BNF1: mais que ce fust; V: Le recuser, mais qu'il fust; BRB, M, K: mais que fust

[13] BNF1: neantmoins, ung chascun

[14] V, BRB, M, K: font à tous; 1545: font alors par

[15] K marginal note: Juramentum judicium

[16] BNF1: et foy de leur; B: et la loy de; S1/2: honneur, sur leur foy et

[17] BNF4: leurs mains

[18] V: par courroux, par faveur, et; 1545: par courroux, faveur ou

[19] This verse is underscored in BL. BNF4: par le droict ou

752  The accusers present[1] new evidence[2]
753  To which the accused respond if they see fit.
754  Then the council assembles another twelve men[3]
755  Who are from the county and location native to
756  And from the same station as those poor captives,
757  To see[4] if, by the proceedings they heard,
758  The prisoners are to be found guilty;
759  But the latter can first, for cause,
760  Remove members of the jury, so long as it done promptly.
761  Nevertheless each one of them is satisfied
762  With the jury-members that the council presents to them,
763  And these then make[5] a solemn promise[6]
764  On their honor and on their word as gentlemen,
765  Placing their hand[7] on the Holy Bible,
766  That neither out of anger, nor favor, nor fear,
767  Will any of them be motivated to judge
768  Other than on the basis of justice and[8] fairness.

---

1  BNF2, S1/2: presented
2  BNF1, S1/2: new things
3  BL: Then the council of twelve, still together; BNF1: Then the council assembles again; BNF4: Then the council and another twelve together; B, V, BRB, K: Then the council of twelve assembles again; S1/2: Then the council assembles twelve lords. The variants of Vat and 1545 appear corrupt. S1 marginal note: "Sentence of death against the four knights"
4  BL: Will see
5  V, BRB, M, K: make to everyone
6  M marginal note in Latin: "Jury oath"
7  BNF4: their hands
8  BNF4: or

---

754:  Carle presumably means to differentiate this panel of twelve men from the grand jury involved in establishing the earlier indictment against the accused; however, this second jury would have been empaneled before testimony was given in the case. The variants here reflect some confusion on the part of later scribes, as well, in grasping the intricacies of the English judicial system.

760:  Carle is not quite right in this matter. The accused had the right to make up to twenty-four peremptory challenges to jurors; they did not have to show cause for these challenges. The jury members who were empaneled included Thomas Wharton, Richard Tempest, William Musgrave, Thomas Palmer, Edward Willoughby, William Sidney, Walter Hungerford, Giles Allington, William Askew, Robert Dormer, William Drewry (or Drury), and John Hampden.

766:  Carle is echoing the words of the oath administered to the jury that required them to judge without regard for "envy, hatred, malice ... love, fear, favour, or affection." See Baker, "Criminal Courts," 33.

| | |
|---|---|
| 769 | Et baisent[1] lors du crucifix l'image,[2] |
| 770 | Et si plaider ilz veulent[3] d'auantage, |
| 771 | Auant[4] que soient les douze retirez,[5] |
| 772 | Ilz le pourront;[6] ainsi[7] sont separez[8] |
| 773 | Ces douze en lieu secret, pour bien[9] congnoistre |
| 774 | Quel droict leur semble en ce cas apparoistre.[10] |
| 775 | Lors qu'ilz se[11] sont trestous en accord[12] mis, |
| 776 | Et que sont tous[13] ensemble d'un aduis, |
| 777 | Estant venuz deuant le tabernacle, |
| 778 | Tout haultement, en publicque spectacle,[14] |
| 779 | S'ilz sont[15] GUILTY ou non, on leur demande. |
| 780 | L'vn[16] dit GUILTY. Soudain la hache grande[17] |
| 781 | Tourne l'endroict du trenchant vers la[18] face                     [25v] |
| 782 | Des prisonniers. Nul[19] n'est lors qui[20] ne face |
| 783 | Plusieurs[21] regretz de veoir[22] le desconfort |

---

1 BNF1: baissent; BNF3, B: prindrent; BNF4, BNF6–7, V, BRB, M, K, 1545: baisant
2 B: Marginal drawing of a cross
3 BNF1–3, BNF6–7, B, V, BRB, M, K: Si plaidoyer ils voulloient; BNF4, S1/2, 1545: Si plaidoyer ils veullent; BNF5: Si plaidoyer y veulent
4 1545: D'avant
5 BRB: Verse 771 missing
6 BNF2–3, BNF6: Ilz ne pourroient; BNF4–5, BNF7, B, S1/2, V, BRB, K, M, Vat: Ils le pourroient; 1545: Ils pourroient
7 BRB: aussy
8 BNF5: retirez
9 BNF1: Les douze en lieu seur, et pour mieulx; BNF2: Ses douze en lieu secret pour mieulx; BNF3: Ces douze au lieu secret pour mieulx; BNF4: Ces douze en lieux pour mieux; B, V: Les douze en lieu secret pour mieulx; BNF5, 1545: Ces douze en lieu où puissent mieulx; BNF6: Les douze au lieu secret pour mieulx; BNF7, S1/2, BRB, M, K, Vat: Ces douze en lieu secret pour mieulx
10 BNF1: Quel droict au cas on doit faire apparoistre; BNF4: à ce cas apparoistre; V, BRB, K: en ces cas apparoistre; 1545: en ce cas mieux apparoistre
11 B: Lors qu'ilz; V: Lesquelz se; BRB, K: Lors que se
12 BNF1: sont ensemble en accord; BNF4–5: sont tous en ung accord; 1545: sont tous en accord
13 BNF1, BNF4, S1/2, V, BRB, M, K: qu'ilz sont tous; Vat: que tous sont
14 BL: spectable (emended to preserve the rhyme); BNF2, BNF7, BRB, K: en public spectacle; BNF5: et en public spectable; M: Verse 778 missing
15 BNF1, S2: S'ilz ont
16 BRB, 1545: L'on
17 BNF6 combines vv. 779–780 to read: "S'ils sont guylty. Soubdain la hache grande"; B combines vv. 779–780 to read: "S'ils sont Guilty; soubdain la grande hache"; Vat originally has after 778: "s'ilz sont guilty. Soudain la hache grande," but this is crossed out and replaced by v. 779.
18 V: leurs; BRB, K: leur
19 V: nuls
20 BNF2, BNF5–6, S1, BRB, Vat: qu'il
21 S1/2: Piteux
22 BNF1, 1545: regrets voyant

769    And they kiss[1] the image of the crucifix,[2]

770    And if they wish[3] to argue the case further,

771    Before the twelve withdraw,

772    They may[4] do so. And so the twelve are

773    Sequestered in a secret place to decide correctly[5]

774    What appears to be just in this case.[6]

775    Once they[7] are all completely in agreement

776    And all are together of one opinion,

777    And they come before the dais in the Great Hall,

778    They are asked out loud, in full view of the public,

779    If the accused are "GUILTY" or not.

780    One says, "GUILTY." Suddenly the great axe[8]

781    Turns its cutting edge towards

782    The face of the prisoners. There is then not a soul who does not experience

783    Much[9] sorrow upon seeing the heavy hearts

---

[1] BNF1: they lower; BNF3, B: they take

[2] B: marginal notation of a cross

[3] BNF1–3, BNF6–7, B, V, BRB, M, K: wished

[4] BNF2–3, BNF6: they could not

[5] BNF1: And so the twelve are sequestered in a safe location, to decide better; BNF2–3, BNF6–7, B, S1/2, V, BRB, M, K, Vat: And so the [these] twelve are sequestered in a secret place to decide better; BNF4: And so these twelve are sequestered in a place to decide better; BNF5, 1545: And so these twelve are sequestered in a place where they can better decide

[6] BNF1: What justice should be done in this case

[7] V: These men

[8] BNF6 and B read at vv. 779–780: If they are guilty; suddenly the great axe

[9] S1/2: Piteous

---

777:    The word Carle uses here is "tabernacle," which meant "pavilion, tent, or hall." The term could also refer more specifically to the dais upon which sat the presider of the trial.

784    De ces seigneurs[1] condamnez à la mort;
785    Laquelle, quant les douze ont rapportee,[2]
786    Le chancelier[3] leur[4] a lors decretee[5]
787    La peine qu'il conuient,[6] selon la[7] loy,
788    Aux condamnez de crime vers[8] le Roy:
789    Premierement, qui est d'estre penduz,[9]
790    Sans estrangler, & puis tous vifz[10] fenduz.
791    En ceste triste & piteuse maniere
792    Sont ramenez[11] en leur[12] prison premiere,
793    Qui n'estoit pas[13] sans estre beaucoup[14] plains.
794    Et mesmement l'on[15] faisoit de grans plains[16]
795    Du Sieur[17] Waston, qui estoit de ieune aage,[18]
796    Yssu de[19] hault & antien lignaige,[20]
797    De[21] bonnes meurs & grace[22] tous passant,[23]          [26r]
798    En lysse, au bal,[24] à[25] saulter triumphant,[26]
799    En ieu de paulme, en[27] grand perfection,

---

[1]  S1/2: Des prisonniers
[2]  BNF5, V, M, K, 1545: raporté
[3]  B: chevalier
[4]  BNF6, 1545: leurs
[5]  BNF5, V, M, K, 1545: decreté
[6]  B: convenoit; S1, BRB, M, K: qui convient
[7]  BNF1–3, BNF5–7, V, BRB, M, K, Vat: leur; 1545: La peine que selon leur
[8]  BNF1: condemnez qui sont envers; BNF2–6, B, S1/2, V, BRB, M, K, Vat: de crime envers;
     BNF7: condemnez envers; 1545: du crime envers
[9]  BL: Verses 788–789 are underscored
[10] 1545: puis apres
[11] BNF4–5: revenuz
[12] B, V, BRB, K: la
[13] V, BRB, M, K: point
[14] BNF4–5, 1545: beaucoup estre
[15] BNF2–3, BNF5–7, B, S1/2, K, Vat: Et mesmement on; V: Et mesme on
[16] BNF1: Et congneut on lors le secret de maintz (a corrupt reading); BNF3: de grand plains; S2,
     K: des grans plains
[17] BNF1–3, BNF5–7, B, S1, V, BRB, M, K, Vat, 1545: Du povre; BNF4: Du bon
[18] BNF1: jeune d'aage
[19] 1545: du
[20] BNF2: et tresancien lignaige; BNF3: hault, tresancien lignaige; BNF4: et bien noble lignaige; B:
     ancien parentaige
[21] S1/2: En
[22] BNF1–2, BNF6, B, V, S1, BRB, K, M, Vat, 1545: graces
[23] BNF5, 1545: tant puissant
[24] BNF1, BRB, M: En lice, en bal; BNF4–5, 1545: En lice ou bal; V: En lice, bal; K: En lysse et bal
[25] BNF3, BNF5–6: et
[26] BNF1–2, BNF4–7, V, BRB, M, K, Vat: saulter effaçant; B: saulter s'efforssant; S1/2: À bataille
     aux lices trespuissant; 1545: saulter tous effaçant
[27] BL, BNF4, BNF7, M, Vat: & (emended for sense as in BNF1, V, BRB, K); BNF2–3, BNF6: de

784    Of these gentlemen[1] who are condemned to death,
785    Which, when the twelve men reported their verdict,
786    The Lord Chancellor[2] then decreed to them
787    To be the appropriate penalty, according to the[3] law,
788    For those condemned of crimes against the king:
789    That is, first, to be hanged without being asphyxiated,
790    And then to be cut open while still alive.[4]
791    In this sad and piteous manner,
792    They were brought back[5] to their first prison,
793    Which happened not without much lamentation,
794    And people especially greatly bewailed
795    Sir[6] Weston, who was of a young age,
796    Born of a noble and ancient lineage,[7]
797    Exceeding everyone[8] in good manners and grace,
798    Triumphing[9] at the list, at[10] dance, and at horse jumping,[11]
799    And perfectly accomplished in tennis,

---

1   S1/2: Of the prisoners
2   B: The knight
3   BNF1–3, BNF5–7, V, BRB, M, K, Vat, 1545: their
4   1545: And then, afterwards, to be cut open
5   BNF4–5: they returned
6   BNF1–3, BNF5–7, B, S1, V, BRB, M, K, Vat, 1545: Poor; BNF4: Good
7   BNF2: and of very ancient lineage; BNF3: and of noble, very ancient lineage; BNF4: and of quite noble lineage; B: and of ancient parentage
8   BNF5, 1545: So strong
9   BNF1–2, BNF4–7, V, BRB, M, K, Vat, 1545: Eclipsing everyone; B: Endeavoring
10  BNF4–5: or
11  S1/2: Very powerful in combat at the list

---

786:    The Lord Chancellor was Thomas Audley.
790:    The normal verdict for acts of treason committed by men was "to be drawn upon a hurdle to the place of execution, … to be hanged by the neck, and being alive cut down, and … privy-members to be cut off, and [the] body to be divided into four quarters." See Baker, "Criminal Courts," 42.

800   Le plus adroict[1] de ceste nation.
801   Et de tous biens tant en luy abondoit[2]
802   Que ce pays tout honoré rendoit.[3]
803   Mais ses vertuz[4] ne peurent[5] rien valoir[6]
804   Pour incliner[7] du prince le vouloir,[8]
805   Qui tant se sent[9] touché de leur[10] offence,
806   Que nul pour eux en ose[11] faire instance,[12]
807   Sinon sa[13] mere, en grant dueil oppressee,[14]
808   Qui humblement au Roy s'est adressee,[15]
809   Sa femme aussi, offrant entierement
810   Sa rente & biens[16] pour son deliurement.
811   Mais le Roy veult que soit executee[17]
812   En leur[18] procez l'ordonnance arrestee.[19]
813   Et si l'argent[20] pour luy eust eu[21] puissance,          [26v]
814   D'escus cent mil eust finé[22] la[23] cheuance.
815   Ainsi[24] sont tous à[25] la prison remis,

---

1  BNF5, BNF7, M, K: Les plus adroictz; V, BRB, 1545: Des plus adroictz
2  BNF1–3, BNF5, BNF7, S2, V, BRB, M, K, Vat, 1545: biens en luy tant abondoit; BNF4: Et tant
   de bien en luy abondoit; BNF6: Et tous bienz en luy tant abondoit; B: Et de tous poinctz en biens
   tant abondoit; S1: biens en luy tant abondit
3  V, BRB, M, K: Qu'en ce pays tout honneur redondoit; S1: rendit
4  BNF2, S1/2: ces vertuz; 1545: vertueulx
5  BNF1: sceurent; V, 1545: peuvent
6  V: voulloir
7  V, K: descliner
8  V: This verse is interpolated in a different ink.
9  BNF4: dict
10  BNF5, S1/2, Vat: son
11  BNF2, BNF6, V, BRB, M, K: eux n'en ose; BNF4 eux n'en osa; BNF5, S1/2: luy n'en osa; B: eux
    n'ose
12  V, BRB, K: l'instance
13  BNF1: la
14  BL: de grand douleur expresse (emended for versification to conform with all others). S1 marginal
    note: Plainte faicte au Roy d'Angleterre pour Oaston
15  BL: faict son adresse (emended to maintain rhyme with v. 807 and to conform with all others);
    vv. 806–808 are partially underscored in BL. V: Verse missing
16  BNF2–3, BNF6: Rentes et biens; BNF4–5, Vat: Ses rentes et biens; S1/2: Leur rente et biens; V,
    M: Sa rente et bien; 1545: Ses biens trestous
17  BNF4: qu'il soit exécuté
18  BNF5, 1545: De leur; S1/2: En son
19  BNF1, BNF3: la sentence arrestee; BNF4: d'ordonnance arresté
20  BNF2–3, BNF6, B: si argent
21  BNF1–2, BNF4: eust eu pour luy; Vat: pour luy eu eust
22  BNF4: finy
23  V, BRB, M, K: de
24  BRB: Aussi
25  Vat: Ainsi tous sont en; all others: sont tous en

800  The[1] most skillful of this nation;
801  And all gifts so abounded in him[2]
802  That this country bestowed every honor on him.[3]
803  But his[4] virtues could be of no value
804  In bending[5] the will of the prince,
805  Who felt[6] so aggrieved by their[7] offense
806  That no one dare[8] stand up for them,[9]
807  Except Weston's mother, who, weighed down by her great grief,[10]
808  Humbly addressed her petition to the king,
809  And also his wife, who offered her[11] entire
810  Wealth and income[12] for his freedom.
811  But the king ordered that the sentence
812  Decreed at their[13] trial be executed.[14]
813  And if money had held any power for him
814  He would have been paid the sum of 100,000 crowns.
815  And so they were all sent back to prison,

---

1  V, BRB, 1545: Among the
2  BNF4: And so many gifts abounded in him; B: And in all points he so abounded in gifts
3  V, BRB, M, K: That every honor of this country overflowed in him
4  BNF2, S1/2: these
5  V, K: In disinclining
6  BNF4: Who said he was
7  BNF5, S1/2: his
8  BNF4–5, S1/2: dared
9  BNF5, S1/2: for him
10  BL: strained by great sorrow; S1 marginal note: "Plea made to the King of England for Weston"
11  S1/2: their
12  1545: Wealth—each and every bit of it—
13  S1/2: his
14  BNF4: But the king wished that he be executed / According to the sentence decreed at their trial

---

810:  Carle is the only source for this information concerning Weston's mother and wife. According to Chapuys, however, the French ambassadors Castelnau and Dinteville were among those who tried to intervene on behalf of Weston. See, on this point, Chapuys's letter to Charles V dated 19 May 1536 in LP 10.908 and CSP, Spain, 5, pt. 2, no. 55. Cf. Husee's letter to Lord Lisle dated 13 May: "in case any do escape it shall be young Weston, for whose life there is importunate suit made." See Byrne, *Lisle Letters*, 3:361. Husee's remark is vague enough to admit the possibility that Weston's mother and wife pleaded with the king; but it is also possible that Carle changed the facts for the sake of adding melodrama to his tale, turning a political plea into a very personal one.

814:  According to David Loades, the sum of 100,000 crowns "would have supported a full household for five or six years." See *Mary Tudor*, 93–94.

816    N'esperant plus secours[1] de leurs amis.
817    Chascun de bien[2] mourir se deslibere,
818    Comme prenant vne mort voluntaire.
819    Chascun vers Dieu eslieue[3] sa pensee,
820    En attendant que leur[4] soit commencee[5]
821    L'heure de mort, & que[6] soient depeschez.
822    Et ce pendant millordz sont empeschez,[7]
823    Selon l'estat dessus mentionné,
824    Pour[8] Rochefort, qui n'est point[9] estonné,[10]
825    Mais de bon cueur attend l'aduenement[11]
826    Ou de sa vie ou du deffinement.[12]
827    Et si iamais au parauant eut[13] force
828    En[14] son couraige, adonc plus se[15] renforce,
829    Et tant plus a le cœur[16] constant & ferme          [27r]
830    Que[17] plus se veoit approcher de son terme.[18]
831    On le voulut,[19] par honneur, exempter
832    De le[20] mener iuger à Wesmester,[21]
833    Et aussi pour la Royne accompaigner,

---

1   1545: ayde
2   S1/2: Chascun d'entre eulx
3   S1/2: eslevoit
4   BRB, Vat: lors; 1545: luy
5   All others but BNF2: annoncee
6   BNF4: qu'ilz
7   B: Verse 822 missing
8   BL: Fort (a corrupt reading, emended for sense as in all but S1/2)
9   BNF5: poinct n'est; V, BRB, K: n'est pas
10  S1/2: Or Rocheffort de riens n'est estonné
11  BNF1, S2: l'avancement
12  BNF5: Ou de sa vie le deffinement; B: Que de sa vie est le definement; S1/2: De delivrance ou
    de son finement; 1545: Ou de sa vie ou diffinement
13  1545: jamais paravant il eust
14  Vat, 1545: À
15  BNF1: il
16  BRB: courage
17  BNF1: Quant
18  S1/2: Verses 829–830 read: Et de tant plus qu'il veoit venir son terme, / De tant plus a le cueur
    constant et ferme
19  BL: On ne voulut (emended for accuracy, to conform with the positive sense present in all other
    readings); BNF5, S1/2, V, BRB, M, K, Vat: On le vouloit; B: On les veult
20  B: les
21  BL, BNF2, BNF6: Remester (emended as in BNF1, BNF5, V); BNF3: Oesmester; BNF4:
    Vymonstier (the word before this is crossed out, as if the scribe is struggling over spelling); S2:
    Oasmaster; Vat: iuger Oesmaster; 1545: Vhemestier; all others as before, v. 710; S1 marginal
    note: Wuestmaster

816   No longer hoping for help[1] from their friends.
817   Each one resolves to die well,[2]
818   As if choosing a voluntary death.
819   Each one raises[3] his thought toward God,
820   While waiting for the hour of their death
821   To begin[4] and to be dispatched to their end.
822   And, in the meantime, the peers of the realm are preoccupied,
823   According to the state of affairs mentioned above,
824   With regard to Rochford, who is not at all[5] daunted,
825   But who is courageously awaiting the outcome[6]
826   Of either life or death.[7]
827   And if he ever before was of strong mettle,
828   He gathers more strength at that moment,
829   And keeps his heart all the more constant and firm
830   Because[8] he sees the end approaching.[9]
831   They had wanted,[10] as a matter of honor, to exempt
832   Him[11] from being taken to be judged at Westminster,[12]
833   And also so as to accompany the queen,

---

[1]  1545: aid
[2]  S1/2: Each one among them resolves to die
[3]  S1/2: raised
[4]  All others but BNF2: To be announced to them
[5]  V, BRB, K: who is not
[6]  S1/2: Verses 824–825 read: Now Rochford is not daunted by anything / But is courageously awaiting the outcome
[7]  BNF5: Or the end of his life; B: Which is the end of his life; S1/2: Of his deliverance or his demise
[8]  BNF1: When
[9]  S1/2: Verses 829–830 read: "And the more he sees the end of his life coming / So much more does he keep his heart constant and firm"
[10]  BL: They had not wanted
[11]  B: Them
[12]  S1: Marginal note: "Westminster"

---

833:   Chapuys also remarks in his letter to Charles V dated 19 May that Rochford and Anne were not tried at Westminster "as the other criminals had been; they were tried within the Tower." See LP 10.908. Chapuys notes, however, that Anne was condemned first. Carle apparently has reversed the order of the trials, presumably for dramatic effect.

834    Que dans la tour on vouloit condamner.[1]
835    Quant, donc, il fut venu[2] en la presence
836    De ces millordz, & qu'en grand reuerence
837    S'est[3] presenté pour estre obeissant
838    À leur auis, l'un[4] vient, la voix haulsant,
839    Qui[5] son meffaict blasme publicquement.
840    Vn aultre apres encor[6] plus asprement,
841    Vn aultre apres[7] ses offenses augmente,[8]
842    Vn aultre apres[9] de nouueau le tourmente.[10]
843    Quand il se[11] veit pressé[12] de tous costéz,[13]
844    Sans se troubler,[14] les a tous escoutéz,
845    Et puis, apres auoir bien retenu                          [27v]
846    De leur discours[15] au vray le contenu,
847    Vn peu pensif auant parler se tient,[16]
848    Et les[17] yeux bas quelque espace retient.[18]
849    Puis sagement[19] en hault les a dressez[20]
850    Vers les millordz, & telz motz prononcez:
851    "Ie n'entendz pas,[21] seigneurs, que de la peine
852    Que[22] ie me voy[23] estre brefue & certaine,[24]

---

[1] BNF1: Que dans le temps on vouloit condamner (a scribal error); B, Vat: Que dedans la Tour on vouloit condamner; S1/2: Que l'on vouloit dans la tour condamner; V, K: Que dedans la Tour l'on vouloit condamner; BRB, M: Qui dans la tour l'on vouloit condamner

[2] BNF1: doncques fut en; B: donques fust venu en

[3] BNF2-3: Fut; BNF7, 1545: C'est

[4] BNF2-4, BNF6-7, B, M: ung

[5] BNF2: Que

[6] BL: apres encores (emended for versification); B: Ung ancoires; 1545: apres blasme

[7] BNF4: aussi

[8] S1/2, Vat: Verse 841 missing

[9] BNF4: Et puis un aultre

[10] S1 adds after v. 842, to complete the rhyme: De dire vray et que point il ne mente; K: Un aultre de nouveau le tourmente

[11] V: Quant se

[12] 1545: veoit presser

[13] S1 marginal note reads: "Defence de Millort de Rochefort"

[14] B: tourbeler

[15] S1/2: leur parler; V, K, Vat, 1545: leurs discours

[16] BNF1, BNF4, BNF7, S1/2: tint; B: "tint" corrected to "tient"

[17] 1545: ses

[18] BNF1: Les yeulx baissez par quelque espace tint; BNF4, BNF7, S1/2: retint

[19] S1/2: gravement

[20] BNF4, V, BRB, M: adressez

[21] BNF1: n'attends riens; BNF2-3, BNF6-7, Vat, 1545: n'attends pas; B, S1/2: n'attends plus

[22] BNF5: Où

[23] BNF6: voye

[24] V, BRB, K: Verse 852 missing; M, Vat: et prochaine

834 Whom they wanted to condemn within the Tower.
835 When, therefore, he was brought before the presence
836 Of these lords and, with great respect,
837 Presented himself to be obedient
838 To their judgment, one of them comes forward, raising his voice
839 And rebukes him publicly for his misdeed,
840 Another, afterwards, even[1] more harshly,
841 Another, afterwards,[2] adds to his crimes,
842 Another, afterwards,[3] torments him anew.[4]
843 When he saw himself hemmed in on all sides,[5]
844 Without getting flustered, he listened to them all
845 And then, after thoroughly mulling over in his mind,
846 With exactitude, the content of their speech,
847 He remains[6] a bit pensive before speaking,
848 And keeps[7] his eyes lowered a little while;
849 Then he soberly[8] looked up and fixed his eyes
850 On the lords and pronounced such words as these:
851 "I do not mean,[9] sirs, that the penalty
852 That I see to be sure and swift[10]

---

[1] 1545: rebukes
[2] BNF4: also
[3] BNF4: And then another
[4] S1/2 and Vat are missing v. 841, but S1 adds after v. 842 (to complete the rhyme): To tell the truth and not lie at all
[5] S1 marginal note reads: "Defense of Lord Rochford"
[6] BNF1, BNF4, BNF7, S1/2: remained
[7] BNF1, BNF4, BNF7, S1/2: kept
[8] S1/2: gravely
[9] BNF1: I expect not a whit; BNF2–4, BNF6–7, Vat, 1545: I do not expect; B, S1/2: I no longer expect
[10] M, Vat: sure and near

---

836:  There were twenty-five peers of the realm serving as judges in the trial against Rochford: Charles, Duke of Suffolk; Henry, Marquis of Exeter; William, Earl of Arundel; John, Earl of Oxford; Ralph, Earl of Westmoreland; Edward, Earl of Derby; Henry, Earl of Worcester; Thomas, Earl of Rutland; Robert, Earl of Sussex; George, Earl of Huntingdon; John, Lord Audeley; Thomas, Lord La Ware; Henry, Lord Mountague; Henry, Lord Morley; Thomas, Lord Dacre; George, Lord Cobham; Henry, Lord Maltravers; Edward, Lord Powes; Thomas, Lord Mount Egle; Edward, Lord Clynton; William, Lord Sandes; Andrew, Lord Wyndesor; Thomas, Lord Wentworth; Thomas, Lord Burgh; and John, Lord Mordaunt. Anne's trial was judged by all of the above plus Henry, Earl of Northumberland, a former suitor of Anne's, who suddenly took ill and was removed before the start of Rochford's trial. On this matter, see LP 10.876.

850:  Carle is the only source for this defense speech, although Chapuys noted (LP 10.908) that "more than 2000" spectators attended the trial.

853    Excusé sois[1] par la triste harengue
854    Que proferer veult ma[2] debile langue.
855    Car[3] si tout seul on m'eut mis & compris[4]
856    En ce meffaict, duquel m'auez[5] repris,
857    Crainte de mort ne[6] m'eust sceu aduancer
858    Pour vn seul mot me[7] faire commancer.[8]
859    Mais cognoissant que la[9] dure infortune[10]
860    Auec ma seur m'est egalle &[11] commune,
861    Contraint ie suis, selon ma conscience,                    [28r]
862    De vous monstrer[12] de nous deux l'innocence.
863    Et combien que tant i'estime[13] & redoubte
864    Voz iugementz, que ne face[14] aucun[15] doubte
865    Que sont pour vous voz raisons apparentes[16]
866    Pour[17] me iuger trouuees suffisantes[18]—
867    Pensantz deuoir, au rapport[19] d'vne femme,

---

[1]  BNF5: Estre absoulz; M, 1545: soye
[2]  V: par ma
[3]  S1/2: Et
[4]  BNF1-3, BNF5, BNF7, S1/2, V, BRB, K, M, Vat: seul je fusse esté compris; BNF4, BNF6: seul je eusse esté compris; B: seul je y fusse esté comprins; 1545: seul en ce feusse comprins
[5]  BNF1: dont vous m'avez; BRB: duquel m'aviez
[6]  BNF3: missing "ne"
[7]  BNF5: ne
[8]  Vat originally skips v. 858, retaining v. 859, but v. 859 is later crossed out and replaced by v. 858 followed by v. 859
[9]  BNF5, V, BRB, M, K, 1545: ma
[10] V, BRB, M, K: fortune
[11] BNF1: Avec ma seur est egalle et; BNF2: Avec ma seur n'est egalle ne; BNF5: D'avec ma seur m'est egalle et; Vat: Aveques ma seur m'est egalle et; 1545: D'avec ma sœur n'est egalle et
[12] BNF1, BNF3-7, B, S1, V, M, 1545: Vous demonstrer; BRB, K: Vous monstrer; Vat: De vous demonstrer
[13] BNF4, K: que tant estime; B, V: que j'estime
[14] BNF1: je face; BNF4: sy ne faiz je; S1/2: je fay
[15] BRB: aucune
[16] BNF1: Que soient raisons, tant soient peu apparentes; BNF2, B, V, M, K: Que soient par vos raisons peu apparentes; BNF3, BNF6-7: Que soient par vous raisons peu apparentes; BNF4: Que ces raisons peu apparentes; BNF5: Que ne soient bonnes ces raisons apparentes; S1/2: Qui soient par vous raisons apparentes; BRB: Que soyent par voz jugements peu apparents; Vat: Que soient par vous voz raisons apparentes; 1545: Que soient par vos raisons apparentes. The variant readings are all corrupt in some way.
[17] BNF2: Peu
[18] BNF2, S1/2: juger trouvees peu suffisantes; BNF4, BRB, M, 1545: juger trouverez suffisantes; Vat: juger trouver et suffisantes
[19] BNF1-2, BNF4, BNF7, B, S1/2, V, BRB, M, K, Vat: Et pour l'advis seullement; BNF3, 1545: Et par l'advis seullement; BNF5: Et pour advis seulement; BNF6: Et à l'advis seullement

853    Should be forgiven[1] by the sad plea
854    That my weak tongue wishes to offer.
855    For,[2] if I alone had been put forth and charged[3]
856    With this crime, for which you have reprimanded me,
857    Fear of death would not have succeeded in bringing forth
858    A single word to make me begin.
859    But knowing that my harsh misfortune
860    Is shared equally[4] with my sister,
861    I am constrained by my conscience
862    To show you[5] that we are both innocent.
863    And, although I so esteem and am in such awe of
864    Your opinions that I have absolutely no doubt
865    That they are, for you, obvious grounds
866    Which you find sufficient[6] to judge me—
867    Such that you think that you are duty-bound, on the word of one
       woman,[7]

---

[1]  BNF5: absolved
[2]  S1/2: And
[3]  All others: if I alone had been charged
[4]  BNF2, 1545: Is not shared equally
[5]  BNF1, BNF3–7, B, S1, V, M, Vat, 1545: To demonstrate for you
[6]  BNF2, S1/2: barely sufficient
[7]  All others: And on the counsel of only one woman

---

867:    While many think this is a reference to George's wife, Jane, within the context of the poem it
        must refer to the sister of the close advisor who made the initial accusation. Rochford might
        also be attempting to point out that normally "two lawful accusers"—and not just one—were
        necessary to bring about a charge. See, on this point, Coke, *Institutes*, 25; and Hill, "Two-
        Witness Rule," 96–99. Furthermore, Rochford may be questioning the reliability of female
        witnesses in particular.

868    Croire de moy vn si grand crime & blasme,[1]
869    Et par l'effect d'vne presomption[2]
870    Determinans[3] ma[4] condamnation—
871    Si toutesfois, seigneurs, puis que scauez[5]
872    Que compaignon long temps tenu[6] m'auez,
873    En mesme estat &[7] mesme authorité,
874    Et ne vouldriez que vostre[8] dignité,
875    Par suspeçon[9] de telle[10] opinion,
876    Fust ainsi mise en disputation,
877    Ie me mettray plus oultre à me[11] deffendre,        [28v]
878    Et de mes faictz telle raison vous rendre,
879    Que certain suis que, quand vous l'entendrez,[12]
880    Tout[13] innocent du crime[14] me rendrez.[15]
881    Mais humblement ie pry la bonté haulte
882    Du Createur, que selon ma defaulte[16]
883    Meritera, il vous[17] vueille inspirer

---

1    BNF1-6, B, S1, V, BRB, M, K, Vat: Croire voullez de moy ung si grant blasme; BNF7: Croire
     vueillez de moy ung si grand blasme; S2: Croirez voulez de moy ung si grant blasme; 1545: Croire
     voulez en moy ung si grand blasme
2    BNF1-7, B, V, BRB, M, K, Vat: Que, pour l'effect de sa presomption; S1/2: Et par l'effect de sa
     presomption; 1545: Que par l'effect de sa presomption
3    BNF1: Determinez; all others: Determiner
4    BNF4: la
5    BNF1: Veu mesmement que vous tous bien savez; all others: Veu mesmement, Seigneurs, que
     bien savez
6    B: eu vous; V: tenuz
7    BNF1: en
8    BNF3, BNF6-7, 1545: Et ne vouldrois que vostre; V: Que ne voldries que une; BRB, M, K: Que
     ne vouldriez que vostre
9    BNF2: sousperon; BNF4: soubspection; BNF5, V: suspition; BNF7: suspecion; B, BRB, K,
     1545: suspection
10   BNF5: de quelque
11   BNF1-2, BNF6, B, S1/2, V, BRB: Si veulx encores plus oultre me; BNF3-5, 1545: Si veulx-ie
     encor plus oultre me; BNF7: Si veulx encor plus oultre me; M, K, Vat: Si veulx-ie encores plus
     oultre me
12   BNF1-2, BNF5-6, B, S1/2, V, BRB, Vat: quant vous m'entenderez; BNF4, BNF7, K, M: quant
     vous m'entenderez; 1545: suis quand vous m'entenderez
13   S1/2: Pur
14   BNF4: de crimes; BNF7, B, M: de crime
15   BNF1, BNF3-7, S1/2, V, BRB, M, K, Vat, 1545: tiendrez; B originally reads "tient" then
     corrected in another hand and ink to "tiendrez" with correction signaled in the margin by two
     parallel bars.
16   BNF2-7, B, S1/2, M, Vat, 1545: que selon que ma faulte; V, BRB, K: que selon ma faulte
17   S1/2: Meritera, tant vous; V: Merite ayt, vous; BRB, K: Merite a, il vous; 1545: Mectra, il vous (a
     corrupt reading)

| 868 | To believe me capable of so great a crime and deserving of blame,[1] |
|---|---|
| 869 | And,[2] on the basis of a single[3] suspicion, |
| 870 | You determine to condemn me— |
| 871 | Yet, gentlemen, since you are aware[4] |
| 872 | That you have long considered me a friend |
| 873 | Of the same status and same authority as you, |
| 874 | And since you would not want[5] your dignity, |
| 875 | On account of such a[6] dubious opinion, |
| 876 | To be disputed in this way, |
| 877 | I shall set out to defend myself still further,[7] |
| 878 | And to give such evidence of my actions |
| 879 | That I am certain that, when you hear it,[8] |
| 880 | You will render me[9] completely[10] innocent of any crime. |
| 881 | But I humbly beseech the great goodness |
| 882 | Of the Creator that, according to whatever my fault |
| 883 | Deserves, He should wish to inspire you |

---

[1] All others: You wish to believe me deserving of such a great blame

[2] All others but S1/2: That

[3] All others: of her

[4] BNF1: Given especially that you are all well aware; all others: Given especially, gentlemen, that you are well aware

[5] BNF3, BNF6–7, 1545: And I would not want

[6] BNF5: of some

[7] All others: Therefore I wish to defend myself still further

[8] All others but BNF3: hear me

[9] BNF1, BNF3–7, B, S1/2, V, BRB, M, K, Vat, 1545: You will hold me

[10] S1/2: clean

884    Que[1] iustement la puissiez[2] declairer."
885    Apres ce[3] dit, il commence à reprendre[4]
886    Les[5] dictz de ceux qui le veullent[6] surprendre,
887    Et leur discours[7] recite asseurement,[8]
888    Et puis à[9] tous respond discrettement,
889    De poinct en poinct, sans nulle[10] ordre confondre,
890    Tant qu'on ne veit onc homme[11] mieux respondre,
891    Non le Maurus, qui sa grande eloquence[12]
892    Et le scauoir qu'auoit en abondance[13]
893    Onc n'employa,[14] en ses[15] cas necessaires,          [29r]
894    Pour mieux respondre[16] à tous ses aduersaires.[17]
895    Et, pour la fin de ses[18] propos, maintient
896    Que, de tous ceulx que la terre soustient,[19]
897    Nul est qui sceust[20] par raison deposer[21]
898    Que d'aulcun[22] cas ilz l'ayent[23] veu abuser
899    Auec la Royne, & qu'il l'a[24] reueree
900    Tousiours en seur & en Dame[25] honoree.
901    Et sur ce poinct, inuocque la clemence

---

1  S1/2: Et
2  BNF1, BNF5, S1/2, 1545: le puissiez; M: la puisse; K: la puissance
3  S1/2: tel
4  BNF4, BNF7: respondre
5  BNF4: Aux
6  M: qu'il le vouloient; all others: qui le voulloient
7  BNF7, M, Vat: Et leurs discours; 1545: En leur discours
8  BNF1: compter asseurement; BNF4: recita seurement
9  BNF4: Et depuis à
10  All others: nul
11  V, K: Tant qu'on voit oncques homme; BRB: Tant qu'on voit homme oncq; 1545: "homme" missing
12  All others: Non pas Maurus mesmes, qui d'eloquence
13  BNF1–3, BNF5–7, B, Vat, 1545: Et de savoir avoit tant d'affluence; BNF4, S1/2, V, BRB, M, K: Et de savoir avoit tant d'influence
14  B: Ne se monstroit; all others: Ne se monstra
15  BNF1–2, BNF4–5, S1/2, V, BRB, K, Vat, 1545: ces
16  BNF1–7, B, V, BRB, M, K, Vat, 1545: Respondant mieulx; S1/2: Mieulx respondant
17  K: à tous ses affaires (a corrupt reading)
18  BNF2, BNF4: ces; BNF3, BNF6: ce
19  K: maintient
20  BNF1, BNF4, V, BRB, M, K: Nul n'est qui sceust; BNF5: Nul est qui peust
21  BNF4, BNF6, B: disposer
22  S2: Et d'aucun; V, BRB: d'ancien
23  BNF1, BNF4, S1/2, V, BRB, M, K: il l'ait; BNF2–3: il ait; BNF5: cas l'ayent; BNF6: ilz ayent; B: lui ont
24  V: mais qu'il l'a; M: et qui la; Vat: et que l'a
25  B: et dame

884    So[1] that you will be able to declare it justly."
885    After this[2] statement he begins to reprise[3]
886    The words of those who wish[4] to take him unawares,
887    And he repeats[5] their speech with confidence.
888    And then he responds to everyone separately,
889    Point by point, without any confusion in the order,
890    Such that you never saw a man respond better:
891    Not even More[6] had ever employed[7] his great eloquence
892    And the knowledge that he possessed in abundance[8]
893    Any better to answer all his adversaries
894    In his[9] most difficult cases.
895    And, at the end of his speech,[10] Rochford maintains
896    That, of all those whom the earth sustains,[11]
897    There is no one who could rightly testify
898    That in any[12] instance did they[13] see him abuse
899    The queen, and[14] that he revered her
900    Always as a sister and as a greatly respected lady.
901    And on this point he invokes the clemency

[1] S1/2: And
[2] S1/2: After such a
[3] BNF4, BNF7: to answer
[4] All others: who wished
[5] BNF1: And to recount; BNF4: And he recited
[6] All others: Not even More himself
[7] All others: shown
[8] BNF4, S1/2, V, BRB, M, K: And his knowledge that had such influence
[9] BNF1-2, BNF4-5, S1/2, V, BRB, K, Vat, 1545: these
[10] BNF2, BNF4: these words; BNF3, BNF6: this speech
[11] K: maintains
[12] V, BRB: a previous
[13] BNF1-4, S1/2, V, BRB, M, K: did he
[14] V: but

894:    More was a renowned lawyer who also defended himself ably but unsuccessfully in his own
        treason trial. Chapuys indicates that Rochford "replied so well that several of those present
        wagered ten to one that he would be acquitted." See LP 10.908; and CSP Spain, 5, pt. 2, no.
        55. Wriothesley also remarks upon Rochford's skillful defense (*Chronicle*, 1:39).

| 902 | De Dieu pour tost en[1] faire l'euidence. |
|-----|-------------------------------------------|
| 903 | Apres auoir son droict bien debattu,[2] |
| 904 | Et les raisons contraires rabattu,[3] |
| 905 | Assemblez sont les iuges pour scauoir |
| 906 | Si viure doit,[4] ou la mort receuoir. |
| 907 | Trouuez se sont d'opinion diuerse,[5] |
| 908 | Mais, à[6] la fin, l'vne l'autre[7] renuerse,[8] |
| 909 | Tant qu'ilz se sont en vne conformez.[9] |
| 910 | Ainsi sortent dont[10] estoient[11] enferméz. |
| 911 | Le millord duc de Norfort,[12] president[13] |
| 912 | Au iugement de ce pauure[14] attendant, |
| 913 | Combien qu'il[15] fust son oncle maternel,[16] |
| 914 | Leur demanda s'il estoit criminel, |
| 915 | Et[17] s'il estoit coulpable ou non prouué.[18] |
| 916 | Vn luy respond[19] que coulpable est trouué.[20] |
| 917 | Quand Rochefort entendit qu'il estoit |
| 918 | À mort iugé, & que plus ne restoit[21] |
| 919 | Que de pourueoir à disposer son ame,[22] |
| 920 | Il ne se meust[23] & les iuges[24] ne blasme, |

[29v]

---

1 BNF1: pour tous pour

2 S1 marginal note reads: "Jugement de mort contre millort de Rocheffort"

3 BNF4: abbatu; S1/2: debatu; V, BRB, K: entendu

4 B: debvoit

5 BNF4: d'opinions diuerse; BNF5: d'opinion contraire

6 BNF6, Vat: en

7 K: l'une à l'autre

8 S1/2: Finablement apres leur controverse

9 BNF1–2, BNF7, B, V, M, 1545: confermez; S1/2: Ils se sont tous en un dict conformez

10 BL, BNF4, B, V, BRB, M, K, Vat: sortant dont (emended for grammar and sense in accordance with BNF1, BNF5); BNF2–3, BNF6: sortant d'où

11 BNF1–3, BNF6, B, V, BRB, M, K: s'estoient; S1/2: Puys sont issuz dont estoient

12 BNF1: "Le" missing; BNF2: Noffert; S1: Noorfort

13 BL: Marginal notation of two crosses. BNF4: Le millord de Norfort le president; 1545: presidant; B marginal note: M. duc de Norfort

14 BNF2: du povre

15 M: qui

16 B: Marginal drawing of a flower

17 BNF2–3, BNF6: Ou

18 BNF1, BNF5, S1/2, V, BRB, K, Vat, 1545: trouvé; M: coulpable trouvé

19 BNF1: L'un luy respond; BNF5: Ung respondit; V: On luy respond

20 BNF1, S2: prouvé

21 K: Verse 918 missing

22 BNF1: et disposer son ame; BNF6: Que disposer à pourvenir de son ame; 1545: ou disposer son ame

23 BNF1–7, B, S1/2, BRB, M, K, Vat: Il ne s'esmeut; V, 1545: Et ne s'esmeut

24 BNF1: ne les autres; BNF5, S1/2, V, M, K, Vat: ne les iuges

902    Of God to make it quickly evident.
903    After carefully examining his reasoning[1]
904    And re-examining[2] the opposite position,
905    The judges assembled to decide
906    If he should live or die.
907    They were found to be of differing opinion,
908    But, in the end, one argument overturns the other,[3]
909    Such that they are all united in a single voice.[4]
910    And so they leave the place where they had been sequestered.[5]
911    My Lord the Duke of Norfolk, who is presiding[6]
912    Over the judgment of this[7] poor man awaiting his sentence,
913    Even though he is the defendant's maternal uncle,[8]
914    Asked them if he was a criminal
915    And[9] if he had been proven[10] guilty or not.
916    One man answers him[11] that he was found[12] guilty.
917    When Rochford heard that he was
918    Condemned to death, and that nothing further remained
919    But to provide for the disposition of his soul,
920    He doesn't get stirred up[13] and doesn't blame the judges,[14]

---

1   S1 marginal note: "Judgment of death made against Lord Rochford"
2   BNF4: breaking down; S1/2: debating; V, BRB, K: hearing
3   S1/2: In the end, after their controversy
4   S1/2: They all conform to one opinion
5   S1/2: Then they go forth from where they were sequestered
6   BL: Marginal notation of two crosses; B marginal note reads: "The Duke of Norfolk"
7   BNF2: the
8   B: marginal notation of a flower
9   BNF2-3, BNF6: Or
10  BNF1, BNF5, S1/2, V, BRB, M, K, Vat, 1545: found
11  BNF5: One responded
12  BNF1, S2: proved
13  All others: He isn't agitated
14  BNF1: the others

---

912:   The Duke of Norfolk served as Lord High Steward for the trial, being in effect its "presi-
       dent," which is the word used by Carle here and in v. 985. The word "attendant," used as a
       substantive and translated here as the man "awaiting" his sentence, is defined in the DMF as
       "celui qui attend de se battre, celui qui attend d'être attaqué" [the one who is waiting to fight,
       the one who is waiting to be attacked]. By using the word in the context of Rochford's trial,
       Carle is perhaps recalling the courtier's prior exploits in the joust or other shows of combat;
       but now, the "attack" is purely a judicial one.
916:   The entire pool of judges would have been polled individually for their verdict, beginning
       with the youngest lord. See, on this matter, Coke, *Institutes*, 30.

| 921 | Mais seullement les prie de tant[1] faire |
| 922 | Enuers le Roy qu'il vueille[2] satisfaire |
| 923 | À ses amis qui luy auoient[3] presté |
| 924 | De leur argent en[4] sa necessité, |
| 925 | Veu mesmement[5] qu'on luy deuoit autant | [30r] |
| 926 | Qu'il en deuoit, & que payé contant[6] |
| 927 | Seroit le Roy de tous ses debiteurs[7] |
| 928 | Qu'il eust esgard[8] aux pauures crediteurs. |
| 929 | Et ce pendant en Dieu[9] deliberoit |
| 930 | Que de bon cueur telle[10] mort souffriroit. |
| 931 | Le president luy a lors[11] proferee |
| 932 | Peine de mort par la loy[12] refferee[13] |
| 933 | Et puis remis est au lieu dont[14] partit. |
| 934 | Soudain apres, vn huissier auertit |
| 935 | La Royne pour au[15] iugement venir, |
| 936 | Qui ne se veult que de Dieu souuenir |
| 937 | Et ne faict cas de chose qui la[16] touche, |
| 938 | Mais plus se tient[17] constante qu'vne souche |
| 939 | Qui ne craint estre aux ventz[18] impetueux. |
| 940 | Elle s'asseure & prent cueur vertueux |
| 941 | Plus que iamais, & ores ne veult craindre | [30v] |
| 942 | Ceux qu'elle a peu[19] auparauant contraindre. |
| 943 | Ainsi s'en vient[20] auec ses damoiselles, |

---

1 BNF1: le prie tant de; BNF5: il les prie de tant; S1/2: les prya de tant
2 S1/2: qu'il luy pleust; M, 1545: qui veuille
3 B: qu'il luy avoit; K: qui avoient
4 BNF4, BNF6, M: à
5 V: mesme
6 BNF1, B, V, BRB, K, Vat: comptant; BNF6–7, 1545: content
7 BNF2: ses crediteurs; S1/2: ces debiteurs
8 BNF2, V: regard
9 S1/2: illec
10 All others but Vat: celle
11 K: luy a alors
12 BNF1: par la mort; S1/2: par le Roy; BRB: "par" missing; 1545: par la reine (a misreading)
13 BNF2–3: inferee; B: preferee; V, BRB, K: arrestee. This is the last line of S1.
14 BNF1, BNF4: remys au lieu dont il; S2: au lieu dont il
15 BNF4: en
16 1545: luy
17 BNF1, S2: se tient plus
18 BNF1: craint gresle ne vent; BNF2–3, BNF7, Vat: craint gresle ou ventz; BNF4–6, B, S2, V, BRB, M, K, 1545: craint gresle ou vent
19 M, K: peult
20 BNF4: vint; BRB: va

| | |
|---|---|
| 921 | But only begs[1] them to do as much as it takes |
| 922 | To motivate the king to pay off |
| 923 | His friends who had loaned him |
| 924 | Some of their money in his moment of need, |
| 925 | Especially given that people owed him |
| 926 | As much as he owed them, and that |
| 927 | The king would be paid off by all who were in his debt, |
| 928 | Should he have consideration for these poor creditors. |
| 929 | And in the meantime he resolved by God[2] |
| 930 | That he would suffer such a[3] death willingly. |
| 931 | The Lord High Steward then pronounced to him |
| 932 | The death penalty as required[4] by law,[5] |
| 933 | And then he was sent back to the place where he had left. |
| 934 | Immediately afterwards, a bailiff notifies |
| 935 | The queen to appear for her judgment; |
| 936 | She wishes only to remember God |
| 937 | And attaches no importance to the matter that touches her, |
| 938 | But remains more steadfast than a tree trunk |
| 939 | That does not fear to be exposed to raging winds.[6] |
| 940 | She steadies herself and takes on a sincere heart, |
| 941 | More than ever before, and she doesn't want to fear now |
| 942 | Those men whom, previously, she had the power to constrain. |
| 943 | And so she comes[7] out with her gentlewomen, |

---

[1] S1/2: begged
[2] S1/2: resolved there and then
[3] All others but Vat: suffer this
[4] BNF2–3: as implied; B: as preferred; V, BRB, K: as ordered
[5] S1/2: by the king. Other variants are corrupt. This is the last line of S1.
[6] All others: does not fear hail or raging winds
[7] BNF4: came; BRB: goes

---

924: Chapuys, too, asserts that Rochford "begged the King that his debts, which he recounted, might be paid out of his goods." See LP 10.908.

935: Anne was brought into the court by the Constable of the Tower, Sir William Kingston, and the Lieutenant of the Tower, Sir Edmond Walsingham.

943: Wriothesley identifies these women as Lady Kingston and Lady Boleyn, Anne's aunt; see *Chronicle*, 1:38. The Harleian Manuscript (Harley 2194, fol. 16r) corroborates this; for a transcription of that text, see Cobbett, *Complete Collection of State Trials*, 410, and *Ballads from Manuscripts*, 1:406. Carle refers to these women here and in v. 1277 as "damoiselles," for which Cotgrave gives this definition: "damoiselle: gentlewoman; anyone under the degree of lady." The term is used to designate a lady-in-waiting and often, but not always, indicates youth. However, Carle elsewhere refers to these same women as "dames," that is, "ladies," generally indicating a higher standing (i.e., vv. 1173, 1183, 1287, and 1303). No doubt, Carle uses these terms interchangeably to suit the necessities of rhyme and meter and not to indicate their actual age or status.

944     Non comme pour defendre ses querelles:
945     Mais elle tient vne grace & maintien
946     Comme venant à l'honneur d'un[1] grand bien.
947     Estant venue, & que l'ont[2] saluee
948     Tous les[3] millordz, ne s'est point[4] oubliee
949     De leur vser d'honnesteté requise.
950     Puis doulcement[5] en sa chaire s'est mise,[6]
951     Où commencent contre elle à disputer,[7]
952     Et plusieurs cas infames imputer.
953     Elle defend son honneur sobrement,
954     Sans se troubler, mais plus constantement[8]
955     En[9] son visaige asseurant[10] sa raison
956     Que ne faisoit[11] par force d'oraison,[12]
957     Car peu parloit: mais qui la regardoit[13]                              [31r]
958     Coulpe de[14] crime en elle n'attendoit.[15]
959     Et quand ouy les iuges ont assez
960     Le demené de ce[16] piteux procez,
961     Ilz luy[17] ont dit que fault que[18] se demette

---

1   BNF5: de
2   BNF1: venu, et qu'ilz l'ont; BNF6: venue, et que l'avoient; S2: venue, elle fust; 1545: venue, et que tout
3   BNF5: Tous ces; S2: Par les
4   S2: et ne s'est
5   B: saigement
6   BNF1: en chaize elle s'est mise; BNF2, BNF6, 1545: en sa chaise s'est mise; B: en sa chaire s'est assise; S2: c'est en sa chaire mise
7   BL: Où l'on commence contre elle à disputer (emended for versification); BNF1: Et commencé ont contredisputer; BNF2: Et commencé ont contre elle à disputer; BNF3, B, V, M, K: Et commence on contre elle disputer; BNF4: Commencé ont à elle disputer; BNF5: On commencea contre elle à disputer; BNF6: Et commencent contre elle disputer; BNF7, S2: Et commencé ont contre elle disputer; BRB: Et commence en contre elle disputer; Vat: Et commence l'on contre elle à disputer; 1545: Et commence encontre elle à disputer
8   BNF1, BNF5: mais bien plus constamment; BNF6, V, BRB, K: mais plus constamment; B: mais plustot constantement
9   BNF5: Par
10  All others: asseuroit
11  B: Plus qu'on n'eust seu
12  BNF4: force de raison
13  1545: la gardoit
14  All others but BNF4–5, Vat: coulpe ne
15  BNF3–6: n'entendoit
16  BNF4: Le demerite de son; S2: La demande de ce
17  1545: Il luy; BRB: "luy" missing
18  BNF1–4, BNF6–7, B, S2, V, K, Vat: qu'il faut qu'el[lc]; BRB: que faut qu'elle

944    Not as though to defend her suit;
945    Rather, she maintains the grace and composure
946    Of someone who was about to receive a great honor.
947    Once she arrived and was greeted
948    By all the lords, she in no way forgot[1]
949    To employ the required courtesy with them.
950    Then she graciously[2] sat down on her chair,
951    Whereupon[3] they begin to argue against her
952    And accuse her of several ignominious charges.
953    She soberly defends her honor
954    Without getting flustered, but more[4] steadfastly
955    Affirming[5] her argument through her countenance
956    Rather than through the power of her speech;[6]
957    For she spoke only a little; but whoever looked upon her
958    Would not expect there to be[7] any criminal guilt[8] in her.
959    And when the judges had heard enough of
960    The dealings of this[9] pitiful proceeding,
961    They told her that she must let go of

---

[1] S2: By the lords, she did not forget
[2] B: discreetly
[3] All others except BNF4–5: And
[4] BNF1, BNF5: but far more
[5] All others: Did she affirm
[6] BNF4: her reasoning
[7] BNF3–6: Would not understand there to be
[8] All others but BNF4–5: any guilt or crime
[9] BNF4: The merit of her; S2: The claim of this

---

950:    This detail is also given in Wriothesley's *Chronicle*, 1:37, as well as Harley 2194, fol. 16r (quoted in Cobbett, *Complete Collection of State Trials*, 410, and *Ballads from Manuscripts* 1:406).

958:    The Harleian MS affirms that, "having an excellent quick wit, and being a ready speaker, [she] did so answer to all objections that had the peers given in their verdict according to the expectation of the assembly, she had been acquitted." See Harley 2194, fol.16r, transcribed in Cobbett, *Complete Collection of State Trials*, 410, and *Ballads from Manuscripts*, 1:406.

962    De la[1] couronne, & qu'en leurs mains la[2] mette,
963    Ce que soubdain a faict sans resister,
964    Sans toutesfois iamais se desister[3]
965    De[4] son propos qu'en vouloir ni par faict[5]
966    Contre le Roy iamais n'auoit meffaict.[6]
967    Apres cela, ordonnent[7] que Contesse
968    Ne sera[8] plus, ne marquise, Princesse[9]
969    N'en tiltre aulcun[10] de dignité donnee[11]
970    Auparauant qu'elle fust couronnee.
971    Elle n'attend plus[12] leur commandement,
972    Mais, renonceant[13] à tous biens promptement,[14]
973    Leur dit que, si par pure volunté[15]                    [31v]
974    Du Roy tenoit marquisat & conté,[16]
975    Ne luy greuoit[17] pour obeir[18] au maistre
976    De reuenir comme elle souloit estre
977    Premierement; mais que, par sa creance,[19]
978    N'a contre luy commis[20] aulcune offence.
979    Pour faire fin au propos commencé,[21]
980    Les iuges ont tant l'affaire[22] aduancé

---

[1]  V, BRB: sa
[2]  B: se
[3]  S2: resister; V: this verse is interpolated in a different ink.
[4]  BRB: En
[5]  BNF5: vouloir ni de faict; 1545: vouloir ay perfaict (a corrupt reading)
[6]  BNF3: n'avoit iamais meffaict; M: iamais n'auroit meffaict; 1545: iamais n'avoit faict (a corrupt reading)
[7]  BL, Vat: ordonne (emended for grammar and sense); B: ordonné fut
[8]  BNF4, Vat: seroit
[9]  BNF1, BNF3-4, BNF6, B, S2, V, BRB, M, K, Vat, 1545: plus, marquise ne princesse; BNF5: Plus ne sera Marquise ne princesse
[10]  BNF5, V, M: Ne tiltre aucun; B: Ne d'aucun tiltre; 1545: Ung tiltre aucun
[11]  BL, V, M, K: de dignité nommee (emended for rhyme); BNF1: ne dignité donnee
[12]  S2: plus que
[13]  BNF5, 1545: renonce
[14]  BNF1: proprement
[15]  BNF1-3, BNF6-7, B, S2, V, BRB, M, K, Vat, 1545: puisque par la volonté; BNF4: que par la bonne volonté; BNF5: Et puis leur deist que par la volonté
[16]  BNF2: tenoit marquise ou conté; BNF4: laissoit marquisat et conté; V, BRB, K: debvoit laisser marquisat et conté; M: debvoit laisser marquisat et conté
[17]  BNF4: grevant
[18]  V, M, K: subvenir; BRB: survenir
[19]  BNF1: loquence; BNF2, S2: science
[20]  BL: commise (emended for grammar to conform with all others but BNF2, BNF7, S2, V, M, Vat, 1545)
[21]  BNF2, BNF6: au proces commencé; S2: aux propoz commencez
[22]  BNF1: ont ce fait tant; BNF7, S2: ont l'affaire tant

962 Her crown and put it[1] in their hands,
963 Which she quickly did without resisting,
964 Yet without ever renouncing
965 Her story that neither in desire nor in deed
966 Had she ever done[2] any wrong towards the king.
967 After that, they order[3] that she shall[4] no longer be
968 A countess, nor a marchioness, nor a princess,
969 Nor hold any title of dignity which she was given[5]
970 Before she was crowned.
971 She waits no longer[6] for their command,
972 But, promptly renouncing[7] all her offices,
973 She tells them that, if purely by the will[8]
974 Of the king did she hold[9] a marquisate and[10] earldom,
975 It would not aggrieve her, so as to obey[11] her master,
976 To revert to what she used to be
977 At first, but that, in her belief,[12]
978 She had not committed a single offense against him.
979 To bring an end to the debate[13] that was begun,
980 The judges put the matter forward, such that,

---

1 B: put herself
2 M: Would she ever have done
3 BL, Vat: he orders; B: it was ordered
4 BNF4, Vat: would
5 BL: to which she was named; BNF1: title, nor any dignity which she was given
6 S2: waits only
7 BNF1: properly renouncing
8 BNF1–3, BNF6–7, B, S2, V, BRB, M, K, Vat, 1545: that since by the will; BNF4: that by the good will; BNF5: And then she told them that by the will
9 BNF4: did she abandon; V, BRB, K: must she abandon
10 BNF2: or
11 V, BRB, M, K: to assist
12 BNF1: words; BNF2, S2: to her knowledge
13 BNF2, BNF6: trial

---

962: This detail regarding the queen's degradation is also found in the letter of Dr. Ortiz to Isabella of Portugal (LP 10.1043) and that of the Bishop of Faenza to Monsignor Ambrogio (LP 10.956).

| 981 | Qu'ilz sont d'auis, pour resolution,[1] |
|---|---|
| 982 | Faire de mort determination. |
| 983 | Apres qu'ilz l'ont[2] coulpable publiee, |
| 984 | Et que luy a peine de mort[3] liuree |
| 985 | Le president, millord duc de Norfort,[4] |
| 986 | Pour endurer de l'espee l'effort, |
| 987 | Ou bien du[5] feu, selon le bon vouloir |
| 988 | Du Roy, n'a faict semblant[6] de se[7] douloir; |
| 989 | Mais eussiez dit qu'elle auoit[8] deuant veu |
| 990 | Le iugement qu'elle a ores[9] receu: |
| 991 | Car en[10] sa face on ne veit[11] changement, |
| 992 | N'en sa façon, ne[12] maintien nullement.[13] |
| 993 | Mais rendit grace[14] à Dieu à ioinctes mains[15] |
| 994 | En luy disant: "Ô pere des humains, |
| 995 | Où est la vie, voye, & verité,[16] |
| 996 | Tu scais si i'ay ceste mort merité." |
| 997 | Puis,[17] se tournant vers les iuges leur dit: |
| 998 | "Dire ne veux iniuste[18] vostre edit, |

[32r]

---

[1] BNF2–3: pour la solucion; S2: sont dedans pour la solucion

[2] S2, V, K: qu'ilz ont

[3] BNF2, S2: qu'on luy à peine de mort; BNF4: que ilz l'ont au poinct de mort; BNF5, Vat: que luy ont peine de mort; BNF6, B: qu'il luy ont peine de mort; 1545: que luy à de peine mort

[4] BNF4: Le president dict Millord du Norfort; V, BRB, M, K: Millord de Norfort

[5] BNF1, BNF3: le; BNF2, BNF6: de

[6] V: faict aulcuns semblant

[7] BNF2: soy; BNF4: s'en

[8] K: qu'elle ait

[9] BNF1–3, BNF6–7, B, S2, Vat, 1545: qu'ores elle a; V, BRB, M, K: que ores a

[10] BNF5: à

[11] BNF3: face on veid; BNF5, BNF7, B, S2: face on ne vit; V, BRB, M, K: face l'on ne veit; Vat: façon ne veit

[12] BNF4: N'a sa façon de; 1545: Ne sa façon ne

[13] V: aulcunement; Vat: seulement

[14] BNF1–3, BNF5–7, B, S2, BRB, M, K: rendoit graces; BNF4: rendant grace; V: rendoit grace; 1545: rendit graces

[15] BNF2–7, B, S2: les joinctes mains; V: à joinct mains; Vat: rendoit à Dieu les joinctes mains (a scribal error)

[16] BNF1: Qui es la voye et vye de verité; BNF2, BNF6: Qui es la vie, la voye, et verité; BNF3, Vat: Qui es la voye, et vye, et verité; BNF4: Qui est la voye, vye, et verité; BNF5, B: Qui es la voye, la vie, et verité; BNF7: Qui es la voye et vie en verité; S2: Qui est la voye, et vye, et verité; V, M: Quy es la voye de vye et verité; BRB, K: Qui es la voye de vie, de verité; 1545: Tu es la voye, et vye, et verité

[17] BNF3: Qui; BRB: Mais

[18] B: inceste (a corrupt reading); V: injust à

| | |
|---|---|
| 981 | They agree, in settling the case, |
| 982 | To make a determination for the death penalty. |
| 983 | After they declared her guilty, |
| 984 | And the death penalty was delivered unto her by[1] |
| 985 | The Lord High Steward, My Lord the Duke of Norfolk,[2] |
| 986 | For her to endure either the violence of a sword |
| 987 | Or else that of fire, according to |
| 988 | The king's pleasure, she made no semblance of grief, |
| 989 | But you would have said that she had foreseen |
| 990 | The judgment that she had now received: |
| 991 | For one saw no change at all in her face, |
| 992 | Nor in her manner, nor in her composure. |
| 993 | But she gave[3] thanks to God, with hands joined in prayer, |
| 994 | Saying to Him: "Oh Father of humankind, |
| 995 | Wherein is the life, way, and truth,[4] |
| 996 | You know if I have deserved this death." |
| 997 | Then,[5] turning towards the judges, she says to them: |
| 998 | "I do not wish to say that your verdict is unjust |

[1] BNF4: And they delivered her to the point of death
[2] BNF4: called the Lord of Norfolk; V, BRB, M, K: The Lord of Norfolk
[3] BNF4: But giving
[4] BNF1: Who art the way and life of truth; BNF2, BNF6: Who art the life, the way, and truth; BNF3, Vat: Who art the way, and life, and truth; BNF4: Who is the way, life, and truth; BNF5, BNF7: Who art the way and life in truth; B: Who art the way, the life, and truth; S2: Who is the way, and life, and truth; V, M: Who art the way of life and truth; BRB, K: Who art the way of life, of truth; 1545: You are the way, and life, and truth
[5] BRB: But

987: See Wriothesley's *Chronicle*, 1:38 as well as Spelman, *Reports*, 71, which states: "The judgment against the Queen was that she should be burned, for that is the judgment against a woman; but because she was Queen the Steward gave judgment that she should be burned or beheaded at the King's pleasure." For the norms concerning punishment of a woman found guilty of treason, see also Baker, "Criminal Courts," 42. Spelman goes on to note that "the justices murmured at this judgment against the queen, for such judgment in the disjunctive had not been seen."

992: Chapuys similarly remarks that "when the sentence was read to her, she received it quite calmly." See CSP, Spain, 5, pt. 2, no. 55. Carle is the only source to provide the text of the queen's allocution speech that followed her sentencing.

996: Anne is here echoing John 14:6: "I am the way, and the truth, and the life." The quotation figures in the text of the *Pasteur évangélique*, a French poem given to Anne in a beautiful presentation copy, which constitutes a meditation on the Pauline doctrine of justification by faith (British Library, Royal 16 E XIII; see fol. 2v of that text). Anne's reaction also recalls that of the biblical Susanna, falsely accused and convicted of adultery: "O eternal God, you know what is secret and are aware of all things before they come to be; you know that these men have given false evidence against me" (Daniel 13:42).

| 999 | Ne presumer que tant soit raisonnable |
|---|---|
| 1000 | Mon seul aduis[1] qu'il doiue[2] estre vallable[3] |
| 1001 | Contre vous tous; & croy[4] que bien scauez[5] |
| 1002 | Raison pourquoy condamnee m'auez,[6] |
| 1003 | Aultre que n'est[7] celle qu'auez deduicte[8] |
| 1004 | Du[9] iugement: car i'en suis du tout quicte,[10] |
| 1005 | Et ne requiers[11] que Dieu me le[12] pardonne, |
| 1006 | Ne pour iamais grace aulcune[13] m'en[14] donne: |
| 1007 | Car i'ay tousiours esté au Roy[15] fidelle. |
| 1008 | Ie ne dis pas[16] que je soys esté[17] telle |
| 1009 | Ne que porté luy ay humilité[18] |
| 1010 | Que ie deuoye,[19] veu son humanité,[20] |
| 1011 | Et grand doulceur dont enuers moy[21] vsoit, |
| 1012 | Et grand honneur[22] que tousiours me faisoit, |
| 1013 | Et que souuent ie n'aye[23] prins fantaisie |
| 1014 | Encontre luy de quelque ialousie:[24] |

[32v]

---

1   BNF7: amys (a corrupt reading)
2   BNF4: qu'il deust; BNF6, M, K, Vat: qui doibve
3   B: "vallable" crossed out and "damnable" written in another hand and ink; S2: lequel n'est pas vallable
4   BNF4: Encontre vous et croist; 1545: Contre vous troys et croy (a corrupt reading)
5   S2: car bien croy asscavez
6   BNF4, BNF6, V, BRB, M: condamné vous m'avez
7   BNF7, B: n'est que
8   BNF4: celle que m'avez dicte; S2: C'est la raison qu'ores aviez desduite; 1545: telle qu'avez desduict
9   BNF1, BNF4–5, B, V, BRB, M, K, Vat, 1545: Au; BNF2–3: En
10  BNF7: car i'en suis de tout quicte; S2: dont je suis necte et quitte; Vat: car je suis de tout quicte; 1545: car ie suis du tout quicte
11  S2: quiers
12  BNF2–6, B, V, BRB, M, K, Vat, 1545: le me
13  BNF2: aulcune grace
14  B, 1545: me donne
15  BNF1–4, BNF7, V, BRB, M, K, Vat, 1545: Car i'ay esté tousjours au Roy; B: Car i'ay esté au Roy tousjours
16  K: plus
17  BL, BNF5–6, Vat, 1545: que i'aye esté (emended for versification as in BNF1–4, BNF7, S1/2, V, K, M); B: pas, pourtant, qu'aye esté; BRB: pas que ne suys esté
18  BNF2: portee luy aye l'humilité; BNF6, B, V, BRB, M, K, Vat: l'humilité
19  BNF2, BNF4–5, BRB, M, Vat: Que je devois; BNF3: Comme je doibs; S2: Que luy devoys; K: Que je debvuoit; 1545: Comme je debvroys
20  BNF4: reverses order of vv. 1009–1010; V: vers son humanité
21  BNF1: dont vers moy il; BNF2–4, BNF6–7, B, S2, V, BRB, M, K, Vat, 1545: dequoy vers moy; BNF5: debvoir enquoy vers moy
22  S2: Aussi l'honneur
23  BNF4: souvent n'aye prins; 1545: souvent qu'aye prins
24  BRB: En contre de luy de quelque fantaisie

999   Nor presume that my opinion alone is so reasonable

1000   That it must be considered valid[1]

1001   Against all of you; and I believe you know full well

1002   The reason why you have condemned me,

1003   Which is other than the one you have deduced[2]

1004   From this trial, for I am clear of all of it.[3]

1005   And I have no need for[4] God to pardon me for it,

1006   Nor ever to grant me any grace for it:

1007   For I have always been faithful to the king.

1008   I do not say[5] that I have been[6] such as I should have been,

1009   Nor that I bore towards him the humility

1010   That I owed him,[7] given his kindness

1011   And the great tenderness with which he treated me,

1012   And the great honor[8] that he always bestowed on me,

1013   And that I didn't often harbor

1014   Some notion of jealousy towards him:

---

[1] B: that it must be considered damnable; S2: Which is not valid

[2] BNF4: the one that you have told me; S2: It is the reason that you now have deduced

[3] S2: trial, of which I am clean and clear

[4] S2: I do not ask

[5] B: I do not say, however; K: I no longer say

[6] BRB: that I have not been

[7] BNF3: As I must do; 1545: As I should do

[8] S2: And also the honor

---

1004:   Ales also reports that Anne's supporters "affirmed that no probable suspicion of adultery could be collected; and that therefore there must have been some other reason which moved the King. Possibly it might be the same as that which induced him to seek for a cause of divorce from his former Queen, namely the desire of having an heir." See "Letter," CSP, Foreign Series, Elizabeth, 1558–59, 1:1303, 529.

| 1015 | En ce congnois[1] qu'en vertu ie failloye,[2] |
|------|---|
| 1016 | Et du[3] deuoir de raison ie partoye.[4] |
| 1017 | Mais au[5] surplus, Dieu soit mon[6] tesmoignage |
| 1018 | Que[7] contre luy n'ay[8] meffaict dauantage, |
| 1019 | Et pour certain plus n'en[9] confesseray |
| 1020 | Le mesme iour que[10] la mort souffriray.[11] |
| 1021 | Et ne pensez que cecy ie[12] vous dye |
| 1022 | Pour quelque espoir de conseruer[13] ma vie: |
| 1023 | Car ie me suis bien aprinse à mourir |
| 1024 | Auec celuy qui de mort peult[14] guarir, |
| 1025 | Qui par sa grace a ma foy retenue,[15] |
| 1026 | Et ma foiblesse au besoing soustenue.[16] |
| 1027 | Mais ie ne[17] suis encores tant rauye |
| 1028 | En tel espoir qu'honneur[18] ne me conuye[19] |
| 1029 | À soustenir ses[20] raisonnables droictz, |
| 1030 | Duquel, seigneurs,[21] peu de compte tiendrois[22] |
| 1031 | Pres de ma fin, s'en vie ie ne l'eusse[23] |
| 1032 | Bien conserué,[24] quelque Royne que fusse. |

[33r]

---

1  BNF5: En quoy congnois; BNF7: En ce craignois
2  All others: que vertu m'est faillye; BNF1: reverses vv. 1014–15; B: Marginal notation of a flower
3  V, 1545: de
4  V, BRB, K: raison suis assaillie; all others: raison suis saillye
5  S2: Et au; V: Mais du
6  BL: Dieu scait mon (emended for sense); BNF1–2, BNF4: Dieu scait le; BNF3, BNF5–7, B, S2, V, BRB, M, K, Vat, 1545: Dieu soit le
7  BNF5: Si
8  BNF5: luy j'ay; V: luy je n'ay
9  B: ne
10 K: quand
11 BNF5: poursuivray
12 BNF4: pensez ores que le
13 BNF5: confirmer; S2: prolonger; V, BRB, M, K: ralonger; 1545: confermer
14 V: me peult
15 S2: a ma vue retenue; V, BRB, K: a ma foy soustenue
16 V, BRB, K: Verse 1026 missing
17 BRB: Mais ne me
18 BNF1, BNF4: En esprit que honneur; BNF2, M: En esperit que honneur; BNF3, BNF5, BNF7, B, Vat, 1545: En l'esperit qu'honneur; BNF6, S2, V, K: En l'esprit que honneur; BRB: En l'esprit que l'honneur
19 BNF1: conduyt
20 BNF4: ces; BNF6: les; S2: mes
21 S2: Et de mon Dieu; V, BRB, M: Desquelz, seigneurs
22 V: tiendroit; Vat: tiendrez
23 BNF1: s'en ma vye ne l'eusse; BNF2–4, BNF6–7, S2, B, V, BRB, M, K, Vat: si en vie ne l'eusse; BNF5: si en vie je l'eusse; 1545: si en vie ne laisse
24 S2: Tousjours fort crainct; 1545: Bien confirmee

1015    In this I know[1] that I failed in virtue,[2]
1016    And I truly strayed from my duty.[3]
1017    But[4] as for the rest, may God be my witness[5]
1018    That[6] I have done no more wrong against him,
1019    And certainly I shall not confess anything further about this
1020    On the very day that I suffer[7] death.
1021    And do not think[8] that I say this to you
1022    Out of some hope of saving[9] my life:
1023    For well have I learned how to die
1024    With the One who can heal death,[10]
1025    Who, by His grace, sustained my faith[11]
1026    And supported my weakness in my moment of need.
1027    But I am not yet so robbed
1028    Of such hope[12] that honor doesn't bid[13] me
1029    To uphold its[14] reasonable rights,
1030    Which, gentlemen, I would hold[15] in little consideration
1031    Near my end, if, during my life, I had not
1032    Fiercely preserved it,[16] as much as any queen who ever lived.

---

1   BNF5: In which I know; BNF7: In this I fear
2   All others: that virtue failed me
3   V, BRB, K: I am truly assailed by my duty; all others: I have truly broken away from my duty
4   S2: And
5   BL, BNF1–2, BNF4: God knows my testimony
6   BNF5: If
7   BNF5: pursue
8   BNF4: think now
9   BNF5, 1545: assuring; S2, V, BRB, M, K: prolonging
10   V: heal my death
11   S2: my sight
12   All others: so ravaged / In spirit
13   BNF1: lead
14   BNF4: these; BNF6: the; S2: my
15   S2: And I would hold God; Vat: you would hold
16   S2: Always greatly feared Him

1033    Et pour ce, veulx[1] que ce[2] dernier parler
1034    Ne soit que pour mon honneur consoler,[3]
1035    Et de mon frere, & de ceulx[4] que iugez
1036    Auez à mort,[5] & d'honneur estrangez,
1037    Tant que vouldrois[6] que les peusse[7] deffendre          [33v]
1038    Et deliurer, pour coulpable me rendre
1039    De mille mortz.[8] Mais[9] puis qu'il[10] plaist au Roy,
1040    Ie recepueray la mort en ceste[11] foy,
1041    Et leur tiendray en leur[12] mort compaignie,
1042    Pour puys apres, en la vie[13] infinie,
1043    Viure auec eulx, en eternel repos[14]
1044    Où priray Dieu[15] pour le Roy & pour vous."[16]
1045    Par ce[17] propos, elle a voulu[18] finir
1046    Sa triste voix,[19] dont nul s'est peu[20] tenir—
1047    Encores[21] ceulx qui luy portoient grand hayne[22]—
1048    D'auoir pitié de ceste paouure[23] Royne,
1049    Qui humblement[24] millordz remerciant,[25]
1050    Et[26] de bon cueur le peuple suppliant[27]

---

1   BL: pource veuil (emended for grammar as in all other manuscripts except S2); S2: veult
2   B: mon
3   BL: conseruer (emended for rhyme); S2: conseiller
4   1545: ce
5   S2: Dignes de mort; V, BRB, K: à tort
6   BNF3, B, M: Tant que vouldroye; S2: Las, bien vouldrois; K: Tantost que vouldrois
7   BNF1: sceusse
8   BNF4: maux; V, M, K: mil mors
9   BNF5: Et; S2: Or
10   M: puis que
11   BNF4, BNF6: à celle
12   BNF3, BNF4: à leur; V, K, 1545: en la
13   BNF1: en la gloire; BNF2: à la vie; BNF6: à leur vie; B: en leur vie
14   BNF4: où le Seigneur de tous (a unique reading that might be preferable insofar as it maintains a rhyme for the eye with v. 1044)
15   BNF4: Je suplieray; BNF6: Pour prier Dieu
16   BNF2: et pour tous; 1545: ou pour vous
17   B, V: ces
18   S2: la royne on veit
19   1545: vie
20   BNF4: se peust; V, BRB, K: se peult
21   1545: Et encores
22   V, BRB, M, K: portoient haine
23   BNF5: de celle povre; S2: d'Anne Boullant la
24   B: tres humblement
25   S2: les millords mercyant; M: myllord remerciant; 1545: Meilhors remercioit
26   S2: Fut
27   S2 adds after this verse: Que mais que soit du monde departie; 1545: supplioit

1033    And for this reason, I wish that this[1] last speech
1034    Serve only to give solace to[2] my sense of honor,
1035    And that of my brother, and of those men whom you have judged
1036    To die[3] and have estranged from their good reputation,
1037    Such that I wish[4] that I had the ability to defend
1038    And deliver them, and take on for myself
1039    A thousand deaths.[5] But,[6] since it pleases the king,
1040    I shall accept death in this faith,
1041    And I shall keep them company in their death
1042    So as, afterwards, in everlasting life,[7]
1043    To live with them in eternal rest,
1044    Where I shall pray to God[8] for the king and for you."[9]
1045    By this remark[10] she wished to finish[11]
1046    Her sad speech,[12] as a result of which no one—
1047    Not even[13] those who bore her great hatred[14]—
1048    Could keep from having pity on this poor queen[15]
1049    Who, humbly[16] thanking the lords,[17]
1050    And heartily begging[18] the people

---

1  B: my
2  BL: to protect; S2: to advise
3  S2: whom you judge / Worthy of death; V, BRB, K: Wrongly
4  S2: Alas, I truly wish
5  BNF4: troubles
6  BNF5: And; S2: Now
7  BNF1: glory
8  BNF4: Live with them where the Lord of all / I shall beseech
9  BNF2: for the king and for everyone; 1545: for the king or for you
10  B, V: these remarks
11  S2: By this remark they saw the queen finish
12  1545: life
13  1545: And not even
14  V, BRB, M, K: bore her hatred
15  S2: pity on Anne Boleyn the queen.
16  B: very humbly
17  M: thanking the lord; 1545: thanked the lords
18  1545: heartily begged

---

1036:   Chapuys also remarked that Anne had said that she "was extremely sorry to hear that others, who were innocent and the King's loyal subjects, should share her fate and die through her." See CSP, Spain, 5, pt. 2, no. 55; and LP 10.908.
1048:   See Ales, "Letter," 529: "all the spectators, even her enemies, and those persons who previously had rejoiced at her misfortune out of their hatred to the doctrine of the religion which she had introduced into England, testified and proclaimed her innocence and chastity."

| 1051 | En leur priere[1] auoir[2] quelque partye, | |
| 1052 | S'en retourna[3] dont elle estoit partye.[4] | |
| 1053 | Les prisonniers, ce pendant, se disposent | [34r] |
| 1054 | Pour[5] bien mourir & leur fardeau[6] composent | |
| 1055 | Pour[7] tost partir de misere profonde, | |
| 1056 | Et voyager au lieu[8] de l'autre monde. | |
| 1057 | Ilz ont receu trestous[9] deuotement | |
| 1058 | Auant mourir le diuin sacrement.[10] | |
| 1059 | Puis, tost apres, on leur a assigné[11] | |
| 1060 | Iour pour souffrir mort, & lieu designé.[12] | |
| 1061 | Et, quand venu fut leur douloureux[13] iour,[14] | |
| 1062 | Par les archiers sont tirez de la tour, | |
| 1063 | Et droict[15] menez au lieu de[16] sacrifice. | |
| 1064 | Lors Rochefort, comme le plus propice | |
| 1065 | Pour ses amys en Dieu reconforter, | |
| 1066 | Les embrassant, les vint[17] admonnester[18] | |
| 1067 | Ensemblement, &[19] puys chascun à part, | |

---

1 BNF1–5, B, S2, V, BRB, M: leurs prieres; 1545: leur proces

2 BRB, V: d'avoir

3 BNF1: Et retourna; V: Puis se tourna

4 S2: Verse 1052 missing; V: s'estoit partie

5 BNF4, S2: De

6 BNF2–3, BNF5–6, B: leurs fardeaux

7 BNF5: De

8 BNF1, B, S2: ès lieux; BNF2–3, BNF5–7, V, BRB, M, K, Vat: aux lieux

9 BNF4: tous bien

10 B: marginal drawing of cross within a circle

11 B: apres leur ont jour assigné; S2: apres comme il fut designé

12 BNF1–7, V, BRB, M, K, Vat, 1545: Jour pour souffrir, et le lieu designé; B: Pour souffrir mort et le lieu designé; S2: Pour souffrir mort jour leur fut assigné

13 BNF1, BNF6, B: le malheureux; BNF2–5, BNF7, V, BRB, M, K, Vat, 1545: leur malheureux

14 S2: Estant escheu adont leur dernier jour

15 S2: D'illec

16 BNF1–3, BNF5–7, B, S2, V, BRB, M: du

17 BNF2: veut; 1545: vient

18 BNF3 follows this verse with v. 1068, followed by v. 1067, then repeats v. 1068. The first instance of v. 1068 is lightly crossed out; BNF6 originally has "reconforter," which is later crossed out with "admonester" in margins; B: Prenoit couraige sans se deconforter

19 B: Les embrassant et; V, BRB, M, K: Ensemble tous et

| | |
|---|---|
| 1051 | To reserve some portion of their prayers for her, |
| 1052 | Returned[1] to the place she had left.[2] |
| 1053 | The prisoners, in the meantime, prepare themselves |
| 1054 | To die well, and they pack up their burden[3] |
| 1055 | For their imminent departure from this profound misery |
| 1056 | To travel towards the dwelling place of the world beyond. |
| 1057 | They—each and every one[4]—devoutly received |
| 1058 | The Divine Sacrament before dying.[5] |
| 1059 | Then, soon afterwards, they were assigned |
| 1060 | The day and designated place to suffer death.[6] |
| 1061 | And when their sorrowful[7] day had come,[8] |
| 1062 | They were taken from the Tower by the archers |
| 1063 | And led straight[9] to the place of sacrifice. |
| 1064 | Thereupon, Rochford, as the most suitable one |
| 1065 | To comfort his friends in God, |
| 1066 | While embracing them, came[10] to exhort them[11] |
| 1067 | Together,[12] and then each one individually, |

---

1  BNF1: And she returned; V: Then she returned
2  S2 is missing v. 1052, but adds another verse after 1050 so that it reads: "Was heartily begging the people / That, when she be departed from this world, / They reserve some portion of their prayers for her"
3  BNF2–3, BNF5–6, B: their burdens
4  BNF4: They all quite
5  B: marginal notation of a cross within a circle
6  S2: Verses 1059–60 read: Then soon afterwards, as it was determined, / the day to suffer death was assigned to them
7  BNF1, BNF6, B: the unhappy; BNF2–5, BNF7, V, BRB, M, K, Vat, 1545: their unhappy
8  S2: Having then fallen upon their last day
9  S2: From there they were led
10  BNF2: wants; 1545: comes
11  B: Took courage without being saddened
12  B: Embracing them; V, BRB, M, K: All together

---

1054:  For an example of these preparations, see LP 10.869, which summarizes a letter written by Francis Weston to his parents and wife, asking them to settle his debts as well as to pardon him for "all the offences I have done to you." Carle uses the word "fardeau" here, literally, according to Cotgrave, "a burden ... truss, pack, bundle." The context suggests both something that is used for travel (in keeping with the journey metaphor in this passage) as well as a difficult load to carry.

1058:  Carle's phrasing refers to the Holy Eucharist, believed to be the Body of Christ and hence to be "divine" or "of God." When administered to someone about to die, the sacrament is often referred to as the "viaticum," suggesting the idea of a journey, an image expressed in Carle's previous verses.

1060:  The men were all beheaded at Tower Hill on 17 May 1536.

| 1068 | De constamment endurer ce depart,[1] |
|---|---|
| 1069 | Et de bon cueur receuoir[2] ceste peine |
| 1070 | Pour auec Dieu gaigner heureuse estraine.[3] |
| 1071 | Lors se[4] baisant, se sont recommandez |
| 1072 | À Dieu, & puys tous pardon demandez.[5] |
| 1073 | Ainsi venuz sont au lieu pour souffrir. |
| 1074 | Rochefort s'est voulu premier[6] offrir, |
| 1075 | Comme portant l'enseigne de victoire |
| 1076 | Contre la mort: car vous ne scauriez croire |
| 1077 | La grand vertu dequoy la mesprisoit,[7] |
| 1078 | Et la façon dequoy[8] se[9] conduysoit. |
| 1079 | Venu qu'il fust[10] en la veue[11] publicque, |
| 1080 | Ne s'essayoit[12] vzer[13] de rethoricque, |
| 1081 | Mais simplement[14] par exhortation[15] |
| 1082 | Ainsi parla: "Amiz, l'intention[16] |
| 1083 | De mes propos[17] icy presentement[18] |

[34v]

---

[1] V originally had "endurer ceste peine," which is later crossed out and corrected to "endurer ce depart" in another ink.

[2] BNF2, B, BRB, M, K: endurer; V: this verse is added in another ink, with the reading "endurer ceste peine"

[3] BL: estrain (spelling emended for rhyme); BNF1, BNF3, BNF5–7, B, S2, M, Vat, 1545: l'heureuse estraine; BNF2: l'heureuse peine (a scribal error); BNF4: Pour en avoir de Dieu l'heureuse estraine

[4] B: les

[5] BNF1: À Dieu et du peuple favorisez (a corrupt reading); BNF4: À Dieu, et puis ont pardon demandez; BNF5: À Dieu. Puis tous le pardon demandez; BNF7: À Dieu, puy à tous pardons demandez; B: À Dieu, et puis ont tous pardon demandez; S2: Et ont à Dieu tous pardon demandez; V, M, Vat: À Dieu, et puis tous pardons demandez; BRB: À Dieu, puis tous pardon demandez; 1545: À Dieu, et puis tout pardon demandez

[6] BNF3, BNF5, B, S2: s'est premier voullu; BNF4: s'est venu premier; BNF6: icy voulu premier; Vat: eust voulu premier. The last two variations are corrupt.

[7] BNF4: dequoy la desprisoit; B: dont il la meprisoit; S2, 1545: dequoy le mesprisoit

[8] B: enquoy; S2: Et le maintien dont il

[9] BRB: la

[10] BNF1: Venu il fut; BNF2: Quand fut venu; BNF5: Et luy venu; BNF7, V, BRB, M, K: Venu quy fut; B: Voyant qu'il fust; S2: Luy parvenue; 1545: Veu qu'il feust

[11] BL: en la voye (emended for sense as in all but BNF5–6, B); BNF1: en veue; BNF3, S2: à la veue; B: en la place

[12] BNF1–4, B, BRB, M, K: Ne s'essaya; BNF6 originally has "Ne cessa la" with marginal correction to "n'essaya user"; BNF7: Ne s'esoyssoit; S2: Il n'essaia; V, 1545: Ne sessa. The readings of BNF6, V, and 1545 are corrupt.

[13] BNF4: d'user

[14] S2, BRB, M, K: seulement

[15] V: Verse 1081 missing

[16] BNF2: l'exortation (a scribal error)

[17] BNF5: Qui me meine; all others: Qui m'a mené

[18] V, BRB, M, K: premierement

1068 To endure this parting[1] with constancy
1069 And to accept[2] this punishment willingly,
1070 So as to gain the gift of God's great blessing.
1071 Thereupon, exchanging a kiss, they recommended each other
1072 To God, and then all asked for pardon.[3]
1073 And so they came to the place for suffering.
1074 Rochford wanted to offer himself first,[4]
1075 As if carrying the sign of victory
1076 Against death, for you would not believe
1077 The great power with which he scorned[5] it
1078 And the manner in which[6] he conducted himself.
1079 Having arrived in full view of the public,[7]
1080 He did not try to use rhetoric,
1081 But, issuing a simple[8] plea
1082 He said this: "Friends, the intent
1083 Of my words[9] here presently[10]

---

[1] V: originally reads: "punishment"
[2] BNF2, B, V, BRB, M, K: endure
[3] BNF4: and then they asked for pardon; BNF7: then they ask pardon from everyone; S2: And they all asked God for forgiveness
[4] BNF4: Rochford came to offer himself first
[5] BNF4: despised
[6] S2: the composure with which
[7] BL, BNF6: Having arrived by the public path; BNF1: He arrived in public view; BNF2: When he arrived in public view; BNF5: And he arrived by the public path; B: Seeing that he was on the public square; 1545: Given that he was in public view
[8] S2, BRB, M, K: But issuing only a
[9] BNF4: That brings me; all others: That brought me
[10] V, BRB, K, M: here in the first place

---

1070: The word Carle uses here, "estraine," is commonly written "estrenne." The expression "bonne estrenne" is defined in the DMF as "good fortune" and is found in a common formula for blessing, "Que Dieu donne bonne/joyeuse estrenne."

1076: Traditionally, the sign of victory against death (and sin) is the cross of Christ. Carle is depicting the scene of this execution (or "sacrifice," as he described it in v. 1063) as a reminiscence of Christ's crucifixion.

| 1084 | N'est pas de faire à vous tous[1] preschement, | |
| 1085 | Mais soustenir la mort qui m'ordonnee[2] | [35r] |
| 1086 | Fut par la loy;[3] & puis qu'abandonnee[4] | |
| 1087 | Tant est[5] ma vie en l'estat que voyez,[6] | |
| 1088 | Ie vous supply, mes derniers motz oyez, | |
| 1089 | Mesmement vous, messeigneurs[7] de la court: | |
| 1090 | Ne vous fiez en ce regne si court,[8] | |
| 1091 | Et n'esperez pas tant à[9] la faueur | |
| 1092 | Des grandz estatz & primie d'honneur[10] | |
| 1093 | Des Roys que[11] plus en celuy ne pensez[12] | |
| 1094 | Qui vous rendra trop[13] mieux recompensez. | |
| 1095 | C'est IESVCHRIST qui m'auoit faict la grace[14] | |
| 1096 | Que[15] ie tenois pres[16] le Roy telle place | |
| 1097 | Qu'auez tous veu,[17] & pour plus m'obliger[18] | |

---

1   BNF1: N'est pour vous faire aucun grant; BNF2–3, BNF7, B, V, BRB, M, K, Vat, 1545: N'est pas pour vous faire aulcun; BNF4: N'est pas pour à vous faire ung; BNF5: N'est pour vous faire quelque grand; BNF6: N'est pour vous faire aulcun; S2: N'est point pour faire à vous un

2   BNF1–2: Mais pour souffrir la mort qui ordonnee; BNF3, BNF5–7, B, V, BRB, M, K, Vat, 1545: Mais pour souffrir la mort qui m'ordonnee; BNF4, S2: Mais pour souffrir mort à moy ordonnee

3   BNF4: Faut par le roy; S2: De par le roy; V, BRB, M, K: par le roy

4   BNF1, BNF4: "qu'" missing; V: "que" interpolated in a different hand

5   BNF3: Tant ay; BNF4: Or est

6   BNF1: vie autant que vous voyez; BNF7: vie en estat que voyez

7   BNF4: Et mesmement vous, messieurs; S2: Vous mesmement, ô Seigneurs; BRB: Mesmement vous, messieurs

8   BNF7: regne qui court

9   BNF1–7, S2, BRB, M, K, Vat: pas tant en; B: point tant à; V: n'esperez tant en

10  BL: primite (a probable mispelling of "primie" or "premie," meaning "recompense" or "reward"); BNF1–6, Vat: Des grans honneurs et privee faueur; BNF7: Verse 1092 missing; B: Des grans honneurs et de privee faueur; S2: Des grans honneurs et haultaine faueur; V, M, K: Des grans honneurs ny aussy en la douceur; BRB: Des grandz seigneurs ne aussy à la douceur; 1545: Des grans honneurs et privé faueur

11  1545: qui

12  BNF5: en celluy que; BNF6: à celluy ne; B: Des rois aussy mais en celuy pensez; S2: Aucuns des roys qu'en Dieu plus ne pensez; V, BRB, K: Des roys mais plus en celuy pensez

13  B: tous

14  S2: Seigneurs, mon Dieu m'avoit faict telle grace

15  S2: "Que" missing

16  BNF4: pour; BNF5, V: vers

17  S2: Comme avez veu; 1545: Qu'avez vous veu

18  B: veu, pour moy plus obliger; V, BRB, M, K: veu, mais pour plus m'obliger

| 1084 | Is not to preach to you all a[1] sermon, |
|------|------|
| 1085 | But to endure[2] the death that was ordered for me[3] |
| 1086 | By law.[4] And since my life is so[5] forsaken |
| 1087 | In the state that[6] you see, |
| 1088 | I beg you, hear my last words, |
| 1089 | Especially you, my lords[7] of the court: |
| 1090 | Do not rely on this kingdom that is so short-lived,[8] |
| 1091 | And do not put[9] so much hope in the favor |
| 1092 | Of great status and in the recompense of honor[10] |
| 1093 | From kings that you no longer think about the One[11] |
| 1094 | Who will give you far[12] greater rewards: |
| 1095 | It is JESUS CHRIST who gave me the grace[13] |
| 1096 | To hold a such a position close to[14] the king, |
| 1097 | As you have all seen;[15] and,[16] to oblige me the more, |

---

1   BNF1: to you any great; BNF2–3, BNF6–7, B, V, BRB, M, K, Vat, 1545: to you any; BNF4: to you a; BNF5: to you some great; S2: Is not at all to preach to you a
2   All others: to suffer
3   BNF1–2: that was ordered
4   BNF4, S2, V, BRB, M, K: By the king
5   BNF4: is now
6   BNF1: To the degree that
7   BNF4: And especially you, men; S2: Especially you, Oh my lords; BRB: Especially you, men
8   BNF7: kingdom that rushes by
9   B: do not in the slightest put
10  BNF1–6, B, Vat, 1545: Of great honors and intimate favor; V, M, K: Of great honors nor in the tenderness; S2: Of any great honors and lofty favor; BRB: Of great lords nor in the tenderness
11  B: From kings, but also think about the One; S2: From kings that you no longer think about God; V, BRB, K: From kings, but think more about the One
12  B: you all
13  S2: Gentlemen, my God gave me such grace
14  BNF4: position for; BNF5, V: position towards
15  S2: As you have seen
16  V, BRB, K, M: but

---

1084:   Cf. *The Chronicle of Calais*, 46: "I am not come hither for to preach, but for to die"; Wriothesley's *Chronicle*, 1:39: "I am come hither not to preach and make a sermon, but to die."
1089:   Cf. *Chronicle of Calais*, 46: "I pray you take heed by me, and especially my lords and gentlemen of the court"; Wriothesley's *Chronicle*, 1:40: "and specially you my masters of the Court."
1092:   Carle uses a variant spelling of the word "premie" here, which Cotgrave defines as "a recompense, guerdon, reward" and the DMF as "recompense, advantage."
1093:   Cf. *Chronicle of Calais*, 46: "beware, trust not in the vanity of the world, and especially in the flattering of the court"; Wriothesley's *Chronicle*, 1:40: "trust on God specially, and not on the vanities of the world." Rochford's words echo those of Psalm 146:3: "Do not put your trust in princes, in mortals, in whom there is no help."

| | | |
|---|---|---|
| 1098 | Et deuers luy tout mon esprit[1] renger, | |
| 1099 | M'auoit donné de sa foy[2] congnoissance. | |
| 1100 | Mais i'ay tant eu en moymesme[3] fiance, | |
| 1101 | Et aux honneurs & biens que i'ay[4] tenu, | [35v] |
| 1102 | Que ie ne l'ay[5] ne sa foy recogneu,[6] | |
| 1103 | Et qu'ay[7] esté comme ceulx qui prescher[8] | |
| 1104 | Veullent[9] la foy, sans point[10] en aprocher. | |
| 1105 | Ainsi,[11] pour mieulx vers[12] luy me ramener, | |
| 1106 | Il luy a pleu[13] mes faultes guerdonner | |
| 1107 | De ceste mort, & me faire sentir | |
| 1108 | Que c'est à luy qu'il se[14] fault conuertir. | |
| 1109 | Ie vous prie, donc,[15] que chacun me[16] contemple, | |
| 1110 | Et que ie soye pour tous[17] certain exemple, | |
| 1111 | Vous suppliant aussi que,[18] d'un accord, | |
| 1112 | Me[19] pardonnez mes[20] faultes en ma[21] mort." | |
| 1113 | Ainsi fina ses[22] propos, & ne dit[23] | |
| 1114 | Qu'enuers le Roy eust meffaict ne[24] mesdit, | |
| 1115 | Mais pria Dieu que le tint[25] longuement | |

---

1  BNF1–2, BNF4, BNF6–7, S2, V, BRB, M, K, Vat: Et devers luy mon esperit; BNF5: Et denvers luy mon esperit; B: Et denvers luy plus mon esprit

2  BNF4: donné de luy la; V, BRB, M, K: de ses faicts

3  BNF2: en moymesme de; B: en moy de luy (a corrupt reading)

4  V, BRB, M, K: biens me suis

5  S2: Que je n'ay Dieu

6  BNF5: de sa foy recogneu; V: Que je ne l'ay en moy ce recognu; BRB, K: en ma foy recogneu; M: ny ma foy recognu

7  BNF1–3, BNF6–7: Et j'ay; BNF4: Car j'ay; BNF5, S2, V, BRB, M, K: Et ay

8  1545: preschent

9  BNF4: Veuille

10  V, BRB, K: plus

11  BNF5–6, V, BRB, M, K: Aussi

12  BNF2: en; BNF4: à

13  BNF4: peu

14  BNF3, BRB, M, K: que se; BNF4, B: qui se

15  BNF1, K: Je prie doncq

16  BNF3, 1545: qu'ung chascun me; S2: que chacun y

17  BNF4: à tous; B: pour vous; V: "tous" missing; K: Et que sois pour tous; 1545: tout

18  BNF5: aussi tous; 1545: ainsi que

19  BNF1, BNF3: Vous

20  BRB: pardonnez à mes

21  BNF5–6, S2, Vat, 1545: à ma; B: à la

22  BNF2, B: ces

23  1545: ce dict

24  BNF5, S2, V, BRB, 1545: ou; K: "ne" missing

25  BL: qu'il le print (emended for sense); BNF2, BNF7, M: qui le tint; BNF3–6, S2, Vat, 1545: qu'il le tint; B: le tenir; V: prye Dieu que le tiengne; BRB, K: prie Dieu qu'il le tient

| | |
|---|---|
| 1098 | And to direct my whole being[1] towards Him, |
| 1099 | He gave me knowledge of His faith.[2] |
| 1100 | But I had such confidence in myself, |
| 1101 | And in the honors and wealth that I held, |
| 1102 | That I recognized neither Him[3] nor His faith,[4] |
| 1103 | And[5] I was like those who wish |
| 1104 | To preach the faith without approaching it in the least.[6] |
| 1105 | And so, to bring me back closer to Him, |
| 1106 | It pleased Him[7] to reward my sins |
| 1107 | With this death and to make me realize |
| 1108 | That it is to Him that one must turn. |
| 1109 | I therefore beg that each one of you contemplate me |
| 1110 | So that I might be for everyone a sure[8] example, |
| 1111 | Beseeching you, too, that, in one accord, |
| 1112 | You pardon my faults at my death." |
| 1113 | Thus he ended his speech,[9] and he doesn't say |
| 1114 | That he had wronged or spoken ill of the king, |
| 1115 | But he prayed that God long keep the king |

---

[1] B: being the more; all others: direct my being
[2] BNF4: of Himself; V, BRB, M, K: of His deeds
[3] S2: neither God
[4] V: That I didn't recognize this in myself; BRB, M, K: nor my faith
[5] BNF4: For
[6] V, BRB, K: approaching it any further
[7] BNF4: He was able
[8] B: for you a sure; 1545: I be a completely sure
[9] BNF2, B: these words

---

1104: Cf. *Chronicle of Calais*, 47: "I did read the Gospel of Christ, but I did not follow it." See also Constantyne's *Memorial*, 65: "if I had lived according to the gospel as I … spake of it, I had never come to this."

1110: Cf. *Chronicle of Calais*, 46: "I pray … that my death may be an example unto you all"; Wriothesley's *Chronicle*, 1:40: "I beseech God that I may be an example to you all, and that all you may beware by me."

1112: Cf. Wriothesley's *Chronicle*, 1:40: "heartily I require [i.e., request] you all to pray for me, and to forgive me if I have offended you."

1116   En vie, en heur,[1] & en contentement.

1117   Et quand il eut dit au peuple assistant,[2]                [36r]

1118   "Priez pour moy," en visaige constant,

1119   En[3] ferme cueur sa teste presenta[4]

1120   Au dur trenchant, qui[5] d'un coup l'emporta.[6]

1121   Les quatre qui deuoint mourir[7] apres

1122   Ne dirent rien,[8] comme si par expres

1123   À Rochefort eussent donné creance

1124   De parler seul[9] selon leur conscience,[10]

1125   Sinon que Marc, qui tousiours percistoit

1126   En[11] son propos, & au peuple attestoit[12]

1127   Que celle[13] mort receuoit iustement

1128   Pour ses[14] meffaictz. Ainsi, finablement,

1129   Apres les[15] quatre, &[16] suyuant leur chemin,[17]

1130   Receut le coup de sa[18] piteuse fin.

1131   La Royne, estant[19] en contemplation

1132   De Iesuchrist & de[20] sa passion,

---

1   BNF1: vye, honneur; BNF4, BNF6, M, K, 1545: vie et heur

2   BNF4: quand eust dit au peuple assistant; BNF5–6: quand dict eut au peuple assistant; S2: Quand il eust dict à ce peuple assistant; Vat: Et quand eut au peuple y assistant; 1545: quand il eut dit au peuple y assistant

3   BNF1, BNF6, S2, V, BRB, K: De; BNF2–3, BNF5, BNF7, M, Vat, 1545: Et

4   BNF6: la teste presenta; B: sa teste a presenté. B adds after v. 1119 (to complete the rhyme with its version of v. 1119): En ne craignant la grande cruaulté

5   1545: que

6   B: Du dur tranchant qui d'un seul coup l'emporta. B adds this verse after v. 1120: Voiant chacun dont grand dueil on en porta. This extra verse is signaled by two parallel vertical lines in the margins.

7   BNF1–2, BNF4, BNF7: qui restoient encor; BNF3: qui estoient encore; BNF5–6, 1545: qui restent encores; B: qui y restoient encor; S2: Ses compaignons estans tous quatre apres; V: Les quattres qui restent apres; BRB, M, K, Vat: qui restoient encores

8   BNF1: ne disans rien; V, BRB, M, K: ne dirent mot; 1545: ne disent rien

9   BNF5: "seul" missing

10  BNF4: sa conscience; 1545: leurs consciences

11  BNF1, V: À

12  BNF2: asseuroit

13  BNF5, Vat: telle

14  BL: Pour les (emended for sense, as in all others).

15  BNF3: le; BRB: ces

16  B: en; 1545: y

17  K: prochain (a corrupt reading)

18  BNF4: le corps ceste

19  S2: estoit

20  K: "de" missing

| | |
|---|---|
| 1116 | In life, in happiness,[1] and in contentment. |
| 1117 | And when, to the people in attendance,[2] he said, |
| 1118 | With a steadfast countenance, "Pray for me," |
| 1119 | With a firm heart he presented his head |
| 1120 | To the sharp blade that carried it off in one blow.[3] |
| 1121 | The four who had to die[4] afterwards |
| 1122 | Said nothing,[5] as if they intentionally |
| 1123 | Had entrusted Rochford |
| 1124 | Alone to speak for their conscience, |
| 1125 | Except for Mark, who still persisted |
| 1126 | In his words and affirmed to[6] the people |
| 1127 | That he received this death[7] justly |
| 1128 | For his misdeeds. And so, at length, |
| 1129 | After the[8] other four, and following their path, |
| 1130 | He received the blow of his[9] pitiable end. |
| 1131 | The queen, who was meditating |
| 1132 | Upon Jesus Christ and His passion, |

---

1 BNF1: in honor
2 S2: to this people in attendance; Vat, 1545: people there in attendance
3 B adds two verses after v. 1119, to read: "And not fearing the great cruelty / Of the sharp blade that carried it off in a single blow / Each one seeing that people bore great grief from it"
4 BNF1–4, BNF7, BRB, M, K, Vat: who still remained; BNF5–6, 1545: who are still remaining; B: who still remained there; S2: All four of his companions remaining; V: The four who stay
5 BNF1: Saying nothing; V, BRB, M, K: Say not a word; 1545: Say nothing
6 BNF2: and assured
7 BNF5, Vat: such a death
8 BRB: these
9 BNF4: His body received this

---

1119: An echo of Psalm 112:7: The righteous "are not afraid of evil tidings; their hearts are firm, secure in the Lord."

1133   En[1] attendant sa[2] iournee derniere,                          [36v]
1134   Se presenta[3] par deuote maniere[4]
1135   Au sacrement. Puis annuncé luy fut[5]
1136   Le iour de mort, dont nullement s'esmeut,[6]
1137   Mais se monstra[7] plus que deuant ioyeuse,
1138   Et si fut tant encores[8] curieuse
1139   Des cinq[9] seigneurs, & de leur asseurance,
1140   Que demander voulut leur[10] patience.
1141   Donc, on luy[11] dit que son frere auoit eu
1142   Plus grand vertu que ne fut onques[12] veu,
1143   Les quatre aussi, mais[13] que Marc dit auoit
1144   Qu'il meritoit la mort qu'il[14] receuoit.
1145   La Royne alors, de[15] face vn peu changee,
1146   "Ne m'a il point[16] (dit elle) deschargee
1147   Auant mourir du publicque diffame[17]
1148   Qu'il m'auoit faict? Las! l'ay peur[18] que son ame
1149   En soit en peine, & que en[19] pugnition                         [37r]

---

[1]  BNF2–3, B, V, M, K, 1545: Et; S2: Qui
[2]  BNF5: la
[3]  BNF5: presentant
[4]  B: Marginal notation of a cross within a circle
[5]  BNF6: denoncé luy fut; B: luy fut anoncé (which results in a disruption in the rhyme)
[6]  B: se meut; B marginal note, signaled by two parallel vertical lines, commenting on the faulty rhyme: "Il y a ici des vers adirés."
[7]  BNF1: Se demonstrant; BNF2, BNF4–6, 1545, S2: Mais se monstroit; BNF3, BNF7, B: Mais se monstrant
[8]  BNF1: Et si fut de son faict; V, BRB, K: encores tant; 1545: fut faict encores
[9]  BNF5: De ces; BNF7, Vat, 1545: De cinq
[10] BNF1–7, B, S2, V, BRB, M, K, Vat: voulut la; BNF6: voullait la; 1545: voulut sa. All but BL invert the order of 1139–40.
[11] All others: Quelcun luy
[12] BNF2: qu'il ne fut onc; BNF5: qu'homme qui fut oncq'; 1545: que oncques ne fut
[13] S2: et
[14] M: qui
[15] BNF6, B: la; BRB: en
[16] BNF3: pas; BRB: "point" missing
[17] BNF2: ce publicque diffame; K: du publicque infame; 1545: du public diffame
[18] S2: Las, je crain; V: m'avoit, helas! J'ay peur
[19] All others: "en" missing

1133   While awaiting[1] her last day,
1134   Presented herself in a devout manner[2]
1135   To receive the Sacrament; then she was told of
1136   The day of her death, about which she was in no way upset,[3]
1137   But she showed herself[4] to be more joyous than before,
1138   Albeit she was still so curious[5]
1139   About the five[6] men and of their steadfastness
1140   That she wished to ask about their forbearance.
1141   Therefore, they tell her[7] that her brother had shown
1142   The greatest strength that was ever seen,[8]
1143   The other four as well, but[9] that Mark had said
1144   That he deserved the death that he received.
1145   The queen, with a slightly changed expression, then says:
1146   "Did he not at all exonerate me,[10]
1147   Before dying, of the[11] public scandal[12]
1148   That he brought on me? Alas, I fear lest his soul
1149   Be in pain because of this, and that

---

1  BNF2–3, B, V, M, K, 1545: And was awaiting; S2: Who was awaiting
2  B: Marginal notation of a cross within a circle
3  B: she was in no way stirred up; B marginal note with two parallel lines: "There are here some verses wanting." The reader has noted that the previous line's inversion resulted in a disruption in the rhyme.
4  BNF1: Showing herself; BNF3, B: But showing herself
5  BNF1: Albeit she was, for her part, curious
6  BNF5: Of these
7  All others: Somebody tells her
8  BNF5: strength of any man ever seen
9  S2: and
10  BNF3, BRB: not exonerate me
11  BNF2: this
12  K: infamy

---

1135:   That is, Holy Eucharist. On Anne's reception of the sacrament, see the letter of Chapuys to Charles V, LP 10.908, also found in CSP, Spain, 5, pt. 2, no. 55. That Anne not only received but also meditated upon the Blessed Sacrament is suggested by a letter from Kingston to Cromwell, which notes that "the Queen hath much desired to have here in the closet [i.e., her oratory] the sacraments." See Ellis, *Original Letters*, 59. The phrasing used by Kingston is ambiguous enough to support the notion of reception as well as meditation upon the Eucharist.

1138:   The expression "et si" here is drawing from its Latin equivalent, "etsi," meaning "albeit, although, even if." The sense is that Anne was, in the midst of her preparations for death, still curious about the comportment of the men who had been convicted with her.

1144:   Cf. Constantyne's *Memorial*, 65: "And Mark said: Masters I pray you all pray for me, for I have deserved the death."

1150    Seuffre de sa faulse confession.[1]
1151    Mais, de mon frere & des aultres, ie croy
1152    Qu'ilz sont[2] deuant la face du grand Roy,[3]
1153    Où, s'il[4] luy plaist, les accompaigneray,
1154    Lors que demain ce[5] monde lesseray."
1155    Le iour apres,[6] attendant qu'approchast
1156    Sa mort,[7] pria que nul ne l'empeschast
1157    Pour ce matin, & qu'on la[8] lessast faire[9]
1158    Avecques[10] Dieu, sans troubler, son affaire.
1159    Ainsi se mist seulle en son oratoire,
1160    Pour confermer[11] sa derniere memoire
1161    En IESVCHRIST,[12] pensant que ce[13] iour deust
1162    Souffrir la mort;[14] mais quand elle aperceut[15]
1163    Que ia passee estoit[16] l'heure donnee,
1164    En son esprit se trouua estonnee,
1165    Et se monstra alors estre[17] ennuyee                        [37v]
1166    Qu'on luy auoit son heure dilayee:[18]
1167    Non que la mort fust d'elle[19] desiree,
1168    Mais luy sembloit[20] qu'elle estoit preparee
1169    Pour bien mourir, & craignoit[21] que longueur[22]

---

[1] BNF2, S2: accusation; BNF5: En souffre par faulse accusation
[2] S2: soient
[3] 1545: davant la grace du Roy
[4] BNF5–6, B: Et s'il; M, K: Où sy
[5] BNF6, S2: le
[6] BNF1, S2: d'apres
[7] BNF1–7, V, BRB, M, K, Vat: Son point; B: Sa fin; S2: Sans fin (a scribal error); 1545: Ce bruit (a corrupt reading)
[8] B: le
[9] S2: Verse 1157 missing
[10] BL, BNF4, BNF7, M, Vat: Avec (emended for versification); S2 adds after 1158: Et que ce jour cherchoit son salut faire.
[11] V, BRB: conformer; 1545: confirmer
[12] BNF3: En son esprit
[13] BRB, K: le
[14] S2: La mort souffrir
[15] BNF5: quand apperceu eut; 1545: "mais" missing
[16] BNF4: ja estoit passee
[17] BNF4, BNF6: Et se monstra lors estre; BNF5: Et se trouva alors estre; S2: Et ce monstra estre adont; 1545: Et ce monstra alors d'estre
[18] BNF6: delaissee; S2: delaydee; V, K, Vat: delayee; 1545: distrahee
[19] BNF1: d'elle fust
[20] BNF1: semblant
[21] BNF1: el' craignoit; B, 1545: et craignant
[22] 1545: langueur

1150 He is suffering punishment for his false confession.[1]
1151 But as for my brother and the other men, I believe
1152 That they are before the face of the Great[2] King,
1153 Where,[3] if it pleases Him, I shall accompany them
1154 Tomorrow, when I leave this[4] world behind."
1155 The next day, while waiting for her approaching
1156 Death,[5] she begged that no one trouble her
1157 During that morning and that they allow her
1158 To manage her affairs with God without being disturbed.[6]
1159 And so she set herself alone in her oratory
1160 To settle her last thoughts
1161 On JESUS CHRIST,[7] believing that this day she must
1162 Suffer death; but when she noticed
1163 That the appointed hour had already passed,
1164 She found herself troubled in spirit
1165 And showed[8] herself then to be vexed
1166 Because her hour had been delayed:
1167 Not because she desired death,
1168 But because it seemed to her that she was prepared
1169 To die well, and she feared that a delay[9]

---

1 BNF2, BNF5, S2: accusation
2 1545: the grace of the
3 BNF5–6, B: And
4 BNF6, S2: the
5 BNF1–7, V, BRB, M, K, Vat: Moment; B: End
6 S2 is missing v. 1157 but adds a line after 1158 to complete the rhyme, so that vv. 1156 forward read: "she begged that no one prevent her / From managing her affairs with God without being disturbed / And that this day she seek to bring about her salvation"
7 BNF3: On her spirit
8 BNF5: found
9 1545: that languishment

---

1152: For this image of God as king, see, *inter alia*, Isaiah 33:22: "the Lord is our ruler, the Lord is our King."
1154: Carle makes it clear that Anne fully expected to be executed the day following the executions of the five men, that is, 18 May.
1164: The expression "troubled in spirit" (Vulg. "turbatus est spiritu") is used with regard to Jesus in foretelling his betrayal. See John 13:21. Similar expressions are found in John 11:33 and 12:27.

1170    Ne l'affoiblist &[1] la mist en langueur.[2]
1171    Ainsi[3] vn peu d'elle[4] se deffioit,
1172    Mais en Dieu seul du tout[5] se confioit,[6]
1173    Tant que, voyant ses Dames[7] tourmentees[8]
1174    De[9] grand ennuy, les a reconfortees[10]
1175    Par plusieurs fois, leur disant que la mort,
1176    Aux vrays[11] Chrestiens, n'a besoing de confort,[12]
1177    Puysque la vie eternelle[13] est aux cieux,
1178    Hors du danger du monde vitieux,
1179    Et pour ce, point[14] ne doiuent sa mort plaindre,[15]
1180    Car elle espoire asseurement attaindre
1181    Aux lieux heureux & de[16] prosperité,                    [38r]
1182    Laissant icy toute infelicité.[17]
1183    Ainsi auoit à ses dames apris[18]
1184    Qu'il[19] fault auoir ce bas monde à despris,[20]

---

[1]  S2: ou
[2]  V, BRB, K: Ne luy changeast son ferme cueur
[3]  V, BRB, M, K: Aussy
[4]  BNF2–3: Ainsi d'elle ung peu
[5]  BNF4: Mais au Sauveur de tout; BNF5: seul elle; B: missing "du tout"
[6]  V, BRB, K: Pource que ainsi delayé on avoit; M: Verse 1172 missing
[7]  BNF3: Tant que voyant ces dames; BNF4: En regardant ses dames
[8]  1545: tournees (a scribal error). B inverts the order of vv. 1172–1173, but this is corrected in the same hand in the margins with a notation of two parallel vertical bars.
[9]  BNF2–3, B, Vat: Du
[10] K: confortees
[11] BNF1–3, BNF5–7, B, V, BRB, M, K, Vat: "vray" missing; BNF4, 1545: bons
[12] BNF5, 1545: reconfort
[13] BNF5: Mais que la vie eternelle; BNF6: Mais que la vie des chrestiens
[14] BNF2: "point" added in another hand; V, K: Et pour ce doncq
[15] BNF1–2, BNF5–6, Vat: ne devoient sa mort plaindre; B: ne doiuent sa mort craindre
[16] BNF5: heureux de grand
[17] V: originally, "infelicité," then changed in the same hand to "infidelité"; BRB: Verses 1179–1182 are missing; K: felicité
[18] BNF1–3, BNF5–7, B, V, BRB, M, K, Vat: Ainsi elle a ses dames bien appris; BNF4: Ainsi elle a aux dames bien appris; S2: En telle sorte a ses dames apris; 1545: Ainsi elle ha à ses dames apris
[19] BNF7, M: Qui
[20] BNF1: avoir de ce monde mespris; BNF2, BNF5–6, B, S2, V, BRB, M, K, Vat: avoir ce bas monde en mespris; BNF3: Qu'il faut mourir, ce bas monde mespris (a corrupt reading); BNF4, BNF7, 1545: avoir ce bas monde à mespris

1170     Might weaken her and[1] put her in distress.[2]
1171     And so she mistrusted herself a little,
1172     But she trusted God alone in everything,[3]
1173     Such that, upon seeing her[4] ladies plagued[5]
1174     By great anguish, she consoled them
1175     Continually, telling them that death,
1176     To true Christians,[6] requires no comforting,
1177     Since eternal life[7] exists in heaven,
1178     Beyond the danger of this wicked world,
1179     And, for this reason, they must not lament[8] her death at all,[9]
1180     For she assuredly hopes to reach
1181     The place of happiness and prosperity,[10]
1182     Leaving all sadness[11] here behind.
1183     In this way, she taught her ladies[12]
1184     That one must have disdain for[13] this lowly world,[14]

---

1   S2: or
2   V, BRB, K: Might change her steadfast heart
3   BNF4: trusted the Savior in everything; V, BRB, K: Because they had delayed in this way
4   BNF3: these
5   BNF4: Looking at her ladies plagued
6   BNF1–3, BNF5–7, B, V, BRB, M, K, Vat: To Christians; BNF4, 1545: To good Christians
7   BNF5: But that eternal life; BNF6: But that Christian life
8   B: not fear for
9   V, K: this reason, therefore, they must not lament her death
10   BNF5: The blessed place of great prosperity
11   V's correction reads: "infidelity"; K: happiness
12   All but S2, 1545: taught her ladies well
13   BNF1–2, BNF5–6, B, S2, V, BRB, M, K, Vat: have scorn for
14   BNF1: this world

---

1170:   Kingston wrote to Cromwell on 18 May that Anne was "very sorry" that her execution had been delayed for she had hoped to be "past [her] pain." He went on to say, in contrast to Carle's reading of the situation, that he believes "this lady has much joy and pleasure in death" because Anne had fallen into laughter, remarking that the "executioner was very good" and that she had "a little neck." See Ellis, *Original Letters*, 64–65. See also Chapuys's letter to Charles V: "She confessed herself yesterday, and communicated [i.e., she received the sacrament of Holy Eucharist, also known as Holy Communion], expecting to be executed, and no person ever showed greater willingness to die. ... And when the command came to put off the execution till today she appeared very sorry, praying the Captain of the Tower that for the honor of God he would beg the King that, since she was in good state and disposed for death, she might be dispatched immediately" (LP 10.908).

1182:   No other sources report this instruction given to her ladies. The *Pasteur évangélique* (a presentation copy of which was made for Anne and Henry) offers a similar meditation on death as a "very desirable friend" that liberates us from our earthly prison (see BL, Royal 16 E XIII, in particular vv. 314–320).

1185    Qui est tout vain, caduc,[1] & transitoire,
1186    Pour aspirer à l'eternelle[2] gloire.
1187    Et tellement les a toutes rauies
1188    Que[3] ne font plus estime[4] de leurs vies,
1189    Mais disent lors[5] que, si Dieu le[6] vouloit,
1190    De viure plus icy ne leur[7] challoit,
1191    Et bien vouldroient s'en aller auec[8] elle
1192    Pour le maintien[9] de sa iuste[10] querelle.
1193    Elle respond[11] qu'il[12] leur failloit attendre
1194    La volunté de Dieu, sans entreprendre
1195    Rien que pour[13] luy, & que l'ayant pour guide,[14]
1196    N'auront iamais à leur besoing[15] d'autre ayde.
1197    Et les[16] prioit qu'eussent en[17] souuenance            [38v]
1198    Ses[18] dictz, mais non sa fragille impuissance.[19]
1199    Par ses sermons ainsi les instruisoit,[20]
1200    En attendant tousiours que venu soit[21]

---

[1]  BNF1: Où tout y est caduc; BNF3–7, B, S2, BRB, M, K, Vat, 1545: Où tout est vain, caduc; V: Où tout est bien caduc
[2]  BNF1: en l'eternelle; V, K, 1545: à eternelle
[3]  BL: Qu'il (emended for grammar and sense)
[4]  BNF2, 1545: Qu'elles ne font plus estime; BNF4: Que ne font nulle estime; BNF5: Qu'elles ne font plus compte; BNF6: Qu'ilz ne font plus compte; B: Que plus ne font estime; S2, Vat: Qu'ils ne font plus estime
[5]  BNF1, V, BRB, M, K: dirent lors; B, S2: disoient lors; 1545: disent tous
[6]  BNF1: "le" missing; BNF2–3: les
[7]  B: vivre icy plus ne leur en; BRB: De vivre icy plus ne leur
[8]  BNF5: vouldroient aller avecques; BNF6: voulloient aller avec
[9]  S2: moien (a scribal error)
[10]  BRB: triste
[11]  BNF1, BNF6, Vat: Elle leur respond; BNF4, S2: Elle leur dist; BNF5, 1545: Et leur respond
[12]  BNF7: qui; M: que
[13]  BNF4: Rien contre
[14]  BNF1: et, l'ayant pour leur guide; 1545: et que l'ayent pour guide
[15]  BNF1–2, BNF4–6, B, V, M, S2: N'auroient jamais affaire; BNF3, BNF7, Vat, 1545: N'auront jamais affaire; BRB, K: N'auroient jamais à faire
[16]  BNF1, Vat: leur; S2: À leur
[17]  BNF5: qu'ilz eussent en; 1545: que eussent à
[18]  S2: Ces
[19]  BNF1: dictz et sa très fragile imprudence; BNF2–4, BNF6, B, BRB, M, K, Vat: mais non sa fragile imprudence; BNF5: non pas sa fragile imprudence; BNF7: mais sa fragile imprudence; S2: dictz et non sa fragile imprudence; V: mais non en sa fragile prudence; 1545: mais non si fragile imprudence
[20]  BL: les confortoit (emended for rhyme as in all others but 1545); 1545: les instuyoit (a corrupt reading)
[21]  BNF1–7, B, S2, V, BRB, M, K, Vat: Et de bon cueur attend que venu soit; 1545: Et de bon cueur a tant que veu soit (a corrupt reading)

| 1185 | Which is completely vain, feeble,[1] and transitory, |
|------|------|
| 1186 | So as to aspire to eternal glory. |
| 1187 | And she so inspired them all |
| 1188 | That they no longer value[2] their own lives |
| 1189 | But say then[3] that, if God so desired, |
| 1190 | They would not care to live here any longer, |
| 1191 | And they would very much like to go away with her |
| 1192 | To support her just[4] cause. |
| 1193 | She answers[5] that they would need to await |
| 1194 | The will of God, without undertaking |
| 1195 | Anything but for[6] Him, and that, having Him for their guide, |
| 1196 | They will never have need of any other aid. |
| 1197 | And she begged them to remember |
| 1198 | Her[7] words, but not her mortal infirmity.[8] |
| 1199 | By her speech she thus instructed[9] them, |
| 1200 | While still waiting for[10] the next day to come, |

---

[1] BNF1: Where everything there is feeble; BNF3–7, B, S2, BRB, M, K, Vat, 1545: Where everything is vain, feeble; V: Where everything is quite feeble

[2] BNF4: they place no value on; BNF5–6: they no longer have regard for

[3] BNF1, B, S2, V, BRB, M, K: said then; 1545: But they all say

[4] BRB: sad

[5] BNF1, BNF6, Vat: She answers them; BNF4, S2: She tells them; BNF5, 1545: And she answers them

[6] BNF4: Anything against

[7] S2: These

[8] BNF1: words and her very weak imprudence; BNF2–4, BNF6, B, BRB, M, K, Vat: but not her weak imprudence; BNF5: words, not her weak imprudence; BNF7: but her weak imprudence; S2: and not her weak imprudence; V: but not in her weak prudence; 1545: but not such weak imprudence

[9] BL: comforted

[10] BNF1–7, B, S2, V, BRB, M, K, Vat: And she courageously awaited

---

1186: Anne's speech to her ladies is somewhat reminiscent of the consoling verses of the Book of Wisdom which proclaims that "though in the sight of others [the righteous] were punished, their hope is full of immortality" (Wisdom 3:4).

1192: Carle's description of Anne's ladies grieving for her coming demise contrasts with Anne's remarks, as recorded by Kingston, that the ladies attending to her in the Tower were not among those most favored by her. See, on this point, Ellis, *Original Letters*, 60.

1198: Cotgrave defines "fragile" as "frail, weak; mortal."

1201   Le iour suyuant, lors que[1] le Capitaine
1202   Dire luy vint[2] que l'heure estoit prochaine,
1203   Et qu'estoit[3] temps qu'elle se[4] disposast.
1204   Elle[5] luy dit que luy mesme aduisast[6]
1205   De[7] s'acquiter de sa charge & deuoir:[8]
1206   Car, de long temps,[9] Dieu a voulu pourueoir[10]
1207   À[11] luy donner couraige & fermeté
1208   Pour resister à plus grand[12] cruaulté.
1209   Ainsi[13] s'en va au lieu de son suplice
1210   Pour obeir au vouloir de iustice,
1211   Tousiours monstrant[14] vn visaige content,[15]
1212   Comme[16] le monde en rien ne regrettant:
1213   Car sa couleur & sa face[17] estoit telle[18]                    [39r]
1214   Que ne fut onc[19] de tous veue si[20] belle.
1215   Par grand doulceur que[21] de ses yeulx rendoit,
1216   En[22] soubzriant, le peuple regardoit,
1217   Auquel,[23] soubdain qu'elle fut[24] arriuee

---

1   BNF1, BNF3, BNF5, BNF7, S2, BRB, M, K, Vat, 1545: suivant et quant; BNF2, BNF4, BNF6: suivant et que; B: suivant auquel; V: suivant ce que quant

2   V, BRB: Dire vint

3   BNF1–3, BNF5, BNF7, B, S2, V, BRB, M, K, Vat, 1545: qu'il estoit; BNF4: qu'il fust; BNF6: qu'il est

4   BNF2: que ce; BNF3, BNF7, B, S2, V, BRB, M, K, Vat: que se; 1545: que si

5   BNF4: Celle; BRB: Et

6   BNF2: s'avisast; V: qu'il luy mesme advisast

7   BNF1: À

8   1545: vouloir

9   BNF2, BNF5–7, B, S2, Vat, 1545: dès longtemps

10  BNF1, BRB: l'a voulu pourveoir; BNF5: a voulu prouveoir

11  BNF1, S2: Et

12  V: grande

13  S2: Adont

14  V: Monstrant toujours

15  BNF1–7, B, S2: constant

16  BNF5, S2: Contre (a scribal error)

17  B: et face s'y

18  BNF7: estoit belle; V, K: estoient telle

19  BNF1, BNF6, B, 1545: oncques

20  BNF4: Qu'elle ne fust oncques veue si; BNF5: Qu'onques n'avoit esté veue si; S2: Qu'elle ne fut oncques veue plus; V: Que ne feust oncques veue de tous plus; BRB: Que ne fut onq veue de tous plus; M: Que ne fust oncques veue de tous si; K: Que ne fust oncq veue de tout plus

21  BNF2, V, BRB, M, K: qui; BNF7: Par grandz doulceurs que; S2: Et par doulceur que

22  BNF4, 1545: Et

23  K: Duquel (a scribal error)

24  S2: Devant lequel elle estant

1201    When[1] the Constable of the Tower
1202    Came to tell her[2] that the hour was near
1203    And that it was[3] time to get prepared.
1204    She[4] tells him that he should himself attend
1205    To fulfilling his charge and duty,[5]
1206    Because, for some time, God had wished to provide for her
1207    By giving her[6] the courage and strength
1208    To withstand the greatest cruelty.
1209    And so[7] she went to the place of her ordeal
1210    To obey the will of justice,
1211    Still showing a serene[8] countenance,
1212    As if she did not grieve for this world in any way;
1213    For her coloring and her face were such[9]
1214    That never before did she seem so[10] beautiful to everyone.
1215    With great[11] gentleness, which she rendered with her eyes,
1216    Smiling[12] all the while, she looked upon the people,
1217    To whom, as soon as[13] she had arrived

---

1  BNF1, BNF3, BNF5, BNF7, S2, BRB, M, K, Vat, 1545: And when; BNF2, BNF4, BNF6: And that; B: At which point
2  V, BRB: Came to say
3  BNF6: is
4  BRB: And she
5  1545: will
6  BNF1, S2: And to give her
7  S2: Thereupon
8  BNF1–7, B, S2: a steadfast
9  BNF7: beautiful
10  S2, V, BRB, K: more
11  S2: And with
12  BNF4, 1545: And smiling
13  S2: In front of whom

---

1203:  Anne's execution took place on 19 May 1536, two days after that of the men accused with her.
1216:  Cf. Harley 2194, fol. 16v, transcribed in Cobbett, *Complete Collection of State Trials*, 411, and *Ballads from Manuscripts*, 407: "This speech she uttered with a smiling countenance." An Imperial account, however, claims that "she looked frequently behind her … and was very much exhausted and amazed." See LP 10.911; *The Pilgrim*, 116; and Gachard, *Analectes historiques*, 17n1, which gives the original French transcription of the text.

| 1218 | Sur l'eschauffault, d'vne grace priuee,[1] |
| 1219 | Sans s'effroyer,[2] a sa voix adressee,[3] |
| 1220 | Qui toutesfois se trouue[4] vn peu pressee |
| 1221 | De la foiblesse en elle dominant.[5] |
| 1222 | Mais peu à peu sa force reprenant,[6] |
| 1223 | Et[7] asseurant sa debille façon, |
| 1224 | Fist de sa voix sortir tel[8] piteux son: |
| 1225 | "Ô mes amys, amis & plus que freres,[9] |
| 1226 | Puis qu'auec vous ie[10] ne puis estre gueres, |
| 1227 | Et que finy est[11] le cours de mes ans,[12] |
| 1228 | Ie vous supply, n'en[13] soyez desplaisans, |
| 1229 | Et me vueillez pardonner de bon cueur |
| 1230 | Si ie n'ay point vzé de la[14] doulceur |
| 1231 | Enuers vous tous, ainsi[15] que ie devoye, |
| 1232 | Veu le pouuoir & moyen[16] que i'auoye.[17] |
| 1233 | Et vous pri[18] tous que, par fraternité[19] |
| 1234 | De chrestienne &[20] vraye[21] charité, |
| 1235 | Me departez[22] vos prieres deuotes |

[39v]

---

1 B: Reclama Dieu et la Vierge sacree. The words "et la Vierge sacree" are underscored, perhaps indicating that the reader noticed that this version is a very weak rhyme, or, possibly, to note this unique depiction of Anne's devotion to the Virgin Mary.

2 BNF3, BNF5–7, S2: Sans s'efforcer

3 B: puis a sa voix dressee; BNF4: elle a sa voix dressee

4 BNF1: Que toutesfoys trouva; V: Que toutesfoys se trouva; BRB, K: Qui toutesfoys se trouva

5 BNF5: De faiblesse en elle demourant; V: Veu la foiblesse en elle dominant; BRB: De sa foiblesse en elle dominant

6 BNF1: sa face reprouvant; B, V: sa face reprenant

7 V, BRB, K: En

8 BNF1: partir ung; BNF2–4, B, V, BRB, M, K, S2: sortir ce; BNF5: sortir un; Vat, 1545: sortir de

9 B: Ô mes amys, et vous aussy, mes freres; S2: Ô mes amys, mes chers et aimez freres; BRB: Ô mes amys et plus que freres

10 V, BRB, K: "je" missing

11 BNF4: Et qu'à la fin est; S2: Et que finir fault

12 1545: mes parens (a corrupt reading)

13 BNF1–4, BNF6–7, B, S2, V, BRB, M, K, Vat: ne; 1545: que ne

14 BNF6: telle

15 BNF1, BNF3–7, B, S2, M, Vat, 1545: selon

16 K: le moyen et pouvoir

17 BNF2–6, S2, Vat, 1545: qu'en avoys; B: qu'avoye

18 1545: Je vous prie

19 B: prie tous que par grand fermeté; K: pri que tous par fraternité

20 BNF1, BNF3–6: De crestienté et; S2: Des vrays chrestiens et

21 M: vray

22 BNF2: Ne departez (a scribal error); BNF3: Me departir; BNF4–5: Me departiez, V: Me despartez de

| 1218 | On the scaffold, with inward grace,[1] |
|---|---|
| 1219 | And without fear,[2] she directed[3] her voice, |
| 1220 | Which nevertheless was a little strained |
| 1221 | By the weakness that held sway over her.[4] |
| 1222 | But, little by little, regaining her strength,[5] |
| 1223 | And[6] emboldening her feeble manner, |
| 1224 | She made her voice emit a piteous sound such as this:[7] |
| 1225 | "Oh my friends, friends and more than brothers,[8] |
| 1226 | Since I can be with you but a short while, |
| 1227 | And finished is[9] the course of my years, |
| 1228 | I entreat you not to be vexed about it. |
| 1229 | And, please, pardon me wholeheartedly |
| 1230 | If I have not treated you all with kindness,[10] |
| 1231 | As I should have done, |
| 1232 | Given the power and means that I had. |
| 1233 | And I beg you all that, in the fellowship[11] |
| 1234 | Of true and Christian[12] charity, |
| 1235 | You favor me with your devout prayers |

---

[1] B: She cried out to God and to the Holy Virgin

[2] BNF3, BNF5-7, S2: Without forcing herself

[3] B: she then directed

[4] BNF5: weakness remaining in her; V: Given the weakness that held sway over her; BRB: From the weakness holding sway over her

[5] BNF1: reproaching her appearance; B, V: regaining control over her appearance

[6] V, BRB, K: While

[7] BNF1, BNF5: emit a piteous sound; BNF2-4, B, S2, V, BRB, M, K: emit this piteous sound

[8] B: Oh my friends, and you, my brothers, as well; S2: Oh my friends, my dear and beloved brothers; BRB: Oh my friends and more than brothers

[9] BNF4: And at its end is; S2: And I must end

[10] BNF6: with such kindness

[11] B: that with great steadfastness

[12] BNF1, BNF3-6: Of Christianity and; S2: Of true Christians and

---

1225:  For the concept of a friend who is more than a brother, see Proverbs 18:24, which Anne echoes here. Carle's version of Anne's scaffold speech differs somewhat from that recorded in other sources such as Hall's *Chronicle*, 819; Wriothesley's *Chronicle*, 1:41–42; and Harley 2194, fol. 16v (recorded in Cobbett, *Complete Collection of State Trials*, 410, and *Ballads from Manuscripts*, 1:406–7).

1235:  Cf. Hall's *Chronicle*, 819: "I heartily desire you all to pray for me"; Harley 2194, fol. 16v: "I bid the world farewell, beseeching me to commend me in your prayers to God" (transcribed in Cobbett, *Complete Collection of State Trials*, 410, and *Ballads from Manuscripts*, 1: 406–7).

1236    Enuers Iesus, affin que, par les nottes[1]
1237    De mes pechez, point ne soit[2] maculee
1238    Mon ame, apres que m'en seray allee.
1239    De vous narrer pourquoy ie suis icy
1240    Ne seruiroit pour moy, ne vous aussi,[3]

At this point, BNF4 inserts seven verses (the last of which is a variant of v. 1241), resuming the poem at v. 1242:

a.    Mais je ne veulx toutesfois oublier
b.    Bien humblement trestous vous supplier
c.    Qu'oncq ne veuillez des choses qu'avez veues
d.    Ou cy apres des autres entendues
e.    Juger la part et me donner sentences
f.    Qui domaiger puissent vos confidences
g.    Car le seul Dieu est vray juge du monde

1241    Parquoy m'en tay.[4] Mais le iuge du monde,[5]
1242    En qui iustice & verité abonde,[6]
1243    Congnoist le tout, lequel d'affection[7]
1244    Ie prie qu'il vueille[8] auoir compassion
1245    De ceulx qui m'ont à ceste mort iugee.                [40r]
1246    Et quand d'icy ie seray[9] deslogee,[10]
1247    Souuienne vous que ie[11] vous recommande
1248    Vostre bon Roy, en qui i'ay veu[12] si grande
1249    Humanité & comble[13] de tous biens,
1250    Craincte enuers[14] Dieu, amour envers[15] les siens,

---

1   BNF4: la notte
2   BNF1–7, B, S2, V, BRB, M, K, Vat: pechez, ne soit point; 1545: pechez, n'en soit point
3   Vat: serviroit que vous ny moy aussi; all others: serviroit pour vous ne moy aussi. This is the last line of BNF5. It is followed by three blank pages.
4   B, 1545: me taiz; BRB, M, Vat: m'en tais
5   S2: mais, las, la deité
6   S2: Où est tousjours justice et verité
7   S2: Congnoist mon cueur, priant d'affection
8   S2: Le doux Jhesus
9   BNF7, K: d'icy seray
10  V: eslongnee
11  S2: Preigne mon ame, atant
12  B: de qui j'ay eu
13  BNF6: Humanité comblé de
14  V, BRB, K: devers
15  BNF1, Vat: amour avec; BNF6: crainte envers (a scribal error); BRB: amour devers

| 1236 | Towards Jesus, so that my soul be not |
|------|------|
| 1237 | Blemished in the slightest by the stains[1] |
| 1238 | Of my sins after I am gone. |
| 1239 | To recount for you why I am here |
| 1240 | Would serve neither me nor you, |

BNF4 inserts seven verses after v. 1240 (the last of which is a variant of v. 1241) and resumes the poem at v. 1242:

| a. | But I do not want, nevertheless, to forget |
|----|------|
| b. | To beg each and every one of you, quite humbly, |
| c. | Never to wish, on the basis of the things that you have seen, |
| d. | Or those which, afterwards, you have heard from others, |
| e. | To determine my part and pass judgments on me |
| f. | That might be detrimental to your trust. |
| g. | For God alone is the true judge of the world |

| 1241 | Which is why I am silent; but the Judge of the world, |
|------|------|
| 1242 | In Whom justice and truth abound, |
| 1243 | Knows all:[2] Whom, out of love, |
| 1244 | I beseech[3] to have compassion |
| 1245 | On those who judged me deserving of this death. |
| 1246 | And when I am removed[4] from here, |
| 1247 | Remember that I recommend to you[5] |
| 1248 | Your good king, in whom I have seen[6] such great |
| 1249 | Kindness and the height of all good things— |
| 1250 | Fear of God, love for his people, |

---

[1] BNF4: the stain

[2] BNF4: He knows all

[3] S2: Verses 1241–1244 read: "Which is why I am silent. But, alas, the Deity, / Wherein there is always justice and truth, / Knows my heart, which, out of love, begs / Sweet Jesus"

[4] V: banished

[5] S2: May He take my soul forthwith. I recommend

[6] B: from whom I have received

---

1240: The variant that follows, from BNF4, is somewhat reminiscent of Anne's speech as recorded in Hall's *Chronicle*, 819: "And if any person will meddle of my cause, I require them to judge the best." Cf. Harley 2194, fol. 16v: "if anyone intend an inquisitive survey of my actions, I entreat him to judge favorably of me, and not rashly to admit any censorious conceit" (transcribed in Cobbett, *Complete Collection of State Trials*, 410, and *Ballads from Manuscripts*, 1: 406–7).

1241: For this image, see, *inter alia*, Isaiah 33:22: "For the Lord is our judge."

1243: Cf. Wriothesley's *Chronicle*, 1:41–42: "as for mine offences ... God knoweth them."

1251    Et[1] grandz vertuz lesquelles ie[2] reserue,
1252    Qu'estes heureux si Dieu vous le[3] conserue.
1253    Priez donc Dieu[4] que longuement le tienne
1254    Auecques[5] vous, & aussi que maintienne[6]
1255    Sa grace pour me tirer auec luy[7]
1256    Et receuoir mon esprit ce iourdhuy."[8]
1257    Ce[9] fut la fin de la foible[10] parolle,
1258    Qui toutesfois le peuple vn peu consolle,[11]
1259    Fort desollé de veoir[12] la paouure Royne
1260    En cest[13] estat, menee en telle[14] peine.
1261    Car n'est aucun[15] qui n'ayt ferme esperance[16]                    [40v]
1262    Que ne sera son esprit en souffrance,[17]
1263    Veu sa[18] grand foy & patience saige,

---

[1]  B: Ses
[2]  B: dire
[3]  BNF1–4, BNF6–7, B, V, BRB, M, K, Vat: le vous
[4]  S2: Or priez Dieu
[5]  V, BRB, M, 1545: Avec
[6]  BNF1: vous; aussi qu'il maintienne; all others: aussi que m'advienne
[7]  BNF1: me retirer à luy; BNR6: me tirer avecques luy; S2: Sa saincte grace afin que ce jourd'huy
[8]  BNF1–7, B, V, BRB, M, K, Vat, 1545: recevoir mon ame ce iourdhuy; S2: Mon ame soit logé avecques luy
[9]  BNF1: Qui
[10]  BNF1–4, BNF7, S2, BRB, K, M, Vat, 1545: sa foible; BNF6: sa fidele
[11]  BNF4: Qui grandement les assistans consolle; 1545: le peuple ainsi consolle
[12]  BNF1: Qui desollé de veoir; BNF4: Fort desolez de veoir; BNF7, M: Fut desolé de veoir; BRB, K: Qui desolé estoit de veoir
[13]  BNF1–4, BNF6–7, B, V, BRB, M, K, Vat, 1545: tel
[14]  BNF1, BNF4, BNF6, Vat, 1545: menee en ceste; BNF2–3, B: mener à ceste; BNF7, S2, V, BRB, M, K: menee à ceste
[15]  BNF4: n'est autruy; S2: Et n'y a nul
[16]  B: bonne esperance; 1545: ferme sperance
[17]  B: Que son esprit ne sera en souffrance; V: en souffisance (a scribal error); S2: Qu'en l'autre monde elle n'aura souffrance
[18]  BNF1: si

1251    And[1] great virtues which I set aside[2]—
1252    That you should be happy if God preserves him for you.
1253    Pray to God, therefore,[3] that He should long keep him
1254    With you, and also that His grace sustain me[4]
1255    So as to draw me towards Him
1256    And receive my spirit[5] today."[6]
1257    This was the end of her feeble[7] speech
1258    Which nevertheless consoles the people a little,[8]
1259    Who were deeply sorry[9] to see the poor queen
1260    Brought to this[10] state in such[11] pain.
1261    For there is no one[12] who does not have firm hope[13]
1262    That her spirit will not be in agony,[14]
1263    Given her[15] great faith and wise patience,

---

[1] B: His
[2] B: I refrain from telling
[3] S2: Now pray to God
[4] All others but BNF1: and also that His grace come to me
[5] BNF1–7, B, V, BRB, M, K, Vat, 1545: my soul
[6] S2: Verses 1254–1256 read: "and also that / His holy grace come to me so that today / My soul be lodged with Him"
[7] BNF6: faithful
[8] BNF4: Which greatly consoles those in attendance; 1545: Which nevertheless thus consoles the people
[9] BNF1, BNF7, BRB, M, K: Who were sorry
[10] BNF1–4, BNF6–7, B, V, BRB, M, K, Vat, 1545: to such a
[11] All others: in this
[12] BNF4: no other
[13] B: good hope.
[14] S2: That she will not experience suffering in the world beyond
[15] BNF1: In light of so

---

1254:   Cf. Hall's *Chronicle*, 819: "I pray God save the King and send him long to reign over you, for a gentler nor a more merciful prince was there never: and to me he was ever a good, a gentle, and sovereign lord"; Wriothesley's *Chronicle*, 1:42: "I beseech Jesu save my sovereign and master the King, the most goodly, noble and gentle Prince that is, and long to reign over you"; Harley 2194, fol. 16v (transcribed in Cobbett, *Complete Collection of State Trials*, 410, and *Ballads from Manuscripts*, 1: 406–7): "I beseech the Almighty to preserve his Majesty long to reign over you; a more gentle or mild Prince never swayed scepter, his bounty and clemency towards me I am sure hath been special"; and Constantyne's *Memorial*, 65: "desiring you all to pray for the King's majesty that he may long reign over you, for he is a very noble prince and fully gently handled me."

At this point, BNF4 adds eight lines (the last four of which are close variants of
vv. 1265–1268), resuming the poem at v. 1269:

a.     Tant que chacun pour sa fin tant constante
b.     Faict jugement de sa vye prudente
c.     Et pense auoir grandement offensé
d.     De tout le mal que d'elle avoit pensé.
e.     Et n'est celuy qui se puisse garder
f.     De se douloir la voulant regarder,
g.     Car de tant plus que d'elle s'accroissoit
h.     Le ferme cœur, tant plus amoindrissoit

1264     Qui surmontoit[1] de femme le couraige.[2]
1265     Ce neantmoins, qui la veult regarder
1266     Par grand pitié ne se scauroit[3] garder
1267     De se douloir,[4] & tant plus que croissoit[5]
1268     Son ferme cœur, tant plus affoiblissoit[6]
1269     Aux assistans, qui[7] ne pouuoient tenir
1270     Leurs[8] pleurs que bien elle a sceu contenir.[9]
1271     Quand la Royne eut elle mesme baissé[10]
1272     Son blanc collet & chapperon laissé[11]
1273     Pour ne donner au coup empeschement,
1274     S'en vint gecter à[12] genoux humblement,
1275     En prununceant ceste voix plusieurs[13] fois:
1276     "Christ ie te pry que[14] mon esprit[15] reçoys!"
1277     Ô grand pitié! l'vne des[16] damoyselles,                    [41r]

---

1   S2: Oultrepassant; V, M: En surmontant
2   BRB: Missing vv. 1261–1264.
3   BNF1: ne scauroit se
4   B: De soy doulloir
5   BNF2: plus se doulloyt
6   BNF1–3, BNF6–7, S2, V, BRB, M, K, Vat, 1545: amoindrissoit; B: s'amoindrissoit
7   V, BRB, K: Le cueur des assistans qui
8   BNF4, BNF6, B, M, Vat, 1545: Les
9   BNF6: elle sceuse contenir; S2: qu'adont elle a sceu soustenir; V, K, M: elle sceut contenir; BRB:
    elle sceut tenir
10  BNF1: Quant a la Royne elle mesme baissé; BNF4: Et quant elle eust elle mesme baissé; S2: La
    Royne enfin son blanc collet baissa
11  BNF1: et son chapperon laissé; S2: Et tout soubdain son chaperon laissa
12  BNF1, BNF3–4, BNF6, B, Vat, 1545: Se vint getter à; BNF2: Se veult getter à; S2: Puis s'est
    jectee à; V, BRB, K: Se vint jecter aux
13  BNF1: la voix par plusieurs; S2: ce parler plusieurs
14  BNF1–4, BNF6, B, V, BRB, M, K, Vat: "que" missing
15  BNF1, BNF3, V, M, 1545: esperit; BNF2: le mien esprit
16  B: l'une de ses

Here, BNF4 adds eight verses (the last four of which are close variants of vv. 1265–1268), resuming the poem with v. 1269:

a.    Such that everyone, on the basis of her mightily steady end,

b.    Judges her life to have been prudent

c.    And believes that they have committed a great offense

d.    In having thought so ill of her.

e.    And there is no one who can keep from

f.    Grieving when they wish to look upon her:

g.    For, as much as her steadfast heart

h.    Grew stronger, so much weaker did grow

1264    Which rose above[1] womanly courage.

1265    Despite this, whoever wishes to look upon her

1266    With great pity could not keep

1267    From grieving, and, just as her steadfast heart

1268    Grew stronger,[2] so, too, did grow weaker[3]

1269    The hearts of those in attendance, who could not hold back

1270    Their[4] tears, which she could so well contain.[5]

1271    When the queen[6] herself had lowered

1272    Her white collar and took off her hood[7]

1273    So as not to impede the blow,

1274    She proceeded to[8] cast herself humbly on her knees

1275    While pronouncing this utterance several times:

1276    "Christ, I beg you to receive my spirit!"

1277    Oh! What great pity! One of the[9] gentlewomen,

---

[1]  S2: Surpassing; V, M: Rising above

[2]  BNF2: just as her steadfast heart did grieve the more

[3]  BNF 1–3, BNF6–7, B, S2, V, BRB, M, K, Vat, 1545: did diminish

[4]  BNF6, B, M, Vat, 1545: The

[5]  BNF6, V, K, M: which she could contain; B: which she could hold back; S2: which she then could contain

[6]  BNF4: When she

[7]  S2: Verses 1271–1272 read: "The queen at last lowered her white collar / And quickly took off her hood"

[8]  BNF2: She wished to; S2: She then

[9]  B: her

---

1272:  Cf. the Imperial account in *The Pilgrim*, 117: "she herself took off her head-dress"; similarly, the *Lettre d'un gentilhomme portugais* states that "with her own hands, she removed her coif from her head."

1276:  Cf. Harley 2194, fol. 16v (also transcribed in Cobbett, *Complete Collection of State Trials*, 411): "kneeling down, with a fervent spirit [she] said: "To Jesus Christ I commend my soul; Lord Jesu receive my soul." See Luke 23:46 and Acts 7:59 for scriptural parallels.

1278  Iectant sans fin[1] larmes continuelles,
1279  Vint au[2] deuant pour faire le seruice
1280  De son dernier & pitoiable office,
1281  Et son visaige a d'un linge voillé.[3]
1282  Lors le ministre en foy fut desollé[4]
1283  Et perturbé[5] de l'execution,
1284  Se contraingnant pour satisfaction,[6]
1285  Le dernier coup d'vne espee visa
1286  Dessus le[7] col, qui tost le diuisa.[8]
1287  La[9] teste & corps furent prins[10] par les dames,[11]
1288  Qu'eussiez iugés estre presque[12] sans ames
1289  Pour la langueur & extresme foiblesse
1290  Enquoy estoient;[13] mais, craignant leur maistresse
1291  Estre tenue & touchee des[14] mains
1292  Indignement des hommes[15] inhumains,
1293  A ce[16] besoing encores s'efforcerent,[17]                    [41v]
1294  Et ce corps mort presque mortes porterent,
1295  Enueloppé d'vne blanche closture,[18]

---

[1]  S2: sans cesse
[2]  BNF4: Vint la devant
[3]  S2: Et de la Royne a la face voillé
[4]  BNF1–4, BNF7, B, M, Vat, 1545: Le maistre allors, luy-mesme desollé; BNF6: Le ministre alors luy mesme desolé; S2: D'un linge blanc. Le maistre desolé; V, BRB, K: Le maistre allors, luy-mesme estonné
[5]  S2: Et fort faché
[6]  BNF1: Et se craignant par satisfaction; V, BRB, M, K: Pour faire fin à la conclusion.
[7]  BNF3: son
[8]  BNF1, BNF6, BRB, 1545: qui soudain devisa; BNF2–4, BNF7, B, M, Vat: que soubdain divisa; S2: Dessus la Royne et son chef divisa; V, K: et soudain divisa
[9]  K: Sa
[10]  1545: "prins" missing
[11]  S2: D'avec le corps qu'adont prindrent ses dames
[12]  BNF2, BNF7, V, BRB, M, K, Vat: jugées presque estre; S2: jugées alors estre
[13]  S2: Où elles sont
[14]  1545: de
[15]  S2: des maistres
[16]  Vat: Adonc (a corrupt reading)
[17]  BNF1: encores se offerent
[18]  BNF1, S2: de blanche couverture

| | |
|---|---|
| 1278 | Endlessly[1] pouring forth continuous tears, |
| 1279 | Came forward[2] to perform the service |
| 1280 | Of her last and piteous office, |
| 1281 | And veiled her face with linen. |
| 1282 | Then the officer, who was assuredly distraught[3] |
| 1283 | And troubled[4] by the execution, |
| 1284 | Forcing himself to fulfill his duty,[5] |
| 1285 | Aimed the final blow of a sword |
| 1286 | Upon her neck, which quickly severed it. |
| 1287 | The[6] head and body were taken by her ladies[7] |
| 1288 | Whom you would have thought to be almost[8] bereft of their souls |
| 1289 | Due to the languishment and extreme weakness |
| 1290 | They were[9] experiencing; but, fearing that their mistress |
| 1291 | Might be taken and touched unworthily by the hands |
| 1292 | Of discourteous men,[10] |
| 1293 | They persevered still[11] in this duty, |
| 1294 | And the nearly dead women carried away this dead body, |
| 1295 | Enveloped in a white shroud, |

---

1  S2: Incessantly
2  BNF4: Came before her
3  BNF1–4, BNF6–7, B, M, Vat, 1545: The officer then, himself distraught; V, BRB, K: The officer then, himself aghast
4  S2: Verses 1281–1283 read: "And veiled the queen's face / With white linen. The officer, distraught / And deeply distressed"
5  BNF1: And fearing to satisfy this duty; V, BRB, M, K: To put an end to this conclusion
6  K: Her
7  S2: Verses 1286–1287 read: "Upon the queen and severed her head / From her body, both of which were then taken by her ladies"
8  S2: to be then
9  S2: are
10  S2: officers
11  BNF1: They offered themselves still

---

1281:  Cf. the Imperial account, in *The Pilgrim*, 117: "One of her attendants gave her a cap into which she gathered her hair. She then knelt; a lady bound her eyes." See also the *Lettre d'un gentilhomme portugais* and *Il Successo in la morte*, both of which depict Anne's attendants as "pouring forth many tears." Ales ("Letter," 529) specifies that Anne "herself arranged her hair, covered her eyes, and commanded the executioner to strike."

1287:  Cf. the Imperial account, in *The Pilgrim*, 117: "When the head fell, a white handkerchief was thrown over it, and one of the four ladies took it up and carried it away. The other three lifted the body, and bore it with the head into the adjoining chapel in the Tower." See also Hannart's letter to the Empress dated 2 June (LP 10.1044): "The Queen's head and body were taken to a church in the Tower, accompanied by four ladies." The *Lettre d'un gentilhomme* and *Il Successo* likewise specify that the queen's head and body were taken to a church in the Tower.

| 1296 | Iusques au lieu de triste sepulture,[1] |
|------|------|
| 1297 | Dedans la tour où estoit prisonniere, |
| 1298 | Qui fut[2] aussi sa demeure[3] derniere. |
| 1299 | Son frere estoit ensepuely aupres,[4] |
| 1300 | Waston, Norris[5] ensemblement apres,[6] |
| 1301 | Bruton &[7] Marc aussi mis en vn couble,[8] |
| 1302 | Faisans d'vn lieu[9] la sepulture double.[10] |
| 1303 | Les dames lors dolentes, separees,[11] |
| 1304 | Sembloient[12] brebis sans pasteur, esgarees, |
| 1305 | Qui toutesfois ne seront[13] longuement, |
| 1306 | Sans reuenir au premier[14] traictement: |
| 1307 | Car ia le Roy s'est mis[15] en fantaisie |
| 1308 | De l'amytié d'vne Dame choisie.[16] |
| 1309 | Et[17] par cecy, monseigneur,[18] accomplye[19]     [42r] |

---

1   BNF2: du triste sepulture; V, BRB, M, K: où fust sa sepulture
2   BNF7: Qui ne fut (a scribal error)
3   1545: demouree
4   V, BRB, K: apres
5   B: Waston, Bruton
6   BNF3, BNF6, K: semblablement apres; V, BRB: semblablement aupres
7   B: Norriz et
8   BL: couple (emended to maintain a stronger rhyme). The scribe of BL may have wished to avoid the image of horses hitched as a pair that the word "couble" generally implies. BNF1: tous en ung couble; BNF2–4, B, 1545: aussi mis en ung comble; BNF7: aussi en ung comble; S2: tous mis en une couble
9   BNF3, BNF6: d'iceulx; Vat, 1545: du lieu
10   V, K, and BRB essentially reverse vv. 1301–1302 as follows: Faisant d'un lieu la [BRB: sa] sepulture ensemble / Avec Bruton et Marcq mis par ensemble. M is missing v. 1302 and renders v. 1301 as follows: Bruton et Marc aussi mis par ensemble.
11   V, BRB, K: lors comme dolentes; 1545: dolentes, separee
12   BNF1, B, V: Semblerent; BNF4: Semblans; 1545: Semblent
13   BNF2: furent; BNF3: seroient; 1545: seroit
14   BNF6: sans recevoir leur premier
15   BNF2–3, BNF6: est mis
16   V, BRB, M, K: Et l'amittié d'une Dame a choisie; 1545: l'amitié d'une chysie (a corrupt reading)
17   BNF4: Est
18   BRB: Monsieur
19   1545: Ends this verse with "monseigneur" and begins the following verse with "accomplie"

1296 Over to the place of somber burial,[1]
1297 Within the Tower where she was a prisoner
1298 And which was also her last abode.
1299 Her brother was buried nearby,[2]
1300 Afterwards, Weston and Norris[3] together,[4]
1301 Brereton[5] and Mark also placed as a pair,[6]
1302 Creating a double grave out of a single space.[7]
1303 Her ladies, who were then grieving and had scattered about,
1304 Seemed[8] like lost sheep, without a shepherd;
1305 Yet, they will not be so[9] for long,
1306 Without reverting to[10] their earlier position,
1307 For the king already fancied
1308 The love of a favored[11] lady.
1309 And by this, my lord,[12] is fulfilled,

---

[1] V, BRB, M, K: place where was her tomb
[2] V, BRB, K: afterwards
[3] B: Weston, Brereton
[4] BNF3, BNF6, K: Weston and Norris similarly afterwards; V, BRB: Weston and Norris similarly nearby
[5] B: Norris
[6] BL: a couple; BNF1: all as a pair; BNF2–4, B, Vat, 1545: also placed in a heap; BNF7: also in a heap; S2: all placed as a pair; M: also placed together
[7] BNF3, BNF6: Making of them a double grave; V, K, BRB: Making of one place their joint grave / With Brereton and Mark placed together; Vat, 1545: Making of the place a double grave.
[8] BNF4: Seeming; 1545: Seem
[9] BNF2: Were not so; BNF3, 1545: would not be so
[10] BNF6: Without obtaining
[11] V, BRB, M, K: And has chosen the love of a
[12] BRB: sir

---

1299: Both Rochford and Anne were buried within the Tower's Chapel of St. Peter ad Vincula.
1302: See Wriothesley's *Chronicle*, 1:40: the men's "bodies with their heads were buried within the Tower of London; the Lord Rochford's body and head within the chapel of the Tower, Mr. Weston and Norris in the church yard of the same in one grave, Mr. Bruton [Brereton] and Mark in another grave in the same church yard within the Tower of London."
1304: Another scriptural echo, this time to the parable of the lost sheep, as recounted in Matthew 18:12–14 and Luke 15:3–7. The particular phrase "sheep without a shepherd" is used repeatedly in the Bible; see Matthew 9:36 as well as Numbers 27:17–18, 1 Kings 22:17, and Judith 11:15.
1308: This is Jane Seymour, to whom the king was betrothed the day after Anne's execution (that is, on 20 May) and whom he married ten days later, on 30 May. Thus, the marriage had already taken place by the time this poem was completed, although it was not announced until 4 June. See on this point Wriothesley's *Chronicle*, 1:43–44. Several of Anne's former ladies continued to serve Jane as their new queen.

| 1310 | Est[1] la grand[2] part de quelque prophetie, |
|------|------------------------------------------|
| 1311 | Laquelle on tient icy pour veritable, |
| 1312 | Pource que n'est[3] aduenu cas notable |
| 1313 | Que bien ne l'aye[4] par icelle congneu[5] |
| 1314 | Au parauant qu'il ne soit aduenu.[6] |
| 1315 | Plusieurs grandz cas sont encores predictz, |
| 1316 | Lesquelz ce[7] peuple asseure par ses[8] dictz. |
| 1317 | Si ie les[9] voy, alors ie les[10] croiray, |
| 1318 | Et bien au long[11] vous en aduertiray:[12] |
| 1319 | Car oncq[13] n'ouy de nouuelles[14] pareilles. |
| 1320 | Aussi dit on[15] que c'est l'an de[16] merueilles. |
| 1321 | Mais ie prie Dieu[17] que tout[18] soit moderé |
| 1322 | Par tel moyen qu'il en soit honnoré. |
| 1323 | Cecy fut faict à Londres, le deuxiesme[19] |
| 1324 | Du moys de Iuing, en l'an trentesixiesme,[20] |
| 1325 | Mille cinq cens, que l'on comptoit ainsi. [42v] |

---

[1] BRB: Et

[2] BNF4: La plus grand

[3] BNF1: Par ce que n'est; BNF4, S2: Parce qu'il n'est; V, M, K: Pour ce qu'il est

[4] BL: l'ayent (emended for grammar)

[5] S2: Que par icelle ils n'ayent bien congneu; V, BRB, M, K: Que bien je l'ay par icelle aperceue

[6] B: qu'il y soit aduenu; S2: qui ne soit aduenu; V, BRB, M, K: Depuis que suis en ce pays venu (these verses are corrupt)

[7] BNF1-2, BNF7: le

[8] B, Vat: ces

[9] BNF3, BNF6: Si je le

[10] BNF1, BNF3, BNF6: alors je le; S2: adont je les; V: adoncq je les; 1545: ailleurs je les (a corrupt reading)

[11] V: au loing

[12] This is the last line of the poem in BRB, which then adds (in prose) the following: Fin. Cecy fut fait à Londres en Angleterre, le deuxiesme du mois de juing en l'an Trentetroisiesme.

[13] BL: oncques (emended for versification)

[14] BNF1-2, BNF6, S2, K, 1545: Car oncq n'advint des nouuelles; BNF3, BNF7, B, M: Car oncq n'advint de nouuelles; BNF4: Car il n'advint oncques choses; V: Car oncques n'advint des nouuelles; Vat: Car onc n'avaient de nouuelles

[15] V, M, K: l'on

[16] BNF1-3, BNF6-7, S2, K, Vat, 1545: des; BNF4: c'est l'annee aux

[17] BNF1, BNF3, BNF6-7, V, B, K, M, Vat: Mais Dieu je prie

[18] BNF1: tant

[19] B: le douziesme; 1545: ce deuxiesme

[20] BNF3: trente et sixieme; S2, V, M: "en" missing. M gives this number as a Roman numeral ("xxxvi").

| 1310 | In large part,[1] some prophecy |
|------|---------------------------------|
| 1311 | That they hold here to be true: |
| 1312 | Because no notable event has occurred |
| 1313 | That really wasn't made known by it[2] |
| 1314 | Before it came to pass. |
| 1315 | Several great matters are still predicted, |
| 1316 | Which this[3] people affirm by their[4] words. |
| 1317 | If I see them[5] then I shall believe them,[6] |
| 1318 | And at length I shall advise you of them,[7] |
| 1319 | For never have I heard such news:[8] |
| 1320 | And so they say that it is the year of wonders. |
| 1321 | But I pray to God that all be allayed |
| 1322 | By such means that He be honored in it. |
| 1323 | This was done in London, the second[9] day |
| 1324 | Of the month of June in the year thirty-six, |
| 1325 | One thousand five hundred, since one counted this way. |

---

1  BNF4: The greater part of
2  S2: That they didn't know well through this one
3  BNF1–2, BNF7: the
4  B, Vat: these
5  BNF3, BNF6: it
6  BNF1, BNF3, BNF6: it
7  BRB: This is the last verse of this manuscript, which adds in prose: "The End. This was done in London in England, the second day of the month of June in the year '33." This date is incorrect, as the executions took place in 1536.
8  BNF1–3, BNF6–7, B, S2, V, M, K, 1545: For never has such news happened; BNF4: For never have such things happened; Vat: For never has there been such news
9  B: the twelfth; 1545: this second

---

1311:  Political prophecies were rampant in Henry's reign. Chapuys, in a letter to Charles V, relates that Cromwell's suspicions regarding Anne's behavior were aroused in part due to "a prognostic made in Flanders threatening the king with a conspiracy of those who were nearest his person" (see LP 10.1069); similarly, Chapuys wrote to Granvelle that Anne herself had often mentioned that there was a prophecy that a queen of England was to be burned, but that she paid it no heed in order to demonstrate her great love to the king (see LP 10.909 and CSP, Spain, 5, pt. 2, no. 54). It is not clear precisely to which prophecies Carle is referring here.

1324:  All manuscripts but BL end the poem with this verse. The extra verses in the BL manuscript are found on the verso of its last folio.

1326   Ie prie à Dieu qu'il vueille auoir mercy
1327   De ceste Royne, aussi de ces seigneurs,
1328   Et auec luy soient en gloire & honneurs. [1]
       FIN [2]

---

[1]   All others: missing vv. 1325–1328
[2]   BNF2, B, Vat: "Fin" missing; BNF2: Vivant in Christo qui credunt in eo; BNF4: Fin de la tragedye; BNF6 adds: Soli deo honor et gloria; B: Louenge à Dieu; "Laus deo" added in a different hand and ink; M: Finis / James tant dheur / Myherne; K: Finis; 1545: Fin de l'Epistre, & Proces criminel de Anne Boullant, Royne d'Angleterre

1326   I pray to God that he should wish to have mercy
1327   On this queen, and also on these gentlemen,
1328   And that they may be with Him in glory and honor.
       THE END[1]

---

[1] BNF2, B, Vat: Missing "The End"; BNF2: Those who believe in Christ shall live in him (transcribed in Latin), a reworking of John 11:26: "Those who believe in me, even though they die, will live, and everyone who lives and believes in me will never die"; BNF4: End of the Tragedy; BNF6: To God alone be honor and glory (transcribed in Latin), a partial quotation of 1 Timothy 1:17: "To the King of the ages, immortal, invisible, the only God, be honor and glory forever and ever"; B: Praise be to God (transcribed in both French and Latin); M: The End (transcribed in Latin) / Never such happiness / Myherne; K: The End (transcribed in Latin); 1545: End of the epistle and criminal proceedings of Anne Boleyn, Queen of England

## Chapter 6

### Afterword

### Reading *The Story of the Death of Anne Boleyn*: An Interpretive Essay

Carle's poem on Anne Boleyn has been widely read (in one form or another) and analyzed by historians from the late sixteenth century to the present day. Those readers of *The Story of the Death of Anne Boleyn*, understandably, have focused on its function as a diplomatic dispatch, sent by the French embassy in London to the court of France back home. They have gleaned from it copious historical details, some of which have no parallel in other known sources. They also have been eager to point out instances where Carle's poem seems to contradict facts drawn from other (perhaps more reliable) sources, including the works of contemporary chroniclers, letters exchanged among those in the know, and dispatches from other foreign ambassadors. Certainly, this diplomatic context—the conventions, expectations, and boundaries of ambassadorial correspondence—must be fully understood and borne in mind by anyone reading Carle's work.

But, of course, Carle has complicated matters by turning his diplomatic correspondence into a long narrative poem, such that this text is much more than an ordinary dispatch, chronicle, or letter. It is clearly intended to be a work of art, and, as such, it demands to be read for its aesthetic qualities. Like any other work of literature, Carle's poem also needs to be read not in isolation but as a text that participates in and is reflective of an array of literary traditions, conventions, and techniques. And yet, this poem has received scant attention from modern literary critics specializing in sixteenth-century poetry.

The purpose of this final chapter is to offer a fuller interpretation of Carle's work qua literary text—that is, as both a poem and a story—yet one that does not relinquish its primary role as a diplomatic dispatch. This chapter will thus first consider evidence of how this text was received and interpreted by its earliest readers, namely its scribes and editors. In so doing, it will tackle the question of textual interpretation and its relationship to genre expectations by surveying the descriptive titles these early readers assigned to the work. Next, this analysis will consider this text with respect to its most basic function as an example of official ambassadorial correspondence. Here the analysis will focus particularly on the ways diplomatic dispatches, by their very nature, might conflict with or conform to the literary pretensions of this work. Attention will next be focused on the particular complications of choosing to write in verse form. Narrative considerations—the domain of storytelling—will then be examined, with special emphasis on Carle's delivery of a message that was unique to him. Next, this study will attempt to disentangle the complex web of competing literary genres of which this poem partakes by reading the work in an intertextual context, striving to identify traces of the many models and influences that can be discerned beneath the poem's surface. It will then consider the poem's very fabric in an attempt to unveil its rich layering of themes, images, devices, and structures that have thus far gone largely unnoticed. Finally, it will offer an assessment of the poem more generally, particularly touching upon the issue of Anne's guilt or innocence as perceived and articulated by Carle's poetic persona, the speaking voice (or "je parlant") of this text.

## Readers' Responses:
## The Question of Genre and Interpretation

Before beginning to tackle the question of how modern-day readers might interpret Carle's unique text, it is useful to survey how its earliest readers approached this same question. While there are few references to Carle's poem that date from the early modern period, there is still some evidence of its reception among its earliest readers: namely, the intitulation imposed on it by its scribes and editors. It should be remembered that the sixteen manuscript versions and single surviving early modern printed edition of Carle's poem do not carry a uniform title crafted by its author; instead, various scribes and editors have taken it upon themselves to introduce the poem with their own descriptive intitulation. Titles, when assigned to a text by a reader rather than by its writer, thus carry special significance and can serve as a kind of shorthand form of critical assessment of the text's place in the literary world.

In the case of Carle's poem, this intitulation most frequently displays an attempt to categorize the text, that is, to assign it to a particular genre or type, based on its conformity to a set of standards gleaned from the reader's experience with previous instantiations of that genre. Once the scribe or editor has used such a designation in the poem's intitulation, this set of standards—or, to use the term developed by Hans Robert Jauss, this "horizon of expectations"—is in turn employed by subsequent readers in their effort to read and interpret the text.[1] As Jauss has explained, "a literary work, even if it seems new, does not appear as

---

[1] See, on the concept of the "horizon of expectations," Hans Robert Jauss, *Towards an Aesthetic of Reception*, trans. Timothy Bahti, intro. Paul de Man (Minneapolis: University of Minnesota Press, 1982).

something absolutely new in an informational vacuum, but predisposes its readers to a very definite type of reception by textual strategies, overt and covert signals, familiar characteristics or implicit allusions."[2] The intitulation assigned to this poem by its various scribes and copyists can thus be read as an indication of these early readers' perception of these signals within the text and their judgment of its affiliation with previously existing genres.

Judging from the earliest records of responses to this text, it seems that reading Carle's work has always been a tricky and confusing matter, for these early readers simply could not agree as to the nature of the work at hand. That is to say, the wide variety of scribal intitulation imposed on this work provides evidence that the text was not read in a uniform fashion but, rather, was perceived, by different readers, as participating in a multitude of genres. In only one instance — namely BnF Fr. 12795, a manuscript now found in Paris — is the title decidedly neutral: "Concerning the Queen of England."[3] Here the scribe provides no hint as to the text's orientation but instead presents the work as a simple factual description. Additionally, another Parisian manuscript, BnF Fr. 12489, carries no intitulation at all and thus is also neutral in orientation. In all other instances, however, the title given to the manuscript by its scribe conveys a nuanced meaning that provides insight into how early readers attempted to interpret the text by assigning it to a specific genre.

While some of these titles recur in multiple manuscripts, others are uniquely manifested in a single text. For example, the manuscript now housed in Munich is titled, on its title folio, *Le Discours de la vie et mort Dame Anna de Boullant, Roÿnne putative d'Angleterre et décapité* [*sic*] *A° 1536.*[4] The term "discours" carries the connotation of a report or relation, but it also suggests the perusal of a problem in one's mind, thus emphasizing a logical examination of the issue at hand.[5] As John Lyons also explains:

> Discourse can . . . be narrative, but it does not pretend to objectivity. Instead it is the vehicle for a personal, subjective expression of belief, experience,

---

[2] See Hans Robert Jauss, "Literary History as a Challenge to Literary Theory," trans. Elizabeth Benzinger, *New Literary History* 2 (1970): 7–37, here 12.

[3] For a complete description of all manuscripts as well as printed editions of this work, consult Chapter 4 above, "Versions of the Text."

[4] This is Munich, Bayerische Staatsbibliothek, Cod. GALL. 105.

[5] See the definition given by Randle Cotgrave in his authoritative early modern French-English dictionary, *A Dictionarie of the French and English Tongues* (1611), intro. William S. Woods (Columbia: University of South Carolina Press, 1950): "a discourse, report, relation, rehearsal of a matter; also a . . . perusal, examination, pondering of things in the mind." Here and throughout, I have modified the spelling of Middle English texts for the ease of the reader.

and judgment. Discourse is the mode in which ethical judgments are made and alternative action is described.[6]

As if to illustrate this subjective mode of expression that emphasizes personal, ethical judgments, the title provided by this scribe describes Anne as the "putative" queen of England. The French term "putative" certainly could suggest this reader's questioning of the royal status of Anne Boleyn and the legitimacy of her marriage to Henry, which was, in fact, annulled before the queen's execution in an effort to illegitimatize Elizabeth and remove her immediately from the royal succession.

Similarly, the manuscript now housed in Brussels and a version related to it found in Karlsruhe, Germany, both use the title "Traictié," meaning "tract" or "treatise."[7] In some cases, this word merely indicates the diminutive nature of the work it describes and could be a synonym for "pamphlet," as Randle Cotgrave indicates.[8] But at other times, such a work is characterized as didactic and thus appears to have some connection to the word "Discours" that is found in the Munich manuscript. A secondary usage of the word also suggests a "narrative development."[9] These three northern exemplars, now located in Munich, Belgium, and Karlsruhe, it will be remembered, constitute a family of manuscripts, when analyzed stylistically and orthographically. But their intitulation is further evidence of their relationship, as each appears to categorize the poem as an analysis of what was clearly a unique event: the unprecedented execution of an anointed queen.

By far the text's most frequent title (one that is found in five different manuscripts) is the one that appears on the copy text used here: "L'Histoire de la mort d'Anne Boulenc, royne d'Angleterre" [The Story of the Death of Anne Boleyn, Queen of England] or, in a variant form, "Histoire de Anne Boullant, royne d'Angleterre" [The Story of Anne Boleyn, Queen of England].[10] When translated this way, these titles clearly remind us that Carle's poem constitutes a narrative or story. Yet, in its original French form, this title is somewhat ambiguous, because the word "histoire" can equally suggest that the poem is in fact a "his-

---

[6] John Lyons, *Exemplum: The Rhetoric of Example in Early Modern France and Italy* (Princeton, NJ: Princeton University Press, 1989), 81.

[7] These are Brussels, Bibliothèque royale de Belgique, MS 19378; and Karlsruhe, Badische Landesbibliothek, Güntersthal 12.

[8] Cotgrave, *A Dictionarie*: "a treatise, pamphlet, small book, or part of a book."

[9] For this secondary meaning, see the *Dictionnaire du Moyen Français*, Version 2015, ATILF–CNRS & Université de Lorraine (hereafter DMF), available at http://www.atilf.fr/dmf: "Développement écrit, notamment développement narratif."

[10] These are London, British Library, Additional 40662; Paris, BnF, Fr. 01742; Paris, BnF, Fr. 02370; Paris, BnF, Lat. 5934; and Paris, BnF, Cinq cents de Colbert 465.

tory," as the very etymology of the word (< Latin *historia*) reveals.[11] When used in the expression "histoire de quelqu'un" or "the story [history] of someone" (as it used four of five times in these manuscripts), it refers to the whole of the events in a person's life, what we might now call a biography.[12] In the other instance, namely "l'histoire de la mort" or "story of the death," the word suggests a history or chronicle of a specific event:[13] namely, the demise of an English queen. The ambiguity of the word "histoire" as both "story" and "history" is critical here: it invites the reader to believe the truth of the tale that is told, but it also allows for a certain amount of license on the part of the teller of this tale to embellish it with details that are not necessarily fully historically accurate. That is to say, the scribes of these manuscripts could have chosen less ambiguous terms to emphasize either the veracity of the diplomat's dispatch or its narrative, literary qualities, but, in referring to the work as "l'histoire," they have left the matter open to the reader's interpretation.

This is certainly not the case in other designations made by other scribes, which more overtly guide the reader to a particular interpretation of the text at hand. Two manuscripts—one found at the Vatican Library ("Tragedie de la femme du Roy d'Angleterre, Anne Boulans" [Tragedy of the wife of the king of England, Anne Boleyn]) and the other at the Bibliothèque nationale in Paris ("Tragedie sur la mort de la royne d'Angleterre, laquelle le roy son mary feit mourir dans la Tour de Londres pour avoir commis adultere" [Tragedy on the death of the Queen of England, whose husband, the king, made her die in the Tower of London for having committed adultery])—each refer to the work as a "tragedy" in their titles.[14] Additionally, this Parisian manuscript and one other (BnF Fr. 02370) each use the expression "Fin de la Tragedie" in their *explicit*, or final words. The manuscripts whose titles refer to the text as a tragedy (unlike the Munich manuscript) also openly declare Anne to be a queen or the wife of the king of England. Indeed, the title assigned to BnF Fr. 10194 is quite expansive, providing a synopsis of the plot by stating, in fine journalistic fashion, how, where, and why Anne died: she was put to death by her husband, the king, at the Tower of London for having committed adultery. We have here an emphasis on the outcome of this tragic story as well as on its dramatic nature. Moreover, the story as outlined here is an indictment not only of Anne's alleged immoral

---

[11] See the DMF definition of "histoire" as "récit d'événements réels ou imaginaires." For an analysis of the intersections between stories and histories, see Hayden V. White, "The Value of Narrativity in the Representation of Reality," in *The Content of the Form: Narrative Discourse and Historical Representation* (Baltimore: The Johns Hopkins University Press, 1987), 1–25.

[12] See the DMF: "Ensemble d'événements concernant une personne."

[13] See the DMF: "Récit de chroniqueur ou d'historien."

[14] These are Rome, Vatican City, Biblioteca Apostolica Vaticana, Reg. lat 1652; and Paris, BnF, Fr. 10194, respectively.

behavior (her adultery) but also of Henry as the principal agent of Anne's demise. The reader is thus prepared to view this poem as inherently sad but also as a work that will encompass a morality tale, one that will convey a measure of *gravitas* befitting the tragic genre as it was defined in classical literary theory and revived in the Renaissance.[15]

Perhaps the most interesting title given to the poem is the one that appears on a manuscript that had once belonged to a religious order, the Discalced Carmelites, before its arrival in the municipal library of Bordeaux. The full title here is "La *pitoiable* description de la *vie et* mort de madame Anne Boulant, en son vivant fesme du roy d'Angleterre, Henry .8. de ce nom *en ses secondes noces*, laquelle fust decolee l'an 1536, **le douzieme de juing**" [The pitiable description of the life and death of Lady Anne Boleyn, in her lifetime the wife of the king of England, Henry the Eighth of that name, in his second marriage, who was beheaded in the year 1536, on the twelfth of June].[16] It is important to notice that certain words here given in italics—"pitiable," "life," "in his second marriage"—are interpolations in a different hand from that of the main text, which suggests that these are the responses of an early modern reader other than the scribe. The date of 12 June, written in a third hand, is an error that shows that this reader has confused the date of Anne's execution with the date of the poem's composition (at least as it is recorded in this manuscript).[17] As it now reads, the full title lends a certain melodramatic air to the text, emphasizing the doleful life of the late queen. It suggests that the poem is not just a classical tale of tragedy; more than anything else, it is a work intended to evoke *pity*, "which in the early modern period channeled its Aristotelian and Senecan roots as a *deliberative* response to *undeserved* suffering."[18] Like the northern manuscripts that refer

---

[15] For a discussion (which is almost contemporaneous with Carle's poem) of the classical tragic genre and its adaptation in French Renaissance literature, see, *inter alia*, Thomas Sébillet, *Art poétique françois* (1548), ed. Félix Gaiffe and Francis Goyet (Paris: Nizet, 1988), 2.8, 161–62.

[16] This is Bordeaux, Bibliothèque municipale, MS 0313.

[17] There is here a further error in dating, insofar as all other versions of this poem give the date of its composition as 2 June, not 12 June. The scribe has therefore misread "deuxieme" for "douzieme," an easy error.

[18] I am grateful to Cynthia Nazarian, who shared this definition with me, which she re-employs in "Montaigne Against Sympathy: On Affect and Ethics in the *Essais*," *Montaigne Studies* 30 (2018): 125–38. Pity, as Nazarian stresses, is distinct from sympathy, insofar as it constitutes an "evaluative response to perceived suffering" (126). For an excellent history of the concept of "pity," especially in classical literature and culture, consult David Konstan, *Pity Transformed* (London: Duckworth, 2001). Konstan (34) stresses that pity was "presumed to be aroused not by the spectacle of misfortune as such, but rather by that of undeserved misfortune." Such an understanding of pity, or *eleos*, is derived from the definition given in Aristotle's *Rhetoric* 2.8.2: "a certain pain at an apparently destructive or painful event happening to *one who does not deserve it . . .*" (italics

to this poem as a "discours" or "traictié," the Bordeaux manuscript thus likewise stresses the role of evaluation and judgment. Moreover, this long title is reminiscent of those attached to certain other melodramatic tales or *histoires tragiques* that proliferated in the early modern period in France.[19] Subsequent readers of this manuscript are thus prepared to empathize with this tragic, pitiable, and (given the Aristotelian meaning of that word) presumably innocent woman who lost her life after having become Henry's wife and queen of England. Her story, according to this manuscript intitulation, thus serves as an example of someone who had first been exalted and then was suddenly brought down from great heights, but undeservedly so, through no real fault of her own.

Another title, this one assigned to a manuscript now located in the municipal library of the northern French provincial town of Valenciennes (and which is also related to the other northern manuscripts found in Belgium and Germany) likewise betrays a decided sympathy for Anne. This title, written in the hand of its scribe, reads: "Pour feu dame Anne de Boullant, jadis royne d'Engleterre, l'an VC trente trois" [For the late lady Anne Boleyn, formerly queen of England, in the year 1533].[20] The word "pour" here is something of a puzzle and could be translated simply as "for," but it may also carry the connotation of "on behalf of" or "in memory of."[21] The issue is further complicated by the fact that a later reader has interpolated the word "Apologie" well to the left of the rest of the title (and this is repeated in the title folio of the manuscript). The word "apology" denotes a defense of some person or action, and clearly this reader has emphasized the poet's overt sympathy toward Anne in the latter half of the poem as well as, perhaps, his critical view of Henry and other subtle images that might indicate Anne's innocence. Subsequent readers of this manuscript, having read this interpolated title, would thus have been prepared to find a view of Anne as a wronged wife who did not deserve the cruel death she endured. Indeed, one early modern reader of this particular manuscript version of the text, Emanuel de Meteren, went on to provide a prose paraphrase of the poem in his own history

---

added). For this definition, consult Aristotle, *On Rhetoric*, trans. George A. Kennedy (New York: Oxford University Press, 2007), 139.

[19] For more on this genre, consult Stéphan Ferrari, "Histoire tragique et grande histoire: rencontre de deux genres," *Dalhousie French Studies* 65 (2003): 18–35. Ferrari defines the "histoire tragique" as a genre unto itself that is marked by "the hyperbolic aesthetic of violence and the horror that characterizes it" and that aims "to arouse in the reader 'fear and pity' [as Aristotle defined tragedy] . . . and thus to lead him towards good" (18; my translation).

[20] This is Valenciennes, Bibliothèque municipale, MS 419.

[21] The title affixed to the first folio of the Munich manuscript described above, "Faict pour deffuncte Anne de Boulland jadis Roynne d'Angleterre," likewise uses this word that could be translated "in memory of."

of England, in the course of which he paints Anne as a Protestant martyr.[22] One can also wonder if it was in fact Meteren himself who discreetly added the word "Apologie" to this title as he read the manuscript for his research or if he himself was inspired by this pre-existing interpolation to arrive at his own apologetic view of Anne.

Two other manuscript versions—sister texts found in the municipal library of Soissons, which open with the designation "Ensuyt le proces de la royne d'Angleterre, de son frere et de quatre chevaliers decapitez en Engleterre, l'an mil cinq cens trente-six en may" [Here follows the trial of the Queen of England and of her brother and four knights beheaded in England in the year 1536 in May]—emphasize the poem's role as a description of court proceedings and thus promise to be a dispassionate presentation of the facts.[23] In this respect, this designation resembles the title given to the work in its only surviving early modern printed edition, *Epistre contenant le proces criminel faict à l'encontre de la royne Anne Boullant d'Angleterre* [An Epistle Containing the Criminal Proceedings Made Against Queen Anne Boleyn of England].[24] Yet the second half of the title found in the Soissons manuscripts complicates the issue by referring to these men as "knights," which, strictly speaking, was not the case. Only one defendant (namely, Francis Weston) had been knighted; moreover, one of those five men accused with Anne was no gentleman at all but, rather, a lowly court musician. By providing this title, however, the scribe is situating the story within the realm of courtly life and may well be, unwittingly or not, conjuring visions of medieval romances. Marginal annotations on one of the Soissons manuscripts likewise insist on the "knighthood" of the men accused with Anne, thus suggesting that some contemporary readers may have seen an inherent analogy between Henry's court and the medieval world of Arthurian romance sadly gone wrong.

The early modern printed text, as mentioned above, also designates the poem as an "epistle" or letter, and, indeed, this is the only version of the text to refer to this aspect of the work. The designation is repeated in the *explicit* of the text, which uses the phrase "Fin de l'Epistre." The unnamed editor here thus twice emphasizes the text's most basic function as a means of communication between two distant places. In assigning the work to a genre that was quite popular in the

---

[22] See Emanuel de Meteren, *L'Histoire des Pays-Bas*, translated from Flemish to French by I. D. L. Haye [Jean de la Haye] (The Hague: Jacobz, 1618), fol. 21r–v. This issue is discussed fully in Chapter 3, above.

[23] These are Soissons, Bibliothèque municipale, MS 201 and MS 202.

[24] Both texts use the French word "proces," which Cotgrave defines as "a case, cause, action, indictment, matter in law," and thus can be translated equally accurately as "trial" or "proceedings." The 1545 printed edition does not give the name of its publisher or place of publication; however, recent scholarship by Raphaël Cappellen suggests that the work was published in Tours by Jean Rousset. See Chapter 4 above, "Versions of the Text," for a complete discussion of this matter.

early sixteenth century, the editor implies that it is related to other verse epistles penned in France at that time by some of that country's leading poets, most notably Clément Marot.[25] But by describing the contents of this epistle as an account of a criminal trial, the editor is perhaps also emphasizing the official, political nature of this work, namely that of a diplomatic dispatch.

Another remnant of early readers' engagement with this text can be found in those versions that carry an *explicit* that may be the work of the scribe or, possibly, an early owner of the manuscript. Three different manuscripts carry an *explicit* that is clearly the handiwork of a Christian believer. The first of these three is found in BnF Fr. 01742, which ends with the Latin phrase "Vivant in Christo qui credunt in eo" [Those who believe in Christ shall live in him]; this is a reworking of John 11:26: "Those who believe in me, even though they die, will live, and everyone who lives and believes in me will never die."[26] A second Parisian manuscript (Colbert 465) ends with the phrase: "Soli deo honor et gloria" [To God alone be honor and glory], which is a partial quotation of 1 Timothy 1:17: "To the King of the ages, immortal, invisible, the only God, be honor and glory forever and ever."[27] A variation of this phrase was frequently used, for example, by Bach at the end of his musical compositions, and it came to be associated with the Protestant Reformation, though it does not necessarily signify that denominational persuasion in all cases. Finally, the Bordeaux manuscript carries the Latin phrase "Laus Deo" [Praise be to God] as well as its French equivalent, "Louenge à Dieu" as an *explicit*. These written interventions, whether by a scribe, patron, or early reader, are likely to be an indication of their writer's own faith; equally, however, they may constitute a genuine response to the text that indicates an appreciation for the profoundly Christian orientation given to this story by its author, Carle.

---

[25] For two works that provide an overview of the French epistolary tradition, see Marc Bizer, *Les lettres romaines de Du Bellay* (Montreal: Les Presses de l'Université de Montréal, 2001); and Katherine Kong, *Lettering the Self in Medieval and Early Modern France* (Cambridge: Brewer, 2010). The epistolary genre will be discussed more fully later in this chapter. For an overview of Clément Marot's works, see M. A. Screech, *Marot évangélique* (Geneva: Droz, 1967); Pauline M. Smith, *Clément Marot: Poet of the French Renaissance* (London: Athlone, 1970); and Ehsan Ahmed, *Clément Marot: The Mirror of the Prince* (Charlottesville, VA: Rookwood Press 2005).

[26] English translations of the Bible here and elsewhere are taken from the New Revised Standard Version as printed in the *Common Bible* (Nashville: Thomas Nelson Publishers, 1989). The equivalent passage from the Latin Vulgate (Vulg.) is: "Qui credit in me, etiam si mortuus fuerit, vivet: et omnis qui vivit et credit in me, non morietur in aeternum." All Latin quotations from the Vulgate are here based on *Biblia sacra juxta vulgatam Clementinam nova editio* (Madrid: Biblioteca de autores cristianos, 1977).

[27] Vulg.: "Regi autem saeculorum immortali, invisibili, soli Deo honor et gloria in saecula saeculorum."

In sum, each of these early readers' responses, whether in the manuscript's title or in its *explicit*, is related to a particular way of reading the poem. They can be thought of as a way of assigning it to a specific genre to help direct the reader's interpretation of what was assuredly perceived to be, then as now, a unique text, one that straddles the domains of fiction and truth, of romance and reality. For, until this time, few works had attempted to tell an essentially true contemporary story in verse form, using the variety of literary strategies that Carle employs.[28] Each of these ways of reading deserves a fuller analysis, to be undertaken in the sections that follow, that will serve to illuminate this text's rich and complex nature.

## The Context of Diplomacy

As has been noted, *The Story of the Death of Anne Boleyn* is essentially a diplomatic dispatch or letter that seeks to inform the French court of the events that had recently taken place in London in May 1536. For this reason, it is worth considering this work within the context of Renaissance diplomacy. This is especially true since, as Timothy Hampton has reminded us, the sixteenth century constitutes a pivotal moment in the history of diplomacy: it witnessed the creation of the "resident ambassador," a man who was looked upon as a representative or, indeed, an embodiment of his nation and its king within the borders of a foreign country.[29] In France, King Francis I (reigned 1515–1547) took an active hand in selecting his diplomatic envoys and most often chose them from among prominent clerics, particularly bishops, whom French kings also traditionally appointed.[30] The French ambassador to England at the time of Anne Boleyn's

---

[28] A notable exception is the work known as *L'Histoire de Guillaume le Maréchal* [The History of William Marshal], which has been called the first — or at least the first surviving — biography of a layman in any of the European vernacular languages. That text, which is written in octosyllabic rhyming couplets, has been thoroughly analyzed by Walter Scott in his unpublished doctoral dissertation entitled "Author, Text, and Audience: The Horizon of Expectations and *L'Histoire de Guillaume le Maréchal* (PhD diss., University of Wisconsin-Madison, 2014). For an English prose translation of the text, see *The History of William Marshal*, trans. Nigel Bryant (Woodbridge, UK: Boydell, 2016). For an edition of the French original, see *L'Histoire de Guillaume le Maréchal, comte de Striguil et de Pembroke, régent d'Angleterre de 1216 à 1219*, ed. Paul Meyer, 3 vols. (Paris: Société de l'histoire de France, 1891–1901). See also *The History of William Marshal*, ed. Anthony J. Holden, trans. Stewart Gregory, and notes by David Crouch, 3 vols. (London: Anglo-Norman Text Society, 2002–2006).

[29] Timothy Hampton, *Fictions of Embassy: Literature and Diplomacy in Early Modern Europe* (Ithaca, NY: Cornell University Press, 2009), 7.

[30] For more on this point, see Loretta T. Burns, "Cleric-Diplomats and the Sixteenth-Century French State," *The Historian* 57 (1995): 721–32, here 721–22. For more

execution, Antoine de Castelnau (d. 1539), certainly conforms to this principle. Castelnau was named Bishop of Tarbes in 1534 and was sent to London to serve as the resident French ambassador in 1535. Traditionally, the ambassador's secretary was likewise a cleric and humanist in his own right, and, as Susan Brigden explains, while "the secretary and the ambassador, of separate status, could not quite be equal friends," the secretary was nonetheless highly respected for his own learning, and the position was certainly a prestigious one to pursue.[31] Several notable writers occupied the station of ambassadorial secretary at one time or another during the Renaissance, including such learned luminaries as Pietro Bembo, Bernardo Tasso, and Niccolò Machiavelli in Italy, and Étienne Dolet, Joachim Du Bellay, and Olivier de Magny among the French. Castelnau's secretary, Lancelot de Carle, the author of this poem, was thus in good company and fits this profile exactly.

The function of an ambassador was to serve as an intermediary between two nations and cultures, and the exchange of letters between a resident ambassador and the court back home was an important tool for accomplishing that task. Above all, the resident ambassador needed to be a keen observer and an excellent listener who could be relied upon to convey news accurately to his prince. Accordingly, as the famed political theorist (and ambassadorial secretary) Machiavelli had suggested, the ambassador needed to "tread the line between rumor and fact";[32] he must sift through an abundance of information, sometimes offered by reliable sources, but at other times generated by persons with their own agenda or by those who were simply not sufficiently well-placed to know the truth of the matter. Additionally, Hampton reminds us, because they were well-trained humanists, ambassadors often actively shaped the narrative of their dispatches and quite naturally would "turn frequently to classical epic and historiography and employ tropes and conventions associated with fiction writing" in telling their stories.[33] From this perspective, the literary pretensions of *The Story of the Death of Anne Boleyn* seem somewhat less surprising. For this text,

on the French bishopric in this time period and its relationship to the monarchy, consult Cédric Michon, *La crosse et le sceptre: Les prélats d'état sous François I$^{er}$ et Henri VIII* (Paris: Tallandier, 2008).

[31] See, on this point, Susan Brigden, *Thomas Wyatt: The Heart's Forest* (London: Faber and Faber, 2012), 324.

[32] See Hampton, *Fictions*, 22. For Machiavelli's diplomatic writings, see Niccolò Machiavelli, *Ritratti e rapporti diplomatici*, ed. Corrado Vivanti (Rome: Riuniti, 2000), here 122. For an English version, see Machiavelli, *The Chief Works and Others*, trans. Allan H. Gilbert, 3 vols. (Durham, NC: Duke University Press, 1989), here 1:116.

[33] Hampton, *Fictions*, 6. For another discussion of fictional tropes and storytelling in the writing of early modern historiography, see William Nelson, *Fact or Fiction: The Dilemma of the Renaissance Storyteller* (Cambridge, MA: Harvard University Press, 1973), especially ch. 2, "The Difference Between Fiction and History," 38–55.

which straddles the worlds of diplomacy and literature, is in some sense merely an exaggerated version of that desire to shape official correspondence according to conventional literary tropes without losing sight of the main goal: to inform the French court of recent news in England that could be of importance to diplomatic relations between the two countries.

And that is exactly what this text purports to do, for its ostensible purpose is to relate the unprecedented events that the French ambassador has just witnessed regarding the demise of an anointed queen. But it is a bit more complicated than that. First, what we have here is not, strictly speaking, the report of the ambassador, Castelnau, but that of his secretary, Carle. We have no way of knowing why Castelnau entrusted his secretary with composing this dispatch in his own voice instead of following the more standard ambassadorial procedure of dictating, or at least outlining, his official version of events, which he would expect his secretary to record and send off to France. In this respect, this text is unique, for, amid the precious few extant exchanges between Castelnau and the French court, no other dispatch displays evidence of the intervention of the secretary's voice, though others may well have been penned by a secretary's hand.[34] Furthermore, the French archives provide no evidence of any other dispatch from any French ambassadorial representative in London giving an account of Anne Boleyn's death.[35] While it is possible, of course, that letters on this event were written and later lost or destroyed, one might also reasonably assume that the text at hand was intended to serve as the official notification of the events of May 1536 on the part of the French embassy and that, for some unknown reason, Castelnau permitted (or even encouraged) Carle to compose the missive himself.

Certainly, the execution of Anne Boleyn was indeed major news and was widely reported by *other* foreign diplomats to their own courts in a timely fashion. But their letters—the best known and most complete of which were written by the Imperial ambassador, Eustace Chapuys (ca. 1490–1556)—while often expressing a sense of astonishment at the events, clearly make no overt claim of literariness.[36] Indeed some reports, particularly those of the Italians, are quite

---

[34] Paul Friedmann writes in *Anne Boleyn: A Chapter of English History, 1527–1536*, 2 vols. (London: Macmillan, 1884), 1:xvii, that "scarcely a letter" of Castelnau remains. For the assertion that ambassadorial secretaries were expected to assume the voice and even the identity of the ambassador, see Bizer, *Les lettres romaines*, 216n145, who quotes from the treatise entitled *The English Secretorie [sic]* of Angel Day (1586): "His pen . . . is not his own, but another's."

[35] The popular historian Alison Weir also notes that there are no extant letters from other French envoys, such as Dinteville, dating from the time of Anne's downfall. See her *The Lady in the Tower: The Fall of Anne Boleyn* (2009; repr. New York: Ballantine Books, 2010), 246.

[36] Chapuys's letters are summarized in the multi-volume historical resource known as *Letters and Papers, Foreign and Domestic, of the Reign of Henry VIII* (hereafter abbre-

brief—just a few sentences in length—and provide few details about the matter.[37] Whether brief or detailed, these foreign diplomatic reports attempted to recount the facts accurately, clearly, and expeditiously. Rhetorically, they are aligned quite closely with chronicles or histories. Indeed, for modern historians, Chapuys's letters, in particular, have become a critical piece of historical evidence for the events of Henry's reign, this despite the diplomat's unmitigated—and unapologetic—sympathy towards Henry's first wife, Catherine of Aragon (aunt to the Holy Roman Emperor, Charles V, whom Chapuys served) and her daughter, Mary.

One way in which Carle's letter differs from those penned by Chapuys and other European diplomats (aside from the obvious fact that it is written in verse) is that the messages from the latter generally indicate their recipient, whereas, in this instance, we do not know for sure to whom Carle's missive was addressed. It is likely that the intended recipient of Carle's letter is not King Francis I himself, however. This can be surmised because Carle consistently calls the *destinataire* (or "addressee") of his missive "Monseigneur" and not "Sire," as he would have done if writing to the king (and, indeed, as Carle's characters address Henry

---

viated as LP), ed. J. S. Brewer, J. Gairdner, and R. H. Brodie (London: Her Majesty's Stationery Office, 1867–1920). This work is now available through an online searchable database: British History Online (https://www.british-history.ac.uk/). For another searchable database available by subscription, which sometimes gives a digitized copy of the original manuscript in addition to the summary made by these Victorian-era scholars, see "State Papers Online: Early Modern Government in Britain and Europe" (https://www.gale.com/intl/primary-sources/state-papers-online). Additionally, slightly different abstracts and, often, transcriptions of many of these letters are available in *Calendar of State Papers* (hereafter abbreviated CSP). This collection of State Papers is also available in digitized format through both British History Online and State Papers Online. For letters pertinent to the fall of Anne Boleyn, see also those that are reprinted in *The Anne Boleyn Papers*, ed. Elizabeth Norton (Stroud: Amberley, 2013). The original letters of Chapuys are written in French (since he was a native Savoyard); Friedmann quotes extensively from the original Middle French in his two-volume work on the fall of Anne Boleyn (cited above). These letters are now housed in the Haus-, Hof- und Staatsarchiv, in Vienna. For more on Chapuys's correspondence, see also Lauren Mackay, *Inside the Tudor Court* (Stroud: Amberley, 2014).

[37] See, for example, London, British Library, Additional 8715 (hereafter Add. 8715), fols. 248v–249r (summarized in LP 10.838) and Add. 8715, fols. 252r–254v (summarized in LP 10.956), both of which are letters written by the Bishop of Faenza to Mons. Ambrogio, dated 10 May and 24 May 1536, respectively. See also London, British Library, Additional 28588 (hereafter Add. 28588), fols. 281r–283v, here 282v (summarized in LP 10.973) from Viscount Hannart to Charles V, dated 26 May 1536; Add. 28588, fols. 284r–285r, here 284v (summarized in LP 10.1043) from Dr. Ortiz to the Empress, Isabella of Portugal, dated 2 June 1536; and Add. 28588, fols. 286r–288r, here 287r–v (summarized in LP 10.1044) from Hannart to Isabella of Portugal, dated 2 June 1536.

VIII within the poem). Nor does Carle use any other term, such as "Roi" [king] or "Prince" (as the famed French poet Clément Marot often addressed Francis I in his verse epistles), which might indicate that the letter was intended for royal eyes. Though the title page of the 1545 print edition identifies the author as the "almoner of the Dauphin," the poem is, nevertheless, also not very likely to have been composed *for* the Dauphin, the eldest son of the king of France. Carle did, indeed, serve as almoner to the Dauphin at the time of the poem's belated *publication*. But he did *not* serve in that capacity at the time of the poem's *composition*, about nine years before.[38] Finally, the term "Monseigneur" was not one that was traditionally associated with the Dauphin at this time. While Marot does once address the Dauphin with the title "Monseigneur" within one of his poems, this honorific did not come to be associated primarily with the Dauphin until much later.[39] In any case, it should be noted that in June 1536, the moment of this letter's composition, the Dauphin was the ill-fated François (who was to die in August of that year) and not Henri, whom Carle later served as almoner and who went on to become King Henry II of France. There would have been no special bond between Carle and the current dauphin, Francis, in 1536, and thus no reason to warrant the assumption that he is the intended recipient of the text. And certainly there would be even less reason to think that Carle was writing specifically for the future Henry II, whose position was, at that moment, of less importance than that of his brother.

There are, however, a few likely suspects to whom Carle (and Castelnau) might have wished to report and who could well be addressed in this fashion. These include various figures associated with the court of France who held positions that one could characterize as broadly "diplomatic" insofar as they were heavily involved in foreign affairs. Principal among these men would be Anne de Montmorency (1493–1567), François, Cardinal de Tournon (1498–1562), and Jean, Cardinal de Lorraine (1498–1550), all of whom were addressed by the title "Monseigneur" by Marot in his epistles. Each of these men had early connections with the court of France and would have known that Anne Boleyn had served

---

[38] Georges-Adrien Crapelet is among those who mistakenly assert that the poem was written for the Dauphin while Carle served as his almoner. See his *Lettres de Henri VIII à Anne Boleyn* (1826; repr. Paris: L'Imprimerie de Crapelet, 1835), xii.

[39] See, on this point, *L'Encyclopédie, ou dictionnaire raisonné des sciences, des arts et des métiers*, ed. Denis Diderot and Jean le Rond d'Alembert (Paris: Briasson, David, Le Breton, and Durand, 1751), 10.670 on the term "Monseigneur": "a title of honor and respect that is used when one writes or when one speaks to persons of a rank or quality" (my translation). The text goes on to specify that the title is bestowed on dukes, peers, archbishops, and bishops, and that, at the present moment, it is used for the Dauphin, though this usage was introduced only during the reign of Louis XIV. A searchable digital copy of this text is available online through ARTFL—Encyclopédie (http://encyclo-pedie.uchicago.edu/).

the French queen, Claude, in her youth, a fact of which the poem implies its intended recipient is well aware (vv. 37–42). Further evidence that the addressee is likely to have been not the king but, rather, one of these other diplomatic figures can be found in other extant letters penned by Carle, now located in the Bibliothèque nationale de France (and reproduced by Tamizey de Larroque in his edition of Guillaume Colletet's biography of Carle): one letter sent to King Henry II in 1553 addresses the monarch as "Sire," while other letters sent to Montmorency and the Cardinal of Lorraine bear the honorific "Monseigneur."[40] Beyond these remarks, however, it is impossible to say for certain for whom Carle wrote this poem.

Yet, although there is clearly some "inscribed reader" of this text to whom Carle is specifically writing, it is evident that the epistle was intended to be read by a far larger audience, despite what the poet says regarding his hope that the recipient will not show his imperfect work to others (vv. 33–36). Indeed, those words are simply an example of both the traditional "modesty topos" and the equally conventional disclaimer that the text one is reading was not intended for publication: neither is to be taken at face value, and each can be found in numerous texts at this time and beyond. As Carle no doubt knew, in the absence of newspapers, which were not yet in use at that time, those who wished to become informed about matters taking place in a foreign land would naturally be interested in reading a letter such as this, which clearly was copied by multiple scribes in the course of the sixteenth century.[41] And, as he was also well aware, other poets, such as Marot, widely circulated their ostensibly "private" verse epistles, addressed to specific royal and noble figures. In this way, Carle appears to be deliberately following the model of France's leading poet, much as he did when he penned his earlier *blasons* in response to Marot's general invitation to engage in what became known as the *Concours des blasons*.[42] Given its topical importance and the sensational story it conveys, Carle could be sure that his half-hearted plea not to show this text to others would be ignored, and that was no doubt his intention all along.

Because the epistle was a genre that could move from the private sphere to the public forum so easily, the art of letter-writing was a serious business that was described at length by many humanist theorists throughout the Renaissance. The most pertinent of these theoretical tracts, at least with regard to the poem at hand, was the *De conscribendis epistolis* [On the Writing of Letters] by the famed

---

[40] See Guillaume Colletet, *Vies des poètes bordelais et périgourdins*, ed. Philippe Tamizey de Larroque (1873; repr. Geneva: Slatkine, 1969), 35–44.

[41] For a study regarding how news was communicated in the early modern era, see Andrew Pettegree, *The Invention of News: How the World Came to Know about Itself* (New Haven: Yale University Press, 2014).

[42] See Chapter 3 above for more on Carle's writing *blasons anatomiques* at Marot's initiative.

Dutch humanist Desiderius Erasmus, which was first published in 1522.[43] Erasmus himself furnishes an example of the way in which private letters, addressed to a specific recipient, were in fact designed for public consumption: his vast Latin correspondence with notable figures of his time, including Thomas More, was quickly published in multiple volumes and known throughout Europe, and he was certainly not alone in this practice of making the private public. Yet, in his theoretical tract, Erasmus stresses the immediacy and intimacy of letters which, unlike public orations or spectacles, are designed to be consumed by a single recipient at a time and not *en masse* by a large audience. As Lisa Jardine has explained, there is always "an expectation that the reader will engage with the legible text as an intimate. . . . Letters convey feeling with immediacy, between a writer and a reader with some kind of mutual investment in the topic."[44] That is, although the letter might be intended to be read by more than its specific recipient, the fact that it does address a single individual creates a palpable and intimate bond between writer and reader in a way that other works do not. Perhaps, then, it is because he had always intended his letter to be read by a larger audience that Carle does not make his specific intended recipient known in a title to the work or in the body of the poem. He may have judged that his text could circulate more broadly and more easily soon after its composition when a specific reader (with whom privileged diplomatic information is being shared) is not named, although that reader is still certainly figured in the body of the text. That is, by not naming a specific interlocutor, Carle could more easily create the illusion, in the mind of his subsequent readers, that this correspondence was somehow addressed to them, too, as Erasmus suggests in this tract.

One of the aims of the epistolary genre as a whole was, once again according to Erasmus, to "make the absent vividly present in writing."[45] Like other foreign envoys then, Carle was tasked with providing a vibrant description of what had taken place in this distant kingdom. In turn, as Seth Lerer asserts, this vivid description, which is a hallmark of Carle's text, renders the letter (and its reading) a kind of "performance for an audience of one, acted out not on the stages of the theater but in the corner of the chamber."[46] In this regard, letters of the early modern period—be they private missives or official governmental correspondence—could be likened to theatrical performances, though perhaps, for modern readers, they might seem more like film scripts where words on a

---

[43] For this work, see Desiderius Eramsus, *De conscribendis epistolis* [*On the Writing of Letters*], in Collected Works of Erasmus 25: Literary and Educational Writings, vol. 3, trans. Craig R. Thompson (Toronto: University of Toronto Press, 1985).

[44] Lisa Jardine, *Erasmus, Man of Letters: The Construction of Charisma in Print* (Princeton, NJ: Princeton University Press, 1993), 151.

[45] See Jardine, *Erasmus*, 153.

[46] See Seth Lerer, *Courtly Letters in the Age of Henry VIII: Literary Culture and the Arts of Deceit* (Cambridge: Cambridge University Press, 1997), 11.

page evoke scenes or vignettes that readers can easily imagine performed before their very eyes. The intrinsic theatricality of letters, which was also noted by Jardine,[47] manifests itself here in the author's efforts to capture and reproduce what is presented as actual dialogue, overheard by a third party or eavesdropper (a word that may have originated from the carved wooden figures perched on the eaves of Tudor great halls, such as those now at Hampton Court Palace). This reporting (or creation) of theatrical-like dialogue could also be construed as a safety measure for writers who, unwilling to commit potentially dangerous words to paper in their own name, could dissociate themselves personally from these thoughts while still evoking them as something that originated with others.[48] This need for protection was acutely felt by ambassadors, in particular, who were advised by Machiavelli to avail themselves, in their letters, of formulae such as "prudent men here judge," rather than overtly expressing their own opinion; in other words, ambassadors were prone to create a "surrogate narrator,"[49] and one possible way to provide these others voices would be through the device of a dialogue or other similarly quoted speech.

Carle's poem takes this advice to the extreme by including verse upon verse of dialogue or quoted speech. Some of these imaginary scenes are evoked not directly but, rather, through the narrative technique of "free indirect discourse," which preserves the first-person perspective of a character's speech yet couches it in the third person: Henry's attempt to placate the crowds clamoring for Mary's return (vv. 643–650) as well Anne's final instruction to her ladies (vv. 1173–1182) are each a case in point. In all these instances, the reader can easily imagine the scene thanks to Carle's lively and dramatic style. But, undoubtedly, the most important—and most dramatic—of all the dialogues that take place in Carle's poem is the critical scene between a brother and his sister who accuses the queen of adulterous behavior. This is quickly followed by another dialogue, one between this brother (accompanied by two other courtiers) and the king himself.

Carle excels at capturing these highly dramatic moments that were no doubt shocking to his early readers. But, while these moments are privileged in Carle's poem, they would not have been the only dramatic scenes to have been played out in the Tudor privy chamber, for, as Lerer asserts, "ruses, lies, and dramatic irruptions are the currency of early Henrician power," lending a certain theatricality to much that took place among courtiers during Henry's reign.[50] It is therefore not surprising that a good deal of Carle's poem is devoted to reporting the ways in which various characters, and most especially the king and his courtiers, assume certain postures as would an actor. At the moment of Anne's coronation, Carle says, the English courtiers, who were fearful of displeasing the king, showed a

---

[47] Jardine, *Erasmus*, 151.
[48] See, on this point, Lerer, *Courtly Letters*, 16.
[49] See, on this point, Hampton, *Fictions*, 22.
[50] See Lerer, *Courtly Letters*, 37.

certain imaginative ingenuity or duplicity in the way they appeared to accept their new queen (vv. 111–116). Anne herself "acts" as if she is hurting when she feels her baby move in her womb (vv. 148–153). But most especially, it is Henry who is a master of artifice in several scenes evoked in the poem. Carle notes that the king dissimulates his anger toward Anne and her alleged lovers before the charges against them are finalized (vv. 475–476, 489). His behavior at the May Day joust was a particularly devious performance of charity and love toward his courtiers through which he "dissembl[ed] their coming ruin" (vv. 507–510, 516). And his address to the crowd that gathered in the streets in hope for Mary's return to the court (vv. 643–650) is clearly a show in which a false promise is made, which the king had no intention of honoring. These feigned postures are minutely noted by Carle, who appears to be well aware of the fact that, as another anonymous writer of the time opined, "the court of England was like a stage."[51]

While theatricality is thus intimately linked to the epistolary genre, another important aspect of diplomatic letters, in particular, is their need to bridge geographical distance, for the space that separates the writer from the reader often constitutes a cultural gap that demands explanation. In this respect, the ambassador's dispatch might be likened to the "traveler's tale," a genre that gained increased popularity during the age of exploration and discovery that was the Renaissance.[52] Like other traveler's tales, Carle's poem is an eyewitness report of life in a foreign land, with its own distinct customs and practices that appear strange to those from other cultural traditions. Carle's job, like that of the narrator of these tales, is to explain these unfamiliar elements to his audience back home. At the same time, it is clear that Carle assumes that France and the French manner of life are the standards by which all things should be judged. His reference to Anne as having so fully assimilated French culture such that she could have been mistaken for a "natural-born Frenchwoman" (vv. 53–54), along with his claim that Anne was beholden to France for the many accomplishments that led to her becoming queen of her own people (vv. 75–80), together betray a decidedly French, chauvinistic perspective.

The characteristic style and content of the traveler's tale is most prominent in the sections of Carle's letter that deal with the governmental and judicial practices of England. To begin with, Carle is careful to note the expansive role of

---

[51] See the Harleian manuscript on the fall of Anne Boleyn (London, British Library, Harley 2194, fol. 16r–v, here 16v), also transcribed in William Cobbett, *Complete Collection of State Trials . . . for High Treason and Other Crimes and Misdemeanors from the Earliest Period to the Present Time*, vol. 1, ed. Thomas Bayly Howell (London: Hansard, 1809), 1:411, and *Ballads from Manuscripts*, vol. 1, pt. 2, ed. Frederick J. Furnivall (London: Taylor and Co., 1872), 407.

[52] For a discussion of how ambassadorial reports were sometimes read as entertaining traveler's tales, see Filippo de Vivo, "How to Read Venetian 'Relazioni,'" *Renaissance and Reformation / Renaissance et Réforme* 34 (2011): 25–59, here 46.

Parliament (v. 189), which would not have been familiar to the average French reader. When describing the trial of Anne and her alleged lovers, he notes that they will be judged by several panels of citizens of comparable rank to that of the accused; this also would have seemed novel to a reader in France, where it was customary for a tribunal or a single judge to hear a case. He goes on to talk about particular rituals that were peculiarly English, especially the ceremonial axe whose blade faces away from the accused before the trial but which is turned in their direction when they are judged to be "guilty," an English word he attempts to teach his French audience (vv. 725–738). He describes how the jury members swear an oath to judge fairly, solemnizing this vow by placing their hand on the Bible and by kissing the crucifix (vv. 763–769). But perhaps his most powerful verses describe the extreme punishment that was normally imposed on those who were convicted of treason: for the French did not usually engage in this practice of hanging convicted men just to the point of asphyxiation and then cutting them open while still alive. It is clear from Carle's description of this practice as a "great and harsh cruelty" (v. 210) and a "horror" (v. 213) that he finds this practice to be excessively punitive. And yet, Carle exhibits a certain fascination with these exotic practices, meticulously describing them despite the shock they evidently aroused.

But unlike carefully crafted traveler's tales that may have been written long after the events they describe—and for a mass audience—Carle's letter to the French court is written within two weeks of Anne's execution. So important was it for him to make this fact known that he inscribes the date of this writing—but, curiously, not his own name (which some medieval and early modern poets *did* occasionally provide in their works)[53]—in his very verses. While Carle's name as poet has consequently been separated from the text at various points in history, the fact of its raw immediacy will never be lost on readers. They can be sure that they are reading a work whose contents are unfiltered by the passage of time and which remain unaffected by subsequent events that might cast a different light on the interpretation of what is unfolding before the poet's eyes. Carle's poem is, essentially, a snapshot of things as they were in the two weeks prior to 2 June 1536, a moment of enormous importance, frozen in time.

## The Complications of Verse: A Barrier to the Truth?

Given its links with the conventions of the "theatrical" epistolary genre and the traveler's tale, Carle's text can clearly be seen as a highly crafted work in its own right, one that took the diplomat's prerogative of shaping his story through the use of literary devices to new heights. Yet it is important to remember that, even

---

[53] See, for example, the Arthurian romance *Erec et Énide*, in which the name of the author, Chrétien de Troyes, appears in the prologue.

when diplomatic correspondence availed itself of literary or historical tropes in telling its story, diplomatic writing, at its heart, still aimed for the truth. That is, while a diplomat might use time-honored devices in his letter or, more prosaically, interject opinion and display a certain amount of bias in his reporting (as Chapuys does repeatedly), he would not—or at least should not—under any circumstances be less than fully truthful when writing to his master. As Hampton again has noted, this point was made quite clearly by Torquato Tasso, who, in his dialogue on diplomacy titled *Il messaggiero* (1580), maintained that "just as a doctor may lie to his patient but the patient should never lie to the doctor, so must the subject always speak the truth to his prince."[54]

In light of this diplomatic context, and in particular the diplomat's need always to speak the truth, it is therefore somewhat surprising that Carle chose to deliver his message through the medium of verse rather than prose. For, as Carle would undoubtedly know, the diplomat's requirement of veracity sits uneasily with the poet's need to accommodate matters of rhyme in casting the story. Indeed, as Adrian Armstrong and Sarah Kay demonstrate in their work on late medieval verse as a medium for the transmission of knowledge, there is an inherent tension between poetry and truth that was recognized and commented upon by poets themselves at this time—and, indeed, since the time of Plato.[55] Given that Carle is writing in the years immediately following the success of the poetic tradition engendered by a group of poets who are the object of Armstrong's and Kay's attention (known as the *Rhétoriqueurs*), it is profitable to consider the analysis of these scholars at some length to provide a sense of what was at stake when Carle made his decision to write in verse.

Armstrong and Kay open their study with an intriguing quotation from one little-known medieval French writer, Nicolas de Senlis (or "Saint-Lis"), who noted that it has long been believed that "no rhymed story is true" [*Nus conte rimés no es verais*].[56] They immediately follow this by a reference to another anonymous French poet who stated (somewhat ironically, in a poem) that telling a story in verse form is an invitation to contaminate it with "a lie for the sake of the rhyme" [*mançonge por fere la rime*].[57] It is for this reason that the latter poet maintains that he will tell *his* story in the manner of the prose *Lancelot*, "where there is not a single word that rhymes" [*ou il n'a de rime un seul mot*], so that he, too, might better tell the truth without falsehoods [*por mielz dire la verité / & por tretier sans*

---

[54] Hampton, *Fictions*, 51. Hampton is here paraphrasing Tasso, "Il messaggiero," in *Prose*, ed. Ettore Mazzali (Milan: Ricciardi, 1959), 69.

[55] See Adrian Armstrong and Sarah Kay, *Knowing Poetry: Verse in Medieval France from the "Rose" to the "Rhétoriqueurs"* (Ithaca, NY: Cornell University Press, 2011).

[56] Armstrong and Kay, *Knowing Poetry*, 1. This contention is found in the *Chronique dite Saintongeaise*, ed. André de Mandach (Tubingen: Niemeyer, 1970), 256.

[57] For this anonymous text, see Paul Meyer, ed., "Prologue en vers français d'une histoire perdue de Philippe-Auguste," *Romania* 6 (1877): 494–98, here 498.

*fauseté*].[58] As Armstrong and Kay show, this common assumption that rhyme is full of lies led to a major literary shift, after the thirteenth century, which saw prose becoming the medium of choice for vernacular histories and, therefore, the realm of fact, whereas verse was coded as "artificial, unreliable, and falsifying."[59] Choosing to write in verse, as Carle did, therefore, might be seen as a subversive act, a sign of the author's desire to mislead his reader by distorting the truth, if not, to put it more bluntly, to embellish it with lies. This would, of course, be in direct conflict with the diplomat's need never to lie to his prince.

At the very least, Carle's decision to deliver his news in verse form hints that the author was not content with merely conveying facts in a dispassionate manner but, rather, had other goals—or other truths—in mind. Indeed, as Armstrong and Kay remind us, once prose became firmly associated with history, the decision to revert to verse was akin to choosing black and white film once color photography became ubiquitous: it was a deliberately "retro" aesthetic choice that advertised the author's concerns with art and artifice.[60] While color film might record events more realistically, black and white film encourages artistic interpretation and a more controlled, personalized presentation of reality. In a similar vein, Armstrong and Kay continue, those late medieval histories—or stories—that are recounted in verse describe events that are explicitly presented as things experienced and remembered: that is, as filtered through the personal lens of the author and other witnesses. Clearly, texts that are characterized by personal reminiscence and other eyewitness reports are subject to other forms of distortion, even if these are not deliberate: for memory can fail and witnesses can produce conflicting accounts of what has transpired.[61] Indeed, at times, the subjective, authorial hand behind texts of this kind is barely concealed and, on the contrary, is often revealed through the frequent intrusion of moral or philosophical commentary on the events described. The narrative "I" that guides the reader through the text does not hesitate to express his opinions regarding the action he describes. This recourse to moral commentary, which character-

---

[58] See Meyer, "Prologue," 498.

[59] Armstrong and Kay, *Knowing Poetry*, 1. For an example of an historiographic work that reverts to the use of verse, see Guillaume de Machaut's *La Prise d'Alixandre* [*The Taking of Alexandria*], ed. and trans. R. Barton Palmer (New York: Routledge, 2002). For an analysis of this work, consult Philip E. Bennett, "Rhetoric, Poetics and History: Machaut's *Prise d'Alixandre* and the Anonymous *Gestes des ducs de Bourgogne*," in *Medieval Historical Discourses: Essays in Honour of Peter S. Noble*, ed. Marianne J. Ailes, Anne Lawrence-Mathers, and Françoise H. M. Le Saux (Reading, UK: University of Reading, 2008), 53–74 [Special issue of *Reading Medieval Studies* 34 (2008)].

[60] Armstrong and Kay, *Knowing Poetry*, 2–3.

[61] For more on texts purporting to give this type of report, see Andrea Frisch, *The Invention of the Eyewitness: Witness and Testimony in Early Modern France* (Chapel Hill: University of North Carolina Press, 2004).

ized poetic narratives at the end of the fifteenth century, further helped "to give heightened definition to verse," as opposed to prose, "as a medium of reflection and enlightenment."[62]

Each of these points made by Armstrong and Kay is relevant to *The Story of the Death of Anne Boleyn*, so much so that their analysis seems tailor-made to help explain Carle's decision to write this dispatch in verse form. Traces of his self-conscious deliberation regarding the use of verse are visible in what one might describe as the prologue of the poem, occupying lines 1–36. This is not surprising, for, as Victor Brombert has reminded us, words located at the threshold of a text acquire a privileged status; they reflect the author's anxieties in beginning his narration, but, at the same time, they provide a key to the interpretation of the text that is to follow.[63] From the very beginning of his poem, in verses 1–5, Carle acknowledges that this unsettling and amazing story is one that he continues to reflect upon, in part because of its unprecedented, "new" nature: he simply does not know what to make of it but continuously tries to make sense of it by turning it over in his mind (vv. 1–5).

He also insists on the personal nature of his story, stating that he writes what he himself has seen or what others have witnessed and conveyed to him:

> J'en escriray ce que i'ay entendu
> Par les raisons que plusieurs m'ont rendu,
> *Puis*, mon Seigneur, ce que i'ay retenu
> Depuis le temps que suis icy venu. (vv. 25–28) Emphasis added.

> [I shall write about what I have heard,
> Through the insights that several people have provided me,
> And *then*, my lord, about what I have remembered
> Since the time that I arrived here.]

By interjecting the temporal adverb "puis" (or "then") at this critical juncture, Carle is also providing a key to the structure of his narration: he will first give Anne's "back-story," describing her life in France and the events leading to her courtship and marriage, culminating in the baptism of her daughter, Elizabeth, all of which occurred prior to Carle's arrival in England (probably in early 1536) and for which he must rely on the reports of others; only *then* will he move on to narrating the events he has personally witnessed since coming to this foreign land. The oft-repeated judgment that Carle "admitted that he was merely versifying rumors he had heard" is thus a decidedly unfair characterization of what Carle says, proffered by those who have missed the importance of that little

---

[62] Armstrong and Kay, *Knowing Poetry*, 2–3.

[63] See Victor Brombert, "Opening Signals in Narrative," *New Literary History* 11 (1980): 489–502.

word, "puis."[64] Carle admits, certainly, that he depends on informants for Anne's early biography, but this is not inconsistent with saying that the description of the events of May 1536 is the handiwork of an eye-witness: Carle himself. Indeed, this two-fold reliance on eyewitness testimony coupled with his own personal experience becomes a hallmark of Carle's narrative strategy throughout his writing career. For, in a later composition, on the death of the Duke of Guise, Carle once again, at the threshold of his text, articulates his dual dependence on reliable and authoritative witnesses on the one hand ("personnages d'authorité, de qui j'en ay entendu l'une partie") and, on the other hand, on what he himself has personally seen and heard ("et l'autre que je l'ay veuë et ouye moy-mesme") in the construction of his narrative, precisely as he does in the opening verses of his poem on the death of Anne Boleyn.[65]

There are several other observations one can make about the inherent tension between truth and fiction that poetry traditionally has generated and how this is manifested in Carle's poem. First, the verse form chosen—decasyllabic rhyming couplets—is one that is in some sense closest to prose and certainly was the form of choice for anyone wishing to produce a verse narrative at this time. Like its medieval counterpart, the octosyllabic rhyming couplet, it was, as Armstrong and Kay remind us, the "*degré zéro* of versification . . . and the form least likely to be sung";[66] thus, while Carle's poem advertises its literary nature, it certainly could not be construed as lyric poetry in the strict sense of that term. More to the point, rhyming couplets would be less vulnerable to the exigencies of rhyme (to the potential detriment of truth) than would be more intricate lyric genres, such as a *rondeau* or a sonnet, which are far more demanding to write.

This observation can be proved by looking at a well-known example from a sonnet penned by the most prestigious poet of sixteenth-century France, Pierre de Ronsard, which purports to reveal the date of his encounter with his beloved

---

[64] For this criticism of Carle's poem as primarily rumor or gossip, see, for example, Retha Warnicke, *Wicked Women of Tudor England: Queens, Aristocrats, Commoners* (New York: Palgrave Macmillan, 2012), 25–26. Perhaps the earliest recorded claim that Carle himself "professes having written from hearsay" is found in the anonymous notice entitled "Poem on the Death of Anne Boleyn," in *The Gentleman's Magazine and Historical Review*, ed. Sylvanus Urban [Edward Cave, pseud.], n.s., 10 (January–June 1861): 189–90, here 190. See also E. W. Ives, *The Life and Death of Anne Boleyn, "The Most Happy"* (2004; repr. Oxford: Blackwell, 2005), who states categorically that Carle "did not himself witness the trial of Anne and her brother," though he "could have attended the trial of the commoners" (60). Ives bases this assumption on the fact that the order of the trials of Anne and George are reversed in Carle's telling (376n59).

[65] See, on this matter, "Lettre de L'Évesque de Riez au Roy, contenant les actions et propos de Monsieur de Guyse, depuis sa blessure, iusques à son trespas," in *Archives curieuses de l'histoire de France depuis Louis XI jusqu'à Louis XVIII*, 1st series, vol. 5, ed. L. Cimber and F. Danjou (Paris: Beauvais, 1835), 171–97, here 175.

[66] Armstrong and Kay, *Knowing Poetry*, 2.

Cassandre at the château of Blois. In the *incipit* or first line of the sonnet, Ronsard acknowledges that this fatal date occurred in "L'an mil cinq cent contant quarante & *six*," that is, in 1546.[67] Now, it is a known fact that the French court was not in residence at Blois in 1546 and that the fateful encounter between Ronsard and Cassandre actually took place in 1545.[68] But the placement of the date in the rhyming position of the first line of his sonnet requires Ronsard to find three other rhyme words in composing these quatrains; and, as any poet would know, there is no rhyme in French for the word "cinq," that is, "five." Thus, as François Rigolot has argued, historical accuracy gives way to poetic expediency, as Ronsard displays no compunction in changing the date to 1546, which opens the door to a host of more easily achieved rhymes in his sonnet: namely "épris," "appris," and "pris."[69] However, in the poem on Anne Boleyn, Carle's choice of employing rhyming couplets requires the poet to find only one pair of rhymes at a time (rather than the quadruple rhyme needed for a sonnet). This would allow him far greater freedom to choose words that reflect historical reality rather than tempting him to "lie for the sake of the rhyme," as Ronsard did and as the anonymous medieval poet quoted above by Armstrong and Kay warned could be the case. In this way, Carle's easier rhymes are more likely to inspire the reader's confidence in the truth of the tale.

Indeed, there is no doubt that the events described in Carle's poem are for the most part verifiably true: that is, there are independent sources, such as letters and other historical documents, which happily confirm the veracity of Carle's tale, with only a few minor exceptions. One could justifiably claim, as well, that Carle's position in the diplomatic corps not only *required* accuracy but also *permitted* him a degree of freedom in truth-telling that English writers on this subject could not enjoy: for in composing a document that was destined to make its way to the continent, rather than remain in the British Isles, Carle could give testimony to things of which others might not dare to speak, in light of the treason laws that forbade slanderous speech aimed at the royal family.[70] By its very

---

[67] Pierre de Ronsard, *Les Amours (1552)*, ed. Paul Laumonier (Paris: Nizet, 1982); this is poem 98.

[68] Laumonier writes in his footnote to this sonnet (97n2) that "according to the *Acts of Francis I* and the *Itinerary of Francis I*, the Court did not spend a single day of 1546 at Blois" (my translation).

[69] François Rigolot, *Poétique et onomastique: L'exemple de la Renaissance* (Geneva: Droz, 1977), 204: "If the date of 1545 is not retained in the text although it was at that date that the court stayed in Blois, it is undoubtedly because, as a savvy poet, Ronsard knew that a rhyme with *cinq* [five] is impossible and that in adding one year he would open up for himself a far richer field for the quadruple rhyme with the word 'six'" (my translation).

[70] This is the claim made by Charles-Hugues Le Febvre de Saint-Marc in his Preface to *Histoire d'Angleterre par M. Rapin de Thoyras, nouvelle édition augmentée des notes de M. Tindal* (The Hague 1749), 1:lxiii. According to Saint-Marc, the author of *L'Histoire*

status as a dispatch, sent from a foreigner to others abroad, the poem enjoyed a certain "diplomatic immunity," so to speak, and could relate the truth in a more direct manner than any English letter could do at that time.[71] This could explain why it is the sole extant source for certain details in the story of Anne Boleyn's demise.

Although Carle alludes to the fact that he is conveying "news" that needs to be dispatched to the court in France, he makes it clear that he is no mere dispassionate reporter but, rather, has been immensely affected by these events. Carle's personal investment in the story and its outcome is evident in passages where he comments on these events. In truth, Carle's personal intervention in the narration is fairly limited: he does not pepper his text with the most visible expressions of eyewitness reporting—the words "I saw" or "I heard" that feature in so many other testimonial texts—such that the reader can never forget the narrator's presence in the story. Instead, Carle's interventions are more subtle and most often take the form of moral judgments and personal interpretations embedded within his retelling of the story. These moral reflections, an example of which is also located in the early verses of the text, can take the form of maxims such as this:

Mais les honneurs & grans exaulcemens
Changent souuent les bons entendemens,
Et plusieurs fois altere la nature
Le changement de bonne nourriture. (vv. 85–88)

[But honors and great exaltation
Often change one's good judgment
And, many times, a change from one's good upbringing
Alters one's character.]

Here Carle opines that extraordinary experiences, such as the sudden acquisition of honors, can change one's very character, and this, he further implies, is a nearly universal truth. That the poem's early readers recognized and appreciated Carle's interjection of moral maxims can be confirmed by a marginal note inscribed in one of the surviving manuscripts of this text now housed in the municipal library at Soissons: there the reader writes the words "Mot doré" [A golden saying] and encases verses 85–86 in quotation marks to note the aptness

---

*de Anne de Boulant* (known in this work via an anonymous manuscript) "could write quite freely, because he was sending his work overseas and . . . he could undoubtedly have apprised us . . . of things which the English historians of that time did not dare say" (my translation).

[71] For a study of the concept of diplomatic immunity in the early modern period, consult Garrett Mattingly, *Renaissance Diplomacy* (Boston: Houghton Mifflin, 1955), 45–51.

of Carle's pithy judgment.[72] Clearly, here and throughout, Carle is not content to narrate just *what* has happened but also endeavors to explain *why* things happened as they did.

All these references to personal reflection, judgment, and point of view near the beginning of this poem verify Armstrong's and Kay's observations regarding the peculiar attributes of historical narrative delivered through the medium of verse composition in an age of prose. But if further proof is needed that Carle was very self-conscious in his deliberate choice to write this missive as a poem, it, too, can be found in the early lines of his text, where he provides his own explicit explanation of why he made this choice (vv. 29–36). Carle makes two claims for his decision in this passage. First, he suggests that there is something in the nature of this particular story—perhaps its universality as a morality tale?—that lends itself to poetry. More importantly, perhaps, the choice is made for the benefit of his reader who will find the story to be less troubling if rendered through the aesthetically pleasing medium of rhyme. The implication is that the inherent pleasure of reading verse will render the awful, violent, and pitiful story that he will recount more palatable. Indeed, later in his career, Carle would say the same thing in the preface to his paraphrase of the book of Ecclesiastes: echoing the modesty topos he also used in the poem on Anne Boleyn, Carle acknowledges his inadequacies in undertaking such a work that challenges his poetic talent, but he justifies his choice of writing the paraphrase in rhyme because he wishes "to temper the severity of the pronouncements with the sweetness of meter" [*temperer la severité des sentences avecques la douceur des nombres*].[73] Thus, although the diplomat cannot alter Anne's story, with its brutal ending, he can at least deliver it in a way that makes the story easier to read.

One could imagine, too, that there probably were more personal reasons that explain Carle's unique choice. For one, Carle arrived in England fresh from his participation in one of the premier poetic contests of the time: the so-called *Concours des Blasons*, which was instigated by Clément Marot in 1535 and which culminated in a series of poems written by various authors on female body parts.[74] Thus it is not too surprising that this young man, who fancied himself a successful poet, having rubbed elbows with the poetic élite of his time, would want to continue his practice of writing rhyme during his time of serving the resident ambassador. And certainly Carle was also aware that this choice would render his text unique in the realm of diplomatic correspondence (certainly with respect to this event, and quite likely on any subject at any point in time). It was

---

[72] This is Soissons, Bibliothèque municipal, MS 201. See fol. 19r for this marginal annotation.

[73] For these remarks regarding Carle's inadequacies and his choice of the verse form, see *L'Ecclésiaste de Salomon, paraphrasé en vers françois, par Lancelot de Carles, Evesque de Riez, avec quelques sonnets chrestiens* (Paris: Nicolas Edoard, 1561), "Au Roy," Aij and B.

[74] See, on this matter, Chapter 3 above.

a way to ensure that this story, as seen through his eyes, would be read by more than the French king and his courtiers, despite his (insincere) request to keep this missive private.

## Telling the Story of Anne Boleyn: The Poem as Narrative

Carle clearly had an eye for what makes a good story and an ear for telling that tale in a compelling fashion. Indeed, in this poem, Carle delivers what in journalistic terms might be called a "scoop": he purports to know exactly how Anne's infidelity came to be known to the king. According to Carle, the queen's downfall came about through a private conversation that took place between one of Anne's ladies-in-waiting and this lady's brother, who happened to be a close advisor to the king. The brother, in turn, shares the story with two other close advisors, and all three men become storytellers in their own right when, together, they relate the tale to Henry. Additionally, we are told that other tales are recounted about Anne and her lovers—specifically by Mark, a court musician, though we do not hear his stories firsthand. This quick succession of multiple overlapping stories creates the impression that the English court is a haven for storytellers: it is rife with gossip, whether based on fact or merely on rumor, which will turn out to have fatal consequences.

The first of these stories begins when the brother, who is counselor to the king, wishes to admonish his sister for showing signs of inappropriate amorous behavior and entreats her to mend her ways before her reputation is ruined (vv. 341–378). There is much that is left unsaid here. First, we do not know what signs prompted the brother to warn his sister about her bad behavior and the potential ruin of her reputation. Some readers have assumed that the obvious sign of the sister's dissolute living was a belly swollen in pregnancy—one that, presumably, resulted from an affair outside of marriage (since carrying her own husband's child would hardly be scandalous).[75] But it is important to note that the fact of her pregnancy is never stated explicitly within the poem. Indeed, a closer look at the text shows that such a reading may be problematic, for several reasons. First, the poet is careful to use a plural form in this passage and speaks of "*many signs* / of loving some *men*" (vv. 344–345), rather than the singular "a sign" and "some man," which one would presume he would use if the reference was to a pregnancy. Instead, the phrasing used here seems to indicate a general-

---

[75] See, for example, George Bernard who says: "What the poet meant by 'showing many signs of loving others by dishonest love' *can only be* that the countess was pregnant. In what other ways does sleeping around affect someone's appearance?" In G. W. Bernard, *Anne Boleyn: Fatal Attractions* (2010; repr. New Haven: Yale University Press, 2011), 154 (emphasis added).

ized inappropriately flirtatious *behavior* with several courtiers (rather than an extra-marital affair with a single lover) and certainly does not explicitly describe a specific change in physical *appearance*.

Furthermore, the warning this brother gives to his sister is expressed in the grammatical mode that is known as the "irréel du présent" to indicate a potential fact that is not actualized. Specifically, the passage uses two verbs in the present conditional mode, "aqueroit" [might acquire] and "blesseroit" [might injure] followed by a verb in the imperfect tense to complete the hypothetical structure. Thus the poet, paraphrasing the brother, declares that the lady *would* be apt to acquire a bad reputation if she didn't soon stop misbehaving. It would be hard to see how withdrawing from sin in the future would save this lady's present "shameful" reputation if she were already visibly pregnant. If that were the case, the damage, presumably, has already been done, and her reputation can no longer be salvaged. In short, reading the passage as a statement of fact cannot be supported by this particular sequence of tenses.

Finally, the sister downplays the significance of her bad behavior, calling it a "petite faulte" [small fault] that is in no way comparable to the greater sin committed by Anne. Clearly, she believes that her brother's admonishment is a disproportionate reaction for so petty a misstep on her part, and she persists in portraying herself as an innocent "dove" in contrast to the infamous "raven" she identifies with Anne. It would be hard to imagine that a pregnancy that occurs outside of marriage could be so easily dismissed as insignificant by this lady. It seems far more likely, again, that the misbehavior in question was indeed a penchant for flirtation, an engagement in amorous trifles, which, while not rising to the level of adultery and the risk of pregnancy, could in fact lead to the loss of her good reputation within the court.

Now, this is not to say that, in actual fact, the sister who delivers this story was not pregnant. It is only to say that Carle, qua poet, does not put that bit of information explicitly in his text. Perhaps Carle, the ambassador's secretary, did not know the identity of the sister (since identified as the Countess of Worcester, who was indeed with child at this time).[76] Nor is this piece of information critical for the purposes of Carle's story: what Carle clearly thought was important was the fact of this dramatic confrontation between siblings (which may have become generally known around court) rather than the specific motivation for it. Indeed, in another literary version of this scene, found in an Italian short story written in the period 1543–1547 by Matteo Bandello, and its French adaptation by François de Belleforest, it was said to be the king himself who instigated the confrontation, asking his counselor to tell his sister to leave the court because of her excessive flirtatious behavior (which Henry did not tolerate because that

---

[76] See Chapter 2 above for a discussion of this lady's identification as the Countess of Worcester.

lady was supposed to be his very own mistress).[77] This somewhat later varying account suggests that the fact of the sister's pregnancy was either not widely known or not considered to be an essential part of the story.

It is also possible that, qua poet, Carle has written verses that are simply grammatically incorrect and that this apparent confusion regarding the proper sequence of tenses could simply be a trace of stylistic inelegance that has crept into Carle's narration. But, if there is indeed confusion here, perhaps it should be viewed more charitably, and more intriguingly, as a deliberate multivalence. At the least, Carle may intentionally be leaving his story open to multiple interpretations, perhaps even equally valid ones. And indeed, this is not the only scene where ambiguous narration can be found in Carle's poem. Carle's deliberate use of the word "signs," without a clear referent, might then be seen as an invitation to view this text as one that thematizes the difficulties of reading and interpretation, as will be analyzed later in this chapter. But within the confines of this text, a univocal interpretation of this scene as a revelation of the lady's pregnancy is unwarranted, both grammatically and semantically, despite what might be known about her real-life situation, gleaned from what literary critics designate as "l'hors-texte," that is, from outside the literary text at hand, through other historical sources.

Regardless of what Carle (and the brother) actually meant, the brother's accusatory words are not answered directly by the sister. Instead, in vv. 363–366, she deliberately changes the subject, diverting attention from her sins to another's so as to diminish the importance of her own faults and erase her lesser sin from their conversation (and from this text). This swerve, or diversion, in the intimate dialogue between brother and sister opens up a space for the story of the queen's misbehavior to emerge (vv. 367–370). As Carle makes clear, the queen's story is told as a *substitute* for the sister's own tale of misbehavior: she does not deny her brother's accusations, nor does she offer any defense or explanation for her actions, but, instead, accuses the queen of worse sins. The sister's "excuse" thus slides directly into another story that is not really her own to tell.

The specific accusation uttered by the sister is precisely the one that carries the most shock-value, that of Anne's incest with her brother, George (vv. 373–

---

[77] For the Italian short story, see Matteo Bandello, "De le molte mogli del re d'Inghilterra e morte de le due di quelle, con altri modi e varii accidenti intervenuti" (novella 62) in *La terza parte de le novelle*, ed. Delmo Maestri (Turin: Edizioni dell'Orso, 1995), 287–93. For an English translation, see "Of the Many Wives of the King of England and the Death of Two of Them" in *The Novels of Matteo Bandello . . . now first done into English . . . by John Payne*, vol. 6 (London: Villon Society, 1890), 103–13 (here, 107–9). See also François de Belleforest, "Mort miserable de deux amans, ausquels le Roy d'Angleterre Henry defendit de se marier ensemble, & autres choses sur la vie dudict Roy" (story 36), in *Le second tome des Histoires Tragiques, extraites de l'italien de Bandel* (Paris: Robert le Mangnier, 1566), 433–62.

376). The words that came tumbling forth from this lady are shocking, not only because of the treacherous and scandalous behavior that they describe but also because they are themselves potentially treacherous, insofar as they could be construed as an example of forbidden discourse and subversive speech. For, as the attentive reader would surely know, remembering what Carle had said less than 200 lines previously, this lady's words might violate a statute that Henry passed in 1534 (about eighteen months after his marriage to Anne) that prohibited citizens from impugning the legitimacy of this marriage or its issue and that had, more broadly, the effect of silencing all of Anne's critics, whose number, according to Carle, was legion (vv. 214–219). This statute was unique in English law, for it radically redefined potential criminal behavior to include not only actions but also mere words.[78] For the first time in English history, a citizen of any rank could be executed just for telling a story, as this woman has dared to do.[79] The choice, for English citizens, was then simple: either conceal their knowledge of things that one really ought not to hide, or speak only in whispers about Anne (vv. 209–213). So, what is remarkable about the disclosure of this lady-in-waiting to her brother is that, unlike others, she speaks openly, defying the law and risking punishment.

Since these are the first examples of quoted speech in the poem, they also call attention to themselves just through that fact. But the reader must acknowledge that these words are problematic: for how can it be that the poet has heard them himself and is able to record them faithfully? Given its subject matter, the dialogue presented here must have occurred behind closed doors, at least figuratively if not literally. Accepting this story as altogether true, therefore, requires accepting the poet to be the most proficient of eavesdroppers. Some historians

---

[78] The Treason Law of 1534 spelled out the possible offenses and punishments already implied in the Act of Succession (formally passed in 1534): "if any person or persons . . . do maliciously wish, will or desire by words or writing, or by craft imagine, invent, practice or attempt any bodily harm to be done or committed to the King's most royal person, the Queen's or their heir's [*sic*] apparent, or to deprive them . . . of the dignity, title or name of their royal estates, or slanderously and maliciously publish and pronounce, by express writing or words, that the King our sovereign lord should be heretic, schismatic, tyrant, infidel or usurper of the crown . . . shall be adjudged traitors; and that every such offence . . . shall be reputed, accepted and adjudged high treason," the penalty for which would be death. See G. R. Elton, ed., *The Tudor Constitution: Documents and Commentary* (Cambridge: Cambridge University Press, 1960), 61–63, here 62.

[79] On this point, see Sharon L. Jansen, *Dangerous Talk and Strange Behavior: Women and Popular Resistance to the Reforms of Henry VIII* (New York: St. Martin's Press, 1996), 77; see also Rebecca Lemon, *Treason by Words: Literature, Law, and Rebellion in Shakespeare's England* (Ithaca, NY: Cornell Univ. Press, 2006), 5.

have, for this reason, seized on this fact to discredit the historical accuracy of the entire poem.[80]

There is no doubt that the dialogue between brother and sister, with its highly theatrical quality, should not be read as if it were a transcript of actual utterances. Indeed, the literariness of this discourse is signaled early on by the maxim proffered by the sister that her brother and other gentlemen of the court are ready to "condemn doves / And pardon infamous ravens" (vv. 361–362). This maxim is a reworking of a quotation taken from the Latin poet Juvenal and thus is a literary allusion that perhaps came more easily from the pen of Carle, a humanist poet who was well versed in the classics, than from the mouth and mind of this ordinary lady-in-waiting.[81] By showing his authorial hand in this way, Carle is reminding his reader that this work occupies a space between truth and fiction insofar as it partakes equally of the divergent genres of diplomatic missive and verse narrative. In other words, what we see here is a prime example of the unresolved tensions between the expectations of diplomatic (or historical) discourse and narrative fiction, or between what is true and what is merely *vraisemblable* or believable.

Carle thus invites his readers to accept these words as true, yet we know that they must be, at least to some extent, imaginative, and thus a fiction. Doubtless, the existence of recreated or imaginative dialogue is a hallmark of this text; it is also a hallmark of the genre we have come to call "historical fiction." By choosing to write his dispatch as a narrative poem that incorporates imaginative dialogue, Carle has anticipated a technique of the modern historical fiction writer who, as Stephen Greenblatt said in his review of Hilary Mantel's *Wolf Hall*, "offers the dream of full access, access to what went on behind closed doors, off the record,

---

[80] See, for example, Ives, *Life and Death*, 60: "Because of . . . the immediacy of his writing, de Carles's account has been assumed to have original authority. Caution should, in fact, have warned otherwise. How could de Carles report events not accessible to the public?" Similarly, Warnicke points to discrepancies between Carle's rendition and the actual facts (such as a change in the chronological order of the trials, which, it is assumed, was enacted for dramatic effect) and wonders "why the entire poem should not be viewed from the perspective of poetic license." Consult Warnicke, "The Fall of Anne Boleyn Revisited," *The English Historical Review* 108.428 (1993): 653–65, here 660.

[81] See Juvenal, *Satires*, in *Juvenal and Persius*, ed. and trans. Susanna Morton Braund, Loeb Classical Library 91 (Cambridge, MA: Harvard University Press, 2004), 2.63: "Dat veniam corvis, vexat censura columbas" [That's a judgment that acquits the ravens and condemns the doves]. The maxim also made its way into the *Adages* of Erasmus, so it is certainly possible that we are to understand that the lady-in-waiting could have been familiar with the proverb as a part of popular wisdom. Nevertheless, given its classical origin, it may well be here to serve as a reminder of authorial presence, especially in this recreated dialogue. For this proverb, see Desiderius Erasmus, *Adagia* [Adages], ed. John N. Grant, trans. Denis L. Drysdall, in Collected Works of Erasmus 35 (Toronto: University of Toronto Press, 2008), no. 3.5.73.

in private, when no one was listening or recording"; the reader is struck by this vivid sensation of lived life, "best summed up in exclamations like 'Yes, this is the way it must have been'; 'This is how they must have sounded.'"[82] Although Carle does not need to bridge a gap created by the passage of time, as does the modern historical novelist, he still is required to convey this sense of vivid believability to an audience that is removed by geographical distance. And, so, it is no wonder that he makes frequent use of the tool of the imagined dialogue to drive home his point.

To return to the text and its unfolding dramatic story, the reader is next allowed to delve into an internal dialogue within the mind of the high-ranking brother, the immediate hearer of this story. For this brother, upon hearing his sister's tale, is confronted with a dilemma that Carle skillfully presents in verses 379–392. The brother well knows that if he repeats his sister's words to the king — if, in effect, he becomes a storyteller in his own right — he would himself be subject to the recently passed treason law and could conceivably lose his head; but if he remained silent and if the story was somehow revealed in another manner to the king — that is, if it becomes someone else's story to tell — he could still be convicted of treason for having access to and hiding such information. Furthermore, the brother is keenly aware that, should he decide to tell the story himself, he would be assuming a role that we know to be very similar to that of the poet: his main concern is to make this outrageous story seem plausible, indeed to make it believable ("de *faire croire*," v. 385, emphasis added). Thus, after weighing his options, the brother decides to speak. But it is important to note that, in so expertly insisting on the brother's dilemma, Carle seems to be suggesting that the king's counselor did not take these accusations lightly, nor were they presented to the king merely to instigate trouble in the royal marriage or to inflict damage upon the reputation of the queen. While the motivations of his sister might still be open to question, Carle is clear that it is duty to his royal master that prompts the brother to reveal the accusations.

Before telling the king, however, the brother enlists the help of two other unnamed men who are also close to the king, to whom he has repeated the sister's forbidden discourse (vv. 394–398). Once again Carle reveals that the brother is concerned about believability and, furthermore, about the matter of authority in storytelling. There is much at stake here, more so than in Carle's own retelling of the tale for a French audience. The solution, for the brother, thus lies in multiplying the potential storytellers: the more who participate in revealing this tale, so his logic goes, the more believable it would be. And by involving these particular storytellers, he can address the matter of authority by invoking the proximity, intimacy, and favored status enjoyed by these two other unnamed men with

---

[82] Stephen Greenblatt, "How It Must Have Been," *The New York Review of Books*, 5 November 2009. For online access, see: http://www.nybooks.com/articles/2009/11/05/ how-it-must-have-been/.

respect to the king. Notably, he does not invite his sister to retell the tale herself. There may be some degree of gender politics at work here, where authority in speech is assumed to be the domain of males, whereas a female witness — even one with first-hand knowledge — may be deemed unreliable in the eyes of court officials. At any rate, the brother avoids any such problem by enlisting the help of two other authoritative males.

The tale that is told by the brother, however, differs from that told by the sister in significant ways. The sister has named only one lover — the queen's own brother, George — and has implicated Mark, the musician, as someone who has more stories to tell. In the brother's retelling of this story to the king, the accusations are broadened to include a vast number of men, too many to tally, he claims (vv. 439–440). The allegations now include not only George but also Henry Norris, the king's groom of the stool (and thus his most intimate associate), as well as Mark himself, who is once again cited as a potential source of further corroboration of this tale. And more details are added, details that mirror the language of the indictments that were eventually drawn up against Anne: the queen is said to be the one who has pursued these men, offering them presents and other welcoming gestures. [83] Yet there is even more to tell, which the brother himself resists revealing, though he knows Henry will eventually hear about it (vv. 441–442).

Carle does not explain why the tale the brother tells Henry is so much more comprehensive — a skeptic would say "hyperbolic" — than the sister's earlier tale told to him. Is this Carle's subtle way of suggesting that the allegations are untrue and that the three men have been convinced, for whatever reason, that it would be beneficial to conspire against Anne and multiply false accusations against her? Or, are we to understand that the brother (perhaps with the help of the other two men) conducted his own investigation prior to revealing the accusations to Henry, and that the result of this investigation was a widening sphere of suspicion? Or, at least, are we meant to assume that the brother took his sister's advice and confronted Mark Smeaton about the matter and that it was the musician who supplied further details about Anne's indiscretions? The text is ambiguous on this point and is certainly open to multiple interpretations. No doubt, there is a certain eagerness in the tone here, implying that the brother has overcome his initial reluctance to speak of these unbelievable charges and perhaps now relishes this opportunity to warn Henry about Anne's infidelities. But this eagerness does not necessarily imply that the brother has embellished the tale without cause: perhaps he did indeed learn new information and saw

---

[83] For these indictments, which specify that Anne, "did falsely and traitorously procure by base conversations and kisses, touchings, gifts, and other infamous incitations, divers of the King's daily and familiar servants to be her adulterers and concubines, so that several of the King's servants yielded to her vile provocations," see LP 10.876; these are also reprinted in Norton, *Anne Boleyn Papers*, 339.

himself as performing an essential duty as a trusted counselor to the king. In any event, when the brother has finished his discourse, Henry is, understandably, shocked by the allegations, or, rather, by this *tale*, for Carle uses the word "récit" here, rather than a word indicating a report or accusation. Yet Henry orders an investigation, reminding the informants that the story had better turn out to be true or their lives would be at risk.

Embedded in the accusations against Anne made by the sister to her brother and the brother to the king is thus another unheard version of the story: the one that would be recited by Mark Smeaton, a Flemish musician who was one of those accused of having committed adultery with the queen. The sister twice refers her brother to Mark (vv. 371–372 and 377–378), who is clearly harboring knowledge about the whole sordid affair. Despite the inherent dangers of divulging this information, Mark, she predicts, will readily recount this explosive story to her brother. It is important to remember that the sister is not explicit about any details except for the accusation of incest between Anne and her brother, George. Thus Mark, at this point in the poem, is not specifically accused and is invoked only as a witness who will confirm the sister's story. Indeed, it would be hard to imagine that the sister could be so confident that Mark would voluntarily incriminate himself by confessing his own involvement with the queen. Yet history does indeed inform us that Mark was the only one of the five men to have confessed to the crime, apparently implicating others in the process. And, furthermore, later in the poem (at v. 1147), Carle makes it clear that Anne herself views Mark as the source of her downfall and the originator of the scandal imputed upon her.

Mark's confession has always been a bit troubling to those who believe in Anne's innocence. Some have assumed that the confession could have been offered only in the course of unspeakable torture. But Carle's poem hints of a different possibility: that Mark was perhaps somewhat proud of having "served" or, to put it more coarsely, "serviced" the queen on three separate occasions (vv. 479–484). There was no need for torture, for Mark willingly engaged in what can be read as a naïve but sadly dangerous act of braggadocio on the part of a foreigner who might not have fully realized what was at stake. It is perhaps for this reason that the sister was so sure Mark would corroborate her story even if it meant he would incriminate himself: the tale itself bestowed on him a certain stature that he did not enjoy in reality. Looking at documents beyond what the poem offers, we know that Mark's lowly status had indeed been made painfully obvious to him only a few days before his arrest. As Anne later told her jailor, William Kingston, she had recently publicly reminded the musician, who, we are to presume, was infatuated with the queen, that she could not speak to him as she would to a gentleman, for he was "an inferior person."[84] By claiming inti-

---

[84] For this story, see John Strype, ed., *Ecclesiastical Memorials, Relating Chiefly to Religion, and the Reformation of It . . . Under King Henry VIII* (Oxford: Clarendon Press,

macy with the queen—whether this claim were true or merely wishful think-
ing—Mark could now establish himself as equal to the gentlemen who stood
accused with him. His story, which ultimately cost him his life, thus bought him
a measure of standing as nothing else could.

Other stories, however, remain untold in this poem. Before the king impris-
ons his faithful servant, Henry Norris, he gives him the opportunity to tell his
story to him personally, with the promise that he would not be harmed should
he tell him "the truth," by which the king presumably means a confession of
guilt. Norris refuses to admit any wrong-doing and is thus summarily locked in
the Tower of London, where he is later joined by several other men who are by
now also suspected of committing adultery with the queen. Things left unsaid
also play a significant role in the scaffold speeches delivered by Anne and her
brother just before their executions, as recorded in this poem. Scaffold speeches
are rather formulaic: prisoners are expected to accept the justice of the law that
condemned them, praise the king, ask others to pray that the monarch be granted
a long life, ask for forgiveness of their sins, and request prayers for their own
soul.[85] This George does, but he omits another crucial component of the stan-
dard speech: namely, he does not admit his guilt in the crime for which he is
charged. This lacuna is noticed by the poet (vv. 1113–1114). Similarly, the poet
makes note of the fact that, in her scaffold speech just before her execution, Anne
refuses to relate to the spectators why she is in this predicament (vv. 1239–1240).
The verb the poet assigns to Anne—"narrer" [to narrate]—is no doubt chosen
to bring home the point that this component is a story left untold. By refusing to
tell their own stories—that is, by maintaining an unconventional and transgres-
sive silence in these circumstances—both Anne and George cast doubt on the
veracity of the tales told by their accusers.

So, are those stories true? This is a far more complex question than one
might think at first blush. Indeed, there are various layers of truth or fiction
that need to be peeled away here. Did the "story" of Anne's infidelity break in
the way that Carle describes, through a conversation between brother and sister?

---

1822), 1.1.436. Kingston's letters were subsequently damaged by fire; they were later
transcribed, with lacunae indicating where they were damaged, in Henry Ellis, *Original
Letters Illustrative of English History*, vol. 2 (London: Harding, Triphook, and Lepard,
1824), 58, for this particular exchange.

[85] For more on the expectations of scaffold speeches, see Nadia Bishai, "'Which
thing had not before been seen': The Rituals and Rhetoric of the Execution of Anne
Boleyn, England's First Criminal Queen" in *The Rituals and Rhetoric of Queenship, Medi-
eval to Early Modern*, ed. Liz Oakley-Brown and Louise J. Wilkinson (Dublin: Four
Courts, 2009), 171–85. Also consult Katherine Royer, *The English Execution Narrative,
1200–1700* (2014; repr. London: Routledge, 2016), 61–84 [ch. entitled "Dressed for
Dying: Contested Visons, Clothes and the Construction of Identity on the Scaffold in
Early Modern England"].

As noted, these circumstances are related only in Carle's poem among contemporary sources, though somewhat later texts — the short stories by Bandello and Belleforest cited above, as well as a French manuscript (dating from the time of Elizabeth I) that partially transcribes Belleforest — give a very similar rendition of events.[86] While some might be tempted, for this reason, to be suspicious of its veracity, at least one historian, namely George Bernard, believes that it is absolutely true. There is no reason to believe, he claims, that Carle invented this episode, for "the details of how Anne's alleged adulteries came to light are . . . incidental" to his purpose; but it is "because of that very marginality that they are the more credible."[87] Nor does Bernard believe there is reason to suspect that Carle (or the French ambassador) was deliberately fed misinformation by highly placed members of the English court, which they would expect him to convey to France. The story does indeed coincide nicely with the "official" version that Henry's right-hand-man and the chief prosecutor in the affair, Thomas Cromwell, tells to the English diplomats stationed in France.[88] Other historians, such as Ives, assert, however, that this coincidence proves merely that Cromwell was himself the ultimate source of the accusations and that Carle was duped into believing this story to be true.[89] But Bernard pointedly wonders why Cromwell would have wanted "to give him *this* story if it were not true."[90] Wouldn't it have been more damning to Anne, he asks, if Cromwell had stated that she had been caught *in flagrante dilecto* rather than resort to this kind of hearsay?

As for the possibility that Carle himself made up the entire episode, with or without Cromwell's help, it is possible to entertain a *tertium quid* that neither Ives nor Bernard has pursued. That is, that Carle learned from some reliable source that one of the queen's ladies — perhaps one whose brother was among

---

[86] For the French manuscript, "A Scandalous Account of K. Henry 8th," see London, British Library, Lansdowne 105, fols. 18r–19v. It is reproduced in Nicholas Pocock, ed., *Records of the Reformation: The Divorce, 1527–1533*, 2 vols. (Oxford: Clarendon, 1870), 2:573–75. See above, Chapter 2, for more on this matter.

[87] Bernard, *Anne Boleyn*, 159–60.

[88] Cromwell writes that the Queen's "abomination both in incontinent living and other offences . . . was so rank and common that the ladies of her privy chamber could not contain it within their breasts. . . . It came to the ears of some of his grace's council, that with their duty to his majesty they could not conceal it from him." See London, British Library, Additional 25114 (hereafter Add. 25114), "Original letters and state papers relating chiefly to the embassies of Stephen Gardiner, Bishop of Winchester, to the courts of Francis I and Charles V: 1527–1545," fols. 160r–161r, here 160r–v, summarized in LP 10.873.

[89] See E. W. Ives, "The Fall of Anne Boleyn Reconsidered," *The English Historical Review* 107.424 (1992): 651–64, here 659: "De Carles is effectively Cromwell with literary embellishments." See also Ives, *Life and Death*, 61: "[Carle's] *Histoire* is, in effect, the government line in translation."

[90] Bernard, *Anne Boleyn*, 158–59; emphasis added.

Henry's close associates—indeed made these accusations, but, for the purpose of adding interest to his story, he made up the high drama of the confrontation between brother and sister, with later texts merely following Carle's lead. Certainly, as we have already noted, the precise wording of the confrontation could not have been known to anyone but the two people involved in this conversation. Moreover, the literary allusion that opens the sister's discourse points to this conversation as being the handiwork of Carle, who embellished it with a sense of dramatic intensity and literary devices of his own design. Indeed, these passages are so dramatic that they appear not unlike a theatrical dialogue that begs to be performed. Thus, while there may have been an accusation originating in Anne's inner circle of ladies-in-waiting, as other texts attest, it may well not have come to light through an encounter between siblings in quite this dramatic a fashion. Yet the scene remains a plausible one and does not contradict any facts known to historians. Indeed, it coincides with the external historical evidence that Mark Smeaton, George Boleyn, and Henry Norris were the earliest to come under suspicion in this affair.

However, even if this dialogue were totally accurate, there is still another layer of truth to be unraveled, and that is precisely this: is the sister herself a reliable narrator? Or was this accusation made, as Carle himself implies, in the heat of the moment to divert attention from her sins to another's? Despite being an admitted sinner, can the sister be a credible witness to someone else's improper behavior? Or is she merely a good storyteller herself? It is tempting to believe that the sister's moral failings deprive her of any credibility, but one must remember that such a tale, if it were thought to be a malicious lie, would have been considered high treason, in light of the laws forbidding negative speech about the queen. Cleverly sidestepping this brotherly admonishment for bad behavior could certainly have achieved by pursuing a less dangerous route. And Mark's corroborating testimony, which she invited her brother to seek, might have gone in yet another direction and have had a far from favorable outcome, from her perspective. The story, if it were not true, would thus have been quite a risky one to tell. From this perspective, it is the very transgressive nature of this speech that makes it more likely to be authentic.

Perhaps a more intriguing possibility to consider here is that the sister's story was not a deliberate fabrication but, rather, a misreading of signs that were ultimately ambiguous. Bernard himself raises this possibility, saying that no one, not even one of Anne's ladies, would have actually witnessed illicit sexual intercourse between the queen and one of her accused lovers.[91] Instead, what many may have seen is simply a series of unusual comings and goings in the queen's chamber at odd times. The lady in question, then, has merely drawn inferences from these signs that she herself thought were reasonable and presented them to her brother

---

[91] Bernard, *Anne Boleyn*, 191.

as actual facts. If this were the case, we once again find ourselves in a middle ground between truth and fiction.

Looking at Carle's poem more broadly, one might say that there is much here that points to reading and misreading signs as a structuring principle of the text. As noted above, the very encounter between the siblings begins by invoking the presence of a sign of dissolute behavior—and one that is ultimately unnamed and thus ambiguous. So there is a sense in which that whole episode serves as a cautionary tale regarding the interpretation of signs that may or may not lead to the truth. Carle's interest in reading signs may well be related to his primary role as a diplomat, for as Hampton again reminds us, there is a "heavily semiotic nature" in diplomacy itself, manifested in "its investment in the production and interpretation of signs," such that "diplomatic actions are understood as symbolic actions. Diplomatic missions are, among other things, mechanisms for producing signification, textual operations in a symbolic drama or mini-narrative."[92]

It is little wonder, then, that elsewhere in the poem, the diplomat Carle alludes to several other "signs" whose interpretation—that is, the story they generate—is problematic. Of course, on the one hand, there are conventional signs with unequivocal meaning, such as the ceremonial axe that is turned away from the defendants before and during the trial but that is abruptly turned towards them if they are condemned. While this sign might require certain information or explanations in order to be interpreted properly—especially by foreigners who would not be familiar with this ritual of English law—it is never ambiguous and can never be misinterpreted by one in the know. On the other hand, Carle's text is replete with other signs that are inherently ambiguous and whose interpretation can be correctly judged perhaps only in hindsight. Here one thinks of Carle's reference to signs that should have forewarned Anne of the tragedy about to befall her—signs, Carle says, that came from God as an invitation to repentance —but that she ignored to her peril: namely, a fire that broke out in her chambers and, more tragically, a miscarriage that she suffered upon hearing the news that Henry had taken a serious fall from his horse.

The fire in Anne's chambers—for which there is no surviving independent corroborating evidence—works particularly well as a symbolic image, for it clearly suggests danger, destruction, and waste. Although Carle does not describe the damage done by this fire, any reader could easily imagine a scene of ruined finery, turned to ashes and dust, a reminder of the vanity of things of this world, which do not endure.[93] Fire is also a conventional symbol for what is evil or dia-

---

[92] Hampton, *Fictions*, 6.

[93] The damage to finery near the queen's bed is described in a passage of Hilary Mantel's *Bring up the Bodies*, which is clearly inspired by Carle's story. But Mantel chiefly uses this incident to cast suspicion on Anne by insinuating that the fire was started by a candle left burning by a night-time visitor to the queen's chambers. See, on this point, Hilary Mantel, *Bring up the Bodies* (2012; repr. New York: Picador, 2015), 157–59.

bolical, and, shortly after this passage, Carle uses the image again to describe Anne's sinful inclinations as a fire that grows ever stronger (vv. 332–334). Ultimately, of course, fire would be associated with the judicial execution of women, and, indeed, the word reappears in v. 987, where Carle reports that Anne could face a fiery death.[94] So, had Anne known how to interpret this portentous sign, Carle implies, she might have been able to repent from her sins, and this conversion, or turning toward God, would have resulted in a diversion from the tragic course on which she had embarked, ultimately leading to a far different outcome. But Anne—unlike the poet himself (who admittedly benefits from hindsight)—fails to read signs properly and, consequently, follows her road to perdition.

There is also another, more intriguing, and quite unlikely reader of signs in the story: the horse that the accused courtier Norris had customarily (and successfully) used in the jousts that Henry often arranged as court entertainment. As Norris prepared to engage in the May Day tournament (which Henry held despite the fact that Mark had already been imprisoned in the Tower), his trusty horse recoiled and refused to take to the list. In Carle's presentation of this scene, this isn't just a matter of an unruly animal, spooked, as horses often are, by random noises or unusual sights. Instead, Carle attributes to the horse some sixth sense, a way of knowing what has happened and what will happen to his unfortunate rider. That is, Carle makes it appear that this horse can read signs of trouble that are not apparent to the poor men—and to Anne—who are all oblivious to their coming demise. Carle is clear on these points. Anne, he says, "doesn't realize just how unfortunate she was / In that the king had been made aware of the secret / Of the whole range of her shameful conduct" (vv. 466–468). And the accused men, he later adds, "did not know / The violent end to which they were destined" (vv. 523–524). In other words, Anne and her alleged lovers have not picked up on signs of trouble—they have not heard or refused to hear the stories told about them by others at the court—and in this they are less proficient readers than Norris's horse, who indeed "knows" that his master's story will end tragically.

Carle does not, of course, explain how this horse "knows" the story of Norris's imminent danger. Traditionally, horses and their riders have been depicted in literature as "two beings in a close connection to each other" who together demonstrate what can be described as an empathetic harmony.[95] This close relationship could explain how Norris's horse might be able to read signs of danger that relate specifically to his master's well-being. Moreover, in some early modern texts, such as Ludovico Ariosto's romance epic, *Orlando furioso*, horses have been endowed with intellect, agency, and self-awareness and can engage "in

---

[94] For more on burning as a traditional sentence for women, see above, Chapter 2.

[95] Juliana Schiesari, "Pedagogy and the Art of Dressage in the Italian Renaissance," in *Animals and Early Modern Identity*, ed. Pia F. Cuneo (Farnham, UK: Ashgate, 2014), 375–89, here 377.

hypothetical reasoning."[96] From this perspective, perhaps, Norris's horse may be attempting to communicate the dangers he perceives through his reasoned interpretation of signs in an effort to save his master's life. But there is more here than just this—impressive though it might be—in Carle's unique account of this horse's refusal to take to the list: for Carle suggests that this horse is a *prescient* animal who can, in some sense, prophesy about events to come.[97] There are very few examples of prescient horses in early modern literature. Perhaps the closest is the horse in Shakespeare's *Richard III* (3.4), which stumbles when in sight of the Tower of London, sensing the danger that will be faced by its rider, who was to be beheaded that morning, a detail that was actually contained in Thomas More's version of the story written around 1513.[98] As is the case in Carle's poem, the significance of the horse's behavior can be ascertained by other characters only in hindsight and only after ill fortune has struck. But the poet—who knows how the story will end—can certainly use such details in shaping his text in order to give a sense of impending doom that hangs in the air. It is probably not coincidental that Carle is our only source for this detail concerning Norris's horse as well as the fire in Anne's chambers, both of which are presented as portents or signs. It is quite possible—perhaps even likely—that both details are fictions, the products of Carle's imaginative poetic license that he constructed in order to fill his poem with "truth" of another kind. But even if they were factually based, it is Carle who has imbued these otherwise random events with meaning.

Norris's horse, as a prescient creature, is related to other references to prophecy found in Carle's text. Certainly, prognostication was rampant in the sixteenth century, the very epoch that saw the publication of the prophecies of Michel de Nostredame (more commonly known as "Nostradamus") in 1555. In England, prophetic pronouncements were made regarding the reign of Henry VIII virtually from its inception.[99] One of the early executions of Henry's reign, that of

---

[96] See, on this point, Bruce Thomas Boehrer, *Animal Characters: Nonhuman Beings in Early Modern Literature* (Philadelphia: University of Pennsylvania Press, 2010), 29–30.

[97] A view of animal foreknowledge as a product of "animals' senses, not their powers of reason" was developed by Sir Kenelm Digby in *Two Treatises* (1644); see, on this point, Erica Fudge, *Brutal Reasoning: Animals, Rationality, and Humanity in Early Modern England* (Ithaca, NY: Cornell University Press, 2006), 183.

[98] See Thomas More's *History of King Richard III*, ed. J. Rawson Lumby (Cambridge: Cambridge University Press, 1883), 49: "Certain is it also that in the riding toward the Tower, the same morning in which he was beheaded, [Lord Hastings's] horse twice or thrice stumbled with him almost to the falling; which thing albeit each man wot well daily happeneth to them in whom no such mischance is toward, yet hath it been, of an old rite and custom, observed as a token often times notably foregoing some great misfortune." I am grateful to Rachel Hile for this reference.

[99] For an overview of political prophecies at this time, see Jansen, *Dangerous Talk*, as well as Tim Thornton, *Prophecy, Politics and the People in Early Modern England* (Woodbridge, UK: Boydell, 2006).

Edward Stafford, the third Duke of Buckingham, came about in 1521 precisely because the duke had allegedly listened to the political prophecies of Nicholas Hopkins (who was executed along with him), which proclaimed that the king would die without an heir.[100] Another well-known seer, Elizabeth Barton, often called "The Holy Maid of Kent," was put to death in 1534 for prophesying that Henry would be subject to the "vengeance of God" should he go forward with his marriage to Anne Boleyn.[101] Indeed, there were many prophecies that purported to concern Anne Boleyn in particular, some of which predicted her demise, others of which foresaw general political and religious upheaval coming about as a result of her elevation as queen.[102] Anne herself was said to have been aware of (but not afraid of) a prophecy that a queen of England was to be burned alive, a fact that was remembered by both Chapuys and the Imperial ambassador to Rome, Pedro Ortiz, in their dispatches.[103] And Chapuys also related that Cromwell himself was impelled to investigate the rumors of Anne's adultery and treasonous behavior toward the king because he remembered that there was a prognostication made in Flanders "threatening the king with a conspiracy of those who were nearest his person."[104] It is no wonder, then, that Carle ends his poem with a reference to the English people's belief that the incredible events of May 1536 were the fulfillment of "some prophecy / That they hold here to be true" and that "several great matters are still predicted" (vv. 1309–1311, 1315). While Carle expresses some skepticism about these predictions, saying that he will believe them when he sees them (v. 1317), he is nevertheless inclined to believe, along with the English people, that this was truly "the year of wonders" (1320). Carle's final verses, then, bear witness to the way that some English people reacted to the events of May 1536 as in keeping with predictions that had

---

[100] For more on this prophecy and execution, see Howard Dobin, *Merlin's Disciples: Prophecy, Poetry, and Power in Renaissance England* (Stanford: Stanford University Press, 1990), 1–2.

[101] See especially Jansen, *Dangerous Talk*, 45–49, for more on this prophecy.

[102] See, for example, Jansen, *Dangerous Talk*, 67–68, regarding the "Bull prophecy" ("When this cow [i.e., Henry] rideth the bull [i.e., Anne Boleyn, or "Bullen," whose family coat of arms features a bull] / Then, priest, beware thy skull"), which was interpreted as a prediction of religious upheaval. For predictions of Anne's demise, including the "H, A, K" drawing depicting a headless queen, see Sharon L. Jansen, *Political Protest and Prophecy under Henry VIII* (Woodbridge, UK: Boydell, 1991), 162; Jansen, *Dangerous Talk*, 69–70; and Thornton, *Prophecy*, 20–21.

[103] For Chapuys's letter to Granvelle stating that Anne herself had often mentioned that there was a prophecy that a queen of England was to be burned, but that she paid it no heed in order to demonstrate her great love to the king, see LP 10.909 and CSP, Spain, 5, pt. 2 (1536–1538), no. 54. For the letter of Pedro Ortiz regarding the prediction that Anne would be burned, see Add. 28588, fols. 284r–285r, here 284v, summarized in LP 10.947.

[104] See Chapuys's letter, summarized in LP 10.1069.

been made over the course of Henry's reign and, in particular, in the years fol-
lowing his courtship of and marriage to Anne Boleyn.

## Shaping Anne's Story: Models and Intertexts

Anne's demise—and indeed the entire plot of this narrative poem—may be
described as "predictable" in another way: in some sense, it was prefigured in
previous literary texts that served as models for Carle to follow in shaping his
story. These intertexts range from popular romances (e.g., the stories of Guine-
vere and Griselda) to biblical episodes (e.g., the story of Susanna and the Elders
and of Christ's passion). In addition to precise texts that offer close thematic or
verbal similarities to Carle's poem, there are also what might be called generic
models that provide structural parallels to *The Story of the Death of Anne Boleyn*,
even when no particular instantiation of a literary tradition, or model text, is
meant to be recalled.

One possible generic parallel or model that was particularly popular at this
time is that of the frame narrative (or "story within a story") as exemplified by
Giovanni Boccaccio's *Decameron*,[105] Geoffrey Chaucer's *Canterbury Tales*,[106] and
Marguerite de Navarre's *Heptaméron*[107] (though this last was not published until
well after Carle's poem was written). In these texts, multiple storytellers relate
their tales, all within an overarching frame (for example, that of the pilgrimage
to Canterbury). These texts are characterized by their polyvocality (or, "polyph-
ony," as one critical assessment suggests).[108] The purpose of the multi-voiced
storytelling in these collections of tales may be simply to furnish amusement or
diversion among speakers engaged in a (sometimes arduous, sometimes boring)
common enterprise, such as Chaucer's pilgrimage; but this storytelling also gen-
erally has a more serious (often, moral) purpose. While Carle does not structure
his poem in exactly this fashion, devising an artificial frame, he nevertheless
allows multiple characters to recount their own tales within the framework of his
own letter. Most notable of these tales, as discussed above, is that of the sister's

---

[105] See Giovanni Boccaccio, *Il Decameron*, ed. Charles S. Singleton, 2 vols. (Bari:
Laterza, 1955), for an Italian edition; for an English version, consult Giovanni Boccaccio,
*The Decameron: A New Translation, Contexts, Criticism*, ed. and trans. Wayne A. Rebhorn
(New York: Norton, 2016).

[106] See Geoffrey Chaucer, *The Canterbury Tales*, ed. Jill Mann (London: Penguin,
2005).

[107] See Marguerite de Navarre, *L'Heptaméron*, ed. Michel François (Paris: Garnier,
1967), for the French edition; for an English version consult Marguerite de Navarre, *The
Heptameron*, trans. P. A. Chilton (New York: Penguin, 1984).

[108] See Lisa Neal and Steven Rendall, "Polyphonic Narrative in Early Modern
France: A Question of Literary History," *Romanic Review* 87 (1996): 297–306.

revelation of Anne's adulteries to her brother and, in turn, that brother's recounting of the story to the king. As in other frame narratives, questions of authority and veracity are pertinent in assessing the scandalous stories that swirl around Anne. Carle, then, may well have drawn from the techniques of these frame narratives in his depiction of an English court in which rumors and gossip abound.

Another significant generic connection may be seen through the way in which Carle's narration recalls the content, scope, and method of a morality tale. To this end, the poem can be likened to the genre known as *de casibus* tragedy, that is, a work retelling the fall of great men or women, in the manner of the famous fourteenth-century Italian writer Boccaccio's collection of tales entitled *De casibus virorum illustrium*.[109] Certainly, like many verse histories of the late Middle Ages and early modern period, Carle's poem demonstrates "a preoccupation with themes of chance, change, and destiny, which in turn provoke moral [or] philosophical . . . reflections";[110] it is ultimately "a moral lesson to display God's hand in determining the affairs of man."[111] But Carle's concern here is the rise and fall not of a collective people (as might be seen in a written history) but, instead, of individuals and, indeed, of one particular individual, Anne Boleyn. Carle thus incorporates aspects of *de casibus* tragedy into his poem to use as a lens through which to produce what can truly be called the first biography of Anne Boleyn. Indeed, to this end, Carle's work conforms to the structure of virtually all conventional biographies that, unlike most of their contemporary counterparts (as Stanley Fish has argued in his critique of modern biographical narrative), made ready use of "master narrative models," including the "providential model . . . and the wheel of fortune model" that provided meaning behind disparate details within their stories.[112] Instead of recounting an array of discrete facts, the way an ambassador's secretary might typically do in an ordinary dispatch, Carle structures his poem in such a way as to make sense of and give shape to the astounding events unfolding before his eyes.

Carle's concern with matters of morality and theology is indeed quite evident from the start. Two related themes—those of *vanitas* and the mutability

---

[109] For this text see Boccaccio, *De casibus illustrium virorum*, ed. Louis Brewer Hall (Gainesville, FL: Scholar's Facsimiles and Reprints, 1962).

[110] Armstrong and Kay, *Knowing Poetry*, 50.

[111] Lacey Baldwin Smith, *Anne Boleyn: The Queen of Controversy, A Biographical Essay* (2013; repr. Stroud: Amberley, 2014), 13. The author is here speaking of the early modern conception of history in general and not in particular about Carle's text.

[112] See Stanley Fish, "Just Published: Minutiae Without Meaning," *The New York Times*, 7 September 1999, available at http://www.writing.upenn.edu/~afilreis/88v/fish-biography.html. For a critique of Fish's piece, see Shirley A. Leckie, "Biography Matters: Why Historians Need Well-Crafted Biographies More than Ever," in *Writing Biography: Historians and Their Craft*, ed. Lloyd E. Ambrosius (Lincoln: University of Nebraska Press, 2004), 1–26.

of fortune (or "the wheel of fortune" alluded to by Fish)—are introduced in the very prologue of the poem, specifically in vv. 11–14 and 16–24. Although both of these themes are prominent in classical literature, there is no doubt that Carle here understands them in a profoundly Christian way. Carle comments, in these verses, on the transformation in this story's outline from "a joyous and fine comedy" to "a sad tragedy." This remark has little to do with the literary meaning of these terms and much to do with Carle's deeply held conviction regarding the continuous mutation of all earthly things: nothing endures in its same shape but, rather, all things eventually become their opposites. The movement described here is certainly that of the Wheel of Fortune, a favorite image of medieval and early modern writers, popularized by the early Christian writer Boethius in his *Consolation of Philosophy*: it is a figure for the belief that those at the peak of good fortune might eventually find themselves at the bottom of despair.[113] While Carle states explicitly (vv. 13–14) that he would have preferred that "the sad conclusion of this play / Were in keeping with its beginning"—that is, that the story would have ended, as classical comedies do, with marriages and births and renewed hope embodied in succeeding generations—he knows that the story of Anne Boleyn is ultimately a tragedy, one that ends with the death of this queen and five men accused with her. The image of fortune's wheel reappears in vv. 275–276, where Carle attempts to explain the cause of Anne's "adverse *fortune*, / Which promptly *brought her down from great heights*." This is Carle's most explicit depiction of the rise and fall of fortune's wheel.

It is important to note, however, that Carle does not really regard Anne's fate to be determined by a capricious goddess Fortuna, as classical writers might have described it. Rather, Carle talks about Anne's ability to choose her own path, to make a free choice regarding her own actions. This is especially evident in the section of the poem that deals with the signs that portend Anne's demise: for Carle makes it clear that these signs were sent by God *to warn her* that she was endangering her very soul, but that she could amend her ways and turn back towards God in an act of repentance (vv. 294–304), which she freely chooses not to do. Path imagery is particularly pertinent in this regard. As early as vv. 81–84, Carle describes Anne as not following the path of virtue shown to her by her "prudent mistress":

> Heureuse estoit, mais encor plus heureuse
> S'elle eust suyuy la voye vertueuse
> Et du chemin eust sceut tenir l'addresse
> Que luy monstroit sa prudente maistresse.

---

[113] For an English translation of that text, see Boethius, *The Consolation of Philosophy*, trans. Victor E. Watts (1969; repr. London: Penguin, 1999). See especially Bk. 2.1 for this image.

> [Happy was she, but happier still would she have been
> If she had followed the virtuous way
> And if she had been able to stay the course
> On the path that her prudent mistress had shown her.]

Here, Carle pronounces Anne "happy," an epithet that she in fact had appropriated for herself in the motto she adopted, "The Most Happy," soon after her coronation.[114] Carle may well be referring to this motto in these verses; but he is even more likely to be alluding to the classical and biblical commonplace "Happy the One" (or "Blessed is the One"), which is found in a host of prior texts, including Horace's *Odes*, the Old Testament books of Job and Proverbs, and, of course, the Beatitudes found in the Gospel of Matthew, all of which attempt to teach the path of true happiness and wisdom. In his particular pairing of the "happy the one" motif with path imagery, Carle is most clearly echoing the words of Psalm 1:1: "Happy are those who do not follow the advice of the wicked, or take the path that sinners tread."[115] Anne's straying from the straight and narrow path showed to her by her royal mistress, Queen Claude of France, whom she served as a lady-in-waiting, does not bode well, Carle implies, for, as Psalm 1 continues, "the way of the wicked will perish" (Psalm 1:6).[116] Instead of following the linear road to happiness, Anne allows the circular movement of Fortune's wheel to come into play, which thus shapes the outcome of this story.

Later in the poem, Carle pairs the theme of inconstant fortune with that of *vanitas*, or the emptiness and worthlessness of life's pleasures. That theme can be traced, in the Judeo-Christian tradition, to the biblical book of Ecclesiastes, which begins with the well-known phrase, "Vanity of vanities! All is vanity" [*Vanitas vanitatum et omnia vanitas*, Ecclesiastes 1:2]. Carle couples the theme of the inconstancy of fortune with that of *vanitas* in a passage where he attempts to explain how Henry's passion for Anne gradually cooled. First, in vv. 283–284, Carle acknowledges that one can attribute this change to "the ordinary reason / Of inconstant and mutable fortune." But he quickly adds a second possibility: that God sometimes "wants to show us / That great honors and wealth are but wind" (vv. 285–286). In other words, earthly treasures are as ephemeral and insubstantial as air. Indeed, this is the very definition of the Hebrew word "hevel," found in Ecclesiastes and translated in the Latin Vulgate as "vanitas": it is a mist, a vapor,

---

[114] This motto encircles a portrait medal of Anne, dating from 1534, a surviving but damaged example of which is found at the British Museum.

[115] Vulg.: "Beatus vir qui non abiit in consilio impiorum, et in via peccatorum non stetit."

[116] Vulg. "Et iter impiorum peribit." For more on Claude de France's reputation as an honorable and virtuous woman, see "The Women of the Court of Francis I: Wives and Mistresses, Sister and Mother," in Kathleen Wellman, *Queens and Mistresses of Renaissance France* (New Haven: Yale University Press, 2013), 111–83, especially 120–24.

or smoke that cannot be grasped or kept.[117] A similar pairing of the *vanitas* and mutability of fortune themes occurs at the very center of the text, in vv. 663–664, in a passage where Anne realizes that "it is no longer the moment to rest upon / The vain hope of this changeable world" and now turns towards God. For Carle, then, these two themes are virtually inseparable and represent the core of the moral lesson he wishes to impart to his audience via this tragic tale.

Beyond the *de casibus* model, there are other specific intertexts that appear to have informed Carle's telling of this tragedy. Perhaps the most significant of these is a tale that stems not from the Bible but from the world of Arthurian romance: the story of the adulterous love between Queen Guinevere and Sir Lancelot, the most favored knight of her husband, King Arthur. The love of Lancelot and Guinevere was outlined in the long, anonymous French prose text commonly referred to as the "Lancelot-Grail" or "Vulgate Cycle." That work is divided into multiple parts, including the prose *Lancelot* (which recounts the earlier days of Lancelot and his love for Guinevere). The final section of the cycle —entitled *La Mort le roi Artu*, which tells of the disastrous consequences of this illicit love—was later reworked for an English audience by Sir Thomas Malory in his fifteenth-century *Morte D'Arthur*. In both its English and French forms, the story enjoyed considerable popularity well into the sixteenth century. Indeed, there is evidence to suggest that Henry himself owned a luxurious French manuscript version of the prose *Lancelot*.[118] A second old-French tale, that of the betrayal of King Marc by his wife Iseut (or Isolde) and her lover, Tristan, provides a further medieval literary model for the queen caught in adultery.[119] For Carle,

---

[117] For more on this topos, including a discussion of the etymology of this word, see Nadia Cernogora, "L'Écriture de la vanité chez les poètes français de l'automne de la Renaissance: Du *memento mori* aux vertiges d'une poétique du vain," *Littératures classiques* 56 (2005): 199–217. For scriptural use of wind as a symbol of delusion and disappointment, see Isaiah 26:18 and 41:29.

[118] For more on the popularity of Arthurian romances at Henry's court, see James P. Carley, *The Books of King Henry VIII and His Wives* (London: The British Library, 2004), 36, which discusses a copy of the prose *Lancelot* apparently catalogued as part of the royal collection housed at Richmond Palace in 1535 (now London, British Library, Royal MS 20. D. IV). Malory's version was printed by William Caxton in 1485 and also enjoyed wide circulation in Tudor society. For more on this point, see Ruth Lexton, "Reading the Adulterous/Treasonous Queen in Early Modern England: Malory's Guinevere and Anne Boleyn," *Exemplaria* 27 (2015): 222–41.

[119] For more on this story and its relationship to the tales of King Arthur, see Reginald Hyatte, "Arthur as Marc's and Tristan's Double in the French *Tristan* Fragments by Béroul and Thomas" in *King Arthur Through the Ages*, ed. Valerie M. Lagorio and Mildred Leake Day, 2 vols. (New York: Garland, 1990), 1:110–26. For a general study of queenship and adultery in medieval romances, see Peggy McCracken, *The Romance of Adultery: Queenship and Sexual Transgression in Old French Literature* (Philadelphia: University of Pennsylvania Press, 1998). McCracken makes the point that adulterous queens,

the similarities between these stories (especially that of Guinevere's love for his namesake Lancelot) and the events of May 1536 must have seemed uncanny. It would be quite easy and inviting, then, for the poet to shape his story using elements from these medieval tales that would have been very familiar to his French audience back home. As Ruth Lexton has argued, "romance tropes provided patterns of interpretation for contemporaries to make sense of what was most likely a rapid and terrifying series of events."[120] Indeed, she further posits that the relevance of the story of Guinevere to Anne's downfall was not only widely perceived by witnesses to this incredible event but also, perhaps, deliberately used by its judicial architects, for "the conceptual groundwork for killing a queen through an accusation of treasonous adultery lay not in legal or historical precedent, but in habits of reading inculcated by late medieval and early modern romance."[121] Unwittingly or not, actors in this astounding drama played out their parts in much the same way that their literary predecessors did, making it only natural for witnesses such as Carle to draw from this tradition in telling this tale.

Certainly, there is no doubt that Henry's court, with its jousts and other nods to chivalry, was itself modeled, in part, on tales from King Arthur, the mythical English king who had so fascinated Henry's father. As will be remembered, Henry VII had arranged for his first son—significantly named Arthur—to be born in Winchester, a city at the time thought to have been associated with the site of Camelot.[122] When Henry VIII inherited the throne, he, too, actively shaped his court according to this model and wished to revive the age of Camelot in his own reign.[123] Still, it is supremely ironic that Henry would be made to follow King Arthur's model quite so far, including playing the role of the cuckolded husband who is yet king.

In his retelling of this story, Carle frequently describes the sights, sounds, pleasures, and behaviors associated with the late medieval or early modern court, beginning with Anne's "training" in courtly pastimes—singing, dancing, conversation, and music (vv. 55–57)—that she learned in the French court while serving Queen Claude of France. Later, he alludes to other courtly activities arranged to honor Anne upon her coronation, including dances, games, hunts, and tournaments (vv. 117–125). Through these early verses (which are certainly irrelevant in a diplomatic dispatch intended to share breaking news about a queen's death), Carle succeeds in reminding his readers that his real-life characters are acting out

---

such as Guinevere and Isolde, are often also portrayed as barren. While Anne was certainly not childless, her inability to produce a male heir has often been cited as one of the key reasons behind her downfall. See also Lexton, "Reading," 233.

[120] Lexton, "Reading," 232–33.

[121] Lexton, "Reading," 223.

[122] See above, Chapter 2, for more on this point.

[123] See, on this point, David Starkey, "King Henry and King Arthur," *Arthurian Literature* 16 (1998): 171–96 (issue edited by James P. Carley and Felicity Riddy).

their parts in a world that could be mistaken for the fictional realm of Arthurian romance, where courtly love and feats of chivalry abound.[124]

Carle draws from Arthurian romance (and other courtly literature, including lyric poetry) particularly in the way he describes his main characters. For example, in explaining Anne's attractiveness, Carle indicates that her allure is a product of her innate gifts coupled with her learned skills (vv. 69–70). He states that one particularly intriguing combination of natural good looks and acquired facility was her ability to excite men simply through the power of her eyes (vv. 62–68). Now, medieval and early modern literature abounds with examples of love that is incited suddenly and irresistibly by a lady simply bestowing a glance upon a hapless male, who is henceforth that lady's obedient servant.[125] Having become adept at this practice, as soon as she returns to England, Anne casts her glance upon the king himself, who is now in her thrall. Indeed, Henry will continue to play the role of the powerless courtly lover or suitor for her attention—and not that of "a king, or a lord, or a husband" (v. 131)—well into his marriage. Through that telling verse, Carle makes clear the extent to which the balance of power in this relationship, as was often the case in medieval romances, has so greatly shifted that a normally powerful king has relinquished all rights of control (be it political, social, or sexual) in favor of his beloved.

The French poet-secretary again looks towards Arthurian romance in his particular depiction of how Anne's adultery became known to Henry and of how Henry reacts towards the "knights" who have betrayed him.[126] In the medieval tale, five knights (all of them brothers) come to learn of Lancelot's betrayal with Guinevere. They argue among themselves regarding whether or not to inform the king that Lancelot has dishonored him. When asked point blank by the king what they were arguing about, two of the five, knowing that such information would tear the kingdom apart, choose to leave the court rather than give Arthur such shocking news, which one brother has denounced as "the worst gossip and

---

[124] For an argument that "the downfall of Anne Boleyn illustrates the persistence of medieval stereotypes, as if the unhappy Queen . . . was also betrayed by the superficial chivalry of Henry's reign," see Camille Naish, *Death Comes to the Maiden: Sex and Execution 1431–1933* (London: Routledge, 1991), 49.

[125] For more on this tradition through the sixteenth century, see Lance K. Donaldson-Evans, *Love's Fatal Glance: A Study of Eye Imagery in the Poets of the "École Lyonnaise"* (University, MS: Romance Monographs, 1980).

[126] As mentioned above, the term "knights" is not used by Carle himself but it is found repeatedly in the French marginalia of the manuscript found in the library of Soissons, thus suggesting that at least some contemporary readers saw an inherent analogy between Henry's court and the medieval world of Arthurian romance. See Chapter 4 above, "Versions of the Text," for more information about the Soissons manuscript. Lexton likewise draws these parallels between Carle's tale and the story of Guinevere, though she focuses on its retelling in Malory's "Slander and Strife" episode rather than on the original Old French narrative. On this matter, see Lexton, "Reading," 236–37.

lies imaginable.”[127] The three brothers who remain go to great lengths to appear reluctant to tell their story, insofar as this denunciation is preceded by a lengthy preamble and has to be drawn from the accusers at the point of a sword. But it is fairly clear that, for at least one of the three accusers, this reluctance is a mere charade and that he had every intention of revealing the adulterous affair despite the horrors that are bound to ensue.

Likewise in Carle’s story, it is three of Henry’s most trusted advisors who break the news to the king. Here the accusation is not made lightly, for the main accuser (that is, the brother of the wayward lady-in-waiting) is shown to have agonized over the decision whether or not to inform the king about what he has heard from his sister (vv. 379–398). Notably, in both Carle’s narration and in the Arthurian romance, the accusers insist that the dreaded accusation is made out of loyalty to the king:

| *The Story of the Death of Anne Boleyn* | *The Death of Arthur* |
|---|---|
| “Si ce n’estoit, Sire, que vous nous estes Beaucoup plus cher que noz biens & noz testes . . . Iamais n’eussons prins ceste hardiesse Vous desclairer ce que vostre honneur presse.” <br><br> [“If it were not, Sire, that you are much dearer to us Than our own goods and our own heads . . . We would never have taken this bold step To declare openly to you something that lies heavy against your honor”] (vv. 403–404 and 409–410) | “Sire,” fet Mordret, “nos le vos avons celé tant comme nos poïsmes; mes or couvient que la verité soit seüe et que nous le vous dions; et de tant comme nous le vous avons celé, si avons nous vers vous esté parjuré et desloial; or nous en aquitons. Si vous disons certeinnement qu’il est einsi.”[128] <br><br> [“Sir,” said Mordred, “we’ve concealed this from you as long as we could; but now the truth must be known, and we must tell it; and by hiding it from you for so long, we’ve been deceitful and disloyal to you. Now we’re doing our duty. And we assure you that it’s the truth.”][129] |

And yet, while there are certainly similarities between these two scenes, there is a significant difference as well. Whereas Mordred characterizes his previous

---

[127] *Lancelot-Grail: The Old French Arthurian Vulgate and Post-Vulgate in Translation,* vol. 4: *The Death of Arthur,* trans. Norris J. Lacy (New York: Garland, 1995), 119.

[128] *La Mort le roi Artu, roman du XIIIᵉ siècle,* ed. Jean Frappier (Geneva: Droz, 1964), 109–10.

[129] *The Death of Arthur,* 119.

*silence* as an act of treachery, the brother in Carle's poem knows that it is *in speaking* that he may indeed be accused of treason and, consequently, lose his wealth and his head, thanks to the series of laws that Henry and his Parliament have passed that prohibit slander of the queen (vv. 386–388).

Additionally, there are very close verbal similarities between the way in which Carle describes Henry's comportment upon receiving the news of his wife's adultery and the analogous scene in *La Mort le roi Artu*:

| *The Story of the Death of Anne of Boleyn* | *The Death of Arthur* |
|---|---|
| De ce recit nouueau & bien estrange<br>Le roy s'estonne *& la couleur luy change*<br>Et *demeura en son esprit doubteux*<br>D'auoir ouy vn propos si honteux.<br>Mais à la fin parlant aux gentilz-<br>  hommes<br>Leur dit ainsi: . . .<br>"En ce m'auez faict seruice aggreable.<br>Mais *s'il aduient que ne soit veritable*<br>*Votre rapport*, ce que croire ne veux,<br>Peine de mort vous aurez en lieu d'eux." | *Quant li rois entent ceste parole, si*<br>*mue couleur et devint pales*, et dist:<br>*"Ce sont merveilles."* Lors commence<br>a penser et ne dit mot d'une grant<br>piece. . . . De ceste chose est li rois<br>pensis et dolenz et tant a malese qu'il<br>ne set qu'il doie fere; et toutevoies<br>quant il parole, si dit: "Se voz onques<br>m'amastes, fetes tant que vous les<br>preigniez prouvez. . . ."[130] |
| [By this unheard of and quite out-<br>  landish tale,<br>The king is astounded, *and his color*<br>  *changes*,<br>And he *remained perplexed* in spirit<br>From having heard such shameful talk.<br>But in the end, speaking to these<br>  gentlemen,<br>He says to them: . . .<br>"In this you have done me a fine<br>  service.<br>But, *if it should happen that your report*<br>*Isn't true, which I wouldn't want to*<br>  *believe* to be the case,<br>You, instead of them, shall suffer pain<br>  of death."]<br>           (vv. 449–454, 459–462) | [When the king heard these words,<br>*he changed color and became pale* and<br>said: *"I can't believe this!"* Then he<br>became pensive and said nothing for<br>a long time. . . . The king was so *pen-*<br>*sive and sad and disturbed* by this that<br>he did not know what to do. Never-<br>theless, when he spoke, he said, "If<br>you ever loved me, do whatever you<br>must to catch them in the act. . . ."][131] |

---

[130] *La Mort le roi Artu*, 109–10.
[131] *The Death of Arthur*, 119.

In both cases, the king's reaction is physically manifested by a change in color on his face, though in Carle's version this sign is somewhat ambiguous. Does Henry blanch in horror, or blush in shame, or, indeed, redden in anger? Carle ultimately leaves this to his reader to interpret. Moreover, the brother's tale, like that of Arthur's knights, further engenders pensive silence and an expressed concern regarding the believability of the charges. Finally, in both instances, these immediate reactions are followed by orders (explicit or implicit) to investigate the matter so that the accusations can be verified.

In the scene depicting the May Day joust, itself another reminiscence of Arthurian romance that was appropriated by Henry in his own court, the power of Anne's glance comes into play again.[132] Anne, Carle reveals, "sat up high and watched / The combatants and often directed / Her sweet glances towards each of them, / To encourage them to be the victor" (vv. 517–520). The principal combatants at this joust, Carle has already informed his readers, were precisely the men who were revealed to be her lovers: her brother, George, and the king's "most beloved" servant, Henry Norris (who, in this respect, is most like Lancelot, highly favored by Arthur). When Henry accosts Norris after the joust, offering him leniency should he confess to having been Anne's lover, Norris responds as would a knight of Arthur's realm: he attempts to invoke the right of *judicium Dei*, that is, a judicial duel whereby, with the help of Divine Providence, the accused, if he wins, would be known to be clear of all wrong-doing. Norris is denied this opportunity, in much the same way as Tristan is prevented from partaking in this legal ritual in lieu of a trial by that other king of French courtly romance, Marc.[133]

Moreover, the sentence imposed on the queen who has been found guilty, in both cases, by a council of lords (with the approval of the king himself) is also similar: Guinevere is to be burned, while Anne is to suffer either by fire or by beheading at the pleasure of the king. At their respective executions, crowds of spectators take pity on the condemned queen, who, despite her anguish, appears more beautiful than ever:

---

[132] For more on the May Day joust as part of a "chivalric revival at the Yorkist court," see Starkey, "King Henry and King Arthur," 189–90.

[133] See *Tristan et Yseut*, ed. J. C. Payen (Paris: Garnier, 1974); the passage in question is found in "Le Tristan de Béroul," vv. 780–793. For more on Marc's refusal to grant Tristan the right of *judicium Dei*, see Hyatte, "Arthur as Marc's and Tristan's Double," 117 and 121.

| The Story of the Death of Anne Boleyn | The Death of Arthur |
|---|---|
| . . . sa couleur & sa face estoit telle *Que ne fut onc de tous veue si belle.* . . . Ce neantmoins, qui la veult regarder Par grand pitié ne scauroit garder De se douloir [et] . . . [les] *assistans . . . ne pouuoient tenir Leurs pleurs* . . . | *Si estoit si bele dame et si avenanz qu'en tout le monde ne trouast l'en si bele ne si avenant* de son aage. . . . Quant . . . cil de la cité la virent venir, lors oïssiez genz crier de toutes parz: "Ha! dame debonere seur toutes autres dames et plus cortoise que nule autre. . . ." Itiex paroles disoient cil de la cité et aloient aprés la reïne *plorant et criant aussi* com s'il fussent hors del sens.[134] |
| [. . . her coloring and her face were such That *never before did she seem so beautiful* to everyone. . . . Despite this, whoever wishes to look upon her With great pity could not keep From grieving, and . . . *those in attendance . . . could not hold back Their tears* which she could so well contain] (vv. 1213–1214, 1265–1267, 1269–1270) | [. . . *She . . . was more beautiful and attractive than any woman* of her age in the world. . . . When . . . the residents of the city saw her coming, then people could be heard crying from all sides: "Oh, lady, you who are more gracious and noble than any other woman. . . ." That is what the people of the city said as they followed the queen, and *they were weeping and wailing* as if out of their minds.][135] |

Despite these similarities, however, the two stories clearly diverge in their *dénouement*: for Guinevere is rescued from the flames by Lancelot, but Anne was indeed executed at the pleasure of the king.[136] For Carle, the model of Guinevere can go only so far in shaping the telling of this tale.

Given its sorrowful outcome, Carle's reworking of the Lancelot-Guinevere story in his poem recalls the way the thirteenth-century Italian writer Dante reuses elements of that tale in Canto 5 of his *Inferno*. There the Italian poet has depicted the real-life adulterous lovers, Paolo and Francesca, as having been

---

[134] *La Mort le roi Artu*, 122.

[135] *The Death of Arthur*, 122–23.

[136] For more on this "last-minute rescue of the condemned queen" as a "centerpiece of the romance of chivalry," see Susan Bordo, *The Creation of Anne Boleyn: A New Look at England's Most Notorious Queen* (2013; repr. Boston: Mariner Books, 2014), 105.

inspired by the fictional story of Lancelot and Guinevere that they read together, alone and unsuspectingly.[137] In their "emulative reading" or performance of the Lancelot story, in which they re-enact the kiss (and, presumably, other intimacies) between the courtly lovers, Paolo and Francesca have blurred the distinction between what is licit (indeed, sometimes encouraged) in the realm of fiction and what is permissible in the world of reality, much to their earthly and spiritual peril:[138] for the Italian couple were discovered *in flagrante delicto* and immediately killed (before they had a chance to repent) by Francesca's enraged and jealous husband (who also happened to be Paolo's brother). For Dante, the fictional world of courtly love, as exemplified in the prose Lancelot-Grail Cycle, constitutes a "negative exemplum": it is meant to be interpreted as a cautionary tale but is instead misread "for personal ends that are egoistic and potentially catastrophic."[139]

Similarly, Carle might be suggesting that Anne Boleyn appeared to embrace courtly models of behavior in real life, believing that, if she were "seized / By some Love . . . / It was entirely permitted to her / To treat her lovers as she pleased" (vv. 267–270). In so doing, she, like Francesca, would have confused the fictional world of courtly romance with the harsh reality of the court of Henry VIII: for, despite what some historians, such as Eric Ives or David Starkey, have maintained, there is no evidence to suggest that the Tudor court itself (notwithstanding its superficial attraction to medieval courtly activities) actually sanctioned behavior that was in keeping with a "game" of courtly love in which the king's men would be expected to play the role of a serious suitor (or lover) to women of the court, including the queen herself.[140] That is to say, while other chivalric values might have found a home in the Tudor court, the principles of

---

[137] For this text, see Dante Alighieri, *Inferno*, trans. Robert Hollander and Jean Hollander (New York: Doubleday, 2000).

[138] For more on this concept of "emulative reading" in the Paolo and Francesca episode, see Donald Maddox, "The Arthurian Intertexts of *Inferno* V," *Dante Studies* 114 (1996): 113–27, here 118.

[139] On these points, see Maddox, "The Arthurian Intertexts," 123 and 118, respectively.

[140] For a claim that courtly love was an acceptable "game" at the Tudor court, see Ives, *Life and Death*, 70–71 as well as Starkey, "King Henry and King Arthur." For a critique of their positions, see Warnicke, "The Conventions of Courtly Love and Anne Boleyn," in *State, Sovereigns and Society in Early Modern England: Essays in Honour of A. J. Slavin*, ed. Charles Carlton, with Robert L. Woods, Mary L. Robertson, and Joseph S. Block (New York: St. Martin's Press, 1998), 103–18; and Warnicke, "Reshaping Tudor Biography: Anne Boleyn and Anne of Cleves," in *Writing Biography: Historians and Their Craft*, ed. Ambrosius, 53–78. As Warnicke writes ("Reshaping," 56): "Almost no other scholar today argues, as Ives has done, that it was an actual, accepted practice at court for older, married women, like Anne Boleyn, to have intimate, potentially sexual relationships with younger men."

"courtly love"—which in almost all cases occurs outside of marriage—would not be part of acceptable social practice in Henry's reign.[141] Essentially, courtly love is a literary construct rather than "an actual social phenomenon."[142] But Anne has inappropriately applied this fictional standard (in which love outside of marriage could prevail, as shown by Lancelot's rescue of his lady Guinevere) to a world in which such behavior inevitably led to the demise of the queen and all five men accused with her. Or, to put it another way, Carle has portrayed Anne in a manner that is bound to recall the world of Arthurian romance, but he does so specifically in order to insist upon the gap between that literary construct and the actual world of the Tudor court.

Literary models of behavior might be brought to bear upon other characters in this story as well. The most notable of these models is perhaps the story of "patient Griselda," which was known to Carle and his French audience (which was thoroughly imbued in Italian Renaissance literature and culture) through a tale told by Boccaccio in his *Decameron*, though it came to be known to the English-speaking world primarily through Chaucer's retelling of the same story in the "Clerk's Tale." In this story, Griselda's husband makes her endure a series of tests in order to prove her love. This includes taking their children away from her and sending them off to their death. Griselda's husband then repudiates her, obtaining a divorce with the intention of remarrying. The story as told by Boccaccio and Chaucer has a happy ending: it is revealed that the cruel husband has not killed his children after all, nor does he remarry. Instead, upon being assured that Griselda's love can withstand the worst treatment imaginable, he takes her back into his home where they live out the rest of their days in loving matrimony.

Griselda's tale is evoked by Carle in two major scenes that are peripheral to Anne's story (and thus to the main point of his dispatch): scenes that describe the ill treatment bestowed by Henry on his forsaken wife, Catherine, and their daughter, Mary. In the first of these vignettes, the reader is transported away from the English court, where Anne now holds sway, to an unnamed location where Catherine lives in exile and where she "tolerated the collapse / Of her condition as patiently / As humanly possible" (vv. 226–228). Carle never comments upon the messy divorce or its theological argumentation undertaken by Henry but, instead, focuses on the human toll of this repudiation, particularly the cruel separation of mother and child that Henry demanded and that Carle

---

[141] For more on the fundamentally adulterous nature of courtly love, see Denis de Rougemont, *L'Amour et l'Occident* (1939; repr. Paris: Bibliothèque 10/18, 1962). For a critique of this work and its followers, see David Lyle Jeffrey, "Courtly Love and Christian Marriage: Chrétien de Troyes, Chaucer, and Henry VIII," *Christianity and Literature* 59 (2010): 515–30.

[142] See, on this point, Warnicke, *Wicked Women of Tudor England*, 24. Jeffrey ("Courtly Love," 517–18) also points out the discrepancy between the fictions of "courtly love" and genuine court culture even in the Middle Ages.

sees as being the cause of the queen's premature death. Unlike Griselda, Catherine is not to be reconciled with her husband, nor would she ever be reunited with her daughter again. Yet, Carle insists, she bears this sorrow patiently until the moment of her death. That Catherine's plight reminded those who knew her story of the tale of Griselda can be discerned from a text written by George Cavendish, who characterized Catherine's behavior as that of "a perfect Griseld."[143] More significantly, it can also be proved by the existence of another long narrative poem, written in English after Mary acceded to the throne and composed on her behalf by William Forrest. This work, known as *The History of Grisild the Second*, explicitly develops an analogy between Catherine and Griselda (as well as between Henry and "Walter," Griselda's husband).[144]

Carle's depiction of Catherine's daughter Mary also partakes of this tradition to some extent, as she, too, is shown to be infinitely patient, virtuous, and forgiving. Mary's reaction to her own mother's passing is a model of the faith-filled Christian understanding of death as a welcome respite from the troubles of this world (vv. 245–250). The French poet also spends considerable time depicting Mary's pastimes in exile, noting both her intellectual and spiritual endeavors in two separate passages (vv. 251–260 and vv. 613–633). Her reaction to Anne's arrest is nothing short of saintly: she offers to pray for her step-mother in her time of need and promises to care for her half-sister Elizabeth out of filial piety.[145] In total, Carle dedicates more than 100 lines to describing Mary's behavior. Perhaps

---

[143] See George Cavendish, *The Life and Death of Cardinal Wolsey*, in *Two Early Tudor Lives*, ed. Richard S. Sylvester and Davis P. Harding (New Haven: Yale University Press, 1962), 38.

[144] See William Forrest, *The History of Grisild the Second: A Narrative, in Verse, of the Divorce of Queen Katherine of Arragon [sic]*, ed. W. D. Macray (London: Whittingham & Wilkins, 1875). For more on this work and its application to Catherine's story, see Carley, *Books*, 123; and especially Ursula Potter, "Tales of Patient Griselda and Henry VIII," *Early Theatre* 5.2 (2002): 11–28; and Carolyn P. Collette, *Performing Polity: Women and Agency in the Anglo-French Tradition, 1385–1620* (Turnhout: Brepols, 2006), 123–40 [ch. entitled "Catherine of Aragon: A New Griselda for a New Polity"].

[145] Some readers, such as Bernard (*Anne Boleyn*, 181), assert that Carle's poem portrays Mary as "implicitly doubting Elizabeth's paternity," an understanding that is presumably based on v. 589: "*si sa fille est au Roy*." The word "si" does indeed most often mean "if," so that the line's translation would normally be "*if* her daughter is the king's." However, in this context, it is clearly used in another sense that was not at all uncommon in the sixteenth century and that draws from its etymological meaning (from the Latin "sic"), signifying "thus," "surely," or "since." See the definition given by Cotgrave: "In the beginning of a speech now and then implies . . . *a kind of certainty* . . . as 'Si advint' . . . *Surely it happened*." Thus the line should be understood to mean "*since* her daughter is the king's." Context dictates that is the only logical interpretation of the word. The poet has already stated that Elizabeth resembles her father more than her mother; thus, it would be inconsistent for him to interject uncertainty in this matter here (which Mary would, of

this was because Mary had been a figure of considerable interest to the French court and was at various times thought to be a potential bride for one or another of the French king's sons—and indeed, briefly, for Francis I himself (after the death of Claude of France). [146] Read as part of a diplomatic dispatch, Carle's interest in conveying news about Mary's status thus appears to be a reflection of the French embassy's continuing preoccupation with attempting to reach an understanding regarding her marriage. [147] Within the poem, however, this focus on Mary affords Carle another opportunity to play with the reader's expectations, for the last we see of Henry's daughter, she is not yet reconciled with her father and continues to live in her own impoverished exile, where she will remain until her father chooses to recall her.

Beyond these medieval and early modern intertexts, there is another story that may have informed Carle's *Story of the Death of Anne Boleyn*, particularly its portrayal of Anne's plight: namely, the biblical tale of Susanna and the Elders. This account of a virtuous woman who is falsely accused of adultery is found in the book of Daniel, but in an appendix that does not appear in the Hebrew Bible. Regardless of its disputed canonical status (at least in the Protestant tradition), the story would have been familiar to Carle and his readers and was depicted in many Renaissance paintings. It is a story of false evidence, of conspiracy among "elders"—who function as judges—but one that ultimately ends in the redemption of the beautiful woman who was unjustly condemned. These elders lusted after Susanna and attempted to coerce her into having sexual relations with them by threatening to accuse her publicly of having a young lover if she did not comply with their desires. Susanna refuses and is brought to trial and quickly found guilty, this despite the fact that "nothing like this had ever been said about [her]" (Daniel 13:27). As in the Guinevere story, the sight of Susanna's plight engendered sympathy among the witnesses, for "those who were with her and all who saw her were weeping" (Daniel 13:33). Throughout her ordeal, Susanna has faith that God, who knows the truth of the matter, will ultimately hear her cry of

---

course, have no way of verifying, in the absence of paternity tests), particularly in a passage that insists on Mary's generous response to Anne's plight.

[146] Mary had been formally betrothed to the Dauphin François when she was just over two years old. Later, in 1527, there had been an attempt to reach an agreement for her to marry the French king's second son, Henri, the Duc d'Orléans, or the king himself. See, on this point, LP 4.3105. Long after these childhood alliances failed, the French continued to propose a prospective marriage between Mary and French royalty. Chapuys, for example, wrote on 16 June 1535 to Charles V saying "I have . . . been told that the thing on which the French insist most is to have the Princess married to their Dauphin [François]." See *Calendar of State Papers, Spain*, 5, pt. 1, no. 174.

[147] A similar point is made by Warnicke, "Conflicting Rhetoric about Tudor Women: The Example of Queen Anne Boleyn," in *Political Rhetoric, Power, and Renaissance Women*, ed. Carole Levin and Patricia A. Sullivan (Albany: State University of New York Press, 1995), 39–54, here 41.

innocence and save her from being put to death. When the verdict against her is announced, Susanna "cried out with a loud voice, and said, 'O eternal God, you know what is secret and are aware of all things before they come to be; you know that these men have given false evidence against me'" (Daniel 13:42). Through the intervention of a young boy named Daniel, who surmises that the judges have lied and tricks them into revealing their perjury by questioning them separately, the truth is eventually revealed, and the judges receive the punishment of death that Susanna herself had escaped through the grace of God.

There are, of course, many differences between the tale of Susanna and that of Anne, but Carle may well be remembering certain details of the biblical story, particularly at the moment when Anne learns of the judgment against her in the courtroom. Her outburst, a moving speech that is not recorded elsewhere, clearly echoes the cries of Susanna: "But she gave thanks to God, with hands joined in prayer, / Saying to Him: 'Oh Father of humankind, / . . . / You know if I have deserved this death'" (vv. 993–996). Anne then turns to her judges, who, though they themselves may not have invented the charges against her, as did the judges or elders in Susanna's case, are nevertheless depicted as concealing the true motivation behind their eagerness to find her guilty: "I do not wish to say that your verdict is unjust / . . . / [but] I believe you know full well / The reason why you have condemned me, / Which is other than the one you have deduced / From this trial" (vv. 998–1004). In the end, of course, Anne is not saved by the God she invokes, and there is much weeping among those who witnessed her execution (vv. 1267–1270). Her story is thus a reversal of Susanna's, in much the same way that the tale of Guinevere's rescue from the flames stands in stark contrast with Anne's fate.

It should be stressed that it is unlikely that Anne, Catherine, and Mary themselves deliberately assumed roles that were modeled on female literary types, such as Guinevere, Griselda, or even Susanna; rather, it is more likely that it is the poet himself who is describing their stories in ways that echo these literary models. But one can more reasonably argue that such may be the case with regard to the behavior of the accused adulterous lovers as they face their execution, which is recounted in a way that recalls the story of Christ's passion. It is not too farfetched to ascribe this self-fashioning to the characters themselves because convicted prisoners quite consciously studied the Passion in preparing for their own deaths, deliberately modeling their behavior on that of Christ, "the normative example of patient suffering and perfect death."[148] Still, it is Carle himself who chooses to frame the scenes of death, burial, and lamentation in ways that explicitly recall the death of Christ, most often through scriptural echoes.

Each of the condemned criminals of this story manifests an admirable approach to death and a thorough knowledge of what was known as the *ars*

---

[148] See Brad S. Gregory, *Salvation at Stake: Christian Martyrdom in Early Modern Europe* (Cambridge, MA: Harvard University Press, 1999), 55.

*moriendi* or "art of dying" well. Several tracts outlining this art (or "craft," as it has also been termed) were available to those who believed that they were approaching their final days and who wished to prepare for it fully.[149] From this perspective, the fact that Anne and her accused lovers are sentenced to death —and therefore know the very day they will meet their maker—gives them a spiritual advantage over others, who "know not the hour" of their demise: for all of the prisoners can—and, in this case, do—thoroughly prepare their mind and soul in advance, ensuring through their prayers and reception of the sacraments that they are ready to be welcomed into the Kingdom of God.[150]

Indeed, Carle pays considerable attention to their preparation for death in the second half of his poem, making frequent use of the term "bien mourir" [to die well] or equivalent expressions.[151] The four commoners, he notes, each resolve "to die well / As if choosing a voluntary death" (vv. 817–818). He likens their preparation for death in terms of preparing for a journey, whereby one must pack one's traveling bag in advance of the trip, in this case from the earthly realm to the world beyond (vv. 1053–1056). Their preparations include the devout final reception of Holy Eucharist (vv. 1057–1058), known in the Catholic tradition as the "Viaticum" (a word that likewise emphasizes the images of roads and journeys), and Carle makes it a point to emphasize that each of the four commoners participates in this practice. Finally, Carle describes their actual journey from their prison to what he calls the "place of sacrifice" (v. 1063), referring to Tower Hill, which they make on that "sorrowful day" [*leur douleureux jour*, v. 1061]. Carle's imagery here, especially the use of the word "douleureux," helps to establish an explicit verbal connection between the death of these men and that of Christ, whose sorrowful procession on the route to his own "place of sacrifice," Calvary, is referred to as the "via dolorosa."[152]

The four commoners were executed on the same day as George Boleyn, Anne's brother, who likewise is described as having accepted his death willingly (v. 930). Though we are not told precisely how George has prepared for his exe-

---

[149] See, for example, *Ars moriendi, that is to saye the craft for to deye for the helthe of mannes sowle*, a tract that was printed by William Caxton around 1491. This work was reproduced by Edward W. B. Nicholson (London: Bernard Quaritch, 1891). Also consult *The Book of the Craft of Dying and Other Early English Tracts Concerning Death*, ed. Frances M. M. Comper (1917; repr. New York: Arno, 1977).

[150] See, on this point, Mitchell B. Merback, *The Thief, the Cross and the Wheel: Pain and the Spectacle of Punishment in Medieval and Renaissance Europe* (Chicago: University of Chicago Press, 1999), who stresses that execution was the "single occasion when a Christian could know the exact moment of his or her death, and thus prepare for grace up until the final blow" (155–56).

[151] See vv. 817, 930, 1023, 1054, and 1169.

[152] The concept of Christ's death as a sacrifice is expounded primarily in the biblical Letter to the Hebrews.

cution, it is clear that his death is also to be compared with the Passion of Christ, since Carle states that Rochford acted "as if carrying the sign of victory / Against death" (vv. 1075–1076): for that phrase is normally associated with the cross of Christ.[153] Moreover, despite his claim not to wish to preach a sermon, Rochford undeniably assumes the role of a preacher, since his final speech, addressed specifically to the gentlemen of the court, aims at teaching them a lesson on the vanity of this world (vv. 1089–1090). His speech is, in effect, a reflection or homily on Ecclesiastes 1:2 (that is, on *vanitas*) as well as on the biblical admonition "trust not in Princes," which was expounded in Psalm 146.[154] Over-attachment to the things of this world was indeed Rochford's most grievous sin: for, as Carle reports, George had exhibited far too great a fondness for earthly glories, paying homage to an earthly king rather than to Christ, the heavenly King (v. 1093). To put it another way, Rochford's behavior might not have been *adulterous*—and indeed he does not admit to that sin—but it was certainly *idolatrous* insofar as he put his hope in (or, in a manner of speaking, *worshipped*) temporal "honors and wealth" (v. 1101), such that he forgot that it was to God "that one must turn" (v. 1108). Yet, at the moment of his death, George presents himself to the executioner with a "firm heart," Carle says, echoing another scriptural passage that likens Rochford to the righteous who are not afraid in the face of adversity.[155]

Carle treats Anne's preparation for death in much the same way. First, she too accepts death willingly (v. 1040) and explicitly states that she has "learned how to die / With the One who can heal death" (vv. 1023–1024), referring to the *ars moriendi* tradition and the redemptive role of Christ's crucifixion. Furthermore, from the moment she learns of her conviction, she quotes from Scripture, extolling the "Father of humankind / Wherein is the life, way, and truth" (vv. 994–995). This verse is an echo of John 14:6 and is also an expression that figures prominently in *Le pasteur évangélique* (a French poem that expounds on the Pauline notion of justification by faith) of which Anne and Henry owned an elaborate presentation copy.[156] Perhaps in reporting that Anne has uttered

---

[153] For an analysis of the cross of Christ as a sign of victory over death, consult, *inter alia*, Alister E. McGrath, *Christian Theology: An Introduction*, 3rd ed. (Oxford: Blackwell, 2001).

[154] Psalm 146:3: "Do not put your trust in princes, in mortals, in whom there is no help" [Vulg.: Nolite confidere in principibus, in filiis hominum, in quibus non est salus].

[155] Psalm 112:7–8: The righteous "are not afraid of evil tidings; their hearts are firm, secure in the Lord. Their hearts are steady" [Vulg.: Ab auditione mala non timebit. Paratum cor eius sperare in Domino. Confirmatum est cor eius].

[156] See John 14:6, "I am the way, and the truth, and the life" [Vulg.: Ego sum via, et veritas, et vita]. The *Pasteur évangélique* is London, British Library, Royal 16 E XIII. For this passage, see fol. 2v. For more on this work, see C. A. Mayer, "Anne Boleyn et la version originale du 'Sermon du bon pasteur' d'Almanque Papillon," *Bulletin de la société de l'histoire du protestantisme français* 132 (1986): 337–46. See also Chapter 2 above for a discussion of this work.

these words, Carle intends for his reader to make a connection between Christ as the "way" and the virtuous path that Anne had been shown to reject earlier (vv. 82–84), for indeed Carle is the only source that describes Anne's allocution speech. Anne is also said to invoke God as her witness that she is not guilty of the charges for which she has been condemned (vv. 1017–1018). Instead, Anne confesses to different sins: her lack of humility towards the king (vv. 1009–1010) and her harboring of jealousy against him (vv. 1013–1014). As Susan Bordo has pointed out, Anne here "shows remarkable insight into the gender politics that undoubtedly played a role in her downfall."[157] Rather than confessing to adultery or treason, Anne acknowledges other failures of virtue, particularly virtues that were of paramount importance to females in the Tudor Age. Anne's lack of humility was a sign of her "not remaining in her proper 'place,'" of not being sufficiently subservient towards Henry, and of implicitly challenging his authority and power, not merely as a king but, more especially, as a husband.[158] Similarly, the infraction of jealousy was unacceptable in a wife who was expected to turn a blind eye toward her husband's infidelities, as Henry himself had made clear to Anne early in his marriage, according to a report by the Imperial ambassador, Chapuys.[159] In confessing these two sins while still in the courtroom, Anne begins to prepare for her impending death even before making a sacramental confession.

But most significantly, in making herself ready for death, Anne meditates on the Passion of Christ and receives the Holy Eucharist (vv. 1131–1135), as the men accused with her had also done. Carle's description of Anne's religious practices, it should be noted, contains no hint of anything other than complete conformity with standard Catholic practice at the time: if Anne had demonstrated evangelical inclinations or "Protestant" sympathies in her lifetime, they were apparently unknown to Carle, who, it will be remembered, was himself a staunch Catholic and would no doubt have commented upon any hint of "heretical" behavior on her part. Instead, Carle emphasizes that Anne is so well prepared by the continuous prayer and meditation in which she engages, within her private oratory (vv. 1155–1162), that she is "troubled in spirit" (v. 1164) to learn that her execution will not take place on the day she had presumed it would, because "it seemed to her that she was prepared / To die well, and she feared that a delay / Might . . . put her in distress" (vv. 1168–1170).[160] Yet Anne soon regains her composure to such an extent that she can instruct her own ladies (who were distraught about her impending execution) that Christians ought not to fear death, which should

---

[157] Bordo, *The Creation of Anne Boleyn*, 84.

[158] Bordo, *The Creation of Anne Boleyn*, 84.

[159] See LP 6.1069 for the letter dated 3 September 1533.

[160] Carle's description of Anne as "troubled in spirit" might be read as an echo of the Vulgate's "turbatus est spiritu" used with regard to Jesus's foretelling of his own betrayal and consequential death. See John 13:21.

be viewed as the beginning of everlasting life (vv. 1174–1182). Here Anne's consoling words echo those of the Book of Wisdom 3.4 (in a passage often read at funeral services) that "though in the sight of others [the righteous] were punished, their hope is full of immortality."[161] Furthermore, on the very day of her execution, Anne maintains a serene countenance (v. 1211) as she awaits the blow from the executioner's sword.

It has sometimes been claimed that the decision to execute Anne with a sword rather than the customary axe was a final gesture of honor towards a disgraced queen on Henry's part or perhaps a nod to her French upbringing, since the swordsman needed to be recruited from Calais, on the continent, to perform this task.[162] But it is also perhaps a symbolic gesture, one that imbues the execution with Christian meaning: for to die by the sword required the accused criminal to kneel upright, *as if in prayer*, rather than be dispatched with one's head bent on the block.[163] It also required perfect composure and the ability to remain completely still "while the swordsman whirled his heavy sword, gathering momentum."[164] Only a truly noble soul could maintain this disciplined posture.[165] Certainly, the artistry of the swordsman would also appear more graceful than the hacking motion of an executioner's axe.[166] For these reasons, execution by the sword was a mark of privilege and status, even from Roman times.[167] But perhaps most importantly, the shape of the sword itself evoked another profoundly Christian symbol, that of the cross, and, indeed, because of the physical resemblance between the sword and the cross, it was a common practice to swear

---

[161] Vulg.: "Et si coram hominibus tormenta passi sunt, spes illorum immortalitate plena est."

[162] It has also been suggested that the sword was a "symbol of Camelot, of a rightful king, and of masculinity." See Leanda de Lisle, *Tudor: The Family Story* (London: Chatto & Windus, 2013), 207.

[163] See, on this point, Samuel Y. Edgerton, "When Even Artists Encouraged the Death Penalty," *Law and Literature* 15 (2003): 235–65, here 244.

[164] Naish, *Death Comes to the Maiden*, 40.

[165] On this point, see also Merback, *The Thief, the Cross and the Wheel*, especially 141–42, as well as Richard J. Evans, *Rituals of Retribution: Capital Punishment in Germany, 1600–1987* (Oxford: Oxford University Press, 1996), especially 55.

[166] See Edgerton, "When Even Artists Encouraged the Death Penalty," 244, who suggests that this hacking motion of the axe "with the headsman chopping downward" is akin to the "unbecoming manner of a peasant splitting wood," whereas the use of the "patrician broadsword" requires a motion comparable to that of an athlete using a tennis racket, "swinging . . . elegantly sideways." This point is also made by Thea Cervone, "'Tucked beneath Her Arm': Culture, Ideology, and Fantasy in the Curious Legend of Anne Boleyn," in *Heads Will Roll: Decapitation in the Medieval and Early Modern Imagination*, ed. Larissa Tracy and Jeff Massey (Leiden: Brill, 2012), 289–310, here 297.

[167] See Naish, *Death Comes to the Maiden*, 40.

upon a sword as if swearing upon a cross.[168] This religious symbolism was probably not lost upon Carle, who makes it a point to mention that Anne "cast herself humbly on her knees" (v. 1274), uttering her final prayer while awaiting the blow of a sword, a substitute for the cross, thus establishing two visual connections with the Christian faith.

Moreover, Anne's calm and fearless acceptance of death, in and of itself, certainly would have been taken as a sign that she had made peace with God: for, as Brad Gregory has reminded us, "dying with a steadfast resolve or patient resignation, evincing neither doubt nor fear regardless of the extent of their suffering" was the mark of a good Christian's death.[169] Not only does Anne approach death calmly, according to Carle; she also embraces it cheerfully: for Carle twice refers to the fact that Anne was smiling and serene as she addressed the crowd (vv. 1211 and 1216). While one other early modern account of Anne's execution interprets her generally happy demeanor on the scaffold as evidence of her devilish nature, for Carle, this detail is surely meant to show that Anne has mastered the art of dying.[170]

As was the case with her brother, Anne's encounter with death is couched in terms reminiscent of the death of Christ himself. First, Anne's final words, as reported by Carle (and many other sources)—"Christ, I beg you to receive my spirit!" (v. 1276)—echo the dying words of Christ—"Father, into your hands I commend my spirit" [Vulg.: "Pater, in manus tuas commendo spiritum meum," Luke 23:46]. This utterance also closely echoes the final words of the first Christian martyr, St. Stephen, who likewise proclaimed "Lord Jesus, receive my spirit" [Vulg.: "Domine Iesu, suscipe spiritum meum," Acts of the Apostles 7:59] at the moment of his execution. Furthermore, the care given to Anne's body before its burial by her attendants is also reminiscent of the Gospel accounts of Christ's burial: just as Joseph of Arimethea was said to have wrapped the body of Jesus in a burial cloth before placing it in a tomb, so too do these ladies carry Anne's body, "Enveloped in a white shroud, / Over to the place of somber burial" (vv. 1295–1296).[171] Finally, these attendants are likened to "lost sheep, without a shep-

---

[168] See, for example, Shakespeare's *Hamlet* 1:5 for an instance of swearing upon a sword as if upon a cross.

[169] Gregory, *Salvation at Stake*, 320.

[170] For this negative interpretation of Anne's demeanor, see the *Chronicle of King Henry VIII . . . Written in Spanish by an Unknown Hand*, trans. and ed. Martin A. Sharp Hume (London: George Bell, 1889), 70: "[she] showed a devilish spirit, and was as gay as if she was not going to die." For the original Spanish text, see *Crónica del Rey Enrico Otavo de Ingalaterra*, ed. El Marqués de Molins (Madrid: Alfonso Durán, 1874), 91: "mostró un ánimo diabólico, que estaba alegre como si no hubiera de morir."

[171] All four gospels mention Joseph of Arimethea's role in preparing the body of Jesus for his burial. See Matthew 27:59–60, Mark 15:46, Luke 23:53, and John 19:40.

herd" (v. 1304), imagery that is used repeatedly throughout the Bible.[172] Here these words imply that these women have lost their guide and teacher, who had recently instructed them about the meaning of death.

## Poetic and Rhetorical Devices: The Fabric of the Text

It should be clear from the above analysis that Carle no doubt shaped his dispatch in accordance with literary models and conventions, from medieval romances to the Bible. But this could certainly have been accomplished by writing his epistle in prose, rather than in verse. Nonetheless, Carle made the extraordinary decision to write this dispatch as a poem, and, in so doing, he opened the door to a host of new ways to convey meaning. Carle was free to exploit poetic and rhetorical devices—that is, structural patterns of repetition at the level of words, images, and sounds—which could be used to reinforce key points and create meanings that are not explicit but that can be read between the lines by the attentive reader. While many rhetorical devices can be applied to prose as well as poetry, some patterns are more easily discernible when they appear in verse compositions. As a classically trained humanist who was already a modestly successful poet, Carle could see in the story of the death of Anne Boleyn a tale that could transcend the news of the moment if it were cast in poetic form.

Before beginning an analysis of the text's specifically poetic qualities, it is necessary to admit that Carle's near-contemporaries, as well as his more modern readers, have not been uniformly positive in assessing his poetic skills. Whereas the Renaissance bibliophile La Croix du Maine, for example, refers to him as a "very excellent poet in Latin and French and quite learned in Greek,"[173] the early modern literary critic and biographer Guillaume Colletet attacks him viciously. Carle's verses, Colletet claims, are so flat and insipid and careless in how they fail to respect the requirements of French versification "that I do not know how it is possible that a scholarly man such as he was, born into a fine family, brought up in the courts of kings and friend to all good poets and all the scholars of his century, was capable of producing such defective verses and, in a word, how such a great prelate could have wished to pass for such a small poet."[174] Even his otherwise sympathetic modern biographer, L.-C. Harmer, states that "as a poet, Lancelot cuts a sad figure" and believes that other versifiers were quite aware

---

[172] For the term "sheep without a shepherd," see, for example, Matthew 9:36 as well as Numbers 27:17–18, 1 Kings 22:17, and Judith 11:15. For the parable of the lost sheep, see Matthew 18:12–14 and Luke 15:3–7.

[173] See François Grudé sieur de La Croix du Maine, *La Bibliothèque du sieur de la Croix du Maine*, vol. 1 (1579; repr. Paris: Abel L'Angelier, 1584), 282 (my translation).

[174] Colletet, *Vies des poètes*, 9 (my translation).

of Carle's deficiencies, but flattered him because they believed they could profit from his closeness to the king.[175]

Carle is indeed no Ronsard; but it is probably unfair to criticize him, as Colletet does, for technical deficiencies in his verse. While it is not always obvious when reading a single version of Carle's poem chosen from the plethora of manuscripts in which it is transcribed (sometimes in very corrupt form), Carle does indeed consistently conform to the most basic requirements of his chosen verse form, the decasyllabic rhyming couplet known in French as *rimes plates*. That is to say, each of his verses, without fail, contains ten syllables when counted according to his consistent practice (and early sixteenth century norms), though in any given manuscript there may be verses that require emendations (drawn from other manuscripts) in order to achieve this consistency. Presumably, those deficiencies are the result of scribal error and do not necessarily reflect Carle's poetic skill. It is true, however, that Carle does not follow the practice of alternating masculine and feminine rhymes (that is, words that end with a silent "e" vs. those that do not) in this text: but this custom did not become a hard and fast rule until later in the century.[176] A good deal of the poetry by Marot and even some of the early verses of Ronsard do not obey this regulation.

More charitable readers than Colletet and Harmer can doubtless find other indices of Carle's poetic sensibilities. For example, Carle frequently takes advantage of poetic techniques to draw attention to particular moments in his account that are especially dramatic or intense. One such technique is known in French as a "coupe," which refers to a division in a verse that is marked by sense (or punctuation). Although the decasyllabic line is normally divided into two parts (with a 4/6 division being the expected pattern), a poet can play with this expectation to suit his own purposes. Carle generally maintains the 4/6 division in his verses but does occasionally make use of the poetic technique of enjambment (running a thought from one line to the next) so that the normal 4/6 division is disrupted. One example of this technique occurs when the wayward sister of the counselor begins to hint that there is a far greater sinner among them:

> Mais on voit bien vne petite faulte
> En moy, laissant vne beaucoup plus haulte
> Qui porte effect de plus gran preiudice. (vv. 355–357)

---

[175] L.-C. Harmer, "Lancelot de Carle: Sa Vie," *Humanisme et Renaissance* 6 (1939): 443–74, here 448 (my translation).

[176] See, on this point, Claude-Gilbert Dubois, *La poésie du XVI^e siècle en toutes lettres* (Paris: Bordas, 1989), 83. See also Sébillet, *Art poétique françois*, 72, where Goyet explains that the alternation of masculine/feminine rhymes became an important rule only around 1555 thanks to the influence of the Pléiade poets.

[But people easily see a small fault
In me, allowing a much higher one
That carries the potential of greater harm.]

The expression "en moy" [in me] is put into relief thanks to this use of enjambment, and it shifts the division of the verse to a 2/8 pattern. More commonly, Carle sometimes interpolates a hard stop after the fourth syllable, again for dramatic effect. This passage where the brother is describing the queen's wanton behavior to the king is a case in point:

Car, quand l'vn a achevé sa journee,
Vn autre apres vient à l'heure assignee,
Et puis un aultre. Ainsi passe le iour
En ce lascif & infame seiour. (vv. 427–430)

[For when one man finishes his job
Another comes along at the appointed hour,
And then another. Thus she spends her day
In this lascivious and infamous employment.]

Similarly, when the guilty verdict is voiced by the jurors who have condemned the commoners, Carle likewise begins a new sentence after the *coupe*:

L'vn dit GUILTY. Soudain la hache grande
Tourne . . . (vv. 780–781)

[One says, "GUILTY." Suddenly the great axe
Turns . . .]

Here the hard stop is given even further emphasis by virtue of the intrusion of the English word "Guilty" (written entirely in uppercase letters in the British Library manuscript) into Carle's otherwise French poem. In both these instances, the extra emphasis at the *coupe* helps the poet hammer home the meaning of his words. One can almost hear the door of Anne's chamber closing as she welcomes another nightly visitor, just as one can imagine the sorrowful hush that followed the pronouncement of guilt as all eyes turned toward the moving axe, which prefigured the beheading of the men deemed guilty.

Carle uses another patterning device, the rhetorical trope known as *anaphora* (the repeated use of the same word or words at the beginning of successive clauses), to evoke the image of a courtroom in which person after person charges Rochford with ignominious crimes:

. . . l'un vient, la voix haulsant,
Qui son meffaict blasme publicquement.
Vn aultre apres encor plus asprement,

Vn aultre apres ses offenses augmente,
Vn aultre apres de nouueau le tourmente. (vv. 838–842)

[. . . one of them comes forward, raising his voice
And rebukes him publicly for his misdeed,
Another, afterwards, even more harshly,
Another, afterwards, adds to his crimes,
Another, afterwards, torments him anew.]

It is easy to imagine, thanks to this device, the aggressive fashion in which multiple accusations are levied against the queen's brother. In another passage, Carle exploits poetic repetition by using internal rhyme to underscore Anne's insistence that she had never done any wrong towards the king: "Contre le Roy iam<u>ais</u> n'au<u>oit</u> meff<u>aict</u>" (v. 966). Although these three words are spelled quite differently, their endings are, in fact, pronounced the same way. While this element is, unfortunately, lost in translation, the triple repetition of the same sound within a single verse allows readers of the original French text to imagine better Anne's persistence in proclaiming her innocence.

Beyond these techniques of poetic repetition, Carle also demonstrates a keen familiarity with the stylistic virtue of "copia," or rhetorical amplification. This technique of literary embellishment was analyzed and encouraged by the Dutch humanist Erasmus in a famous work, entitled *De copia*, which had been published multiple times in the years before the French poet composed this text. One passage where Carle applies this technique is in a series of verses where he extols the virtues of Mary, Henry's elder daughter. Just as Erasmus, in the *De copia*, had provided 200 variations of the sentence "As long as I live, I will preserve your memory,"[177] so too did Carle find multiple ways to describe Mary's steadfast comportment after she learns of Anne's arrest:

But at all times she always conducted herself
In the same way, whether in adversity
Or in the season of prosperity.
And she showed herself to behave completely in a single manner,
Be it in good fortune or bad.
And, what is more, on account of sadness or loss,
The color in her face never changed. (vv. 594–600)

---

[177] See Desiderius Erasmus, *De duplici copia verborum ac rerum comentarii duo* [Copia: Foundations of the Abundant Style], trans. Betty I. Knott, in Collected Works of Erasmus 24: Literary and Educational Writings, vol. 2 (Toronto: University of Toronto Press, 1978), 348.

While these verses might seem, at first glance, to be merely redundant and a sign of the poet's weakness, they should be read, instead, as an effort to conform to the humanist ideals of composition that circulated in his time.

Carle's poem is also notable for its remarkable structure that highlights a Renaissance concern for symmetry, balance, and proportion. It has often been noted that Carle's sympathies in depicting Anne shift dramatically in the later part of the text:[178] while he had earlier described Anne as an evil person who is full of malice (vv. 335–336), Carle clearly takes pity on the condemned queen who has now turned toward God, renouncing the things of this world. What has not been sufficiently emphasized, however, is that this shift takes place exactly at the numerical midpoint of the poem, which is composed of 1320 "canonical" verses found in multiple manuscripts. For it is at verse 660, precisely the beginning of the second half of the poem, where Carle speaks of Anne's newfound trust in God, that the poet also begins to pepper his poem with words such as "poor" and "pitiable" to describe not only Queen Anne but also all the men accused with her and the sorrowful treatment they must endure.[179] By beginning his more compassionate account of Anne at the midpoint of his story, Carle is engaging in a time-honored technique that could be found in other texts, such as Chrétien de Troyes's *Yvain, ou le chevalier au lion* [Yvain, or the Knight of the Lion] in which the worldly knight Yvain undergoes a spiritual awakening once he meets a remarkable lion, an encounter that takes place exactly at the center of the work.[180]

The contrast between the poet's treatment of Anne in the first and second halves of his poem is just one example of what can be called Carle's "doubling" technique, whereby descriptions of two people or events — sometimes separated by many verses — are meant to recall (and, consequently, give added meaning to) each other. One of the most intriguing, but subtle, contrasts (and one that is difficult to convey through translation) is that between Carle's description of the abandoned and impoverished Catherine on the one hand and, on the other hand, Anne's wanton behavior with multiple lovers, as depicted by the advisor to the king. Queen Catherine, Carle says, "estoit de tous honneurs <u>priuee</u> / Qu'elle viuoit comme femme <u>priuee</u>" [was so deprived of every honor / That she lived like a private citizen] (vv. 229–230). The epithet that Carle uses, "femme privée,"

---

[178] See, for example, Bernard, *Anne Boleyn*, 159.

[179] See vv. 756, 783, 791, 912, 960, 1048, 1130, 1259, 1277, and 1280 for these empathetic terms. The midpoint is at v. 665 in BL and this edition.

[180] See Chrétien de Troyes, *Le Chevalier au lion, ou le roman d'Yvain*, ed. David F. Hult (Paris: Livre de Poche, 1994). For an extensive discussion of the importance of midpoints in medieval literature, see Karl D. Uitti, "'Cele [qui] doit estre Rose clamee' (*Rose*, vv. 40–44): Guillaume's Intentionality," in *Rethinking the "Romance of the Rose": Text, Image, Reception*, ed. Kevin Brownlee and Sylvia Huot (Philadelphia: University of Pennsylvania Press, 1992), 39–64, especially 51.

is intended to mean that Catherine lived as a woman who was no longer in the public sphere: she did not function as a queen and was all but forgotten by the English court. Several verses later, when Carle quotes the speech of her accuser, Anne is described as living "en la façon d'vne femme publicque," which is rendered here as "in the manner of a street-walker" (v. 426); literally, however, Anne is a "public" woman who is potentially the property of any man who wants to use her. By employing the two antithetical epithets, "femme privée" and "femme publique," at comparable locations at the end of a verse to describe these two women, Carle no doubt intends for his readers to realize that these two queens are polar opposites in their behavior and reputation.

Another doubling that appears in this poem juxtaposes the behavior of Anne and her step-daughter, Mary. Carle's descriptions of the pastimes that Anne perfected in France—those pleasant but frivolous diversions that were valued at court, such as singing, dancing, conversation, and music (vv. 55–58) —are certainly meant to be contrasted with the learned and serious pursuits in which Mary engages, which include spiritual readings, needlework, and various other studies such as astronomy, philosophy, foreign languages, mathematics, and literature (see vv. 251–254 and 615–624). Furthermore, Anne's iniquitous daily activities (described by her accuser, vv. 424–430) constitute an even greater contrast with Mary's virtuous interests.

Yet, Carle hastens to add, Mary's intellectual activities are not exactly in keeping with traditional expectations for women, such that Mary is portrayed as learned beyond what is expected—or indeed fitting—for her sex. Certainly, it was important for young women to avoid idleness, which can lead to all sorts of vices (which, Carle goes on to say, is Mary's chief motivation for engaging in these activities). But the ideal occupation for Mary, Carle would assume, is domestic handiwork, not reading and studying. This is not the only time that Carle comments on traditional expectations for female comportment: he makes a similar comment regarding Anne's "great faith and wise patience, / Which rose above womanly courage" (vv. 1263–1264) at the time of her execution. Once again, Carle engages in a doubling technique, this time showing Anne and Mary to be more alike than different. Importantly, although both Mary and Anne are shown as behaving in ways that defied gender conventions, Carle does not condemn either woman for surpassing the limitations imposed on them through societal expectations and clearly wants to emphasize their ability to cope with their respective trials and adversity, no matter how that is achieved.

A further way that Anne and Mary are shown to be unexpectedly alike is in the attitudes towards death that each professes. While Mary was said to have responded to her own mother's demise by invoking death as a respite from this sorrowful life (vv. 245–250), Anne likewise teaches her distraught ladies-in-waiting that death, to Christians, is the beginning of eternal life with God (vv. 1175–1185). These lessons are hardly original, and indeed a similar meditation upon death as a "very desirable friend" who liberates us from the prison of earthly life can be found in the text of the *Pasteur évangélique*, the French poem of which Anne and Henry owned a fine presentation copy.[181] Once again, Carle is the only source that reports Anne's long—and completely orthodox—theological lesson given to her ladies, which, given this uniqueness, may not reflect historical reality. Indeed, historical sources have indicated that Anne was not particularly fond of the women who were sent to attend her in her final days.[182] Yet this vignette, which portrays an intimate bond between the queen and her troubled ladies, provides Carle with a way to show Anne's piety as well as to put her execution in a Christian perspective, ventriloquizing words attributed to her instead of using his own voice to make this key argument. But equally important, it serves to show that Mary and Anne, though perhaps bitter enemies in life, each arrived at a Christian understanding of the redemptive nature of death and suffering that leads to a new life in the world beyond.

The technique of doubling in poetic narration is also employed with respect to Anne and George, for the purpose, once again, of teaching a theological lesson. The speeches made by both Anne and George, in either their defense presentation before the jury reaches its verdict (in the case of George) or in their allocution speech, after their conviction is announced (in the case of Anne), as well as their final scaffold speeches, are clearly meant to mirror each other. Moreover, within his transcription of these speeches, Carle allows Anne and George to share his penchant for doubling, for each of them develops at length a unique juxtaposition that encompasses the whole of the point they wish to make. George's scaffold speech focuses on the contrast between the kingdoms of earth and the Kingdom of God. He warns other gentlemen of the court not to rely so heavily on "the recompense of honor / From kings" (or, more to the point, from King Henry) that they begin to neglect the King whose rewards are greater than those of this realm (vv. 1090–1094). To make this fact even more evident, Carle allows Anne to pick up on this imagery when she is told of her brother's stoic manner at the moment of his death: for she states that she hopes that George is now before the "face of the Great King" (v. 1152) in his heavenly abode.

---

[181]  For this passage, see Royal 16 E XIII, fols. 10v–11r.

[182]  See, on this point, the report of Anne's jailor Kingston as recorded in Ellis, *Letters*, 2.60 and Strype, *Ecclesiastical Memorials*, 1.1.435. The latter reads: "[Anne] took notice of divers women set about her [in the Tower] that she liked not; saying, 'I think much unkindness in the King, to put such about me as I never loved.'" For an argument that, after Anne's complaint, "Henry VIII appointed four of Anne's favourite attendants to accompany her to the scaffold," among whom may have figured Elizabeth Holland (to whom, apparently, Anne gave a precious Book of Hours, in which she and Henry had previously exchanged love notes), see Sylwia Sobczak Zupanec, "An Overlooked Connection of Anne Boleyn's Maid of Honour, Elizabeth Holland, with BL, King's MS. 9," *The Electronic British Library Journal*, 2017, Article 7, p. 5.

Likewise, Anne's scaffold speech centers on the contrast between "the Judge of the world / In Whom justice and truth abound" (vv. 1241–1242) and the earthly judges "who judged me deserving of this death" (v. 1245). The latter, whose sense of judgment she implicitly calls into question, like those judges or elders in the parallel story of Susanna analyzed above, will in turn require compassion from God for this failing, she states. In juxtaposing both the king and judge imagery used in the scaffold speeches of George and Anne, Carle is evoking yet another biblical echo, taken from Isaiah 33:22: "For the Lord is our judge, the Lord is our ruler, the Lord is our King."[183] In this way, Carle implies, these two condemned souls have come to understand a scriptural truth that others in Henry's court could not so easily express.

Carle's fondness for doubling and his appreciation for symmetry and balance can be found on a smaller scale as well, indeed within the confines of a single verse. Specifically, at vv. 1294–1296, Carle describes the most poignant scene of his story, the preparation of Anne's body for burial by her ladies-in-waiting: "Et ce corps mort presque mortes porterent / Enueloppé d'vne blanche closture / Iusques au lieu de triste sepulture" [And the nearly dead women carried away this dead body, / Enveloped in a white shroud, / Over to the place of somber burial]. The exquisitely balanced verse 1294 juxtaposes Anne's dead body ("corps mort") with the image of the nearly dead women ("presques mortes") who, despite being bereft of their souls, force themselves to perform their final duty. Thanks to its exceptionally balanced composition, this verse calls attention to itself and thus to the brave action of Anne's ladies who, as Thea Cervone has put it, "almost experience death with her."[184] Carle's explanation that these ladies perform this duty because they are loathe to let "unworthy men" touch their queen shows, according to Cervone, that he has understood their gesture to be one of "feminine empowerment."[185] For, she further explains, Anne's attendants "circumvent the violent male element inherent in the scene" (set in motion by Anne's husband and finalized by her executioner and other male authorities present at the execution) and "replace it with a compassionate and feminine image of sisterhood, empathy, and loyalty."[186] All this is underscored through the balanced verbal repetition of verse 1294, which establishes an equivalence between the lifeless queen and her female servants who have lost their will to live, yet carry on.

An even better example of balanced repetition can be found at the beginning of the poem. In introducing his story, Carle admits that the unprecedented events he will describe have been "Tristes aux vns, & et aux autres ioyeuses," a line that, respecting Carle's syntax, translates as "sad to some and to others joyous" (v. 2). Carle here changes the normal syntax of the phrase, as it would

---

183 Vulg.: "Dominus enim iudex noster, Dominus legifer noster, Dominus rex noster."
184 Cervone, "'Tucked beneath Her Arm,'" 298.
185 Cervone, "'Tucked beneath Her Arm,'" 298.
186 Cervone, "'Tucked beneath Her Arm,'" 299.

have been rendered in ordinary prose discourse, by inverting the position of the words "joyous" and "others." This, in turn, allows Carle to use the rhetorical device of "chiasmus" (< Greek, "cross"), a "crossed" or inverted repetition of two verbal structures. In this case, the chiasmus is achieved by flanking the similar expressions "aux vns" [to some] and "aux autres" [to others] with the antithetical adjectives, "tristes" and "joyeuses" [sad and joyful]. The ensuing verse thus conforms to a crisscross pattern of adjective/noun // noun/adjective (or, to put it more schematically, an A-B-B-A pattern). While this device is common enough in literary texts of all kinds, during the Renaissance it was often used to insert a verbal "sign of the cross" into the text, to mark the work as profoundly Christian in orientation.[187] It was particularly used, understandably, to evoke Christ's crucifixion or death on the cross and thus to suggest themes of sin and redemption. This could certainly be the case here, for there is no doubt that such theological concerns were of paramount importance to Carle, who may well have wished to mark the beginning of his text with a cross, just as a priest marks the Gospel before proclaiming it.

## Conclusion:
## Interpreting *The Story of the Death of Anne Boleyn*

In light of all these literary conventions and devices, how exactly is a reader to understand the meaning of *The Story of the Death of Anne Boleyn*? More specifically, what, if anything, does this poem tell us about the guilt or innocence of that disgraced queen? It is important to remember that Carle never states explicitly whether or not Anne is guilty. This is indeed beyond his purview: he can report only what he has seen and what he has learned about this incredible story, and this would certainly preclude giving eye-witness testimony to the queen's improprieties or stating categorically that she never engaged in such behavior. There is a fact of the matter here to which virtually everyone, including Carle, is no longer (or, perhaps, never was) privy. Nevertheless, the text reveals certain meanings to those who make an effort to interpret this poem as a cultivated reader of the sixteenth century would do.

Certainly, Carle initially portrays Anne as capable of having committed these crimes and others. With regard to the issue of illicit sexual behavior, Carle states that Anne was given the "leisure, means, and freedom / To take her pleasure as she wished" (vv. 263–264) and "to treat her lovers as she pleased" (v. 270). More generally, he makes it clear that, even when given the chance to repent (when confronted with signs of danger to her soul that she ought to have

---

[187] For more on the Christian meaning of the rhetorical device of chiasmus, see Ryan McDermott, *Tropologies: Ethics and Invention in England c. 1350–1600* (Notre Dame, IN: University of Notre Dame Press, 2016), 197–210, especially 200.

recognized), she did not "forsake engaging in / Her first—and bad—way of living" (vv. 330–331). Carle also suggests that Anne's bad behavior encompassed more than sexual improprieties when he states that "the evil that tainted her / And the malice hidden in her spirit" (vv. 335–336) grew continuously, like a fire that smolders and eventually burns out of control. Based on these verses and others in his poem (e.g., vv. 212–213 and 611–612), one can presume that Carle, like many people at the time, considered Anne to be the one ultimately behind the ill treatment of Catherine and Mary as well as the executions of Thomas More and the Carthusian martyrs.[188] It is for these reasons, presumably, that Warnicke considers Carle's poem to reflect "the heightened nature of [the] hostility" towards Anne, which, she claims, was rampant within the French embassy at the time.[189]

Carle's depiction of Anne's evil and malice are no doubt rather damning statements. Yet they all seem to be forgotten in the second half of the poem, in which Carle gives a far more sympathetic portrayal of Anne. The queen is not just unfortunate: she is *pitiable*, and that word must be understood in its classical meaning (which persisted through the sixteenth century) of someone who does not deserve the misfortune he or she is suffering. Moreover, Carle's use of scriptural imagery—particularly that drawn from the story of Christ's Passion—reinforces this notion that Anne and the men executed with her are, like Christ, sacrificial victims who do not merit being put to death. Now, it could well be that Carle believed, as many people do, that the taking of life by the state, at least in these circumstances, was unwarranted. If this is so, then Carle might still believe in Anne's guilt and yet be moved to pity, seeing her death as undeserved suffering, because her crime did not rise to the level of meriting execution.

---

[188] See, for example, the account of the Carthusian martyrs by Dom Maurice Chauncy (1509–1581) in which he states: "There was one Anne, a wretched woman, surnamed Boleyn. Bellona we may name her not inaptly, Bellona goddess of war, for of the grievous ecclesiastical war which followed she was the origin and cause"; found in Dom Maurice Chauncy, *The Passion and Martyrdom of the Holy English Carthusian Fathers*, ed. G. W. S. Curtis, trans. A. F. Radcliffe, intro. E. Margaret Thompson (London: Society for Promoting Christian Knowledge, 1935), 48–49. See also Michel de Castelnau, who writes that Catholics blamed Anne "for being the cause of the repudiation of another queen, for being a Lutheran, for having Henry change his religion, and especially for having put to death Thomas More, Chancellor of England, one of the greatest figures of his time" [my translation]; found in Michel de Castelnau, *Mémoires de Messire Michel de Castelnau . . . ausquelles sont traictées les choses plus remarquables qu'il a veuës . . . en France, Angleterre, et Escosse* (Paris: Sebastien Chappelet, 1621), 56–57. Additionally, Chapuys blames Anne for Henry's cruelty towards Mary and Catherine; see especially LP 6.351, where Chapuys notes in a letter to Charles V dated 15 April 1533: "Although the King himself is not ill-natured, it is this Anne who has put him in this perverse and wicked temper and alienates him from his former humanity."

[189] See, on this point, Warnicke, "Conflicting Rhetoric," 41.

Indeed, regardless of whether or not Carle was sufficiently convinced that Anne was guilty of adultery, he still might have believed that, from the moment she repented of her ways, she deserved mercy rather than punishment. At any rate, Carle is clearly moved by Anne's death and that of the men accused with her and believes that they have mastered the "art of dying" enough to deserve his prayers for the salvation of their souls, as is clearly expressed in the final verses that appear only in the British Library manuscript of this text: "I pray to God that he should wish to have mercy / On this queen, and also on these gentlemen, / And that they may be with Him in glory and honor" (vv. 1326–1328).

This rather ambiguous interpretation of Carle's perception of Anne's guilt or innocence may well be the best reading that can be derived from the poem in the form that has most often survived. But four of the previously unknown verses of the Parisian manuscript BnF Fr 10194 (here transcribed as BNF4), discussed in Chapters 3 and 4 above, alter this reading in a dramatic fashion. There, the poet describes the reaction of the crowd who witnesses Anne's final moments, declaring that "everyone, on the basis of her mightily steady end, / Judges her life to have been prudent / And believes that they had committed a great offense / In having thought so ill of her" (inserted after v. 1264). If these verses are indeed Carle's and not the work of a later scribe—and the manuscript itself gives no indication that they are "interpolations" rather than part of the integral text—then it would seem that Carle is, in effect, engaging in an act of self-accusation, for surely he had, earlier in his poem, thought ill of Anne. And he must be understood to be part of the group that comprises "everyone" who has now changed their mind about her, confessing that he, along with everyone else, has erred in judging her.

It is important to note that here, Carle is going far beyond saying that Anne has merely *repented* of her sins and that, consequently, she has shown herself capable of redemption and therefore deserving of God's mercy (and the public's prayers). Instead, Carle explicitly states that Anne's life has been "prudent." This is a word that appears multiple times in the course of Carle's poem, most notably in the passage that describes the way of life embraced by Claude de France, Anne's "prudent mistress" (v. 84), and Mary's dedication to the pursuit of virtuous pastimes. While, earlier, Carle may have called into question Anne's prudence, specifically her ability to follow the example of Claude de France, he now, along with the other witnesses to her demise, believes that she had indeed been endowed with this virtue. Having prudence, one of the four cardinal virtues, of course, does not imply that Anne was sinless. But this virtue, which can be defined as having the ability to discern the proper course of action and correct behavior, certainly would preclude her having committed such grievous sins as adultery and incest: for prudence, as Thomas Aquinas and other medieval theologians declared, was the particular virtue needed for "holding the passions and the appetites in check."[190]

Carle did not come to this conclusion of Anne's innocence by way of legal evidence that was submitted in her trial. Instead, he, along with everyone else, derived this new estimation of Anne's innocence on the basis of her comportment when facing death. For, according to the customary beliefs of the time, a smiling face and a willingness to accept death fearlessly were signs that indicated that the condemned person was, in fact, innocent. As Katherine Royer explains, it was traditionally accepted that the crowds witnessing the executions of criminals could form a judgment—or indeed, construct a "reading"—of the "state of [the] soul [of the accused criminals] from their physical demeanor," such that the condemned person's body "became a window to the state of his soul and, by implication, his guilt or innocence."[191] Now, of course, modern witnesses to such a sight would not necessarily reach the same conclusion, for we no longer believe that such outward signs permit us to read the state of a dying person's soul. But for Carle and his contemporaries, this was the only conclusion to draw.

While these verses were apparently excised from all other surviving manuscripts, it seems likely, for the reasons outlined in Chapters 3 and 4 above, that it is precisely this version of the text that came into Henry VIII's hands in 1537.[192] It is no wonder, then, that Henry was livid and demanded that all copies of this poem be destroyed and that its author be punished. For he, like other readers of his time, would have realized that Carle ultimately portrayed an innocent Anne who was wrongly convicted and executed, this despite the poet's earlier references to her malice and his convincing account of the accusations brought against her by a close counselor and his sister. If we are to read Carle's poem the way it was read in the sixteenth century, this is the conclusion we too must draw.

---

[190] For more on the evolving understanding of prudence in the Middle Ages and early modern periods, see John Martin, "Inventing Sincerity, Refashioning Prudence: The Discovery of the Individual in Renaissance Europe," *The American Historical Review* 102 (1997): 1309–42, here 1323–24.

[191] Royer, "Dressed for Dying," 72–73. Royer also notes (71) that spectators similarly formed their judgment concerning the guilt or innocence of the condemned in part based on the semiotics of their dress. It is notable that Carle (like Chapuys) does not describe Anne's dress on the scaffold, though other accounts do.

[192] These reasons include the fact that this is the only manuscript version that refers to Carle by name in its intitulation, which also designates the poem as a "tragedy." These two details are alluded to in Henry's letter to Stephen Gardiner, which was written upon receipt of what he thought of as a book full of malice. For this letter, see Add. 25114, fols. 267r–268v. For a synopsis, see LP 12.2.78. Furthermore, later correspondence on the part of William Paget regarding this book refers to the author as a prothonotary, another designation found in the intitulation of this version of the text. See Kew, National Archives, SP, 1/177, fols. 33v–35r. Paget's letter is summarized in LP 18.1.381 and a facsimile is available via State Papers Online. For more on this matter, see Chapter 3 above.

As can be seen from the above analysis, Carle has taken an active role in shaping and interpreting, rather than merely reporting, the events of May 1536. Although he appears, in the prologue of his poem, to dread undertaking this task, which will require him to reflect further upon these haunting memories, he knows that his diplomatic position requires him to give a full account. Carle admits at the beginning of his poem that he is perplexed by what he has just witnessed: the world has not seen the likes of this story, which, as he realizes, does not fit neatly within a single literary genre, since it begins so promisingly, like a comedy, but ends as a tragedy. In saying this, Carle reveals that he has tried to make sense out of what he sees by analyzing these events as one would read a literary text. His ultimate conclusion that Anne was misjudged is another act of reading, this time of the visible signs Anne displays at her execution. Reading and interpreting signs and texts is thus at the very heart of this story, and one of the conclusions to be drawn from it is that the proper reading of signs is an activity that is fraught with difficulty. Carle's emphasis on reading and interpreting meaning—in essence, on semiotics—provides a further insight into his decision to convey this unique story to his French audience back home by creating a literary text, and, in particular, a poem: for, this medium is one that has long been recognized as one that advertises its very literariness. It is the very nature of poetry to convey meaning through signs and symbols, through metaphors and similes, through what is not explicit but remains implicit. Poetry is thus the perfect outlet through which to express the high emotions of this dramatic story as well as to explore the moral meanings behind this tragedy.

Recognizing the literariness of Carle's text need not diminish its value as an historical document, however. Indeed, as Natalie Zemon Davis has shown, in contrast to the advice given to students of history in her generation, it is no longer desirable "to peel away the fictive elements in our documents so we could get at the real facts."[193] Davis's approach to history, which lets "the 'fictional' aspects of [historical] documents be the center of analysis" is a fruitful one.[194] As she has shown, "fiction" does not necessarily equate to "feigned elements." Instead, Davis focuses on elements suggested by the "broader sense of the root word *fingere*, their forming, shaping, and molding elements: the crafting of a narrative," an approach that leads her to conclude that "the artifice of fiction [does] not necessarily lend falsity to an account."[195] From this perspective, Carle's text is a gold-mine: for, in the hands of a skilled historian, the artifice of Carle's unapologetically literary account can reveal truths that other, unadorned reports simply cannot provide.

---

[193] Natalie Zemon Davis, *Fiction in the Archives: Pardon Tales and Their Tellers in Sixteenth-Century France* (Stanford: Stanford University Press, 1987), 3.

[194] Davis, *Fiction in the Archives*, 3.

[195] Davis, *Fiction in the Archives*, 3–4.

The impulse to write of these events in a tragic and poetic mode was one
that Carle shared, apparently, with Henry VIII himself: for the Imperial ambas-
sador, Chapuys, wrote that the king had revealed to the Bishop of Carlisle that
he "long expected the issue of these affairs, and that thereupon he had before
composed a tragedy, which he carried with him; and so saying, the King drew
from his bosom a little book written in his own hand, but the Bishop did not
read the contents."[196] No one knows exactly what Henry wrote on this matter,
or what literary form it actually took, but Chapuys conjectured that "it may have
been certain ballads that the King has composed."[197] In any case, both Carle and
Henry apparently recognized the suitability of turning to literary forms to cap-
ture the events of May 1536.[198] Henry's "tragedy" no longer exists, but Carle's
work, despite Henry's efforts to eradicate it, is a survivor. *The Story of the Death
of Anne Boleyn* testifies to Carle's decision to eschew the conventional form of a
diplomatic dispatch—written in the immediate aftermath of what must have
seemed to be a series of astounding events—and to construct a *sui generis* work
that bridges the worlds of diplomacy and poetry, truth and fiction. It is a text
whose novel form and content thus fittingly convey the unprecedented nature of
these "cas nouueaux et choses merveilleuses" that make up the story of the life
and death of Anne Boleyn.

---

[196] LP 10.908, Chapuys to Charles V, dated 19 May 1536; see also CSP, Spain, 5,
pt. 2 (1536–1538), no. 55.

[197] LP 10.908 and CSP, Spain, 5, pt. 2 (1536–1538), no. 55.

[198] For a discussion of this lost work and how "literary forms were seen as suitable
vehicles for even the most important of political expressions" in the Henrician era, see
Greg Walker, *Plays of Persuasion: Drama and Politics at the Court of Henry VIII* (Cam-
bridge: Cambridge University Press, 1991), 21. See also Lerer, *Courtly Letters*, 118–21,
for an analysis of how this lost work intersects with other "tragedies" of Henry's acquain-
tance.

# BIBLIOGRAPHY

## I. Manuscripts

### A. Manuscript Versions of Carle's Poem

Bordeaux, Bibliothèque municipale, 0313
Brussels, Bibliothèque royale de Belgique, 19378
Karlsruhe, Badische Landesbibliothek, Güntersthal 12
London, British Library, Additional 40662
Munich, Bayerische Staatsbibliothek, Cod. GALL 105
Paris, Bibliothèque nationale de France, Colbert 465
Paris, Bibliothèque nationale de France, Fr. 01742
Paris, Bibliothèque nationale de France, Fr. 02370
Paris, Bibliothèque nationale de France, Fr. 10194
Paris, Bibliothèque nationale de France, Fr. 12489
Paris, Bibliothèque nationale de France, Fr. 12795
Paris, Bibliothèque nationale de France, Lat. 5934
Rome, Vatican City, Biblioteca Apostolica Vaticana, Reg. lat. 1652
Soissons, Bibliothèque municipale, 201
Soissons, Bibliothèque municipale, 202
Valenciennes, Bibliothèque municipale, 419

### B. Other Manuscripts Consulted

Cambridge, Corpus Christi College, 119
Kew, National Archives, KB 8/8
Kew, National Archives, KB 8/9
Kew, National Archives, SP 1/129
Kew, National Archives, SP 1/177
London, British Library, Additional 19398
London, British Library, Additional 25114
London, British Library, Additional 28585
London, British Library, Additional 28587
London, British Library, Additional 28588
London, British Library, Additional 6113

London, British Library, Additional 6297
London, British Library, Additional 8715
London, British Library, Cotton Cleopatra E.VI
London, British Library, Cotton Titus B/I
London, British Library, Cotton Vespasian F/XIII
London, British Library, Egerton 2403
London, British Library, Harley 2194
London, British Library, Harley 368
London, British Library, Harley 6561
London, British Library, Lansdowne 105
London, British Library, Lansdowne 261
London, British Library, Royal 16 E XIII
London, British Library, Royal 20 B XVII: 1529–1530
London, British Library, Royal 20 B XXI
London, British Library, Royal 20 D IV
Paris, Bibliothèque nationale de France, Dupuy 373
Paris, Bibliothèque Sainte-Geneviève, 3986 (4)
Rome, Vatican City, Biblioteca Apostolica Vaticana, Lat. 3731, pt. A

## II. Bibliographic Databases and Full-Text Sources

Bibliothèque nationale de France: Archives et manuscrits http://archivesetmanu-
    scrits.bnf.fr/
Bibliothèque nationale de France: Gallica http://Gallica.bnf.fr/
Calames: Catalogue en ligne des archives et des manuscrits de l'enseignement
    supérieur http://www.calames.abes.fr/pub/
Catalogue Collectif de France [CCFr] http://ccfr.bnf.fr
Google Books http://books.google.com
Hathi Trust Digital Library http://hathitrust.org
Internet Archive http://archive.org
Jonas = Répertoire des textes et des manuscrits médiévaux d'oc et d'oïl. Section
    romane, notice de "Histoire de la royne Anne Boullant d'Angleterre, Lance-
    lot de Carles" http://Jonas.irht.cnrs.fr/
Joubaud, Pascal, and Claire Sicard. Demêler Mellin de Saint-Gelais. Carnet de
    recherche Hypothèses, http://demelermellin.hypotheses.org/
Manuscrits Médiévaux d'Aquitaine http://manuscrits-medievaux.fr
NuBis: Bibliothèque numérique, University of Paris https://nubis.univ-paris1.fr/
Parker Library on the Web (Manuscripts in the Parker Library at Corpus Christi
    College, Cambridge) http://parker.stanford.edu
Project Gutenberg http://gutenberg.org

The Renaissance in Print: Sixteenth-Century French Books in the Douglas Gordon Collection (University of Virginia) https://www.lib.virginia.edu/rmds/collections/gordon/index.html

Schoenberg Database of Manuscripts, University of Pennsylvania https://sdbm.library.upenn.edu

State Papers Online: Early Modern Government in Britain and Europe https://www.gale.com/intl/primary-sources/state-papers-online

Universal Short Title Catalogue www.ustc.ac.uk

WorldCat https://www.worldcat.org/

## III. Transcription and Translation Tools

The ARTFL Project. University of Chicago. *Dictionnaires d'autrefois*. https://artfl-project.uchicago.edu/content/dictionnaires-dautrefois

Buat, Nicolas, and Evelyne Van den Neste. *Dictionnaire de paléographie française*. 2011. Paris: Belles Lettres, 2013.

——. *Manuel de paléographie française*. Paris: Belles Lettres, 2016.

Cotgrave, Randle. *A Dictionarie of the French and English Tongues*. London: Adam Islip, 1611. Reproduced in a facsimile edition, introduced by William S. Woods. Columbia: University of South Carolina Press, 1950.

*Dictionnaire du Moyen Français*. Version 2015. ATILF–CNRS & Université de Lorraine. http://www.atilf.fr/dmf

Gougenheim, Georges. *Grammaire de la langue française du seizième siècle*. Paris: Picard, 1973.

Greimas, A. J. *Dictionnaire de l'ancien français jusqu'au milieu du XIVe siècle*. Paris: Larousse, 1968.

Oxford English Dictionary. https://www.oed.com

Rickard, Peter. *La langue française au seizième siècle*. Cambridge: Cambridge University Press, 1968.

## IV. Printed Primary Sources, Including Histories before 1800 and Reference Works

Ales (Alesius), Alexander. "Letter to Queen Elizabeth." In *Calendar of State Papers, Foreign Series, Elizabeth 1558–59*, 1:1303, 524–34.

Amyot, Thomas, ed. "Transcript of an Original Manuscript Containing a Memorial from George Constantyne to Thomas Lord Cromwell." *Archaeologia, or Miscellaneous Tracts Relating to Antiquity* 23 (1830): 50–78.

*The Anne Boleyn Music Book (Royal College of Music MS 1070)*. Edited by Thomas Schmidt and David Skinner, with Katja Airaksinen-Monier. Oxford: Diamm Publications, 2017.

Aristotle. *On Rhetoric.* Translated by George A. Kennedy. New York: Oxford University Press, 2007.

*Ars moriendi, that is to saye the craft for to deye for the helthe of mannes sowle* [1491]. Edited by Edward W. B. Nicholson. London: Bernard Quaritch, 1891.

*Ballads from Manuscripts.* Edited by Frederick J. Furnivall. Vol. 1. Pt. 2. London: Taylor and Co., 1872.

Bandello, Matteo. "De le molte mogli del re d'Inghilterra e morte de le due di quelle, con altri modi e varii accidenti intervenuti." In *La terza parte de le novelle.* Edited by Delmo Maestri, 287–93. Turin: Edizioni dell'Orso, 1995. Translated as "Of the Many Wives of the King of England and the Death of Two of Them." In *The Novels of Matteo Bandello . . . now first done into English . . . by John Payne,* 6 vols., 6:103–13. London: Villon Society, 1890.

Belleforest, François de. "Mort miserable de deux amans, ausquels le Roy d'Angleterre Henry defendit de se marier ensemble, & autres choses sur la vie dudict Roy." In *Le second tome des Histoires Tragiques, extraites de l'italien de Bandel.* 433–62. Paris: Robert le Mangnier, 1566.

Bentley, Samuel. *Excerpta historica or, Illustrations of English History.* London: Bentley, 1831.

*Biblia sacra juxta vulgatam Clementinam nova editio.* Madrid: Biblioteca de autores cristianos, 1977.

*The Bibliographer's Manual of English Literature.* Vol. 1. Edited by William Thomas Lowndes. Revised by Henry G. Bohn. London: Henry Bohn, 1858.

*Bibliotheca bibliothecarum manuscriptorum nova.* Vol. 2. Edited by Bernard de Montfaucon. Paris: Briasson, 1739.

*Bibliotheca Towneleiana: A Catalogue of the Curious and Extensive Library of the Late John Towneley . . . Sold by Auction by R. H. Evans.* London: Bulmer, 1814.

*Bibliothèque municipale de Bordeaux. Catalogue des manuscrits.* Vol. 1. Edited by Jules Delpit. Bordeaux: Delmas, 1880.

*Blasons anatomiques du corps féminin.* Edited by Julien Gœury. Paris: Flammarion, 2016.

*Blasons anatomiques du corps féminin.* Paris: Charles Langelier, 1543.

Boccaccio, Giovanni. *De casibus illustrium virorum.* Edited by Louis Brewer Hall. Gainesville, FL: Scholar's Facsimiles and Reprints, 1962.

———. *Il Decameron.* Edited by Charles S. Singleton. 2 vols. Bari: Laterza, 1955.

———. *The Decameron: A New Translation, Contexts, Criticism.* Edited and translated by Wayne A. Rebhorn. New York: Norton, 2016.

Boethius. *The Consolation of Philosophy.* Translated by Victor E. Watts. 1969. London: Penguin, 1999.

*The Book of the Craft of Dying and Other Early English Tracts Concerning Death.* Edited by Frances M. M. Comper. 1917. Reprint, New York: Arno, 1977.

Bourgueville, Charles de. *Les recherches et antiquitez de la province de Neustrie.* Caen: Jean de Feure, 1588.

Brantôme, Pierre de Bourdeille, Seigneur de. *Œuvres complètes*. Vol. 3. Edited by Ludovic Lalanne. Paris: Renouard, 1867.

Burnet, Gilbert. *The History of the Reformation of the Church of England*. 2nd ed. Pt. 1. London: Chiswell, 1681.

———. *The History of the Reformation of the Church of England*. Pt. 3. Edited by Rev. E. Nares. New York: Appleton, 1843.

Byrne, Muriel St. Clare, ed. *The Lisle Letters*. 6 vols. Chicago: University of Chicago Press, 1981.

*Calendar of State Papers, Foreign Series, Elizabeth 1558–1559*. Edited by Joseph Stevenson. London: Her Majesty's Stationery Office, 1863. Online access at British History Online: https://www.british-history.ac.uk/cal-state-papers/foreign/vol1 and State Papers Online: Early Modern Government in Britain and Europe https://www.gale.com/intl/primary-sources/state-papers-online.

*Calendar of State Papers, Spain*. Edited by G. A. Bergenroth, Pascual de Gayangos, and Martin A. S. Hume. Vols. 2–7. London: Her Majesty's Stationery Office, 1866–1899. Online access at British History Online: http://www.british-history.ac.uk/search/series/cal-state-papers-spain and State Papers Online: Early Modern Government in Britain and Europe https://www.gale.com/intl/primary-sources/state-papers-online.

*Calendar of State Papers, Venice*. Edited by Rawdon Brown. London: Her Majesty's Stationery Office, 1867–1873. Online access at British History Online: http://www.british-history.ac.uk/search/series/cal-state-papers-venice and State Papers Online: Early Modern Government in Britain and Europe https://www.gale.com/intl/primary-sources/state-papers-online.

Carle, Lancelot de. *Le Cantique des Cantiques de Salomon, paraphrasé en vers françois, par Lancelot de Carle, Evesque de Riez*. Paris: Vascosan, 1562.

———. *Les Cantiques de la Bible, traduits selon l'hébreu, par Lancelot de Carle, Evesque de Riez, plus deux hymnes qui se chantent en l'Eglise*. Paris: Vascosan, 1562.

———. *De Carles' Trial and Death of Queen Anne Boleyn translated into Modern English*. Translated by Margaret Bolton. CreateSpace Independent Publishing Platform, 2015.

———. *L'Ecclésiaste de Salomon, paraphrasé en vers françois, par Lancelot de Carles, Evesque de Riez, avec quelques sonnets chrestiens*. Paris: Nicolas Edoard, 1561.

———. *Epistre contenant le proces criminel faict à l'encontre de la royne Anne Boullant d'Angleterre, par Carles aulmosnier de Monsieur le Daulphin*. On les vend à Lyon, pres Nostre Dame de Confort. [Tours: Jean Rousset]. 1545. In 8°.

———. "Histoire de Anne Boleyn jadis royne d'Angleterre, exécutée à mort à Londres, le 19ᵉ jour de mai, l'an 1536," in Crapelet, *Lettres*, 165–214.

———. *Lanceloti Carlæi Rhegiensium pontificis, ad Janum Carlæum, fratris filium, sermo*. Paris: Vascosan, 1560. Translated by Carle in the same volume as *Exhortation ou parenese . . . à son neveu*.

————. "Lettre de l'Evesque de Riez au Roy, contenant les actions et propos de Monsieur de Guyse, depuis sa blessure, iusques à son trespas." In *Archives curieuses de l'histoire de France depuis Louis XI jusqu'à Louis XVIII*, 1st series, vol. 5. Edited by L. Cimber and F. Danjou, 171–97. Paris: Beauvais, 1835.

————. "Poème sur la mort d'Anne Boleyn, par Lancelot de Carles." In Ascoli, *La Grande-Bretagne*, 231–73.

————. *Recueil des derniers propos que dit et teint feu tresillustre prince, Messire François de Lorraine Duc de Guyse . . . prononcez par luy devant son trespas à Madame la Duchesse sa femme, Monsieur son filz, Messieurs les Cardinaulz ses freres, & à plusieurs assistans à l'heure de son trespas*. Paris: Jacques Kerver, 1563.

Castelnau, Michel de. *Mémoires de Messire Michel de Castelnau . . . ausquelles sont traictées les choses plus remarquables qu'il a veuës . . . en France, Angleterre, et Escosse*. Paris: Sebastien Chappelet, 1621.

*Catalogue des actes de François I⁰ʳ*. Vol. 3. January 1535–April 1539. Paris: Imprimerie nationale, 1889.

*Catalogue des livres de la bibliothèque de feu M. le duc de la Vallière*. Pt. 1, Vol. 2. Edited by Guillaume de Bure. Paris: de Bure, 1783.

*Catalogue des livres rares et précieux de M. \*\*\* [Heiss] . . . dont la vente se fera le lundi 7 Mars 1785*. Paris: de Bure, 1785.

"Catalogue des manuscrits de Jean et Pierre Bourdelot: Concordance." Edited by Elisabeth Pellegrin. *Scriptorium* 40 (1986): 202–32.

"Catalogue des manuscrits de Jean et Pierre Bourdelot, médecins parisiens." Edited by H. Omont. *Revue des bibliothèques* 1 (1891): 81–103.

*Catalogue des manuscrits de la Bibliothèque royale de Belgique*. Edited by J. Van den Gheyn. Brussels: Henri Lamertin, 1907.

*Catalogue descriptif et raisonné des manuscrits de la Bibliothèque de Valenciennes*. Edited by Jacques Mangeart. Paris: Techener, 1860.

*Catalogue général des manuscrits des bibliothèques publiques de France*. Vol. 3: Soissons. Paris: Plon, 1885.

*Catalogue général des manuscrits des bibliothèques publiques de France*. Vol. 23: Bordeaux. Edited by Camille Couderc. Paris: Plon, 1894.

*Catalogue général des manuscrits des bibliothèques publiques de France*. Vol. 25: Valenciennes. Edited by Auguste Molinier. Paris: Plon, 1894.

*Catalogue of the Library of the late Richard Heber, Part the Sixth, which will be sold by auction by Mr. Evans*. London: W. Nicol, 1835.

*Catalogus codicum manu scriptorum bibliothecae Regiae Monacensis*. Vol. 7. Munich: Regia Palmiana, 1858.

Cavendish, George. *Metrical Visions Concerning the Fortunes and Fall of the Most Eminent Persons of His Time*. In *The Life of Cardinal Wolsey and Metrical Visions by George Cavendish*, edited by Samuel Weller Singer. Vol. 2. Chiswick: Whittingham, 1825.

————. *The Life and Death of Cardinal Wolsey*. In *Two Early Tudor Lives*, 3–193.

Chaucer, Geoffrey. *The Canterbury Tales*. Edited by Jill Mann. London: Penguin, 2005.

Chauncy, Dom Maurice. *The Passion and Martyrdom of the Holy English Carthusian Fathers*. Edited by G. W. S. Curtis. Translated by A. F. Radcliffe. Introduced by E. Margaret Thompson. London: Society for Promoting Christian Knowledge, 1935.

Chrétien de Troyes. *Le Chevalier au lion, ou le roman d'Yvain*. Edited by David F. Hult. Paris: Livre de Poche, 1994.

Christine de Pizan. *The Boke of the Cyte of Ladyes*. Translated by Brian Anslay. Edited by Hope Johnson. Tempe, AZ: ACMRS, 2014.

*The Chronicle of Calais in the Reigns of Henry VII and Henry VIII to the Year 1540*. Edited by John Gough Nichols. London: Camden Society, 1846.

*Chronicle of King Henry VIII of England . . . Written in Spanish by an Unknown Hand*. Translated and edited by Martin A. Sharp Hume. London: George Bell, 1889. Original Spanish text: *Crónica del Rey Enrico Otavo de Ingalaterra*. Edited by El Marqués de Molins. Madrid: Álfonso Durán, 1874.

*Chronique dite Saintongeaise*. Edited by André de Mandach. Tubingen: Niemeyer, 1970.

Cobbett, William. *Complete Collection of State Trials . . . for High Treason and Other Crimes and Misdemeanors from the Earliest Period to the Present Time*. Vol. 1. Edited by Thomas Bayly Howell. London: Hansard, 1809.

Coke, Edward. *The Third Part of the Institutes of the Laws of England: Concerning High Treason, and Other Pleas of the Crown, and Criminall [sic] Causes*. London: Flesher, 1644.

Colletet, Guillaume. *Vies des poètes bordelais et périgourdins*. Edited by Philippe Tamizey de Larroque. 1873. Reprint, Geneva: Slatkine, 1969.

*The Common Bible, NRSV*. Nashville: Thomas Nelson Publishers, 1989.

Constantyne, George. See under Amyot.

Crapelet, Georges-Adrien, ed. *Lettres de Henri VIII à Anne Boleyn*. 1826. Reprint, Paris: L'Imprimerie de Crapelet, 1835.

Dante Alighieri. *Inferno*. Translated by Robert Hollander and Jean Hollander. New York: Doubleday, 2000.

Des Masures, Louis. *Œuvres poétiques*. Lyon: Jean de Tournes, 1557.

*Dictionnaire bibliographique, historique et critique de livres rares . . . dont les auteurs ne sont pas connus*. Pt. 2. Edited by Abbé R. Duclos. Paris: Cailleau, 1790.

*Dictionnaire des manuscrits . . . existants dans les principales bibliothèques d'Europe*. Paris: Migne, 1853.

Dolet, Étienne. *Stephani Doleti Galli aurelii carminum libri quatuor [Epigrammata]*. Lyon: Dolet, 1538.

Du Bellay, Joachim. *Œuvres complètes*. Vol. 2. Edited by Marie-Dominique Legrand, Michel Magnien, Daniel Ménager, and Olivier Millet. Paris: Champion, 2003.

Du Verdier, Antoine. *La bibliothèque d'Antoine du Verdier*. Lyon: Honorat, 1585.

Ellis, Henry. *Original Letters Illustrative of English History.* Vol. 2. London: Harding, Triphook, and Lepard, 1824.

Elton, G. R., ed. *The Tudor Constitution: Documents and Commentary.* Cambridge: Cambridge University Press, 1960.

*L'Encyclopédie, ou dictionnaire raisonné des sciences, des arts et des métiers.* Edited by Denis Diderot and Jean le Rond d'Alembert. Paris: Briasson, David, Le Breton, and Durand, 1751.

Erasmus, Desiderius. *Adagia* [Adages]. Edited by John N. Grant. Translated by Denis L. Drysdall. In Collected Works of Erasmus 35. Toronto: University of Toronto Press, 2008.

———. *Correspondence of Erasmus: Letters 842–992 (1518–1519).* Translated by R. A. B. Mynors and D. F. S. Thomson. Annotated by P. G. Bietenholz. In Collected Works of Erasmus 6. Toronto: University of Toronto Press, 1982.

———. *De conscribendis epistolis* [On the Writing of Letters]. Translated by Craig R. Thompson. In Collected Works of Erasmus 25: Literary and Educational Writings, vol. 3. Toronto: University of Toronto Press, 1985.

———. *De duplici copia verborum ac rerum comentarii duo* [Copia: Foundations of the Abundant Style]. Translated by Betty I. Knott. In Collected Works of Erasmus 24: Literary and Educational Writings, vol. 2. Toronto: University of Toronto Press, 1978.

Forrest, William. *The History of Grisild the Second: A Narrative, in Verse, of the Divorce of Queen Katharine of Arragon* [sic]. Edited by W. D. Macray. London: Whittingham and Wilkins, 1875.

[Fox, Edward?]. *Gravissimae atque exactissimae illustrissimarum totius Italiae et Galliae academiarum censurae.* London: Thomas Berthelet, 1530. Translated as *The Determination of the moste famous and mooste excellent universities of Italy and Fraunce.* London: Thomas Berthelet, 1531.

Fox [Foxe], John. *Book of Martyrs, or, a History of the Lives, Sufferings, and Triumphant Deaths of the Primitive as well as Protestant Martyrs.* Edited by Charles A. Goodrich. Hartford: Eli Hall, 1833.

*French Vernacular Books: Books Published in the French Language before 1601.* Edited by Andrew Pettegree, Malcolm Walsby, and Alexander Wilkinson. Vol. 1 (A–G). Leiden: Brill, 2007.

Gachard, [Louis Prosper]. *Analectes historiques.* Brussels: Hayez, 1856.

Giovio, Paolo. *Descriptio Britanniae, Scotiae, Hyberniae et Orchadum.* Venice: Michele Tramezzino, 1548.

Hall, Edward. *The Lives of the Kings: Henry VIII.* Edited by Charles Whibley. 2 vols. London: T. C. Jack and E. C. Jack, 1904.

———. *The Union of the Two Noble and Illustre Fameles of Lancastre & Yorke.* In *Hall's Chronicle Containing the History of England . . . to the End of the Reign of Henry the Eighth.* 1548. Edited by Henry Ellis. London: Johnson et al., 1809.

Halliwell Phillips, J. O., ed. *The Love Letters of Henry VIII to Anne Boleyn, With Notes*. Boston: John W. Luce, 1906.

Hamy, A. *Entrevue de François Premier avec Henry VIII*. Paris: Gougy, 1898.

*Die Handschriften der Badischen Landesbibliothek in Karlsruhe*. Vol. 13. Edited by Armin Schlechter and Gerhard Stamm. Wiesbaden: Harrassowitz, 2000.

*Hécatomphile, Les fleurs de poésies françaises, Blasons du corps féminin*. Lyon: François Juste, 1536–1537.

Henry VIII. *Assertio septem sacramentorum adversus Martinum Lutherum*. Antwerp: Michel Hillen, 1522.

———. *Assertio septem sacramentorum, or Defence of the Seven Sacraments*. Edited by Louis O'Donovan, S.T.L. New York: Benziger, 1908.

[———?]. "A Glasse of the Truthe." In *Records of the Reformation: The Divorce, 1527–1533*. Vol. 2. Edited by Nicholas Pocock, 385–88. Oxford: Clarendon, 1870.

*L'Histoire de Guillaume le Maréchal, comte de Striguil et de Pembroke, régent d'Angleterre de 1216 à 1219*. Edited by Paul Meyer. 3 vols. Paris: Société de l'histoire de France, 1891–1901.

*The History of William Marshal*. Edited by Anthony J. Holden. Translated by Stewart Gregory. Notes by David Crouch. 3 vols. London: AngloNorman Text Society, 2002–2006.

*The History of William Marshal*. Translated by Nigel Bryant. Woodbridge, UK: Boydell, 2016.

Juvenal. *Satires*. In *Juvenal and Persius*. Edited and translated by Susanna Morton Braund. Loeb Classical Library 91. Cambridge, MA: Harvard University Press, 2004.

La Croix du Maine, François Grudé sieur de. *La Bibliothèque du sieur de la Croix du Maine*. Vol. 1. 1579. Reprint, Paris: Abel L'Angelier, 1584.

*"Les lamentations" de Matheolus et le "Livre de leesce" de Jehan Le Fèvre de Ressons*. Edited by Anton-Gérard Van Hamel. 2 vols. Paris: E. Bouillon, 1892–1905.

*Lancelot-Grail: The Old French Arthurian Vulgate and Post-Vulgate in Translation*. Vol. 4. *The Death of Arthur*. Translated by Norris J. Lacy. New York: Garland, 1995.

Latymer, William. "William Latymer's 'Cronickille of Anne Bulleyne.'" Edited by Maria Dowling. *Camden Miscellany* 30, Camden Fourth Series 39, 23–65. London: Royal Historical Society, 1990.

Le Grand, Joachim. *Histoire du divorce de Henry VIII, Roy d'Angleterre, et de Catherine d'Aragon*. 3 vols. Paris: Martin and Boudot, 1688.

*Letters and Papers, Foreign and Domestic, of the Reign of Henry VIII*. Edited by J. S. Brewer, J. Gairdner, and R. H. Brodie. 21 vols. London: Her Majesty's Stationery Office, 1846–1932. Electronic access available at *British History Online*: http://www.british-history.ac.uk/search/series/letters-papers-hen8 and State Papers Online: Early Modern Government in Britain and Europe https://www.gale.com/intl/primary-sources/state-papers-online.

*Lettre d'un gentilhomme portugais . . . sur l'exécution d'Anne Boleyn.* Edited by Francisque Michel. English translation by Viscount Strangford. Paris: Silvestre, 1832.

Machaut, Guillaume de. *La Prise d'Alixandre* [*The Taking of Alexandria*]. Edited and translated by R. Barton Palmer. New York: Routledge, 2002.

Machiavelli, Niccolò. *The Chief Works and Others.* Translated by Allan H. Gilbert. 3 vols. Durham, NC: Duke University Press, 1989.

———. *Ritratti e rapporti diplomatici.* Edited by Corrado Vivanti. Rome: Riuniti, 2000.

Mantel, Hilary. *Bring Up the Bodies.* 2012. Reprint, New York: Picador, 2015.

*Manuel du libraire et de l'amateur de livres.* Edited by Jacques-Charles Brunet. Vol. 1. Paris: Didot, 1860.

*Manuscripts of J. Eliot Hodgkin. Fifteenth Report.* Appendix, Pt. 2. London: Her Majesty's Stationery Office, 1897.

Marguerite de Navarre. *L'Heptaméron.* Edited by Michel François. Paris: Garnier, 1967.

———. *The Heptameron.* Translated by P. A. Chilton. New York: Penguin, 1984.

Marot, Clément. *Œuvres poétiques.* Vol. 2. Edited by Gérard Defaux. Paris: Classiques Garnier, 1993.

Merriman, Roger Bigelow, ed. *Life and Letters of Thomas Cromwell.* 2 vols. 1968. Reprint, Oxford: Clarendon, 2000.

Meteren, Emanuel de. *L'Histoire des Pays-Bas.* Translated from Flemish to French by I. D. L. Haye [Jean de la Haye]. The Hague: Jacobz, 1618.

Meyer, Paul, ed. "Prologue en vers français d'une histoire perdue de Philippe-Auguste." *Romania* 6 (1877): 494–98.

Montaigne, Michel de. *Les Essais de Michel de Montaigne.* Edited by Pierre Villey and V.-L. Saulnier. Paris: Presses universitaires de France, 1965. Translated by Donald M. Frame as *The Complete Essays of Montaigne.* 1958. Reprint, Stanford: Stanford University Press, 1975.

More, Thomas. *History of King Richard III.* Edited by J. Rawson Lumby. Cambridge: Cambridge University Press, 1883.

———. *Utopia.* Translated by Dominic Baker-Smith. London: Penguin, 2012.

*La Mort le roi Artu, roman du XIIIᵉ siècle.* Edited by Jean Frappier. Geneva: Droz, 1964.

"The Noble Triumphant Coronation of Queen Anne, Wife unto the Most Noble King Henry the Eighth." In *Tudor Tracts, 1532–1588.* Edited by A. F. Pollard, 9–28. Westminster: Archibald Constable, 1903.

Norton, Elizabeth, ed. *The Anne Boleyn Papers.* Stroud: Amberley, 2013.

*Notice des principaux articles des livres de la bibliothèque de feu M. Mouchard . . . dont la vente se fera . . . le mercredi 12 février 1783.* Edited by Guillaume de Bure. Paris: de Bure, 1783.

*Nouvelles recherches bibliographiques pour servir de supplément au manuel du libraire.* Vol. 1. Edited by Jacques-Charles Brunet. Paris: Silvestre, 1834.

*The Oxford Dictionary of National Biography [ODNB]*. Online access at www. oxforddnb.com.

*The Pilgrim: A Dialogue on the Life and Actions of King Henry the Eighth*. By William Thomas. Edited by J. A. Froude. London: Parker, Son, and Bourn, 1861.

Pocock, Nicholas, ed. *Records of the Reformation: The Divorce, 1527–1533*. 2 vols. Oxford: Clarendon, 1870.

Poulton, Mike. *Bring up the Bodies*. In *Wolf Hall and Bring Up the Bodies: The Stage Adaptation*. 2013. Reprint, New York: Picador, 2014.

Rapin de Thoyras, Paul de. *Histoire d'Angleterre par M. Paul Rapin de Thoyras, nouvelle édition augmentée des notes de M. Tindal*. Edited by M. de S. M. [Charles-Hugues Le Febvre de Saint-Marc]. With notes by [Nicolas] Tindal. Vols. 1 and 6. The Hague, 1749.

*Repertorium bibliographicum, or, some account of the most celebrated British libraries*. London: William Clarke, 1819.

*Romanische Handschriften der Grossherzoglich Badischen Hof- und Landesbibliothek, Karlsruhe*. Edited by Ferdinand Lamey. Karlsruhe: Ch. Th. Groos, 1894.

Ronsard, Pierre de. *Les Amours (1552)*. Edited by Paul Laumonier. Paris: Nizet, 1982.

———. *Œuvres complètes*, Vol. 8. Edited by Paul Laumonier. 3rd ed. Paris: Didier, 1973.

Roper, William. *The Life of Sir Thomas More*. In *Two Early Tudor Lives*, 197–254.

Sander, Nicholas. *Rise and Growth of the Anglican Schism*. Translated by David Lewis. London: Burns and Oates, 1877.

Sébillet, Thomas. *Art poétique françois*. Edited by Félix Gaiffe and Francis Goyet. Paris: Nizet, 1988.

Shakespeare, William. *Henry VIII, or All is True*. Edited by Jay L. Halio. 2000. Reprint, Oxford: Oxford University Press, 2008.

Singer, Samuel Weller, ed. *The Life of Cardinal Wolsey by George Cavendish*. 2nd ed. London: Harding and Lepard, 1827.

Spelman, Sir John. *The Reports of Sir John Spelman*. Edited by J. H. Baker. Vol. 1. London: Selden Society, 1977.

Stemmler, Theo, ed. *Die Liebesbriefe Heinrichs VIII an Anna Boleyn*. Zurich: Belser, 1988.

Strype, John. *Ecclesiastical Memorials, Relating Chiefly to Religion, and the Reformation of It . . . Under King Henry VIII*. Vol. 1, Pt. 1. Oxford: Clarendon, 1822.

*Il successo in la morte della regina de Inghilterra*. Bologna: Giovam Battista di Phaelli, 1536. Another edition printed without place of publication, 1536.

Tamizey de Larroque, Philippe, ed. *Sonnets inédits d'Olivier de Magny*. Paris: Lemerre, 1880.

Tasso, Torquato. "Il messaggiero." In *Prose*, edited by Ettore Mazzali. Milan: Ricciardi, 1959.

*Tristan et Yseut.* Edited by J. C. Payen. Paris: Garnier, 1974.

*Two Early Tudor Lives: The Life and Death of Cardinal Wolsey* by George Cavendish and *The Life of Sir Thomas More* by William Roper. Edited by Richard S. Sylvester and Davis P. Harding. New Haven: Yale University Press, 1962.

Vives, Juan Luis. *The Education of a Christian Woman: A Sixteenth-Century Manual.* Edited and translated by Charles Fantazzi. Chicago: University of Chicago Press, 2000.

Wood, Mary Anne Everett, ed. *Letters of Royal and Illustrious Ladies of Great Britain.* 3 vols. London: Colburn, 1846.

Wriothesley, Charles. *A Chronicle of England during the Reigns of the Tudors from A.D. 1485 to 1559.* Edited by William Douglas Hamilton. Vol. 1. London: Camden Society, 1875.

Wyatt, George. "Extracts from the Life of the Virtuous Christian and Renowned Queen Anne Boleigne." In *The Life of Cardinal Wolsey*, ed. Singer, 417–49.

Wyatt, Sir Thomas. *The Complete Poems.* Edited by R. A. Rebholz. 1978. Reprint, London: Penguin, 1997.

## V. Secondary Sources

Adams, Tracy. "Anne Boleyn: Seductress or Scholar?" In *The Female Beauty Systems: Beauty as Social Capital in Western Europe and the United States, Middle Ages to the Present.* Edited by Christine Adams and Tracy Adams. 48–74. Newcastle upon Tyne: Cambridge Scholars Publishing, 2015.

Ahmed, Ehsan. *Clément Marot: The Mirror of the Prince.* Charlottesville, VA: Rookwood Press, 2005.

Ambrosius, Lloyd E., ed. *Writing Biography: Historians and Their Craft.* Lincoln: University of Nebraska Press, 2004.

Armstrong, Adrian, and Sarah Kay. *Knowing Poetry: Verse in Medieval France from the "Rose" to the Rhétoriqueurs.* Ithaca, NY: Cornell University Press, 2011.

Ascoli, Georges. *La Grande-Bretagne devant l'opinion française depuis la Guerre de Cent Ans jusqu'à la fin du XVIᵉ siècle.* Paris: Librairie universitaire J. Gamber, 1927.

Audin, Jean-Marie Vincent. *Histoire de Henri VIII et du schisme d'Angleterre.* Vol. 2. Paris: L. Maison, 1847. Translated by Edward G. Kirwan Browne as *The Life of Henry the Eighth, and History of the Schism of England.* London: Charles Dolman, 1852.

Babelon, Jean-Pierre. "Les derniers moments du duc François de Guise, d'après un manuscrit de Lancelot de Carle (février 1563)." *Comptes rendus des séances de l'Académie des Inscriptions et Belles-Lettres* 131 (1987): 597–608.

Baker, J. H. "Criminal Courts and Procedure at Common Law, 1550–1800." In *Crime in England, 1500–1800*. Edited by J. S. Cockburn, 15–48. Princeton, NJ: Princeton University Press, 1977.

Bapst, Edmond. *Deux gentilshommes-poètes de la cour de Henry VIII*. Paris: Plon, 1891.

Benger, Elizabeth. *Memoirs of the Life of Anne Boleyn, Queen of Henry VIII*. 3rd ed. London: Longman, Rees, Orme, Brown, and Green, 1827.

Bennett, Philip E. "Rhetoric, Poetics and History: Machaut's *Prise d'Alixandre* and the Anonymous *Gestes des ducs de Bourgogne*." In *Medieval Historical Discourses: Essays in Honour of Peter S. Noble*. Edited by Marianne J. Ailes, Anne Lawrence-Mathers, and Françoise H. M. Le Saux, 53–74. Reading, UK: University of Reading, 2008. [Special issue of *Reading Medieval Studies* 34 (2008)].

Bernard, G. W. *Anne Boleyn: Fatal Attractions*. 2010. Reprint, New Haven: Yale University Press, 2011.

———. "Anne Boleyn's Religion." *The Historical Journal* 36 (1993): 1–20.

———. "The Fall of Anne Boleyn." *The English Historical Review* 106.420 (1991): 584–610.

———. "The Fall of Anne Boleyn: A Rejoinder." *The English Historical Review* 107.424 (1992): 665–74.

———. *The King's Reformation: Henry VIII and the Remaking of the English Church*. New Haven: Yale University Press, 2005.

Bishai, Nadia. "'Which thing had not before been seen': The Rituals and Rhetoric of the Execution of Anne Boleyn, England's First Criminal Queen." In *The Rituals and Rhetoric of Queenship, Medieval to Early Modern*. Edited by Liz Oakley-Brown and Louise J. Wilkinson, 171–85. Dublin: Four Courts Press, 2009.

Bizer, Marc. *Les lettres romaines de Du Bellay*. Montreal: Les Presses de l'Université de Montréal, 2001.

Blaisdell, Charmarie Jenkins. "Renée de France between Reform and Counter-Reform." *Archiv für Reformationsgeschichte—Archive for Reformation History* 63 (1972): 196–225.

Blumenfeld-Kosinski, Renate. "Jean Le Fèvre's *Livre de leesce*: Praise or Blame of Women?" *Speculum* 69 (1994): 705–25.

Boehrer, Bruce Thomas. *Animal Characters: Nonhuman Beings in Early Modern Literature*. Philadelphia: University of Pennsylvania Press, 2010.

Bordo, Susan. *The Creation of Anne Boleyn: A New Look at England's Most Notorious Queen*. 2013. Reprint, Boston: Mariner Books/Houghton Mifflin Harcourt, 2014.

Borman, Tracy. *Thomas Cromwell: The Untold Story of Henry VIII's Most Faithful Servant*. New York: Grove, 2014.

Brigden, Susan. "Sir Francis Bryan." In *The Oxford Dictionary of National Biography*. www.oxforddnb.com.

———. *Thomas Wyatt: The Heart's Forest.* London: Faber and Faber, 2012.

Brombert, Victor. "Opening Signals in Narrative." *New Literary History* 11 (1980): 489–502.

Brooks, Jeanice. *Courtly Song in Late Sixteenth-Century France.* Chicago: University of Chicago Press, 2000.

Burns, Loretta T. "Cleric-Diplomats and the Sixteenth-Century French State." *The Historian* 57 (1995): 721–32.

Cappellen, Raphaël. "Le mystère des origines. *L'Isle Sonante* dans son contexte tourangeau (1544-1562). *L'Année rabelaisienne* 5 (2021): 49–94.

Carley, James P. *The Books of King Henry VIII and His Wives.* London: The British Library, 2004.

———. "'Her moost lovyng and fryndely brother sendeth gretyng': Anne Boleyn's Manuscripts and Their Sources." In *Illuminating the Book: Makers and Interpreters; Essays in Honour of Janet Backhouse.* Edited by Michelle P. Brown and Scot McKendrick, 261–80. London: The British Library, 1998.

Cernogora, Nadia. "L'Écriture de la vanité chez les poètes français de l'automne de la Renaissance: Du *memento mori* aux vertiges d'une poétique du vain." *Littératures classiques* 56 (2005): 199–217.

Cervone, Thea. "'Tucked Beneath Her Arm': Culture, Ideology, and Fantasy in the Curious Legend of Anne Boleyn." In *Heads Will Roll: Decapitation in The Medieval and Early Modern Imaginations.* Edited by Larissa Tracy and Jeff Massey, 289–310. Leiden: Brill, 2012.

Chamard, Henri. "Sonnets chrétiens inédits de Lancelot de Carle, Évêque de Riez." In *Mélanges offerts par ses amis et ses élèves à M. Gustave Lanson.* Edited by Gustave Lanson, 87–97. Paris: Hachette, 1922.

Chapman, Hester W. *Anne Boleyn.* London: Jonathan Cape, 1974.

Childs, Jessie. *Henry VIII's Last Victim: The Life and Times of Henry Howard, Earl of Surrey.* 2006. Reprint, London: Vintage, 2008.

Collette, Carolyn P. *Performing Polity: Women and Agency in the Anglo-French Tradition, 1385–1620.* Turnhout: Brepols, 2006.

Cunningham, Sean. *Prince Arthur: The Tudor King Who Never Was.* Stroud: Amberley, 2016.

D'Aubigné, Jean-Henri Merle. *History of the Reformation in Europe in the Time of Calvin.* Vol. 5: *England, Geneva, Ferrara.* New York: Carter, 1876.

Davies, C. S. L. "Representation, Repute, Reality." *The English Historical Review* 124.511 (2009): 1432–47.

———. "Tudor: What's in a Name?" *History* 97.1 (2012): 24–42.

Davies, Catharine. "Sir Richard Page." In *The Oxford Dictionary of National Biography.* www.oxforddnb.com.

Davis, Natalie Zemon. *Fiction in the Archives: Pardon Tales and Their Tellers in Sixteenth-Century France.* Stanford: Stanford University Press, 1987.

de Vivo, Filippo. "How to Read Venetian 'Relazioni.'" *Renaissance and Reformation / Renaissance et Réforme* 34 (2011): 25–59.

Defaux, Gérard, and Michel Simonin, eds. *Clément Marot, "Prince des poëtes françois" 1496–1996*. Actes du colloque international de Cahors en Quercy, 21–25 mai 1996. Paris: Champion, 1997.

Delaruelle, Louis. "Un dîner littéraire chez Mellin de Saint-Gelays." *Revue d'histoire littéraire de la France* 4 (1897): 407–11.

Denny, Joanna. *Anne Boleyn: A New Life of England's Tragic Queen*. 2004. Reprint, Cambridge, MA: Da Capo Press, 2006.

Dillon, Janette. *Shakespeare and the Staging of English History*. Oxford: Oxford University Press, 2012.

Dixon, William Hepworth. *History of Two Queens: I. Catherine of Aragon, II. Anne Boleyn*. Vol. 6. Leipzig: Bernhard Tauchnitz, 1874.

Dobin, Howard. *Merlin's Disciples: Prophecy, Poetry and Power in Renaissance England*. Stanford: Stanford University Press, 1990.

Dolan, Frances E. *Marriage and Violence: The Early Modern Legacy*. Philadelphia: University of Pennsylvania Press, 2008.

Donaldson-Evans, Lance K. "'Le Blason du beau tetin': Une relecture." In Defaux and Simonin, *Clément Marot, "Prince des poëtes françois,"* 645–55.

———. *Love's Fatal Glance: A Study of Eye Imagery in the Poets of the "École Lyonnaise."* University, MS: Romance Monographs, 1980.

Dowling, Maria. See Latymer, "Chronickille."

Dubois, Claude-Gilbert. *La poésie du XVIᵉ siècle en toutes lettres*. Paris: Bordas, 1989.

Dwyer, Richard A. "Scriveners' Tales: Scribal Versions of the French Prose Romances." In *King Arthur Through the Ages*. Edited by Valerie M. Lagorio and Mildred Leake Day. 2 vols. 1:99–109. New York: Garland, 1990.

Edgerton, Samuel Y. "When Even Artists Encouraged the Death Penalty." *Law and Literature* 15 (2003): 235–65.

Edwards, John. *Mary I: England's Catholic Queen*. New Haven: Yale University Press, 2011.

Eisenstein, Elizabeth L. *The Printing Revolution in Early Modern Europe*. 2nd ed. Cambridge: Cambridge University Press, 2012.

Elton, G. R. *England Under the Tudors*. 3rd edition. London: Routledge, 1991.

Evans, Richard J. *Rituals of Retribution: Capital Punishment in Germany, 1600–1987*. Oxford: Oxford University Press, 1996.

Everett, Michael. *The Rise of Thomas Cromwell: Power and Politics in the Reign of Henry VIII*. New Haven: Yale University Press, 2015.

Fernández-Armesto, Felipe. "Eustache Chapuys." In *Contemporaries of Erasmus: A Biographical Register of the Renaissance and Reformation*, 3 vols. Edited by Peter G. Bietenholz and Thomas B. Deutscher, 1:293–95. Toronto: University of Toronto Press, 1985.

Ferrari, Stéphan. "Histoire tragique et grande histoire: rencontre de deux genres." *Dalhousie French Studies* 65 (2003): 18–35.

Fish, Stanley. "Just Published: Minutiae Without Meaning." *The New York Times*, 7 September 1999. http://www.writing.upenn.edu/~afilreis/88v/fish-biography.html.

Fletcher, Catherine. *The Divorce of Henry VIII: The Untold Story from Inside the Vatican*. New York: Palgrave Macmillan, 2012.

Fox, Julia. *Jane Boleyn: The Infamous Lady Rochford*. 2007. Reprint, London: Phoenix, 2008.

Fragonard, Marie-Madeleine. "Lancelot de Carle, l'institution ecclésiale, la Bible et la poésie." In *Poésie et Bible de la Renaissance à l'âge classique (1550–1680)*, Actes du colloque de Besançon des 25 et 26 mars 1997. Edited by Pascale Blum and Anne Mantero, 161–82. Paris: Champion, 1999.

Freeman, Thomas S. "Research, Rumour and Propaganda: Anne Boleyn in Foxe's 'Book of Martyrs.'" *The Historical Journal* 38.4 (1995): 797–819.

Friedmann, Paul. *Anne Boleyn: A Chapter of English History, 1527–1536*. 2 vols. London: Macmillan, 1884.

Frisch, Andrea. *The Invention of the Eyewitness: Witnessing and Testimony in Early Modern France*. Chapel Hill: University of North Carolina Press, 2004.

Froude, James Anthony. *The Divorce of Catherine of Aragon: The Story as Told by the Imperial Ambassadors Resident at the Court of Henry VIII*. New York: Scribner, 1891.

———. *History of England from the Fall of Wolsey to the Death of Elizabeth*. Vol. 1. Leipzig: Brockhaus, 1861. Vol. 2. London: Parker & Son, 1856.

Fudge, Erica. *Brutal Reasoning: Animals, Rationality, and Humanity in Early Modern England*. Ithaca, NY: Cornell University Press, 2006.

*The Gentleman's Magazine and Historical Chronicle*. Edited by Sylvanus Urban [Edward Cave, pseud.]. Untitled notice on the report of Sharon Turner to the Royal Society of Literature. n.s., 97 (January–June 1827): 623.

Giry-Deloison, Charles, ed. *1520: Le Camp du drap d'or: La Rencontre d'Henri VIII et de François I^er*. Paris: Somogy, 2012.

Gorris, Rosanna. "'Un franzese nominato Clemente': Marot à Ferrare." In Defaux and Simonin, *Clément Marot, "Prince des poëtes françois,"* 339–64.

Greenblatt, Stephen. "How It Must Have Been." *The New York Review of Books*, 5 November 2009. http://www.nybooks.com/articles/2009/11/05/how-it-must-have-been/.

Gregory, Brad S. *Salvation at Stake: Christian Martyrdom in Early Modern Europe*. Cambridge, MA: Harvard University Press, 1999.

Gunn, S. J. *Charles Brandon, Duke of Suffolk, c. 1484–1545*. Oxford: Blackwell, 1988.

———. "Henry VII." In *The Oxford Dictionary of National Biography*. www.oxforddnb.com.

Guy, John. *The Children of Henry VIII*. Oxford: Oxford University Press, 2013.

———. *A Daughter's Love*. 2008. Reprint, London: Harper Perennial, 2009.

———. "Footnotes on a Scandal." Review of Weir, *The Lady in the Tower. Sunday Times* (London), 1 November 2009.

———. *Henry VIII: The Quest for Fame.* London: Allen Lane, 2014.

———. *Thomas More.* New York: Oxford University Press, 2000.

Gwyn, Peter. *The King's Cardinal: The Rise and Fall of Thomas Wolsey.* 1990. Reprint, London: Pimlico, 2002.

Hampton, Timothy. *Fictions of Embassy: Literature and Diplomacy in Early Modern Europe.* Ithaca, NY: Cornell University Press, 2009.

Harmer, Lewis C. "Lancelot de Carle et les hommes de lettres de son temps." *Bibliothèque d'humanisme et Renaissance* 7 (1945): 95–117.

———. "Lancelot de Carle: Sa vie." *Humanisme et Renaissance* 6 (1939): 443–74.

Head, David M. *The Ebbs and Flows of Fortune: The Life of Thomas Howard, Third Duke of Norfolk.* 1995. Reprint, Athens: University of Georgia Press, 2009.

Hill, L. M. "The Two-Witness Rule in English Treason Trials: Some Comments on the Emergence of Procedural Law." *The American Journal of Legal History* 12.2 (1968): 95–111.

*Histoire de la Bibliothèque de l'Arsenal.* Edited by Henry Martin. Paris: Plon, 1900.

Horrox, Rosemary. "Arthur, Prince of Wales." In *The Oxford Dictionary of National Biography.* www.oxforddnb.com.

Hughes, Jonathan. "Sir Francis Weston." In *The Oxford Dictionary of National Biography.* www.oxforddnb.com.

Hunt, Alice. *The Drama of Coronation: Medieval Ceremony in Early Modern England.* Cambridge: Cambridge University Press, 2008.

Hyatte, Reginald. "Arthur as Marc's and Tristan's Double in the French *Tristan* Fragments by Béroul and Thomas." In *King Arthur Through the Ages.* Edited by Valerie M. Lagorio and Mildred Leake Day. 2 vols. 1:110–26. New York: Garland, 1990.

Ives, E. W. *Anne Boleyn.* 1986. Reprint, Oxford: Blackwell, 1987.

———. "Anne Boleyn and the Early Reformation in England: The Contemporary Evidence." *The Historical Journal* 37 (1994): 389–400.

———. "Anne Boleyn and the *Entente Évangélique.*" In *François I^er et Henri VIII: Deux Princes de la Renaissance (1515–1547).* Edited by Roger Mettam and Charles Giry-Deloison, 83–102. Lille: L'Institut de recherches historiques du Septentrion, 1995.

———. "Anne Boleyn on Trial Again." *The Journal of Ecclesiastical History* 62 (2011): 763–77.

———. "Faction at the Court of Henry VIII: The Fall of Anne Boleyn." *History* 57.190 (1972): 169–88.

———. "The Fall of Anne Boleyn Reconsidered." *The English Historical Review* 107.424 (1992): 651–64.

———. "Henry Norris." In *The Oxford Dictionary of National Biography.* www.oxforddnb.com.

———. "Henry VIII." In *The Oxford Dictionary of National Biography*. www. oxforddnb.com.

———. *The Life and Death of Anne Boleyn, "The Most Happy."* 2004. Reprint, Oxford: Blackwell, 2005.

———. "William Brereton." In *The Oxford Dictionary of National Biography*. www.oxforddnb.com.

Janes, Regina. *Losing our Heads: Beheadings in Literature and Culture*. New York: New York University Press, 2005.

Jansen, Sharon L. *Dangerous Talk and Strange Behavior: Women and Popular Resistance to the Reforms of Henry VIII*. New York: St. Martin's Press, 1996.

———. *Political Protest and Prophecy under Henry VIII*. Woodbridge, UK: Boydell, 1991.

Jardine, Lisa. *Erasmus, Man of Letters: The Construction of Charisma in Print*. Princeton, NJ: Princeton University Press, 1993.

Jauss, Hans Robert. "Literary History as a Challenge to Literary Theory." Translated by Elizabeth Benzinger. *New Literary History* 2 (1970): 7–37.

———. *Towards an Aesthetic of Reception*. Translated by Timothy Bahti. Introduced by Paul de Man. Minneapolis: University of Minnesota Press, 1982.

Jeffrey, David Lyle. "Courtly Love and Christian Marriage: Chrétien de Troyes, Chaucer, and Henry VIII." *Christianity and Literature* 59 (2010): 515–30.

Knecht, R. J. *Renaissance Warrior and Patron: The Reign of Francis I*. Cambridge: Cambridge University Press, 1994.

Kong, Katherine. *Lettering the Self in Medieval and Early Modern France*. Cambridge: Brewer, 2010.

Konstan, David. *Pity Transformed*. London: Duckworth, 2001.

Langbein, John H. *Prosecuting Crime in the Renaissance: England, Germany, France*. Cambridge, MA: Harvard University Press, 1974.

Leckie, Shirley A. "Biography Matters: Why Historians Need Well-Crafted Biographies More Than Ever." In *Writing Biography*, ed. Ambrosius, 1–26.

Lemon, Rebecca. *Treason by Words: Literature, Law, and Rebellion in Shakespeare's England*. Ithaca, NY: Cornell University Press, 2006.

Lerer, Seth. *Courtly Letters in the Age of Henry VIII: Literary Culture and the Arts of Deceit*. Cambridge: Cambridge University Press, 1997.

Leroy, Aimé. "Manuscrits de la bibliothèque de Valenciennes." *Archives historiques et littéraires du Nord de la France et du Midi de la Belgique*, n.s., 5 (1844): 361–70.

Lexton, Ruth. "Reading the Adulterous/Treasonous Queen in Early Modern England: Malory's Guinevere and Anne Boleyn." *Exemplaria* 27 (2015): 222–41.

Lingard, John. *A History of England, From the First Invasion by the Romans*. Vol. 4. 5th ed. Paris: Galignani, 1840; and Vol. 6. 2nd ed. London: Mawman, 1823.

Lipscomb, Suzannah. "The Fall of Anne Boleyn: A Crisis in Gender Relations?" In *Henry VIII and the Court: Art, Politics and Performance*. Edited by Thomas Betteridge and Suzannah Lipscomb, 287–305. Farnham: Ashgate, 2013.

———. *1536: The Year that Changed Henry VIII*. Oxford: Lion Hudson, 2009.

Lisle, Leanda de. *Tudor: The Family Story*. London: Chatto & Windus, 2013.

*Literary Gazette and Journal of Belles Lettres, Arts, Sciences, etc.* London: Moyes, 1826. No. 517 (Saturday, 16 December 1826): 789–90.

Loades, David M. *The Boleyns: The Rise and Fall of a Tudor Family*. Stroud: Amberley, 2011.

———. *Henry VIII*. Stroud: Amberley, 2013.

———. *Mary Tudor: A Life*. Oxford: Blackwell, 1989.

Lyons, John. *Exemplum: The Rhetoric of Example in Early Modern France and Italy*. Princeton, NJ: Princeton University Press, 1989.

MacCulloch, Diarmaid. *Thomas Cranmer: A Life*. New Haven: Yale University Press, 1996.

———. *Thomas Cromwell: A Life*. London: Allen Lane, 2018.

Macdougall, Norman. *An Antidote to the English: The Auld Alliance, 1295–1560*. East Linton: Tuckwell, 2001.

Mackay, Lauren. *Among the Wolves of Court: The Untold Story of Thomas and George Boleyn*. London: I. B. Tauris, 2018.

———. *Inside the Tudor Court*. Stroud: Amberley, 2014.

Mackintosh, Sir James. *History of England, from the Earliest Times, to the Year 1588*. Philadelphia: Carey, Lea, and Blanchard, 1834.

Madden, Frederick. *Privy Purse Expenses of the Princess Mary, Daughter of King Henry the Eighth, Afterwards Queen Mary*. London: Pickering, 1831.

Maddox, Donald. "The Arthurian Intertexts of *Inferno V*." *Dante Studies* 114 (1996): 113–27.

Martin, John. "Inventing Sincerity, Refashioning Prudence: The Discovery of the Individual in Renaissance Europe." *The American Historical Review* 102 (1997): 1309–42.

Mattingly, Garrett. *Catherine of Aragon*. London: Jonathan Cape, 1942.

———. *Renaissance Diplomacy*. Boston: Houghton Mifflin, 1955.

May, Steven W., and Heather Wolfe. "Manuscripts in Tudor England." In *A Companion to Tudor Literature*. Edited by Kent Cartwright, 125–39. Oxford: Wiley-Blackwell, 2010.

Mayer, C. A. "Anne Boleyn et la version originale du 'Sermon du bon pasteur' d'Almanque Papillon." *Bulletin de la société de l'histoire du protestantisme français* 132 (1986): 337–46.

———. "'Le sermon du bon pasteur': Un problème d'attribution." *Bibliothèque d'humanisme et Renaissance* 27 (1965): 286–303.

McCracken, Peggy. *The Romance of Adultery: Queenship and Sexual Transgression in Old French Literature*. Philadelphia: University of Pennsylvania Press, 1998.

McDermott, Ryan. *Tropologies: Ethics and Invention in England c. 1350–1600*. Notre Dame, IN: University of Notre Dame Press, 2016.

McGrath, Alister E. *Christian Theology: An Introduction*. 3rd ed. Oxford: Blackwell, 2001.

Merback, Mitchell B. *The Thief, the Cross and the Wheel: Pain and the Spectacle of Punishment in Medieval and Renaissance Europe*. Chicago: University of Chicago Press, 1999.

Michon, Cédric. *La crosse et le sceptre: Les prélats d'état sous François I^er et Henri VIII*. Paris: Tallandier, 2008.

Murphy, Virginia. "The Literature and Propaganda of Henry VIII's First Divorce." In *The Reign of Henry VIII: Politics, Policy and Piety*. Edited by Diarmaid MacCulloch, 135–58. New York: St. Martin's Press, 1995.

Naish, Camille. *Death Comes to the Maiden: Sex and Execution 1431–1933*. London: Routledge, 1991.

Nazarian, Cynthia. "Montaigne Against Sympathy: On Affect and Ethics in the *Essais*." *Montaigne Studies* 30 (2018): 125–38.

Neal, Lisa, and Steven Rendall. "Polyphonic Narrative in Early Modern France: A Question of Literary History." *Romanic Review* 87 (1996): 297–306.

Nelson, William. *Fact or Fiction: The Dilemma of the Renaissance Storyteller*. Cambridge, MA: Harvard University Press, 1973.

Paget, Hugh. "The Youth of Anne Boleyn." *Historical Research* 54.130 (1981): 162–70.

Pettegree, Andrew. *The Invention of News: How the World Came to Know about Itself*. New Haven: Yale University Press, 2014.

Picot, Émile. *Les Français italianisants au XVI^e siècle*. Vol. 1. Paris: Champion, 1906.

Piggot, John. "The Character of Mary Tudor," *Fraser's Magazine*. Vol. 12 (July–December 1875): 457–74.

"Poem on the Death of Anne Boleyn." *The Gentleman's Magazine and Historical Review*, edited by Sylvanus Urban [Edward Cave, pseud.], n.s., 10 (January–June 1861): 189–90.

Potter, Ursula. "Tales of Patient Griselda and Henry VIII." *Early Theatre* 5.2 (2002): 11–28.

Pugh, T. B. Review of Ives, *Anne Boleyn*. In *Welsh History Review* 14 (1989): 638–40.

Reid, Jonathan A. *King's Sister—Queen of Dissent: Marguerite of Navarre (1492–1549) and Her Evangelical Network*. 2 vols. Leiden: Brill, 2009.

[Reiffenberg, Baron de]. "Poème manuscrit sur Anne de Boleyn, par un auteur contemporain." *Le bibliophile belge* 1 (1845): 455–62.

———. Review of Aimé Leroy, *Archives historiques et littéraires*. In *Le bibliophile belge* 3 (1846): 158.

Rex, Richard. "John Fisher [St. John Fisher]." In *Oxford Dictionary of National Biography*. www.oxforddnb.com.

———. *Tudors: The Illustrated History*. 2002. Stroud: Amberley, 2014.

Richardson, Glenn. *The Field of Cloth of Gold*. New Haven: Yale University Press, 2013.

Rigolot, François. *Poétique et onomastique: L'exemple de la Renaissance*. Geneva: Droz, 1977.

Robinson, W. R. B. "Patronage and Hospitality in Early Tudor Wales: The Role of Henry, Earl of Worcester, 1526–49." *Bulletin of the Institute of Historical Research* 51 (1978): 20–36.

Robison, William B. "Sir Anthony Brown." In *Oxford Dictionary of National Biography*. www.oxforddnb.com.

———. "Sir William Fitzwilliam." In *Oxford Dictionary of National Biography*. www.oxforddnb.com.

Rougemont, Denis de. *L'Amour et l'Occident*. 1939. Reprint, Paris: Bibliothèque 10/18, 1962.

Rouget, François. "Un évêque lettré au temps des Valois: Lancelot de Carle (vers 1500–1568)." *Seizième siècle* 11 (2015): 119–34.

Royer, Katherine. *The English Execution Narrative, 1200–1700*. 2014. Reprint London: Routledge, 2016.

Saunders, Alison. "Sixteenth-Century Collected Editions of *Blasons anatomiques*." *The Library*, series 5, 31.4 (1976): 351–68.

Scarisbrick, J. J. *Henry VIII*. 1968. Reprint, London: Penguin, 1974.

Schauer, Margery Stone, and Frederick Schauer. "Law as the Engine of State: The Trial of Anne Boleyn." *William & Mary Law Review* 22 (1980): 49–84.

Schiesari, Juliana. "Pedagogy and the Art of Dressage in the Italian Renaissance." In *Animals and Early Modern Identity*. Edited by Pia F. Cuneo, 375–89. Farnham, UK: Ashgate, 2014.

Schmid, Susan Walters. "Anne Boleyn, Lancelot de Carle, and the Uses of Documentary Evidence." PhD diss., Arizona State University, 2009. Includes a translation of Carle's poem.

Schofield, John. *The Rise and Fall of Thomas Cromwell, Henry VIII's Most Faithful Servant*. 2008. Reprint, Stroud: The History Press, 2011.

Scott, Walter. "Author, Text, and Audience: The Horizon of Expectations and *L'Histoire de Guillaume le Maréchal*." PhD diss., University of Wisconsin-Madison, 2014.

Screech, M. A. *Marot évangélique*. Geneva: Droz, 1967.

Sherman, William H. *Used Books: Marking Readers in Renaissance England*. Philadelphia: University of Pennsylvania Press, 2008.

Smith, Lacey Baldwin. *Anne Boleyn: The Queen of Controversy, A Biographical Essay*. 2013. Reprint, Stroud: Amberley, 2014.

———. "English Treason Trials and Confessions in the Sixteenth Century." *Journal of the History of Ideas* 15 (1954): 471–98.

Smith, Pauline M. *Clément Marot: Poet of the French Renaissance*. London: Athlone, 1970.

Starkey, David. *Henry: Virtuous Prince.* 2008. Reprint, London: Harper Perennial, 2009.

———. "King Henry and King Arthur." *Arthurian Literature* 16 (1998): 171–96. Issue edited by James P. Carley and Felicity Riddy.

———. *Six Wives: The Queens of Henry VIII.* 2003. Reprint, London: Harper Perennial, 2004.

Starkey, David. With D. A. L. Morgan, John Murphy, Pam Wright, Neil Cuddy, and Kevin Sharpe. *The English Court: From the Wars of the Roses to the Civil War.* London: Longman, 1987.

Strickland, Agnes. *Lives of the Queens of England.* 4th ed. Vol. 2. London: Hurst and Blackett, 1854.

Takenaka, Koji. "Lancelot de Carle et le récit des dernières paroles du duc François de Guise." *Cahiers d'études françaises Université Keio* 19 (2014): 112–28.

Tamizey de Larroque, Philippe. "Du poème de Lancelot de Carle sur Anne de Boleyn." In Guillaume Colletet, *Vies des poètes bordelais et périgourdins*, 29–34.

Taylor, Andrew W. "*Ad Omne Virtutum Genus*'? Mary Between Piety, Pedagogy and Praise in Early Tudor Humanism." In *Mary Tudor, Old and New Perspectives.* Edited by Susan Doran and Thomas Freeman, 103–22. New York: Palgrave Macmillan, 2011.

Telle, Émile. "Étienne Dolet et Thomas More," *Moreana* 9.36 (1972): 33–38.

Thomson, Patricia. *Sir Thomas Wyatt and His Background.* London: Routledge and Kegan Paul, 1964.

Thornton, Tim. *Prophecy, Politics and the People in Early Modern England.* Woodbridge, UK: Boydell, 2006.

Thurley, Simon. *Houses of Power: The Places That Shaped the Tudor World.* London: Transworld, 2017.

Trinquet, Roger. "La Lettre sur la mort de La Boétie, ou Lancelot de Carle inspirateur de Montaigne." In *Mélanges d'histoire littéraire (XVI^e–XVII^e siècle) offerts à Raymond Lebègue par ses collègues, ses élèves, et ses amis.* Edited by Raymond Lebègue, 115–25. Paris: Nizet, 1969.

Turner, Sharon. *The History of the Reign of Henry the Eighth.* 3rd ed. Vol. 2. London: Longman, Rees, Orme, Brown, and Green, 1828.

Tytler, P. Fraser. *Life of Henry the Eighth.* London: Nelson, 1854.

Uitti, Karl D. "'Cele [qui] doit estre Rose clamee' (*Rose*, vv. 40–44): Guillaume's Intentionality." In *Rethinking the "Romance of the Rose": Text, Image, Reception.* Edited by Kevin Brownlee and Sylvia Huot, 39–64. Philadelphia: University of Pennsylvania Press, 1992.

Van Rhee, C. H. "Litigation and Legislation: Civil Procedure at First Instance in the Great Council for the Netherlands in Malines (1522–1559)." Brussels: Archives générales du royaume et archives de l'état dans les provinces, 1997.

Vignes, Jean. "Paraphrase et appropriation: Les avatars poétiques de l'Ecclésiaste au temps des Guerres de Religion (Dalbiac, Carle, Belleau, Baïf)." *Bibliothèque d'humanisme et Renaissance* 55 (1993): 503–26.

Vincent, Nicholas. *Magna Carta: A Very Short Introduction.* Oxford: Oxford University Press, 2012.

Vose, Heather M. "Marguerite of Navarre: That 'Righte English Woman.'" *Sixteenth Century Journal* 16 (1985): 315–34.

Walker, Greg. *Plays of Persuasion: Drama and Politics at the Court of Henry VIII.* Cambridge: Cambridge University Press, 1991.

———. "Rethinking the Fall of Anne Boleyn." *The Historical Journal* 45 (2002): 1–29.

———. *Writing Under Tyranny: English Literature and the Henrician Reformation.* Oxford: Oxford University Press, 2005.

Warnicke, Retha M. "Anne Boleyn's Childhood and Adolescence." *The Historical Journal* 28 (1985): 939–52.

———. "Conflicting Rhetoric about Tudor Women: The Example of Queen Anne Boleyn." In *Political Rhetoric, Power, and Renaissance Women.* Edited by Carole Levin and Patricia A. Sullivan, 39–54. Albany: State University of New York Press, 1995.

———. "The Conventions of Courtly Love and Anne Boleyn." In *State, Sovereigns and Society in Early Modern England: Essays in Honour of A. J. Slavin.* Edited by Charles Carlton, with Robert L. Woods, Mary L. Robertson, and Joseph S. Block, 103–18. New York: St. Martin's Press, 1998.

———. "The Fall of Anne Boleyn Revisited." *The English Historical Review* 108.428 (1993): 653–65.

———. "Reshaping Tudor Biography: Anne Boleyn and Anne of Cleves." In *Writing Biography*, ed. Ambrosius, 53–78.

———. *The Rise and Fall of Anne Boleyn: Family Politics at the Court of Henry VIII.* Cambridge: Cambridge University Press, 1989.

———. *Wicked Women of Tudor England: Queens, Aristocrats, Commoners.* New York: Palgrave Macmillan, 2012.

Weir, Alison. *The Lady in the Tower: The Fall of Anne Boleyn.* 2009. Reprint, New York: Ballantine Books, 2010.

Wellman, Kathleen. *Queens and Mistresses of Renaissance France.* New Haven: Yale University Press, 2013.

White, Hayden V. "The Value of Narrativity in the Representation of Reality." In *The Content of the Form: Narrative Discourse and Historical Representation* (Baltimore: The Johns Hopkins University Press, 1987). 1–25.

Whitelock, Anna. *Mary Tudor: Princess, Bastard, Queen.* 2009. Reprint, New York: Penguin, 2016.

Wiatt, William H. "Sir Thomas Wyatt and Anne Boleyn." *English Language Notes* 6 (1968): 94–102.

Williams, Deanne. "The French Education of Anne Boleyn." Paper presented at the Sixteenth Century Studies Conference. New Orleans, October 2014.

Wooding, Lucy. *Henry VIII*. 2nd ed. London: Routledge, 2015.

Yandell, Cathy. "Iconography and Iconoclasm: The Female Breast in French Renaissance Culture." *The French Review* 83 (2010): 540–88.

Zupanec, Sylwia Sobczak. "An Overlooked Connection of Anne Boleyn's Maid of Honour, Elizabeth Holland, with BL, King's MS. 9." *The Electronic British Library Journal* (2017), Article 7: 1–6.

# INDEX